Fifteenth Edition

Texas Public School Organization and Administration 2016

A Project of
Texas Council of Professors
of Educational Administration

D0992827

James A. Vornberg, Editor
Wesley D. Hickey, Editor

Kendall Hunt
publishing company

Cover images courtesy of Eubanks Harris Roberts Craig Architects, Inc.
Main cover photo: Dr. Bryan C. Jack Elementary School, Tyler ISD
Photographer: Carrol Sinclair

Small top photo: Bullard Elementary School, Bullard ISD
Photographer: Alan Roberts

Small middle photo: Lindale ISD Performing Arts Center, Lindale ISD
Photographer: Alan Roberts

Small bottom photo: Horace H. Clarkston, Sr. Elementary School, Tyler ISD
Photographer: Alan Roberts

Architects for the projects:
Eubanks Harris Roberts Craig Architects, Inc.
1530 East Grande Boulevard
Tyler, TX 75703
903-534-0995
www.eharchitects.com

www.kendallhunt.com
Send all inquiries to:
4050 Westmark Drive
Dubuque, IA 52004-1840

Dedication

The editors of *Texas Public School Organization and Administration* dedicate this edition to Dr. Morgan Moses, former professor and department chair in the College of Education at Stephen F. Austin State University. Dr. Moses impacted administrators throughout Texas with his professionalism and personality that exhibited a personal care for those with whom he worked. Educational leadership lost one of its greatest advocates with his death on April 17, 2014.

CONTRIBUTORS

The Texas Council of Professors of Educational Administration is a professional organization made up of professors who prepare leaders for the schools in Texas and across the nation. Membership is from forty-one institutions of higher education, the Texas Education Agency, and the Texas Higher Education Coordinating Board. Website: www.tcpea.org

Melissa Arrambide
Assistant Professor of Educational Leadership
Texas A&M-Commerce

Rolando Avila
Lecturer of History
The University of Texas-Pan American

Julia Ballenger
Associate Professor of Educational Leadership
Texas A&M University-Commerce

Charles Barké
Chair and Professor of Psychology
The University of Texas at Tyler

Rosemary Barké
Senior Lecturer of Psychology
The University of Texas at Tyler

Carrie Y. Barron Ausbrooks
Associate Dean of the College of Education and
Health Professions
University of Texas at Arlington

Don Beach
Professor of Educational Leadership
Tarleton State University

Danna Beaty
Associate Professor of Educational Leadership
Tarleton State University

Gary Bigham
Associate Professor of Education
West Texas A&M University

Arthur Borgemenke
Assistant Professor of Educational Leadership
Texas A&M-Commerce

Brian Brown
Visiting Assistant Professor
The University of Texas at Arlington

Casey Brown
Associate Professor of Educational Leadership
University of Texas at Arlington

Maria de Lourdes Viloria
Assistant Professor of Educational Leadership
Texas A&M International University

Stacey Edmonson
Dean of the College of Education
Sam Houston State University

Shelley Garrett
Director of Student & Family Services
Rockwall ISD

Phillip Gilbreath
Director of Career and Technical Education
Garland ISD

Viveca Grant
Clinical Professor
Prairie View A&M University

Pamela Gray
Assistant Professor of Educational Leadership
Sam Houston State University

Wesley D. Hickey, editor
Chair and Associate Professor of Educational
Leadership
The University of Texas at Tyler

Chuck Holt
Assistant Professor of Educational Leadership
Texas A&M University-Commerce

Jennifer Jones
Assistant Professor of Educational Leadership
The University of Texas at Tyler

Timothy Jones
Principal Consultant
Education Management

Kriss Kemp-Graham
Assistant Professor of Educational Leadership
Texas A&M University-Commerce

Elisabeth Krimbill
Stone Oak Elementary Principal
North East ISD

Christine McNichols
Assistant Professor of Counseling
The University of Texas at Tyler

Gary Miller
Assistant Professor of Educational Leadership
The University of Texas at Tyler

Susan Nix
Chair and Professor of Educational Leadership
West Texas A&M University

Yanira Oliveras-Ortiz
Assistant Professor of Educational Leadership
The University of Texas at Tyler

Anita Pankake
Professor of Educational Leadership
University of Texas-Pan American

Lillian Poats
Dean of the College of Education
Texas Southern University

Alfredo Ramirez, Jr.
Associate Professor of Educational Leadership
Texas A&M International University

Thomas Ratliff
State Board of Education Member
District 9

Pauline Sampson
Professor of Educational Leadership
Stephen F. Austin State University

Ross Sherman
Dean of the College of Education
and Psychology
The University of Texas at Tyler

Nathan Templeton
Assistant Professor of Educational
Leadership
Texas A&M University-Commerce

David P. Thompson
Professor of Educational Leadership
The University of Texas at San Antonio

Ray Thompson
Assistant Professor of Educational
Leadership
Texas A&M University-Commerce

Vance Vaughn
Associate Professor of Educational Leadership
The University of Texas at Tyler

James A. Vornberg, editor
Professor Emeritus of Educational Leadership
Texas A&M University-Commerce

Nicole Walters
Associate Dean of the School of Education
University of St. Thomas

Mark Weber
Associate Professor of Educational Leadership
Tarleton State University

Pam Winn
Assistant Professor of Educational Leadership
Tarleton State University

Karl Witt
Assistant Professor of Counseling
The University of Texas at Tyler

PAST PRESIDENTS OF TEXAS COUNCIL OF PROFESSORS OF EDUCATIONAL ADMINISTRATION

1974–1976	Barry B. Thompson	Pan American University
1976–1978	Robert Hefner	Southwest Texas State University
1978–1979	Harold Hawkins	Texas A&M University
1979–1980	Kelly Hamby	Abilene Christian University
1980–1981	Bill Strong	Texas Southern University
1981–1982	A. Lynn Turner	East Texas State University
1982–1983	Hoyt Watson	North Texas State University
1983–1984	Fred Harvey	Texas A&I University
1984–1985	Audean Allman	Texas Southern University
1985–1986	John Beck	Southwest Texas State University
1986–1987	James A. Vornberg	East Texas State University
1987–1988	Weldon Beckner	Texas Tech University
1988–1989	Bob Thompson	Lamar University
1989–1990	William Kurtz	Southwest Texas State University
1990–1991	Lawrence Lane	University of Texas at San Antonio
1991–1992	Carole Veir	University of Texas at Austin
1992–1993	Kip Sullivan	Sul Ross State University
1993–1994	Linda Avila	Southwest Texas State University
1994–1995	Jim Merchant	Sam Houston State University
1995–1996	Mike Boone	Southwest Texas State University
1996–1997	Joe Claudet	Texas Tech University
1997–1998	David P. Thompson	Texas A&M University-Commerce
1998–1999	Edward H. Seifert	Texas A&M University-Commerce
1999–2000	Elaine Wilmore	University of Texas at Arlington
2000–2001	Nora Hutto	University of Houston-Victoria
2001–2002	Linda Garner	Prairie View A&M University
2002–2003	Michael Stevens	West Texas A&M University
2003–2004	Judy Adkinson	University of North Texas
2004–2005	Sandra Harris	Lamar University
2005–2007	Stacey Edmonson	Sam Houston State University
2007–2008	Julia Ballinger	Stephen F. Austin State University
2008–2009	Lloyd Goldsmith	Abilene Christian University
2009–2010	Timothy B. Jones	Sam Houston State University
2010–2012	Casey Graham Brown	Texas A&M University-Commerce
2012–2013	Russ Higham	Tarleton State University
2013–2014	Lloyd Goldsmith	Abilene Christian University
2014–2015	David P. Thompson	University of Texas at San Antonio
2015–2016	Vance Vaughn	The University of Texas at Tyler

Executive Directors

2002–2007	Charles W. Blanton	Texas A&M University-Commerce
2009–2015	Stacey Edmonson	Sam Houston State University
2015–Present	Art Borgemenke	Texas A&M University-Commerce

CONTENTS

PART III THE SUPERINTENDENT   275

14 District Leadership in Texas   277
◆ *Wesley D. Hickey, Pauline M. Sampson, and Jennifer Jones*

15 Financing Texas Public Schools   291
◆ *Chuck Holt*

16 School District Business and Financial Operations   311
◆ *Timothy B. Jones*

17 The Superintendent and Human Resources   325
◆ *Chuck Holt*

APPENDICES

PREFACE

Texas public schools continue to be excellent places for educational achievement, and much of this is due to excellent administrators. The requirements for schools continue to change, but the leadership within them adapts with a focus on doing what is right for students. The 84th legislature, new federal points of emphasis, and local school board initiatives create an ongoing professional tension that continues the discussion toward better schools.

The 15th edition of *Texas Public School Organization and Administration* has provided important updates to the ever-changing environment of education, and along with addressing new laws, has added chapters in urban education and counseling. Urban education is a challenge that is often different from suburban and rural schools, as the issues of poverty and safety are often more prominent. Tragedies within our schools have made counseling services a vital part of any educational plan, including the recognizing of students who are struggling psychologically. Addressing these students lawfully and ethically makes for a safer and more nurturing school.

Texas Public School Organization and Administration (15th ed.) continues its role as an important reference in the development of principals and superintendents. This is why we have continued an online component that provides PowerPoint templates, guiding questions or case studies, and TExES formatted questions. These supporting documents are there to assist professors and prepare students.

There may be nothing more important to society than our next generation of educational leaders. *Texas Public School Organization and Administration* (15th ed.) is proud to play a small role in this mission.

PART I

FOUNDATIONS

THE ORGANIZATIONAL STRUCTURE OF GOVERNMENT AND ITS ROLE IN TEXAS PUBLIC EDUCATION

Carrie Y. Barron Ausbrooks ◆ *Nathan R. Templeton*

The organization and governance of education in America is unique among the nations of the world. It is a responsibility of the state in which the schools are located; it is given to local decision-making, and yet its impact is national and international in scope. No other nation places the responsibility for the education of its citizens at such a grass roots level (Klein, 2011; U.S. Department of Education, 2009a).

As a function of the state government, education is a major focus of state officials since many state resources are allocated to advance the development of young citizens. State government in Texas—the lawmakers, the administration, and the court system—is no exception. Biennially, the Texas Legislature grapples with its financial responsibility for education. Several times in recent years, the governor has appointed various committees to explore better ways of administering and improving the schools. Since 1975, Texas courts have also been dealing with the challenge of equitable allocation of resources among the districts across the state to meet the requirements of state court decisions. To date, however, the issue of "equality of educational opportunity" remains unresolved (Gamoran & Long, 2006).

This chapter explores the dynamics of the educational system as of the end of the 84th session of the Texas Legislature in the summer of 2015, including waivers that provided some relief from the No Child Left Behind Act in 2013 and 2015.

◆ HISTORICAL CONTEXT FOR AMERICAN PUBLIC SCHOOLING

The movement in the United States from having private and parochial schools only for the privileged to providing free public schools for all, i.e., "universal education," was a difficult one, which had varying manifestations in different parts of the country. The central argument in favor of public schools was that the development and perpetuation of American democratic society and ideals depended upon an educated citizenry. In addition, the argument was made that only through free public secular schools could the principle of separation of church and state be maintained to avoid the problems endemic to European countries. The basic arguments against free schooling and public control of schools were that (1) such schools would undermine private interests and initiative and (2) the wealth of the privileged would be taxed to provide education for the lower classes of the society who could not benefit from education. The thrust of this argument was that education should be reserved only for those who were intellectually able to profit from it and financially able to pay for it. Religious groups argued that secular, and therefore "godless," schools would destroy the religious and moral foundations of society. In addition, they argued that publicly financed schools would threaten and eventually destroy the financial resources of existing private and religious school systems.

The development of free public schools in Texas followed a similar pattern. Public education in Texas is believed to have begun in 1854. However, progress was slow, and many of the efforts to address education through the legislature were thwarted by racial and political issues. It was not until World War I that Texas public education finally came "of age" with the passage of compulsory attendance law in 1915 and the provision of free textbooks to public school students (McCleskey, Dickens, & Butcher, 1975). Many of the subsequent changes in public education throughout the nation occurred as a result of considerable influence from the federal government, the courts, and public pressure for educational reforms, which will be discussed in greater detail throughout this book.

◆ THE STRUCTURE OF GOVERNMENT AND SOURCES OF LAW RELEVANT TO EDUCATION

In the United States, there are two basic structures of government: a federal system of government and 50 state systems of government quite similar in structure to that of the federal government. Table 1.1 shows a comparison of the two government structures. Additionally, there are four basic types, or sources, of law relevant to education existing at both the federal and state levels of government: (1) constitutional law, (2) statutory (legislative) law, (3) administrative (executive) law, and (4) judicial law. A discussion of each source of law at each level of government follows.

Constitutional Law

As its name implies, constitutional law at the federal level of government is composed of provisions contained in the U.S. Constitution. It is the supreme law of the nation that cites American philosophy of government; defines the structure and specifies the powers and duties of government; separates the federal government into three distinct branches (legislative, executive, and judicial); and defines the rights, privileges, immunities, restrictions, and guarantees granted to the people and all states. Article I creates the legislative branch of government and endows it with the power to make written law; Article II creates the executive (administrative) branch of government and vests it with the power and duty to administer the law and run the government; and Article III creates the judicial branch of government, which is given the power and responsibility of settling controversies arising under the Constitution and U.S. statutory and administrative laws. Some of the important U.S. Constitutional provisions relevant to education are listed in Table 1.2.

TABLE 1.1
Comparison of Federal and Texas State Government Structure

Federal Government	*Texas State Government*
LEGISLATIVE	

The legislative branch of government makes the laws.

• Article I of the U.S. Constitution authorizes the legislative branch of government, specifically Section 1 and Sections 8, 9, and 10.	• Article 2, Section 1 of the Texas constitution delineates the powers of the state government, dividing it into three departments–legislative, executive and judicial. Article 3 authorizes the legislative branch of Texas state government.
• At the federal level, the authority at the legislative branch is vested in the U.S. Congress.	• State authority at the legislative branch is vested in the Texas Legislature.

EXECUTIVE

The executive branch of government enforces (administers) the laws.

• Article II of the U.S. Constitution authorizes the executive branch of federal government.	• Article 4 of the Texas constitution authorizes the executive branch of Texas state government.
• Federal authority at the executive branch rests with the U.S. President.	• State authority at the executive branch rests with the Governor.

JUDICIAL

The judicial branch of government interprets the law.

• Article III of the Constitution invests the judicial power of the United States in the federal court system.	• The Constitution and laws of each state establish the state courts. Article 5 of the Texas constitution authorizes the judicial branch of the state's government.
• Article III, Section 1 specifically creates the U.S. Supreme Court, vesting the authority at the judicial branch of federal government in the U.S. Supreme Court.	• The authority in the judicial branch of Texas state government lies in the Texas court system, which includes two courts of final jurisdiction–the Texas Supreme Court and the Texas Court of Criminal Appeals– the Courts of Appeals, the District Courts, County Courts, Commissioners Courts, Courts of Justices of the Peace, and any other courts provided by law.

At the state level, constitutional law is derived from each state's constitution and is known as the supreme law of each state. Like the U.S. Constitution, each state's constitution provides the philosophy of the state's government, specifies the structure and functions of state government and its officials, and defines the rights, privileges, immunities, etc. of individuals in the

---

TABLE 1.2
Important U.S. Constitutional Provisions

Article I, Section 8. "The Congress shall have Power to lay and collect Taxes . . . to pay the Debts and provide for the common Defense and general Welfare of the United States. . . ."

Amendment I. "Congress shall make no law respecting an establishment of religion, or prohibiting the free exercise thereof; or abridging the freedom of speech, or of the press; or the right of the people peaceably to assemble, and to petition the Government for a redress of grievances."

Amendment IV. "The right of the people to be secure in their persons, . . . papers, and effects, against unreasonable searches and seizures, shall not be violated and no Warrants shall issue, but upon probable cause, supported by Oath or affirmation, and particularly describing the place to be searched, and the persons or things to be seized."

Amendment V. "No person shall be held to answer for a capital, or otherwise infamous crime, unless on a presentment or indictment of a Grand Jury . . .; nor shall any person . . . be compelled in any criminal case to be a witness against himself, nor be deprived of . . . liberty, or property, without due process of law; nor shall private property be taken for public use without just compensation."

Amendment VI. "In all criminal prosecutions, the accused shall enjoy the right to a speedy and public trial, by an impartial jury of the State and district wherein the crime shall have been committed, which district shall have been previously ascertained by law, and to be informed of the nature and cause of the accusation; to be confronted with the witnesses against him; to have compulsory process for obtaining Witnesses in his favor, and to have the assistance of counsel for his defense."

Amendment VIII. "Excessive bail shall not be required, nor excessive fines imposed, nor cruel and unusual punishments inflicted."

Amendment X. "The powers not delegated to the United States by the constitution, nor prohibited by it to the States, are reserved to the States respectively, or to the people."

Amendment XIV, Section 1. "All persons born or naturalized in the United States, and subject to the jurisdiction thereof, are citizens of the United States and of the State wherein they reside. No State shall make or enforce any law which shall abridge the privileges or immunities of citizens of the United States; nor shall any State deprive any person of life, liberty, or property, without due process of law; nor deny to any person within its jurisdiction the equal protection of the laws."

---

state. Although similar in content and purpose to the U.S. Constitution, the state constitution is subordinate to it and cannot contain provisions contrary to those in the U.S. Constitution.

Statutory or Legislative Law

The second source of law is statutory law, sometimes referred to as legislative law. It is the written law enacted by the elected representatives of government at both the federal and state levels. At the federal level, statutory law is created by the U.S. Congress as authorized by Article II of the U.S. Constitution, and at the state level, it is created by the state legislature as authorized by provisions in the state constitution.

Federal Statutory Law

Federal statutory laws are called public laws and are made by Congress, which is authorized to do so via Article I of the U.S. Constitution. The full text of federal statutes (laws) can be found in the Congressional Record. These statutes are codified and published by the federal government in the United States Code (U.S.C.). Table 1.3 contains some of the federal statutory laws important to education.

TABLE 1.3
Important Federal Statutes

Civil Rights Act of 1964, Title VI, 42 U.S.C. §2000d. (P.L. 88-352). This law prohibits against exclusion of participation in, denial of benefits from, or discrimination against persons on the basis of race, color, or nation origin in any program receiving federal financial assistance.

Civil Rights Act of 1964, Title VII, 42 U.S.C. §2000e. (P.L. 88-352). The law prohibits discrimination in employment or employment practices on the basis of race, color, religion, gender, or national origin under any program receiving federal financial assistance.

Title IX, Discrimination Based on Sex, 20 U.S.C. §1681. This law prohibits against exclusion of participation in or denial of benefits or discrimination against persons on the basis of gender in any program receiving federal financial assistance.

Education for All Handicapped Children Act of 1975, 20 U.S.C. §1401. (P.L. 94-142). [This law was renamed in 1990 to the Individuals with Disabilities Act (IDEA)]. This law requires all programs receiving federal financial assistance to provide handicapped children with free education that is appropriate and designed to meet their needs. In 1991, the law was renamed the Individuals with Disabilities Education Act, and on January 7, 1997, this law was again amended by Congress with provision that improved the programs and services to the handicapped and disabled. The Equal Pay Act of 1963, 20 U.S.C. §206. Requires all employees subject to the Fair Labor Standards Act to provide equal pay for men and women performing similar work.

Family Educational Rights and Privacy Act [Buckley Amendment], 20 U.S.C. §1232g. Prescribes the conditions and requirements for inspection, review, and release of educational records of children (including the psychiatric or psychological testing of children) and families participating in federally assisted programs.

Section 504, Rehabilitation Act of 1973 (Public Law 93-112). This law provides that no qualified handicapped student shall, on the basis of handicap, be excluded from participation in or be discriminated against in any program receiving federal assistance.

The Americans with Disabilities Act of 1990. This law enlarged the scope of Section 504 by protecting individuals with disabilities from discrimination by employers and providers of public services.

No Child Left Behind Act of 2001 (Public Law 107-110). This law redefined the role of the federal government in K–12 education toward improving academic achievement for all American children by requiring greater accountability for educational results, increased flexibility for state and local control, increased educational choice options for parents and students, and greater focus on effective instructional methods. The Act was reauthorized in 2007.

attorney general's opinions are not legally binding either on the governmental officials, agencies requesting them, or on the courts, they carry a great deal of influence, especially in those situations in which there is no authoritative interpretation or decision by the courts. However, there is an exception to the advisory (nonlegally binding) opinions of the attorney general with regard to the Texas open records law. The statute states that if a state governmental body receives a written request for information that it feels is not public according to the law, and there has been no previous determination that the information falls within one of the exceptions specified by law, the governmental body must within at least 10 days request an opinion from the attorney general to determine whether the information falls within that exception. Upon receipt of the request, the attorney general must provide an opinion not later than 45 days following receipt of the request (Government Code §§ 552.301, 552.306). However, if a decision is not requested from the attorney general, the information is presumed to be public information and must be provided (Government Code § 552.302). Also, if a governmental body refuses to request an attorney general's opinion or to supply the public information, the attorney general may seek a writ of mandamus that compels the governmental body to make the information available for public inspection (Government Code § 552.321). The attorney general's opinion stands as an authoritative and binding interpretation of this legal question facing the state, its agencies and officials. A more thorough discussion of the roles and functions of the Texas Education Agency, local school districts, and their officials in Texas are provided in subsequent chapters of this book.

Judicial Law

The fourth source of law, judicial law, is the law of the courts; i.e., the decisions rendered by the judges of both the federal and state courts. The courts use both the common law and case law in reaching their decisions. Common law is composed of traditions, folkways, and mores, which have been handed down primarily from the English legal system. It derives its authority from "usage and customs of immemorial antiquity" (Black, Nolan-Haley, & Nolan, 1991) and/or judgments rendered by the courts that have recognized such usage and customs. In essence, common law is based on all the statutory and case law of England and the American colonies before and after the American Revolution. Case law, on the other hand, is the accumulation of law from previous issues or disputes that have been resolved by the contemporary court systems of the United States. When a rule of law is established in a case for the first time, thereafter it is considered a precedent. Once a precedent is established, it may serve as an example or authority for resolving cases of a similar nature by a subsequent or lower court. A basic principle of case law is the use of precedents by the courts whereby they attempt to decide issues on the basis of principles established in previous legal cases or disputes of a similar nature. Although precedent does not bind the judges, it is considered highly influential in the judicial decision-making process.

Federal Judicial Law

The federal courts operate as the judicial arm of the federal government and have jurisdiction over U.S. constitutional law, federal legislative law, and federal administrative law issues. The U.S. Constitution authorizes the existence of the federal court system, which derives its powers from the Constitution and from subsequent legislation passed by the U.S. Congress.

Article III, Section 1, of the Constitution provides for the establishment of the judicial branch of government through the creation of one Supreme Court of the United States in which it vests the judicial power of the United States.

Acting within the authority of this constitutional provision, the U.S. Congress passed the Judiciary Act of 1789, which provided for a Supreme Court consisting of a chief justice and five associate justices. Additionally, this act divided the nation into 13 judicial districts, which were further divided into three circuits: southern, middle, and northern. Subsequent expansion of the nation from the original 13 states resulted in Congress authorizing the appointment of circuit judges who rode the circuit once every two years. In 1891, however, Congress established nine intermediate appellate courts of appeals, which were staffed with their own judges, and in 1911, Congress enacted the Judicial Code, which established a three-level hierarchical system of federal courts. The latest revision of the structure of the federal courts was in 1982 when Congress authorized the creation of the 12th circuit court of appeals (a split in the fifth circuit court of appeals). Moreover, Congress created other specialized courts that have specific functions.

A person involved in a dispute or controversy concerning a constitutional issue or a federal law (statutory or administrative) may seek a resolution through the federal courts. The case will be tried in the federal district court of jurisdiction. In Texas, there are four federal district courts—Northern, Southern, Eastern and Western. If either the plaintiff or defendant is dissatisfied with the decision of the federal district court, they may appeal to the U.S. Court of Appeals in that jurisdiction. (Texas is in the Fifth Circuit.) If the appeal is accepted, i.e., the court grants *certiorari*, the case is reviewed and a decision is reached. Again, if either party, the plaintiff or defendant, in the case is dissatisfied with the decision of the U.S. Appeals Court, an appeal can be made to the U.S. Supreme Court; however, *certiorari*, i.e., a successful appeal to the U.S. Supreme Court, is rarely granted except in those cases or issues of national significance.

The basic function of the federal courts is to settle disputes between two or more parties as permitted by the Constitution and the laws enacted by Congress. The types of disputes that can be resolved by the federal courts are set forth in Article III, Section 2, of the U.S. Constitution which states:

> The judicial power [of the federal courts] shall extend to all Cases, in Law and Equity, arising under this Constitution, [and] the Laws of the United States . . . to Controversies to which the United States shall be a Party;— . . . [and] between Citizens of different States . . . the supreme Court shall have appellate Jurisdiction both as to Law and Fact, with such Exceptions, and under such Regulations as the Congress shall make.

The hierarchical organizational structure of the federal court system serves two important purposes. First, the U.S. Supreme Court and the U.S. Circuit Courts of Appeals can remedy improper judicial conduct (of the trial judge, attorneys, and jury) and correct judicial errors that have been made in reaching decisions in the U.S. District Courts. Second, these higher courts of appeals serve to assure uniformity of decisions within their jurisdiction by reviewing cases where two or more lower courts have reached different or conflicting decisions. The D.C. Circuit is the most important federal appellate circuit, for it is located in Washington and hears cases that deal with the government. For additional information on the federal court system, go to http://www.uscourts.gov.

State Judicial Law

The state constitutions and state legislatures in each of the 50 states provide the structure and functions of the judicial system. All state constitutions provide for a court of final jurisdiction, i.e., a state supreme court, except for New Hampshire where the highest court was established by the state legislature in accordance with authority granted under its state constitution.

State judicial systems are not identical, but they are similar in their general structure and functions (in fact, they are similar to the federal judicial system in structure). Figure 1.1 compares the structure of the federal and Texas state court systems. For additional information on the court system in Texas, go to http://www.txcourts.gov/. Let us now turn our attention to the influence of federal and state government over education.

◆ FEDERAL GOVERNMENT INVOLVEMENT IN EDUCATION

During the formation of the United States, as a result of a national interest in education the Continental Congress enacted the Ordinance of 1785. It provided that "there shall be reserved the lot No. 16 of every township for the maintenance of public schools, within said township," in the land of the Northwest Territory later known as the states of Indiana, Illinois, Michigan, Ohio, Wisconsin, and a part of Minnesota. Two years later, the Ordinance of 1787 was passed, which provided for the sale of land by federal contract to the Ohio Development Company that reserved a certain township in each territory for the endowment of a university, and expressed the national policy toward education which stated that "Religion, morality and knowledge being necessary to good government shall forever encouraged."

The original U.S. Constitution did not include a provision for a national system of education. Despite the efforts of Presidents Jefferson (1806) and Madison (1817), the adoption of a constitutional amendment granting the federal government control over education in

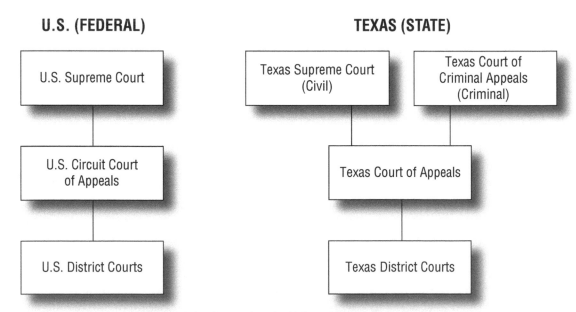

Figure 1.1 Comparing the U.S. and Texas Court Systems

the nation (Quattlebaum, 1952) was neither seriously considered nor adopted. Therefore, by interpretation of the Tenth Amendment to the U.S. Constitution, education should be a state function.

Even though the federal government is precluded from directly participating in or controlling public and private education in the 50 state systems, this does not and has not prevented the national government from becoming involved and influential in education. The federal government influences education in four ways:

- Through the application and guarantees of the U.S. Constitution that are enforced by the courts via judicial review as explained in Chapter 1;
- By providing federal aid to the states and school districts in a variety of ways. For instance, under the authority of Article I, Section 8 of the U.S. Constitution, Congress can levy taxes to provide for the general welfare and common defense of the United States. Acting under this authority, Congress has passed a host of legislation that established programs with incentives and categorical grants aimed at influencing the states to develop and implement special educational programs for specific populations of students or for other particular purposes that serve the national interest;
- By the studies and reports issued by federal government commissions on education appointed by the President, cabinet members, or Congress; and
- By the administrative and regulatory functions of various agencies of the federal government, such as the U.S. Department of Education, over programs funded by Congress.

Federal government support and influence over education emanates from the following sources: (a) federal grants to the states and educational agencies, which are provided for under the implied authority given to Congress by the General Welfare Clause of Article I, Section 9, Clause 1, of the U.S. Constitution; (b) interstate and intrastate standards or regulations that Congress imposes upon the states under the authority of the Commerce Clause of Article I, Section 8, Clause 3 of the U.S. Constitution; and (c) federal court judicial review; i.e., the right under common law for the federal courts to review state laws and actions which are charged with conflicting with or violating the constitutionally protected rights and freedoms of individuals or states. A brief discussion of each of these powers and sources of federal government influence follows.

The General Welfare Clause

Article I, Section 8 (Clause 1) of the Constitution, states "The Congress shall have power to lay and collect taxes . . . and provide for the common defense and general welfare of the United States . . ." This constitutional provision has served as the legal foundation upon which Congress has relied to pass laws and appropriate federal tax monies to support and influence education within the states. As a result of this constitutional provision, states may enter into contracts with the federal government and its agencies (most specifically, the Department of Education) for federal funds for specific educational purposes. However, once a state government or any of its agencies accepts federal monies, whether as a grant or as a result of a contract with a federal governmental agency, it is bound by all federal laws, rules, regulations, guidelines, procedures, etc., (i.e., federal administrative laws) associated with the monies.

There have been many unsuccessful challenges to the right of the federal government to provide public tax monies to the states under Article I, Section 8, Clause 1 as well as many unsuccessful challenges to the right of the federal government to enforce compliance with federal laws associated with government grants and contracts [U.S Department of Education (USDE), 2009]. These two issues are at the center of most of the conflicts and misunderstandings concerning the federal role and influence over education in the states.

The Commerce Clause

Under the implied powers of the Commerce Clause, Article I, Section 8, Clause 3, which states that Congress shall have the power "[t]o regulate Commerce . . . among the several States . . ." the federal government has influenced education in the states through congressional legislation primarily in the areas of employment, labor regulations, and transportation. The broad interpretation concerning the meaning of commerce was explicated by Chief Justice Marshall in *Gibbons v. Ogden* in which he ruled in the majority opinion of the Court that ". . . Commerce among the states must, of necessity, be commerce within the states . . . The power of Congress, then, whatever it may be, must be exercised within the territorial jurisdiction of the several states . . . It is the power to regulate; that is, to prescribe the rule by which commerce is to be governed. This power, like all others vested in Congress, is complete in itself, may be exercised to its utmost extent, and acknowledges no limitations other than those prescribed in the Constitution . . ."

In the *National League of Cities v. Usery* case, a challenge was made concerning the applicability of the 1974 amendments to the Fair Labor Standards Act to the states which extended wage and hour standards to almost all public employees, including school district employees. While admitting that the amendments were within the scope of the Commerce Clause, the Supreme Court held that the Tenth Amendment to the U.S. Constitution was violated. The decision enunciated a restrictive view of the Commerce Clause and interpreted the Tenth Amendment as a clear limiting force upon the power of Congress to regulate activities of a state government or its agencies. However, in *Garcia v. San Antonio Metropolitan Transit Authority* (1985), the Supreme Court overturned the ruling in the *National League of Cities v. Usery* case. The Court ruled that the federal government does have the authority to enforce the Commerce Clause found in Article I, Section 3, of the U.S. Constitution. The majority opinion delivered by Justice Blackmun stated that:

> Insofar as the present cases are concerned, then, we need go no further than to state that we perceive nothing in the overtime and minimum-wage requirements of the FLSA [Fair Labor Standards Act] as applied to SAMA [San Antonio Metropolitan Transit Authority], that is destructive to state sovereignty or violative of any constitutional provision.

Judicial Review

The third basic source of federal influence over education in the states is through the federal courts. A basic power of the federal courts is the right of judicial review—the power of the courts, and ultimately the U.S. Supreme Court, to review and declare both federal and state laws unenforceable for being in violation of the U.S. Constitution. Also, those individuals who feel that their constitutionally protected rights and freedoms have been violated by a state agency or its officials can seek redress in federal court in the form of damages under the Civil Rights Act of 1871 (42 U.S.C. § 1983) which states:

> Every person who, under color of any statute, ordinance, regulation, custom, or usage, of any State or Territory, subjects, or causes to be subjected, any citizen of the United States or other person within the jurisdiction thereof to the deprivation of any rights, privileges, or immunities secured by the Constitution and laws, shall be liable to the party injured in an action at law, suit in equity, or other proper proceeding for redress.

Professor Charles L. Black (1960) of the Yale Law School eloquently explained the nature of judicial review:

> In the course of a judicial proceeding, it may happen that one of the litigants relies on a statute or other governmental pronouncement which the other litigant contends to be repugnant to some provision of the Constitution. It is the task of the court to determine what the law is. If the constitution is a law of superior status, then the rule of the Constitution, and not the rule of the statute or other governmental pronouncement, is the correct rule of law for application to the case before the court. The Court, under our system, therefore, considers itself bound to follow the rule of the Constitution, and so to treat the other rule as a nullity. (p. 12)

The U.S. Supreme Court, in the case of *Marbury v. Madison*, established the power of judicial review over federal statutes. Congress passed the Judicial Act of 1801 on February 3 of that year, which relieved Supreme Court judges of circuit court duty, increased the number of circuit court judges, and created a number of minor judicial positions. President Adams, during his last 16 days in office, proceeded to fill the newly created 67 judgeships with people loyal to his political party. Upon taking office, the incensed Jeffersonian party repealed the Judiciary Act of 1801 on March 8, 1802, which in effect restored the Judiciary Act of 1789. As a result, the Supreme Court judges were returned to circuit court duty and all of the newly created judgeships and positions were abolished.

When the Supreme Court convened, the case of *Marbury v. Madison* was on the docket. Marbury was one of the judges appointed by President Adams under the Judiciary Act of 1801 whose commission was not delivered by James Madison, the Secretary of State when Jefferson took office as President of the United States. Marbury filed a suit asking the Supreme Court to issue a *writ of mandamus* to compel the issuance of his commission as judge. The right to issue such a writ was conferred upon the Supreme Court by the Judiciary Act of 1789. Chief Justice Marshall of the Supreme Court, speaking for the majority of the Court, ruled that even though the issuance of the *writ of mandamus* was a proper remedy in this case, the section of the Judiciary Act of 1789 granting the Supreme Court the authority to issue such a writ was void. Thus, the doctrine of judicial review, that is, the power of the Supreme Court to declare laws of Congress unconstitutional, was established. A portion of Chief Justice Marshall's opinion that dealt with the issue concerning the power of the federal courts to invalidate acts of Congress follows:

> It is emphatically the province and duty of the judicial department to say what the law is. Those who apply the rule to particular cases, must of necessity expound and interpret that rule. If two laws conflict with each other, the courts must decide on the operation of each . . . So if a law be in opposition to the Constitution; if both the law and the Constitution apply to a particular case,

so that the court must either decide that case conformably to the law, disregarding the constitution, or conformably to the Constitution, disregarding the law, the court must determine which of these conflicting rules governs the case. This is the very essence of judicial duty . . . [1 Cranch 137; 2 L.Ed. 60 (1803)]

◆ FEDERAL LAWS AND CONSTITUTIONAL PROVISIONS

Although the U.S. Constitution contains no reference to education, its first 10 amendments (the Bill of Rights) and the Fourteenth Amendment assure state control of education and the secularization of public education in the respective states. The First and Fourteenth Amendments of the Constitution have had a definite impact on education. The First Amendment guarantees to each individual (including students and personnel) the right to freedom of religion, expression (speech and press), association (right to peaceably assemble), and the right to petition the government for a redress of grievances. The Fourteenth Amendment specifically defines citizenship in the states and nation, makes the U.S. Constitution (especially the Bill of Rights) applicable to the states and prohibits the states from denying to any person equal protection under the laws or depriving them of their life, liberty, or property without providing due process of law. Based upon these two amendments, the federal courts (especially the Supreme Court) have rendered many important decisions influencing the direction and implementation of education in the states. Among these are decisions concerning the rights of parents to send their children to private or parochial schools, the use of public funds to support private and religious education, prohibiting the teaching or practice of religion in public schools, and providing all students with equal access to public educational facilities.

◆ SELECTED FEDERAL COURT DECISIONS AFFECTING EDUCATION IN THE STATES

Table 1.4 lists some of the important U.S. Supreme Court decisions that have affected public education, specifically with regard to parental rights, the use of public funds to support private or religious schools, religion in public schools, and equal access to education. Other important case law and legal concepts are discussed in subsequent chapters of this book.

TABLE 1.4
Selected Supreme Court Rulings Affecting American Public Education

---

Pierce v. Society of Sisters. The law passed by the Oregon Legislature in 1922 [268 U.S. 510 (1925)]requiring all children to attend public school was unconstitutional.

Cochran v. Louisiana State Board. A state law that provides that textbooks purchased with of Education [281 U.S. 370 (1930)] public funds may be furnished to students attending parochial schools does not violate the U.S. Constitution.

Everson v. Board of Education. A New Jersey school district could use locally raised [330 U.S. 1 (1943)] public tax monies to reimburse parents for bus fares expended to transport their children to parochial schools.

Aguilar v. Felton. New York City's program that sent public school teachers [473 U.S. 402 (1985)] into parochial schools to provide "neutral" remedial education to disadvantaged children pursuant to Title I of the Elementary and Secondary Education Act of 1965 was in violation of the Establishment Clause of the U.S. Constitution.

Agostini v. Felton. The Court overturned its decision in the Aguilar v. Felton [521 U.S. 203 (1997)] case.

School District of Abington. The recitation of prayers that are demanded, encouraged, Township v. Schempp and/or held by school personnel violates the Establishment Murray v. Curlett Clause of the First Amendment.[374 U.S. 203 (1963)].

Zorach v. Clausen. Releasing children from public school to attend religious [343 U.S. 306 (1952)] exercises is permissible within state laws and school board policies and rules.

People ex rel. McCollum v. Board. Religious instruction cannot be conducted on public of Education of School District school property. No. 71, Champaign, Illinois [333 U.S. 68 (1948)]

Lemon v. Kurtzman. Established a test to determine whether a law or practice [403 U.S. 602 (1971)] will withstand an establishment clause challenge: it must have a secular purpose, its primary effect is to neither advance nor inhibit the practice of religion and it does not result in excessive government entanglement with religion.

Stone v. Graham. Placing the Ten Commandments in public school class [449 U.S. 39 (1980)] rooms or on the walls in public schools is unconstitutional.

Wallace v. Jafree. The addition of the phrase "or prayer" to the law [105 S.Ct. 2479 (1985)] authorizing silent meditation was an unconstitutional attempt by the state legislators to restore prayer to public schools.

Edwards v. Aguillard. A state statute that requires that creation science be [107 S.Ct. 2573 (1987)]taught when evolution is taught violates the Establishment Clause of the U.S. Constitution.

Lee v. Weisman. Prayer at school functions such as extra-curricular [504 U.S. 577 (1992)] activities, graduation ceremonies, athletic events, etc. is impermissible unconstitutional activity. However, student-initiated and student-conducted prayer that does not have the coercion or encouragement of school officials is permissible.

Santa Fe ISD v. Doe. A school policy that permits student-initiated prayer at [120 S.Ct. 2266, *2273 (2000)] football games violates the Establishment Clause of the U.S. Constitution.

Brown v. Board of Education of Education. The maintenance of "separate but equal" schools for Topeka, Kansas White and Black students is unconstitutional and must be [347 U.S. 483 (1954)] corrected.

Brown v. Board of Education. De jure segregation must be corrected with "all deliberate Topeka, Kansas, Brown II speed." The Court placed desegregation of schools in [394 U.S. 294 (1955)] each community under the jurisdiction of the federal district courts.

Mitchell, et al. v. Helms, et al. Used a modified Lemon test in ruling that some direct, U.S. 793; 120 S.Ct. 2530; 147 L.Ed. nonincidental 530 U.S. 793; 120 S.Ct. government aid to 2d 660; 2000 U.S. LEXIS 4485 religious schools is permissible under the Establishment Clause so long as the aid is made available to both religious and secular beneficiaries on a nondiscriminatory basis. The Court found that with respect to governmental aid to religious schools, neither the divertibility nor the actual diversion of the aid to religious indoctrination violates the Establishment Clause so long as the aid is not itself unsuitable for use in the public schools because of religious content and eligibility for aid is determined in a constitutionally permissible manner.

Parents' Rights to Choose Public or Private Schools

In the seminal case, *Pierce v. Society of Sisters*, the Supreme Court ruled that the law passed by the Oregon legislature in 1922 requiring all school-aged children to attend public school was unconstitutional. The court reasoned that such a law denied parents the right to control the education of their children and that the law, in effect, deprived the private schools of their property without due process as guaranteed under the Fourteenth Amendment. Because of this ruling, children can meet the requirements of compulsory school attendance by attending either public or private schools. Thus, two systems of education—public and private—have continued to coexist in the United States. This ruling also strengthened a state's authority to enact compulsory school attendance policy; regulate all of its schools, both public and private; and specify curriculum requirements.

Use of Public Funds for Private or Religious Education

There have been numerous cases adjudicated before the federal courts involving the use of public funds to support private or religious education directly or indirectly. Prominent among them are the *Cochran* and *Everson* cases. In the *Cochran v. Louisiana State Board of Education* case, the Supreme Court held that a state law that provided for furnishing textbooks to children attending parochial schools that were purchased with public monies did not violate the U.S. Constitution. Further, in the *Everson v. Board of Education* case, the Supreme Court ruled that a New Jersey school district could use locally raised public tax monies to reimburse parents for bus fares expended to transport their children to parochial schools. In both of these cases, the Court based its decision on the "Child Benefit Theory," which played a very important role in settling issues related to state provision of financial support to parochial school students. The Court held that where the state legislation is primarily for the benefit of the student rather than for the parochial school, the aid would be upheld. The effect of this ruling was to strengthen a state's authority to regulate all of its schools, both public and private, and to specify curriculum requirements.

Over the years, the highest courts in some states, e.g., Alaska, Wisconsin, Oklahoma, Delaware, and Oregon, have struck down laws authorizing either transportation or textbooks for children attending parochial (denominational) schools. However, on June 23, 1997, the U.S. Supreme Court appears to have heralded a new era of cooperation and communication between public and private school officials (*Agostini v. Felton*). In this case, the court held that New York City's program that sent public school teachers into parochial schools to provide "neutral" remedial education to disadvantaged children pursuant to Title I of the Elementary and Secondary Education Act of 1965 did not violate the Establishment Clause of the First Amendment to the U.S. Constitution. Applying the *Lemon* Test, the Supreme Court admittedly reversed its decision on the previous case involving this issue (*Aguilar v. Felton*). In litigation in 2000 (*Mitchell v. Helms*), the Supreme Court was asked to render a decision regarding the constitutionality of Chapter 2 of the Educational Consolidation and Improvement Act of 1981 (20 USCS 7301-7373) under which Louisiana Parish loaned materials to private schools. The court applied a modified *Lemon* Test ruling that this practice, as applied under Chapter 2, did not violate the Establishment Clause of the First Amendment. It reasoned that the legislation had a secular purpose, having neither the effect of advancing nor endorsing religion. The court's decision did not result in religious indoctrination by the government; recipients were not defined by reference to religion, and it did not create excessive government entanglement with religion.

More recently, the constitutionality of providing parents with publicly funded vouchers reached the forefront at both the state and federal levels. Voucher programs give public funds to parents, in the form of a voucher, which enables them to select a public or private school for their children. In some cases, the private schools may include sectarian schools. Various states have enacted statutory provisions ranging from prohibiting vouchers altogether to restricting them to public schools (Kemerer, 1997). For example, in Ohio in 1995, the Cleveland city school district came under state control because of the poor performance of the district's schools. Ohio, then, implemented a program providing tuition scholarship vouchers to some students residing in the Cleveland school district enabling them to attend participating public or private schools selected by their parents. Both public and private schools were eligible to participate in the program, which included tuition assistance to parents based upon financial need, and parents had complete discretion as to where they spent the scholarship funds. By the 1999–2000 school year, 82% of the participating private schools were religiously affiliated, and none of the adjacent public schools chose to participate. In addition, 96% of the students participating in the program enrolled in religiously affiliated private schools. As a result, a group of Ohio taxpayers sued to bar the implementation of the scholarship program because it violated the Establishment Clause of the First Amendment of the U.S. Constitution (*Zelman v. Simmons-Harris*, 2002). The Supreme Court disagreed, ruling that the Ohio program providing tuition aid in the form of scholarship vouchers for some students to attend a public or private school of their parent's choosing did not violate the Establishment Clause of the First Amendment.

In the second special session of the 79th Texas Legislature, a joint resolution was proposed calling for the amendment of Section 7 of the Texas constitution, which stipulates that "No money shall be appropriated, or drawn from the Treasury for the benefit of any sect, or religious society, theological or religious seminary; nor shall property belonging to the State be appropriated for any such purposes." The proposed amendment was designed to prohibit the appropriation of public funds for, or authorization of, a publicly funded voucher program "under which state or local public revenue is used to pay all or any part of the costs of a student's attendance at a private school" (H.J.R. 27, 2005). The amendment was referred to the Select Committee on Public Education Reform where no further action was taken. In 2009 during the 81st session, Texas legislators sought to amend Chapter 29 of the Education Code by adding Subchapters J and K that would allow specified students to use state-funded vouchers to attend public or private schools. Specifically, legislators proposed four bills that would (1) create a public education voucher pilot program for certain children (HB 41), create a school choice program for certain students with disabilities (HB 716), address accessibility for certain students with autism or autism spectrum disorder (SB 1301), and enhance services for certain students with autism or autism spectrum disorder as well as training and support for educators who serve students with autism (SB 2204).

During the 83rd legislative session (2013), the issue of vouchers re-emerged amid unwavering opposition. Three voucher bills were proposed but did not pass: (1) creation of Equal Opportunity Scholarships through private companies in exchange for tax credits for donations to a third-party entity responsible for awarding the scholarships; (2) creation of a traditional voucher system for students with disabilities; and (3) implementation of Taxpayer Savings Grants to provide students with vouchers equaling 60% of the average amount of per-student expenditure in Texas. As predicted by some legislative observers, the issue of vouchers emerged again during the 84th legislative session (2015). The Senate debated three school voucher bills, all of which failed to pass. Senate Bill 4 (SB 4) would have allowed students in low-income districts to transfer to private or religious schools by allowing tax credits for business who donated money to private school scholarships. Senate Bill 276 (SB 276), a more traditional voucher bill, would award state money to pay private school tuition in the form of grants. The third bill, Senate Bill 642 (SB 642), was designed to fund private school tuition scholarships by giving tax credits to businesses that donated to a nonprofit scholarship fund. The continued proposal of school voucher bills for consideration by the Texas Legislature underscores a consistent interest of proponents to include vouchers as part of the school choice landscape. It remains to be seen how the courts will rule in litigation concerning school vouchers in Texas.

Religion in Public Schools

The First Amendment to the U.S. Constitution requires that the government remain neutral in matters of religion. Sometimes the issue of neutrality is not clear, which has presented a challenge for the courts. While the Court has held that Bible reading in public schools for academic or literary purposes is constitutional, it has also held that it is unconstitutional for religious purposes (*School District of Abington Township v. Schempp* and *Murray v. Curlett*). The Court has ruled that the recitation of prayers that are demanded, encouraged, or held by school personnel violates the Establishment Clause of the First Amendment to the U.S. Constitution. In earlier years, the Supreme Court ruled that it is permissible within state laws and school board policies to release children from public school to attend religious instruction (*Zorach v. Clausen*) but that religious instruction cannot be held on public school property (*People ex rel. McCollum v. Board of Education of School District No. 71*, Champaign, Illinois).

In 1971, the Supreme Court developed a set of guidelines, called the *Lemon* Test, for determining the constitutionality of a law or practice in the public schools (*Lemon v. Kurtzman*). Under these guidelines, a law or practice must satisfy all three of the following conditions in order to pass constitutional muster: (1) its purpose must be secular in nature and intent; (2) its primary effect must neither advance nor inhibit the practice of religion; and (3) it must not result in excessive government entanglement with religion. Using the *Lemon* Test, the Court has ruled that placing the Ten Commandments in public school classrooms or on the walls in the public schools is unconstitutional (*Stone v. Graham*). The U.S. Supreme Court also applied the *Lemon* test in each of the following cases.

In 1992 (*Lee v. Weisman*), the Supreme Court ruled that prayer at school functions such as extra-curricular activities, graduation ceremonies, athletic events, etc. is an impermissible unconstitutional activity. However, student-initiated and student-conducted prayer that does not have the coercion or encouragement of school officials is permissible so long as it is not proselytizing, it is nonsectarian, and does not bear the imprimatur of the school or its officials (*Jones v. Clear Creek I.S.D.*, 1992; *cert. denied*, 1993). In another case regarding student-initiated prayer (*Santa Fe ISD v. Doe*, 2000), the Supreme Court ruled that a policy that permits student-initiated prayer at football games violates the First and Fourteenth Amendments to the U.S. Constitution. It reasoned that such a policy establishes an improper majoritarian election of religion and creates the perception of school district endorsement of student prayer.

In 1985, the Supreme Court was petitioned to rule on an Alabama statute authorizing public schools to set aside time for silent meditation or prayer (*Wallace v. Jafree*). The court concluded that the addition of the phrase "or prayer" to the law authorizing silent meditation was an unconstitutional attempt by the state legislators to restore prayer to its public schools. Similarly, a 2001 case (*Doe v. School Board of Ouachita Parish, et al.*) challenged a Louisiana statute that required school authorities to allow students and teachers to observe a "brief time in prayer or meditation." The circuit court ruled that the statute failed the secular prong of the *Lemon Test* and was, therefore, unconstitutional. During the 78th Legislative session in 2003, the Texas Legislature passed Senate Bill 83, which amended Section 25.082 of the state's education code. Among the changes was the addition of a provision for 1 minute of silence during which students may "reflect, pray, meditate, or engage in any other silent activity" that is not disruptive or distracting to others.

The parents of two minor children brought an action against Governor Perry challenging the constitutionality of the Texas minute of silence provision as violative of the Establishment Clause of the First Amendment (*Croft v. Perry*, 2009). Although similar to the *Ouachita Parish* case (*Doe v. School Board of Ouachita Parish, et al.*, 2001), the Fifth Circuit Court took a different approach than the U.S. Supreme Court, following the lead of the Eleventh Circuit and the Fourth Circuit courts (*Brown v. Gwinnett Country School Dist, 1997 and Brown v. Gilmore*, respectively). The court admittedly had the most difficulty with the secular legislative purpose prong of the *Lemon* test, given the evidence in the legislative history that some legislators were motivated to restore religion and prayer to Texas public schools. Nevertheless, the Fifth Circuit Court ultimately deferred to "the stated legislative intent . . . to promote patriotism and allow for a moment of quiet contemplation," both of which are deemed to be secular, and ruled in favor of the governor.

A second provision of the amendment to Section 25.082 of the Texas education code is a requirement that students in all public schools pledge allegiance to both the U.S. flag and the state flag each day to inculcate patriotism among public school students. Throughout the years, the courts have ruled on the constitutionality of such a practice. An important case addressing this issue is the *West Virginia Board of Education v. Barnette* case (1942) in which the U.S. Supreme Court struck down the resolution of a West Virginia board of education that required the flag salute as a regular activity in the public schools. All teachers and students were required to honor the nation by saluting the flag. Refusal to salute the flag was regarded as an act of insubordination punishable by expulsion. Readmission required compliance, and a student who had been expelled was considered "unlawfully absent" and his or her parents or guardians were subject to prosecution, fine, and incarceration. In overruling its decision in the *Gobitis* case, the Supreme Court held that compelling the flag salute and pledge by school authorities is a violation of the First and Fourteenth Amendments to the U.S. Constitution. It reasoned that neither the domestic tranquility nor war effort depended upon coercion of children to participate in a ceremony that would result in their fear of spiritual condemnation. Such would only defeat the purpose of the requirement and would be inconsistent with the purpose of the Constitution.

In 2004 (*Elk Grove Unified School District v. Newdow*), the Supreme Court was asked to rule on the constitutionality of a school district policy requiring teachers to lead willing students in reciting the Pledge of Allegiance, which includes the words "under God." The court sidestepped this issue by ruling that Newdow did not have standing to sue on his daughter's behalf. However, in separate concurring judgments, justices expressed the views that the policy neither violated the Establishment Clause nor the Free Exercise Clause since the practice was a patriotic exercise, rather than a religious one. In 2004 (*Frazier v. Winn*), a student, through his parents, challenged the provision of the Florida Pledge of Allegiance statute (Fla. Stat. Section 1003.44(1)) that requires all students to stand at attention during recitation of the pledge of allegiance, including students whose parents excused them from reciting the pledge. The Eleventh Circuit Court ruled that it is unconstitutional to require all students to stand at attention for the pledge of allegiance, but in recognizing the right of parents to control the upbringing of their children, ruled the requirement of parental consent constitutional.

In the spring of 2007, during its 80th session, the Texas Legislature passed House Bill 1034 by an overwhelming majority. The bill amends Section 3100.101 of the Government Code to insert the phrase "one state under God" in the pledge of allegiance to the Texas flag. Of the 13 states that have additional pledges unique to their individual states, five states— Kentucky, Louisiana, Mississippi, Tennessee, and Texas—reference "God" or divine grace. In an action separate from the minute of silence challenge, parents on behalf of their minor children brought legal action against the governor alleging that the insertion of "under God" in the Texas Pledge of Allegiance is an unconstitutional establishment of religion (*Croft v. Perry,* 604 F.Supp.2d 932) in violation of the Establishment Clause of the First Amendment. Using the *Lemon* test and finding no evidence of a legislative intent to establish religion by inserting the phrase "under God," the district court ruled in favor of the governor.

The Religious Viewpoints Antidiscrimination Act, or the Schoolchildren's Religious Liberties Act (H.B. 3678), was also passed during the 80th legislative session, effective with the 2007–2008 school year. The Act requires a school district to adopt a limited open forum and prohibits school officials from discriminating against students' voluntary expression of religious viewpoints, including class assignments, organization of religious groups and activities, and graduation and other school events. Through the Act, the legislature sought to clarify "the first amendment rights of students at school by codifying current court decisions regarding religious expression" (H.B. 3678, 2007). During the summer of 2007, the U.S. Supreme Court was asked to rule on the right of school principals to restrict student speech when a student refused to remove a banner, "Bong Hits for Jesus," which he hung at a school-sponsored, school-supervised event. The court ruled that school authorities do not violate the First Amendment when they prohibit student views that promote illegal drug use (*Morse v. Frederick,* 2007).

In a similar case in the southeast Texas town of Kountze, a group of cheerleaders asked the courts to determine whether banners containing bible verses displayed at football games is protected free speech. In 2012, the district initially determined that the banners could not be displayed after a complaint from the Freedom from Religion Foundation. Following debate at state and national levels the school district changed its position and allowed the banners, stipulating retention of the right to limit the content on such banners based on the view that they are government speech rather than private speech. In May of 2013, a state district judge ruled the banners were permissible, but was silent as to whether the district could regulate their content. At the state appellate level, the court ruled the lawsuit moot because the district had already amended its policy. The case is scheduled to be argued before the Texas Supreme Court in early 2016.

Equality of Student Access to Public Education

Some of the most pertinent uses of the Fourteenth Amendment to the U.S. Constitution have been via decisions by the Supreme Court in desegregation cases. At one time, there were 11 southern states with statutory laws mandating separation of the races, which is defined as *de jure* segregation. However, in most of the other states, there was evidence of racial separation called *de facto* segregation that occurs because of housing patterns, economic circumstances, religious and other preferences, etc., rather than as a direct result of statutory or administrative law. The judicial pronouncement in the *Brown v. Board of Education of Topeka, Kansas* case was that the maintenance of "separate but equal" schools for Black and White students was unconstitutional and had to be corrected. Furthermore, in its companion case, *Brown II, (Brown v. Board of Education of Topeka, Kansas, [1955]),* the court stated that *de jure* segregation (segregation by law) had to be corrected with "all deliberate speed." The Court also placed the desegregation of schools in each community under the jurisdiction of the federal district courts.

In 1964, the passage of the Civil Rights Act by Congress served to strengthen the impact of federal judicial decisions with regard to religious freedom and desegregation. In recent years, courts have been asked to rule on issues regarding whether or not school districts have met requirements for unitary status. In deliberating the issue, the courts have considered whether vestiges of past discrimination have been eliminated to the extent practicable (*Belk, et al. v. The Charlotte-Mecklenburg Board of Education*) and whether the school district has complied in good faith with the desegregation order (*Lee v. Alexander City Board of Education*). Courts have also used the *Green* factors in determining whether unitary status has been achieved. For example, in the *Lee* case, in addition to the constitutional standards, the Alexander City School Board was required to comply with a 1988 consent decree under which the district was to take specified actions to address areas in which further action was found to be required. The areas included students within schools and instruction; faculty hiring, assignment and promotion; administrative hiring, assignment and promotion; student discipline; extracurricular activities; dropout and graduation rates; and special education. The district court declared the Alexander City School System unitary, returning control to the school district, in all areas except hiring and promotion of higher-level administrators, rendering it partially unitary. Although it commended the board on its efforts to end *de jure* segregation in Alexander City, the court noted that since 1970, a Black principal had never been appointed at any district school, nor had there ever been more than one Black administrator employed at one time in the central administration. In June 2007 (*Parents Involved in Community Schools v. Seattle School District; Meredith v. Jefferson County Public Schools*), the U.S. Supreme Court ruled that school districts' use of race to assign students to schools violated students' equal protection rights. Although the district's goal was to ensure that schools' racial composition mirrored that of the district, the Court was not persuaded that racial balancing should become constitutional simply by labeling it "racial diversity."

The foregoing court cases highlight some of the most important issues the federal courts have been petitioned to resolve. Religion in public schools and ensuring that all children have equal access to education continue to be two controversial issues over which the federal courts exert considerable influence.

◆ FEDERAL LEGISLATION AFFECTING ELEMENTARY AND SECONDARY EDUCATION

Acting under the authority of Article I, Section 8, of the U.S. Constitution, Congress has passed legislation that has aided and influenced American education. However, the federal government interest and influence in education began long before the Constitution was adopted.

The land ordinances of the 1700s were Congress' initial means of funding and supporting education in the new nation. After 1800, as new states joined the newly formed United States, each received land grants for schools. These laws and policies, which came without any explicit constitutional authority to do so, established federal involvement in public education.

In response to public demands for improved and expanded agricultural, mechanical, and scientific educational programs in the nation's colleges and universities, Congress passed the Morrill Acts of 1862 and 1890. These laws provided land and federal funding for support of land grant colleges that specifically emphasized agriculture, mechanical arts, and military science. The second Morrill Act (1890) provided federal funds for these land grant institutions of higher learning.

Since the early 1900s, federal government involvement in education has been through the passage of legislation aimed at providing incentives (e.g., seed money, matching grants, and categorical grants) to the states and local educational systems for special programs that address the national interests, goals, and purposes. For instance, during the Great Depression between 1933 and 1938, a series of legislation was passed, and appropriations made, creating such programs as the Civilian Conservation Corps (CCC), the National Youth Administration (NYA), Federal Emergency Relief Administration (FERA), Public Works Administration (PWA), and the Works Progress Administration (WPA), which provided educational training and work for unemployed youth and adults, including rural teachers and other professionals. Those programs also provided money for the construction of public and school buildings but were terminated by the mid-1940s when the nation was facing the crisis of World War II.

At the end of World War II and the Korean Conflict, the United States entered into a Cold War with Russia. When the former Soviet Union launched Sputnik in 1957, the perception was that the nation needed a better educational system to effectively close the scientific gap between these two nations. There was tremendous pressure for the federal government to become more involved in funding education in the states. Congress responded by passing the National Defense Education Act (NDEA) of 1958, which emphasized the importance of education to the nation's defense. As part of this act, Congress provided funding for educational programs that emphasized instructional improvement in science, mathematics, foreign languages, and other critical subjects.

With the emergence of the civil rights movement in the 1960s, the emphasis shifted to equal rights for minorities, ending poverty, achieving racial integration of schools, and improving the education received by the "culturally and socially" disadvantaged. President Lyndon B. Johnson declared a "War on Poverty" under the umbrella of what he envisioned as the "Great Society." On August 20, 1964, Congress passed the Economic Opportunity Act (P.L. 88-452), which was designed to provide equality of opportunity for education, training, and employment. With the passage of this policy, the Head Start Program provided preschool education to disadvantaged poor children and families and other community-based programs. It was also under this policy that Congress passed the Elementary and Secondary Education Act (ESEA) of 1965 (P.L. 89-10) and the Civil Rights Act of 1964 (P.L. 88-352), which provided that all federal programs that were supported by federal monies must be operated and administered without discrimination. Later, Congress passed a series of legislation to support equal rights to educational opportunities, including the Emergency School Aid Act (ESAA) and the Bilingual Education Act in 1968.

In order to encourage the education of handicapped children, Congress passed three laws: Section 504 of the Rehabilitation Act of 1973 (P.L. 93-112), the Education for All Handicapped

Children Act (P.L. 94-142) in 1975, and the Americans with Disabilities Act of 1990. In 1990, P.L. 94-142 was amended and its name was changed to the Individuals with Disabilities Education Act (IDEA); in 1997, the IDEA was reauthorized making substantial changes to many aspects of the original law. The Americans with Disabilities Act of 1990 was a civil rights act that enlarged the scope of Section 504 of the Rehabilitation Act and was designed to protect the individuals with disabilities from discrimination by employers as well as state governments and their agencies. In 1981, with the passage of the Educational Consolidation and Improvement Act (ECIA), the focus of federal funding to states for educational purposes shifted from categorical to block grants, and states were granted more authority in regulating and managing federal funds and programs.

During President William Clinton's administration in 1994, Congress passed the Improving America's Schools Act (which reauthorized the ESEA and established the principle that disadvantaged children should achieve to the same challenging academic standards as other children) and the Goals 2000: Educate America Act (which supported state and local reform efforts based on challenging academic standards and assessments linked to those standards). These efforts began the transformation of the federal role in education by supporting the establishment of higher standards and the clear expectation that all children would reach those standards. Both laws built upon the premise that students and schools rise to the expectations and standards set for them. Therefore, these two laws not only complemented and accelerated existing reforms in many states but also provided a catalyst for change in states that had not yet established high academic standards.

Building on the 1994 reauthorization of the ESEA, President Clinton sent the Educational Excellence for All Children Act of 1999 (U.S. Department of Education, 1999) to Congress. The purpose of this legislation was to reaffirm the critical role of the federal government in working with schools, school districts, and states to foster educational excellence for all children based on a commitment to high classroom standards; improvement of teacher and principal quality to ensure quality instruction for all children; strengthening accountability for results; and ensuring safe, healthy, disciplined, and drug-free educational environments to which all children feel connected, motivated, and challenged to learn and where parents are welcomed and involved. To ensure that state policies and practices promote high-quality education for all children, ESEA requires that states receiving grants under this act adopt policies and programs to incorporate the above themes.

On January 8, 2002, President George W. Bush signed the No Child Left Behind Act (NCLB) into law. It was the most comprehensive reauthorization of the ESEA since 1965. This legislation expanded the initiative begun by President Clinton and ushered the nation into a new era of educating American children with federal government support. It also redefined the federal government's role in K-12 education with respect to the improvement of the academic achievement of all American children based on four principles: greater accountability for results; expanded state flexibility and local control; expanded educational choice options for parents and students, particularly those attending low-performing schools; and emphasis on teaching methods proven effective, with a particular focus on reading.

To meet the NCLB accountability requirements, states must implement statewide public school accountability systems affecting all public school students. Schools and districts failing to make adequate yearly progress (AYP) toward statewide proficiency goals will be subject to corrective action and restructuring methods designed to redirect efforts toward meeting state standards. The Act provides states and school districts greater flexibility in how they may utilize education funds, in exchange for stronger accountability for results. For example, states and local districts may transfer up to 50% of funding they receive under four major state grant programs—Teacher Quality State Grants, Educational Technology, Innovative Programs, and Safe and Drug-Free Schools—or to Title I (U.S. Department of Education, 2007).

NCLB significantly increases educational choices available to parents of students attending Title I schools failing to meet state standards. Specifically, local districts must give these students an opportunity to attend a higher performing public school, which may include public charter schools, within the district. The district is responsible for providing transportation to the chosen school and, if necessary, may use a minimum of 5% of its Title I funds for this purpose. To ensure that local districts provide meaningful choices, NCLB requires districts to spend a maximum of 20% of their Title I funds for school choice and supplemental educational services to eligible students. In order to stimulate improvement among low-performing schools, the supplemental service requirements provide that schools failing to make AYP for 5 years may be reconstituted under a restructuring plan.

Some educational observers have praised NCLB for raising awareness about educational inequalities nationwide. The law insists that all students are entitled to highly qualified teachers and has generated greater efforts to recruit teachers in areas where students have been impacted by high teacher turnover. However, despite its intent, some education observers maintain that funding supporting the law is insufficient to implement the law's requirements fully, while others point out that NCLB is not mandatory. School districts are not required to follow its mandates if they elect to forego the funding it provides. There is also a growing concern as to its ability to produce the human intellectual capital needed in order for the nation to remain competitive in the twenty-first century. After nearly 14 years since NCLB was signed into law, some decry its emphasis on testing, narrowing of the curriculum, and the practice of unfairly labeling many schools as failures, which makes it even more difficult for them to attract and retain qualified teachers. They assert that NCLB's requirement for disaggregating data by race tends to create incentives for schools to eliminate students at the bottom of each subgroup (Gamoran & Long, 2006; Henry, 2007).

Conversely, other observers admit that NCLB requires state governments to establish educational standards, but assert that it does not include provisions for addressing mediocre or ridiculous standards, although it includes sanctions if the standards are not met (Darling-Hammond, 2007; Finn, 2008). Building on the belief that the role of the federal government is to "support reform by encouraging bold, creative approaches to addressing underperforming schools, close the achievement gap, strengthening the field of education, reducing the dropout rate, and boosting college access," Arne Duncan, Education Secretary, convened a series of stakeholder meetings in Washington, DC from October to December 2009 to solicit public input as to how NCLB should be revised. His remarks on NCLB are available at http://www.ed.gov/news/speeches/2009/09/09242009.html (U.S. Department of Education Press Release, 2009). Speaking at an event celebrating the 50th anniversary of Congress passing ESEA, Secretary Duncan outlined the need for revisions to NCLB. His remarks are available at http://www.ed.gov/news/speeches/remarks-us-secretary-education-arne-duncan-50th-anniversary-congress-passing-elementary-and-secondary-education-act (U.S. Department of Education Press Release, 2015).

Although NCLB is still considered law, waivers have become more common as schools fail to meet the increasing standards. On September 30, 2013, Texas received approval to waive many NCLB requirements. This waiver eliminated the AYP designations and requirements to use 20% of Title I funds for supplemental instruction provided by external entities.

The 15% poorest performing schools will still require sanctions, and the state must address issues with their teacher and principal evaluations.

In 2014, Texas was asked to provide the USDE by May 2, 2014, an amended request incorporating final guidelines for teacher and principal evaluation and support systems that met the requirements of ESEA flexibility, including the use of student growth as a significant factor in determining a teacher's or principal's summative evaluation rating (TEA, 2014). Although Texas submitted the documentation to USDE on May 2, 2014, state agency leaders wanted an additional year in which to refine the teacher and principal evaluation systems being piloted. Therefore, Texas requested and was conditionally granted a continued waiver in May 2014 to continue piloting the evaluation systems. Through TEA, the state submitted final evaluation protocols to USDE in December 2014. In January, 2015, U.S. Assistant Secretary of Education Deborah S. Deslisle replied, "Texas has not yet adopted guidelines for teacher and principal evaluation and support systems that meet all requirements of ESEA flexibility, nor does it have a process for ensuring that each district in Texas develops, adopts, pilots, and implements teacher and principal evaluation and support systems consistent with those guidelines as required by ESEA flexibility" (D. S. Delisle, personal communication, January 7, 2015) On June 2, 2015, Texas resubmitted its flexibility request complete with detailed plans to implement teacher and principal evaluation systems (TEA, 2015). A copy of the Texas reply is available from http://www2.ed.gov/policy/elsec/guid/esea-flexibility/flex-renewal/index.html?exp=0.

In July of 2015, the U.S. Senate passed the Every Child Achieves Act (S.B. 1177) designed to reauthorize the Elementary and Secondary Education Act (ESEA). Proponents believe if enacted, the bill will significantly reduce the role of the federal government in public education and give states more flexibility in the process. Other observers are more reserved in their predictions of its effects. For a summary of the bill, go to http://www.help.senate.gov/imo/media/The_Every_Child_Achieves_Act_of_2015--summary.pdf. The text of the bill may be accessed at http://www.help.senate.gov/imo/media/S_EveryChildAchievesActof2015.pdf.

◆ REGULATORY FUNCTIONS OF THE U.S. DEPARTMENT OF EDUCATION

Over the years, various commissions, appointed by the President or by cabinet members, most notably the U.S. Department of Education, have examined issues and produced reports that have influenced education across the nation. In 1867, congressional law created the first Department of Education, and President Andrew Johnson appointed Henry Barnard as the first U.S. Commissioner of Education. This new department was attached to the Department of Interior instead of being granted cabinet level status. Its major functions under the direction of its Commissioner were:

- collecting such statistics and facts as shall show the condition and progress of education in the several states and territories;
- diffusing such information respecting the organization and management of schools and school systems, and methods of teaching, as shall aid the people of the United States in the establishment and maintenance of efficient school systems; and
- otherwise [promoting] the cause of education throughout the country (Quattlebaum, 1952).

On February 25, 1870, U.S. Senator George F. Hoar of Massachusetts introduced a bill to create a national educational system. The bill, H.R. 1326, specifically called for a national system of compulsory education, appointment of a state superintendent of national schools in each state by the President, and for dividing the states into school districts along congressional district lines. The bill also included the appointment of a division inspector and a local superintendent of national schools within each district who were appointed by the Secretary of Interior. Although this bill aroused somewhat positive reactions in the northern states, reactions in the South were considerably more negative amid concerns that it would destroy local control over education and inflame racial tensions and issues. Such concerns still exist today because of the concern that federal aid means federal government control accompanied by loss of state and or local autonomy over a function that is reserved to the states. The Hoar Bill neither received adequate support, nor was it ever enacted by Congress (Knight, 1953).

Between 1867 and 1953, the U.S. Office of Education went through numerous name changes and primarily performed only those duties and functions assigned to it by the original law. On April 11, 1953, with the passage of Public Law 83-13, Congress created the U.S. Department of Health, Education, and Welfare (HEW) and the Office of Education became an integral unit of this cabinet-level department, with the Commissioner of Education as its executive officer. In 1979, under Public Law 96-88, the Department of Education Organization Act, passed by Congress and signed into law by President James Carter on October 17, 1979, granted authority to establish a cabinet-level U.S. Department of Education with a Secretary of Education as its executive officer. On May 4, 1980, the U.S. Department of Education became formally operational under its first secretary, Shirley M. Hufstedler.

When President Ronald Reagan was elected in November 1980, he appointed Terrell H. Bell to serve as the Secretary of Education. In his first "State of the Union" address to Congress in January 1981, President Reagan reaffirmed his intent to dismantle the U.S. Department of Education, deferring responsibility for education to local school systems, teachers, parents, citizens, boards, and state governments. He asserted, "[b]y eliminating the Department of Education we can . . . ensure that local needs and preferences rather than the wishes of Washington determine the education of our children." The President's effort at eliminating the U.S. Department of Education created considerable debate and resistance by Congress, and many others in the educational profession, as well as the public. The issue was finally dropped, and the U.S. Department of Education survived.

Today, as a cabinet-level agency of the executive branch of the federal government, the U.S. Department of Education has experienced a substantial increase in its responsibilities. For example, it is responsible for (1) establishing policies on federal financial aid for education and distributing and monitoring the funds expended; (2) collecting data on American schools and disseminating research; (3) focusing national attention on key educational issues; and (4) prohibiting discrimination and ensuring equal access to education. Through these responsibilities, it assists the President in executing national policies and implementing laws enacted by Congress. The officials of the Department of Education also have the authority and responsibility, as do the officials of other cabinets and agencies of the federal government, for drafting regulations, guidelines, and procedures to implement federal laws that create and fund federal programs. Once drafted, the regulations are submitted to the appropriate congressional committees for approval, published in the Federal Register, and eventually inserted into the Federal Administrative Code to carry the weight of administrative law.

States and local agencies are required to submit proposals and plans to the various departments and agencies in order to acquire federal program monies. If the proposals and plans are accepted and approved, the state or local agency enters into a contract with the federal agency pledging to comply with the federal law and agency regulations, guidelines, and procedures. The administering federal agency has the authority and responsibility to perform periodic audits to ensure that the legislation and regulations are being followed by the state or local agency receiving the federal monies.

Figure 1.2 depicts the current organizational structure of the U.S. Department of Education. Its mission under President Obama's administration is to promote student achievement and preparation for global competitiveness by fostering educational excellence while ensuring equal access. This mission is carried out in two major ways: (1) through the leadership of the Secretary and the Department in the ongoing dialogue about how to improve the results of our educational system for all students and (2) by pursuing the goals of access and excellence through the administration of programs that address every area of education, ranging from preschool education through postdoctoral research.

In 2009, as with previous presidential administrations, the Department of Education underwent organizational changes to reflect the goals and objectives of the new administration. For example, the Office of Communications and Outreach was established to provide leadership for the Department of Education in communications and outreach activities. It was designed to engage a wide variety of stakeholders, e.g., the public, education, community, business, parent, academic, student, and other groups, including the media, intergovernmental and interagency organizations, and public advocacy groups in the federal education agenda.

Risk Management Service is charged with "identifying risks and taking effective action to manage and mitigate risks that may adversely affect the advancement of the Department's mission" (U.S. Department of Education, 2009). Four teams assist this office in carrying out its responsibilities:

- Grants Policy and Procedures Team
- Program Risk Management and Monitoring Team
- Management Improvement Team
- Customer Service Team

The Office of Planning, Evaluation and Policy Development (OPEPD) serves to advise the Education Secretary on all matters relative to the policy development and review; performance measurement and evaluation; budget processes and proposals (U.S. Department of Education, 2009). The Office of Safe and Drug-Free Schools is the principal advisor to the Education Secretary concerning matters regarding safe and drug-free schools and character education programs. It represents the Department of Education at national and international meetings relative to safe and drug-free schools and character education. The Office also administers, coordinates, and recommends policy for improving the quality and excellence of programs and activities designed to provide financial assistance for drug and violence prevention activities as well as those that provide for the health and well being of elementary and secondary students and those in institutions of higher education.

The Office of English Language Acquisition advises the Education Secretary on matters concerning the education of linguistically and culturally diverse students. The office is responsible for administering specified programs authorized under Title III of the No Child Left Behind Act of 2001 (NCLB) and for administering the foreign language assistance program

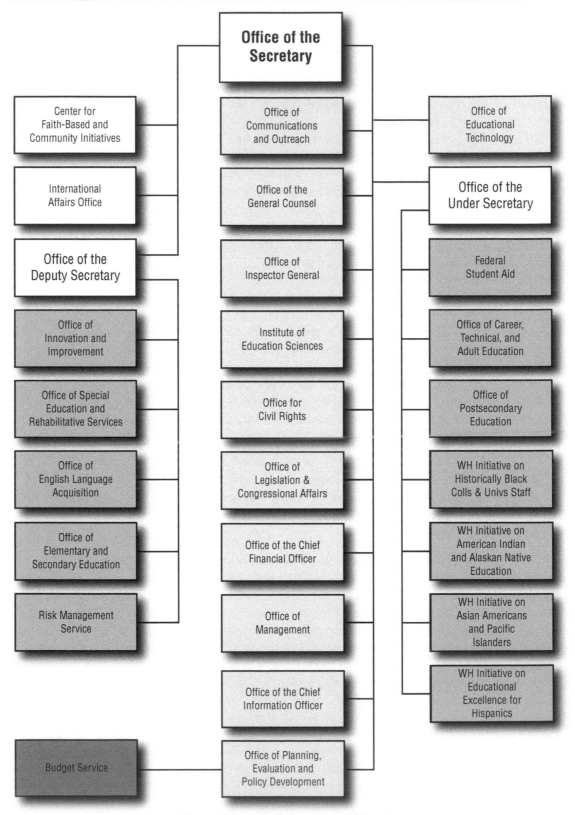

Figure 1.2 U.S. Department of Education

authorized by Title V or NCLB. In addition, it develops and implements "policy and National dissemination reports of the bilingual education programs that serve the limited English proficient (LEP) children and adults (U.S. Department of Education, 2009). For a comprehensive overview of all Department of Education offices, go to http://www.ed.gov/about/offices/list/index.html?src=ln.

◆ LEGAL BASIS FOR STATE CONTROL OVER EDUCATION

During the colonial period, before the adoption of the U.S. Constitution, parents were primarily responsible for educating their children. Since the colonial educational system was modeled after the English educational system, only the children of the privileged and upper classes received formal education, which was provided either by private or religious institutions. The children of the poor and lower classes received little, if any, formal education. Although there were some laws with regard to education, American schools throughout the colonies were essentially private or church-related institutions, which were few in number and selective in their enrollment practices.

Thomas Jefferson was among the first public figures to propose a system of free public education. In a letter to George Wythe in 1786, he wrote in support of a bill for general education. He stated that:

> I think by far the most important bill in our whole code is that for the diffusion of knowledge among the people. No other sure foundation can be devised for the preservation of freedom and happiness . . . Preach, my dear sir, a crusade against ignorance; establish and improve the law for educating the common people.

Jefferson's plan for education was not passed, but the new philosophy of universal education began to spread and take root. Advocates for state-supported education began to emerge, and a conflict between church-supported and public-supported education developed into bitter struggles in some of the states of the new nation. One of the strongest advocates for state-supported education was Horace Mann, who influenced the development of free secular public schools supported by state and local community taxes.

After the adoption of the U.S. Constitution in 1787, which made no provision for education as a permissible function of the federal government, the responsibility for education essentially became a state function. The Tenth Amendment to the U.S. Constitution specifically states "all powers not delegated to the federal government, nor prohibited by it to the States, are reserved to the States or to the people, respectively." Therefore, acting under interpretation of the Tenth Amendment, all of the states through their constitutions have taken on education as a state function. For example, the Texas constitution of 1876 instituted the legal basis for the establishment of and control for a public school system in the State of Texas. Article VII, Section 1, of the Texas constitution reads:

> A general diffusion of knowledge being essential to the preservation of the liberties and rights of the people, it shall be the duty of the Legislature of the State to establish and make suitable provisions for the support and maintenance of an efficient system of public free schools.

In fact, the Texas Legislature sought to reinforce that sentiment by grounding the mission of the state's public education on "the conviction that a general diffusion of knowledge is essential for the welfare of this state and for the preservation of the liberties and rights of citizens" (TEC § 4.001). It follows, then, that the authority for designating education as a state function is clearly specified in the constitutions of each state, which also grants the state legislature the authority to establish and maintain the state educational system and to determine its structure and standards by legislative law.

◆ STATE LEGISLATIVE CONTROL OVER EDUCATION

Education is a state function that is primarily under the plenary control of the state legislature. The broad power of the state legislature extends over public schools as well as private and parochial schools. Additionally, state court decisions have supported state legislative control over education.

Acting under authority of the Texas constitution, the Texas Legislature has passed laws governing education in the state. For example, the Legislature established the Foundation School Program (TEC Chapter 42) and the following state policy regarding education (TEC § 42.001):

> (a) It is the policy of this state that the provision of public education is a state responsibility and that a thorough and efficient system be provided and substantially financed through state revenue sources so that each student enrolled in the public school system shall have access to programs and services that are appropriate to the student's educational needs and that are substantially equal to those available to any similar student, notwithstanding varying local economic factors. (b) The public school finance system of this state shall adhere to a standard of neutrality that provides for substantially equal access to similar revenue per student at similar tax effort, considering all state and local tax revenues of districts after acknowledging all legitimate student and district cost differences.

The Texas Legislature also passed laws that guaranteed, to each eligible student, adequate resources for a basic instructional program and facilities suitable to the student's educational needs (TEC § 42.002). Through the public school accountability system (TEC Chapter 39), the Legislature established school accreditation standards, a system of rewards for achieving the standards, and sanctions for non-compliance to ensure that school districts provide an adequate education.

During its 84th session (2015), the Legislature changed how truancy will be managed by school officials and the judiciary through passage of HB 2398. The bill redefines and decriminalizes truant conduct and amends Chapters 25, 7, and 33 of the Texas education code relative to compulsory school attendance, parents contributing to student's non-attendance, duties and authority of school attendance officers, and school district referrals. Emphasis is on prevention and intervention. The bill (effective September 1, 2015) also amends relevant chapters in the Code of Criminal Procedure, Family Code, and the Government Code. Additional information, including an overview, is available at http://www.txcourts.gov/publications-training/training-materials/truancy-reform.aspx.

Also, the Legislature created a 14-member State Board for Educator Certification (SBEC), 11 of whom are appointed by the governor with the consent of the senate, to grant educators greater authority to govern the standards of their profession (TEC §§ 21.031–21.045).

State control over education in Texas was demonstrated emphatically when the U.S. Supreme Court ruled in the *San Antonio v. Rodriguez* case in 1973 that even though the method of financing education in the state was "chaotic and unjust," it did not violate any provision of the U.S. Constitution. The Court further ruled that if the method of financing education in the state were to be remedied, it would have to be done by the state court or the legislature. Thus began efforts by the Texas Legislature to establish equality of educational opportunity throughout all school districts. In addition, the most recent struggles over school reform and the efforts of achieving equality of educational opportunity in the state were initiated by the State District Court ruling in the *Edgewood v. Kirby* case of 1987 that the financing system violated both Article I, Section 3 (the equal protection clause) and Article VII, Section 1 of the Texas constitution. Since that landmark court decision, the state legislature, in its subsequent sessions, has attempted to meet the provisions specified by state courts.

◆ STATE REGULATORY CONTROL OVER EDUCATION

The Texas Legislature also created the Texas Education Agency (TEA). This hierarchical administrative governmental structure is authorized to implement, administer, and regulate the state-mandated educational function in the local school districts of the state. An important part of its responsibility is to make rules and regulations governing education in the state, which are compiled in the official state publication, Title 19 Education, Texas Administrative Code. Subsequent revisions of the Texas Education Code by the Texas Legislature diminished some, although not all, of the regulatory control over education by the TEA. This agency and its responsibilities will be discussed in greater detail later in this book.

At the local school district level, school districts exist as quasi-municipal corporations; i.e., legal extensions (arms or agencies) of the state. Therefore, their boards of trustees are considered state officials with specific administrative duties, responsibilities, and functions mandated by law. The Texas Education Code § 11.151(b), states:

> The trustees as a body corporate have the exclusive power and duty to govern and oversee the management of the public schools of the district. All powers and duties not specifically delegated by statute to the agency or to the State Board of Education are reserved for the trustees, and the agency may not substitute its judgment for the lawful exercise of those powers and duties by the trustees.

In addition, the trustees have the authority to "adopt rules and bylaws necessary to carry out the powers and duties" as stipulated in the statute (TEC § 11.151(d)). Moreover, the district superintendent and campus principals function as extensions of the local school board through the general duties and authority granted to them through TEC § 11.201 and § 11.202.

◆ SUMMARY

The purpose of American education is to ensure that American democratic values, codified by the nation's founders in the U.S. Constitution, are inculcated in its citizenry. Therefore, the federal government has a stake in the American educational system and continues to exert considerable influence over education in the 50 states through federal programs, federal legislation and U.S. Constitutional provisions enforced through judicial review in the federal courts. Indeed, one could say that the federal and state governments and their organization form the structure upon which public education rests. The three branches of the federal government—legislative, executive, and judicial—are reflected in the structure of the Texas state government. Similarly, the four sources of law relative to education parallel the tripartite federal and state government structures. Sources of constitutional and statutory law are reflective of the legislative branch of federal and state government, administrative law reflects the executive branch of government, and judicial law parallels the judicial branch of government.

Due to the expense of offering quality education, one might consider the federal government as the "best" or most logical source of revenue and assistance for education. However, this has not been the case. In fact, the federal government's contribution to national education remains minimal (~8%) and is primarily in the form of categorical aid; i.e., aid for a specific government purpose and program that cannot be used to lower the state or local government burden of supporting education in the state. Few would argue that federal government involvement in, and assistance to, education is desirable, but most would prefer that it come without federal government "red tape" (regulations, etc.) and control. This rarely happens, for as is often said, the one who has the gold makes the rules. Additionally, there are the rights of individuals to consider—students, teachers, individuals with special needs, etc.—as guaranteed by the U.S. Constitution, made applicable to the states by the Fourteenth Amendment, and enforced through the federal courts.

Although the Texas constitution empowers the State Legislature to make the state's laws, the details of the legislation are not formed at that level. The ultimate authority for education rests with state and local educational agencies (including school districts). That is why administrative law is so important. It is the law developed by administrative agencies to carry out the provisions of statutory law. Therefore, administrative law has the most direct impact on the daily operation of public schools, typically in the form of school board policy. The superintendent is the educational leader and chief executive officer of the school district. State law (made by the Texas Legislature as codified in the Texas Education Code) grants the superintendent the authority to provide the leadership, direction and oversight of a school district. The principal has similar responsibilities at the school campus level, with emphasis on instructional leadership. Thus, at the local school district level, superintendents and principals are responsible for implementing administrative law. Their ability to do so is crucial in today's climate of increased responsibility and accountability for school improvement; hence the importance of developing a working knowledge of the structure of federal and state government, the role each plays in the education of children, the sources of law, and the purpose and implications of each.

◆ REFERENCES

Black, C. L. (1960). *The people and the court*. New York: The Macmillan Company.

Black, H. C., Nolan-Haley, J. M. & Nolan, J. R. (1991). *Black's Law Dictionary* (Abridged 6th ed.). St. Paul, MN: West Publishing Company.

Darling-Hammond, L. (2007, May 2). Evaluating 'No Child Left Behind.' *The Nation*. Retrieved from http://www.thenation.com/article/evaluating-no-child-left-behind/

Finn, C. (2008, March 30). 5 myths about No Child Left Behind: Myths about the education law everyone loves to hate. *Washington Post*. Retrieved from http://www.washingtonpost.com/wp-dyn/content/article/2008/03/28/AR2008032802976.html

Gamoran, A., & Long, D. A. (2006). Equality of educational opportunity: A 40-year retrospective (WCER Working Paper No. 2006-9). Madison: University of Wisconsin–Madison, Wisconsin Center for Education Research. Retrieved from http://www.wcer.wisc.edu/publications/workingPapers/papers.php

Henry, P. (2007). The case against standardized testing. *Minnesota English Journal, 43*(1), 39–71.

Kemerer, F. R. (1997). State Constitutions and School Vouchers. 120 Ed. Law Rep. [1]. St. Paul, MN: West Publishing Company.

Klein, A. (2011, February 23). Obama's 2012 plan shelters education. *Education Week,* pp. 1–31, 3p.

Knight, E. W. (1953). *Readings in educational administration.* New York: Henry Holt and Company, pp. 458–463.

McCleskey, C., Dickens, E. L., & Butcher, A. K. (1975). *The government and politics of Texas* (5th ed.). Boston, MA: Little, Brown and Company.

Quattlebaum, C. A. (1952). *Federal educational activities and educational issues before congress.* Washington, DC: United States Government Printing Office.

Texas Education Agency. (2015a). *Briefing book on public education legislation—84th Texas legislative session.*

Texas Education Agency (2015b). *TEA submits waiver renewal application.* Retrieved from http://tea.texas.gov/Texas_Schools/Waivers/NCLB-ESEA_Waiver_Information/

U.S. Department of Education. (1999). *Regarding the educational excellence for all children Act of 1999.* Retrieved from http://listserv.ed.gov/archives/edinfo/archived/msg00458.html

U.S. Department of Education. (2007). *Brown v. Board of Education 50th Anniversary Commission.* Retrieved from http://www.ed.gov/brownvboard50th.

U.S. Department of Education. (2009a). Offices and Coordinating Structure. Retrieved from http://www.ed.gov/about/offices/or/index.html?src=ln

U.S. Department of Education (2009b, September 24). *Secretary Duncan says rewrite of 'No Child Left Behind' should start now; reauthorization can't wait. Next version of the federal K-12 law should drive school reforms that prepare students for success,* Retrieved from http://www.ed.gov/news/pressreleases/2009/09/09242009.html

U.S. Department of Education (2009c). *The federal role in education.* Retrieved 2009 from http://www.ed.gov/about/overview/fed/role.html?src=ln

U.S. Department of Education. (2009d). *White House initiatives on educational excellence for Hispanic Americans.* Retrieved from http://www.ed.gov/about/inits/list/hispanic-initiative/index.html

U.S. Department of Education. (2015). *Remarks by U.S. Secretary of Education Arne Duncan on the 50th Anniversary of Congress Passing the Elementary and Secondary Education Act.* Retrieved from http://www.ed.gov/news/speeches/remarks-us-secretary-education-arne-duncan-50th-anniversary-congress-passing-elementary-and-secondary-education-act

◆ LEGAL REFERENCES

1 Cranch 137; 2 L.Ed. 60 (1803).

20 USCS 7301-7373.

Agostini v. Felton, 521 U.S. 203 (1997).

Aguilar v. Felton, 473 U.S. 402 (1985).

Belk, et al. v. The Charlotte-Mecklenburg Board of Education, 2001 U.S. App. LEXIS 20712.

Brown v. Board of Education of Topeka, Kansas, 347 U.S. 483 (1954).

Brown v. Board of Education of Topeka, Kansas, 349 U.S. 294 (1955).

Brown v. Gwinnett County School Dist, 112 F.3d 1464 (11th Cir. 1997).

Brown v. Gilmore, 258 F.3d 265 (4th Cir. 2001).

Carrollton-Farmers Branch I.S.D. v. Edgewood I.S.D. and Alvarado I.S.D., 826 S.W.2d 489, 35 Tex. Sup.J. 374 (Tex., 1992).

Cochran v. Louisiana State Board of Education, 281 U.S. 370 (1930).

Croft v. Perry, 604 F.Supp.2d 932 (U.S. Dist. 2009).

Croft v. Perry, 562 F.3d 735 (5th Cir. 2009).

Doe v. School Board of Ouachita Parish, et al., 274 F.3d 289 (5th Cir. 2001).

Edgewood I.S.D. v. Kirby, 777 S.W.2d 391, 33 Tex. Sup. Ct. J. 12 (Tex., 1989).

Elk Grove Unified School District v. Newdow, 124 S.Ct. 2301 (2004).

Everson v. Board of Education, 330 U.S. 1 (1947).

Every Child Achieves Act – 2015 – S.B. 1177, 114th Congress (2015).

Frazier v. Winn, 535 F.3d 1279 (11th Cir. 2008).

Garcia v. San Antonio Metropolitan Transit Authority, 471 U.S. 1049 (1985).

Gibbons v. Ogden, 9 Wheaton 1; 7 L.Ed 23 (1824).

H.B. 1034, 80th Leg., Reg. Sess. (Tex. 2007).

H.B. 3678, 80th Leg., Reg. Sess. (Tex. 2007).

H.B. 2398, 84th Leg. Reg. Sess. (Tex. 2015)

H.J.R. 27, 79th Leg., 2nd Spec. Sess. (Tex. 2005).

Jones v. Clear Creek I.S.D., 977 F.2d 963 (5th Cir. 1992).

Jones v. Clear Creek I.S.D., cert. denied, 508 U.S. 967 (1993).

Lee v. Alexander City Board of Education, 2002 U.S. Dist. LEXIS 17853.

Lee v. Weisman, 112 S.Ct. 2649 (1992).

Lemon v. Kurtzman, 403 U.S. 602 (1971).

Marbury v. Madison, 1 Cranch 137 (1803).

Meredith v. Jefferson Co. Pub. Sch., 6 F.3d 513 (6th Cir. 2005), U.S. 2007.

Minersville School District v. Gobitis, 310 U.S. 586: 60 S.Ct. 1010; 84 L.Ed. 1375; 1940 U.S. LEXIS 1136; 17 Ohio Op. 417; 127 A.L.R. 1493.

Mitchell v. Helms, 120 S.Ct. 2530 (2000).

Morse v. Frederick, No. 551, slip op._ (U.S. 2007),

Morse v. Frederick, U.S. LEXIS 8514, (June 25, 2007)

National League of Cities v. Usery, 426 U.S. 833 (1976).

Parents Involved in Community Schools v. Seattle Sch. Dist. No. 1, 426 F.3d 1162 (9th Cir. 2007, WL 1836531).

People ex rel. McCollum v. Board of Education of School District No. 71, Champaign, Illinois, 333 U.S. 68 (1948).

Pierce v. Society of Sisters of the Holy Names of Jesus and Mary, 268 U.S. 510 (1925).

San Antonio I.S.D. v. Rodriguez, 411 U.S. 1 (1973).

Santa Fe Independent School District v. Doe, 120 S.Ct. 2266, 2272 (2000).

School District of Abington v. Schempp and Murray v. Curlett, 374 U.S. 203 (1963).

Stone v. Graham, 449 U.S. 39 (1980).

Wallace v. Jafree, 105 S.Ct. 2479 (1985).

West Virginia School Board v. Barnette, 63 S.Ct. 1178 (1943).

Zelman v. Simmons-Harris, 122 S.Ct. 2460 (2002).

Zorach v. Clausen, 343 U.S. 306 (1952).

GOVERNING AND SUPPORTING EDUCATION IN TEXAS

The Texas Education Agency and Educational Service Centers*

Stacey Edmonson ◆ *Pamela Gray*

Although the Texas Legislature has broad control of public education within the state, the legislature operates normally only 5 of every 24 months and sets broad policy through the laws that organize and enable the constitutionally authorized schools in the public sector. Consequently, the legislature arranged for administrative direction of the state's public schools by authorizing the Texas Education Agency (TEA), which included the Texas Commissioner of Education, the staff of the Agency, and also the State Board of Education (SBOE), to set policy in many areas of education. Established in 1949, TEA has undergone considerable changes with the responsibilities designated to these three components. Once appointed by the SBOE, the Commissioner since 1986 is more independent of the board and sets many of the policies as an important member of the government headed by the state's governor. The Agency's staff works under the direction of the Commissioner to administer the laws and the policies set within the board's authority as well as those set by the legislature.

Education Service Centers (ESCs) began in 1967 to offer various services to the school districts in the state by helping them develop their programs and the support structure that enabled them to meet the requirements of the modern schools that were desired by the citizens. With close to 50 years of growth and service, ESCs have also undergone considerable change during the last 20 years to make them leaner and more supportive of the TEA in their quest to implement the legislature's directives as well as meeting school district needs in a decentralized manner. These two important organizations, TEA and ESCs, strive to make education in

*Joe Neely and Virgil Ed Flathouse authored the chapter on Education Service Centers in previous editions of this book. Their earlier research is acknowledged and appreciated and used in parts of this chapter. Alice Fisher and Nora Hutto are also acknowledged as former contributors.

Texas more thorough and effective as they align to support the state's more than 8,500 schools. The purpose of this chapter is to provide an increased understanding of the roles of The TEA and the ESCs.

◆ TEXAS EDUCATION AGENCY

Today more than 5.1 million students attend Texas public schools. The TEA serves 1,247 school districts and charter schools (TEA, 2015a), with a mission to "provide leadership, guidance, and resources to help schools meet the educational needs of all students and prepare them for success in the global economy" (TEA, 2015b, p. 11). As the state has raised educational standards and increased its ability to measure student achievement by individual district, campus, and student, oversight by the State has been achieved by collection of the data into the Public Education Information Management System Data. The No Child Left Behind Act increased the responsibility of school districts for improving student learning as accountability for student achievement increased. A new emphasis was placed upon teacher certification in both content knowledge and pedagogy so that students may reach the higher levels of learning necessary to function in a global society. The statutory responsibility of TEA is specified by TEC 7.021(a) and (b). These statutes explain that the Agency shall:

- Administer and monitor compliance with education programs required by federal or state law, including federal funding and state funding for those programs.
- Conduct research, analysis, and reporting to improve teaching and learning.
- Conduct hearings involving state school law at the direction and under the supervision of the Commissioner.
- Establish and implement pilot programs established by the title.
- Carry out the duties relating to the investment capital fund under Section 7.024.
- Develop and implement a teacher recruitment program as provided by Section 21.004.
- Carry out duties under the Texas Advanced Placement Incentive Program under Subchapter C, Chapter 28.
- Carry out power and duties relating to adult and community education as required under Subchapter H, Chapter 29.
- Develop a program of Instruction in driver education and traffic safety as provided by Section 29.902.
- Carry out duties assigned under Section 30.002 concerning children with visual impairments.
- Carry out power and duties related to regional day school programs for deaf as provided under Subchapter D, Chapter 30.
- Establish and maintain an electronic information transfer system as required under Section 32.032, maintain and expand telecommunications capabilities of school districts and regional ESCs as required under Section 32.033, and establish technology demonstration programs as required under Section 32.035.
- Review school district budgets, audit reports, and other fiscal reports as required under Sections 44.008 and 44.010 and prescribe forms for financial reports made by or for school district to the Commissioner or the Agency as required under Section 44.009.
- Cooperate with the Texas Higher Education Coordinating Board (THECB) in connection with the Texas Partnership and scholarship program under Subchapter P, Chapter 61.

The TEA has an important role in the education of all children of the state. In fact, TEA serves students, teachers, administrator, ESCs, communities, and families. Specifically, roles and responsibilities of TEA include:

- Administers the distribution of state and federal funding to public schools;
- Administers the statewide assessment program and accountability system;
- Provides support to the SBOE in the development of the statewide curriculum;
- Assists the SBOE in the instructional materials adoption process and managing the instructional materials distribution process;
- Administers a data collection system on public school information;
- Performs the administrative functions and services of the State Board for Educator Certification (SBEC);
- Supports agency operations, including carrying out duties related to the Permanent School Fund; and
- Monitors for compliance with certain federal and state guidelines. (TEA, 2015c)

In addition, the Agency operates under two major goals:

1. Provide education system leadership, guidance, and resources.
   Specifically, TEA will provide leadership, guidance, and resources to create a public education system that continuously improves student performance and supports public schools as the choice of Texas citizens. The Agency will satisfy its customers and stakeholders by promoting supportive school environments and providing resources, challenging academic standards, high-quality data, and timely and clear reports on results.
2. Provide system oversight and support.
   TEA will sustain a system of accountability for student performance that is supported by challenging assessments, high-quality data, high qualified and effective educators, and high standards of students, campus, district, and agency performance (TEA, 2015a, p. 41).

The P-16 Initiative in Texas: Closing the Gaps

A relevant and important component of achieving TEA's goals is evidenced by progress on the Closing the Gaps initiative. Closing the Gaps by 2015 was implemented in October 2000 by the THECB with the goal of closing the gaps in student participation, student success, excellence, and research. The plan includes strategies for reaching the goals, target strategies, and an annual performance measuring system. The P-16 Initiative is an effort to work with stakeholders collaboratively to foster a more integrated education system, while addressing issues of college readiness standards, teacher education, and educational resources. The goals include:

- Expanding access to early learning for children aged 3–5 years and improve their readiness for kindergarten.
- Smooth student transitions from one level of learning to the next.
- Close the achievement gap between White and minority students.
- Upgrade teacher education and professional development.
- Strengthen relationships with families and schools.

- Create a wider range of learning experiences and opportunities for students in the final 2 years of high school.
- Improve college readiness and college success.
- Other activities including raising scholarships, creating promotional campaigns, and providing incentives or recognition awards for high academic performance. (THECB, 2009).

The THECB provided an update on the status of the initiative in the June 2015 Closing the Gaps 2015 Progress Report. The report notes that goal attainment has been mixed. The state met the goal of 210,000 undergraduate degrees in 2011 although African American and Hispanic graduation rates continue to trail those of other students. This progress measure and coordination with the THECB demonstrate an important component of how TEA's responsibilities extend beyond the overall oversight of K-12 schools and into broader educational contexts.

❖ THE COMMISSIONER OF EDUCATION

The office of the Commissioner of Education was first created in 1871 as the State Superintendent of Public Instruction. The position remained for 2 years, and then the SBOE was established with new authority to hire a secretary. In 1884, the law was again rewritten, mandating election of a state superintendent to supervise the common system school (Eby, 1925). Roles of the superintendents were not clearly delineated until the 1949 Gilmer-Aiken Bill (Blake, 1996). Senate Bill 115 (1949) reorganized ". . . the state administration of education through consolidation and rationalization of the existing education divisions of the state into one central education agency . . . composed of the [elected] State Board of Education" (Yoes, 1969, p. 49).

The law established that the Commissioner worked for the SBOE and served as the chief executive officer of the TEA. The Commissioner was responsible for promoting efficiency and improvement in the state's public school system; recommending policies, rules, and regulations necessary for educational progress; and supplying the SBOE with information needed in its deliberations (TEA, 1980). The only statutory requirement to serve as the Commissioner of Education at this time is that he or she be a citizen of the United States.

The Commissioner of Education, Michael L. Williams, was appointed by Governor Rick Perry on September 1, 2012, and approved by the Texas Senate. Commissioner Williams serves as the head of TEA. The executive leadership of the Commissioner's office includes the Chief Deputy, who is responsible for all ESCs, the Deputy Commissioner of Policy and Programs, who oversees rule making; and the Deputy Commissioner of Finance and Administration. Commissioner Williams announced his resignation effective January 1, 2016, which will pave the way for a new agency leader.

The Texas Education Code (2015) states in Section TEC 7.003 provides that the Commissioner of Education serves as the educational leader of the state, executive secretary of the SBOE, and executive officer of TEA. The Commissioner provides leadership for the direction of public education in Texas and responsibilities include:

- Overseeing the distribution of state funding to public schools.
- Administering the statewide accountability system.
- Administering the statewide assessment program.

- Overseeing the development of the statewide curriculum.
- Managing the textbook adoption and distribution process.
- Administering a data collection system on public school students, staff, and finances.
- Monitoring for the compliance with certain federal and state guidelines.
- Administering the distribution of state and federal funds.

◆ THE STATE BOARD OF EDUCATION

In addition to the TEA and the Commissioner, a third primary partner impacting Texas public schools is the SBOE. The first state board, empowered in 1871, consisted of the superintendent of public instruction, governor, and the attorney general. The first board "was empowered to act in place of the legislature in school affairs" (Eby, 1925, p. 159). Duties of the first board were:

1. To adopt all necessary rules and regulations for the establishment and promotion of the public schools.
2. To provide for the examination and appointment of all teachers.
3. To fix the salaries of teachers.
4. To define the state course of study.
5. To select textbooks and apparatus for the schools.
6. To prescribe the duties of the board of directors of the several school districts (Eby, p. 159).

In 1873, a new board was formed composed of the governor, comptroller, and the secretary of state (Blake, 1996). Difficulty in finding time and money to operate led to a reorganization of the SBOE by the Legislature in 1928. A nine-member board was appointed by the governor and approved by the senate. Reversal to an elected SBOE resulted with the passage of the Gilmer-Aikin Bill in 1949 (Tolson, 1975). This bill established the election of SBOE members from congressional districts. By 1980, the Board had grown to 27 members. In 1984, HB 72 was passed, requiring a 15-member board appointed by the governor. This particular board served only 4 years when the law changed the process of appointment and re-instituted the election as the process for determining state board members. The public voters in Texas voted to elect 15 members from SBOE districts across the state. At the same time, the role of the SBOE changed from policy making to implementation of legislative policy (Blake, 1996).

The current board serves most of its functions through three committees: instruction, school initiatives, and school finance/permanent school fund. The Committee on Instruction has primary responsibility for issues dealing with curriculum and instruction, student testing, vocational and special education programs, and alternatives to social promotion. Primary responsibility for the preliminary work on issues dealing with school finance, vocational and special education programs, and the Permanent School Fund rests with the Committee on School Finance/Permanent School Fund. The Committee on School Initiatives deals with issues such as charter schools, the long-range plan for public education and rules proposed by the State Board of Educator Certification.

Establishing policy and providing leadership for the Texas public school system are the responsibilities of the SBOE. By adopting policies and setting standards for educational programs, the SBOE provides the direction necessary to enable Texas public schools to prepare today's schoolchildren for a successful future. As part of its efforts to provide the best possible education to public school students, the SBOE designates and mandates instruction in the knowledge and skills that are essential to a well-balanced curriculum. The SBOE approves and determines passing scores for the state-mandated assessment program, currently the State of Texas Assessments of Academic Readiness. In its other activities, the SBOE oversees the investment of the Permanent School Fund, approves the creation of charter schools, and adopts regulations and standards for the operation of adult education programs provided by public school districts, junior colleges and universities (SBOE, 2007). The SBOE has recently examined and made decisions regarding critical items including social studies curriculum/textbooks, evolution, and sex education.

A person is eligible to serve on the SBOE if he or she has resided in his or her respective district for 1 year, is a qualified voter of the district, and is at least 26 years old. SBOE members serve staggered 4-year terms and may not hold another public office. No compensation is given, although a member's expenses may be reimbursed. Statute requires at least four meetings a year, held in Austin. The Governor, with approval of the Senate, appoints the chair of the SBOE.

State Board for Educator Certification

Although the names may sound similar, the SBOE and the SBEC are two very distinct entities. The Texas Legislature created SBEC in 1995 to recognize public school educators as professionals and to grant educators the authority to govern the standards of their profession. SBEC oversees all aspects of the preparation, certification, and standards of conduct of public school educators (TEA, 2015d). SBEC's responsibilities include educator preparation, assessment, accountability, certification, and professional discipline. SBEC works with and approves all entities that prepare educators for certification in Texas, including universities, community colleges, alternative teacher certification programs, and alternative administrator certification programs. SBEC is also responsible for the development and administration of all certification examinations that must be passed by educators in Texas. Results of these certification examinations are used to monitor the quality of educator preparation programs. In addition, SBEC is responsible for issuing all educator credentials (certification) to those individuals who have completed the appropriate requirements. This also includes issuing emergency permits and advising school districts on hiring appropriately certified personnel. SBEC must also monitor the professional conduct of Texas educators and enforce both disciplinary rules and the Educators' Code of Ethics in order to ensure the well-being and safety of Texas school children. Effective September 1, 2005, the SBEC staff became a part of the TEA and under the direction of the Commissioner. Consequently, the Commissioner appoints the head administrator to carry out the policies of the SBEC and the Board itself does not select the director for this agency as in the past.

◆ EDUCATION SERVICE CENTERS

Located statewide in 20 geographical regions, the ESCs represent a key link in the overall support of management of the public education system in Texas. From an inauspicious beginning in 1967—storing and distributing technology-based educational materials as a minor part of the federal Elementary and Secondary Education Act of 1965 (ESEA)—the ESCs have evolved into a multimillion dollar operation, employing over 4,000 personnel throughout Texas. The 20 regional ESCs provide direct support and assistance to local school districts and campuses. Since 1965 federal funds have been sent to states through the Elementary and Secondary Education Act, with the intent of increasing performance of all students regardless of their race, gender, or socioeconomic level. With the No Child Left Behind Act funding can be sent from the federal government to the states and directly to school districts, which allows districts to design their own plans for campus improvement and professional growth of teachers. Since 1990 the role of regional ESCs has been that of assistance from the TEA to school districts. Educational Service Centers are located in proximity to local school districts and have provided information, models of best practice for improved student learning, and a knowledgeable source of support.

From a limited beginning in the mid-1960s, the ESCs have developed over almost five decades into large and complex organizations that play a crucial role in promoting quality of services assisting school districts and charter schools in their mission in educating the children of Texas. The ESCs have three primary roles: (1) improve student performance, (2) promote economic efficiency of member school districts, and (3) provide support for the implementation of statewide initiatives enacted by the Legislature or the Commissioner of Education (TEC § 8.002). By virtue of their profile as intermediary units in the public education system, ESCs are uniquely positioned to address the needs of individual school districts and charter schools in a cost-effective manner. Cost savings have resulted on multiple levels by the ESCs, assistance in implementing the initiatives and mandates of the state, thus allowing the central education bureaucracy to depend on ESCs to provide a helping role and avoid one of regulation.

ESCs have received both strong praise and criticism throughout their history. They serve in supportive roles for school district and charter school operations and seldom assume high-profile postures. The fact that the ESCs operate in a role that is largely invisible to the general public may contribute to their difficulty in fostering a consistently strong positive image. While the quiet nature of their role may enhance the value of their services to the local district that is ultimately accountable to its taxpayers, it also increases the perceived lack of ESC accountability by members of the general public and their elected representatives. Efforts to combat this perception have resulted in the process to develop, implement, and refine a comprehensive strategic plan that identifies not only the strengths of the ESCs but also the future challenges they face.

ESC Support to School Districts

The fundamental mission of the ESCs is clearly outlined in statute (TEC § 8.002), and reads as follows:

1. Assist school districts in improving student performance in each region of the system;
2. Enable school districts to operate more efficiently and economically;
3. Implement initiatives assigned by the Legislature or the Commissioner.

These are purposefully broad mandates, and their implementations by the ESCs are as diverse as the clientele served. While each ESC is constricted by certain statewide policies and procedures, each one also enjoys a degree of autonomy and flexibility in the fulfillment of its mission.

Services to improve student and school district performance are the driving forces behind the ESCs, as evidenced in the statutory mission previously stated. Additional statutes reflect this emphasis on performance and spell out certain services that every ESC must offer for purchase by the school districts. These services are referred to "core services" and are described in Sections 8.051 and 8.121 of the Texas Education Code as follows:

(1)   training and assistance in teaching each subject area assessed under Section 39.023:
(2)   training and assistance in providing each program that qualifies for a funding allotment under Section 42.151, 42.152, 42.153, or 42.156;
(3)   assistance specifically designed for a school district rated academically unacceptable under Section 39.054 (a) or a campus whose performance is considered unacceptable based on the indicators adopted under Section 39.051;
(4)   training and assistance to teachers, administrators, members of district boards of trustees, and members of site-based decision-making committees;
(5)   assistance specifically designed for a school district that is considered out of compliance with state or federal special education requirements, based on the agency's most recent compliance review of the district's special education programs; and
(6)   assistance in complying with state laws and rules.

Each ESC must develop an impressive array of services and products to have at its disposal in order to adequately serve its districts and charter schools, remain competitive, justify its existence, and fulfill its mission. This array of services includes such areas as staff development, assessment, instruction, health and safety, technology, certification, administration, business support, and specialized services.

Special mention must be made of the role that ESCs play in the implementation of legislative or commissioner initiatives. These are special programs initiated by the Legislature or the Commissioner of Education that have statewide implications for education. While selected agency staff may have oversight over these programs, the actual implementation and management of them are transferred to the personnel in selected ESCs. An example of such initiative follows:

> Texas Reading, Math, and Science Initiative: This program was authorized by the 80th session of the Texas Legislature in 2007 to improve student performance in Reading, Math, and Science areas. Out of the federal funds appropriated for this initiative (both state and federal funds were appropriated), the Commissioner could allocate an amount not to exceed $5,000,000 in each fiscal year of the biennium for the development of educator training programs at the ESCs in a manner that ensured access for small and mid-size school districts and charter schools. (General Appropriations Act [HB1], 80th Session, 2007, Rider 40, pp. 111–113)

Each ESC has its own customized webpage that lists its wide variety of services offered, as well as a wealth of other pertinent information about the ESC and its operations, with numerous links to relevant websites which facilitate the search for information. Anyone may access any ESC's webpage through the TEA webpage or may go directly to the ESC web address.

Governance, Fiscal Support and Accountability of ESCs

Originally supported through Title III federal funds, ESCs have become supported by multiple sources as the Centers grew and matured. At one time, a considerable portion of their support came from the Foundation School Program; however, today state revenues comprise ~12% of

ESCs funding while federal support in terms of grants, etc. is ~45% and local revenues from school districts is above 40% of their funding. Districts are not required to buy consultant or support services from their ESCs but may chose to purchase services from another center or an outside source.

ESCs are quasistate agencies and employees are not legally state employees; however, the employees are considered such when it comes to influencing political activities and legislation. ESCs are nonregulatory in responsibility, although they frequently provide services to districts to meet the ESCs' obligations required by state law and policies. The Commissioner of Education has the ultimate responsibility for the ESCs' operations and administration, even though the ESCs are regional in design. General everyday operations actually are the responsibility of an elected board, chosen by the school district boards of those districts within the ESCs' territory. This board has great input on the decision of employing a director for the ESC. Also included on the board is an appointed nonvoting representative of the charter schools within its territory.

Like schools, ESCs are responsible for accountability of programs within the districts that they serve. Consequently, they must be successful in assisting with the effectiveness and efficiency of the districts served. These include student performance, effectiveness and efficiency of school operations resulting from their services including program support, technical assistance, shared services, results of grants contracts, and also client satisfaction with their services. As a result the last 10 years of ESCs existence have seen these centers become significantly more accountable for the results of their services.

◆ THE LEGISLATIVE BUDGET BOARD

The Legislative Budget Board (LBB) is a permanent joint committee of the Texas Legislature that develops budget and policy recommendations for legislative appropriations for all agencies of state government, as well as completes fiscal analysis for proposed legislation. The LBB also conducts evaluations and reviews for the purpose of identifying and recommending changes that improve the efficiency and performance of state and local operations and finances.

The impetus for the creation of the LBB was twofold: (1) escalating state government expenditures after the end of World War II and (2) a recommendation from the State Auditor's Office for the creation of a legislative committee for the continuous review of state spending. Thus, the 10-member LBB was created by statute in 1949 and since that time, the legislation required all state agencies to submit their budget requests to the LBB for review and recommendations.

The composition of the LBB includes the Lieutenant Governor, Speaker of the House of Representatives, Chair of House Committee on Appropriations, Chair of the House Committee on Ways and Means, and the Chair of Senate Finance Committee. In addition, the Speaker appoints two House members, and the Lieutenant Governor appoints three Senate members (Williams, 1966). The primary purpose of the LBB is the development of budget and policy recommendations for legislative appropriations, completes fiscal analyses for proposed legislation, and conducts evaluations and reviews to improve the efficiency and performance of state and local operations. The Board provides the Texas Legislature with the recommended state budget, prepared by the LBB staff, at the beginning of each legislative session, which occurs in early January of odd-numbered years. The Board's authority is broad and its influence on state government spending is significant.

The LBB has a wide range of responsibilities that are intended to serve the fiscal policy and analysis needs of the Texas Legislature. These responsibilities incorporate those mandated by general law, those directed by the General Appropriations Act, and those that have been designated by the Board and its staff. The following is a summary of significant responsibilities assigned by statute to the LBB:

- Adopt a constitutional spending limit (Section 316, Government Code; Article 8, Section 22, Texas Constitution);
- Prepare a General Appropriations Bill draft (Section 322.008(a), Government Code);
- Prepare a budget estimates document (Section 322.008(c), Government Code);
- Prepare a performance report (Section 322.011(c), Government Code;
- Guide, review, and finalize agency strategic plans (Section 2056, Government Code)
- Prepare fiscal notes, impact statements (Section 314, Government Code); and
- Take necessary budget execution actions (Section 317, Government Code) (LBB Responsibilities, 2015).

The LBB provides a wide range of services and informative documents that are not required under general law. During the interim, the LBB is responsible for the following:

- Provide assistance to standing and special committees, as requested.
- Inform the Legislature about significant budget and performance developments among state agencies.
- Provide Fiscal Size-up, which summarizes important fiscal actions of the prior legislative session.
- Describe the purpose and services of state agencies.
- Provide comparative information on Texas state government.
- Provide assessments of state agency performance. (LBB Responsibilities, 2015)

During the legislative session, the LBB supports the legislative appropriations process by providing staff resources for the House Appropriations Committee, the Senate Finance Committee, and the Conference Committee on Appropriations. Staff support takes the form of tracking committee decisions, answering inquiries from committee members, and performing analyses. The LBB staff records committee-funding decisions in order to produce bill texts and summaries for each step of the appropriations process.

In summary, the role of the LBB has varied somewhat through the years with expansion of that role coming first through legislation enacted in 1973, the Board continues to have great authority and influence over all state agencies. Included among them is the impact on all areas of education due to the fiscal implications. The adage "He who holds the gold, rules," is not quite appropriate but with the LBB preparing a recommended budget for each agency and also assisting in its evaluation, great influence accrues. The TEA, the SBOE, and the Commissioner receive appropriations necessary to perform their assigned tasks. All three entities must work together to meet the statutory requirements established by the legislature.

◆ CONCLUSION

Because Texas is a large, diverse state, the responsibility of educating the state was originally somewhat decentralized as a necessity with local school boards responsible for operating the dispersed districts/schools. With highly developed programs that were more recently mandated by federal and state initiatives, greater expectations for schools and students ensued. These mandates include the educational initiatives of the Legislature and the Commissioner as well as the promotion of economical and efficient management practices in the schools. Over the years, the relationship of the legislature, the governor, the SBOE, the Commissioner of Education, and the staff of TEA have been subject to the political pressures of party politics and the stress of the cost of providing adequate services in educating the youth of Texas. Consequently over the last 60 years, these relationships between the above political players have moved from being somewhat decentralized to more centralized in controlling the various factors impacting the educational processes involved.

The roles of the Governor and Commissioner of Education are crucial in defining the direction of educational programs and initiatives for the State of Texas. Working with the Governor, SBOE, State Board of Educator Certification, and the LBB, the impact of the Commissioner and TEA upon local school districts is tremendous. The curriculum and assessment component required for graduation from high school, and grade level and accountability testing has been a primary focus for school districts. The ongoing analysis of fiscal accountability and school improvement planning are placing increased accountability and compliance with legislative intent upon school districts.

As causative change agents, the Texas ESCs are strategically positioning themselves to provide improved and extended services to students, teachers, administrators, and boards of trustees in school districts and charter schools of all sizes. These services are designed to develop the collective potential of their clientele in order for them to successfully confront the continuing challenges that face public education. School districts have greater control and flexibility, while accountability for student success is non-negotiable. The expectations of increased student learning, increased accountability for student learning, and fiscal integrity places great responsibility upon the local school district for student success.

◆ REFERENCES

Blake, M. (1996). The state agency and governance of Texas education. In James A. Vornberg (Ed.), *Texas Public School Organization and Administration: 1996.* Dubuque, Iowa: Kendall/Hunt.

Eby, F. (1925). *The development of education in Texas.* New York, NY: MacMillan.

General Appropriations Act, HB1, 80th Session of the Texas Legislature, Rider 40, pp. 11–13.

Legislative Budget Board (2015). Retrieved from http://www.lbb.state.tx.us/responsibilities.aspx

No Child Left Behind (2001). Public Law 107–110.

Texas Education Agency. (1980). Texas Education Agency: Leadership for the public school system. In C.W. Funkhouser and I.N. Bruscemi (Eds.), *Perspectives on Schooling for Texas Educators.* Dubuque, IA: Kendall/Hunt.

Texas Education Agency (2015a). *Texas Education Agency Strategic Plan for the Fiscal Years 2015–2019.* Austin, TX: Texas Education Agency.

Texas Education Agency (2015b). *2014 Comprehensive Biennial Report on Texas Public Schools.* Austin, TX: Texas Education Agency.

Texas Education Agency (2015c). *Welcome and overview.* Retrieved from http://tea.texas.gov/About_TEA/Welcome_and_Overview/

Texas Education Agency (2015d). *State Board for Educator Certification*. Retrieved from http://tea. texas.gov/index2.aspx?id=3461&menu_id=865&menu_id2=794

Texas Education Code (2015). Retrieved from http://www.statutes.legis.state.tx.us/?link=ED

Texas Higher Education Coordinating Board (2015). *Closing the Gaps 2015 Progress Report*. Retrieved from http://www.thecb.state.tx.us/reports/PDF/6696.PDF?CFID=29816651&CFTOK EN=75833403

Tolson, D. F. (1975). The role of Senator. In S. M. Aikin, Jr. *The Development of Public Education in Texas, 1933–1974*. Ann Arbor, Michigan; University Microfilm Instructional.

Williams, T. E. (1996). Available online at http://www.lbb.state.tx.us

Yoes, E. D. (1969). Public education in Texas (1910–1966). In Charles W. Funkhouser & John N. Brusceni (Eds.), *Perspectives on Schooling for Texas Educators* (1981). Dubuque, Iowa: Kendall/Hunt.

RACIAL AND ETHNIC GROUPS IN TEXAS

Who Are They?

Lillian B. Poats ◆ *Viveca A. Grant* ◆ *Nicole Walters*

Texas is one of the most racially and culturally diverse states in America. Although many racial and ethnic groups are currently represented in Texas, the most prominent ethnic minority groups are Mexican Americans, African Americans, Native Americans, and Asian Americans, primarily Chinese and Vietnamese. Each group has made significant contributions to the growth and development of Texas and America. To understand and be better able to assist in more effective educational program planning, school administrators, teachers, and others who work in Texas schools need to know about culture and cultural diversity. They need information and understanding of the varied histories, cultures, hopes, and aspirations these groups have for themselves and for their children and youth. Following is a series of brief vignettes focusing on each of the above groups.

◆ AFRICAN AMERICANS

Education is for improving the lives of others and for leaving your community and world better than you found it.

—Marian Wright Edelman

Gay (1977, p. 34) stated that despite a wealth of a sociological, anthropological, and historical data to the contrary, some people still believe that (1) Black Americans are just Americans without a discernible past beyond their arrival on the American scene as slaves, and (2) Blacks have no values or lifestyle other than those they share with the common American culture.

Highly developed kingdoms existed in various parts of Africa hundreds of years ago. The kings of the ancient empire of Ghana came to power about the year 700. However, their power tended to decline in the 1000s, and their capital was destroyed in the western Sudan and in Congo at the mouth of the Congo River. Also, African kingdoms of antiquity were responsible for some outstanding accomplishments in commerce, construction, agriculture, arts and crafts, and education. Africans also helped design and build some of the great pyramids of Egypt.

Between 1200 and 1600, an African Arabic university flourished at Timbuktu in West Africa and became famous throughout Spain, North Africa, and the Middle East. Each tribe had its own language, religion, and customs. The family was important everywhere in Africa.

Beginning in the late 1500s, White settlers from European nations established colonies in many African countries. Many of these European nations engaged in the slave trade, and during a 400-year period, 1400 through 1800, they carried hundreds of thousands of Africans to North and South America. Gay (1977) further suggested that to understand fully the essence of Blacks' presence in the history and culture of the United States, there is a need to examine both the enculturative and the acculturative dimensions, that is, the results of the pull of the integrative forces and the push of the segregated forces operating upon Black Americans. To the extent that both of these elements are explored, a real understanding of what it means to be Black in America can be achieved. The development of a clear understanding is often impeded in American society because of the images of African American's portrayed by the media. The absence of any real interaction or determination to learn about another race makes it difficult to develop an understanding of what it means to be Black in America. Such awareness is necessary if one is to understand the diversity and similarities of Black Americans within the context of the American diaspora. Furthermore, plausible questions could also be raised about cultural parallels between Blacks in the United States, the Caribbean, and South America, including the extent to which African retentions are noted in contemporary Black American lifestyles, and the degrees of acculturation and assimilation among Blacks in the United States. Brought to the New World as slaves, Africans reacted to situations in different ways. Their reactions were varied and essentially were a function of many interactive factors, including their particular African backgrounds, their time of arrival, geographical location, how the plantation on which they lived was organized and operated, the numerical ratio of Whites to Blacks, and the extent of contact between Blacks and Whites, and between Blacks and Blacks.

Understandably, then, the first generation of Blacks probably felt a greater compulsion to try to transplant African customs and traditions in America than did later generations. They had no other language, religion, or values. Another series of factors and circumstances that, in part, explain Black behavior in America is significant at this point. Blacks in the United States did not assimilate into the structure of mainstream society to the extent that Blacks did in Latin America. With respect to the different styles of cultural adaptations, which emerged among different groups of Blacks in the New World, the same culturally cultivating processes—enculturation and acculturation—took place simultaneously in North and South America. Although slavery in South America was equally dehumanizing, as cruel and immoral as in the United States, some conditions did exist that created a sociopolitical climate generally more conducive to both the survival of African traditions—the enculturative process—and the assimilation of Africans into European customs and culture, the acculturative process. Among these conditions were the concentration of large numbers of Blacks in the same area; the constant influx of other Blacks directly from Africa, which contributed to the continuation and revitalization of African customs and traditions; the tendency to keep Black families together; the idea of inferiority of Blacks was less pervasive; and many African descendants intermarried with Europeans and Indians (especially in Brazil). While most colonists abolished slavery during the 1800s, many of the economic, social, and political developments that accompanied slavery continue to present day.

The history of Blacks in America is the history of the American racial dilemma. For centuries, Blacks have seen themselves through the revelation and measurement of White people who have looked on them with sentiments ranging from amused contempt and pity to fear and hatred. To the Romans, slaves were merely vulgar and conquered people who were not accorded the rights and privileges of Roman citizenship. The Greeks looked on slaves as unfortunate citizens of their plundered lands who failed to cultivate their minds and desires and were thus reduced to that lowly but necessary state. But in America, slaves were property and were not even considered human beings. With the Emancipation Proclamation came the vain search for freedom. For more than three centuries on this continent, Blacks have been denied equal access to education, economic security, and other societal advantages and generally have been relegated to menial levels of work or joblessness, which, to a great extent, continue to result in conditions of poverty, disunion, and misery for countless millions. It must be recognized, however, that throughout their struggle, Blacks have wanted to be both Black and American, with pride in both. Blacks have always felt that their African heritage had something to offer America, as did the European ethnic cultures. Consistent with cultural pluralist thinking, African Americans, not unlike Irish Americans, is unique and different and is desirous of remaining that way. This diversity is America's greatness. This diversity is America!

◆ AFRICAN AMERICANS IN TEXAS

On going to school

I would come home with five A's and a B, and my father would say, Why do you have a B?
—Barbara Jordan

Students in public schools in Texas have become majority minority. Based on information in the 2014 Texas Education Agency report, the racial make-up is 52% Hispanic, 13% Black, and 29% White. Unfortunately, in some instances, statistically African American students are an invisible group of students in Texas public schools. In Texas public schools, regardless of African American students zip code or socioeconomic status, African American students are placed at a higher rate in special education classes, suspended, expelled, and pushed out (dropout) of school at a higher rate than any other group of students. A dropout is defined as a student who is enrolled in public school in Grades 7–12, does not return to public school the following fall, is not expelled, and does not: graduate, receive a GED certificate, continue school outside the public school systems, begin college, or die. The TEA report shows that the longitudinal dropout rate for the Class of 2014 Grade 9 cohort was 6.6% (the same percentage as the Class of 2013), with the rate for Asian students at 2.4%, White students at 3.6%, Hispanic students at 8.2% and African American students at 9.8% (McMillion, Wright, & Merrill, 2015). Texas public schools need to value and address the identity crisis development of African American males.

Recognizing an identity crisis of an African American male in sports does not benefit the group. Sadly, in Texas it seems the focus is to make money for educational institutions starting in high school, continuing through college and ultimately to the multibillion dollar industry in the National Football League and National Basketball Association. It is imperative that African American Adolescent Males are helped to overcome the struggles of an identity crisis because of alarming national statistics. These categories include: low academic achievement, high rates of being victims and perpetrators of homicides (Fox & Swatt, 2008), declining rates for life expectancy (Anderson, 2006), high numbers of youth engaging in gang activities (Hill,

Howell, Hawkins, & Battin-Pearson, 1999), high numbers of delinquency (Toldson, Sutton, & Brown, 2012), and growing rates of suicide (Poussaint & Alexander, 2000). The rates of incarceration, conviction, and arrest are the highest for AAAMs compared to every other demographic group in the nation (Gilgoff, 2007). African American males are also least likely to be hired and most likely to be unemployed (Hornor, 2002). AAAMs, in comparison to their peers, are more likely to drop out of school and less likely to graduate from high school (Brown, 2005). These quality-of life indicators considered to be the identity development crisis among the African American Adolescent Male population (Hatcher, Williams, & Hanes, 2015)." For Texas to continue to flourish economically amongst other states education institutions have to provide a top education to all students.

◆ AFRICAN AMERICANS ACHIEVING EDUCATIONAL EXCELLENCE

Education is the key to unlock the golden door of freedom.

—George Washington Carver

Achieving educational excellence for African Americans starts from birth and continues through college completion. The American Dream has been the belief that education paves the way to success in our society. Education opens the door of success for students living in poverty or a desire to move to a higher socioeconomic group. Obtaining the education needed to attain good jobs and opportunities is still not a reality for too many African Americans in our nation. Students at any age, from birth through adulthood, deserve opportunities that enable them to be successful at school and prepare for careers they desire, that will support them and their families (The White House Initiative on Educational Excellence For African Americans, 2015).

Key components of achieving excellence for African Americans are equity, quality early learning, K-12 reforms, STEM, college and career readiness and mentoring programs.

Equality of opportunity which is a vital American value cannot be attained without equity in education. Regardless of wealth, race, language, gender, disability, etc. must have the chance to learn and achieve. Too many students, especially in underserved communities, lack access to a quality education. A quality of education includes high-quality preschool, strong teachers and school leaders, rigorous course offerings, high standards, robust enrichment both in and outside of school, safe environments, the support of caring adults, and affordable higher education.

◆ QUALITY EARLY LEARNING

Education is the most powerful weapon which you can use to change the world.

—Nelson Mandela

Much of the achievement gap we see between different groups of children develops well before they enter kindergarten. It is more difficult to close the achievement gap than it is to prevent the achievement gap. Parents and caregivers are the first teachers a child has before attending kindergarten. One of the first steps, to achieving educational excellence is partnering with communities to show them what quality early learning resembles.

Quality early learning is imperative because from birth until age 5, a child's brain develops more than at any other period in life. Research indicates that too many African American children, especially from families with low incomes, are not attending early education programs. High quality early education gives African American students an increased chance to succeed in school and life. When students miss early learning and development opportunities, it results in more money being spent to catch and close the achievement gap.

◆ K-12 Reforms

A little learning, indeed, may be a dangerous thing, but the want of learning is a calamity to any people.

—Frederick Douglass, Address, Washington, DC

Currently, there is a high need for K-12 Reforms in America because the National Center for Education Statistics (2015) Reports that 53% of African American fourth graders are reading below grade level nationally, 44% of African American eighth-graders are reading below grade level, and 74% of students who cannot read well by the end of third grade do not do well in later grades and often drop out before earning a high school diploma. The United States has one of the highest high school dropout rates in the world. There have been breakthroughs in closing achievement gaps in graduation rates between African Americans and their White counterparts, but there is still a long way to go. The graduation percentage rate growth over the past 2 years has improved. African American growth rate is 3.7% and White growth rate is 2.6% (U.S Department of Education, 2010). Of African American students who complete high school and attend college, half are required to take remedial courses and nearly half never graduate. A college degree or advanced certificate represents the entry ticket to rewarding careers. The "achievement gap" is one of the most disturbing phenomena in American education. Teachers want to close the gap in their own schools, but because the gap is rooted in longstanding and widespread problems, the task sometimes feels like a monumental undertaking (Hawley, 2009).There is an achievement gap, but addressing the achievement gap should not be the primary focus. The priority should include meeting African American students where they are and teaching them with high expectations. Caring about students, valuing and believing in student achievement will yield positive results and ultimately close the achievement gap.

◆ College and Career Readiness

I think going to college for that one year was probably the best thing I have ever done.

—Carmelo Anthony

There are two national goals and one is that all adult Americans pursue at least 1 year of higher education or career training, and that America regains its role as the world leader in college completion. Historically, education determines the future success and wealth of a nation. Teaching is very important in educating all students because having a great teacher; school leader and school administrator make a big difference in how well students perform in school and in life. While 16% of students in the U.S. identify as African American, only 7% of teachers identify as African American. Unfortunately, less than 2% of the nation's educators are African American men and most of those are on secondary campuses (The White House Initiative on Educational Excellence For African Americans, 2015).

It is imperative that schools support a college completion culture in the African American community in three important ways:

1. Talk to students about the fact that they can go to and graduate from college.

   African American students must believe they are smart enough to graduate from college.

   Students need to be engaged in discussions about campus life and the benefits of higher education. Include parents or guardians in discussions about reassuring their child about the possibility of going to college. If the parents or guardians do not believe this possibility, help them understand all students are capable of meeting high expectations (The White House Initiative on Educational Excellence For African Americans, 2015).

2. Include in the curriculum taking students to visit colleges and universities. Attend institutions of higher education in the African American community or city. Plan a trip to a higher education campus, walk around the campus, talk to students, let them eat on campus and help the students imagine learning and succeeding in college (The White House Initiative on Educational Excellence For African Americans 2015).

3. The last important way is to support the students. Inform them about how scholarships are awarded which includes the importance of maintaining good grades and conduct. The cost of higher education should not prevent African American students from achieving their dreams of attaining a high-quality education and degree. Ensuring that students know about college preparation and financial aid resources available at StudentAid.gov will guide them in the right direction in reaching a bright future (The White House Initiative on Educational Excellence For African Americans, 2015).

◆ AFRICAN AMERICANS, EDUCATION AND EQUAL EDUCATIONAL OPPORTUNITY

Our progress as a nation can be no swifter than our progress in education. The human mind is our fundamental resource.

—John F. Kennedy

Contrary to the beliefs of many, a significant number of Blacks have always viewed the acquisition of an education as a means of escape from their plight, as a means of hope. Hilliard (1984) suggested that it is only a temporary loss of memory that causes one to forget that African people were brought here in chains, but were nevertheless very richly endowed. African captives were not ignorant, savage, or pagan. Some knew the Quran from memory and could write in Arabic. Some could read and write indigenous West African scripts. All were highly educated and profoundly religious, sharing in a very complex culture, a culture that had allowed survival for thousands of years. Some Africans had even made Atlantic Ocean crossings and were in America long before the time of Columbus. Others had arrived here before the time of Christ, leaving their portraits carved in stone in Mexico and their writing in other places as well (Fell, 1976; Van Sertima, 1976).

It took an educational effort that was systematic, intensive, and unparalleled in the history of the world to erase these memories, to cloud vision, to impair hearing, and to impede the operation of the critical capacities among African Americans. Once reference points were lost, African Americans as a people became like a computer without a program, a spacecraft without a homing device, a dependent without a benefactor.

To understand what is happening to African Americans as a people (not as a minority or as poverty-stricken or as individuals) and especially what is happening to African Americans in education, one must start at the beginning and try to grasp the whole story. There is a need to view the whole story in order to see the patterns, which give us the essence of what is happening. To fail to perceive the pattern is to raise one's susceptibility to the seductiveness of attractive but false issues. Jean Piaget calls this capacity in young children conservation; that is, being able to see the changes in form may not mean that there are changes in the form of African American education, but few changes in substances. Of particular interest that despite the fact that we have embarked on a major accountability movement creating changes in curriculum, teaching strategies and assessment, minority children seem to remain at the bottom of the learning curve. Most data from 1970 to present show either flat achievement or gains canceled by losses. It seems that the achievement gap between minority and White students, which narrowed in the 1980s, has either stopped or begun to widen again (Manno, 1998). One might argue that such changes are merely superficial and do little to address the real needs of students. Educational opportunity remains a concern as the gaps between advantaged and disadvantaged students remain huge, with devastating effects on minority children as they seek to move up in society. In *A Nation Still at Risk*, Allen (1998) suggests that millions of Americans, mainly the children of the poor and minorities, do not enjoy full participation in the educational system. They are stuck with what "the system" dishes out to them, and all too often they are stuck with the least qualified teachers, the most rigid bureaucratic structures, the fewest choices, and the shoddiest quality. Those Parents who yearn for something better for their children lack the power to make it happen. They lack the power to shape their own lives and those of their children.

The first thing that any educator or citizen needs that would attempt to solve our educational problems is a clear sense of history. In the latter regard, DuBois (1973), Bullock (1970), Woodson (1969), Bond (1972), King (1971), Spivey (1978), and many others have given us all that we need to see certain key patterns. For example, in Bullock's *A History of Negro Education in the South* (1970), the following points were noted: He described the educational system that was designed for slaves, noting the changes that took place following episodes such as Nat Turner's fight for freedom. The first adjustment that slave owners far and near made after the fight was to change the nature of the educational system for the slave. The Slave Codes were set up to enhance this intellectual containment, among other things. After slavery, the Freedman's Bureau and its successor, African American private education efforts, and publicly supported education that was inspired and initiated in the south mainly by African Americans (DuBois, 1973), began to show remarkable results. African Americans excelled very quickly wherever literacy training was offered. The fear was not that African Americans could not learn; the fear then and later was that they would.

Bullock picks as his next major point the 1964 Civil Rights Act, a comprehensive piece of legislation that included provisions for mechanisms that were designed to reduce inequities, including inequities in the schools. We must point out that it also took several major court cases to try to accelerate the equity process: *Hobson v. Hartsen* to outlaw the tracking system in Washington, DC; *Larry P. v. Wilson Riles* to outlaw the use of I.Q. testing for placing Black children into classes for the mentally retarded in California; the Ann Arbor Joiner decision on Black language to require educators to take Black language diversity into account in the schools; *Debra P. v. Turlington* to prevent the denial of diploma to Blacks who failed tests that did not match the schooling that they were offered, and many others. All these efforts were required after the Brown decision. They still are required and necessary now.

In 1968, Professor Charles V. Hamilton of Roosevelt University captured the essence of the time at the height of the upheavals of the 1960s led by African American dissidents. His now widely quoted article appeared in the Harvard Educational Review and was titled Race and Education: A Search for Legitimacy. His analysis was astute. While it was noted and quoted, these authors do not believe that most of us comprehended the full implications of his comments. To be sure, Hamilton directed his attention to the crux of the problem. He revealed that African Americans were looking for a liberating, meaningful, quality education and that they were questioning the capacity of the schools, all schools, to deliver such an education.

In his short article, Hamilton made many key points:

1. African American parents, students, and educators in the 1960s were asking questions about the education systems that were fundamentally different from those who were being reared by traditional educators who were conducting the national dialogue. In effect, African Americans were questioning the legitimacy of educational institutions while traditional educators were merely questioning the efficiency of those institutions.

2. As a result of such questioning, a tension arose between the two groups. One group saw community control of schools as the answer and thus would build their own institutions. The other groups perceived school integration as the way and would have Black and White students share in the same process, whatever it was. More significantly, however, the process itself was not questioned.

3. African Americans had made explicit demands about African and African Americans' cultural awareness being given equal importance as equal as was that given verbal and computational skills. It is important to note that this notion was not a demand that cultural awareness be substituted for academic and intellectual skills, as some antagonists tried to suggest. African Americans wanted both skills and awareness.

Then, as now, a plethora of commissions were reporting on education. By the same token, the reports did not deal with the specific problems of African Americans, even though African Americans were then, as now, the most educationally depressed group. This insensitivity at the highest level was an integral catalyst that prompted African Americans to believe that the schools would fail them, especially as matters stood then. Hamilton perceived the basic focus of the reports as how to do a more efficient job of the same thing the schools had been doing. As Hamilton expressed it, institutions only became legitimate in the eyes of their people when the people believed that the institution's service was appropriate for them. At that point, they can give the institution their loyalty and allegiance. Needless to say, when African Americans looked at the schools, they saw no payoff for themselves, especially the payoffs they expected—academic excellence and positive self-images. It was this latter factor, especially, that the traditional experts failed to address then, just as they have failed to address it in the most recent state of reports.

To buttress his analysis, Hamilton compared the results of the reports of the National Association of African American Educators with the Coleman Report, the African history and culture demands by students with the Civil Rights Commission's emphasis on Racial Isolation in the Schools, and the Harlem branch of the Congress on Racial Equity's demands for independent community schools with the Chicago Board of Education's Redmon Report. What he found was that Blacks and Whites are worlds apart in their definitions of the problem and in their visions of a solution. Hamilton summarized the views of 800 African American educators as follows:

1. They wanted to control their own schools;
2. They wanted parents to be deeply involved in the schools and in a working alliance with their children's teachers;
3. They wanted to have schools that were designed for maximum positive psychological impact through the careful use of staffing patterns, holidays, group solidarity and pride, Black curriculum perspectives, and evaluation criteria; and
4. They wanted appropriate curriculum and instructional materials.

Hamilton's own model for change highlighted three key points:

1. He challenged the notion that integrated education was synonymous with quality education;
2. He felt that the school in predominantly African American communities should be the focal point for both school and community activities; and
3. He felt that schools should belong to the communities in which they were located.

It must be remembered that problems in education are inseparable from problems of the larger society. That is to say, the type of education that is offered will always fit the socio-politico-economic context. If there is oppression in the general society, the schools supported by that society would be a part of the oppression. Hilliard (1984) described the specific features of the system that were used to oppress African Americans. Six of the steps used were the following:

1. African American history and culture were suppressed and distorted.
2. African American group identities were suppressed.
3. White supremacy was taught in the schools, churches, the mass media, and so forth.
4. All African American social institutions, as well as the larger societal institutions, were controlled by European Americans.
5. Systematic steps were taken to ensure that African Americans could not accumulate resources.
6. African Americans were physically segregated from European Americans.

The battle against the last step in the aforementioned system has been waged since 1954. The courts have ruled against segregation. Legislation and regulations have outlawed segregation, even though the present national leadership appears to be openly hostile to equity protections. Yet, five of the six features mentioned earlier have received little systematic attention. Apparently, it was believed that desegregation and integration alone would and could remedy all of the ills of the system. Indubitably, though, education has an active role to play in reversing all of the six mechanisms and their effects. For example, without a clear sense of history, without a clear cultural consciousness, and without a clear sense of identity, group unity and self-help, then, other than on an individual basis, are impossible to achieve. In the past, any educational effort that fostered these things was destroyed immediately.

To be sure, African Americans have been derailed in efforts to rebuild a group capacity for rebuilding. Sometimes remedies for past injustices have been pursued; yet, ironically, these have worked against the development of a fundamental asset—namely, a strong sense of group unity. If the past two decades have taught nothing else, they should have shown us clearly that African Americans cannot depend upon others, no matter how sympathetic, to sustain an effort that will change the basic conditions of life for the masses of African Americans. In the final analysis, the real measure of progress will not be the condition of the few but the many.

It is because of these points that it is clear that Hamilton was right in 1968 and is right now. Like DuBois, Woodson, and Garvey before him, Hamilton saw that it was not where one sat but rather what one received where he sat that mattered. Being miseducated in integrated schools was not really different from being miseducated in segregated schools. Certainly no one can condone or permit the evil system of legally and morally sanctioned segregation of schools to thrive. Yet community schools are not segregated schools unless enforced legal protections to maintain free access to housing, jobs, and schools are missing. Likewise, it would be inane to contend that simply because a school is predominantly African American, then it is segregated. We create and live in a fog of conceptual confusion whenever we use terms that cause us to lose sight of all the elements in the problem, especially to the extent that we subsequently accept incomplete remedies to that problem.

Again, Hamilton reminds us that integration as experienced in America is not necessarily synonymous with quality education. To wit, Hamilton's vision of a quality education is one wherein the school belongs to a community and wherein the school becomes the center of a myriad of hosts of related community activities. To implement such a situation, then, means drawing on strength that flows out of group unity. It also clearly suggests that the community must be valued. To this end, community involvement is critical as schools seek to create effective learning environments. The traditional approach in America has been to discredit the community, value system, and lifestyles of individuals in minority schools. This approach does not work in contemporary education. School leaders must understand that effective learning can only occur when we embrace the culture and community of the students. When we focus on respect and understanding of the learner, we can significantly enhance the learning environment.

A Nation Still at Risk (Allen, 1998) evaluates the current risk by indicating.

> we face a widening and unacceptable chasm between good schools and bad, between those youngsters who get an adequate education and those who emerge from school barely able to read and write. Poor and minority children, by and large, go to worse schools, have less expected of them, are taught by less knowledgeable teachers, and have the least power to alter bad situations.

This information reiterates the thinking of Witty (1982) who suggested that a review of public school education activity from around the nation over the past few decades did not give us a great cause for hope. For example, the African American principal is now a dying breed in many communities where once he/she was previously in abundance. In addition, the National Teacher Examinations, along with other state licensing examinations, have been used to deny licensure to disproportionately large numbers of African American teachers, to deny initial employment to others, to deny tenure to others, and to evaluate programs of teacher education in Black colleges. Likewise, many Black colleges are being threatened with the loss of accreditation or authorization to offer teacher education programs because of the test scores of their graduates. Yet no one has shown that the content of this national examination are related to better teaching. The net result of use of the teacher examinations is that fewer African American teachers will be employed in the nation's schools and offering no guarantee that our children will learn better as a result.

Finally, it must be understood that Black people have left indelible marks on the pages of American history and continue to exert significant influence on the shaping of American culture. This reality needs to be judiciously considered as this nation begins to think about restructuring American education so that its underlying principles are more compatible with the ethnic, cultural, and social characteristics of our pluralistic society. Black Americans are indeed bicultural. As such, they share and practice some of the values, behaviors, institutions, and beliefs of the common American culture, while at the same time, they engage in an alternative lifestyle resulting from Black culture. As Gay (1977, pp. 51–55) explained: The realities and influence of Black American heritage, the nature of Black life, and the presence and influence of Blacks in American history and generally in American life posit several important educational implications. First, teachers and other school personnel need to develop a better understanding of the concept of culture. Educators also need to understand that despite changes over time, the original heritages and historical experiences of ethnic groups still have significant impacts upon the lives and identification processes of members of these groups today. Students have a right to be proud of their ethnic and cultural identity. The inclusion of this element in school programs as legitimate curriculum content is fundamental to providing quality education. School leaders should understand why ethnic and cultural diversity has been a vital, catalytic force in American life and culture of the past, how it can be so in the present and the future. Moreover, they need to learn how to use information about different ethnic groups and their cultural experiences in the process of analyzing the social, interactional, and instructional dynamics of multiethnic classrooms. Second, not only Blacks, but all students need to receive instruction in Black American heritage and culture. This content should become an integral part of the total school curriculum—that is, appropriately incorporated in all subjects and learning experiences for all students at all grade levels. Third, the heritage and experiences of Black Americans are complex and multidimensional. A one-dimensional, single-subject approach to the study of Black American life is inadequate for the task. Fourth, to teach Black students most effectively and to implement the best multicultural education programs possible require more than curricular changes. Black students and their teachers who come from different ethnic and experiential backgrounds may look at the same situations and see different meanings to them. These behaviors stem from differing perceptions and referential codes. A fifth implication, learning style differences, is closely related to the foregoing. Black students are likely to be more inclined toward learning in social-group settings instead of in the formal, individualistic environments generally prevalent in American schools. Undoubtedly, this predilection reflects the cultural and historical emphases of Black Americans on cooperation, communalism, and mutual aid in work situations, or what Lerone Bennett describes as "the responsibility of each to all and all to each" (Bennett, 1975, p. 136).

Among the thousands of African Americans who have made Texas their home—some less important, others more important than those cited above—many individuals have made contributions in exploration, colonization, and the growth of Texas further under Spanish and then under Anglo control. Admittedly, over the past 30 years, the situation of African American Texans has improved legally, socially, politically, and to a lesser degree, economically. Today, many closed doors of opportunity have opened into positions of wealth, power, and prominence for them in the state and in the nation. Somewhat ironically, attitudes of the people now seem to change slower than do the laws. The trend, to be sure, is steady and unmistakable. Unlike some other ethnic groups in Texas, African Americans were forced to abandon the heritage of their native land. Fortunately like most groups, they developed an indigenous culture in their new home, and the state and the nation are the richer for this cultural enrichment and development.

◆ MEXICAN AMERICANS

In the early 1800s, as White settlement expanded across the western frontier, Anglo settlers eventually came into contact with Hispanics in the Southwest. Thus was born a familiar story about the Southwest. Powerful Anglo settlers, imbued with the notion of manifest destiny (a belief that destiny ordained their expansion all the way to the Pacific Ocean), came into contact with an established but weaker Hispanic community. The powerful group wanted, and got, the land of the weaker one. In 1830, Anglo colonists outnumbered Mexicans in what is now Texas by six to one. By 1836, Texas had so many Anglos that it eventually broke away from Mexico and sought to establish a separate republic. The historic battle at the Alamo in 1836 in what is now San Antonio was, indeed, lost by the colonists (Anglos and numerous persons of Spanish American origin); however, 6 weeks later Sam Houston and his Anglo troops defeated Mexican President General Santa Anna's and ultimately achieved independence.

According to Tenorio (1977), many Tejanos (persons of Spanish-Mexican heritage) supported the new Republic of Texas. Three of them signed the Texas Declaration of Independence and one became the first vice president of Texas. By 1845, Texas had become part of the United States. Later, in 1848, the United States launched an expansionist war against Mexico. As a result, Mexicans living north of the new border became known as Mexican Americans. While they were given assurances of fair treatment, particularly regarding their land holdings, they instead met with racism and suffered exposure to feelings of discrimination and denial. In many areas, these feelings are believed to have continued to the present time. Tenorio (1977) further suggested that when Americans of Spanish-Mexican-Indian heritage in 1848 sought citizenship status, they brought with them vestiges of the system of social stratification that had been imposed on them by Spanish rule of more than 300 years. Needless to say, becoming American citizens did not change this system. The original rulers who had been born in Spain were known as peninsulares. They were replaced after the Mexican Revolution (1810–1824) by the creoles (Mexicans born of Spanish parents). During the nineteenth century, most Mexican Americans were mestizos (children of Spanish and Indian parents). Below this latter group in the social and economic status were the Indians, known as indios and indigenous.

On the other hand, the frontier contact between Anglos and Hispanics appears similar to that which existed between White settlers and Native Americans. However, Mexican labor was incorporated into the economy of the Southwest later in the twentieth century; and so Mexican Americans—meaning Hispanos of the borderlands and immigrants from Mexico—were never excluded from the larger society to the extent that Native Americans were. Of the approximately 20 million persons of Spanish origin in the United States, persons of Mexican origin account for more than 12.5 million, according to the U.S. Bureau of the Census. Therefore,

Mexican Americans, a heterogeneous group in itself, represent ~60% of the total population of Spanish extraction, the largest single group of Spanish Americans (Johnson, 1976).

At the time of earliest contact, early in the nineteenth century, it is estimated that the Hispanic community of the Southwest numbered no more than 200,000 persons. Hraba (1979) noted that this community was composed of three economic classes: elite landlords who possessed large tracts of land and could trace their property rights back to the Spanish land grants in the New World; a large class of poor Mexican Indian laborers; and a small number of middle-class merchants, small ranchers, and farmers. Early in the twentieth century, in connection with both the growth of the Southwest as an economic empire and with the Mexican Revolution (1910), the Spanish-speaking community of the Southwest was fraught with immigrants from Mexico. McWilliams (1968) estimated that fully 10% of the Mexican people immigrated into the United States early in this century; the vast majority of them took up work in the Southwest. This immigration pattern continues even to this day. Thus, America's second largest minority group, as Mexican Americans are sometimes called, is unique among ethnic groups in America inasmuch as it is both indigenous and immigrant in character.

Much of the area in America's Southwest, which now includes the states of Texas, California, New Mexico, Nevada, Arizona, and Colorado, once was part of the Hispanic domain, which originally was based in Mexico. The names of some of these states and several cities within them reflect historic Spanish and Mexican influences: Amarillo, Atascadero, Alamagordo, Los Alamos, Pueblo, San Francisco, Los Angeles, and Sacramento are a few examples of these Spanish and Mexican place names.

The Mexican American Family Structure

Among Mexican Americans, the family's role is significantly important and is very traditional. For one thing, the Mexican American family is structured with the father as patriarch. Moreover, family relationships are close, and children are accorded love, warmth, and attention. Regarding adherence to ethnic values and mores, Castaneda (1974) opined that these attributes would likely vary in strength depending on the community and family from which a child comes. Thus, values are strongest in traditional (in urban barrios and in rural colonies) where family values are almost identical with those in Mexico. On the other hand, in dualistic communities, there is some adaptation to Anglo American values and some maintenance of traditional Mexican values. In traditional communities, however, Mexican American values have become amalgamated with American values.

Another significant aspect of Mexican Americans' family structure is the continuity fostered by at least 300 centuries of a similar culture and language. Lourdes Miranda King (in Johnson, 1976) suggested that of any single ethnic minority, the Spanish Americans have resisted melting by refusing to abandon their cultural and linguistic heritage. The Spanish language has persisted, despite the overwhelming attempts to assimilate forcibly the Spanish American linguistically. Historically, however, economic, social, political, and legal pressures have been exerted in an attempt to eradicate the Spanish language from ethnic communities. Some southwestern states and the state of California have ruled unlawful the use of Spanish as the language of instruction. Once again, this posture is characterized by a lack of understanding and respect for their heritage. The outdated "melting pot" model forced the educational arena to frown upon the use of a second language. This lack of understanding on the part of administrators has exacerbated this problem and created communication disjoints with Hispanic families.

Educational Needs of Mexican Americans

Provisions for the education of Mexican American children must take into account the social, cultural, economic, and educational characteristics of the Mexican American population. Although they are represented across the economic spectrum, generally they come from poor and/or low-income levels; they have a lower level of educational attainment than does the overall population; they were either born into or now live in a different cultural environment from the vast majority of students with whom they interact; in many cases they are not White by American standards but rather perceive themselves as non-Black; they live within a conflict of cultural and social values with those they are expected to accept and embrace in school and those they learn at home; and, in many cases, they speak only a foreign language—Spanish.

Griggs and Dunn (1995) examined the learning styles of Hispanic American students and found that larger numbers of Hispanic students prefer the following:

1. Cool environment
2. Conformity
3. Peer-oriented learning
4. Kinesthetic instructional resources
5. High degree of structure
6. Late morning and afternoon peak energy levels
7. Variety as opposed to routines
8. Field-dependent cognitive style

Being cognizant of these differences may allow an educator to create a more responsive environment. They also suggest that educators need to be aware of self-image problems of Hispanic American students that may result from a rejection of their ethnicity and from attempts to conform to the larger Anglo culture. Effective educators minimize the conflict and create a learning environment where these differences are celebrated and conflict due to traditional expectations is minimized.

Hispanic students were considerably more segregated in Texas, which had the second highest population of Hispanics during the 1970s. While Texas did experience some desegregation of Hispanic students during the 1980s the level of segregation has increased during the 1990s (Orfield, 2001). Orfield also reports "Texas had the nation's second highest dropout rate by some measures, which rose significantly for Latino students following the imposition of a high school graduation test in the early 1980s." Evidence exists that the isolation and segregation of Hispanic students has had detrimental effects. Hispanics have the highest dropout rate of any ethnic group in this country. It is reported that one half of all Mexican American and Puerto Rican students do not graduate from high schools (National Council of La Raza, 1989). Also of concern is the fact that Hispanic students are increasingly isolated from Whites, and are more highly concentrated in high poverty schools, than any other group of students (Orfield, Bachmeier, James, & Eitle, 1997).

Bilingual Education Efforts

In a critical case, the U.S. Supreme Court of Appeals for the 10th Circuit upheld the earlier *Serna v. Portales* Municipal Schools Decision, which held bilingual-bicultural education is a right of non-English-speaking children under Title VI of the Civil Rights Act of 1964. Earlier, in a similar case, *Lau et al. v. Nichols et al.*, the San Francisco school systems were required to provide English language instruction for approximately 1,000 students of Chinese ancestry who did not speak English.

Although the debate continues, these cases provide a solid legal base for enforcing the principle of special obligations to non-English-speaking children nationally via the provision of equal educational opportunity. Likewise, one can reason that the academic failures of these children are due primarily to an educational system whose practitioners have refused to intervene in the cycle of exclusion, which has been their fate. As indicated in the Kerner Report, the problem is the one who causes it, the prejudiced and biased non-disadvantaged, and the White "people responsible for the poverty of those" disadvantaged.

For years, the response to this educational dilemma has been to establish English as a Second Language (ESL or ESOL) programs with in schools. The object of this approach was to increase the English language skills of non-English-speaking children. Studies by Lambert (1955) in Canada have shown that students who learn to read first in their native language have an advantage over students who must learn first in English. To be sure, the child who learns to read first in Spanish is also learning a writing system, that is very regular, with close correspondence between sounds and letters. Certainly bilingual education is not a panacea for all Spanish or Mexican American children, but it does represent a degree of hope. King (1976) continued pointing out that a well-conceived bilingual, bicultural education program will be successful only if it also takes into account cognitive styles as the Spanish American child performs better in situations de-emphasizing competitiveness and asserting cooperation, on tasks requiring visual, rather than the auditory, and with textbooks that reflect their reality.

In 1968, the U.S. Office of Education defined bilingual, bicultural education as the use of two languages, one of which is English, as mediums of instruction for the same pupil population in a well-organized program that encompasses the entire curriculum and that includes the study of history and the cultures. Krashen (1997) suggests the best bilingual education programs include all of these characteristics: ESL, instruction, sheltered subject matter teaching, and instruction in the first language. Non-English speaking children initially receive core instruction in the primary language along with ESL instruction. As children grow more proficient in English, they learn subjects using more contextualized language (e.g., math and science) in sheltered classes taught in English, and eventually in mainstream classes. In this way, the sheltered classes function as a bridge between instruction in the first language and in the mainstream.

Irrespective of the selected structure, the value of a full bilingual, bicultural education program, accompanied by appropriately prepared teachers and materials, community involvement and participation, and high expectations and commitment, will achieve the desired results and outcomes. The current high-stakes testing environment challenges bilingual education programs because of the focus on test scores. The need for students to perform on tests given in English outweighs the intention to create a true bilingual learning environment.

While proponents of bilingual, bicultural approaches advocate expanding such programs, those opposed continue to question their efficacy. In any case, administrators and teachers, as they increase in sensitivity, must understand that there is no one model of the Mexican American. It must be equally clear, too, that negative stereotypes, often obtained from American movies and otherwise, are equally unjustified. Characterization of Mexican Americans as lazy, indolent, and lacking motivation perpetuates labeling that is erroneously applied by those who lack insight and/or understanding of the values, lifestyles, folkways, and mores of Mexican Americans. Administrators are challenged to seek out accurate information that will assist them in better understanding all cultures.

◆ NATIVE AMERICANS IN TEXAS

Native Americans, the first Americans and Texans, have a special uniqueness in America by virtue of being the pre-Colombian inhabitant and possessor of the American continents. In addition, the Indian, by right of the U.S. Constitution and other national treaties and policies has a special relationship with the federal government.

Native Americans, usually identified by tribe, oftentimes have been described as a unitary group. This belief and/or attitude persisted for a number of reasons. There are many in America who do not realize that Indians are quite variable, and that the Native Indian American culture is not one culture but many, often at opposite ends of a continuum of human behavior. To be sure, Native Americans are different, not only from non-Indians but also tremendously different among various tribal groups and subgroups.

Historical Issues

In 1528, the Karankawas were the first Texas Indians to become acquainted with the Europeans who would eventually take over their homeland. In a report titled the Indian Texans (1970), the Karankawas greeted survivors of the Narvaez expedition, which was shipwrecked on an island off the Texas coast with awe and delight. Four survivors, three Spaniards and one Negro, were enslaved until they won the respect of the Indians as medicine men and traders. Eventually, these four escaped and made their way along the coast, where they were also received as healers by various tribes. This first encounter with unarmed civilized men gave the Indians the false idea of the peaceful intentions of all White men and a great respect for the magic of their religion. One of the survivors of this 6-year adventure across Texas, Cabeza de Vaca, later published an account of the adventure, which is still one of the most valuable sources of information on Texas Indians of this period. Native Indian American people are extremely diverse and vary in lifestyles and languages. Native Americans in Texas have left an outstanding legacy in those who now reside there. In recent decades, the Native Indian American population in Texas has shown a significant increase. In 1900, the state had only 470 persons of Native American ancestry; in 1920, 2,109; in 1940, 4,103. The 1960 Census showed a population of 5,750, of whom 4,101 were urban and 1,649 were rural. The 2000 Census data report a population of 118,362 or 0.6% of the total population of Texas. According to the 2000 Census Report, individuals were allowed to self identify for the first time with more than one race, and this has continued. As result of self-identification with multiple race categories, the American Indian and Alaskan native population has increased almost twice as fast as the total U.S. population growing by 18%. More significantly, however, are the thousands of Native Americans who, over the years, have left the reservations, secured educations, and made a place for themselves in the trades, businesses, and professions. Every major Texas City has a number of Native Americans who achieved notable success.

Educational Needs of the Native Indian American

These students have a unique cultural heritage that should not be ignored, but expecting less is detrimental. Respecting the culture within an environment of high expectations is important in preparing Native Indian American students for future challenges. An appreciation for and sensitivity to these cultural differences by school leaders and other school staff personnel may be helpful in undoing some of the paternalistic, prejudicial, and presumptuous educational practices of the past. While there are exceptions, many schools that teach Native Americans are subject to criticism that the curriculum is irrelevant to their needs.

Although many Native Indian American parents agree that the mastery of English is important, some schools approach this problem by using programs of teaching English as a second language. However, the lack of trained teachers limits this approach. Additionally, the materials often have a strong Spanish-English bias, which may not be applicable for use with Native Americans. Some educators resist bilingualism because they still believe in the melting pot theory, with Native Americans being subjected to a one-way assimilation.

Special consideration must be given to the needs of teachers and others who work with Native Americans. They need to be sensitized to the sociocultural differences they encounter with Native Americans. This is not only a problem to be addressed by teacher-training institutions but also by administrators and supervisors who provide in-service training for teachers and generally facilitate the instructional process.

Many Native Indian American children differ from others in their level of acculturation. Historically, they have learned by doing, primarily because culture and language had not been reduced to writing. Therefore, teaching approaches that failed to take into account such learning style differences tended to project Native Americans as intellectually inferior and/or academically inept.

A multisensory approach that permits learning to occur in varied ways is preferred. The intent is to promote a learning environment responsive to students' needs. Positive learning growth promotes improved feelings and attitudes toward self, toward others, and toward learning. An enriched learning program using a multiplicity of approaches and materials should provide rewarding experiences for teachers and students. Native Indian American researchers, scholars, and educators are only now beginning to show a concerted effort to establish criteria for the selection of varied educational materials to be used with Native Indian American students. Some suggested criteria to be used are as follows:

1. Is the material accurate? Does the material accurately depict Native Indian Americana as they are rather than a projection of generalized stereotypes?
2. Does the material contribute to a positive self-image of the Native American? Does the experience represent an enhancing force as opposed to a degrading or ego-assaulting experience?
3. Does the material depict the Native American as a person of worth, whose culture has a right to exist on an equal basis in a world of many cultures?
4. Does the material contribute to an understanding that Native Americans had substantial roles of lasting impact on developing the American continents?

Finally, there are many factors that influence the learning environment of and for Native Americans, including the social atmosphere of the school and the administrative practices and policies that prevail. It is reasoned that the continuation of the progress made will require the collective efforts of school boards, the community, accrediting agencies, universities, Indian parents and students, and enlightened activists.

◆ ASIANS IN AMERICA

An oft quoted statement, taken from the tablet at the base of the Statue of Liberty beckons "Give me your tired, your poor, your huddled masses yearning to breathe free, the wretched refuse of your teeming shore. Send these, the homeless, tempest-tost to me; I lift my lamp beside the golden door." Apparently U.S. state and local lawmakers do not take into account the countless thousands of immigrants who respond to this appeal, seeking to escape tyranny, poverty, and other oppressive conditions in their native lands. Not all immigrants were or are welcome; many did not or do not possess the desired attributes or background for easy blending, and many came and continue to come with different notions of the meaning of America.

Such is the case with Asians and other ethnic minority groups including Haitians, Mexicans, Jamaicans, and Africans who do not possess the proper Caucasian background. Until after World War II, many immigrants from Asia were not kept on Ellis Island, in the shadow of the Statue of Liberty, but in the detention barracks on Angel Island near San Francisco's Alcatraz, a notorious prison. This racist attitude toward Asian refugees, in particular, led to the U.S. Congress passing, in 1882, the Chinese Exclusion Act, whereby the immigration of Chinese laborers was suspended for ten years. In 1892, the Geary Act extended these exclusion laws for another ten years. In 1902, the exclusion of Chinese immigrants was extended indefinitely, a curious posture when one considers that the greatness America has achieved attested to by many, is said to be due in great part to its diversity, openness, and willingness to accept all who would come.

Answers to questions regarding Asian migration to America are plentiful. Some Asians (specifically the Chinese) came as contract laborers with the intent of returning to their home country, while others arrived with the hope of permanent residence. On the other hand, many came for economic and educational opportunities with the hope of participating in the "American Dream."

The Chinese

The first Asians in Texas were the Chinese who worked on the railroads and in the mines, and those who followed held the traditional occupations of launderers, restaurateurs, truck farmers, and household servants. These were the same kind of occupations held by their countrymen in other parts of the United States. These were not necessarily the jobs they wanted, but local racism and discrimination kept them from many opportunities, and their mobility to gain citizenship limited possibilities in positions that restricted aliens. For example, New York prohibited noncitizens from participating in 27 occupations. During this period, before and following World War II, many states would not allow aliens to become doctors, lawyers, architects, even barbers, all activities that require a certificate or license. Further, many labor unions would not accept Chinese as members, keeping them in low-skill and/or semiskilled trades.

In Houston, conditions were very much like those described earlier. Accordingly, the restaurant and grocery business became the main economic activities of the Chinese. While in 1940, only 2.8% of the Chinese employed in America were in technical or professional fields, in Houston, for example, over 500 students at the University of Houston were studying science, engineering, or computer science; over 250 were studying business, economics, or accounting; whereas pharmacy and architecture had 50 students each. These numbers have continued to grow at universities throughout the State of Texas.

The Vietnamese

Vietnamese refugees migrated to America in two waves. The first wave consisted of mostly military personnel, civil servants, teachers, farmers, fishermen, employees of Americans, and Catholics. Recognizing that their middle and upper class lifestyles would not be compatible under a communist regime, these refugees feared reprisal and personal harm. The second wave occurred after the American military forces pullout in 1975.

Comparatively, there were vast differences in the demographic makeup of those in the first and second waves. In the first wave 49% were under 36 years of age and in the second wave 58%. The average family size was four in the first group, and four to five in the second. Forty-one percent were Catholic and 47% Buddhist in the second. Regarding education level, 48.8% of the first wave attended over 4 years of college, compared to 29.1% in the second.

Of these immigrants, who settled in Texas, Houston received a sizable proportion of this exodus. From fewer than 100 before 1975, there are presently more than 100,000 Indochinese in the Houston area alone. Houston has the second largest urban concentration of Indochinese in the United States, behind only Los Angeles. Why Houston? The reasons for the choice have been numerous and sometimes interacting. Some came as wives and family of ex-servicemen or on a temporary basis. Some came due to the semitropical nature of the city and, like other Americans; they were drawn by job opportunities.

Education and Language

Education and language are two examples of the problems and achievements of the Indochinese community. Not withstanding the length of time in the United States, many still express frustration with English. For those who came from Vietnam in the early years, the transition to English was made easier because the Vietnamese language had been Romanized under the French; many were educated in European-styled schools and some had dealt with Americans during the war. Regardless of their condition upon arrival, the refugee has generally displayed an intense desire to learn English in order to obtain a job and enter into the mainstream of his community.

Relative to education, the learning process takes place on three levels. On the most fundamental level is English language instruction. Once the language issue is satisfied, considerable progress is often realized and manifested in academic awards, outstanding grades and college entrance for many of these youngsters. On another level are adults who seek both language and skill training. English classes are provided by local school systems and volunteer agencies and vary in length. A third element is the regular college student, where there continues to be significant growth of the Indochinese, mostly Vietnamese students. It must be noted that Asians have earned the label of the super minority group because of their academic success in American schools. Research, however, suggests that this may not be the case for all Asians. Of interest is the fact that academic success may be a factor of increased socioeconomic status. Asians who do not enjoy the privilege of higher socioeconomic status often experience the same challenges of other minority groups in education.

Lesbian, Gay, Bisexual, and Transgender Students in Texas Cultural proficiency, support, and understanding are tenets of addressing and understanding diverse populations, which include Lesbian, Gay, Bisexual, and Transgender (LGBT) students. Schools are institutions of learning and serve as a microcosm of the wider lens of the world in which students co-exist daily. The climate and health of a school reinforce the thinking and behaviors of all stakeholders. Most teachers and administrators will agree that they work hard to make the learning environment a safe and nurturing place for all learners. But despite their best efforts, increasingly, LGBT students—including those who are thought to be—face the harsh reality of non-acceptance, bullying, and in some cases, disruption of academic progress. With heightened stressors, LGBT are most likely to experience negative educational outcomes.

With over 15,000 self-identified LGBT students, increasing resources for support within and outside of school continue to present an ongoing need. It is of salient understanding that creating an educator generated and student-centric focus on creating a supportive environment improves the educational trajectory for all students—not just LGBT. This need is not steeped in political ideology or rhetoric; rather, it is about providing support to one of the most vulnerable student population currently in today's schools.

In 2001, Governor Rick Perry signed the James Byrd Jr. Hate Crimes Act, which criminalized violent or coercive action against other Texas residents on various immutable traits, including sexual orientation. While school districts in Texas continue to dialogue on their best approach, some, such as the Keller Independent School District in Keller, Texas, will decide whether to include nondiscrimination protection for gender identity, gender expression, and sexual orientation in several district policies. Presenting knowledge of awareness and eliciting best practices from approved resources show meaningful practices that promote genuine inclusivity. Educators need to be able to address the aforementioned issues that may arise related to LGBT students. With an increase in hate crimes against LGBT, legislation has been a key proponent to take a stance that such behaviors will not be tolerated.

◆ CURRENT ISSUES AND TRENDS IN EDUCATION

We live in an increasingly diverse world where culture and language continue to underpin the critical nature of its existence as it relates to education. With an emphasis on global thinkers, shrinking the digital divide, and the rapidity of industrialization, one must understand the fundamentals of its intersection as it relates to today's learners. Advancements in technology have made the world appear smaller and increased the interaction between students not only in Texas but alsofrom all over the world. In order to maintain social mobility and opportunity as viable possibilities, educators must find ways to address current issues and trends.

Socioeconomic Status (SES)

It is no surprise that children raised in poverty are much less likely to have their needs met than their more affluent peers are, and as a result, are subject to significant consequences. In many poor households, parental education can be considered substandard, time is short, and the attunement process of student's education may be at risk. Those who offer care and support within these households may feel overwhelmed or overworked and are unable to extend school to home relations so needed for academic success. One study found that only 36% of low-income parents were involved in three or more school activities on a regular basis, compared with 59% of parents above the poverty line (U.S. Department of Health and Human Services, 2015). School facilities can also be resource deprived, where students do not receive adequate supplies, technology infrastructure is weak.

The Digital Divide

The ability to access computers and digitized learning has become increasingly important as it relates to acquisition of information because it allows students to completely immerse themselves in the community and world around them. While technology continues to advance with new mechanisms for learning, not everyone has access. The idea of the Digital Divide refers to the growing gap between the underserved members of our society, especially the poor, those in rural, elderly, and handicapped portion of the population who do not have access to computers or the internet; and the wealthy, middle-class, and young Americans living in urban and suburban areas who have access. Widening levels of education seem to magnify the Digital Divide; households with higher levels of education are increasingly more likely to use computers and the Internet. It has been observed that those with college degrees or higher are 10 times more likely to have internet access at work as than those with only a high school education. In addition, in direct correlation to education, the levels of household income also play a significant role in the widening gap. With the technology continuing to change and adapt, the issue of the Digital Divide simply cannot be ignored. In our society, where the distribution of wealth is already heavily unbalanced, access to computers and the Internet is unbalancing the situation even more. Significant efforts must be put into place to mitigate the widening of this gap. With socio-economic disparities present in today's society, the Digital Divide is compounding its effects. Identifying the gaps that exist within the Digital Divide presents a real opportunity to lift people out of poverty and provide real solutions to support a generation of skilled workers prepared to take on global demands.

Mentoring Programs

Most adults can think of at least one caring parent, guardian, mentor, teacher, neighbor or coach who played a positive role in shaping their future as a child. It is imperative, in the institutions of education, partnering with businesses and community leaders be a priority. These positive partnerships will be invaluable in making a difference in the lives of children and young adults. These mentors will realize that they have the ability to make a difference in the world. Allowing mentors to stand in the gap and support African American education excellence is priceless.

STEM

At a time when STEM knowledge is essential for twenty-first century jobs, a recent study of the computer science Advanced Placement exam found that, in 11 states, no African American students took the exam and in eight states, no Hispanic students took the exam. In 2009, in STEM fields, Blacks received only 7% of bachelor's degrees, 4% of master's degrees and 2% of doctorates. In 2011, 6% of STEM workers were Black, increasing from 2% in 1970. In 2011, women with a science or engineering bachelor's degree who were employed full-time, year-round in STEM occupations earned $16,300 more per year than women who had a bachelor's degree in science or engineering but were not employed in STEM occupations. The projected percentage increases in STEM jobs for 2010–2020 are: 14% of All Occupations, 16% Mathematics, 22% Computer Systems Analysts, 32% Systems Software Developers, 36% Medical Scientists and 62% Biomedical Engineers. (The White House Initiative on Educational Excellence For African Americans, 2015) It is imperative that African American students excel in the STEM fields in school to be prepared to major in those areas in college. These improvements in STEM education can only happen if African Americans, Hispanics and other underrepresented groups in the STEM fields-including women, people with disabilities, and first-generation Americans participate and succeed.

◆ REFERENCES

Allen, J. (1998) *A nation still at risk: An education manifesto.* Washington, DC: Thomas B. Fordham Foundation.

Anderson, J. L. (2006). An evaluation of African-American adolescent health status with gender comparison. *California Journal of Health Promotion, 4*(2), 168–174.

Bennett, L. (1975). *The shaping of black America. Chicago*: Penguin.

Bond, I. L (1972). *Black American scholars: A study of their beginnings.* Detroit, MI: Delamp.

Boutte, G. S. (2001). *Resounding voices: School experiences of people from diverse backgrounds.* Boston: Allyn & Bacon.

Brown, D. F. (2005). The significance of congruent communication in effective classroom management. *The Clearing House, 79*(1), 12–15.

Bullock, H. (1970). *A history of negro education in the south from 1619 to the present.* New York: Praeger.

Casteneda, H. (1974). *The structure of morality.* Springfield, MO: Thomas Publishing.

DuBois, W. E. B. (1973). *Black reconstruction in America: An essay toward a history of the part which black folk played in the attempt to reconstruct democracy in America, 1860–1880.* New York: Athenaeum.

Fell, B. (1976). *America B.C.: Ancient settlers in the new world.* New York: Quadrangle/New York Times Book.

Fox, J., & Swatt, M. (2008). *The recent surge in homicides involving young Black males and guns: Time to reinvest in prevention and crime control.* Boston, MA: Northeastern University.

Gay, G. (1977). Chinese Americans. In M. J. Gold, C. A. Grant, & H. N. Rivlin (Eds.), *In praise of diversity: A resource book for multicultural education.* Washington, DC: Teacher Corps-Association of Teacher Educators.

Gilgoff, J. (2007). *Boyz 2 Men: Responsible empowerment for inner-city adolescent males.* Retrieved from http://www.niost.org

Griggs, S., & Dunn, R. (1995). Hispanic-American students and learning style. *Emergency Librarian, 23*(2): 11–16.

Hamilton, C. (1968). *Race and education: A search for legitimacy.* Cambridge: Harvard Educational Review.

Hatcher, J., Williams, H., & Hanes, J. (2015). The African-American adolescent male identity development crisis: A mixed-methods design exploring the relationships between ethnic identity development status and academic achievement. *Journal of African American Males in Education, 6*(1), 27–27.

Hawley, W. (2009). Reaching students where they are. *Teaching Tolerance,* (36), 37–40.

Hill, K., Howell, J., Hawkins, D., & Battin-Pearson, C. (1999). Childhood risk factors for adolescent gang membership: Results from the Seattle social development project. *Journal of Research in Crime and Delinquency, 36*(3), 300–322.

Hilliard, A. (1984). *Race and education: A search for legitimacy revisited.* Paper presented at the Clifton M. Claye Educational Leadership Symposium at Texas Southern University, Houston, Texas.

Hornor, L. L. (2002). *Black Americans: A statistical sourcebook.* Information Publications: Palo Alto, CA.

Hraba, J. (1979). *American ethnicity.* Itasca, IL: F. K. Peacock Publishers.

Johnson, H. (1976). *Ethnic American minorities: A guide to media and materials.* New York: R. R. Bowker.

King, K. (1971). *Pan Africanism education: A study of race, philanthropy, and education in the southern states of America and east Africa.* Oxford: Clarendon Press.

Krashen, S. (1997). Why bilingual education? *Eric Digest* No ED403101.

Lambert, H. (1955). *Our language: The story of the words we use.* New York: Lothrop Lee and Shepard.

Lourdes, M. K. in Johnson (1976). *Ethnic American minorities: A guide to media and materials.* New York: R. R. Bowker.

Manno, B. V. (1998, June 15). How to fix anation still at risk. *Investor's Business Daily.*

McMillion, R., Wright, B., & Merrill, A. (2015, August). Secondary school completion and dropouts in Texas public schools. (Document No. GE1560107) Retrieved, from http://tea.texas.gov/acctres/dropcomp_index.html

McWilliams, C. (1968). *Noah from Mexico: The Spanish-speaking people of the United States.* New York: Greenwood Press.

National Center for Education Statistics. (2015). State dropout and completion data. *Common Core of Data.* Retrieved from https://nces.ed.gov/ccd/drpcompstatelvl.asp

National Council of LaRaza. (1989). *Multiple choice: Hispanics and education.* Washington, DC: Author.

Orfield, G. (2001). Schools more separate: Consequences of a decade of resegregation. Cambridge, MA: The Civil Rights Project, Harvard University.

Orfield, G., Bachmeier, M. D., James, D. R., & Eitle, T. (1997). Deepening segregation in American public schools: A special report from the Harvard Project on school desegregation. *Equity and Excellence in Education, 30*(2), 5–24.

Poussaint, A., & Alexander, A. (2000). *Lay my burden down: Unraveling suicide and the mental health crisis among African-Americans.* Boston, MA: Beacon.

Sance, M. (1975). *The African-American Texans.* San Antonio, TX: Institute of Texan Cultures.

Spivey, D. (1978). *Schooling for the new slavery: Black industrial education, 1868–1915.* Westport, CT: Greenwood Press.

Tenorio, A. (1977). The Puerto Ricans. In M. J. Gold, C. A. Grant, & H. N. Rivlin (Eds.), *In praise of diversity: A resource book for multicultural education.* Washington, DC: Teacher Corps-Association of Teacher Educators.

The White House Initiative on Educational Excellence For African Americans. (2015). *U.S. Department of Education.* Retrieved from sites.ed.gov/whieeaa/

Toldson, I., Sutton, R., & Brown, R. (2012). Preventing delinquency and promoting academic success among school-age African American Males. *Journal of African American Males in Education, 3*(1), 12–28.

U.S. Department of Health & Human Services. (2015). 2015 Poverty Guidelines. *Office of the Assistant Secretary for Planning and Evaluation.* Retrieved from https://aspe.hhs.gov/2015-poverty-guidelines

Van Sertima, I. (1976). *They came before columbus.* New York: Ronald Press Company.

Vonder Mehden, F. R. (1982). *Indo-Chinese in Houston.* Houston: Houston Center for the Humanities and National Endowment for the Humanities.

Witty, E. (1982). *Prospects for black teachers preparation, certification, and employment.* Washington, DC: ERIC Clearinghouse on Teacher Education.

Woodson, C. (1969). *The miseducation of the negro.* Washington, DC: The Associated Publishers.

Educational Leadership: Historical Perspectives and New Approaches

Julia Warren Ballenger

Leadership and the study of this phenomenon date back over 5,000 years to ancient Egyptians and continue to be a recurrent theme in the literature. Since the beginning of civilization, Egyptian rulers, Greek heroes, and biblical patriarchs all have one thing in common—leadership (Wren, 1995). Writers have sought answers to the question of who becomes a leader and why? Plato believed only a select few with superior wisdom should be leaders. Aristotle agreed with this thought and stated that some people are marked for enslavement and others to command. Similarly, Machiavelli believed that some people are inherently weak and dishonest; thus, leaders are necessary to maintain stability. These historical perspectives continue to influence our thinking about leadership (Stogdill, 1974).

Debates on educational leadership include whether leadership is inherit. The research by Bennis and Nanus (1985) dispels the myth that leadership qualities are something of which one must be born. These researchers argued that whatever natural endowments one brings to the role of leadership, they can be enhanced. Thus, Bennis and Nanus concluded that nurture is far more important than nature in determining who becomes a successful leader.

This is why leadership is one of the most complex and multifaceted phenomena in research. The word leader was in the Oxford English Dictionary in the 1300s; however, the concept of leadership has only existed in research since the late 1700s (Stogdill, 1974). Burns (1978) noted that leadership is one of the most observed and least understood concepts on earth. This purpose of this chapter is to examine the evolution of leadership and focus on its role in education.

◆ Definition of Educational Leadership

Educational leadership is a complex phenomenon. For example, leadership may be described as traits, skills, behaviors, influence, and action and also be defined as relationships with an individual or group. These definitions differ in many respects, including who exerts influence, and the intended purpose and outcome of the behavior (Yukl, 2002). Some researchers emphasized the action element of leadership. Smith and Piele (2006) emphasized the different ways leaders act, as some actions are based on style and others, in part, on the choices made to achieve organizational goals. These behaviors involve a delicate balancing act as school leaders get pulled in different directions. Smith and Piele noted, "What gives coherence to this act of leadership is the leader's sense of purpose" (p. 103).

Blumberg (1989) described this feeling of purpose in a story of a sculptor who explains that the statue is already somewhere in the block of stone. His job is to chip away the parts that do not belong. Blumberg stated,

> The same applies to education. It is as though for every school building, there's a beautiful school in there somewhere and, if you keep on chipping away, you will find it. But you have to know what you are looking for. (p. 103)

This type of action leads a principal or superintendent to a purpose. Leadership is not merely an action, it is the process that matters and makes a difference in the lives of others.

Rost (1991) synthesized the literature written from 1900 to 1990, finding more than 200 different definitions of leadership. Rost's work provides a clear history of the definition of leadership throughout the last century.

1900–1929. The definition of leadership appearing in the first three decades of the twentieth century emphasized control and centralization of power. Moore (1927) defined leadership as "the ability to impress the will of the leader . . . and to induce obedience, and respect" (p. 124).

1930–1940. During this timeframe, the definition of leadership moves from an emphasis on domination to influence. Traits became the focus of defining leadership, and the group approach came to the forefront (Hemphill, 1949).

1950–1960. Three themes dominated leadership during this period, which consisted of what leaders do in groups, relationships, and collaborations based on the behavior of the leader. The tumultuous 60s saw harmony among leadership in schools. Thus, leadership was defined as "acts by persons that influence others in a shared direction" (Seeman, 1960, p. 53).

1960–1970. During this period, the styles approach emphasized the behavior of the leader. The focus was on what leaders do. Leadership comprised two dimensions: One on task and the other on the people or interpersonal dimension (Yukl, 2002).

1980–twenty-first Century. During this period, the concept of leadership continued to focus on getting followers to do what the leader wants to be done. In the 1980s, the word "influence" became famous in defining leadership (Yukl, 2002).

Leadership is defined in many different ways. However, most definitions share the assumption that leadership is an influence process. One thing that leadership scholars can agree is the lack of a standard definition of leadership.

◆ LEADERSHIP VERSUS MANAGEMENT

Controversy exists about the differences between leadership and management. Bennis and Nanus (1985) and Yalenik (1977) noted that leadership and management are qualitatively different and mutually exclusive. They proposed that managers value stability, order, and efficiency; whereas, leaders value flexibility, innovation, and adaptation. Bennis and Nanus (1985) stated, "Managers are people who do things right and leaders are people who do the right things" (p. 21). That is, managers are concerned about how things get done; they try to get people to perform better. Leaders are concerned about what things mean to people; they try to get people to reach consensus related to the most important things to be done (Bennis & Nanus, 1985).

Empirical research does not support associating leadership and management with different types of people. Scholars such as Bass (1990a), Mintzberg (1973), and Rost (1991) viewed leading and managing as distinct roles, processes, and relationships. In the earlier work of Mintzberg on the nature of managerial work, leadership was identified as one of the administrative functions. This feature of leadership focused on motivating subordinates and creating favorable conditions for the environment. Kotter (1990) described leadership and management in terms of their processes and intended outcomes.

Rost (1991) addressed management as a relationship between managers and subordinates. Rost described leadership as influence between leader and followers and noted that while leaders and followers influence each other, managers function as leaders only if they have this type of power.

◆ EVOLUTION OF LEADERSHIP APPROACHES

The historical development of leadership theory originated from the Galton's Great Man theory. Researchers focused on great men (and some women) in the world. Heroes, royalty, and successful individuals are thought to possess innate talents and abilities that set them apart from others, which enables them to achieve great success (Northouse, 2012). Since the Great Man theory, many approaches to leadership have evolved. This section will include an overview of the leadership approaches.

Leadership: Trait Approach

The Great Man theory subsequently gave rise to the Trait theory in the 1920s and 1930s.

The trait approach was one of the earliest perspectives for studying leadership. Many studies were conducted during the 1930s and 1940s to identify traits that made leaders different from other individuals. The primary purpose of the trait approach was that leaders had to possess some universal characteristics that made them leaders. For the most part, traits were viewed as present at birth. However, this thinking did not take into account the various situations faced by leaders nor the differences in types of followers. Additionally, no attempt was made to measure leader performance (Hollander & Offermann, 1990).

Stogdill (1948) reviewed 124 trait studies conducted from 104 to 1948. Relevant traits reviewed were intelligence, alertness to the needs of others, self-confidence, and the desire to accept responsibility. Several decades later, in 1974, Stogdill reviewed 163 trait studies conducted from 1949 to 1970. Many of the same traits, as well as new ones, were found to be related to leader effectiveness. However, Stogdill (1974) noted that evidence did not support universal leadership traits. Possession of some traits increased the likelihood that a leader would be effective, but these traits did not guarantee effectiveness.

Leadership: Skills Approach

Leadership conceptualized as skill shifts the thinking from a focus on traits to an emphasis on skills and abilities. Katz (1955) identified a three-skill approach to leadership. This approach stated that three leadership skills can be acquired: Technical, human, and conceptual. Technical skills consist of knowledge about a particular type of work, a specialized area, or product. Human skills are the ability to understand and work with people, unlike technical skills that focus on working with things. Leaders with human skills create an atmosphere of trust. Lastly, conceptual skills are the ability to work with ideas and concepts. Conceptual skills are essential for creating a vision for an organization.

Leadership: Behavior

Unlike the trait approach, the behavioral approach makes an effort to identify what good leaders do on the job and then draws correlations between these specific behaviors and their leadership effectiveness. This approach was well received by practicing managers because of its ease of implementation and the empirical base. The Ohio State and Michigan State studies identified two critical leadership behaviors: initiating structure and consideration (Yukl, 2002)

The behavioral approach to leadership is heuristic. That is, it provides a conceptual map to use to understand the complexities of educational leadership. Leaders can determine how they come across to others in light of the task and relationship dimensions. However, critics state that the behavioral approach does not demonstrate how leader behaviors serve as a consistent link between task and relationship behavior and outcomes such as productivity and job satisfaction (Northouse, 2012).

Leadership: Situational Approach

The situational era marks a vast step forward by acknowledging the importance of factors beyond the leader and followers. This approach proposes that effective leadership required an understanding of the situaltion and an appropriae response, rather than certain traits of the leaders (Grint, 2011).

The situational leadership theory evolved from a task-oriented versus people-oriented leadership continuum (Bass, 2008). This model was originally developed by Hershey and Blanchard (1969, 1979, 1996). Hersey and Blanchard (1993) reported that the situational leadership model has been used in training programs of more than 400 of the Fortune 500 companies. However, a general criticism of this model is its consistency and ambiguity. It is not clear how commitment is combined with competence to form the different levels of development (Nicholls, 1985).

Leadership: Transactional versus Transformational

According to Burns (1978), transactional leadership involves exchanges between leaders and their followers. Transactional leaders exchange things of value with members to advance their own and their follower's agenda (Kuhnert, 1994). Transactional leadership consists of three factors: (1) contingent reward, (2) management-by-exception, and (3) laissez-faire. The contingent reward factor is an exchange process between leader and followers. From this perspective, the leader obtains agreement from followers on what must be done and what the payoffs will be for people doing it. The management-by-exception factor consists of two forms of action: active and passive. The leader who uses the active form of management-by-exception watches followers closely for mistakes. A leader using the passive form intervenes after standards have not been met or problems have occurred. The final factor, laissez-faire leadership represents the absence or avoidance of leadership characterized by avoidance of responsibility, disorganization, and little direction and support. Laissez-faire leaders adopt a hands-off, let-things-ride approach (Northouse, 2016).

In contrast, transformational leaders "attempt and succeed in raising colleagues, subordinates, followers to a greater level of awareness about issues of consequence" (Bass, 1985, p. 13). Transformational leaders accomplish this action through four factors. Northouse (2016) called these factors the *Four I's*: (1) idealized influence; (2) inspirational motivation; (3) intellectual stimulation; and (4) individual consideration. Idealized influence means behavior that inspires others to follow. These leaders usually exhibit high standards of moral and ethical conduct. The second factor, inspirational motivation, is characteric of leaders who communicate high expectations to followers. Leaders inspire followers to become committed to and a part of the shared vision of the organization. Intellectual stimulation, factor 3, includes leadership that stimulates followers to challenge their assumptions, beliefs, and values as well as those of the leader. Factor 4, individualized consideration, means that leaders care about follower's needs and the needs of the organization. The transformation leader exhibits each of these factors to varying degrees to bring about the desired organization outcomes through their followers (Bass, 1985, 1990a, 1990b).

Transformation leadership has its critics. Some of the critics say that researchers have not established that transformational leaders can transform individuals and the organization. Others posit that transformational leadership is too broad, making it difficult to define its parameters. Many of these criticisms remain relevant today (Yukl, 1999, 2011).

Leadership: Instructional

Effective educational leaders makes a difference in improving learning. According to Leithwood, Seashore-Lowis, Anderson, and Wahstrom (2004), "Leadership not only matters, it is second only to teaching among school-related factors in its impact on student learning" (p. 3). How do quality leaders achieve this impact on student learning? According to DeVita, president of the Wallace Foundation, leaders accomplish this task by:

> (a) setting directions and establishing high expectation, and using data to track progress and performance; (b) developing people by providing teachers and others the necessary resources and support, and (c) making the organization work through creating an infrastructure that supports rather than inhibits effective teaching and learning. (Leithwood et al., 2004, p. 1)

Hallinger and Leithwood (1998) contended that instructional leadership functions focus directly on teaching and learning. Instructional leadership is conceptualized as (1) defining the school's mission, (2) managing the instructional program, and (3) promoting a positive school culture. Today, instructional leadership is more involved. It requires leaders who have knowledge of adult learning principles and can connect with the larger community all under the spotlight of high-stakes testing (Smith & Piele, 2006).

Leadership: A Team Approach

Due to increasingly complex tasks, more globalization, and the flattening of organizational structures, more work is done through teams. A team is an structural group that is composed of members who share common goals, which are interdependent, and coordinate their activities to accomplish these goals (Wageman, Gardner, & Mortensen, 2012). Team leadership is process oriented. For teams to be successful, the organization culture needs to be supportive of member involvement, collaborative work, and shared decision making.

Hackman (2012) identified six enabling conditions that lead to effective team function.

- Is it a real team?
- Does it have a compelling purpose?
- Does it have the right people?
- Are the norms of conduct clear?
- Is there support from the organizational context
- Is there team-focused coaching?

Similar to Hackman's (2012) enabling conditions for effective teams, Larson and LaFasto (1989) identified eight features consistently associated with team excellent. These characteristics include: (1) clear, elevating goals, (2) results-driven structure, (3) unified commitment, (4) collaborative climates, (5) standards of excellence, (6) external support, and recognition, and (7) principal leadership.

Leadership has been studied in many different ways. The overview of the research revealed numerous definitions of leadership and a many leadership approaches.

◆ NEW FACES, NEW APPROACHES

The traditional leadership approaches research focused on white leaders who were male. Women and people of color come to leadership positions with different sets of experiences, values, beliefs, and attitudes. These various experiences may give rise to a unique perspective on leadership (Smith & Piele, 2006).

Females and People of Color in Educational Leadership

Some of the new faces in educational leadership are women and people of color. The knowledge based on women's leadership in education is a relatively recent development. According to Shakeshaft (1989), the research on women's leadership that emerged in the 1970s was a response to the androcentric research dominating the field of educational leadership at that time. Two chapters in the *Handbook for Achieving Gender Equity through Education*, written by Shakeshaft, Brown, Irby, Grogan, and Ballenger (2007), include a review of the research on women educational leaders in PK to 16. From this comprehensive review, Grogan and Shakshaft (2011) identified five approaches of women educational leadership. These approaches include: leadership for learning, leadership for social justice, relational leadership, spiritual leadership, and balanced leadership. While Grogan and Shakeshaft acknowledged that not all women value these approaches, they felt confident enough with the research to categorize these themes as five common approaches to leadership among women.

Grogan and Shakeshaft (2011) posited that women leadership is purposeful and conclude that these five approaches and values represent a shift away from thinking of leadership as residing primarily in an individual. These authors stated, "Women leadership of schools and districts in the United States suggest a new leadership emphasis that relies on different perspectives to craft new solution so problems" (p. 3). Thus, many women leaders seek various ideas across the globe and use these ideas in framing and addressing issues quite differently from traditional leadership approaches (Grogan & Shakeshaft, 2011).

Founded on equity and social justice perspectives, Brown and Irby (2006) developed the synergistic leadership theory (SLT). According to Brown and Irby (2006), SLT states that female leaders may be impacted by external forces, organizational structures, beliefs, attitudes, and values in different ways from male leaders. As a result, female leadership behaviors may interact with the factors of the theory in ways unlike the leadership behavior of men.

The SLT is the first gender-inclusive leadership theory that includes attributes, experiences, and abilities inherent in both male and female leaders (Irby, Brown, & Duffy, 1999). Brown and Irby included female leaders in developing this theory. By acknowledging a range of behaviors and organization structures inclusive of women, the SLT reflects females' leadership experiences (Brown & Irby, 2006). However, in the field of educational administration, gender research usually focuses on women in management and is mostly conducted by women. Brown and Irby (2006) indicated that the knowledge of women in leadership roles and how they lead my increase the number of women in educational leadership.

Leadership for Social Justice

Social justice is often used as a catchphrase and defined in many ways. Lyman, Strachan, and Lazaridou (2012) defined social justice through actions. The action is central to social justice leadership. Action informs social justice leadership theories and these theories inform actions. The literature on social justice leadership points to change, resistance, critique, all of which require action (Rapp, 2002). Thus, social justice can be defined from a variety of approaches. The statement from the *Annual Report of the Aboriginal and Torres Strait Islander Social Justice Commission* describes social justice in a nontheoretical and practical way:

> Social justice is what faces you in the morning. It is awakening in a house with adequate water supply, cooking facilities, and sanitation. Social justice is the ability to nourish your children and send them to a school where their education not only equips them for employment but reinforces their knowledge and understanding of their culture inheritance. It is the prospect of genuine employment and good health; a life of choices and opportunity, free from discrimination. (Dodson, 1993, p.1)

Beliefs, attitudes, and values impact social justice work. Shields (2004) exclaimed, "I believe firmly that social justice and academic excellent must not be seen as competing goals, but must go hand in hand . . . Academic success must be for all students" (p. 9). Social justice for leadership is about doing what is right. Social justice also involves working for the rights of individuals and people.

Doing what is right means different things to different people. Doing what is right also has several antecedents. Recognition and distribution are two antecedents of doing what is right.

North (2008) noted, "recognition as cultural groups competing for respect and dignity and redistribution as socioeconomic classes demanding equitable sharing of wealth and power" (p. 29). The concept of redistribution in social justice may be a barrier to privilege and entitlement. When people lose rights and privileges due to oppressive systems, others may benefit, often unknowingly, from the same system (Blankstein & Houston, 2011).

Rawls (1971) described social justice as fairness in the distribution of societal goods. However, Fraser (1997) argued that we must recognize diverse identities over the distribution of material goods and services. According to Marshall and Olivia (2010), administrator preparation programs that focus on social justice attempt to integrate concern for poverty and care for diverse identities. The recognition of differences coupled with caring and critique are actions for sundry individualities. Starratt (1994) approaches social justice differently. He described the three-pronged approach of what he calls the ethical school, which fosters ethics of care, critique, and justice. Starratt's framework for social justice leadership, care, justice, and critique combine to form a human, ethical response to unethical situations that school leaders may face (Marshall & Oliva, 2010).

Bogotch (2002) noted, "There can be no fixed or predictable meaning of social justice prior to actually engaging in educational leadership practices" (p. 153). Furthermore, Bogotch acknowledged that by connecting social justice with the educational leadership field we can direct our actions toward creating new and just communities and schools.

◆ CONCLUSION

The broad eras of leadership theories have been discussed using an evolutionary developmental approach. This review of leadership approaches reveals new directions for the future of practicing educational leaders. The old view of educational leadership dealt with dominating followers through authority and control. The new view of leadership calls for flexibility, adaptability, a team approach, and virtuous leadership. Leaders must empower others and place increasingly more emphasis on servantship. Leaders must take on a more collaborative view of leadership, in which leader influence is distributed across all levels of an organization (Osborn, Morris, & Connnor, 1984)

Perhaps the greatest challenge for educational leaders and their graduate students is to influence others to do the right things for all children and youth. Doing the right thing for every child is leading for social justice. Fullan (2003) argued that social justice leadership requires reassertion of the moral purpose of leadership. Leadership matters, Sergiovanni (1992) described purpose and responsibility of leadership best in the discussion of the head, heart, and hand of leadership. Unmistakably, there is value understanding what we call the hand of leadership. Behaviors exhibited by leaders that reflect a concern for task and concern for people are essential in certain circumstances. Sergiovanni reminds us that the hand alone is not powerful enough to account for what leadership is. If we want to understand all of what leadership is about, we have to examine the heart and the head of leadership.

The heart of leadership is about personal vision. However, leadership is more than one's own view. The head of leadership has to do with the mindscapes, or theories of practice that leaders develop over time. Reflection, combined with personal vision, becomes the basis of leadership actions. If the heart and the head are separated from the hand, the leader's actions, decisions, and behaviors cannot be understood (Sergovanni, 1992).

◆ REFERENCES

Bass, B. M. (1985). Leadership: Good, better. Best. *Organizational Dynamics, 13*(3), 26–40.

Bass, B. M. (1990a). *Bass and Stogdill's handbook of leadership* (3rd ed.), New York, NY: The Free Press.

Bass, B. M. (1990b). From transactional to transformational leadership: Learning to share the vision. *Organizational Dynamics, 18,* 19–31.

Bass, B. M. (2008). *The Bass handbook of leadership: Theory research & managerial applications* (4th ed.). New York, NY: Free Press.

Bennis, W., & Nanus, B. (1985). *Leaders: The strategies for taking charge.* New York, NY: Harper & Row.

Blumberg, A. (1989). *School administration as a craft: Foundations of practice.* Boston, MA: Allyn & Bacon.

Bogotch, I. E. (2002). Educational leadership and social justice: Practice into theory. *Journal of School Leadership, 12*(2), 138–156.

Brown, G., & Irby, B. J., (2006). Expanding the knowledge base: Socially just theory in educational leadership programs. In F. Dembowski (Ed.), *Unbridled spirit* (pp. 7–13). Lancaster, PA: Proactive Publications.

Burns, J. M. (1978). *Leadership.* New York, NY: Harper & Row.

Dodson, M. (1993). *Annual report of the Aboriginal and Torres Strait Islander Social Justice Commission.* Retrieved from http://www.austlii.edu.Au/au/other/IndigLRes/1993/3/index

Fullan, M. (2003). *Leadership and sustainability: Systems thinkers in action.* Thousand Oaks, CA: Corwin.

Grint, K. (2011). A history of leadership. In A. Bryman, D. Collinson, K. Grint, B. Jackson, & M. Uhl-Bien (Eds.), *The SAGE handbook of leadership* (pp. 3–14). Thousand Oaks, CA: Sage.

Grogan, M., & Shakeshaft, C. (2011). *Women and educational leadership.* San Francisco, CA: Jossey-Bass.

Hackman, J. R. (2012). From causes to conditions in group research. *Journal of Organizational Behavior, 33,* 428–444.

Hallinger, P., & Leithwood, K. (1998). *Unseen forces: The impact of social culture on leadership, 73*(2), 126–151.

Hemphill, J. K. (1949). *Situational factors in leadership.* Columbus Ohio State University, Bureau of Educational Research.

Hersey, P., & Blanchard, K. H. (1969). Life cycle theory of leadershp. *Training & Development Journal, 23*(5), 26.

Hersey, P., & Blanchard, K. H. (1979). Life cyle theory of leadership. *Training & Development Journal, 33*(6), 94.

Hersey, P., & Blanchard, K. H. (1980). The management of change. *Training & Development Journal, 34*(6), 80.

Hersey, P., & Blanchard, K. H. (1993). *Management of organizational behavior: Utilizing human resources* (6th ed.). Englewood Cliffs, NJ: Prentice Hall.

Hollander, E. P., & Offermann, L. R. (1990). Power and leadership in organizations: Relationships in transition. *American Psychologist, 45,* 179–189.

Irby, B. J., Brown, G., & Duffy, J. (1999). *A feminine inclusive leadership theory*. Paper presented at the Annual Meeting of the American Educational Research Association, New Orleans, LA.

Kanter, R. (1985). *Change masters: Corporate entrepreneurs at work*. New York, NY: Touchstone Press.

Katz, R. L. (1955). Skills of an effective administrator. *Harvard Business Review, 33*(1), 33–42.

Kotter, J. P. (1990). *A force for change: How leadership differs from management*. New York, NY: The Free Press.

Kuhnert, K. W. (1994). Transforming leadership: Developing people through delegation. In B. M. Bass & B. J. Avolio (Eds.), *Improving organizational effectiveness through transformational leadership* (pp. 10–25). Thousand Oaks, CA: SAGE.

Larson, C. E., & LaFasto, F. M. (1989). *Teamwork: What must go right/what can go wrong?* Newbury Park, CA: SAGE.

Leithwood, K., Seashore-Lewis, K., Anderson, S., & Wahstrom, K. (2004). *How Leadership Influences Student Learning: Review of Research*. Wallace Foundation.

Lyman, L. L., Strachan, J., & Lazaridou, A. (2012). *Shaping social justice leadership: Insights of women educators worldwide*. New York, NY: Rowman & Littlefield Education.

Marshall, C., & Oliva, M. (2010). *Leadership for social justice: Making revolutions in education* (2nd ed.). New York, NY: Allyn & Bacon.

Mintzberg, H. (1973). *The nature of managerial work*. New York, NY: Harper & Row.

Moore, B. V. (1927). The May conference on leadership. *Personnel Journal, 6*, 124–128.

Nicholls, J. R. (1985). A new approach to situational leadership. *Leadership & Organization Development Journal, 6*(4), 2.

North, C. (2008). What is all this talk about "social justice"? Mapping the terrain of education's latest catchphrase. *Teachers College Record, 110*(6), 1182–1206.

Northouse, P. G. (2012). *Leadership: Theory and practice* (3rd ed.). London: Sage.

Northouse, P. G. (2016). *Leadership: Theory and practice* (7th ed.). London: Sage.

Osborn, R. N., Morris, F. A., & Connor, P. E. (1984). Emerging Technologies: The challenge of leadership theory. In J. G. Hunt, D. M. Hosking, C. A. Shriesheim, & R. Stewart (Eds.), *Leaders and managers. International perspectives on managerial behavior and leadership*. New York, NY: Pergamon Press.

Rapp, D. (2002). Social justice and the importance of rebellious oppositional imaginations. *Journal of School Leadership, 12*(4), 226–245

Rawls, J. (1971). *A theory of justice*. Cambridge, MA: Belknap Press of Harvard University Press.

Rost, J. (1991). *Leadership for the twenty-first century*. New York, NY: Praeger.

Seeman, M. (1960). *Social status and leadership*. Columbus Ohio State University, Bureau of Educational Research.

Sergiovanni, T. (1992). *Moral leadership: Getting to the heart of school improvement*. San Francisco, CA: Jossey-Bass.

Shakeshaft, C. (1989). *Women in educational administration*. Newbury Park, CA: Sage.

Shakeshaft, C., Brown, G., Irby, G., Grogan, M., & Ballenger, J. (2007). Increasing gender equity in educational leadership. In S. Klein, B. Richardson, D. A. Grayson, L. H. Fox, C. Kramarae, D.

Pollard, & C. A. Dwyer (Eds.), *Handbook for achieving gender equity through education.* (2nd ed.). (pp. 103–129). Florence, KY: Lawrence Erlbaum.

Shields, C. M. (2004). Good intentions are not enough: Leadership for social justice and academic excellence. *New Zealand Journal of Educational Leadership, 19,* 7–20.

Smith, S. C., & Piele, P. K. (2006). *School leadership: Handbook for excellence in student learning* (4th ed.). Thousand Oaks, CA: Corwin.

Starratt, R. J. (1994). *Building an ethical school: A practical response to the moral crisis in schools.* London: Falmer Press.

Stogdill, R. (1948). Personal factors associated with leadership: A survey of the literature. *Journal of Psychology, 25,* 35–71.

Stogdill, R. (1974). *Handbook of leadership: A survey of theory and research.* New York, NY: Free Press.

Wageman, R., Gardner, H., & Mortensen, M. (2012). The changing ecology of teams: New directions for teams research. *Journal of Organizational Behavior, 33,* 301–315.

Wren, J. T. (1995). *The leaders' companion: Insights on leadership through the ages.* New York, NY: The Free Press.

Yukl, G. (1999). An evaluation of conceptual weaknesses in transformational and charismatic leadership theories. *The Leadership Quarterly, 10*(2), 285.

Yukl, G. (2002). *Leadership in organizations* (5th Ed.). Upper Saddle River, NJ: Prentice-Hall.

Yukl, G. (2011). Contingency theories of effective leadership. In A Bryman, D. Collinson, K. Grint, B. Jackson & M. Uhl-Bien (Eds.). *The SAGE handbook of leadership* (pp. 286–298). Thousand Oaks, CA: Sage.

Yalenik, A. (1977). Managers and leaders: Are they different? *Harvard Business Review, 55,* (May–June), 67–78.

ETHICS AND SCHOOL ADMINISTRATION

Don M. Beach ◆ *Mark Weber*

Educational administrators face many difficult challenges in meeting the needs of their communities, and perhaps no challenge today causes such apprehension as the area of ethics. Colgan (2004) noted that

> . . . in a time of increased public scrutiny, many who have authority for the day-to-day operation of school districts and school buildings—superintendents, business officials, administrators, and principals—are being accused of ethical lapses or worse. The result is often the loss of public trust . . . (p. 5)

Giacalone and Thompson (2006) devoted a special issue of *Academy of Management Learning & Education* to "ethics and social responsibility." In discussing this topic, they noted that, "The search for a better understanding of ethics and ethical conduct has been a frustrating endeavor and challenge . . ." (p. 261). In elaborating on this theme, they noted how often "allocating culpability" or blaming others becomes a part of a typical response, rather than acting responsibly. Hartman (2006) even questioned, "Can we teach character?" Giacalone and Thompson concluded,

> An erosion of ethical values and standards has . . . shift[ed] society from a focus on the dignity and uplifting for all into a 'me-first' mentality . . . In reality the values that an individual holds fast are central to . . . character and . . . behaviors. (p. 261)

Badaracco (2006) in working with leaders from many backgrounds concluded:

> The basic challenges of leaders . . . reflect two fundamental, enduring aspects of leadership. One is the humanity of leaders—the hopes and fears, traits and instincts of the human nature we all share. The other is the unchanging agenda of leadership, in all times and places: developing a goal, a plan, a purpose, or an ideal and working with and through other people to make it real—in a world that is often uncertain, recalcitrant, and sometimes perilous. (p. 6)

Paul and Elder (2006) have noted that,

> The ultimate basis for ethics is clear: Human behavior has consequences for the welfare of others. We are capable of acting toward others in such a way as to increase or decrease the quality of their lives. We are capable of helping or harming [and] understanding when we are doing one and when the other." (p. 4)

More recently, Glanz (2009) has observed that, "Resolving ethical dilemmas is no easy task, and there are no ready-made recipes to follow. A principal . . . will be challenged to think on his or her feet when confronting situations that require ethical decision making" (p. 24). This chapter provides background information and models that school administrators can use when identifying and resolving ethical issues on their campus or in their district.

Since the Athenian philosopher Aristotle defined the "Golden Mean," societies have struggled with the application of ethical principles in a dynamic and fluid environment where often the understanding of what is "right and wrong" are relative. Aristotle's premise was that the greatest happiness was the ultimate good not only for the individual, but also the community as well. Current ethical dilemmas or situations present ambivalent messages that require administrators to critically examine their beliefs about what is right and good. Herein is the daily dilemma; "the principal, representing a significant administrative unit within the district, is in a highly visible position of leadership, and faces situations day after day that can test moral and professional behavior" (Drake & Roe, 2003, p. 33). In examining the role of ethics in educational administration, it has become clear that educational leaders need a way of conceptualizing the various components of morals, values, and virtues. As MacIntyre (1966) has said:

> We cannot expect to find in our society a single set of moral concepts . . . Conceptual conflict is endemic in our situation because of the depth of our moral conflicts. Each of us therefore has to choose both whom we wish to be morally bound and by what ends, rules, and virtues we wish to be guided. (p. 268)

In Texas, there are more than 1,000 school districts with several million students, 500,000 certified teachers, more than 11,000 principals and thousands of support staff. In addition, there are parents, grandparents, and a myriad of other community members contributing to the educational community. Issues that confront school leaders can seem never ending and involve cultural, gender, and socioeconomic concerns, as well as reporting financial and student achievement data. Nash (2002) found that administrators can spend as much as half of their work day making ethical decisions.

Public school administrators, then, must find their way through this complex and often shifting environment to make decisions that are not only good for each student, simultaneously contributing to the greater good. In their book *Ethics in Educational Leadership Programs*, Beck and Murphy (1994) identified two themes impacting educational administration. First, the education process itself is vested in moral character. Second, "is the belief that educators must become aware of the ethical implications of their work and they must continually strive to make and be guided by morally sound decisions . . ." (p. 1).

The importance of ethical behavior has also been reinforced in the standards of the Interstate School Leaders Licensure Consortium (ISLLC), developed by the Chief State School Officers. These standards state, "A school administrator is an educational leader who promotes the success of all students by acting with integrity, fairness, and in an ethical manner."

◆ DEFINITION OF ETHICS

Aristotle began the discussion of what has come to be known as ethics. He attempted to define the standard of the good and explain what makes an act right or wrong. Aristotle sought to answer the question, "Is there an absolute, universal standard of right and wrong, or are all such standards relative to a particular time and culture, or even to individual desires and preferences?" (Hocking, 1962, p. xv). Adams and Maine (1998) defined ethics or ethical behavior as "the standards and values that people use to judge what is right and good or worthwhile—their moral standards" (p. 1).

White and Wooten (1986) noted that ethical behavior is shaped by the intersection of four constructs: values, norms, science, and laws, which serve to shape responses to ethical dilemmas or situations. Adams and Maine (1988) have suggested that ethics provides a way of (1) examining the issues; (2) understanding the aspects involved; (3) considering various ways to judge and resolve problems; and (4) wrestling with which solutions seem best. Therefore, "to be effective, when confronted with a confounding ethical dilemma, administrators should know in advance how they would react . . ." (Colgan, 2004, p. 6). In his book *Courage: The Backbone of Leadership*, Lee (2006) has observed two types of ethics. One is "formal ethical codes that are published"; the other is "internal ethical codes that reflect . . . actual core values" (p. 36). Citing examples from business such as the Enron scandal, he concluded three things:

1. Ethics is not right or wrong; it's just a code.
2. An ethics code is only as good as its sponsor's informal, cultural code of actual practice.
3. A gap between formal and informal codes can be institutionally and professionally fatal. (p. 37)

Meara, Schmidt, and Day (1996) differentiate between principle ethics and virtue ethics. Corey, Corey, and Callanan (2007) explained principle ethics as a set of obligations and methods as ways of: "(a) solving a particular dilemma or set of dilemmas and (b) establishing a framework to guide future ethical thinking and behavior . . . to answer the question 'What shall I do?'" (p. 15). They further noted that virtue ethics involve character traits and nonobligatory ideals and asks, "Am I doing what is best?" For Corey et al (2007), "Even in the absence of an ethical dilemma, virtue ethics compels the [administrator] to be conscious of ethical behavior" (p. 15). Using Meara et al. ideas, Corey et al have suggested that, "it is not a question of subscribing to one or the other form of ethics. Rather, professional[s] . . . should strive to integrate virtue ethics and principle ethics to reach better ethical decisions and policies" (p. 15). Even if school leaders have a professional code of ethics, that code is not as important as the informal cultural code. If the informal code is one that permits or allows "small inaccuracies" then there is a gap that can prove fatal.

◆ ETHICS AND DECISIONS

How then does one begin to make decisions that are for the good of the school if every community member has his or her own definition of what is good and right with regard to a given student and/or situation? Given the myriad of cultural, religious, political, and public beliefs, the administrator must be able to recognize and deal with these positions that are often in conflict. Mirk (2009), drawing upon the work of the Institute for Global Ethics has suggested five key recommendations for "a new type of leader" (p. 20). Mirk's summary of the recommendations included:

> (1) lead from your core values-integrity is essential; (2) have the courage to connect—resist the temptation to impose beliefs; (3) do your homework-get to know others and their thinking; (4) model your outcomes-demonstrate and try new things; and (5) lean on others for support-seek out others and build a culture of integrity. (pp. 20–23)

Mirk (2009) describes a principal who asks three questions as grounded. These questions include: "Who am I? What do I believe? [and] What am I here in school for?" (p. 18)

Shapiro and Stefkovich (2010) have proposed an ethical decision-making model for school leaders that centers on the best interest(s) of the student. In achieving the best interest of the student, personal codes of ethics, standards of the profession, professional codes of ethics, and ethics of the community interact with professional judgment, professional decision making, and even conflicting codes to produce a result. No wonder educational leaders have a difficult task. There may even be disagreement or conflict in what constitutes the best interest of the student. Shapiro and Stefkovich suggest that school leaders use the ethics of justice, the ethics of critique, the ethics of care, and the ethics of the profession to make decisions. The ethics of justice focuses on respect for individuals and for freedoms, rights, and laws. The ethics of critique challenges the status quo and not only critically examines the laws but the processes as well. The ethics of care takes into account concern, connection, and compassion in responding to moral dilemmas. The ethics of the profession incorporates ethical frameworks and perspectives in arriving at decisions specifically related to the education enterprise.

As Kidder (1995) pointed out, with the recognition of one's own core values. Without this understanding, school administrators will not be able to recognize when ethical dilemmas occur, much less be able to deal with them. If, however, administrators have well-grounded morals and ethics and the ability to analyze conceptually the many situations that occur everyday in the school setting, ultimately the good for every student will be served. Rebore (2001) said, ". . . if the decisions of administrators are not prompted by their core values, their decision making will be dislocated from their genuine selves and certainly will be manipulated by circumstances and whims" (p. 74). Behr (1998) also noted that value-centered leadership creates a sense of community and organizational integrity based on shared goals, values, and commitments.

Kidder (1995) correctly pointed out that few people have trouble with the "right vs. wrong" choices faced in life. With few exceptions, most people would agree that lying, killing, and stealing are wrong. The dilemmas faced by today's administrators are often the "right vs. right" choices, such as when the right of the individual and the right of the school clash or when the rights of two individuals are in conflict. When speaking of "right," the concept is not of a constitutional right but the correctness for the individual or institution. Kidder (1995) categorized the really tough choices into four general categories called "dilemma paradigms." These include: truth vs. loyalty, individual vs. community, short-term vs. long-term, and justice vs. mercy. The administrator must be able to analyze the situation and apply basic ethical principles to make the appropriate decision in tough situations. Reinhartz and Beach (2004) noted that, "For school leaders, ethical behavior involves providing not only vision and inspiration, but a purpose or meaning to the educational process" (p. 47), and Yates (1999) said that, "Good leaders must first be good people" (p. 57).

To make good decisions, administrators need to understand each of the four dilemma paradigms. Each category requires some basic definitions for common understanding and discussion. Truth is conformity with facts or reality, while loyalty involves allegiance to another person, government, or a set of ideas to which one owes fidelity. The *truth vs. loyalty* dilemma can arise in situations involving job references or the seemingly innocuous parental request for a particular teacher. If an administrator has a faculty member who is not perceived as an effective teacher or struggles with classroom management, what is the ethical response to a letter of reference that best serves the truth test while also doing what is best for the teacher and school? The situation could require the administrator to withhold some parts of the truth to support and be loyal to the individual faculty member. To do otherwise could undermine faculty morale and affect school culture and climate.

The *individual vs. community* dilemma can be seen in schools when the need of an individual student conflicts with the overall needs of the school. For example, a high school student might need an advanced math class such as calculus to meet the minimum requirements for college entrance, but the school is small and does not have the resources to provide the class. Both the individual and the institution are "right," and an administrator has an ethical responsibility to each. A different type of individual vs. community dilemma occurs when an individual is suspected of taking something from the class and the entire class is punished.

The *short-term vs. long-term* dilemma can be seen when some schools push for immediate "exemplary status" at the cost of long-term educational goals. Administrators are faced with making short-term decisions to quickly raise test scores to meet state performance standards, while recognizing the long-term development of the school and the needs of the students may not be met. Both are "right" but both seemingly cannot be done without some sacrifice.

The final dilemma is *justice vs. mercy*. On the surface, this appears to be an easy dilemma to identify and resolve. When school policies and protocols require that administrators give swift justice to thwart inappropriate or unwanted behaviors, this can sometimes clash with the need for mercy. All students can make mistakes on the road to adulthood and deserve a "second chance." However, the demands of the school may require zero tolerance, a term that is usually understood as being merciless since there are no exceptions to the rule. Stories abound about students who, through no direct fault of their own or with deliberate intention, break a rule. One example occurred when a student moved his grandmother over the weekend and a butter knife fell out of the boxes and was left in his truck. When the knife was discovered at school, he violated the policy of "no knives at school" and, as a result, was sent to in-school suspension because of the zero-tolerance policy. This application of the policy could be seen as justice without mercy.

Simply recognizing that dilemmas exist will not suffice when the administrator must make tough decisions. Kidder (1995) provided three tenets that offer guidance for administrators in making tough decisions. First, do what is best for the greatest number of people, and second, follow one's highest sense of principle. The last tenet is to do what one would want others to do to them.

To do what is best for the greatest number of people is called ends-based and was proposed by the English philosopher Jeremy Bentham (1789). The focus is on the institution as opposed to the individual. As such, the administrator must decide at which point the "right" of the school as an institution supersedes the right of an individual, whether it is a student, faculty member, or community member. One example of this situation occurs when offering classes for either remediation or for enrichment. When public schools have limited financial resources for instruction, administrators have the difficult choice of deciding how to use school funds for the "greatest good." Should funds be spent on remediation and support, enrichment, advanced classes, nonacademic electives, or reducing teacher/student ratios? To resolve this dilemma, school administrators must balance what is best for the campus corporately and students individually, sometimes requiring them to make decisions based on district policy or rules governing the distribution of government monies in place of the "rightness" of the situation.

Ultimately, administrators must fall back upon their own sense of core values and follow their highest principles. This approach is called rule-based thinking and was proposed by the German philosopher Immanuel Kant, who originally called his concept "categorical imperative." This concept requires one's actions to follow an inner conscience driving those actions. To accomplish this second step in resolving ethical dilemmas, administrators not only must understand their own core values but also must have personal integrity and honesty.

Finally, if neither of the previous approaches provides the answer, administrators must ask if the action is what they would want others to do unto them. This is called care-based thinking and arises from the writings of Confucius, who said, "Here certainly is the golden maxim; do not do to others that which we do not want them to do unto us." This precept requires administrators to imagine themselves as the object of the focus rather than the agent of the action.

Before an administrator can begin the process of making an ethical decision, there is perhaps a fourth tenet that is not only the most important, but must underlie everything the administrator does. That overarching tenet is that all decisions, all steps, and all principles must be based on personal traits of integrity, honesty, and forthrightness. Without honesty and truthfulness, ethical decision making becomes an intellectual process rather than an ethical choice.

Kidder (1995) also suggested a series of steps to follow in order to resolve ethical dilemmas. Each step is based upon the ability and willingness of administrators to be honest and truthful in searching for the right decision. The first step is to determine if a situation entails a moral or ethical dilemma. In many situations, the issues are superficial and may involve behaviors associated with manners or social conventions, or they may center on economic, technological, or aesthetic concerns. Second, after determining if a dilemma exists, then administrators must determine if there is a moral or ethical responsibility for action required in the situation. Administrators must understand that in almost every situation, depending on one's analytical predisposition, one could dismiss an obligation based upon ends-based thinking. Honesty and integrity, however, require administrators to assess each situation within the professional responsibilities of the public school administrator rather than doing what is personally or politically expedient.

The third step in resolving ethical dilemmas is to gather all of the relevant data. In schools, when a decision does not have to be made immediately to make an appropriate decision administrators need as much information as possible otherwise risking reducing the process to the realm of speculation and the theoretical. Since school decisions involve people, administrators must gather as much information as possible to make an informed decision.

Once all relevant information has been gathered, administrators must then make the test for right vs. wrong or right vs. right. To assess the right vs. wrong dilemma, the first test is a legal test. Was breaking the law involved? If the answer is yes, then administrators must enforce the laws and codes that are applicable. If there is some question about the legality of the situation, Kidder (1995) provides three additional tests. First, administrators should apply the "stench" test. This test involves moral intuition and asks: Does this go against your internal moral principles? What is your gut reaction to the situation? A second test is called the "front-page" test. If the decision was made public, what would be the result? Would you have qualms? Would you be embarrassed about the decision? The final test is called the "mom" test. Administrators have to ask themselves: What would your mother do or think about my actions and/or decisions?

Ultimately, administrators must make decisions based on personal ethics and integrity after they have engaged in an exhaustive effort to determine the facts through rigorous reasoning. Sometimes, after going through the process, administrators may regress to what Kidder (1995) calls the "quasi-academic" mind set causing them to confuse analysis with action and fail to move from theoretical reasoning to the practical solution. Contemporary society requires public school administrators to make decisions that are not only tough but often far-reaching. No decision in education can be made in isolation or without consequences. School administrators must first embrace an awareness of their own locus of morality, their own value system, and then proceed to make decisions in the best interests of all concerned.

As detailed earlier, educators are often confronted with dilemmas like the one above. Since the educational environment is becoming increasingly litigious, are current ethical foundations becoming inadequate? How does an administrator determine if certain conduct is ethical? Are there certain rules of moral conduct that should not be broken under any circumstance? Or, should the rules be broken if the outcome of the conduct would lead to positive results? Over thousands of years, great philosophers have debated these issues, without a resultant set of coherent beliefs about moral conduct that is satisfactory to all. Indeed, what may be moral to one person would not be moral to another. As suggested earlier, there are systems of ethical conduct or ethical theories that have developed over time. Some of these theories are apropos to the discussions in this chapter and beg for a more thorough explanation.

Although many philosophers use morals and ethics interchangeably, morality is a social convention with rules dependent upon cultural expectations (Pojman, 2002). Morality, as defined by Beauchamp and Bowie (1983), "refers to traditions of belief about right and wrong conduct" (p. 1). Ethical theory, on the other hand, is the study of the nature of moral principles, dilemmas, and decisions.

The section on ethical theory will discuss the two most prominent ethical systems of moral thinking: teleology and deontology. Although they may be presented as such (see Table 5.1),

ETHICAL THEORY

Marcella is an intelligent young lady who works very hard for her good grades. She is the oldest of six children in a family that is very poor, but all members of the family are considered honest, fair, and hard working. Marcella and her siblings qualify for the school's free-lunch program, but have chosen to take odd jobs with the school to earn money for the school's lunch program. On this particular day, Marcella is working for the school. She has volunteered her time before school to sell spirit buttons. Money from the sale will add to the fund that purchases school supplies for indigent children. Marcella was unaware that the principal observed her taking money from the cash bag and placing it in her purse. After confronting her, Marcella remorsefully admits that she took the money to pay for her lunch on that day because she gave her lunch money to her younger sister, who was attending an elementary school field trip. She intended to return the money during the next morning's spirit ribbon sale, which is after her pay period for working after school. Can the principal trust Marcella as she works for the school? What is the principal to do?

TABLE 5.1
Ethical Systems

Ethical system	Teleology	Deontology	Axiology
Descriptor	Ends-based	Rules-based	Care-based
Ethical theories	Utilitarian	Objectivism	Values
Moral focus	Ultimate consequences	Duty bound to rules and principles	Character of the decision maker

these systems are not mutually exclusive (Cahill, 1981). Additionally, a third, less established, system of moral thinking called axiology will be presented. Concomitant with these systems, Section II will introduce related ethical theories. It is important to note that each theory has its own variation, which often leads to overlap among the theories. It is doubtful that even a full understanding of ethical systems and theories will lead to a truly consistent means of making decisions. Yet, "the awareness of a duty which is higher than mere convenience or greater than the mere survival of the school is being asked" (Craig, 1993, p. 25).

Teleology and Utilitarianism (End-Based Ethics)

Teleology (teleo is Greek for "end") is the doctrine of the study of ends or final causes (Oxford English Dictionary [OED], 2005). Teleology is often referred to as ends-based ethics, as presented earlier, because it is predicated on the basis that an action is right if it leads to the best balance of good consequences or the least balance of bad consequences. In other words, the moral worth of actions or decisions is determined solely by the consequences of the actions or decisions. Although there are several ethical theories related to teleological systems, the most widely studied is utilitarianism (Hitt, 1990).

Utilitarians want to maximize the good and minimize the bad. Adler and Cain (1962) noted that "[t]his utilitarian moral criterion is that the rightness or wrongness of human conduct is to be determined by its effect on happiness—ultimately, on the happiness of the greatest number of persons" (p. 261). Happiness, as observed by the preeminent utilitarian, John Stuart Mill, is more than the egocentric euphoria, but it is seeking pleasure and goodness (e.g., kindness, productivity, and efficiency) over pain (e.g., unkindness, worthlessness, and indigence). According to Mill, it is "the objective results, not the personal motivations of action [that] make the ethical difference" (p. 264). Furthermore, Mill observed that not every ethical dilemma requires the decision maker to consider society in its entirety. The decision maker need only consider the persons involved in a specific situation.

On a broader scale, the utilitarians ascribe to the belief that the purpose of morality is social good produced by sensitivity to the needs of others. Conversely, the social good is achieved by controlling the activities that cause harm to others (Beauchamp & Bowie, 1979).

Utilitarians are classified into two types—act-utilitarians and rule-utilitarians. *Act-utilitarians* see rules as guidelines and not valid in every circumstance. Therefore, "an act is right if and only if it results in as much good as any available alternative" (Pojman, 2002, p. 111). For example, an act-utilitarian educator might consider Marcella's work for the school (and her apparent remorse) as overriding the educator's "stealing is bad" rule. In essence,

Marcella's helping the school and younger sibling is a greater good than punishing her for stealing.

Rule-utilitarians, on the other hand, believe that there are some maxims that should not be compromised. These maxims, e.g., do not lie, do not cheat, do not steal, do not change because of particular circumstance. In instances where these maxims may conflict, the rule-utilitarian would then have to decide which rule took priority (Beauchamp & Bowie, 1979). According to Pojman (2002), for rule-utilitarians "an act is right if and only if it is required by a rule that is a member of a set of rules whose acceptance would lead to greater utility for society than any available alternative" (p. 112). In Marcella's case, the rule-utilitarian would have to consider which rule took priority—"stealing is bad," or "concern for the welfare of others is good."

Deontology and Objectivism (Rules-Based Ethics)

Deontology (from the Greek "that which is binding") is the science of duty; the area of knowledge that focuses on moral obligations (OED, 2005). Deontology is predicated on natural laws or divine laws. The rules are the standards for which individuals act and make their decisions. Prominent philosopher Immanuel Kant argued ethical truths and moral principles are universal and established by reason (or natural law) (Hitt, 1990). Whereas followers of teleology argue that a particular act always has the potential to be right or wrong and followers of deontology argue that some acts are intrinsically right or wrong (Cahill, 1981).

Objectivism, sometimes referred to as rules-based ethics, is the most predominant ethical theory credited to deontology. Bauchamp and Bowie (1979) asserted that objectivism is "independent of the concept of good, and . . . actions are not justified by their consequences" (p. 31). Apart from utilitarianism where consequences of the act or decision are important, with objectivism the importance of the motive affects the act or decision. To the objectivist, the motive, duty, or obligation is important in ethical decision making.

Natural laws, or reasoned principles, that form the foundation for objectivism may be specific to the decision maker or generally applicable to all. An individualistic principle might well be to *always* put the needs of others before his or her own needs. Preserving human dignity and worth would be a more universally accepted principle. For other objectivists, the ethics are founded on divine law—laws established by a supreme being, or stated in a religious code. Cooper (1982) offered some proverbs that are indicative of rules, or laws:

> "Honesty is the best policy."
> "Truth will win out."
> "Never fight a battle that you can't win."
> "My country, right or wrong." (p. 14)

Moral absolutism, an extreme objectivist viewpoint, is based upon the idea that there are "nonoverrideable [sic] moral principles" (Beckner, 2004, p. 50). For instance, the moral absolutist who believes that stealing is wrong would likely argue that it is impermissible to steal even to save a life. An objectivist might feel duty bound to punish Marcella for stealing, regardless of the reason for the theft or the consequences of the punishment.

A discussion of duty, rules, and principles naturally leads us to consider established, enforceable professional rules. For example, zero-tolerance policies have their roots in objectivism, as do codes of ethics. Although Kidder (1995) contends that codes of ethics are typically "shared reference points" (p. 99), Texas educators have codified a set of ethical guidelines so they are rules to be followed. In a sense, the enforceable ethics code is a set of guidelines so broadly agreed upon that the behavior is mandated. (See the Educator's Code of Ethics in Appendix)

Differing from utilitarianism, objectivism offers a more structured framework for ethical behavior. However, the adherence to rules and duty can be messy, as well. By whose authority do we accept the rules? What if we have conflicting rules? Should rules change to adapt to changing situations?

Axiology and Values (Care-Based)

Axiology, or care-based ethics, is the study of values (OED, 2005). Beckner (2004) noted that "value ethics tries to describe the good or virtuous person and show how such a person may be developed" (p. 72). Kidder (1995) argued that central to care-based ethics is the philosophical concept of reversibility. The ethical test for reversibility is "putting yourself in another's shoes and imagining how it would feel if you were the recipient, rather than the perpetrator, of your actions" (p. 25).

Unlike teleology and deontology, which have prescriptive tendencies, axiology has less clearly defined formal procedures. Teleology and deontology emphasize principles, where axiology emphasizes the development of the decision maker (Jordan & Meara, 1990). Axiology requires a significant understanding of morality "implicit in the multifarious character of our human engagements" (Becker, 2004, p. 271).

Still, Becker (2004) contended that the "dynamic context" of professional organizations requires that the decision maker "take into consideration all sorts of competing tensions that are unique to [a] specific circumstance" (pp. 273–274). Consequently, the rightness or wrongness of a decision relating to an ethical dilemma relates specifically to the context of the moral complexities involved in a professional environment. Ergo, virtue is highly personal, and establishing fixed moral standards becomes quite difficult. It is not to say, however, that the personal nature of the virtue allows for arbitrary decisions. It simply means that the decisions are based upon the context of the ethical dilemma.

Central to axiology is the value system of the decision maker. What values are good, or right? Again, this is a topic that has been debated for centuries by some of the most notable philosophers. Aristotle, and others, claimed that prudence, justice, temperance, and fortitude were the traditional virtues. Others have added loyalty, compassion, humility, and courage. Beckner (2004) argued that what makes a decision virtuous is the motive, or character, of the decision maker. He defined character as "the ability to make the best decision when a decision is required" (p. 79). Acquisition of character in order to make the best decision is dependent upon experience and observation.

Drawing from these prominent scholars, Starrat (1994) posited that an ethical person possesses developed qualities of autonomy, connectedness, and transcendence. *Autonomy* refers to the independent, individual ability to act without the direction of an outside force or influence. Autonomous acts are intentional acts, not routine responses, or impersonal reactions. The knowledge of oneself, and the knowledge to act autonomously, comes from intuition and imagination as well as scientific knowledge. *Connectedness* refers to an awareness and sensitivity to others involved in the circumstance. This connectedness implies an understanding of the individuals involved, the environment, and the culture of the setting.

Transcendence is going beyond the ordinary. It is "engaging our lives with other people" (p. 38), sacrificing self-interests for the benefit of others, and rising above common expectations in our actions.

Given the lack of a "menu" or prescribed flowchart for decision making, it is easy to see how axiological systems are more difficult to understand than the more prescriptive teleological and deontological systems. Yet, considering the complexity and sophistication of society, a discussion and consideration of values of decision makers is vital. In section III, values-based ethics is considered within the same decision-making model with ends-based ethics or rules-based ethics.

Given an understanding of some of the background of ethical theory, a study of current ethical dilemmas in a precise and subtle nature can begin. As Pojman (2002) commented, "with the onset of pluralism and the loss of confidence in traditional authorities, a rational approach to ethics is vital for us to survive and thrive" (p. xviii).

◆ ETHICAL DECISION MAKING

As articulated earlier, ethical behavior is promulgated and supported by a complex system of balances and counterbalances that ebb and flow with differing moral conflicts and ethical dilemmas. Future educational leaders must master and operationalize the ethical pedagogy necessary to make sound and appropriate decisions.

In Texas, and across the country, a steady whirlwind of criticism about public schools and public school administrators continues. The community trust enjoyed in the past has been steadily eroding. Confidence in university-based principal preparation programs has likewise diminished. The alternative preparation wave has reached the shores of educational leadership. At the heart of this controversy are the parametric dimensions of what principals need to know to be effective school leaders, and the processes and skills they must master.

The literature on effective school leaders indicates they must be competent managers, effective instructional leaders, and human relations experts. What has been fuzzy in the public education arena is a clear and concise body of knowledge about *how* decisions are made, in particular, ethical decisions that might help win a public trust that has been dissipating rapidly.

The Legal Connection

As discussed early in this chapter, the legal questions in decision making are generally questions of right versus wrong and easier to decide. The dilemma of right versus right in ethical practice is more of a challenge. At times the correct legal answer itself presents a morale conflict for many. A good example is the *Plessy v. Ferguson* (1896) case in which the U.S. Supreme Court established the doctrine of "separate but equal." It took the conscience of a country and the struggle of a civil rights movement to right that legal wrong. Administrators may experience this same type of dilemma when dealing with issues related to church and state, language, culture, etc.

The Formative Process

One might make the case that ethics and school reform actions sometimes seem to take different trajectories. Yet, the ethical process and the action process blend together almost as a natural progression. Figure 5.1 shows that ethics is founded on core values typically representing

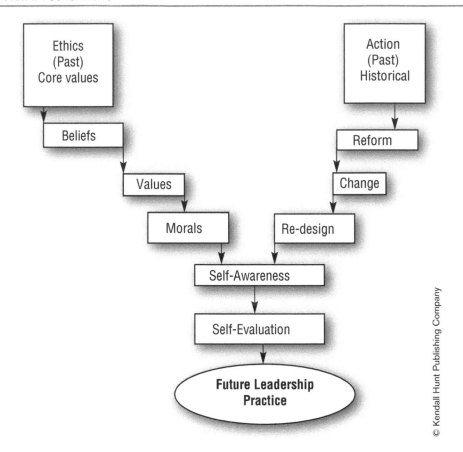

Figure 5.1   Re-Culturing Future Leadership Practice Through Ethics and Action.

the past in terms of formative development. Where the administrator was raised during childhood and the family values transmitted to him or her at a young age are only two of the many variables defining the character of the administrator. Character development, both innate and acquired, defines the individual in terms of beliefs, values, and morals determining, to a great extent, how solutions to difficult ethical conflicts are viewed.

The action process has a similar past in historical practice that likewise guides ideas about reform, change, and redesign. The focal point is the transgression at the level of self awareness and self evaluation, individually or as a group. The end result is a homogenized solution to an ethical dilemma.

Heifetz and Linsky (2002) suggested the need for administrators to "anchor" themselves. They further suggest that "the self relies on our capacity to witness and learn throughout our lives, to refine the core values that orient our decisions—whether or not they conform to our expectations" (p. 187). Furthermore, administrators need to distinguish between the self and the administrative role; the latter of which cannot be anchored.

Kidder (1995, p. 212) presented three previously unanticipated conditions that could shape future ethics. His first condition is that "we will face entirely new ethical issues." Second, "we will live in an age of increasing moral intensity." And third, "we will experience unprecedented pressures to drop out of society and make a separate peace."

The Ethical Questions

Many ethical dilemmas are encased in issues such as loyalty, community, justice, mercy, religion, relationships, finances, responsibilities, role conflict, policy making, morality, and gender, to name a few (Beckner, 2004). There are many models, guidelines, and codes that can be followed to make sound decisions. Hodgkinson (1991) suggested the consideration of the following questions:

1. What are the values in conflict in the given case? Can they be named?
2. What fields of values are most affected or most salient?
3. Who are the value actors?
4. How is the conflict distributed interpersonally and intrapersonally?
5. Is the conflict interhierarchical or intrahierarchical on the value paradigm?
6. Are ends seeking to dictate means? Or are means subverting ends?
7. Could the conflict be apparently resolved by removing a value actor or group of actors?
8. What are the metavalues?
9. Is there a principle that must be invoked or can that be avoided?
10. Can the conflict be resolved at a lower level of the paradigm?
11. Can the tension of non-resolution be avoided (i.e., must the conflict be resolved now)?
12. What rational and pragmatic consequences follow from possible and probable scenarios?
13. What bodies of value consensus and political relevance are involved? Both within and without the organization?
14. To what extent does one have control over the formative and informative media in the case (press, radio, television, lines of communication, informal organization, etc.)?
15. How does one analyze the state of the effect, and affect control, amongst the parties to the case?
16. What is the analysis of commitment (using the paradigm)?
17. What is the interest of the commons, the collectivity? How can higher level interest be invoked? And how high need one go?
18. What, in the end, is my true will in the case before me? (pp. 136–137)

The Culturally Diverse Environment

Today's school administrators must be sensitive and cognizant of the cultural maze our society has become. The country, and even more so the state of Texas, has evolved from a melting pot to a salad bowl society. A society that once placed great value in the creation of a homogeneous culture now recognizes cultural diversity as strength, where differences (including language) are respected and accepted.

As administrators wrestle with the relatively easy questions of right versus wrong, the true ethical dilemmas, as noted earlier, are better categorized as *right versus right* decision making. The fact that currently in Texas the majority of school children in public schools come from a minority population dictates that many educational decisions are embedded in the fabric of cultural differences.

For example, state policy makers are currently struggling with an equitable way to fund public schools. Different funding mechanisms suggest that funding preferences are culturally and demographically dependent. Additionally, acceptance by state leaders for a two-way dual language model for children is indicative of recognition of the ethnic diversity in the state.

In public schools a similar conflict between right versus right occurs daily as administrators and teachers make academic decisions concerning the degree of inclusion in regular education programs by handicapped, migrant, bilingual, low socioeconomic, and minority children. As noted earlier, the decision-making process to determine the most important right allows administrators to solve issues based on the following principles: "Do what is good for the greatest number" (teleology); "Follow only the principles that you want everyone else to follow" (deontology); and "Do to others what you would want them to do to you" (axiology).

Table 5.2 shows the extension of the six steps for decision-making process by Bazerman (1986) as well as the nine steps of ethical decision making (Kidder, 1995) and the five cultural safeguards as envisioned by Gonzalez. Importantly, administrators need to extend their decision-making process beyond the ethical realm to include the impact of the outcomes of decisions on students, teachers, and community members in a culturally diverse environment. In safeguard number one, the administrator identifies which culture sensitive issues, if any, are involved. For this the administrator needs to be sensitive to student and staff differences and must understand that this type of awareness starts at the top and sets the tone for a healthy school environment.

TABLE 5.2
Extending the Decision-Making Model to Accommodate Ethical and Cultural Considerations

Six Steps for Decision Making (Bazerman, 1986)	*Nine Checkpoints for Ethical Decision Making (Kidder, 1995)*	*Five Cultural Safeguards*
1. Define the problem	1. Recognize that there is a moral issue.	1. Identify the culture-sensitive issues involved.
2. Criteria identification	2. Determine the actors.	2. Identify the cultural/equity foundations that need to be respected/protected.
3. Criteria weighing	3. Gather the relevant facts.	3. Apply principle of benefits maximization and principle of equal respect.
4. Generate alternatives	4. Test for right-versus-wrong issues.	4. Walk through options and predict its culture/equity effects.
5. Rank alternatives	5. Test for right-versus-right paradigms.	5. Evaluate the effect on cultural equity.
6. Implement decision	6. Investigate the "trilemma" options.	
	7. Make a decision.	
	8. Re-visit and reflect on the decision.	

Safeguard number two allows the administrator to identify the cultural or equity foundation being jeopardized. Knowing the basic foundations is important because they may deal with cultural integrity associated with language, physical appearance, history, customs, traditions, safety, and welfare.

In safeguard number three, the administrator weighs the effect of the principle of benefit maximization with the principle of equal respect. The principle of maximization may be a threat to basic rights, permitting schools to trade the welfare of some for the welfare of others. The principle of equal respect, however, does not have such drastic consequences and allows decision makers to respect the rights of others without trading rights for welfare (Strike, Haller, & Soltis, 1988). Looking at all possible options and predicting the degree of damage or harm to culture and equity in a diverse environment is the essence of safeguard number four. The decision to take the best possible option is many times found above and beyond the administrator's theoretical, empirical, and experiential knowledge base. The last safeguard is an assessment of the outcome of the decision (with cultural and equity implications). Has the issue been resolved or have new ones been created? What is the new direction in terms of continuing the evolution of mutual respect and understanding? The ethical goal for school administrators is to become advocates of equality for all and to develop a conscience for quality school environments in the future. Students, teachers, and administrators living in a global village, where the world seems smaller and moves more rapidly due to technological developments, must build a synergistic environment of interdependence. This synergistic environment must build on respect and acceptance through an ethical and conscious morality of decision making (Tiedt & Tiedt, 1990).

If the administrator accepts the premise that values drive beliefs, attitudes, and actions, which are derived primarily from culture, then it becomes important to understand cultural backgrounds to determine the reasons for people's behaviors. In doing so, the administrator may be able to predict people's reactions to administrative decisions. Administrators must know that values shape attitudes and beliefs about work, success, wealth, authority, equity, competition, and other components of the contextual work environment. Values govern how one expects to be treated, how one treats others, communicates, negotiates, processes information, and makes decisions. Leadership styles and the willingness of individuals to be led have tremendous implications for school administrators as managers and instructional leaders (Scarborough, 1998).

In the wake of school violence like the incident at Littleton, Colorado, which dealt with possible cultural differences between students, it is important to note and appreciate the complex campus environments that administrators have helped to create. These school environments are large impersonal schools where non-ethnic as well as ethnic differences have the potential to manifest themselves in violent behavior. The principal will continue to be held accountable for interpreting and understanding cultural diversity in the realm of youth behavior and the legal and ethical codes will continue to be debated in terms of school administrator expectations. Tomorrow's administrators do not have to be bilingual, but they must be bicultural.

◆ REFERENCES

Adams, D. M., & Maine, E. W. (1998). *Business ethics for the 21st century*. Mountain View, CA: Mayfield Publishing.

Adler, M. J., & Cain, S. (1962). *Ethics: The study of moral values*. Chicago: Encyclopedia Britannica, Inc.

Bazerman, M. H. (1986). *Judgment in managerial decision making*. New York: John Wiley and Sons.

Beauchamp, T. L., & Bowie, N. E. (1979). *Ethical theory and business* (2nd ed.). Englewood Cliffs, NJ: Prentice-Hall, Inc.

Beck, L. G., & Murphy, J. (1994). *Ethics in educational administration programs: An expanding role.* Thousand Oaks, CA: Corwin.

Becker, M. (2004). Virtue ethics, applied ethics and rationality twenty-three years after virtue. *South African Journal of Philosophy, 23,* 267–281. Retrieved from EBSCOhost database.

Beckner, W. (2004). *Ethics for educational leaders.* Boston: Allyn & Bacon.

Behr, E. T. (1998). Acting from the center. *Management Review, 87,* 51–60.

Cahill, L. S. (1981). Teleology, utilitarianism, and Christian ethics. *Theological Studies, 42,* 601–629. Retrieved from EBSCOhost database.

Colgan, C. (2004). The ethical choice. *American School Board Journal, 191,* 5, 4–6.

Cooper, T. L. (1982). *The responsible administrator: An approach to ethics for the administrative role.* Port Washington, NY: Kennikat Press.

Corey, G., Corey, M. S., & Callanan, P. (2007). *Issues and ethics in the helping professions* (7th ed.). Belmont, CA: Brooks/Cole.

Craig, R. P. (1993). Ethical and moral theory and public school administration. *Journal of School Leadership, 3,* 21–29.

Drake, T. L., & Roe, W. H. (2003). *The principalship* (6th ed.). Upper Saddle River, NJ: Merrill Prentice Hall.

Giacalone, R. A., & Thompson, K. R. (2006). From the guest co-editors: Special issue on ethics and social responsibility. *Academy of Management Learning & Education, 5*(3), 261–265.

Glanz, J. (2009). Decisions you can live with. *Principal Leadership, 10*(2), 24–28.

Greenberg, R. A., & Baron, J. (2000). *Behavior in organizations* (7th ed.). Upper Saddle River, NJ: Merrill Prentice Hall.

Hartman, E. (2006). Can we teach character? An Aristotelian answer. *Academy of Management Learning & Education, 5*(1), 68–81.

Heifetz, R. A., & Linsky, M. (2002). *Leadership on the line.* Boston: Harvard Business School Press.

Hitt, W. D. (1990). *Ethics and leadership: Putting theory into practice.* Columbus, OH: Battelle Press.

Hocking, W. E. (1962). Preface. In M. Adler & S. Cain (Eds.) *Ethics: The study of moral values.* Chicago: Encyclopedia Britannica.

Hodgkinson, C. (1991). *Educational leadership: The moral art.* Albany, NY: State University of New York Press.

Jordan, A. E., & Meara, N. M. (1990). Ethics and the professional practice of psychologists: The role of virtues and principles. *Professional Psychology, 21,* 107–114.

Kidder, R. M. (1995). *How good people make tough choices: Resolving the dilemmas of ethical living.* New York: Fireside.

Lee, G. (2006). *Courage: The backbone of leadership.* San Francisco, CA: Jossey-Bass.

MacIntyre, A. (1966). *A short history of ethics.* New York: Macmillan.

Meara, N. M., Schmidt, L. D., & Day, J. D (1996). Principles and virtues: A foundation for ethical decisions, policies, and character. *The Counseling Psychologist, 24*(1), 4–77.

Mirk, P. (2009). Ethics by example. *Principal Leadership,* 18–23.

Nash, R. J. (2002). *"Real world" ethics: Frameworks for educators and human service professionals.* New York: Teachers College Press.

Oxford English Dictionary. (2005). [Electronic version.] Oxford, England: Oxford University Press.

Paul, R., & Elder, L. (2006). *Understanding the foundations of ethical reasoning.* Dillon Beach, CA: Foundation for Critical Thinking

Plessy v. Ferguson, 163 U.S. 537 (1896).

Pojman, L. P. (2002). *Ethics: Discovering right and wrong* (4th ed.). Belmont, CA: Wadsworth/ Thomson.

Rebore, R. W. (2001). *The ethics of educational leadership.* Upper Saddle River, NJ: Merrill Prentice Hall.

Reinhartz, J., & Beach, D. M. (2004). *Educational leadership: Changing schools, changing roles.* Boston: Allyn & Bacon.

Scarborough, J. (1998). *The origins of cultural differences and their impact on management.* Westport, CT: Quorum Books.

Shapiro, J. P., & Stefkovich, J. A. (2010). *Ethical leadership and decision making in education: Applying theoretical perspectives to complex dilemmas* (3rd ed.). New York: Routledge.

Starrat, R. J. (1994). *Building an ethical school: A practical response to the moral crisis in schools.* London: Routledge-Falmer.

Strike, K. A., Haller, E. J., & Soltis, J. F. (1998). *The ethics of school administration.* New York: Teachers College Press.

Tiedt, P. L., & Tiedt, I. M. (1990). *Multicultural teaching: A handbook of activities, information, and resources.* Boston: Allyn & Bacon.

White, L. P., & Wooten, K. C. (1986). *Professional ethics and practice in organizational development: A systematic analysis of issues, alternatives, and approaches.* New York: Praeger.

Yates, A. C. (1999). Good leaders must first be good people. In L. Orozco (Ed.), *Educational Leadership* (pp. 46–49). Chicago: Coursewise Publishing.

LEADING AND MANAGING THE CHANGE PROCESS

Essential Roles for School Leaders

Danna Beaty ◆ *Anita Pankake*

It is always safe to assume, not that the old way is wrong, but that there may be a better way.
—Henry F. Harrower

If anything is likely to stay the same in education, it is change! Year in and year out, decade after decade, changes of all sorts have been proposed to improve schools. Hanson (2003) noted "schools have changed in almost all aspects of their historical composition, including curricular programs, physical designs, instructional methodologies, and procedures of policy formation" (p. 296). Some of these changes have come rapidly; others have had long and difficult journeys. Schools have seen many changes and are likely to see many more. The primary difference for the future relates to pace. The rapidity with which changes are proposed and required will probably increase. As Rebore (2011) put it, "Change is not only continual, but also accelerative . . ." (p. 1). The obvious conclusion is that change is and will continue to be a constant focus of conversation and a catalyst for action among school leaders, i.e., school professionals, parents, and the public and private sectors of our society.

It is imperative that school leaders know as much about the change process as possible if they are to lead and manage it effectively. Change issues from the past, the present, and the projected future are important topics for schools leaders to study. The history of change in education is replete with good ideas that failed to move into an effective practice. Why did some changes find their way into the operation of schools and others did not? What are the various sources of change proposals? Why do some people resist change and others embrace it? What influences whether or not something gets initiated? Knowledge about these issues can help school leaders assure that needed changes are proposed, adopted, and successfully implemented, and, perhaps just as important, that changes not needed are avoided.

Once a change has been initiated, how can it be sustained and become a part of "the way we do business"? How can changes that are no longer relevant and, in fact, may even be damaging to current purposes be discarded? What is the systemic nature of change? Why is it important for school leaders to understand and plan for this? Initiating, implementing, institutionalizing, and, when appropriate, resisting changes in education are all part of the role responsibilities of school leaders.

Much has been written about change and how to plan, implement, and sustain it. The purpose of this chapter is to provide the reader with a general overview of planned change in organizations. To accomplish this, the first section defines change types and offers a brief history of planned change in education. Some general vocabulary and concepts regarding the phenomenon of change are included. Next, information regarding selected change models is presented to provide an overview of what is available and identify sources for additional information. Third, some important considerations for school leaders in their efforts to initiate and implement successful changes are presented. Finally, the chapter closes with a section regarding the future of change in education. Following the reference list is an offering of some additional resources (readings, videos, articles, and Websites) for those wanting to know more.

◆ DEFINING CHANGE AND REVIEWING ITS HISTORY

Most areas of study have a vocabulary of terms used in unique ways to help in defining and understanding the central concepts in the field. So, it is with the study of change. Some of the terms found in the literature on change can be helpful in understanding the phenomenon of change and what has been learned about it.

Unplanned and Planned Change

First, it is important to differentiate between change and planned change. Change, as a general happening, implies that things are different than they were. It implies no judgement of good or bad, effective or ineffective, just different. Hanson (2003) referred to such change as spontaneous and defines it as, "an alteration that emerges in a short time frame as a result of natural circumstance and random occurrences" (p. 297). There is no coordinated intent to bring about these changes; they "just happen." Nelson and Quick (2000) labeled such changes as unplanned. They see unplanned changes as those that are imposed on the organization from the outside and are generally unforeseen. These changes will occur no matter what we do—we will get older, prices will increase, personnel will transfer in and out of the school, etc. These are the kinds of things that just happen. When they do, leaders must respond.

Planned change on the other hand refers to intent. Early in the organized study of change, Chin (1967) noted planned changes are "where there is a deliberate attempt to bring about change" (p. 39). According to Hanson (2003), planned change is "a conscious and deliberate attempt to manage events so that the outcome is redirected by design to some predetermined end" (p. 297). Nelson and Quick (2000) also used the term planned change and differentiated it from unplanned change. Like Chin (1967) and Hanson (2003), Nelson and Quick (2000) defined planned change as that which results from a deliberate decision to alter the organization. They go on to declare the obvious, "Not all change is planned" (p. 603).

Planned change is generally that which captures the attention of school leaders because of the specified direction or valued outcome involved. For those who value a particular idea, a planned change in that area will be a welcomed effort. For anyone who does not value that particular outcome or advocates a different outcome, the planned change will cause resistance, if not real controversy.

Change and Progress

Change merely means that things are different than they were—not better or not worse, just different. Synonyms for the word change include: modification, alteration, shift, and movement. However, the kind of changes of interest in education are generally proposed with the intent of making things better or causing improvement in the current situation, whatever it may be, i.e., making progress. Rarely does someone propose a change with the intent of making things worse—however, while it may not be their intent, it may well be the result. It is important that school leaders recognize that making progress requires change, but all changes do not necessarily result in progress.

Change Agent

Various authors have identified a number of roles essential in the change process. Especially important in planned change is the change agent. According to Trybus (2011), all leaders must be the agents of change and educational leaders are no exception (Jazzar & Algozzine, 2006). Nelson and Quick (2000) defined change agent as "the individual or group that undertakes the task of introducing and managing a change in an organization" (p. 609). Change agents can be internal or external to the organization. Additionally, Hanson (2003) noted that "The roles and responsibilities of the change agent vary from complex to simplistic and tough to permissive, depending on the demands of the situation and the individuals involved" (p. 323). School leaders often volunteer for or are assigned this role. When school leaders lead and manage change, they are serving as change agents in their organizations. Jazzar and Algozzine (2006) state that educational leaders in the twenty-first century will need to change agent and must be aware that the "road to improvement will not be well paved" (p. 176).

Selected Characteristics of Change: Potency and Complexity

Potency of change refers to, "the degree to which a change requires a significant departure from existing conditions" (Hanson, 2003, p. 306). The potency of the change relates to its complexity. "Change can be of a relatively small scope . . . a fine-tuning of the organization or the making of small improvements. Change also can be of a larger scale, such as the restructuring of an organization" (Nelson & Quick, 2000, p. 608). The greater the complexity, the greater the potency. Complexity, according to Fullan (2001a), refers to "the difficulty and extent of change required of the individuals responsible for implementation (p. 78). Similarly, Hanson (2003) suggested that the level of potency is "the degree to which resources, time, energy, power and goodwill are involved in a change initiative . . . the energies and resources available to do battle" (p. 306). An example in education would be Cuban's (1988) first- and second-order changes. He described first-order changes as focused on fixing various parts of the existing system. Second-order changes, on the other hand, are focused on entirely restructuring the system. Second-order changes would have much greater potency than first-order changes. More recently, Fullan (2001b) made similar differentiations using the terms reorganizing and reculturing.

Systemic

The dictionary defines systemic as, "of or pertaining to a system" and a system is "a group of interacting, interrelated or interdependent elements forming a complex whole" (Houghton-Mifflin, 1982, p. 1234). Organizations (classrooms, schools, districts, communities, etc.) are systems in their own right and subsystems of larger entities in which they operate. Because the elements of systems are interacting, interrelated or interdependent, any change has consequences in other parts of the whole. Realizing this is essential in successfully planning and implementing change. Change agents need to be aware of the possible consequences—positive and negative—of their actions. No change occurs in isolation; changing one part of the system will results in changes in other parts of the system. "Everything in this world is connected with everything else in a delicate and complex web of interrelationships" (Rifkin, 1980, p. 226).

The History of Planned Change in Education

The focus of this chapter is planned change—change with a deliberate direction, a valued outcome. The history of studying (researching) planned change in education is relatively brief. Such study has occurred for only the past 40–45 years. During that time, much has been learned about how change in education has fared and what accounts for its successes and failures. Fullan (2001a, 2007) marked the beginning of wide-scale planned change in education with the launch of Sputnik by the Russians in 1957. According to Spring (1978), this was a major part of the reason that the National Defense Education Act was passed. The NDEA provided money for specific educational purposes and programs. Certainly changes in education occurred prior to this event. However, two elements involved at this point were unprecedented—there was a focus on large-scale changes in education across the nation and large amounts of federal funds were made available for use in accomplishing these advocated (categorical) changes (Fullan, 2001a; Spring 1978). Fullan (2001a, 2007) called this period of multiple, large-scale, national reform initiatives the "adoption era." The large amounts of money available generated many change proposals in the funded areas. Larger amounts of money were being allocated for the development of major curriculum reforms to be disseminated to the schools.

Unfortunately, after a bit more than a decade of such design and adoption efforts, there was little evidence that anything had changed. Little implementation had occurred. Fullan (2001a, 2007) labeled this period (1970s) "failed implementation" for obvious reasons. Because of the pressure on schools to be innovative, many schools adopted reforms but were unable to fully implement them. Often general trappings were adopted by the schools, but no real changes ever occurred at the instructional level. Fullan (2001a) claimed, "The history of implementation research is not pleasant. It shows that planned change attempts rarely succeed as intended" (p. 10); in 2007, he simply stated, "Putting ideas into practice was a far more complex process than people realized" (Fullan, 2007, p. 5).

There was a renewed interest in large-scale change in the 1980s motivated by the effective schools movement. While some pockets of successful change were reported, there was little evidence that any general, large-scale impact was occurring in the schools of the nation. Early in this period, 1983, The National Commission on Excellence in Education issued its report titled *A Nation at Risk*. Following the publication of this indictment of public education, a flood of reform proposals appeared from a variety of sources including educators, the business community, and public and private foundations. Fullan (2001a, 1992) labeled this period of change "intensification and restructuring." The term intensification was used to describe those change proposals that focused on increased definition of existing elements of the system (increased requirements for graduation, longer school days/years, mandated textbooks, and/or teaching practices). The increased definitions were accompanied by more frequent monitoring and evaluations. Restructuring change proposals were focused on power structures and relationships within the organization, collaborative cultures for professional staff, and new roles and relationships for teachers, school administrators, and central office staff.

The 1990s brought a renewed interest in large-scale reform and that interest continues into this new millennium. However, whether evaluating each of the periods included in the study of planned change individually or looking at the history as a whole, the ratio of initiated changes to successfully implemented ones is not encouraging. More initiations have been generated and proposed than have been successfully implemented. Most educators are able to nod knowingly at this statement; each year seems to bring yet another list of change proposals intended to improve the schools. Carpenter (2000) counted some 315 "good ideas" in a single year's issues of the *Kappan* journal. Educators and those interested in education are not at a loss for "good ideas"; rather, knowledge and skills regarding how to put good ideas into practice—how to make real change happen—is where the need lies. Unfortunately, according to Fullan (2006),

> Even reform efforts that had millions of dollars and political will behind them along with focusing on many of the right strategies (standards, assessment aligned with standards, curriculum revision, plenty of professional development for teachers and principals and even professional learning communities) have failed to make much of an impact in the classroom. (p. 2)

As a consequence of this disappointing initiation to implementation ratio, change proposals are often viewed with suspicion. This suspicion stems from so many proposed changes having been shooting stars—coming on the scene with great brightness and then within a short period of time burned out and faded from sight. Certainly these feelings have accompanied the No Child Left Behind Act of 2001 and continue as its reauthorization is considered (Spelling, 2007). Some say that No Child Left Behind Act of 2001 has caused significant progress in schools, others would argue that while there may be changes most could not be called progress. Thus, the current legislative activity regarding change mimics the past in almost every way.

During the four decades of study of planned change, we have learned a great deal about the process of change. Some major elements of this learning are described in the section that follows. Again, the warning is given, this is only a brief overview; school leaders are encouraged to pursue other resources to gain an in-depth knowledge.

◆ CHANGE MODELS

During the 40–45 year history of the study of planned change in education numerous change models have been developed and advocated to help schools leaders understand why and how change happens and indicate the actions they should take to ensure successful implementation. This section is divided into two parts. The first part is a quick review of two of the pioneering research efforts done in the formal study of change. These two works, Lionberger's Stages of Change and Lewin's Force-Field Analysis, provided a basic foundation for much of the more recent formulations of models for change. The second part takes up a brief discussion of three of the more contemporary change models, Fullan's Three I Model, Hall and Hord's Concerns-Based Adoption Model, and Bridges' Transitions Model.

Pioneering Research in the Formal Study of Change

Lionberger's Stages of Change

Some of the pioneering work in understanding the processes involved in getting individuals to implement change came not through education or even business but through Lionberger's work with the U.S. Office of Agriculture. The focus was on trying to get farmers to change their practices. Over some 13 years of efforts, Lionberger identified several phases or stages through which the farmers moved into learning to accept and use the new idea. The five stages identified through the research were awareness, interest, evaluation, trial, and adoption. Awareness involves the stage at which an individual is introduced to the new ideas, practice or product. This stage provides some general information. The second stage is Interest. Here, the individual becomes interested in the innovation and wants to learn more about it. In order to learn, the individual will actively seek additional information. Evaluation is the stage at which the individual tries to determine whether or not the innovation has merit for him or her. Trial involves the person trying the innovation, and adoption is the point at which the innovation is accepted and put into "full-scale" use (Bagin, Gallagher, & Kindred, 1994; Gwin & Lionberger, 1999; Rollins, 1993).

These stages do not always follow in discrete steps, nor are they experienced by all people. Different information sources were found to have greater impact at different stages in the process. Mass media is helpful at the first two stages (Awareness and Interest), but friends and neighbors become increasingly important throughout Awareness, Interest, Evaluation, and Trial stages. At the last stage (Adoption), personal experience becomes the most important source of information with friends and neighbors falling to second in influence (Gwin & Lionberger, 1999).

Bagin, Gallagher, and Kindred (1994) reviewed these information influences as important for use in school community relations issues. However, the stages identified by Lionberger and the sources of media influencing each of these stages provide an excellent model for understanding the change process and selecting actions for initiating and implementing change successfully. The relevance of this early work can be seen today in various discussions of formulating strategies for change, identifying perceptions of credible sources of change for different role groups, disseminating information, and formulating shared meaning of proposed changes.

Lewin's Force-Field Analysis

One of the most commonly offered change models is Kurt Lewin's Force Field Analysis which was developed in the early 1950s (Henson, 2010). According to Nelson and Quick (2000), "Lewin developed a model of the change process that has stood the test of time and continues to influence the way organizations manage planned change . . . " (p. 616). Lewin viewed the organization as existing in a state of equilibrium or status quo. This state was the result of the balance generated by two opposing sets of forces—driving forces and resisting or restraining forces. As long as each set of forces remains in balance, the organization exists in a state of equilibrium. Lewin's change model employs changing the balance in these two opposing sets of forces to bring about change.

The model has three basic stages—unfreezing, changing (moving, also called molding), and refreezing. In order to unfreeze the organization, an imbalance between the driving and restraining/resisting forces must be created. This can be done by increasing the driving forces (those forces in support of a change in the organization), decreasing the restraining/resisting forces (those forces working to resist change in the organization) or some combination of the two. When this imbalance of the forces occurs, the status quo or equilibrium is unfrozen allowing the organization to change. During the changing phase (moving), the organization adopts and begins using something new—technologies, strategies, materials, new norms of behavior, new attitudes and values, new mission, etc. When the change has been adopted and implemented, the driving and resisting/restraining forces are allowed to come back into balance, i.e., refreeze, with the organization now operating at a new changed level.

Owens (2001) asserted that the real value of force-field analysis is "diagnostic" (p. 209). As change agents move through the process of identifying the driving and resisting forces keeping the organization in equilibrium, they are diagnosing the current status of the organization. Additionally, as they examine each element of the sets of forces to determine how it might be increased or decreased in order to allow the unfreezing to begin, analytical and diagnostic skills are necessary. A great deal is learned about the organization through these two stages of the model; this knowledge can be used to determine new structures that are needed in order to refreeze the organization (i.e., bring equilibrium back) at the newly established levels following the change implementation (Owens, 2001; Pankake, 1998).

Three Contemporary Models for the Change Process

Fullan's Three I Model

Fullan's (2007) model of change is often referenced as the "Three I Model—Initiation, Implementation, and Institutionalization". In *The New Meaning of Educational Change*, Fullan (2007) devoted one of three major sections of the book to describing the various components of this model. In this work, he offers concentric circles to illustrate an overview of the change process. The center circle contains the outcomes of the change process—student learning and organizational capacity. The three phases of the change process—initiation, implementation, and institutionalization—are located in the next circle out. Dual-pointed arrows are set in between each of the three phases indicating mutual influence between and among them. Fullan noted that this is a "general image of a much more detailed and snarled process" (2007, p. 67). Activity can and will be occurring in all three phases simultaneously—change is not a linear process.

Initiation is the first phase of Fullan's three I's. Other labels given to this phase of the process include mobilization and adoption. He defines initiation as "the process leading up to and including the decision to proceed with implementation" (p. 53). Numerous factors influence whether or not this phase of the process is successful. Fullan (2001a) identified and discussed eight factors influencing initiation decisions: (1) the existence and quality of innovations, (2) access to innovation, (3) advocacy from central administration, (4) teacher advocacy, (5) external change agent, (6) community pressure/support/apathy, (7) new policy—funds, and (8) problem-solving and bureaucratic orientation.

While too detailed to discuss all eight in this overview, an example of one of these factors influencing initiation decisions relates to community. Whether a community is putting pressure on the schools to adopt or resist initiating a particular change can exercise a great deal of influence on the initiation phase of the change process. Some communities demonstrate little or no interest in the schools and the changes they propose; in such communities those individuals internal to the school operations are the major influence on initiation decisions with little or not input from the school community, Fullan (2001a) describes each of these eight factors and the research available on each.

The second phase in Fullan's model refers to implementation. He (Fullan, 2001a) described implementation as consisting of "the process of putting into practice an idea, program, or set of activities and structures new to the people attempting or expected to change" (p. 69). The time here includes the initial years of use when attempts to put the innovation into practice are being made. This phase of the process becomes more complex than the initiation phase. However, implementation is essential if the ideas are to become actual practices and real changes are to be accomplished. Fullan (2001a) identified three major sources of influence on the implementation process: (1) characteristics of the change itself, (2) local characteristics, and (3) external factors. Each of these three areas has elements within them, some of which Fullan identifies and discusses:

1. Characteristics of the change itself—need, clarity, complexity, quality/practicality;
2. Local characteristics—district, community, principal, and teacher; and
3. External factors—government and other agencies.

He cautions, however, that his lists are not exhaustive and change agents and advocates need to be attuned to additional influences operating in any particular implementation effort.

The third and final phase in Fullan's model of change is institutionalization. Other terms used in referencing this phase are continuation, incorporation, and routinization. Whatever the term used, the reference is to whether or not the change becomes part of the system or disappears as one more failed attempt. Fullan pointed out that in fact institutionalization involves a decision to adopt; in essence, the process has come full circle. Changes that have been adopted and implemented may or may not be continued. Reasons for this may be that the innovation may be replaced by newer ideas, there may be insufficient funds to support the continuation, or the project's advocate may be lost for one reason or another.

The three phases of change that Fullan identified overlap and influence each other. Change is not a linear process; elements of implementation for the change may be just getting underway, when new adoption decisions are needed regarding other elements of the same change. Boards and superintendents may be declaring plans to continue with a particular project at the same time that classroom teachers have lost interest in that project and begun looking for new practices to initiate. Planning for the change process is important; however, no plan can be written that takes all of these multiple and simultaneously operating elements into account. Even if that could happen initially, as things got underway, the resulting variations would scuttle the attempt to "plan for everything." Still planning for change is important and consideration must be given to each phase of the process. Fullan (2001a) offered some important assumptions for planners of successful change through a "do" and "don't" list.

Concerns-Based Adoption Model

The Concerns-Based Adoption Model or CBAM has developed through some 30 years (Hall & Hord, 2001). The model has three major elements: individuals who implement change, change facilitators who assist with the change process, and a system of resources for support. These elements exist in a unique organizational environment or culture; that organization exists in a larger environment composed of a variety of influences including the district, community, local, state and federal government agencies, economics, etc.

Over the years, three diagnostics tools have been development to assist change facilitators with the process: Stages of Concern, Levels of Use, and Innovation Configurations. According to Hall and Hord (2001), the use of these tools can help assure that resources are matched to the needs of those expected to implement the change.

- Stages of Concern refers to the seven categories of concerns individuals move through as the change process unfolds—Awareness, Information, Personal, Management, Consequence, Collaboration, and Refocusing. By knowing what concerns individuals have, change facilitators can offer assistance that meet these needs and help move the individual from a focus on self to one on the impact of the change.

- Levels of Use focuses on what the implementers are doing, or not doing, in relationship to the innovation. Levels of use describe to what extent individuals are actually using the proposed change: Level I—Orientation, Level II—Preparation, Level III—Mechanical Use, Level IV—Routine Use and Refinement, Level V—Integration, and Level VI—Renewal. Knowing the level of use of a group or individual attempting to implement change informs the change facilitators about the kinds of assistance (time, coaching, information, staff development, etc.) most needed and useful in their efforts.

- Innovation configurations are used to describe the innovation as it will look when it is fully implemented. An innovation configuration is a means for bringing clarity to change. Hall and Hord (2001) have developed a process that can be used to describe any innovation and assess the different configurations that are likely to evidence themselves during implementation—Innovation Configuration Map.

Over the 30 years, the developers of CBAM have seen some major themes or principles emerge. These principles represent the patterns that have appeared repeatedly in the research conducted and examined; they underlie all of the components of the model itself, recommendations for actions based on the model and the development of the diagnostic tools. The 12 principles of the Concerns-Based Adoption Model are:

- Change is a process, not an event.
- There are significant differences in what is entailed in development and implementation of an innovation.
- An organization does not change until the individuals within it change.
- Innovations come in different sizes.
- Interventions are the actions and events that are key to success of the change process.
- Although both top-down and bottom-up change can work, a horizontal perspective is best.
- Administrator leadership is essential to long-term change success.
- Mandates can work.
- The school is the primary unit for change.
- Facilitating change is a team effort.
- Appropriate interventions reduce the challenges of change.
- The context of school influences the process of change.

Details on the model, the tools, and the principles are discussed in Hall and Hord's (2001) latest work, *Implementing Change: Patterns, Principles, and Potholes*, as well as in earlier works such as, Taking Charge of Change (1987) and Change in Schools: Facilitating the

Process (1987). Additional documents about and training on this model are available through the Southwest Educational Development Laboratory in Austin, Texas.

Bridges' Managing Transitions Model

William Bridges (2003) developed a model of the change process that while focused on the individual is easily applicable to groups and organizations. The name, Transitions Model, is derived from his assertion that "It isn't the changes that do you in, it's the transitions" (Bridges, 2003, p. 3). He differentiates between the change, itself, and the transitions that change requires by stating that change is situational, but the transitions are psychological. With the focus on these psychological aspects of transitions, Bridges identified three phases that individuals go through in coming to terms with the various changes that occur in people's lives.

Three phases of transitions of Bridges are labeled: (1) Ending, Losing and Letting Go, (2) The Neutral Zone, and (3) The New Beginning. It is helping people move through these transitions that is the real challenge of change. His descriptions of each of the phases are as follows:

- *Ending, Losing, and Letting* Go. Letting go of the old ways and the old identity people had. This first phase of transition is an ending, and the time when you need to help people to deal with their losses.
- *The Neutral Zone.* Going through an in-between time when the old is gone but the new isn't fully operational . . . it's when the critical psychological realignments and repatternings take place.
- *The New Beginning.* Coming out of the transition and making a new beginning. This is when people develop the new identity, experience the new energy, and discover the new sense of purpose that make the change begin to work (Bridges, 2003, pp. 4–5).

Bridges provides great detail regarding the issues involved in each of the transition phases. Important here is the link between the first phase, Ending Losing and Letting Go, and the resistance to change that often arises in even those changes that are rationally known to be good for the individual, group or organization. "Before you can begin something new, you have to end what used to be . . . If things change within an organization, a least some of the employees and managers are going to have to let go of something" (Bridges, 2003, p. 23). This is labeled in the literature on resistance to change as vested interest. Among the suggestions, Bridges offers for planner of change in helping people move through this phase are: (1) describe the change in as much detail as you can; (2) identify what other changes will occur because of this change (this relates directly to the notion of changes being systemic); (3) identify just who is going to have to let go of something (who has a vested interest in the way things are remembering that this may not immediately be obvious to the planners of the change); realize that some loses will be psychological rather than concrete or tangible; and finally, try to identify if there is something in the new way that will replace the losses that individuals will experience with the change.

In the second phase of transition (The Neutral Zone) is when the new way isn't fully established and some of the old way is still in place. This relates directly to the implementation phase of Fullan's Model and the point he refers to as the "implementation dip" (Fullan, 2001a, 2007; Henson, 2010). This is the time when things sometimes become more difficult before they get easier. This is a point at which giving up is a real possibility; leaders' attention to this phase is essential. This neutral zone may last a short time or it may extend for months or even years. Recognizing this phase, it's pitfalls and it's timeline line is necessary for the new way to ultimately succeed. When leaders are truly aware of these realities, patience will be required, monitoring with feedback will be essential (Pankake, 1998), and continuing communication with those affected by the change is necessary.

According to Bridges, final phase (The New Beginning) "will take place only after [employees] have throught the wilderness and are ready to make the emotional commitment to do things the new way and see themselves as new people" (p. 58) He also asserts that at this point, new energy and commitment are generated for the new way at this point. The New Beginning is the point at which the change has become the new way of doing things or as Fullan's Model labels it, institutionalization.

While models are helpful in giving a general sense of planning for change, developers caution that each change and the organization in which it is undertaken is unique. Models can provide guidelines, but not recipes. As Hanson (1996) noted, "The trick is to identify a specific strategy for implementing a specific innovation in a specific organizational environment" (p. 285).

◆ IMPORTANT CONSIDERATION FOR SUCCESSFUL CHANGE

The history of education is replete with proposals regarding "what oughta be in schools" and/ or "what schools oughta be." However, out of the myriad changes proposed, few have found their way to institutionalization. Why? One contributing factor is that while assertions about knowing what to change are common, instances where leaders have made use of what is known about how effective change happens are much more rare. Failure to access and utilize this body of knowledge is unacceptable. Some important considerations to assist school leaders in successfully initiating, implementing, and maintaining change follow.

First, change is unlikely to succeed if there is no apparent need for it. Change agents have a moral responsibility to propose changes that are needed and whenever possible not waste time, money, and people's energy on unnecessary changes. School leaders can prepare for change by making sure that the proposed changes are needed and that those who will have to do the changing see the need and the benefits that changing will bring. Changes are rarely implemented unless there is a perceived need for them. However, even when a need can be seen, those who must implement the change need to be unhappy or dissatisfied enough with the way things are to make the sacrifices needed to change things. Sometimes, the need is not perceived to be great enough to merit the effort. Several of the models for change reference the importance of need. They also refer to this condition with various terms, sense of urgency being one such term.

Even when need is established and everyone agrees that change is needed, that is not enough to make change happen. Miles and Louis (1990) pointed out that desire or will is important but it must be accompanied by the skill to implement the proposed change. There is a difference between wanting to and knowing how to do something. Knowing this about the change process leads to recognizing the importance of staff development as a means of supporting the initiation and implementation of change.

Another important finding from the study of planned change relates to the issue of time. Based on the research of some 40–45 years, the importance of allowing enough time for change to occur has become evident. According to Fullan (2001a), the following estimates for change in a school have been gleaned from the research, "you can turn around an elementary school in about three years, a high school in about six years, and a school district (depending on size) in about eight years" (Fullan, 2001a, p. 17). Sadly, such time periods are rarely allocated when change proposals are proposed. There are all sorts of elements in the system working against this time requirement being met. For example, school leadership and governance are not configured to assist in supporting change for the time needed. Superintendents' tenure in large school districts averages less than 5 years and small district often experience high turnover—serving as entry level positions for initial training experience for the position (Lunenburg & Ornstein, 2000). School board elections occur annually. With a change in one or both of these sources of leadership, the entire outcome of a change initiative could be determined.

This issue of needed time feeds directly into another important element required for successful initiation and implementation of change, advocacy. Changes that have an advocate are those that are most likely to succeed. Advocacy can come from several sources. If changing the school system is the intent, there must be an advocate at the district level. Primary to the successful change of any sort at the school level is the principal. The literature on change and school improvement repeatedly identifies the support and advocacy of the principal as key to any initiatives for school improvement. Finally, if instructional changes are to succeed, then the advocacy for the change from teachers is necessary. Teachers advocating a change are the most credible source from the perspective of another teacher. And, of course, broad scale community support is desirable, probably necessary and perhaps one of the most potent advocacy sources.

Planned change involves valued outcomes and deliberate directions. Because not everyone agrees on what outcomes are most valued and what directions should be pursued, not surprisingly, planned changes are often resisted. People resist change for a variety of reasons. When people are asked to change, they must alter or abandon what is known and what is comfortable. Fear of the unknown is a powerful source of resistance. Individuals will remain in difficult, even dangerous situations, rather than risk the "unknown." Social agencies find this to be true in case of abuse; the victim will often express a desire to "go home" even if the abuse is likely to continue. Evidently, this difficult but known situation is better than the unknown of foster and/or custodial care. In education some teachers will change schools rather than teach a grade or subject they haven't ever taught; others may well teach any grade or subject as long as they get to stay at the school they know. Fear of the unknown is only one of many reasons individuals resist proposed change (Hanson, 1996; Harvey, 1990 for additional discussion on resistance to change; Pankake, 1998). School leaders must remember that people who resist change do so for reasons that make a great deal of sense to them. Rather than being surprised or angry about expressions of resistance, school leaders need to gather this information and use it as a way of learning about other perspectives, possible problems with proposed plans, needs for additional information and training, and other important issues for successful change.

Hanson (1996, 2003) and Pankake (1998) pointed out that resistance to change can come from the organization as well as the individual. Sustaining change in organizations requires that the context of the organization adjust to accommodate the changes in behavior. A major reason for the lack of behavior changes in individuals after they have received training is that they return to the same environment they left. While they may have new knowledge and skills and a desire to behave differently, the same policies, procedures, rewards systems, supervision structure, etc. remain in place. Consequently, not only will the new knowledge, skills, and behaviors not be reinforced or supported, they may well be punished (Mager & Pipe, 1970). Other times, multiple changes are adopted in a school or district during the same time period that they are working at cross-purposes. Examples might include: "advocating an integrated curriculum but retaining content-specific testing, trying to implement a performance-based or portfolio system to assess student learning but retaining the standard letter grading report card system, [or] encouraging a variety of means for professional development growth opportunities but rewarding only formal graduate credit options" (Pankake, 1998, p. 140).

The first principle of CBAM (Hall & Hord, 2001), change is a process, not an event, may be one of the two most important considerations that school leaders can practice when planning and implementing change. Change takes time and involves people; it won't happen at the next board meeting, or at the start of the second semester or any other chronological point we would like to identify. The information presented here has been intended to help make this principle clear and encourage school leaders to behave in ways that indicate they understand what it means.

Finally, changes in schools should be advocated or resisted based on the benefits they generate for the education of the students they serve. Proposed changes in structures, schedules, parking lot assignments, faculty work cultures or anything else should eventually link back to some educational benefit for students. Keeping the focus on the middle circle of Fullan's Model, i.e., the outcomes of student learning and organization capacity, will assure that change proposals are valid and the school well-led.

◆ THE FUTURE OF CHANGE IN EDUCATION

According to James (1996) "systemic change is the change style of the future" (p. 120). Systemic change, she says, is different from incremental change. Rather than a one step at a time cadence, systemic is experienced as a "total transformation." She declares systemic changes to be "very powerful," often requiring a complete change, that is, a 180-degree turn, from the current operation. She asserts that while the steps in incremental and systemic change are the same, the rate of system change is much more rapid.

Systems' thinking is identified again as crucial for staff development (Sparks & Hirsch, 1997). Sparks and Hirsch (1997) identified systems thinking as one of the powerful ideas influencing major shifts in professional development. First, staff development will provide a means for helping everyone, at all levels of the organization understand and begin to use systems thinking in their work. Second, there will be a realization that systemic change will be helped through staff development operating as an integral part of the system rather than an isolated, disconnected activity.

Senge (1990) identified systems thinking as "the fifth discipline" for the creation of learning organizations. He identified five dimensions that enhance an organization's capacity to become a learning organization—systems thinking, personal mastery, mental models, building shared vision, and team learning. He emphasizes that the five must "develop as an ensemble" and that the integration of these new tools is a challenge. "This is why systems thinking is the fifth discipline" (Senge, 1990, p. 12).

More and more writers in the areas related to school restructuring (organizational theory, organizational development, change, leadership, and professional development) focus on systems thinking and systems change. For those who want to lead organizations into the future, there is an increasing expectation that the preferred goal is toward becoming learning organizations. Senge (1990) described a learning organization as one "where people continually expand their capacity to create the result they truly desire, where new and expansive patterns of thinking are nurtured, where collective aspiration is set free, and where people are continually learning how to learn together" (p. 3). Obviously, both the potency and rapidity of change are increased with such a focus. There are major consequences for the role responsibilities of school leaders with an increase in this type of change.

◆ SUMMARY

Educational leaders must view leading change as an essential role responsibility. Restructuring, transforming, school improvement, professional development and other terms frequently heard into today's educational conversations all imply change—change in structure, change in form, change in performance and change in knowledge and skills! Change is a given not a perhaps. Things in education will change whether we lead them or are led by them. The more educational leaders can know about how and why changes are initiated, implemented and institutionalized, the more confidently they can accomplish their role. The more school leaders can understand the mistakes of the past and gain insights from the lessons learned the more confident they can be that history will not repeat itself. The more sensitive educational leaders can be regarding the human aspects of the change process, the more probable will be success. Knowing what resources are available to assist in learning about and understanding the dynamics of change and the change process is an important objective for educational leaders' continued professional development.

◆ REFERENCES

Bagin, D., Gallagher, D. R., & Kindred, L. W. (1994). *The school and community I* (5th ed.). Needham Heights, MA: Allyn and Bacon.

Bridges, W. (2003). *Managing transitions: Making the most of change* (2nd ed.). Cambridge, MA: Da Capo Press.

Carpenter, W. A. (2000). Ten years of silver bullets: Dissenting thoughts on education form. *Kappan, 81*(5), 383–389.

Chin, R. (1967). Basic strategies and procedures in effecting change. In E. L. Morphet & C. O. Ryan, *Planning and effecting needed changes in education* (pp. 39–57). Denver, CO: Reports prepared for the third area conference, Designing Education for the Future: An Eight-State Project.

Cuban, L. (1988). A fundamental puzzle of school reform. *Kappan, 70*(5), 341–344.

Fullan, M. (1992). *The new meaning of educational change.* New York: Columbia Teachers College Press.

Fullan, M. (2001a). *The new meaning of educational change* (3rd ed.). New York: Columbia Teachers College Press.

Fullan, M. (2001b). *Leading in a culture of change.* San Francisco: Jossey-Bass.

Fullan, M. (2006). Leading professional learning. *School Administrator, 63*(10), 10–14. Retrieved from http://www.education.nt.gov.au/__data/assets/pdf_file/0011/4205/leading_prof_learning.pdf

Fullan, M. (2007). *The new meaning of educational change* (4th ed.) New York: Teachers College Press.

Gwin, P., & Lionberger, H. F. (1999). *Speeding adoption of new technology in rural America.* University of Missouri-Columbia. MO: University Extension.

Hall, G. E., & Hord, S. M. (2001). *Implementing change: Patterns, principles, and potholes.* Boston: Allyn and Bacon.

Hanson, E. M. (1996). *Educational administration and organizational behavior* (4th ed.). Needham Heights, MA: Allyn and Bacon.

Hanson, E. M. (2003). *Educational administration and organizational behavior* (5th ed.). Needham Heights, MA: Allyn and Bacon.

Harvey, T. R. (1990). *Checklist for change: A pragmatic approach to creating and controlling change.* Boston: Allyn and Bacon.

Henson, K. T. (2010). *Supervision: A collaborative approach to instructional improvement.* Long Grove, IL: Waveland Press.

Houghton-Mifflin Company. (1982). *The American heritage dictionary* (2nd ed.). Boston: Author.

James, J. (1996). Thinking in the future tense: A workout for the mind. New York: Simon & Schuster, Inc.

Jazzar, M., & Algozzine, B. (2006). *Critical issues in educational leadership.* Boston: Pearson.

Lunenburg, F. C., & Ornstein, A. (2000). *Educational administration: Concepts and practices* (3rd ed.). Belmont, CA: Wadsworth.

Mager, R. F., & Pipe, P. (1970). *Analyzing performance problems or 'You really oughta wanna.'* Belmont, CA: Pitman Learning, Inc.

Miles, M. B., & Louis, K. S. (1990). Mustering the will and skill for change. *Educational Leadership, 47*(8), 57–61.

National Commission on Excellence in Education. (1983). *A nation at risk.* Washington, DC: Author.

Nelson D. L., & Quick, J. C. (2000). *Organizational behavior: Foundations, realities & challenges* (3rd ed.). Cincinnati, OH: South-Western College Publishing.

Owens, R. C. (2001). *Organizational behavior in education: Instructional leadership and school reform* (7th ed.). Boston: Allyn and Bacon.

Pankake, A. M. (1998). *Implementation: Making things happen.* Larchmont, NY: Eye on Education.

Rifkin, J., & Howard, T. (1980). *Entropy: A new world view.* New York: Viking Press.

Rebore, R. W. (2011). *Human resources administration in education: A management* approach (7th ed.). Boston: Allyn and Bacon.

Rollins, T. (1993). Using the innovation adoption diffusion model to target educational programming. *Journal of Agricultural Education, 134*, 46–54. Retrieved from http://pubs.aged.tamu.edu/jae/pdf/vol34/34-04-46.pdf

Senge, P. M. (1990). *The fifth discipline: The art & practice of the learning organization.* New York: Doubleday.

Sparks, D., & Hirsh, S. (1997). *A new vision of staff development.* Alexandria, VA: Association for Supervision and Curriculum Development.

Spelling, M. (2007). *Building on results: A blueprint for strengthening the no child left behind act.* Washington, DC: U.S. Department of Education.

Spring, J. (1978). *American education: An introduction to social and political aspects.* New York: Longman.

Trybus, M. A. (2011). Facing the challenge of change: Steps to becoming an effective leader. *Delta Kappa Gamma Bulletin*, pp. 33–36.

7

Texas Politics and the Governance Process in Public Education

Gary Miller ◆ *Thomas Ratliff*

To fully understand the governance model of Texas public schools, one must first look at the jurisdictional boundaries between the Federal Government, Texas Legislature, Texas Commissioner of Education, and State Board of Education. Each has its role to play in many of the day-to-day decisions our schools face.

◆ The Federal Government

Pursuant to the Tenth Amendment to the United States Constitution and Article VII of the Texas Constitution, the Texas Legislature is responsible for the structure and operation of the Texas public school system.

Constitutionally speaking, the federal government cannot have anything to do with public education. However, there are some exceptions when issues cross over into civil rights or other federal laws. The most recognized example of this in public education is the Education of All Handicapped Children Act of 1975; known later as the Individuals with Disabilities Education Act (IDEA) and finally IDEA 2004 when reauthorized and signed into law by President George W. Bush on December 3, 2004. IDEA 2004 encompasses a series of amendments to the law, including the definition of "highly qualified teacher." Without question, this federal legislation revolutionized the teaching of special education in the United States.

The Elementary and Secondary Education Act (ESEA), signed into law by President Lyndon Baines Johnson in 1965, focused on providing a "full educational opportunity" to students traditionally underserved (U.S. Department of Education, 2015). The law provided federal grants to state educational agencies with the purpose of improving the quality of elementary and secondary education by focusing on serving low-income students, purchasing books, creating special education centers, and creating scholarships for low-income college students (U.S. Department of Education, 2015).

In 2002, Congress reauthorized ESEA giving it a new name, No Child Left Behind (NCLB). The Federal Government dangled billions of dollars in front of states to encourage them to adopt the program. These financial enticements were quite effective. However, 14 years later, states are wondering if the federal money is worth the cost of implementation and compliance. Changes are taking place in NCLB legislation, the Obama administration began offering greater discretion to states in 2012 in exchange for improved quality of instruction and rigorous state-developed plans designed to increase achievement of all students (U.S. Department of Education, 2015). To date, 42 states including the District of Columbia and Puerto Rico have received waivers from NCLB governmental measures (U.S. Department of Education, 2015).

Regardless of political ideology, most members of Congress agree on limiting federal requirements coupled with states being front and center in developing school rating systems based on performance, graduation rates, identifying low-performing schools and designing and implementing interventions to improve them (Hyslop, 2015). With this belief in mind, Secretary Duncan has called for replacing NCLB with new ESEA legislation, including curtailing the seemingly endless prescriptive measures and reporting requirements (Hyslop, 2015).

NCLB requires standardized testing in grades 3–8 throughout the nation. In Texas, elementary and middle school students must take 17 standardized tests. Deemed an excessive amount of testing, Representative Dan Huberty filed House Bill (HB) 742 during the 84th legislative session seeking to reduce the number of standardized tests by eliminating the social studies exam in grade 8 (Huberty, 2015). Addressing this matter Representative Huberty said, "As a parent of three children in public school, who are all subject to these tests, I know firsthand the frustration and exhaustion that comes from these excessive standardized tests." Unfortunately, the bill did not survive the legislative session.

HB 743 is another education-related billed filed by Representative Huberty and supported by the Senate and House (Huberty, 2015). Governor Greg Abbott signed the bill into law on June 19, 2015. This legislation reduces the amount of time a student can spend completing a standardized test. HB 743 stipulates that 85% of students in grades 3–5 are able to take the test within 120 minutes and 85% of students in grades 6–8 can complete the test within 180 minutes (Huberty, 2015). Additionally, the amount of time allowed for administration of an assessment may not exceed 8 hours and must occur on only 1 day. These new requirements offer much-needed relief.

◆ THE TEXAS LEGISLATURE

The Constitution of the State of Texas adopted on February 15, 1876, provides the foundation for the laws governing the state, declaring Texas free and independent, subject only to the Constitution of the United States (Ericson & Wallace, 2010). Article VII of the Texas Constitution of 1876 affirms:

> A general diffusion of knowledge being essential to the preservation of the liberties and rights of the people, it shall be the duty of the Legislature of the State to establish and make suitable provision for the support and maintenance of an efficient system of public free schools.

The Constitution of 1876 drastically changed the system of governance concerning education founded in the previous Constitution of 1869 by adding provisions that made the directive for maintaining an efficient system possible, namely through the creation of the Perpetual School Fund (Ericson & Wallace, 2010). Additionally, the Constitution abolished the office of state superintendent; founded a board of education composed of the governor, comptroller, secretary of state; eliminated compulsory attendance; provided for segregated schools; and made no provisions for local school taxes (Ericson & Wallace, 2010).

Although school districts are structural creations of the state and routinely permitted to exercise considerable autonomy in the name of local authority, the Texas Legislature still maintains considerable control. The Texas Legislature determines which courses are subject to standardized testing in high school, student-teacher ratios, school finance formulas, number of instructional minutes, teacher salary schedules, school start date, and many more decisions. The Texas Legislature was responsible for the 15 End of Course (EOC) tests, but also responsible for reducing that number down to five in 2013. Though state governments appear stronger than ever, it has not exempted them from civic scrutiny when it comes to educational matters (Herrington & Fowler, 2003). Heightened political instability around education and state policymaking indicate just how far our state government is from effectively exercising governance responsibility when it comes to accountability reforms.

This year the Texas Legislature took a step in the right direction regarding the accountability system. The previous system was 100% driven by the standardized test results. With the passage of HB 2804, the new accountability system will be 55% related to test measures (i.e., gaps and growth), 35% related to certificates earned, AP scores, dual credit courses and other elements, 10% related to non-STAAR high school academic measurements, and 10% related to community and student engagement (Aycock, 2015). While this is far from perfect, it is certainly heading in the right direction.

One of the biggest remaining pieces of accountability that needed addressing took a half-step step towards improvement. HB 1164 requires that TEA conduct a pilot program to replace the current timed writing assessment with a "portfolio" system that looks at a student's body of work throughout the year (VanDeaver, 2015).

HB 1164 states:

A writing sample submitted by a student in connection with an assessment instrument administered under this section may not be used to assess the student's writing for purposes of accountability under this chapter or for purposes of grade promotion or graduation criteria.

To evaluate student achievement in writing, each school district shall assess secondary-level courses in accordance with the essential knowledge and skills for writing. A district may use any method the district determines appropriate for assessing students under this section, including portfolio assessment.

This evaluation appears to be a much more accurate and relevant way to assess a student's writing skills. There are very few professions where the first draft of anything submitted is the final version, much less under a time sensitive deadline.

Some may question the usefulness of portfolio assessments in evaluating students or schools because one school might require one kind of writing project, while another school require an entirely different project with different grading criteria (Mathews, 2004). Thus, the argument continues, portfolio assessments present difficulties when analyzing student performance because of a lack of project uniformity and grading standard equality. In order for student portfolios to have value over standardized testing, they must be objective and based upon a systematic diagnostic approach in terms of individual and school feedback.

THE TEXAS COMMISSIONER OF EDUCATION

The powers and duties of the commissioner include serving as the educational leader of the state and carrying out the directives imposed by the State Board of Education or the Texas Legislature. Under Chapter 39, Public School System Accountability, of the Texas Education Code, the Commissioner determines the administration dates of the statewide assessment program and its criterion-referenced assessment instruments (i.e., State of Texas Assessments of Academic Readiness or STAAR). With the passage of HB 2804 (Aycock, 2015), the legislature has significantly restricted the commissioner's role in the accountability system. The remaining jurisdiction of the commissioner is limited to the creation and administration of the standardized tests, along with setting the "passing" standard or "cut score" for STAAR/EOC tests.

THE STATE BOARD OF EDUCATION

The policy-making body of the Texas Education Agency (TEA) is the Texas State Board of Education (SBOE), comprised members elected from fifteen single-member districts. The governor appoints one member to chair the board. In 2011, the 82nd Legislature enacted legislation specifying the single-member district's current configuration (Texas State Library and Archives Commission, 2015). Since 1995, the SBOE has seen its jurisdiction curtailed by the Texas Legislature.

The SBOE has been limited to adopting the TEKS, approving textbooks and charter schools, approving or rejecting proposed SBEC rules, and managing the Permanent School Fund (PSF). In 2012, the SBOE fulfilled its legislative obligation of passing rules to implement HB 5 (Aycock, Deshotel, Davis, Villarreal, & Callegari, 2013), the new graduation requirements, and endorsement categories. Overall, these rules have gotten very high marks.

With the passage of SB 313 (Seliger, 2015), along with SBOE members expressing concern, the SBOE is poised to undertake a significant effort at reducing the length of the TEKS for the core subject areas. Interested parties on all sides of the public education debate agree on one thing—standards are too long. The length of the standards do not allow enough time for teachers to comprehensively cover the material or for students to master the content, often leading to remediation in later grades.

LOCAL SCHOOL BOARDS

The educational policy-making organization for Texas public schools districts is the local Board of Trustees. As of 2003–2004, there were 1,241 public school districts in Texas (U.S. Department of Education, n.d.), each with a school board of elected officials, totaling over 7,000 members across the state, who truly believe they have "local control." Unfortunately, this is not the case concerning many of the decisions facing schools. Some notable examples of legislative authority by the state include: student–teacher ratios for K-5, school start date, courses required for graduation, transportation requirements, and base pay for teachers.

THE LEGISLATIVE PROCESS

From the time of filing in either the House of Representatives or Senate to final passage and transmittal to the governor, a bill has many hurdles to overcome. Although legislative bills progress in a seemingly sequential fashion aimed for efficiency, the governmental process in practice is quite burdensome and designed to kill bills, not pass them. For an excruciatingly detailed explanation of this legislative process visit: www.tlc.state.tx.us/pubslegref/gtli.pdf to read the "Guide to Texas Legislative Information (Revised)" published by the Texas Legislative Council (2015). As summarized in the following, it becomes apparent there are many obstacles to navigate in avoiding the governor's veto pen. Here is the abbreviated version:

1. The week after the November election, members of the legislature can begin prefiling bills for consideration during the upcoming session. Keep in mind that these bills do not get a "head start" as the legislature cannot consider them until the beginning of session in January of odd numbered years.

2. Legislators may file bills for the first 60 days of the 140-day session. The later in session the bill is filed, the less likely it is to pass due to time constraints and the necessary hurdles to clear in a compressed amount of time.

3. Once filed, a bill must go through the following steps
   - read and referred to committee;
   - heard in a public hearing, with public testimony;
   - sent to the calendars committee (House bills) or placed on the Intent calendar (Senate bills);
   - read a second time and voted on by the full House or Senate;
   - read a third time and voted on by the full House or Senate; and
   - sent to the other chamber and the process starts over.

4. By the time a bill reaches the governor's desk, it has been read aloud on the House and Senate floor three times and been through two public hearings with members of the public allowed to testify or register their position on the bill.

5. Keep in mind, if the Senate amends a House bill, or vice versa, the originating chamber accepts the amendments or the bill goes to a conference committee made up of five members of each chamber to work out the differences. Both chambers must then vote on the final product.

Only when a bill survives all of the aforementioned steps, does it go to the governor's office for consideration. The governor has 10 days to veto a bill if the bill arrives "on his desk" prior to the last ten days of the legislative session. However, if a bill arrives during the last ten days of the session, the governor has 20 days to veto the bill. The Texas governor does not have a "pocket veto" (i.e., a tactic allowing an official with veto power to exercise that power over a bill by taking no action), as the case in some states. If the governor does not veto or sign the bill, it will become law "without his signature" which does not mean the bill is any less of a law than those bills he signs. It is noteworthy; many bills become law without the governor's signature as the governor typically signs "major" pieces of legislation.

◆ POLICY FORMATION

Bills originate from an idea. Elected officials come across ideas while confronted by "real world" experiences and in the most unexpected places. Ideas can start in the classroom, coffee shop, football game, or even at the high school One Act Play contest. These random encounters are sometimes the most powerful way to spark action. Other, more formal means of bringing ideas forward, include public testimony at a hearing in the capitol, an email from a concerned parent, a letter from a student, or a meeting with an association like the Texas Elementary Principals and Supervisors Association (TEPSA) or the Association of Texas Professional Educators (ATPE). There really is not a "best" way to get an idea in front of a policy maker.

The key ingredient to any advocacy is authenticity and credibility. When approaching a policy maker, concerned citizens really have to focus on two questions, "What is the problem you are trying to solve?" and "Does this person have the authority to solve it?" No matter how compelling a story or how supportive the policy maker wants to be, it must be clear they have the authority to do something about it before asking someone for help. Many times elected officials get bombarded with letters, emails or calls about a particular issue that is not within their jurisdiction. This is frustrating for both the requestor and elected official.

Upon identifying the appropriate governmental body (e.g., legislature, SBOE, Congress, TEA, and school board), there are a few things to keep in mind:

1. Very few, if any, elected officials will understand the issue as well as a concerned citizen who lives with and see these issues on a daily basis. There is no substitute for that experience. Advocates must try to convey their concerns and potential solutions in great depth to help the elected official understand the larger picture. Once achieving support, dive deeper. Attempting to overwhelm an official all at once is frustrating and both parties will likely come away from the meeting disappointed.

2. Unless the elected official serves on the committee referring the bill or issue, it is very likely that he or she will follow the lead of a member of that committee. In the legislature, there is an old saying, "follow the jockey, not the horse" when it comes to voting on bills. When there are literally thousands of bills filed every session, a legislator cannot possibly read and understand each one with a degree of specificity or knowledge he or she would like. Members will work with their colleagues known to be more experienced in an issue and have similar ideology. Follow that legislator or "jockey," not the specific bill or "horse" on a particular issue.

   Members of a committee have influence beyond the committee hearings. For example, the nine members of the House Public Education Committee carry far more weight on the House floor than just their nine votes, especially the committee chairman. This is both a blessing and a curse. Those who have successful meetings with members of a committee know their advocacy is having far more impact than just those meetings. If, however, the meetings do not go so well, the hill becomes much steeper to climb. Obviously, just because a bill passes out of committee does not guarantee success on the House or Senate floor because dynamics change and the process can have strong personalities at each step along the way. Counting chickens before they hatch and not giving up because of one bad committee meeting or hearing are important factors to keep in mind. Remember, a bill has to successfully pass through both chambers.

3. Advocates should not let perfect be the enemy of good. Voltaire, Aristotle, and Confucius all agree on this principle. What does it mean in this context? When an advocate approaches a policy maker about a particular problem, they should be open to the likelihood that there may be more than one solution. In addition, being aware of the possibility, or even the probability, that they will not get everything requested. Remember the words of Lao Tzu (Chinese philosopher 604 BC-531 BC), "A journey of a thousand miles begins with a single step." Even if not solved immediately, continuing to make the situation better is preferable. The over reliance on standardized

testing did not happen overnight and the solution will not happen overnight either. It is amazing the accomplishments achieved through steady incremental changes over each legislative session.

4. Most importantly, advocates should not take things personally. This is probably the hardest thing for most supporters to remember. Whether a policy maker agrees or disagrees with an advocate's position on an issue or whether the "problem" needs to be "solved" has nothing to do with the role as a parent, educator, or life-changer. Most people have a tendency to get personally involved with issues near to them. One of the things that make educators great is their passion for helping children. That same passion can also cause a strong emotional attachment to an issue resulting in either being very excited or deeply wounded, depending on the passage or failure of the bill. To the extent possible, advocates have to separate who they are as a person or an educator and their role in supporting a particular cause.

◆ POLICY-MAKING AND IMPLEMENTATION

Policy-making and implementation have a cyclical process, just like the legislative sessions that come around every odd numbered year. It begins with recognizing a public problem or issue and moves towards an organized call to government action (Texas Politics Project, 2015). From agenda setting to policy formulation and adoption, the process culminates in policy implementation and evaluation (Texas Politics Project, 2015). When the legislature leaves town, there is a lot of sawdust to clean up—a result of the proceedings of the governmental machinery.

The Texas Education Agency, State Board of Education, and local school boards across the state begin interpreting and implementing new laws, often times before school starts—less than 90 days after the legislative session. This is the beginning of the next story told; where the "rubber meets the road" and the legislative concepts are subjected to real life. There are always trade-offs in public policy; furthermore, defining values and objectives can be difficult, especially when time is a limiting factor (Texas Politics Project, 2015).

Instead of a thorough study of every policy option, usually a much more constrained process of "successive limited comparison" occurs (Texas Politics Project, 2015). This propensity toward incrementalism policy development building on existing policies, fine-tuning them through a continuous evolutionary process frequently causes irritation among those who feel that the government is apathetic and unresponsive (Texas Politics Project, 2015).

Policy-making and implementation, if done well, can go smoothly and painlessly. On the other hand, there can be bumps along the way that can either be temporary or knock the process in the ditch. Here are a few keys to help minimize the size of the bumps.

- If there are uncertainties about the legislative intent, ask questions.
- If it is a change that directly affects children, talk to parents early and often.
- If it will change other programs, make note of those changes.

These seem like basic concepts, but require viewing through a political filter for a complete understanding.

First, many times, problems become worse if people try to guess what the legislature meant, rather than verifying the intent. With time and resources being all too precious, no one should spend time heading off in the wrong direction. Knowing the path and then following it is imperative—there are many resources available to corroborate the meaning. Groups like the Texas Association of School Administrators (TASA), Texas Association of School Boards (TASB), a school attorney, and even the legislator who wrote the bill are great places to start.

Second, as the school environment changes, so can a parent's relationship with their child's school. In some situations, there are levels of distrust or even conspiratorial atmospheres. When parents perceive information is not forthcoming, they may become more suspicious. Early and open communication will not solve this every time, but it can keep a trying situation from becoming an impossible one. The most recent example of this is the whole dust up over CSCOPE, a curriculum used by many districts that was claimed to be un-American by a small group of activists. Assuredly, no one wants to go there. All it takes is for one child to go home and tell their mom or dad about the new things happening at school to start a chain reaction. An ounce of prevention is worth a pound of cure, every single time.

Third, when an elected official is required to say "yes" to something, it forces them to say "no" to something else. Oftentimes, saying "no" to something affects a child and their parents. That is when the phone starts to ring. Wise officials document the actions and reactions to new legislation. It will help tell the story the next time the legislature comes to town. There is absolutely no substitute for experience on the ground and the more detailed, the better.

◆ TRENDS IN EDUCATION POLICY: KEY ISSUES

School Vouchers

Legislation about school vouchers is as predictable as bluebonnets along a central Texas highway. They bloom with such fanfare and beauty; talked about and photographed by admirers. However, as soon as the heat turns up, they fade and wither seemingly overnight. Vouchers, or "taxpayer savings grants," are in an odd political predicament these days. Voucher supporters have to walk a fine line between supporting vouchers and transparency versus simply supporting vouchers and blindly trusting those institutions receiving them. The legislature has to be "conservative" enough to support vouchers, but not so "conservative" that they want transparency and accountability to follow the tax money being sent to the private education institutions. Right now, moderate Republicans, most Democrats, and many Tea Party legislators find themselves on the same side of this issue, but for different reasons. Democrats know losing students will result in the loss of funding; hurting school districts' balance sheets. Frankly, this is the weakest argument in a GOP-controlled legislature. It is no different in a competitive market, if the customer is lost; so is the money they bring. Moderate Republicans are happy to put public schools up against any other kind of school, as long as there is a level playing field (accountability, transparency, regulations, requirements, etc.). Tea Party Republicans so far have agreed with the concerns about accountability and transparency.

The major problem with all of this is the private schools do not want any of those rules and requirements. That is why they became private schools; they do not want to be business partners with the State of Texas. Voucher legislation will continue popping up and then dying on the vine for the immediate future.

Early Childhood Education

Investing in high-quality preschool education has finally garnered enough political capital and friends in high places to take a good first step this year. Most experts agree that early childhood education pays huge dividends, especially in the later years of schooling. Mathis' (2012) study, "Research-Based Options for Education Policymaking: Preschool Education," reported there is near unanimous agreement that high-quality preschool programs more than pay for themselves in economic and social benefits, including fewer grade retentions, less special education, higher graduation rates, and increased college attendance rates.

When Governor Abbott came out and publicly supported pre-kindergarten programs, it all but assured some version of success because the biggest stumbling block to passing this type of bill in the past have been the "conservative" legislators. These legislators believe children should be home with their mother or at a faith-based pre-kindergarten program. The difficulty faced by many families is working parents who are either not at home or cannot afford a private pre-kindergarten program.

Aimed at improving early childhood education, Governor Abbott signed into law HB 4 at an Austin early childhood center proclaiming "nothing but green lights" on May 28, 2015 (Svitek, 2015). This early education boost, for children whose parents cannot afford to stay at home or the cost of a private facility, closes the gaps between the "haves" and the "have-nots" in schools. Without this support, a learning gap that exists between these children and their school peers will only widen as the years progress. While funding a half-day pre-kindergarten program is a step in the right direction, in actuality Texas needs full-day programming for it to be meaningful to the 60.2% of children—approximately three in five students, who are economically disadvantaged in our schools (Texas Education Agency, 2015). As learned in the Policy Formation section earlier, advocates cannot let perfect be the enemy of good and this piece of legislation provides a good, but not perfect, funding source that will help a lot of children benefit from the positive effects found in high-quality early childhood education programs.

Truancy

The state's school attendance laws define the number of absences a student can accumulate in a school year, the mandatory age a child begins school, and the age a child can legally drop out. Truancy laws were one area requiring much needed attention during the 84th legislative session, resulting in the passage of House Bill 2398 (White, 2015) making truancy a civil matter. Before this legislation, Texas was one of only two states that prosecuted minors for truancy in adult criminal court (Jones-McClure, 2015). "Failure to Attend School" is a Class C misdemeanor punishable by fines, arrest, and possible jail time—all which can hinder college and career prospects (Jones-McClure, 2015). Texas Appleseed, an advocacy organization for truancy reform, reported that in 2013, Texas filed ~115,000 truancy charges, more than twice the number cases in all other states combined (Semiens, 2015).

School districts handing out tickets for truancy and other offenses had risen exponentially in some areas of the state, becoming a major concern. In fact, it had become quite the revenue source for some districts. Many times students received a ticket and had their "judgment" rendered without due process. As expected, some parents did not care for this practice very much and they got the ear of the Texas Legislature. The passage of House Bill

2398 (White, 2015) curtails these practices making truancy a civil matter, schools are now required to take steps to address student truancy problems before referring them to court. Moreover, if the school determines truancy is a result of pregnancy, homelessness, being the primary income earner for the family, or being in a state foster program then a school cannot refer the student to court. It is hopeful this legislation will restore some balance in truancy enforcement across the state.

Charter Schools

Like vouchers, charter schools enjoy a certain amount of political support around the Texas Capitol. Though publicly funded, charter schools are subject to fewer state regulations than traditional public schools (Texas Association of School Boards, 2009). There are several types of charter schools in Texas including: school district campus and campus program charters, open-enrollment charter schools, and home-rule charter schools. Open-enrollment charter schools are by far the most common form of charter school in Texas (Texas Education Agency, 2011). In 2014, the Texas Education Agency reported 588 charter schools with a total enrollment of 202,972 students (Texas Education Agency, 2015). By comparison, that same year, there were 7,986 public schools with a total student enrollment of 4,932,908 (Texas Education Agency, 2015). Between the 1998–1999 and 2008–2009 academic years, students attending charter schools expanded by 736% (Texas Education Agency, 2011). Despite this rapid growth, enrollment remains relatively small with 4% of Texas students attending a charter school.

Members from both sides of the aisle support charters as educational centers of innovation—not constrained by instructional methods and other state mandates typically imposed on traditional schools. However, not everyone is convinced charter schools perform better than traditional schools. Admittedly, there are some charter schools doing a wonderful job and traditional public schools are not the best choice for every child. In the "Evaluation of Texas Charter Schools 2009–2010 Executive Summary," researchers generally found no statistically significant difference between the performance of charter schools students and the performance of students at matched traditional public schools (Texas Education Agency, 2011). Furthermore, when comparing open-enrollment charters to matched traditional public schools, there were no reliable differences in TAKS accountability ratings, including passing rates and test scores (Texas Education Agency, 2011).

However, the report "2014 Snapshot: School District Profiles" (Texas Education Agency, 2015), covering a wide range of data released by the Texas Education Agency, tells a rather different story. In summary, public schools have higher graduation rates, fewer dropouts, smaller classes, outperform charter schools on the STAAR/EOC exams, lower teacher turnover, better teacher pay, and spend less money on central administration.

The authors support private schools, home school, and charter schools along with parent's ability to choose what is best for their child. What the authors do not support is blind allegiance to a particular group of schools without the facts to back up that loyalty. The authors hope this helps explain their skepticism about the success of the charter school movement overall. Ironically, it was Bill Ratliff, father of chapter author Thomas Ratliff, who authorized legislation in 1995 creating home-rule school districts granting them freedom from many state mandates, thus ushering in open-enrollment charter schools in Texas (Ratliff, 2015). In the interest of full disclosure; however, it was to keep the political winds from blowing a voucher bill out of the legislature at the request of Governor George Bush.

Curriculum Adoption

Oftentimes negative attention prompts a swifter response; over the last several years, this appears to be the case regarding curriculum adoption with all of the attention it has received. The State Board of Education is the entity most responsible for curriculum adoption in Texas. The Texas Education Agency is heavily involved before, during, and after the adoption of the Texas Essential Knowledge and Skills (TEKs), but the ultimate decision rests with the 15-member SBOE.

Since 2010, the SBOE has become acutely aware of the issue of curriculum standards that are too long. Rather than being a mile wide and an inch deep, interested parties from many sides of the public education debate agree the TEKS should be narrower and deeper. Many of our courses have standards that require teachers and students to move too quickly through the content. This approach does not allow time for students to master the concepts, but merely learn them long enough to take a test, leading to remediation issues the following years. This topic had its fair share of attention this past legislative session and, in fact, the legislature sent Senate Bill 313 (Seliger, 2015) to the Governor that would require the SBOE to shorten the standards in the Foundation Curriculum. Unfortunately, the bill was vetoed; although a significant majority of the SBOE is committed to this effort and will begin working on this in the near future. In his remarks addressing this matter, Governor Abbott (Abbott, 2015) said the following:

> While Senate Bill 313 is intended to provide additional flexibility to school districts when purchasing classroom instructional materials, the bill potentially restricts the ability of the State Board of Education to address the need of Texas classrooms. Portions of Senate Bill 313 may have merit, but serious concerns were raised about other parts of the bill. I look forward to working with the Legislature and other stakeholders to ensure this issue is vigorously evaluated before next Session. (para. 2)

Instructional Materials

Living in a "post-CSCOPE" world has shown that controversy over instructional materials can be elevated into the town square almost overnight. This attention and scrutiny does not always come from parents in the district, but many times from local community members or political agitators hundreds of miles away. At any rate, instructional materials are no longer just a discussion for teachers. With the passage of SB 6 in 2011, school districts have much more latitude over the materials in the classroom and whether those materials are paper or digital, state adopted or not (Shapiro, 2011). This is a good thing. Districts have always had the ability to purchase whatever books they choose, it was just a question of using state funds to purchase them rather than the more limited local funds. The key is having 100% TEKS coverage with whatever materials a district chooses.

As a member of the State Board of Education representing District 9, author Thomas Ratliff, has always felt that the SBOE should be a filter for content used in the classroom, but not the *only* filter, trusting the 7,000+ elected school boards and 1,000+ superintendents along with their teams to choose what is best for their district. This trust in local community members trumps any elected official whose office is in Austin, including members of SBOE. What is the reason for placing such a high value? Local stakeholders just have one district to worry about; they know the families, the students, and their stories. Each member of the SBOE represents hundreds of school districts. District 9, for example, has 180 school districts. When it comes to representing communities in their districts, elected officials at the state and federal level will never possess the same level of understanding as those who locally govern, nor should they pretend they have that capability.

◆ GETTING INVOLVED TO MAKE YOUR VOICE HEARD

Public Education is a sleeping political giant. With the sheer numbers of teachers and staff, along with associated family members, the public education community could elect, or un-elect, any Texas elected official—but they do not. The reason why is simple, as a group they do not vote. The turnout among the education community and its supporters is borderline embarrassing. Consequently, communities are stuck with elected officials who do not support education initiatives at the capitol as much as they should, unless they are asking for votes. If local education interests ever hope to increase or maintain any political momentum, they simply have to get supporters of education to the ballot box.

Now, as with almost every rule there is an exception. In Thomas Ratliff's 2010 election over Dr. Don McLeroy (the 10-year incumbent), there were 116,204 total votes cast. The margin of victory was 402 votes across 31 counties. That is 50.17%–49.83%. Talk about your slimmest of margins! Support came from educators and public education supports across East and Northeast Texas. Groups like Texas Parent PAC, Raise Your Hand Texas, and others are influencing political campaigns and thus the makeup of the House and Senate. Others such as Texans Advocating for Meaningful Student Assessment (TAMSA) are making a big difference in the bills that make it through the process.

Case in point, HB 5 (Aycock et al., 2013) enacted in July 2013 would not have been possible without the support of TAMSA and others pushing for testing and graduation reforms from the living rooms and minivans across the state. HB 5 required the Commissioner of Education to adopt a transition plan beginning with the 2014–2015 school year replacing the Minimum High School Program (MHSP), Recommended High School Program (RHSP), and Distinguished Achievement Program (DAP) with the Foundation High School Program with options for endorsements, distinguished level of achievement and performance acknowledgements. Legislators knew that these efforts were not simply from the "talking heads" or trade associations around Austin. This was real and it was big, the kind of effort educational interest groups can exert.

Though not easy, these are the kind of results achievable if the education community will stay engaged and active. Everyone has a job, family, and a life beyond the issues of state and federal governance. The evidence is clear, everyday people are making a difference in the lives of millions of students, both in the classroom and out, and will always overpower any politician's career or press conference. Politics should take a back seat; however, just like family trips, we cannot ignore the back seat. Every now and then, we have to look back there and say, "Don't make me pull this car over!"

◆ REFERENCES

Abbott, G. (2015). Governor Abbott vetoes Senate Bill 313. *Office of the Governor.* Retrieved from http://gov.texas.gov/news/veto/21098

Aycock, J. (2015). HB 2804. *Texas Legislature Online.* Retrieved from http://www.legis.state.tx.us/billlookup/text.aspx?LegSess=84R&Bill=HB2804

Aycock, J., Deshotel, J., Davis, J., Villarreal, M., & Callegari, B. (2013). HB 5. *Texas Legislature Online.* Retrieved from http://www.capitol.state.tx.us/BillLookup/Text.aspx?LegSess=83R&Bill=HB5

Ericson, J., & Wallace, E. (2010). Constitution of 1876, Handbook of Texas Online. *Texas State Historical Association.* Retrieved from https://tshaonline.org/handbook/online/articles/mhc07

Herrington, C., & Fowler, F. (2003). Rethinking the role of states and educational governance. *Yearbook of the National Society for the Study of Education,* 102: 271–290.

Huberty, D. (2015). Representative Huberty again files legislation for student testing relief. Retrieved from http://www.danhuberty.com/representative-huberty-files-legislation-student-testing-relief/

Hyslop, A. (2015). Let's make a deal: The ESEA compromise Congress should make. *Ahead of the Heard, Bellwether Education Partners.* Retrieved from http://aheadoftheheard.org/lets-make-a-deal-the-esea-compromise-congress-should-make/

Jones-McClure (2015). Texas legislature decriminalizes truancy. *Annotations O'Connor's Online.* Retrieved from http://annotations.jonesmcclure.com/2015/06/24/texas-legislature-decriminalizes-truancy/#sthash.bijgguzX.dpbs

Mathews, J. (2004). Portfolio assessment. *Education Next Summer, 4,* 3. Retrieved from http://educationnext.org/portfolio-assessment/

Mathis, W. (2012). Research-based options for education policymaking: Preschool education. *National Education Policy Center.* Retrieved from http://nepc.colorado.edu/files/pb-options-3-earlyed.pdf

Ratliff, B. (2015). Bill Ratliff: Bill doesn't solve home-rule law's problems; it makes them worse. *The Dallas Morning News.* Retrieved from http://www.dallasnews.com/opinion/latest-columns/20150510-bill-ratliff-home- rule-bill-strays-from-original-intent.ece

Seliger, K. (2015). SB 313. *Texas Legislature Online.* Retrieved from http://www.legis.state.tx.us/tlodocs/84R/billtext/html/SB00313I.htm

Semiens, A. (2015). Report: Texas prosecutes more truancy cases than all other states combined. *Texas Observer.* Retrieved from http://www.texasobserver.org/report-texas-prosecutes-truancy-than-all-other-states-combined/

Shapiro, F. (2011). SB 6. *Texas Legislature Online.* Retrieved from http://www.legis.state.tx.us/billlookup/History.aspx?LegSess=82R&Bill=SB6

Svitek, P. (2015). Abbott signs pre-k bill considered top priority. *The Texas Tribune.* Retrieved from http://www.texastribune.org/2015/05/28/abbott-signs-pre-k-bill-considered-top-priority/

Texas Association of School Boards (2009). Charter schools in Texas: Facts and Figures. Retrieved from https://www.tasb.org/Legislative/Issue-Based-Resources/documents/charters.aspx

Texas Education Agency (2011). Evaluation of Texas charter schools 2009–10: Executive summary. *State of Texas Education Research Center at Texas A&M University.* Retrieved from tea.texas.gov/WorkArea/DownloadAsset.aspx?id=2147502002

Texas Education Agency (2015). Snapshot 2014 summary tables: State totals. Retrieved from http://ritter.tea.state.tx.us/perfreport/snapshot/2014/sumtables.html

Texas Legislative Council (2015). Guide to Texas legislative information (Revised). *Prepared by the Research Division of the Txas Legislative Council.* Retrieved from http://www.tlc.state.tx.us/publegref/gtli.pdf

Texas Politics Project (2015). Education. *The Texas Politics Project at the University of Texas at Austin.* Retrieved from http://www.texaspolitics.utexas.edu/educational-resources

Texas State Library and Archives Commission (2015). Texas State Board of Education: An inventory of State Board of Education minutes and agenda at the Texas State Archives, 1950–2005. Retrieved from http://www.lib.utexas.edu/taro/tslac/30140/tsl-30140.html

U.S. Department of Education (2015). Elementary and Secondary Education Act. Retrieved from http://www.ed.gov/esea

U.S. Department of Education (n.d.). Rural education in America. *National Center for Educational Statistics.* Retrieved from https://nces.ed.gov/surveys/ruraled/TablesHTML/5localedistricts.asp

VanDeaver, G. (2015). HB 1164. *Texas Legislature Online.* Retrieved from http://www.legis.state.tx.us/tlodocs/84R/billtext/html/HB01164I.htm

White, J. (2015). HB 2398. *Texas Legislature Online.* Retrieved from http://www.legis.state.tx.us/billlookup/History.aspx?LegSess=84R&Bill=HB2398

8

DEVELOPMENT AND USES OF THEORY FOR EDUCATIONAL LEADERS

Anita Pankake ◆ Rolando Avila

Theory can help educational leaders generate possible solutions to problems in organizations. Once a problem is recognized as resistant to solution through established policies or procedures, theory can offer several possible actions to consider. No single theory in educational administration, or any field, can explain or predict all possible administrative or organizational behavior. In fact, theories are continually open for question, modification, and/or verification through research. You could say, they are always "under construction." Theories evolve over time as research adds to the knowledge base and directs the thinking of theorists.

Using theories, incomplete though they are, as a means to describe, understand, or predict some portion of organizational and individual behavior is very valuable. Thus, knowledge of theories can be useful to practicing administrators. In fact, there are few tools as useful as good theory when school leaders are faced with a complex problem. If a theory is not useful in practice, then it is not a good theory.

◆ WHAT IS A THEORY?

There are numerous definitions of theory. The *American Heritage Dictionary* provides two distinctively different ones. Theory is (1) "systematically organized knowledge applicable in a relatively wide variety of circumstance," and (2) a "guess based on limited information or knowledge" (p. 126). These definitions illustrate the range of meanings associated with the term theory. This chapter employs a definition of theory that relates directly to the uses educational leaders can make of it. Consequently, theory, in this chapter, is defined as an interrelated set of "proven" statements or hypotheses that describe, explain, account for, and/or predict an empirical phenomenon.

The purpose of this chapter is to help practicing public school administrators and those preparing themselves to enter the field to understand that theory and practice are not mutually exclusive. In this chapter, educational leaders learn how the intelligent use of theories can assist in improving their practice and better serve the organizations in which they work. This chapter (1) introduces the notion of theory in educational leadership; (2) provides a historical framework through which the development of both leadership and organizational theories; and (3) briefly describes the conceptual elements of some selected leadership and organizational theories within designated periods of development. Throughout the chapter, practical examples demonstrating how the theory can be usefully applied are offered.

It is virtually impossible to discuss leadership without also addressing organizations; leadership and organizations are linked. Organizations are led, leaders influence how organizations function, and the purpose and dynamics of organizations can influence the leader's style and performance; one can know little about one without also having some knowledge of the other. Theories in these two dimensions of the human enterprise have a reciprocal and mutually dependent relationship.

Based on earlier works, leadership and organizational theories are grouped into four essential time periods of development (see Table 8.1). In Table 8.1, the first three major periods in the development of organizational and leadership theory in western culture are (1) Classical

TABLE 8.1
The Four Major Periods of Administrative Theory

Period	*Leadership*	*Organization*	*Authority*	*Reward*	*Major Contributors*
Classical (1890–1935)	Top-Down	Machine-like with a formal structure	Coercive with rules	Economic	Taylor Fayol Gulick Weber
Human Relations (1935–1950)	All directions	Organism with an informal structure	Group norms	Social and psycho-log-ical	Mayo, Roethlis-berger, & Dickson Lewin Follett
Behavioral Sciences (1950–1980)	Consideration of all major elements	Attempt to reconcile previous approaches	Systems theory	Intrinsic & extrinsic	Getzels & Guba Blake & Mouton Barnard Senge
Modern Day (1980–present)	Inclusive of all stakeholders	Adapts to change	Bridging generation gaps	Commitment to others; legacy	Zenger Northouse Colvin Rossi Fullan Rawls Dantley & Tillman

(Modified from Lunenburg & Ornstein, 1996; Lutz, Watt, & Combs, 2006; Pankake, 2012; Watt & Pankake, 2008, 2010.)

Period, which began with the Industrial Revolution and continued as dominant through the 1930s; (2) Humanistic or Human Relations period, which became popular in the mid-1930s; and (3) Behavioral Sciences Period, which attempted to combine elements of both the classical and the human relations theories to give consideration to the organization and the workers. A fourth period is currently developing, although it has not been formally named, the reference in this chapter will be to the Modern Day Period. The theories in this category seem to deal with greater degrees of complexity and give greater recognition to the influence of elements outside the organization. In the figure that follows, a few contributors and specific theories are identified for each period.

Describing and discussing all of the contributors and theories for each period would be impossible in the scope of this chapter. As a result, only a few of the theories from each period are highlighted and have applications explained. Deciding which theories to include was challenging. Those selected are one that are widely used or accepted. In every case, the treatment is brief and in no way a comprehensive explanation. Even so, reviewing some of the most common theories of leading and organizing provides an important framework for the practical application of the theories presented.

Presenting the general thinking about leadership prior to the eras of theory development (i.e., Trait and the Great Man theories) seems appropriate to do prior to discussing the selected theories from each period. Because these paradigms have a long history and still thrive in our collective thinking about leaders, the information on them provides a larger historical perspective.

◆ HISTORICAL OVERVIEW

Even before the classical organizational period, theories such as the "Great Man" and Trait Theories were introduced; these theories were based on the ideas that leaders were born with certain characteristics that destined them to become leaders. Most everyone has heard and/or used the description "born leader". Hegel (1837) and Carlyle (1841) suggested leaders inherently had certain personality and behavioral traits that made them great leaders. Both the Great Man and Trait Theories assume that leaders are born with specific traits that make them great leaders; consequently, if an individual is not born with these traits, she or he will not become a great leader. These ideas were developed as theories in the early 1900s and reemerged in the early 1980s (Conger, 1990, 1999). In fact, trait theory perspectives have never gone away completely.

Great Man Theory

Originally coined by Thomas Carlyle, the Great Man Theory is the notion that everything good or bad is the creation of a few effective people. Great Man theory posits that leadership is inherent—that great leaders are born—not made. The Great Man Theory portrays leaders as heroic and destined to rise to leadership when called upon. The term Great Man was used because, at the time, leadership was thought of primarily as a male quality, such as in military leadership. The Great Man theory points to people such as George Washington and Abraham Lincoln. Within the scope of this theory, even less popular leaders like Adolf Hitler and Joseph Stalin have been recognized for their leadership traits. As support for the premises of the Great

Man theory of leadership, one must recognize the lasting mark that some ancient "great men," including Moses, Gautama Buddha, Jesus, and Mohammed, have had on the world.

Trait Theory

Trait Theory is similar in some ways to "Great Man" theories; it assumes people have inherent qualities and traits that make them function better in leadership positions. Trait theories often identify particular personality or behavioral characteristics shared by leaders; examinations of trait theory elements were among the first systematic studies of leadership (Northouse, 2013). Stogdill (1948), in his review of several works on Great Man Theories, identified the following traits of great leaders: (1) capacity, including intelligence, judgment, and verbal facility; (2) achievement, including scholarship, knowledge, and even athletic accomplishments; (3) responsibility, including dependability, aggressiveness, and self-confidence; (4) participation, such as sociability, cooperation, and humor; and (5) status, such as socioeconomic status and popularity. Hanson (2003) noted that Stogdill dismissed isolated traits as having any predictive significance, but when viewed in these clusters or groups of traits they could influence the individuals seeking leadership responsibilities. McCall and Lombardo (1983) researched another trait theory perspective by looking at both success and failure of leaders. They identified several primary traits by which leaders could succeed or fail: (1) emotional stability and composure; (2) calm, confident, and predictable, particularly when under stress; (3) admitting error; (4) owning up to mistakes rather than putting energy into covering up; (5) good interpersonal skills; (6) ability to communicate and persuade others without resort to negative or coercive tactics; (7) intellectual breadth; and, (8) ability to understand a wide range of areas, rather than having a narrow (and narrow-minded) area of expertise.

A recent resurgence of trait theory has emphasized character rather than a focus on inherent traits with many researchers emphasizing visionary and charismatic leadership in their research (Northouse, 2013). In this approach, the leader's role is to help followers reach their full potential, examples being leaders such as Mahatma Gandhi, Martin Luther King, Jr., and Nelson Mandela. In specific formal organizations, there have been similar acclaims for individuals such as Lee Iaccoca, Jack Welch, Vince Lombardi, Herb Kelleher, Colin Powell, and others.

According to trait theories, leadership is defined as a talent that select individuals possess. Trait theories suggest that leadership is restricted to those who may have certain unique physical, personality, and ability characteristics (Bryman, 1992). Ongoing leadership research, however, has failed to find any consistency in specific traits that characterize leaders (Gibb, 1954). Even today, however, we continue to be influenced in our thinking about who can be a leader based on characteristics such as height, gender, racial or ethnic background, and wealth and family background. These are physical characteristics that even today drive perceptions about leadership ability.

◆ THE CLASSICAL PERIOD (1890–1935)

The "classical" theory period of theory development tends to view mankind as a machine and people as replaceable parts in that machine. Each function, role, or task in the organization is reduced to its smallest elements. This paradigm assumes that the parts equal the whole and there is one best way to do a specified job. When the job is done in the prescribed way, then it will be done in the most effective and efficient manner possible and everyone will "profit." However, in reality, it does not always work that way.

The two dominant and enduring theories of this period are scientific management and bureaucratic theory. Both emerged as natural outgrowths of the Industrial Revolution and both survived into the twenty-first century as major models for organizing and explaining organizational behavior. Remnants of each can be found in educational organizations today.

Scientific Management

Scientific management was the work of Frederick Taylor (1856–1915) and was intended to provide the technological steps to correct dysfunctions in organizations. Noticing that everything did not operate as well as expected, Taylor, a mechanical engineer, studied the process of loading pig-iron onto freight cars (Taylor, 1947). From this and other studies, he devised a system that reduced any job to its smallest separate parts (or motions) and then described the most efficient way to get that job accomplished (in the least amount of time). Thus was born the time-motion model of organizing a job within an organization. Taylor established four principles of scientific management: (1) scientific job analysis; (2) selection of personnel; (3) management cooperation; and (4) functional supervising. Taylor felt that the scientific management approach would help workers perform to their full potential.

Taylor's scientific management was first adopted by American business as a way to cure its own ills and then by American education as a way to make common cause with the business values in American culture and its local school boards (Callahan, 1962). The principles of this theory included the identification of the "one best way" to do a job, the training of workers to perform the job using this identified "best way," the tacit agreement that workers did the labor and managers made the decisions. Schools today continue to search for the "one-best way" in all parts of the organization—whether it is the "one-best-way" to teach reading, to determine accountability, to schedule the high school, to serve food in the cafeteria, to address student absences and tardies, to train staff, etc. In this search for the "one-best-way" schools, often eliminate options that are good for some situations but not all and require everyone to adopt the same procedures, which sometimes make things worse rather than better.

Bureaucratic Theory

The German sociologist Max Weber developed bureaucratic theory. His purpose was to develop the "ideal typical" rational organizational model. Bureaucracy in its true sense is a very functional process. In Weber's "ideal typical" bureaucracy, the organization is operated through: (1) a hierarchy of roles or positions with each incumbent chosen because of her/his clear ability, (2) a system of rules (of which everyone is aware and generally accepts), (3) impersonality (which treats everyone fairly and alike), and (4) specialization through a division of labor (which permits everyone's particular talent and ability to be used to its fullest extent). Weber intended bureaucracy to operate a complex organization rationally, efficiently, and reliably (see Blau, 1956; Weber, 1964). Hanson (2003) noted, "Bureaucratic structure and administration are designed to routinize problem solving – to treat incoming questions and issues in a programmed, systematic way that will draw upon a minimum of human and material resources" (p. 16).

Unfortunately, the implementation of Weber's ideas has resulted in organizational operations far from what he intended. Rather, many organizations have experienced a variety of dysfunctions stemming from the very elements that Weber believed to be ideal. For example, organizations are often burdened with a morass of rules and regulations (commonly referred to as "red tape"), some of which even conflict with each other. This situation can result in slowing down or even the blocking of getting things accomplished. Another dysfunction that emerges is related to the specialized job responsibilities of the employees in bureaucracies assume. Who has not stood in the "wrong line," filled out the "wrong form," been sent to another work area because "we don't deal with that"?

Schools, school districts, state departments, and the U.S. Office of Education have many characteristics of Weber's bureaucracy. Rules are everywhere and while the intent is to have the rules to assist in the smooth and efficient operation of the organization and its various processes, which intent is often obscured and even obstructed by the rules themselves. For example, schools have attendance policies for both staff and students. The intent of such policies is to make sure that compulsory student attendance laws are observed and that students attend school regularly to receive the necessary instruction to achieve the learning standards set and to assist the community and parents in assuring that minors are in safe, secure environments under the supervision of adults. Attendance policies for staff are intended to ensure that various functions of the organization have qualified individuals in place to carry them out. Thus, the many rules of attendance have a positive and productive intent. Unfortunately, committees and task forces at all levels of the organization spend hours and hours creating rules to govern such issues as what constitutes a reasonable number of days of absence before some harm comes to the student or staff member and the organization, which reasons for absence are acceptable and which are "unexcused," and what sanctions will be implemented if someone "misses too many days, for the wrong reasons." To implement all of these rules and regulations, schools and districts have created attendance offices, truancy officers, time cards, sign in sheets, tardy slips, early bells, late bells, hall sweeps, doctors' excuses, failure criteria based on "excessive absences" and more. As Weber theorized, rules and specialization help with the efficient operation of the organization; unfortunately, they can also become obstacles to achieving the intended outcomes.

Other theorists contributed during the classical period to the concepts of bureaucratic-type management of complex organizations. Three of these individuals deserve mention here. Henri Fayol (1949) lived from 1841 to 1925 and developed a category of elements for administering complex organizations. As a coal-mining firm manager, Fayol attributed his success to a set of principles and functions that he believed all managers needed to perform. These principles emphasized chain of command, allocation of authority, order, efficiency, equity and stability.

Gulick, working in the early 1900s, expanded Fayol's categories in collaboration with Urwick (1929) to include planning, organizing, staffing, directing, coordinating, reporting, and budgeting, or the unpronounceable acronym of "POSDCoRB." Gulick and Urwick also popularized the concepts of organizational charts, line-staff administration (those who command or direct and those who support), and span of control (the number of persons that can be reasonably supervised by a single person). A quick look on the Website of most any school district will reveal that these concepts are still used in both describing and operating the functions of the organization.

In summary, classical management theories emphasized efficiency in job performance and organizational functions without regard to social or psychological needs of workers. These theories were also built on the premise that workers were motivated extrinsically, particularly by money, in order to perform specific tasks.

Leadership in the classic organizational framework is not complicated. In fact, the entire emphasis of this perspective is to limit any variance by developing policies, rules, and procedures to address every situation; discourage (even disallow) individual thinking; and, expect that leaders behave according to standard operating procedures (SOP), no exceptions. Additionally, leaders are to be aloof and separate from their employees and constituents, demonstrating some sort of caring or compassion is frowned upon since the efficiency and rationality of the decisions would likely be affected. Locating individuals in classroom and locating school and district leadership positions who subscribe to this theory to guide their behavior, even today, is not a difficult task – just ask students about teachers, teachers about principals, and principals about superintendents! The classical "man as machine" models of organization dominated thinking about leadership and organizations for nearly 50 years, and, as noted earlier, remnants of this way of organizing still persist in schools today.

◆ HUMAN RELATIONS PERIOD (1935–1950)

As a reaction to the extreme depersonalization that resulted from the classical period of leadership and organization, the period of Human Relations emerged. The Human Relations period emerged through some surprising results of research focused on increased productivity, as defined by the scientific management perspective. These findings presented a challenge to the general negative situation for workers that was being produced by efficiency studies to the extreme, extrinsic rewards as the sole motivator, and close supervision by an unemotional manager; the challenge spawned a new management perspective focusing on "the important of social-psychological needs of the worker and his or her group" gained popularity. Hanson (2003) described the human relationship ideology as promoting

> the view that the most satisfying organization would be the most efficient. Instead of attempting to quash the informal groups, their basic needs are recognized and brought into harmony with the goals of the organization . . . methodology emphasizes that by practicing democratic principals of management and advocating employee participation in structuring the work environment and in establishing open channels of communication, management and workers could resolve their differences in a spirit of good will and cooperation. (p. 48)

Perhaps first among those who recognized that something else was needed was Mary Parker Follett. Ahead of her time, both as a professional female and as an insightful observer of human organizations, Follett (1924) emphasized that the key to any successful organization was building and maintaining a process that sustained human relationships and dealt effectively with conflict without compromise. Seldom has Follett been given the recognition she deserves; yet, much of what is "preached" and "practiced" in organizational leadership today has roots in her writings.

Follett recognized conflict as a common element in human relations. She regarded conflict as a necessary condition for movement and improvement. She saw the function of administration as a matter of (1) maintaining direct contact among the responsible people, (2) coordination of early stages of the process, (3) reciprocal and interactive relationships among all situational factors, and (4) a continuing process, not a means-end entity (Metcalf & Urwick, 1940). She contended that compromise was a poor way to handle conflict because when two parties compromised, both parties lost; they tended to resent what they had given up, which, often caused a festering, residual resentment, capable of creating a new and more difficult conflict. Instead Follett proposed the concept of "power with" rather than "power over" in an attempt to stress the importance of teamwork and collaboration between the leader and followers (Follett, 1949). These terms are still often heard in leadership workshops today.

A group of studies, often called the "Hawthorne Studies," conducted by Elton Mayo and F. J. Roethlisberger and carried out and reported by Roethlisberger and Dickson (1939) had a significant influence on changing the focus of leading and organizing from the needs of the organization to the needs of the individuals in the organization. At the time of these studies, students and scholars of administration and organizations were beginning to understand that the concepts of scientific management and bureaucracy did not adequately describe organizational behavior. Mayo and those who worked with him became convinced that workers were motivated by more than a mere paycheck and that something more than bureaucratic rules, technical specification, and management decisions were involved in the organizational behavior of workers. The "Hawthorne Studies" demonstrated that workers were more than cogs in a machine to be assembled, instructed, and supervised. Results of their research firmly showed that workers formed groups, established norms, and responded to the organization mostly as groups rather than as individuals.

Another influential thinker during this period was Kurt Lewin, who conducted experiments on leadership style and planned change during World War II. His studies began in 1939 when he was asked to address employee turnover. His work initiated a scientific understanding of the management of people in industry, and became an action research approach (Lewin, 1953 as cited in Burnes, 2007). These studies continued from 1939 to 1947 and resulted in various ideas and practices including: group decision-making, self-management, leadership training, changing stereotypes, and overcoming resistance to change (Burnes, 2007). Most importantly, Lewin's studies focused on the importance of changing group behavior rather than individual behavior.

◆ BEHAVIORAL SCIENCES PERIOD (1950–1980)

Behavioral Sciences Leadership Theories

Behavioral leadership theories assume that effective leaders use certain behaviors consistently and that good leadership is rooted in behavior that can be learned and is not necessarily inherent. Three, of the many, behavioral leadership theories are discussed here. They are Fiedler's Contingency Leadership Theory, Path-Goal Theory, and Situational Leadership Theory. These three theories often overlap philosophically and have some similarities. They all recognize that different leadership behaviors are needed in different situations. A major difference between them focuses on changing the leader when the situation changes versus the leader changing his or her behavior depending on the situation.

Contingency Leadership Theory

Fiedler's (1964) contingency theory model purports to determine whether leadership style is task or relationship oriented, and whether the situation matches the style. In Fielder's contingency theory of leadership, the success of the leader is a function of various contingencies including subordinates, tasks, and/or group variables. The effectiveness of specific leader behaviors is contingent upon the demands of the situation. Contingency theory stresses using different styles of leadership appropriate to the needs of the different organizational situations. In addition, Fiedler asserts that group performance is contingent on the leader's psychological orientation and on three contextual variables: group atmosphere, task structure, and leader's power position. With Fiedler's perspective, different individuals would be selected depending on the situation in which the leader must function. As Northouse (2013) puts it: "To understand the performance of leaders, it is essential to understand the situations in which they lead. Effective leadership is *contingent* on matching a leader's style to the right setting" (p. 123).

Within Fiedler's Contingency Theory, leadership styles are defined as task motivated or relationship motivated. Task-motivated leaders are primarily concerned with completing the task, or reaching a goal. Relationship-motivated leaders are more concerned with developing important interpersonal relationships. Fielder measured the leader styles through the Least Preferred Co-Worker (LPC) Scale. The LPC measures the leader's style by asking him/her to describe a coworker with whom they had difficulty completing a task (Northouse, 2013). Those who score high on the scale are considered relationship motivated, while those who score low are identified as task motivated (Fiedler & Garcia, 1987).

An application of these concepts is used regularly in schools and districts when consideration is given to which individuals would be the best leader for working with a situation. Principals often think this through when a particular group of students have needs that a specific teaching style can best address. Superintendents use this theory when they review the organizational culture, the school community context, a school's unique problems, personnel, and school demographics in considering who might be the best fit as the principal in that situation. Using Contingency Theory, it is likely that if the situation changes significantly, a new principal with a different style would be sought. Another example might be when teacher leaders are asked to facilitate the accomplishment of a task with other teachers. In this instance, the teacher leader has no positional power and is therefore more focused on the group atmosphere and task. He/she must use behaviors in that situation that will develop strong peer-relationships, causing the group to work willingly to achieve the goal.

Path-Goal Theory

Martin Evans and Robert House developed the Path-Goal Theory, which hypothesizing that the leader's behavior has an effect on the subordinate's motivation to achieve a goal. Evans and House identified four specific leadership behaviors that characterize the model: (1) directive leadership; (2) supportive leadership; (3) participative leadership; and (4) achievement-oriented leadership. Research has shown that a single leader can use all four of these leadership behaviors in various situations. Unlike the Contingency Theory of leadership, Path-Goal suggests that leadership behavior is adaptable (Downey, Sheridan, & Slocum, 1975).

At a later time, House (1996) made a major overhaul of the theory. An expansion of the number of leadership behaviors and outcome variables, a modernization of the situational concepts, and the development of some 26 specific propositions or hypotheses were among the changes made. The major concepts of the reformulated theory were leader behavior, situations factors, and hypotheses. Hoy and Miskel (2008) identified the model's overall proposition as "the subordinate's satisfaction and individual and work unit effectiveness increase as leaders engage in behaviors that complement the task environments and subordinates' abilities and compensate for deficiencies" (p. 442). They go on to point out that House's reformulation postulates that it is unlikely that any one leader will possess all of the various leadership behaviors, but that some behaviors can be substituted for others.

Application of House's work would imply that any one individual might be a satisfactory choice as a leader in most any school or school administrative function. This person would be able to adapt his/her leadership behaviors to best address the majority of situations encountered in their job assignment. However, a situation could arise in which the incumbent might not possess the behaviors needed to address a particular set of circumstances. For example, leadership in the schools of New Orleans following the damage of hurricane Katrina might require leaders other than those who were in the schools prior to the storm; or, a school district that had operated with sufficient tax revenue, might need a different leader if a drastic decrease in funding is experienced. Path-Goal Theory acknowledges that while these incumbents demonstrated leadership behaviors with some range of adaptability, the presentation of an exceptional or extreme situation might reach beyond their adaptability and require they be replaced by individuals with different ranges of behaviors.

Situational Leadership Theory

Hersey and Blanchard's (1969) Situational Leadership model states that leaders should select one of four leadership styles that fits the employees' maturity level in a given situation. This model expanded the notion of relationship and task dimensions to leadership and added a readiness dimension. This theory implies that different situations demand different kinds of leadership and that leadership style should be matched to the maturity or developmental level of the subordinates. It further implies that a single individual, i.e., the leader, can adopt and adapt his/her style to make the best match for the situation.

As the subordinates' developmental levels increase, leadership should be more relationship motivated than task motivated. For four degrees of subordinate maturity, from highly mature to highly immature, leadership can consist of *Delegating to, Participating with, Selling* ideas to, and *Telling* subordinates what to do. Leaders using the Situational Leadership approach must be very flexible and able to diagnose where subordinates are in their development level. The leader must then adapt his/her leadership style to match the subordinate's level.

Hambleton and Gumpart (1982) conducted an industrial study on the Situational Leadership theory and found that managers who correctly applied Hersey and Blanchard's model had higher performing subordinates than those who did not use this model. In a study of elementary school principals, who were tested before and after the Hersey–Blanchard framework training, these administrators were perceived as more effective 3 years after the training than before the training; however, there were no significant differences in principals' effectiveness immediately after the training (Pascarella & Lunenburg, 1988).

In each situation, the leader must modify his/her approach to best address the needs of the subordinates involved. *Telling* is a style that the leader would want to assume when working with veteran subordinates on a new or unique task or with new teachers on a standard task. In both cases, the followers need direction to assist them in knowing what to do. Both *Selling* and *Participating* involve subordinates' opinions and participation to a greater degree. When using a *Selling* style, the leader will have made a decision and will then work with his/her followers to convince them to accept and implement it; with *Participating*, the leader will bring information about a decision that needs to be made to the followers and seek their input and help in making that decision. A *Delegating* style is best used when the followers are mature in their jobs and have the commitment to pursue the desired goal. This would be an instance appropriately described as the leader outlining the desired result and then "getting out of the way." The followers assume the leadership of their own work and need little or no direction from the leader.

In Situational Leadership Theory, the same leader uses all four styles as is appropriate for the situation. The leader must be able adjust his/her style to fit the situation that infers a level of flexibility on the part of the leader's behavior, as well as, well-developed skills in task analysis. An additional implication is that the leader is well acquainted with the individuals with whom they work and have a relatively comprehensive knowledge of the work to be done. The leader's appropriate choice of behavior is the desired outcome with the application of this theory, however, that behavior will only occur when careful consideration of various context variables has been done.

◆ BEHAVIORAL SCIENCE MODELS

The behavioral science approach attempts to reconcile conflict or differences between the classical and human relations approaches. Chester Barnard is often credited with being the first to introduce the behavioral science approach. He was known for development of the cooperative system, which was an attempt to integrate human relations and classical management through a focus on efficiency and effectiveness (Barnard, 1938). Several models that extended Barnard's basic premises are introduced in the following paragraphs. These models introduce new behavioral approaches to management and leadership.

Getzels–Guba Model

Toward the end of the Human Relations Period, Getzels and Guba (1957) blended the concepts of the classical and human relations period into a macrotheory accounting for administrator and organization behavior. In 1958, Getzels presented their work in a schematic model to which. Kimbrough and Nunnery (1988) later referred to as a systems theory.

As with most macrotheories, the Getzels–Guba model describes the universe of organizational behaviors, but leaves out the numerous social science concepts that account for the rich variation among those behaviors. This makes the model universally useful in describing behavior and simultaneously useless in predicting behavior or assisting an administrator in deciding what might be done. The major concepts in the Getzels–Guba model are (1) nomothetic (bureaucratic) concerns and (2) idiographic (personal) concerns. The blends of these two produce organization behavior. Most of the vast research this model generated in the 1960s and 1970s resulted in the notion that administrative behavior, in order to be helpful, was neither "nomothetic" nor "idiographic" but "transactional." Thus, successful administrators relied sometimes on bureaucratic criteria and at other times considered human criteria in making decisions, depending on the situation.

Two– and Three-Factor Models

Some theories of leadership and organization behavior define the constructs in terms of the interaction among two or three factors. For example, the Getzels and Guba model, as previously explained, involved two "ideal typical" concepts along a continuum (i.e., nomothetic and idiographic) measured from high to low. The theory assumed the interaction of several elements along each point on the continuum. The interaction of the two concepts resulted in "organizational behavior," the output variable, which, in turn, influenced original inputs. Research using the model produced the concept of "transaction," a third factor. Another important dimension of this model is the context in which this transaction occurs. For example, the students entering the school (inputs) are influenced during their time in the organization. When they exit the organization and return to the community, they are the output of the system known as school.

Another example of a two-factor model is the Leadership Behavior Description Questionnaire (LBDQ). The LBDQ was initially developed for military use, but was later modified for use with school administrators (Halpin, 1956). It has two continua, which are initiation of structure (i.e., "sets deadlines") and consideration of subordinates (i.e., "listens to subordinates"). The instrument is used to measure leadership behavior as an output. Effective leaders tend to be high in both initiation and consideration, but must be at least high in initiation. While scoring high in consideration alone will not guarantee leadership behavior, nonleaders are those who tend to score low in both dimensions.

Theory X and Y

This theory, proposed by McGregor (1960), follows the same pattern as any two-factor theory, and explains the motivation of workers based on the administrators' perceptions of the workers' nature. A manager with a Theory X perspective assumes workers will do as little as possible and require pressure or prodding in order to get their best effort, with some clear reward if they behave "correctly." A manager with a Theory Y perspective assumes that workers are self-motivated and self-actualized and will meet or exceed goals, if expected to do so and when given the necessary support and encouragement. These two perspectives direct the behavior of the managers (from classroom to board room); the actions that a manager having a Theory Y perspective might take are totally different than the actions of a manager with a Theory X perspective. Add Ouchi's (1981) Theory Z (a creative combination of X and Y) to Theory X and Y and one has a three-factor model, not unlike the Getzels–Guba model of nomothetic, idiographic, and transactional behaviors.

Blake/Mouton Grid

Developed as a means of organizational development (OD) in industry, the Blake/Mouton (1964) grid has been used to enhance leadership development for over 50 years. More specifically, it has been largely used with administrators to assist them in seeing the difference in the way they perceive themselves as managers as opposed to the way others see them as managers. The feedback from others is used to motivate the administrator to seek leadership development. Blake and Mouton posited a two-dimensional nine-point scale, one horizontal along a concern for people (from [9] high to [1] low) and the other vertical along a concern for production (from [9] high to [1] low). This provides a 9 × 9 or 81-cell grid where a 9, 1 is very high in people concern and very low in production concern and 1, 9 is very low in people concern and very high production concern. Little research has been done with the grid, and no data are available on its reliability and validity (personal letter from authors, 1989). Similarities between concern for people with consideration and Theory Y, and the concern for production with initiation of structure and Theory X can easily be seen.

General Systems Theory

Everything deserving consideration under the label "systems" model owes its origin to Ludwig von Bertalannfy (1968). At a very rudimentary and basic level von Bertalannfy's notions of general systems deal with the differences between relatively open versus relatively closed systems. A system is defined as an organization or organism that exchanges interactions within its specified boundaries more often that it does across its boundaries. In school, a classroom is a system exchanging within its boundaries more often than with other classroom systems. However, a school can be studied as a system exchanging interactions more within than across the boundaries of the school. School districts can also be studied as systems exchanging interactions more often within the organizational boundaries but also exchanging across boundaries with its community. The more open the system, the more often it exchanges across boundaries with other systems. The more closed the system, the less frequently it exchanges across boundaries. A totally closed system does not exchange interactions and will progress toward entropy or death (Rifkin & Howard, 1980).

A simplistic system model could be composed of two systems. System A exchanges inputs and outputs with system B. Each may also be a subsystem of a larger system (i.e., two classrooms A & B in their environment, a school). A's output becomes an input for B, and vice versa. The inputs received by each system are processed for meaning and implications and are used to produce and modify future outputs (i.e., teacher A hears from teacher B about a fire drill at 9:20, and does not begin the reading lesson at 9:20 as previously planned). Such exchanges help each system survive within its environment. These elements help explain and, to some extent, predict the behavior of the system. Prediction, in general systems theory, is in terms of "equifinality." That is, if everything remains as it is now, some predictable state will occur at a definable time. Dickens, without intending to do so, defines equifinality and general systems when Scrooge asks, "are these the things which must be or may be only?" and is told, "if these shadows remain unchanged the boy will die." But in open systems things can change. Inputs can be processed and, thus, change future outputs and future conditions. The boy did not die! Nor was the reading lesson interrupted by a fire drill!

Homans (1950, 1960) sets forth what may be considered the basic work on small groups and their behavior, sometimes called "interaction theory" (Turner, 1974). Homans (1950) defines the three basic elements of human behavior (in groups) as (1) activity, (2) interaction, and (3) sentiment. Activities are the things people do. Interaction is the process of one person providing a stimulus for another and the other responding. Sentiment is the exchange of feelings. For example, two people can go fishing (activity). One can fall out of the boat and the other save the first person (interaction). The first person can express gratitude and the other receives it and both become friends (sentiment). The three elements are interactive. The more one element increases, the more likely the others are to increase and vice versa. These behaviors are governed in groups, by group norms. Group norms are defined as behavior people expect from others, a shared sentiment, and which individuals sanction when behavior becomes too deviant. Homans' work (1960) goes quite beyond the simplistic model presented here, dealing with complicated concepts of human behavior such as justice and fair exchange.

In order to look at how larger social systems behave with other larger systems we turn to Loomis (1960). Again, Loomis is not the only option available, merely the choice for this chapter. Larger systems means, for example, a metropolitan school district dealing with a large teacher union in a major city, or an influential church in the community dealing with the school district about library book selection.

Loomis' title (1960) is informative: *Social Systems: Their Persistence and Change*. Much of American sociology has been described as conservative by focusing on "persistence" or status quo rather than change. In spite of the rhetoric to the contrary, American social science and public education have tended toward the preservation of the status quo. This is one reason why real reform of education is so difficult. Loomis defines various factors that influence the manner in which one group of individuals can be predicted to behave when confronted with another group with somewhat different goals. These include the potential of the group, the group's history, its institutionalization, its perception of territoriality, and its boundary maintenance.

Loose Coupling

Although many would agree that various organizational behaviors in public schools could be accounted for by bureaucratic theory, at least as many others would not. As the ideal typical bureaucracy is the "iron cage" for humanity, the fact that everything in public schooling is not bureaucratic is probably for the best. Weick (1983) suggested the concept of loose coupling as an alternative to bureaucracy. Perhaps loosely coupled is the opposite, the antithesis, of bureaucratic or a tightly coupled system.

Loosely coupled organizations behave according to the concepts of General Systems Theory (Weick, 1985). Therefore, it has been suggested that we did not need a new theory to account for loosely coupled behavior (Lutz, 1982). What was clearly needed, however, was a concept to call attention to the fact that school organizations often do not behave according to the rules of bureaucracy, are often unpredictable, and those unpredictable behaviors often allow the organization to survive and succeed when tight coupling would contribute to its failure and demise. Loosely coupled organizations:

- encourage subunits to maintain somewhat separate identities and individualities;
- develop only generalized organizational goals with broad parameters;
- permit subunits to develop different goals within defined broad parameters; and
- evaluate accomplishment and redistribute resources based on such goal differentiation and flexibility, sometimes through informal, rather than formal arrangements.

Because of this loose coupling arrangement, subunits can better respond to a varied and ever-changing environment, providing greater opportunity for their survival and the survival of the larger organization. Such organizations are, however, less predictable and often experience more difficulty in effecting system-wide organizational change as the subunits are free to resist or even subvert top-down efforts to change.

A popular name among systems theorists today is Peter Senge. Senge's seminal work, *The Fifth Discipline* (1990), has brought increased attention to systems theory. While systems theory is only one of five elements (systems thinking, personal mastery, mental models, building shared vision, and team learning) required for a learning organization, its inclusion precipitated an increase in the conversation among educators about systems theory. More and more school leaders were discussing the need for systemic thinking and systemic change. Senge's work in *The Fifth Discipline* puts systems theory to work in its own right and in conjunction with other theories.

According to Smith (2001), Senge argues that a key problem with much that is written about and done in the name of management is that rather simplistic frameworks are applied to complex systems. Senge asserts that we tend to look at the organization part by part rather than focusing the whole; this, in turn, causes a failure to see organization as a dynamic process. With our short-term views, we rarely see the consequences of some of our most important decisions. Sometimes the result of a decision made today will not reveal itself for months or years; even, then the consequence may be in an area that seems totally unrelated to the area and intent of the original actions. Senge (1990) points out that

> The systems viewpoint is generally oriented toward the long-term view. That's why delays and feedback loops are so important. In the short term, you can often ignore them; they're inconsequential. They only come back to haunt you in the long term. (p. 92)

In schools, an application of this theory is often seen when leaders in districts and individual schools make decisions that will bring about an immediate increase in student learning as measured by standardized tests. Such decisions bring the desired results in the short term; however, in the long term, consequences have been experienced in plateauing of measured achievement, in a decrease in performance on other measures, and in increased stress resulting in absences among both students and staff.

Understanding and applying systems thinking is not easy. However, if the effort is not made to do just that, then school leaders will continue to make decisions without realizing the consequences to other parts of the organization. Additionally, they will, themselves, be dealing with problems in their own purview, generated by decisions made in other parts of the organization.

◆ MODERN DAY THEORY (1980–PRESENT)

The modern workplace is becoming more and more diverse with regard to gender, ethnicity, age, race, and socioeconomic status. A recent focus of leadership research has been on closing the leadership gap with regard to multigenerational diversity in the workplace. School leaders are faced with working together with students, teachers, and staff, and need to understand and respect each other's ideas and opinion (Rossi, 2007; Sessa, Kabacoff, Deal, & Brown, 2007). It is important for the leader to establish relationships with stakeholders of all age groups, and this often requires more open lines of communication than has traditionally been the case.

According to Colvin, Demos, Mero, Elliott, & Yang (2007), the command and control model of leadership is no longer effective in today's information-based economy. In order to reach desired results, leaders must limit dictatorship styles and in turn build working relationships with employees that foster positive learning and working environments (Colvin et al., 2007). Zenger, Ulrich, & Smallwood (2000) suggest that modern day leadership should focus on teamwork, improve interpersonal relationships, and build self-awareness. According to Northouse (2007), leadership in organizational groups or work teams has become one of the most popular and rapidly growing areas of leadership theory and research. Team Leadership consists of organizational groups of people working together equally to reach a common goal. Examples of team leadership include project management teams, task forces, work units, standing committees, quality teams, and improvement teams.

Transformational Leadership

Downton first coined the term, Transformational Leadership, in 1973; however, James McGregor Burns (1978) is most often credited with the development of the concepts that make up transformational leadership. Burns made a distinction between transactional leadership and transforming leadership. In transactional leadership, both leaders and followers are motivated to action by an expectation of an exclusive benefit. In contrast, Burns describes transformational leadership as involving leaders who tap into the motives of followers in order to reach organizational goals. The purpose of transformational leadership is to raise the level of motivation and morality of both the leader and follower. Others, particularly, Bernard Bass (1985), have added to Burns' ideas and have attempted to operationalize these concepts. Bass developed a more expanded and refined version of transformational leadership by giving followers' needs more attention than the leader's. He explained that transformational leadership raises followers' levels of consciousness about the importance of goals, gets followers to become "team players" rather than place their own interests above those of others, and moves followers to address higher level needs (Bass, 1985, 1990).

Bass contrasts Burns' Transformational Leadership which focuses on setting goals, providing the resources to meet the goals, and assessing success in reaching the goals with Laissez-faire leadership that provides little to no direction of any sort. Transformational leadership is seen in all types of organizations from sports teams, to corporations, to the military and in schools as well. Those schools that excel in their work with students even though a variety of financial, social, physical and demographic issues work against them are examples of transformational leadership in education. The leadership in those schools is able to bring the teachers, students, and community members together in such a way that they go beyond expectations. In the early research on effective schools, these were identified as the "maverick schools."

Including followers in genuine ways in the operation and management of the school is a basic element of transformational leadership. Deal (1993) believed that in order to have participatory management, the character or culture of the school must be transformed. Deal suggested that most problems within schools are social, not technical problems and in order to transform the organization, the basic character or culture must be changed. This is not an easy task as shared values, rituals, symbols, and mindsets are deeply rooted in the institution's culture.

Synergistic Leadership Theory

Synergistic Leadership Theory (SLT) (Irby, Brown, Duffy, & Trautman, 2002) seeks to help answer the voices of women and minorities that must be heard by developing an alternative to traditional theory, although not a replacement for these theories. What SLT does attempt to do is to offer a point of view that accommodates both men and women's perspectives as they work in leadership roles in organizations, especially organizations that work in areas of social justice and impact programs and institutions of importance to the development of society, particularly as it is known in the twenty-first century. Most of the classical theories in leadership were developed looking only at male behavior; whereas SLT was developed using qualitative derived ideas tested using triangulation. SLT is relational and interactive as contrasted with being linear. SLT has four interacting factors: (1) leadership behavior, (2) organizational structure, (3) external forces, and (4) attitudes, beliefs, and values.

Brown and Irby (2003) developed SLT. They viewed the four factors as four stellar points of a tetrahedron with six interacting pairs or sets of factors that can be examined. Situated experiences may be viewed as inside or outside the tetrahedron, whether the events or interactions are inside the planes of the figure or outside the planes of the figure. The tetrahedron can be rotated so no point becomes the focus. Consequently, multiple perspectives can be examined in a dynamic environment, in which none of the four stellar points take precedence over the other, but can be used to better understand the interplay between the leader's behavior, the environment, the organizational factors, and the attitudes, beliefs and values of the individuals and of the organization. Although the developers were attempting to develop a theory that had characteristics of understanding and included women's behavior within the leadership scheme, the theory actually accommodates both genders and consequently opens up many possibilities in examining organizational and leadership behavior.

Servant Leadership

Servant leadership's development is credited to Robert Greenleaf, who published his essay, "The Servant as Leader" in 1970. Although Greenleaf's work appeared in 1970, it was not until the new millennium that his ideas were popularized in business and well into the first decade of the new millennium before education recognized and embraced them. Servant leadership is a philosophy that supports people who choose to serve first and then lead as a way of expanding service to individuals and institutions. Greenleaf acquired the idea of servant-as-leader after reading Herman Hesse's *Journey to the East in* which he identifies Leo as a servant for a group of men who are on a journey. Everything goes well until Leo disappears and the group falls apart. Later, one of the men finds Leo as a great and noble leader.

Servant-leaders may or may not hold formal leadership positions. Servant-Leadership encourages collaboration, trust, foresight, listening, and the ethical use of power and empowerment. Greenleaf developed 10 principles of the servant leader. These include listening, empathy, healing, awareness, persuasion, conceptualization, foresight, stewardship, commitment to the growth of people, and building community (Greenleaf, 1977).

The actions of the servant leader are often required when school and districts are embroiled in situations that require difficult decision that will affect a variety of both internal and external publics. For example, the closing of a school is a deeply emotional issue for students, parents, teachers, and others. The servant leader knows and recognizes the feeling involved, but also sees the need for the action and the focus on the future. Relevant to the current financial difficulties in many school districts, the servant leader may have the best combination of perspective and skills to guide the organization through the actions needed to cut costs without damaging what is the best for students' learning.

Participative Leadership

Participative leadership involves encouragement and facilitation by the leader for others to participate in making decisions that would otherwise be made by the leader alone. This involvement of multiple stakeholders improves the understanding of the issues involved by those carrying out the decisions. Participative leadership has also been called empowerment, joint decision making, democratic leadership, Management by Objective, and power sharing. Even when it is not necessary to consult with others before making a decision, a leader may still do so in order to obtain the benefits of participation. Potential benefits of participation include better decisions and greater acceptance of decisions by people who will implement them or be affected by them (Yukl, 2002).

A popular strategy for operationalizing participative leadership in education is site-based decision making. A site-based council or team is generally made up of a variety of representatives from different roles. There may classroom or subject/grade level representatives, parents, and/or community representatives, students may be represented, administrators, student services support personnel and noncertified, staff representatives, and others. A once centralized decision making role that has given way to site-based decision making is professional development. Rather than decisions regarding content, scheduling, and resource allocations being made wholly at the central office, many districts have made all or some of this decision making a school site responsibility. This action acknowledges that the individuals at the school are in the best position to make decisions about their professional development needs. The site-based decision-making team at a school may request input from faculty and staff regarding needs based on student learning data, safety issues, change initiatives, etc., listed in the school's improvement plan. Based on the school's goals and the identified needs, the personnel at the school determine what professional development activities are best for the students and staff. While central office officials will retain decision making responsibility for professional development that addresses district issues and various mandates, what is best for the individual school is a decision this is delegated to those who have a personal stake in this unit of the organization.

◆ CHANGE LEADERSHIP THEORY

Formal research and theory development regarding change in education has been ongoing for more than 50 years. Without question, change is constant, especially in this time of state and federal mandates, increasing privatization and alternative vendors for the schooling process, and the cultural and demographic dynamics in the country. Change will happen no matter what leaders do or do not do. The key for effective leaders is to create the kind of change that best serves the needs of the entire organization. Among the most prominent names in contemporary writing and research on change theory in educational organizations is Michael Fullan. Fullan (1992) examines the relationship between educational leaders and organizational change. Fullan's (2007) "Three I Model" simplifies the change process into three stages: initiation (adoption of a new program), implementation (putting a new program into action), and institutionalization (a new program becomes a lasting part of the organization). Institutionalization is necessary for reform to make an effective and lasting difference. Unfortunately, very few new programs make it to the institutionalization stage.

Two other aspects of change and change leadership on which Fullan has written are the Tri-level model and sustainability. The Tri-level model makes the point that long-term, deep changes need the three governing levels of education (local, state. and federal) to be in coordinated in their efforts. To illustrate, Fullan, Cuttress, and Kilcher (2005) the following as "a trilevel lens on a problem":

- What has to happen at the school and community level?
- What has to happen at the district level?
- What has to happen at the state level? (p. 58).

Fullan advocates this trilevel approach as the means to develop better organizations and systems at while simultaneously developing individuals. This perspective provides the entree for understanding Fullan's concept of sustainability.

In his book, *Leadership and Sustainability: System Thinkers in Action*, Fullan (2005) discusses the concept of sustainability and elaborates extensively on the roles, responsibilities, and actions of each of the three levels (local, district, and state) of the trilevel model. He identified eight elements of sustainability and goes on to link these first to the trilevel model and ultimately to advocacy for developing individuals as systems thinkers at each level of the model.

Other researchers in the area of change theory and research in education include Hall and Hord (2014), Hargreaves (2009), Elmore (2004) from among many. Writers and researchers in other fields have also influenced the thinking of educational leaders in the area of change theory. Among the many authors are Bennis (2009), Bridges (2009), Lewin (as described in Nelson & Quick, 2000), and Kotter (2012).*

Social Justice Leadership

A perspective of long standing, but recently receiving increased attention in the literature and research regarding leadership and organizations is social justice. The term social justice can be found in myriad publications related to education and elsewhere. Without some historical perspective, social justice might appear to be a contemporary idea in its formulation. Not so.

Often, Rawls' work, *A Theory of Justice (1971)*, is viewed as the foundation for the many questions, conversations and conflicts between traditional and contemporary thinking in this area of organizing and leading. "Thousands of essays and scores of books have appeared, defending Rawls, criticizing Rawls, seeking to go beyond Rawls" (Anderson, 2003, p. 40). Early in *A Theory of Justice,* Rawls stated: "A theory however elegant and economical must be rejected or revised if it is untrue; likewise laws and institutions no matter how efficient and well-arranged must be reformed or abolished if they are unjust" (Anderson, 2003, p. 42). Rawl's larger goal was to create or identify "normative principles" that would be used to evaluation political institutions and guide public life. To this end, Rawls declared that, "Justice is the first virtue of social institutions, as truth is of systems of thought," and he labeled this theory "justice as fairness" (Anderson, 2003, p. 42).

According to McKenzie et al (2008, as cited in Dantley & Tillman, 2010), "Notions of social justice are varied, complex and contested." In fact, Novak (2000) claimed the trouble with social justice begins with its meaning. He references Friedrich Hayek's (Hayek was a major social theorist and political philosopher of the twentieth century) work in this area,

> . . . whole books and treatises have been written about social justice without ever offering a definition of it. It is allowed to float in the air as if everyone will recognize an instance of it when it appears. This vagueness seems indispensable. The minute one begins to define social justice, one runs into embarrassing intellectual difficulty. (Hayek as cited in Novak, 2000, p. 11)

Even so, efforts continue to define and describe social justice and social justice leadership. Tillman (2002) offered insights to a possible definition of social justice, i.e., "Generally, social justice theorists and activists focus their inquiry on how institutionalized theories, norms, and practices in schools and society lead to social, political, economic and educational inequities" (as cited in Dantley & Tillman, 2006, p. 20).

---

*The authors listed have numerous publications in addition to the ones listed here.

Similarly, Lupton (2005) notes social justice in education refers to both the opportunities and the processes necessary to provide them in a quality way.

> Social justice in education demands, at the very minimum, that all students should have access to schools of the same quality." (p. 589).

For the most part, the contemporary use of the term social justice infers criticism and sometimes even an indictment of the manner in which educational entities are organized and led. This has resulted in the study and advocacy of social justice leadership.

Definitions of social justice leadership vary among scholars. According to Dantley and Tillman (2006), "Leadership for social justice interrogates policies and procedures that shape schools and at the same time perpetuate social inequalities and marginalization due to race, class, gender, and other markers of difference" (p. 31). Advocating for social justice requires leaders who are relentless in the pursuit of "a more equitable and socially just society" (Dantley & Tillman, 2006, p. 31). They identify schools as important places for doing this work and educational leaders as the ones who must begin this work.

Although early American leaders like Thomas Jefferson envisioned a democratic nation buttressed by an educated populace, the history of the American people has been fraught with various inequalities. Certainly, the institution of slavery, which lasted for more than 200 years, created a system that barred millions of African Americans from education. Unfortunately, even after slavery was abolished by constitutional amendment in 1865, the legacy of inequality remained strong for more than 100 years including the U.S. Supreme Court decision of *Plessy v. Ferguson* (1896), which legalized segregation. In like manner, massive immigration waves before the American Civil War (1861–1865) and again at the end of the nineteenth century introduced millions of people to the growing nation that were different to the older immigrants. The differences in language, dress, religion, and culture became the defining characteristics between the haves and the have nots, because the great equalization power of education was not equally accessible to all. If educational leaders are to live up to the democratic principles on which the nation was founded, they will have an unrelenting desire to create educational opportunities for all students. In this way, Social Justice leaders will benefit the entire nation by facilitating all dimensions of student growth. After all, since educational access many times determines standards of living, equal educational opportunities equate to social justice.

Brooks' (2012) words provide an appropriate closing to this section on social justice. He states:

> Social justice is many things to many people . . . . Social justice can be as quiet and calm as a teacher's caring and compassionate look and as unrelenting as the storm of fury unleashed on a racist educator by someone bold enough to confront them. To be sure, it is a combination of these things to some, these things and more to others and none of them to many more. (p. xii)

The areas of social justice and social justice leadership will continue to be defined, studied, advocated, argued and denigrated within education through a variety of lenses. Social justice concerns permeate not only education, but also social, political, and economic dimensions of our world. This section of the chapter on the *Development and Uses of Theory for Educational Leaders* is one that will change with each edition of this text. There is much more to come in this area of theory development and use; it is definitely an area to which educational leaders must stay attuned as they engage in daily practice and anticipate the future.

◆ SUMMARY

A lot has been said about organizations and leaders, and yet there is so much more that could be said. Hopefully, what has become apparent through this presentation is that the questions from long ago still persist. As Bennis (1959) stated so well,

> These studies of leadership raise[s] the fundamental issues that every group, organization, nation, and group of nations has to resolve or at least struggle with: What are the sources of power? Can all the various kinds of leaders be accounted for under one frame of reference? (p. 261)

Even as the busy school administrator and those aspiring to be school administrators read works that focus on the "10 mistakes" or the "7 secrets," some sort of "moving food" or the myriad other forms of do's and don'ts that appear on the nation's book shelves, theory is at play. Each and every one of these works is founded on one or more leadership and/or organizational theories. Whether we know it or not, we use theories routinely. School leaders need to become more aware of the theories that do exist and begin to use them to improve their own skills of predicting and explaining of what goes on in school. While none of the theories presented have their origins in schools, schools have adopted or been forced to accept the theoretical constructs in formulating their management and operations as organizations. Each of the theories for organizing has implications for the leadership action required and leaders can have significant influence or the organizing of the workplace.

◆ REFERENCES

Barnard, C. (1938). *Functions of the executive*. Cambridge: Harvard University Press.

Bass, B. M. (1985). *Leadership and performance beyond expectations*. New York: Free Press.

Bass, B. M. (1990). From transactional to transformational leadership: Learning to share the vision. *Organizational Dynamics, 18* (3), 19–36.

Bennis, W. G. (1959). Leadership theory and administrative behavior: The problem of authority. *Administrative Science Quarterly, 4*(3), 259–301.

Bennis, W.G. (2009). *On becoming a leader* (4th ed.). New York, NY: Basic Books

Bertalannfy, L. von (1968).General systems—a critical review. In Buckley, W. (Ed.) *Modern Systems Research for the Behavioral Scientist*. Chicago: Aldine.

Blake, R. R., & Mouton, J. S. (1964).*The managerial grid*. Houston, TX: Gulf.

Blau, P. M. (1956). *Bureaucracy in modern society*. New York: Random House.

Bridges, W. (with Susan Bridges). (2009). *Managing transitions: Making the most of change* (3rd ed.). Philadelphia, PA: Da Capo Press.

Brooks, J. S. (2012). Preface: Educational leadership and social justice: Paths to the present, possibilities for the future and future (pp. xi–xiii) In E. Murakami-Ramalho & A. Pankake (Eds.), *Educational leaders encouraging the intellectual and professional capacity of others: A social justice agenda*. Charlotte, NC: Information Age Publishing, Inc.

Brown, G., & Irby, B. (2003). The synergistic leadership theory: Contextualizing multiple realities of female leaders. *Journal of Women in Educational Leadership, 1* (1): 101–116.

Bryman, A. (1992). *Charisma and leadership in organizations.* London: Sage.

Burnes, B. (2007). Kurt Lewin and the Harwood studies: The foundations of OD. *The Journal of Applied Behavioral Science, 43*: 213–231.

Burns, J. M. (1978). *Leadership.* New York: Harper and Row.

Callahan, R. E. (1962). *Education and the cult of efficiency.* Chicago: University of Chicago Press.

Carlyle, T. (1841). *Lectures on heroes and hero worship.*

Colvin, G., Demos, T., Mero, J., Elliott, J., & Yang, J. (2007). Leader machines. *Fortune, 156* (7), 98–106.

Conger, J. (1990). The dark side of leadership, *Organizational Dynamics*, 19, 44–55.

Conger, J. (1999). Charismatic and transformational leadership in organizations: An insider's perspective on these developing streams of research, *Leadership Quarterly*, 10, 145–169.

Deal, T. E. (1993). The culture of schools. In M. Sashkin & H. J. Walberg (Eds.), *Educational leadership and school culture.* Berkeley, CA: McCutchan.

Downey, H. K., Sheridan, J. E., & Slocum, J.W. (1975). Analysis of relationships among leader behavior, subordinate job performance, and satisfaction: A path-goal approach. *Academy of Management Journal, 18*, 253–262.

Downton, J. V. (1973). *Rebel leadership: Commitment and charisma in a revolutionary process.* New York: Free Press.

Elmore, R. (2004). *School reform from the inside out: Policy, practice and performance.* Cambridge, MA: Harvard Education Press.

Fayol, H. (1949). General and industrial management. (C. Stoars Trans.). London: Pitman.

Fiedler, F. E. (1964). *A contingency model of leadership effectiveness. Advances in experimental social psychology* (Vol. 1, pp. 149–190). New York: Academic Press.

Fiedler, F. E., & Garcia, J. E. (1987). *New approaches to leadership: Cognitive resources and organizational performance.* New York: John Wiley.

Follett, M. P. (1924). *Creative experience.* New York: Longmans.

Follett, M. P. (1949). The essentials of leadership. In L. Urwick (Ed.), *Freedom and coordination.* London: Management Publications Trust, pp. 47–60.

Fullan, M. (1992). *The new meaning of educational change.* New York: Columbia Teachers College Press.

Fullan, M. (2005). Leadership sustainability: Systems thinkers in action. Thousand Oaks, CA:Corwin Press.

Fullan, M. (2007). *The new meaning of educational change.* New York: Columbia Teachers College Press.

Fullan, M., Cuttress, C., & Kilcher, A. (2005, Fall). 8 forces for leaders of change. *Journal of Staff Development, 26*(4), 54–58, 64.

Getzels, J. W. (1958). Administration as a social process. In A. W. Halpin (Ed.). *Administrative theory in education* (pp. 150–165). New York: MacMillan.

Getzels, J. W., & Guba, E. G. (1957). Social behavior and the administration process. *School Review, 65*, 423–441.

Gibb, G. A. (1954). Leadership. In G. Lindzey (Ed.), *Handbook of social psychology* (Vol. II, pp. 877–920). Reading, MA: Addison-Wesley.

Greenleaf, R. K. (1977). *Servant leadership: A journey into the nature of legitimate power and greatness*. New York: Paulist Press.

Hall, G. E. & Hord, S. H. (2014). *Implementing change: Patterns, principles, and potholes* (4th ed.). New York, NY: Pearson.

Halpin, A. W. (1956). *The leadership behavior of school superintendents*. Columbus, Ohio: College of Education, Ohio State University.

Hambleton, R. K., & Gumpart, R. (1982). The validity of Hersey and Blanchard's theory of leadership effectiveness. *Group and Organization Studies, 7*, 225–242.

Hanson, E. M. (2003). *Educational administration and organization behavior* (5th ed.). Boston: Allyn and Bacon.

Hargreaves, A. & Shirley, D. L. (Eds.) (2009). *The fourth way: The inspiring future for education change* (4th ed.). Thousand Oaks, CA: Corwin.

Hegel, W. F. (1837). *The philosophy of history*. (Ontario J. Sibree, Tran., 2001). Kitchener Batoche Books.

Hersey, P., & Blanchard, K. H. (1969). Life cycle theory of leadership. *Training and Development, 23*(5), 26–34.

Homans, G. C. (1950). *Human groups*. New York: Harcourt, Brace, and World.

Homans, G. C. (1960). *Social behavior: Its elementary form*. New York: Harcourt, Brace, and World.

House, R. (1996). Path-goal theory of leadership: Lessons, legacy, and a reformulated theory. *The Leadership Quarterly, 7*(3), 323–352.

Hoy, W. K. & Miskel, C. G. (2008). *Educational administration: Theory, research and practice*. (8th ed.). New York: McGraw-Hill.

Irby B. J., Brown, G., Duffy, J. A., & Trautman, D. (2002). The synergistic leadership theory. *Journal of Educational Administration, 40*(4), 304–322.

Kimbrough, R. B., & Nunnery, M. Y. (1988). *Educational administration: An introduction* (3rd ed.). New York: MacMillan.

Kotter, J. P. (2012). *Leading change* (with a new Preface by the author). Cambridge, MA: Harvard Business Review Press.

Loomis, C. P. (1960). *Social systems: Essays on their persistence and change*. New York: Von Norstrand.

Lunenburg, F. C., & Ornstein, A. C. (1996). *Educational administration: Concepts and practices* (2nd ed.). Belmont, CA: Wadsworth.

Lupton, R. (2005). Social justice and school improvement: Improving the quality of schooling in the poorest neighbourhoods. *British Educational Research Journal, 31*(5), 589–604.

Lutz, F. W. (1982). Tightening up loose coupling in higher education. *Administrative Science Quarterly, 27*(4), 643–669.

Lutz, F. W., Watt, K. M, & Combs, J. P. (2006). Practical theory in educational administration. In J. Vornberg (Ed.), *Texas Public School Organization and Administration*: 2006 (10th ed.) (pp. 269–300). Dubuque, IA: Kendall Hunt.

McCall, M. W., Jr., & Lombardo, M. M. (1983). *Off the track: Why and how successful executives get derailed*. Greensboro, NC: Centre for Creative Leadership.

McGregor, D. M. (1960). *The human side of enterprise*. New York: McGraw-Hill.

Nelson, D. L., & Quick, J. C. (2000). *Organizational behavior: Foundations, realities & challenges* (3rd ed.). Cincinnati, OH: South-Western College Publishing.

Northouse, P. G. (2007). *Leadership theory and practice*. Thousand Oaks, CA: Sage Publications.

Northouse, P. G. (2013). *Leadership theory and practice* (6th ed.). Thousand Oaks, CA: Sage Publications.

Novak, M. (2000). *Defining social justice. First things.* Retrieved from http://www.firstthings.com/article/2000/12/defining-social-justice-29

Ouchi, W. (1981). *Theory Z: How American business can meet the Japanese challenge.* Reading, MA: Addison-Wesley.

Pascarella, S. V., & Lunenberg, F. C. (1988). A field test of Hersey & Blanchard's situational leadership theory in a school setting. *College Student Journal, 21,* 33–37.

Rifkin, J., & Howard, T. (1980). *Entropy: A new world view.* New York: The Viking Press.

Roethlisberger, F. J., & Dickson, W. J. (1939). *Management and the worker.* Cambridge, MA: Harvard University Press.

Rossi, J. (2007). What generation gap? *Training and Development, 61*(11), 10–11.

Senge, P. M. (1990). *The fifth discipline: The art and practice of the learning organization.* New York: Doubleday Currency.

Sessa, V., Kabacoff, R., Deal, J., & Brown, H. (2007). Research tools for the psychologist manager: Generational differences in leader values and leadership behaviors. *Psychologist-Manager Journal, 10*(1), 47–74.

Smith, M. K. (2001). Peter Senge and the learning organization. *The encyclopedia of informal education.* [www.infed.org/thinkers/senge.htm. Last update: August 23, 2007]

Stogdill, R. M. (1948). Personal factors associated with leadership: Survey of literature. *Journal of Psychology, 25,* 35–71.

Taylor, F. W. (1947). *Scientific management: The principles of scientific management.* New York: Harper and Row.

Turner, J. (1974). *The structure of sociological theory.* Homewood, IL: Dorsey Press.

Urwick, L. F. (1929). *The meaning of rationalisation.* London: Nisbet & Co.

Watt, K. M., & Pankake, A. (2010). The practical application of theory for educational leaders. In James A. Vornberg (Ed.), *Texas Public School Organization and Administration* (pp. 273–298). Dubuque, IA: Kendall Hunt.

Weber, M. (1964). *The theory of social and economic organization.* New York: Free Press.

Weick, K. (1983). Administering education in loosely coupled schools. *Phi Delta Kappan, 63* (10), 673–676.

Yukl, G. (2002). *Leadership in organizations.* Delhi, India: Pearson Education.

Zenger, J., Ulrich, D., & Smallwood, N. (2000). The new leadership development. *Training & Development, 54,* 22–28.

PART II

THE PRINCIPAL

THE PRINCIPAL

Campus Leadership

Ray Thompson ◆ *Susan Nix*

Leaders become great, not because of their power, but because of their ability to empower others.

—John Maxwell

Pick up a newspaper, listen to broadcast news, read a book on educational leadership, and each source will make a case for the difficulty of becoming a school leader for multiple reasons, including the scope of the position and the necessary skills needed for success. Why then, would anyone want to earn a graduate degree and certification to become a school principal? John Maxwell's (2011) quote is especially important because Texas' school administrators are expected to manage a campus, but more critically, they are viewed as instructional leaders, which entails empowering teachers and staff to accomplish data-based goals for the teaching and learning processes.

The purpose of this chapter is to provide aspiring administrators insights into the evolution of the principalship and the current status and expectations of school administrators in Texas, inspiring and encouraging the journey. Texas Statutory law is emphasized because it drives actions and responsibilities from the school district and campus perspectives. Particular attention is given to upcoming changes in teacher and principal appraisal processes and responsibilities.

◆ HOW DID WE GET HERE?

Historically, "the word principal appeared in Horace Mann's report to the Massachusetts School Board in 1842" (Matthews & Crow, 2003, p. 18). The word was used in the teaching ranks to describe a teacher with small administrative duties, similar to those responsibilities of a headmaster. "The term Principal Teacher was a common designation for the controlling head of the school in the early report of school boards, indication that teaching was the chief duty" (Pierce, 1935, p. 11). Over time as the population in American cities grew and as student enrollment in urban schools increased, the term principal emerged to describe an individual, usually a teacher, with administrative responsibilities. The early understanding of school leadership envisioned the principal primarily as an authoritative, efficient manager of the building, class schedules, student discipline, and financial resources. Over time, the areas of management and supervision served to establish the role of the principal as a separate and distinct position (Matthews & Crow, 2003). By the mid-1970s, the principal's role shifted to include supervising teacher quality and student learning. This shift was then followed by a push for principals to differentiate among teachers based on their developmental level. An effective principal adapted his or her leadership practices for each teacher's needs and monitored the teacher's progress toward certain goals or standards.

The trend of shared school leadership in the last two decades projected a new focus on the principal's role in leading instruction on the campus. With this new focus, an effective principal not only sets high expectations and articulates a strong vision but also models good instruction, observes and coaches teachers, and provides them with opportunities to reflect on and improve their practices. The most recent conceptualization of school leadership views an effective principal as one who creates a professional learning community by sharing authority and distributing leadership roles to teachers whose skills and capacities match with the task at hand (Walker, 2002).

In recent decades, the Texas Legislature has been at the forefront of educational reform to impact the school principal. In 1984, the Texas Legislature passed House Bill 72 (HB72), enacting numerous far-reaching public education reforms. Included in HB72 was a pay raise for teachers, a public school finance overhaul to provide money to property-poor school districts, and accountability measures designed to improve the academic achievement of students. Sweeping education reforms included a 22:1 student-teacher cap on enrollment in kindergarten through fourth grade and a "no pass-no play" rule that prohibited students from participating in extracurricular activities in the event of failing academic performance. These educational laws either directly or indirectly impacted the work of the principal (Texas Education Agency, 2004).

The Texas Education Agency enacted major accountability decisions, which has impacted the education reform effort, In 1985, the legislature passed the Texas Educational Assessment of Minimum Skills; in 1990, the Texas Assessment of Academic Skills; in 2001, the Texas Assessment of Knowledge and Skills; and in 2014, the State of Texas Assessment of Academic Readiness.

In 1995, the Texas Education System was reformed by the enactment of Senate Bill 1 (SB1). This created a massive effort to rewrite the Texas Education Code. SB1 is of particular interest to the campus principal for it granted teachers the authority to remove disruptive students from class as well as the power of the teacher to veto a disruptive student's return to class. Furthermore, student suspension time was decreased under the no-pass/no-play rule from 6 weeks to 3 weeks. These are examples of the intent of SB1 to eliminate some state-mandated rules and give back more authority to the local school district. Other elements of SB1 included granting the authority to the State Board of Education for open-enrollment charter schools. Also, the appointment of the Commissioner of Education would rest with the governor of the state (Texas Education Agency, 2004).

In 1999, the Texas Legislature enacted House Bill 4, which established the Student Success Initiative. This measure required students to pass state tests at certain grade levels in order to be promoted to the next grade. The impact of education reform efforts has propelled the campus principal into the forefront of education leadership as an instructional leader (Texas Education Agency, 2004).

Due to these legislative enactments, the campus principal affects the local campus through policy interpretation, resource allocation, and community relations. The principal manages the pragmatic day-to-day school activities, from the classroom to the gym, and juggle competing priorities to provide high-quality educational services to students. In the face of a myriad of duties and expectations, campus leadership is the second most influential school-level factor on student achievement, after teaching quality (Leithwood, Louis, Anderson, & Wahlstrom, 2004; Waters, Marzano, & McNulty, 2003). The traditional views of the principal as the authoritative school manager who focuses on the efficient management of instruction have been extended to include the principal as a learning leader who shares decision making with teachers and actively facilitates professional communities of reflective practitioners (Darling-Hammond, LaPointe, Meyerson, & Terry Orr, 2007; Davis, Kearney, Sanders, Thomas, & Leon, 2011; Lambert, 2002; The Wallace Foundation, 2008). According to DiPaola and Hoy (2008), supervision, professional development of teachers and teacher evaluation are the responsibilities of the principal. Implied, is that principals help teachers so that teachers, in turn, will improve student's learning through instructional best practices. The role of the principal in contemporary America has evolved to instructional or learning leadership. Above and beyond the practice of supervising and evaluation new and experienced teaching, was that of improving students learning, which according to DiPaola and Hoy (2008), is the "ultimate test of the effectiveness of teachers, principals, and schools" (p. 1). Cuban (1998) noted that the principal had a political role as a communicator with the central office staff.

◆ THE TEXAS PRINCIPAL

Principal Expectation as Defined by the Texas Education Code

In 1995, the 74th Texas Legislature enacted TEC 11:202. This legislation details the expectations of the principal. In the state of Texas, the principal shall

1. except as provided by Subsection (d), approve all teacher and staff appointments for that principal's campus from a pool of applicants selected by the district or of applicants who meet the hiring requirements established by the district, based on criteria developed by the principal after informal consultation with the faculty;
2. set specific education objectives for the principal's campus, through the planning process under Section 11.253;
3. develop budgets for the principal's campus;
4. assume the administrative responsibility and instructional leadership, under the supervision of the superintendent, for discipline at the campus;
5. assign, evaluate, and promote personnel assigned to the campus;
6. recommend to the superintendent the termination or suspension of an employee assigned to the campus or the nonrenewal of the term contract of an employee assigned to the campus; and
7. perform other duties assigned by the superintendent pursuant to the policy of the board of trustees (Texas Education Code 11:202, 1995).

The role of campus planning and the site-based decision-making is described in the Texas Education Code 11.253. The principal is charged to direct the planning and site decision-making that supports improved student performance at each campus. The campus-level committee and the principal will review, develop, and revise the campus improvement plan. This plan shall address improving student performance for all student populations.

Principal Expectation as Defined by the Texas Administrative Code

The Texas Administrative Code (TAC) stated the leadership compliance expectation of a campus principal. Those leadership standards include the following: "instructional leadership; administration, supervision, and communication skills; curriculum and instruction management; performance evaluation; organization; and fiscal management" (Texas Administrative Code Title 19, Part 7, Chapter 241: Rule 241.1, 2009; Texas Education Code. 21/046, 1995).

The leadership standards in the TAC (2009) are reflected in the principal certificate standards (TAC, 2009), as adopted by the State Board for Educator Certification in 1999 and are the basis for the standard Principal Certificate, which consists of seven learner-centered standards: Values and Ethics of Leadership, Leadership and Campus Culture, Human Resources Leadership and Management, Communications and Community Relations, Organizational Leadership and Management, Curriculum Planning and Development, and Instructional Leadership and Management. (Texas Administrative Code, Title 19, Part 7, Chapter 241: Rule 241.1, 2009; Texas Education Code §21.3541, 2014). These leadership standards serve as the foundation for the individual assessment, professional growth planning, and continuing professional education activities required by §241.30 of this title for Educator preparation programs."The knowledge and skills identified in this section must be used by an educator preparation program in the development of curricula and coursework and by the State Board for Educator Certification" (Texas Administrative Code, 2009).

Principal Expectations as Defined by the Texas State Board of Education

Aspiring principal candidates must show mastery on the Texas Examinations of Educator Standards (TExES) Principal Exam. Principal candidates will be examined over three domains: Domain I: School-Community Leadership; Domain II: Instructional Leadership, and Domain III The Administrative Leadership domain I contains three competencies over which a candidate will be examined (State Board for Educator Certification/Texas Education Agency, 2010).

Domain I: School-Community

Competence 001 states that the principal must have an understanding of the campus culture and possess the skill to shape the campus culture by implementing a vision of learning that supported by the school community.

The focus of Competency 002 is the principal's communication and collaboration with the members of the school community. The principal knows how to communicate and collaborate with all members of the school community. The principal is tasked with enjoining community diverse needs in the effort to promote student success.

Competency 003 centers on integrity and, fairness in an ethical and legal. The principal knows how to act with integrity, fairness and in an ethical and legal manner.

Domain II: Instructional Leadership

The competences comprising Domain II focus on the abilities of the principal to improve student performance by demonstrating the ability to facilitate planning, promote an effective instructional program, and implement a staff evaluation and development system. Four competences are delineated as the map to accomplish these outcomes.

Competency 004 taps into the knowledge of the principal for the understanding and implementation of curricula and strategic plans that enhance teaching and learning. Alignment of curriculum instruction, resources and assessment are essential, as well as the skill to use varied assessments to measure student performance.

The organization and communication skills of the principal are necessary to achieve the aspirations of Competency 005, which calls upon the principal to develop and implement an instructional program that seeks the support of the staff with the end result of increased student learning.

Competency 006 addresses the ability of the principal to select a staff evaluation model and implement it in a manner that results in improved performance of all educators. The principal is challenged to apply the legal expectations for personnel management in the selection and supervision of staff.

Decision making and problem solving are central to Competency 007. The organization abilities of the principal are evident in the development of an effective learning environment.

Domain III: Administrative Leadership

Administrative Leadership centers on campus administration for the purpose of ensuring for students and stakeholders a safe, learning environment. There are two competencies in which the aspiring candidate must demonstrate mastery. Competency 008 tasks the principal with leadership and management skills in the areas of financial management, personnel, and technology use.

Competency 009 calls upon the principal to demonstrate leadership and management in administration of the campus physical plant and support systems. The objective of competency 009 is to ensure a safe and effective learning environment.

In the development of the aforementioned competencies, descriptive statements were used to illustrate the knowledge and skills expected of the principal. Each competency contains a number of descriptive statements of knowledge and skills for which the principal candidates are expected to demonstrate mastery on the TExES Principal Exam (State Board for Educator Certification/Texas Education Agency, 2010).

◆ THE TEXAS PRINCIPAL OF TODAY

Leadership Skills

Institutions of higher education are tasked with preparing the next generations of aspiring administrators. In order for principals to gain leadership skills, first the state has to provide the educational structure to facilitate this process. Title 19 of the TAC addresses education (http://texreg.sos.state.tx.us/public/readtac$ext.viewtac). The Higher Education Coordinating Board is Part I of Title 19 and provides the rules upon which public institutions of higher education are governed. Educational Leadership programs in Texas are required to prepare aspiring principals according to Title 19, Part 7, Chapter 228 of the Texas Administrative

Code (http://texreg.sos.state.tx.us/public/readtac$ext.ViewTAC?tac view=4&ti=19&pt=7&ch =228&rl=Y).

Standards for the principal certificate are specified in Title 19, Part 7, Chapter 241, Rule §241.15 (Texas Administrative Code, 2009) and include seven learner-centered statements. Those statements are the basis for the Texas State Board of Education principal certification and include nine competencies (or skills statements) in three domains with additional detailed sub-statements as mentioned previously. Each competency starts with the phrase, "The principal knows how to . . . " The three domains include those phrases and are categorized as (1) Communication and Community Leadership; (2) Instructional Leadership and (3) Administrative Leadership. Graduate school candidates for educational leadership, upon completion of their program of study, must demonstrate their knowledge and skills on the state assessment to receive the principal certificate allowing them to practice as school administrators in Texas.

Those prescribed skills are comprehensive and demanding of a certain expertise and they are categorized expediently into three domains. The first domain, Communication and Community Leadership, embraces the notion of shaping a campus culture supported by the school community and it requires skillful communication skills to respond to the diverse needs of the campus with ethics and integrity, and within three competencies. The second domain, Instructional Leadership, features four competencies that articulate the intricacies of teaching and learning, including professional development and teacher appraisal, and problem-solving skills, all to ensure an effective learning environment. The third domain, Administrative Leadership, addresses the additional aspects of safety, infrastructure, finances, and technology to again ensure an effective learning environment. The domain structure organizes the leadership skills into a manageable package for the sake of assessment for certification. The principal who finds him or herself lacking in any of these areas, unless improvement can be made, will not be a school administrator for long.

Academic Responsibilities

As has been stated previously, the primary responsibility of the principal is instructional leadership, which encompasses academics. At first glance of Table 9.1, the Waters and Cameron Table of Leadership Responsibilities (2007), two items (5 and 7) seem most directly related to the academic responsibilities of the school principal because they deal directly with curriculum, instruction and assessment, which is the business of schools. Item five addresses professional involvement with curriculum, instruction, and assessment, in particular, the design and implementation of teacher practices.

Curriculum addresses what is taught. Instruction addresses how the curriculum is taught and assessment addresses the success of the learners as a result of the effectiveness of the curriculum and instruction. According to item seven, the principal is responsible for knowing curriculum, instruction, and assessment practices in order to provide guidance for teachers. Both of these responsibilities clearly identify the instructional knowledge base necessary to guide teachers toward the vision of a school that of the education of young people. As a result of monitoring and evaluating the educational practices of teachers, principals are aware of the reality of both short- and long-term accomplishments for them and their students. Texas provides the comprehensive curriculum in the form of the Texas Essential Knowledge and Skills (TEKS) and can be found on the Texas Education Agency Website at: http://tea.texas.gov/ index2.aspx?id=6148. Teachers are required to teach the curriculum for which each of them is certified by the state of Texas and hired to teach by a school district.

TABLE 9.1
Waters and Cameron Leadership Responsibilities

Leadership Responsibilities	*(Extent to which the principal. . .)*
1. Culture	fosters shared beliefs and a sense of community and cooperation
2. Order	establishes a set of standard operating procedures and routines
3. Discipline	protects teachers from issues and influences that detract from teaching time or focus
4. Resources	provides teachers with necessary materials and professional development
5. Involvement in curriculum, instruction, and assessment	Is directly involved in the design and implementation of Curriculum, Instruction, & Assessment
6. Focus	Establishes clear coals and keeps those goals in the forefront of the school's attention
7. Knowledge of curriculum, instruction, and assessment	Is knowledgeable about current Curriculum, Instruction and Assessment practices
8. Visibility	Has quality contact and interactions with teachers and students
9. Contingent rewards	Recognizes and rewards individual accomplishments
10. Communication	Establishes strong lines of communication with teachers and among students
11. Outreach	Is an advocate and spokesperson for the school to all stakeholders
12. Input	Involves teachers in the design & implementation of important decisions and policies
13. Affirmation	Recognizes and celebrates school accomplishments and acknowledges failures
14. Relationship	Demonstrates an awareness of the personal aspects of teachers & staff
15. Change agent	Is willing to and actively challenges the status quo
16. Optimize	Inspires and leads new and challenging innovations
17. Ideals/beliefs	Communicates and operates from strong ideas/beliefs about schooling
18. Monitors/evaluates	Monitors the effectiveness of school practices & their impact on student learning
19. Flexibility	Adapts his/her leadership behavior to the needs of the current situation & is comfortable with dissent
20. Situational awareness	Is aware of the details & undercurrents in the running of the school and uses this information to address current & potential problems
21. Intellectual stimulation	Ensures faculty & staff are aware of the most current theories/practices & makes the discussion of these a regular aspect of the school's culture

Academic responsibilities also include assuring necessary resources for teachers to enhance the learning environment. Couple that with authentic and appropriate professional development or intellectual stimulation, as it is listed on this table, and the principal has an awareness of the potential for a positive impact on student learning as a direct result of focused and appropriate professional development. As a part of that process, the principal has to be open to new and challenging innovations that will further develop teachers and students enabling them to reach their potential in the teaching and learning process of education. Teacher appraisal plays a critical role in the improvement and growth of professional skills, which impacts student learning. Principals necessarily receive training that facilitates this teacher growth and the expected student success.

Many of the other responsibilities listed on this table facilitate the environment that encourages academic success as the primary focus of public schools in Texas. Additionally, the Texas Principal Standards from the TAC (Chapter 149) includes these five responsibilities:

1. Instructional Leadership—to ensure every student receives high quality instruction
2. Human Capital—to ensure there are high quality teachers and staff in every classroom throughout the school
3. Executive Leadership—to model personal responsibility and relentless focus on improving student outcomes
4. School Culture—to establish and implement a shared vision and culture of high expectations for all staff and students
5. Strategic Operations—to implement systems that align with the school's vision and mission and improve the quality of instruction.

Clearly, the Texas Principal Standards articulate the expectation of leadership responsibilities that will ensure teacher and student success.

Extracurricular Activities

The campus principal is central to the organization and the implementation of extracurricular activities. In Texas, schools participate in the University Interscholastic League (UIL), which is an organization for athletic, musical, and academic contests for students in public and private schools. The UIL was originally conceived in 1904 by Dr. S. E. Mezes, president of The University of Texas. From the desire to be of service to the state of Texas, William Sutton, dean of the school of education described the "Wisconsin Plan in 1909 to the University of Texas Board of Regents. Funds were allocated for the implementation of the UT Extension Bureau. From these beginnings, the UIL emerged into an interschool organization for the purpose of assisting schools in competitive endeavors (http://www.uiltexas.org/history).

While the school superintendent has specified responsibilities as stated in the 105th Edition of the Constitution and Contest Rules, the role of the campus principal assumes is one of compliance and administration of the extra-curricular activities. With the oversight of the superintendent, the principal implements the contest and provides the management of all UIL contests on his/her campus, particularly enforcing the regulations and rules of student eligibility. Assuming these duties includes submission of documents for student's grades, attendance, and accounting for UIL activity funds. Consequently, the principal causes all forms and paperwork to be properly completed for the campus.

Effective administration of the UIL programs requires a thorough understanding by the principal of school district policies on extra-curricular activities, e.g., transportation and fundraising. Imperatively, the principal stays abreast of all local and legal school district policies, the Constitution and Contest Rules, and applicable rules of the Texas Administrative Code.

Additionally, the principal assists with the annual orientation of UIL directors, sponsors, advisers, and coaches regarding League rules, expectations regarding appropriate conduct during UIL contests, goals, and purposes and must report any violation of the Constitution and Contest Rules to the superintendent. The campus responsibilities assumed by the principal includes assisting with completion of Professional Acknowledgement Form for all athletic coaches and sponsors on a campus, providing input on event schedules, avoiding scheduling extracurricular activities or public performances the day or the evening before the administration of the State of Texas Assessments, and submitting all recommendations of employment of coaches, directors, and sponsors to the school superintendent.

Importantly, the campus principal assumes his/her responsibilities for UIL and other extracurricular events seriously. To do so ensures that students experience healthy educational experiences, good sportsmanship, and cooperation throughout competition. Failure to do so may prevent a student from the opportunity of participation, suspension of a campus, or assessment of some other penalty. The UIL provides a number of guidelines that are essential to the administration of extracurricular activities. These include, but are not limited to, safety training, sport season date, safety training for participants, practice limits, and guidelines for booster organizations (Sorenson, 2014).

The University Interscholastic League (UIL) provides a number of informational materials to assist the campus principal. These include event videotapes, films on athletic tournament and games rules, clinics, and regional conferences, UIL contests materials, and a plethora of library resources. A complete listing of rules for UIL activities, standards of eligibility, and administrator responsibilities are contained in the Constitution and Contest Rules. Participating schools and students are must comply with these rules (http://www.uiltexas.org/about). Notably, UIL is not the only extracurricular program over which principals preside but it is statewide, making it worthy of extensive explanation.

Best Practices

Leadership really matters. According to Shelton (2011), principal leadership is second in importance only to classroom teaching. Mendels reached the conclusion that "a major reason for the attention being paid to principals is the emergence of research that has found an empirical link between school leadership and student achievement" (2012, p. 54). Educational leadership is at the forefront of educational reform as evidence that "23 states of the United States enacted 43 laws regarding leadership in the 2010 legislative session" (Mendels, 2012, p. 58).

Why are principals central to campus education and student learning? Shelton (2011) suggests the following reasons. Good principals attract quality teachers, ensure that excellent teaching and learning occurs, share a compelling vision, shares authority, and accepts the responsibility for student learning. Mendels (2012) advances the notion that knowing what makes good leaders is different from putting into action what one knows. At the heart of educational leadership is collaboration. The campus principal working collaboratively with classroom teachers is essential to unleashing the potential of the two. While teachers are the deliverers of instruction, the principal is the instructional leader. The effective principal guides and facilitates teachers to better instruction and student learning.

In 2013, The Wallace Foundation solicited responses from teachers regarding the benefits of good principal leadership. The overriding research question was, "What do effective principals do?" Five best practices of the principal emerged from their research. These are: "(1) shaping a vision of academic success for all students, (2) creating a climate hospitable to education, (3) cultivating leadership in others, (4) improving instruction, and (5) managing people, data and process to foster school improvement" (The Wallace Foundation, 2013, p. 4). It was concluded that the campus principal, who masters these practices, provides students a quality education environment to learn, achieve, and succeed. Therefore, effective school leadership does rank as a top priority for school improvement.

Accordingly, Sergiovanni and Green (2015) agree that leadership from the campus principal significantly influences the quality of a student's education. Although a practitioner, the principal utilizes theories of practice to inform his/her practices and produce quality learning. In order to bring these practices to realization, the principal masters knowledge in the "areas of change, decision making, communication, and conflict management" (Sergiovanni & Green, 2015, p. 89). Research by Brown (2012) discovered seven practices that cultivate effective school. These practices are "(1) leadership; (2) professional development; (3) student intervention; (4) collaboration; (5) curriculum alignment; (6) data analysis; and (7) organizational structure" (Sergiovanni & Green, 2015, p. 210). Positive changes in teachers and students are realized when these practices are foundational.

In like manner, Good (2008) subscribes to the view that the personal leadership of the campus principal results in increased student performance. Improved principal leadership results from compelling best practices for improving one's personal leadership skills. These best practices include regular communication with one's supervisor about instruction leadership capacity, weekly visiting the classroom, demonstrating a working knowledge of educational trends and best practices, and regularly implementing a best practice. Additionally, Good (2008) suggests best practices is evidenced by participating with one's teachers in meetings, developing a facilitation program for administrators and faculty, and engaging with teacher professional development training. Importantly, Good notes that a principal should seek and establish a mentor relationship with one who exposes effective leadership. The principal models a commitment to leadership goals and aspirations (Good, 2008).

Best practices inherently imply the application of a value-added teacher appraisal system as one of the critical administrative skills used to improve teachers and their practices. Currently, across the nation, teacher appraisals have been critiqued and found lacking (Doyle & Han, 2012; Glazerman, et al., 2011; Goe, Holdheide, & Miller, 2011; Osborne, 2012; Springer, et al., 2007) since most teachers receive excellent evaluations, yet the education system is not perceived as graduating more or better students. Therefore, similar to other states, the Texas Legislature began the process of changing the teacher evaluation system, previously named Professional Development and Appraisal System (PDAS) (TASB, 2015). The new system, called Teacher Evaluation and Support System (T-TESS) is currently being piloted across the state with modifications as a result of that practical application and will be implemented in 2017 (TEA, 2014). Meanwhile, appraisal trainers are being taught so the massive undertaking of certifying all school administrators currently certified in the PDAS will be able to continue that critical role as a teacher appraiser. Only time will tell if the T-TESS is more effective than the PDAS in teacher improvement leading to student success. Implementation of best practices has the potential for a positive effect on teachers with an accompanying increase in student achievement.

◆ THE TEXAS PRINCIPAL IN THE FUTURE

This decade in public education is one filled with angst and excitement; angst because of the increased scrutiny and comparison of schools across the nation and globally; and excitement because change is occurring on an almost daily basis as education leaders apply research-based methods to improve the teaching and learning experience.

Much research is being conducted to inform our knowledge of schools and, in particular, school leadership. Fullan (2013) identified eight "policy drivers" (p. vii) intended to facilitate "whole-system reform" (p. vii), four of which are deemed right and the other four are considered wrong. Bambrick-Santoyo (2012) asserts that research identifies effective schools, but not leadership actions that accomplished those successes. Marshall (2009) identifies instruction as the "single-most important factor in student achievement (as quoted by Bambrick-Santoyo, 2012, p. 4). The Mid-continent Research for Education and Learning (Waters & Cameron, 2007) considered "the effects of classroom, school and leadership practices on student achievement" (p. 1). Statistically significant effects were found in a group of quantitative studies conducted by multiple researchers (Marzano, 1998; Marzano, Gaddy, & Dean, 2000). As a result, a meta-analysis was conducted of 69 studies with a focus on the impact of school-level leadership on student achievement (Waters, Marzano, & McNulty, 2003). The strength of a meta-analysis is its focus on relationships between dependent and independent variables. The Waters et al. (2003) study resulted in three critical findings. A statistically significant finding was the relationship between student achievement and school-level leadership. The meta-analysis specifically identified 21 leadership responsibilities "with statistically significant correlations to student achievement and 66 practices or behaviors for fulfilling these responsibilities" (Waters & Cameron, 2007, p. 3). In higher education, professors and program directors have been referring to school principals as instructional leaders for years. The Waters and Cameron (2007) meta-analysis validated the use of that term, and as a result, has a "well-defined set of research-based leadership responsibilities and associated practices correlated with student achievement" (p. 3). See *Leadership Responsibilities* (Table 9.1) from Waters and Cameron (2007).

Principal Appraisal

The state of Texas recognizes the importance of the school principal's role in the success of students and teachers. The 82nd Regular Legislative Session resulted in a statute that "established school leadership standards" (TEA, 2013). Those five standards were completed in 2013 and are as follows: (1) Instructional Leadership; (2) Human Capital; (3) Executive Leadership; (4) School Culture; and (5) Strategic Operations. A committee made of education professionals spanning the state and beyond developed the most recent principal evaluation system and called it the Texas Principal Evaluation and Support System, or T-PESS, which is expected to be piloted for two years, from 2014 to 2016 and then implemented in 2017.

The annual principal evaluation process is referred to as a Systematic Delivery Model (TEA, 2015) and includes seven steps: orientation, self-assessment goal setting, pre-evaluation conference, mid-year evaluation meeting, consolidated performance assessment, end-of-year performance discussion, and final evaluation goal setting. The five Texas principal standards can be implemented with five expected professional outcomes: (1) common vocabulary associated with professional practice; (2) identification of a pathway for professional improvement; (3) reduction of instructional variability; (4) increase in instructional quality; and (5) student achievement. This new model of principal evaluation parallels the also newly developed teacher appraisal system. Both appraisal systems require goal setting and reflection to monitor forward momentum on the goal setting component. They also involve more extensive interaction with the most immediate supervisor. For the teacher, this means he or she will meet with the principal to discuss and set goals at the classroom level. Simultaneously, the principal will be conferencing to set professional goals for the campus with the district superintendent.

As a result of the research resulting in the Texas Principal Evaluation and Support System (T-PESS), 21 Leadership Responsibilities were identified by Waters and Cameron (2007). Those leadership responsibilities, shown in Table 9.1, came about as a result of the meta-analysis of "school-level leadership and its effects on student achievement" (Waters & Cameron, 2007, p. 2) and correlated with statistical significance to student achievement, including "66 practices or behaviors for fulfilling those responsibilities" (Waters & Cameron, 2007, p. 3). This body of work clearly substantiates the use of the identifier of "instructional leadership" for the responsibility of the school principal. Table 9.2 illustrates the clear link between the National Standards from Interstate School Leaders Licensure Consortium (2015) and the Texas principal standards, further validating the frameworks of each.

TABLE 9.2
Comparison of Standards With T-PESS

ISLLC (2015) National Standards NEW	Texas Principal Standards (TAC Chapter 149) Commissioners Rules AND T-PESS	Texas State Board for Educator Certification (TAC Chapter 241)	TExES Competencies for Principal Certification
1. . . .Shared vision. . .	4. School culture	1. Values/ethics 2. Leadership & campus culture	001: Campus culture 003: Integrity/ethics/legal 007: Organizational decision-making/problem-solving
2. . . .Support instruction & assessment	1. Instructional leadership	5. Organizational leadership & management 6. Curriculum planning/development 7. Instructional leadership/management	004: Design/implementation of curriculum/strategic plans 005: Advocate/nurture/sustain instructional program 006: Implement staff evaluation/development system

3. . . .Professional skills & practices	2. Human capital	3. Human resources management	006: Implement staff evaluation/development system
4. . . .Caring & inclusive community	4. School culture	2. Leadership & campus culture	005: Advocate/nurture/ sustain instructional program
5. . . .Coordinate resources, time, structures & roles	3. Executive leadership 5. Strategic operations	3. Human resources management 6. Curriculum planning & development 7. Instructional leadership/ management	004: Design/ implementation of curriculum/strategic plans 005: Advocate/nurture/ sustain instructional program 006: Implement staff evaluation/development system 007: Organizational decision-making/ problem-solving 008: Effective leadership and management 009: Principles of leadership and management to physical plant and support systems
6. . . .Engage families & outside community	4. School culture	2. Leadership & campus culture 4. Communications & community relationships	002: Communicate/ collaborate with community
7. . . .Administer & manage operations	3. Executive leadership 5. Strategic operations	5. Organizational leadership & management	007: Organizational decision-making/ problem-solving 008: Effective leadership and management (budget, etc.) 009: Principles of leadership and management to physical plant and support systems

The Texas Principal in 2017

The position of school principal requires an increased understanding of the laws impacting schools. Fortunately, Texas has a system for disseminating those laws originating from the federal government and state into policy and procedures. And, because local control dominates, schools interpret the laws and publish policy manuals for ease of use by education stakeholders. Critical to policy manual use is the understanding that laws take time to make their journey from the Texas Legislature to the school district. This means that district administrators must remain aware of the recent past, present, and future of law as it impacts schools in Texas.

Typically, school leaders first become knowledgeable about school law when taking classes for the required graduate degree and certification. However, the application of those laws is more often required once in the administrative position. Therefore, this means continued readings and briefings from lawyers specializing in school law, to enhance the administrators' success in this aspect of the leadership position. Additionally, the TAC (http://texreg.sos .state.tx.us/public/readtac$ext.viewtac) can be accessed online easily and provides important information for all school entities in Texas. If the standards for the principal changed, this is the online location for finding those new standards.

Currently, multiple important bills are in process to become part of administrative practice. One of the most important ones is Senate Bill 1383, codified as Texas Education Code (TEC) Section 21.3541, and enacted by the Texas legislature in 2011 which directed the Texas Commissioner of Education to create a principal appraisal system (Principal Appraisal Report, 2014). This report and more information including the Texas Principal Evaluation and Support System (T-PESS) can be found on the Texas Education Agency page: (http://tea.texas.gov/ Texas_Educators/Educator_Evaluation_and_Support_System/Texas_Principal_Evaluation_ and_Support_System/. According to this online information, the T-PESS has been piloted and will continue into the 2015–2016 school year with an expected implementation in the 2016–2017 school year. Meanwhile, the TEA will continue receiving input about the T-PESS and use that information to refine the process before the final rollout. An FAQ document is available online at the aforementioned Website. Additionally, the Region 13 Education Service Center at http://www4.esc13.net/pdas/ contains the same documents and information about the principal evaluation system. Important to the principal is the understanding that laws take time to become policy at the local level; therefore, it is imperative that all school administrators have an understanding of what has been passed by the state legislature and what is in the process of being codified and made into policy for school boards and districts.

As has been identified previously in this chapter, law is a dynamic process, changing the landscape for educators. Additional multiple bills are set to impact school districts and administrators as a result of decisions made in the 84th Texas legislature session. Three tables identify the particular categories in alphabetical order and across three tables as provided by the Texas Association of School Administrators (TASA, 2015). Each subcategory shows the individual bill, either from the Texas House or Senate. Access to the individual bills is easily reached online at http://billtracker.tasanet.org/. When entering the bill type and number, more detailed information is provided online, including the list of actions that led to the final passage of the bill. At any given time, the school district administrators need to follow actions by the Texas legislature sessions to remain aware of impacts on district policy and students, ultimately (Tables 9.3–9.5).

TABLE 9.3
84th Legislative Session: Education-Related Bills Passed Related to Accountability, Assessment, Certification, and Curriculum

Accountability	Assessment	Certification	Curriculum
Accountability System Redesign (HB 2804)	Individual Graduation Committees (SB 149)	Superintendent Certificate Waiver (SB 168)	TEKS Review (SB 313)
Campus-District A-F Ratings (HB 2804)	College Prep Test Endorsement (HB 2349)	Mental Health Training Requirement (SB 674)	Dual Credit (HB 2812; HB 505; SB 1004; HB 18)
Campus Turnaround (HB 1842)	CLEP Testing (SB 453)	Educator Criminal History (HB 1783)	Instruction in HS, College & Career Prep (HB 18)
Innovation Zones (HB 1842)	EOC Testing Exemptions (HB 1613)	Bilingual Certification (HB 218)	Educator Input into IEP (SB 1259)
Dropout Rates (HB 1867)	TSI Assessment Exemption (SB 1776)	CTE Certification (HB 2205)	Mental Health Professions Information (HB 1430)
		Junior ROTC Teaching Certificate (SB 1309)	PE Curriculum for Students with Disabilities (HB 440)

TABLE 9.4
84th Legislative Session: Education-Related Bills Passed Related to Safety, Early Education, Paperwork Reporting, and School District Operations

Discipline/Safety	Early Education Initiatives	Paperwork Reporting	School District Operations
Campus Behavior Coordinator (SB 107)	High-Quality Pre-K (HB 4)	Duplicate Paperwork (HB 1706)	Local Breakfast Programs (HB 1305)
School Crime Reporting (HB 1783)	Math Achievement Academies (K-3) (SB 934)	Electronic Reports to Parents (HB 1993)	Minutes of Instruction/ School Calendar (HB 2610)
School Officer Training (HB 2684)	Literacy Achievement Academies (K-3) (SB 925)	Notice to Foster Parents (HB 1804)	Accommodations for Breastfeeding Employees (HB 786)

School Marshal Notification (SB 996)	Reading Excellence Teams (Grade 3) (SB 935)	Information Printed on HS Diplomas (HB 181)	School/Municipal Facility Agreements (SB 810)
Video Cameras in Special Ed Classrooms (SB 507)	Reading-to-Learn Academies (Grades 4–5) (SB 972)		Bodily Injury Insurance (HB 744)

TABLE 9.5

84th Legislative Session: Education-Related Bills Passed Related to Funding, Staff Development, Student Health, and Truancy

School Funding	*Staff Development*	*Student Health/ Well-Being*	*Truancy*
Public Education Budget (HB 1)	Counseling Academies (HB 18)	EpiPens (SB 66)	(HB 2398) decriminalizes truancy . . .
Flexible School Day ADA (HB 2660)	CPE for Defibrillator Training (HB 382)	Homeless Students (HB 1559), (SB 1494)	
Instructional Materials Allotment (SB 313)	Mental Health First Aid Training (HB 133)	Meal Grace Period (HB 3562)	
Off-Campus Instruction Programs/ ADA (HB 2812)	Youth Suicide Prevention Training (HB 2186)	Sunscreen (SB 265)	
Counseling Academies (HB 18)		Vapor Products on School Property (SB 97)	
Mental Health First Aid Training (SB 133)			

The breadth of the bills passing the 84th Texas Legislature (http://www.tasanet.org/cms/lib07/TX01923126/Centricity/Domain/329/84th_session_bills.pdf) spans a plethora of impacts from accountability and assessment to student health and truancy. Some of the laws will impact daily district policy. For example, the most obvious is School Funding, which includes Guaranteed Yield increases for both 2016 and 2017 and $40.6 million for math and reading academies. This is just two examples of impacts of funding changes in a list of many from House Bill 1.

It would not be reasonable to address each item that passed the 84th Legislature for schools in one book chapter. What is critical, is that any school administrator keeps up with expected changes and knows where to find them online to learn about them and to share them with all school stakeholders, including teachers, parents, and community members.

◆ CONCLUSION

The expectations of the school principal have changed from that of a building manager to instructional leader. The campus principal of today faces new and greater challenges, increased high-stake testing and accountability, complex social environments, and advances in technology. In this context, the campus principal has the opportunity to provide the necessary leadership to mold schools into dynamic learning communities in challenging and exciting times.

This chapter provided the view of a principal as one whose role has changed over time. The role of the principal is defined by the Texas Education Code, Texas Administrative Code, and the State Board of Education Certification. The quality of principals demands more than managerial skills of overseeing, directing, and controlling. The principal assumes the responsibility for the operation of the entire school and its stakeholders. Instructional leader, visionary, change agent, innovator for improved student learning, and collaborator are the hats that the campus principal now wears. Values of trust, authenticity, inclusion, empowerment, and professionalism define the context of a successful principal's leadership. Supervisory knowledge and skills are critical to the success of the building principal and an awareness of the constant scrutiny by all stakeholders is necessary to maintain a dynamic balance of interaction in the education community. Ever mindful of the impact of decisions made at the federal, state, and local levels, the district administrative team, including the building principal works to empower others with the end result of a high quality of student success and pride in work well done for now and the future.

◆ REFERENCES

Bambrick-Santoyo, P. with Peiser, B. (2012). *Leveraging leadership: A practical guide to building exceptional schools.* San Francisco, CA: Jossey-Bass.

Brown, A. A. (2012). *Turnaround Schools: Practices used by national recognized principals to improve student achievement in high poverty school.* Dissertation, University of Memphis.

Cuban, L. (1998, January 28). *A tale of two schools: How progressives and traditionalists undermine our understanding of what is "good" in schools.* Retrieved from http://www.edweek.org/ew/articles/1998/01/28/20cuban.h17.html

Darling-Hammond, L., LaPointe, M., Meyerson, D., & Terry Orr, M. (2007). *Preparing school leaders for a changing world: Executive summary.* Stanford, CA: Stanford University, Stanford Educational Leadership Institute.

Davis, S., Kearney, K., Sanders, N., Thomas, C., & Leon, R. (2011). *The policies and practices of principal evaluation: A review of the literature.* San Francisco: WestEd.

DiPaola, M. F., & Hoy, W. K. (2008). *Principals improving instruction.* Pearson Education, Inc.: Boston. Retrieved from www.ccsso.org/content/pdfs/isllcstd.

Doyle, D., & Han, J. G. (2012). *Measuring teacher effectiveness: A look "Under the Hood" of teacher evaluation in 10 sites.* New York, 50CAN; New Haven, CT: ConnCAN and Chapel Hill, NC: Public Impact.

Fullan, M. (2013). *Motion leadership in action.* Thousand Oaks, CA: SAGE Publications.

Glazerman, S., Goldhaber, D., Loeb, S., Raudenbush, S., Staiger, D., Whitehurst, G. J., & Croft, M. (2011). *Passing muster: Evaluating teacher evaluation systems.* Washington, D. C.: Brown Center on Education Policy at Brookings Institution.

Goe, L., Holdheide, L., & Miller, T. (2011). *A practical guide to designing comprehensive teacher evaluation systems: A tool to assist in the development of teacher evaluation systems*. Retrieved from http://www.lauragoe.com/LauraGoe/practicalGuideEvalSystems.pdf

Good, R., (2008, April). Sharing the secrets. *Principal Leadership, 8*(8), 46–50. Retrieved from http://eric.ed.gov/?id=EJ789940

Interstate School Leaders Licensure Consortium. (2015). *ISLLC Standards*. Retrieved from http://coe.fgcu.edu/faculty/valesky/isllcstandards.htm

Lambert, L. (2002). Toward a deepened theory of constructivist leadership. In L. Lanbert, D. Walker, D. P. Zimmerman, J. E. Cooper, M. D. Lambert, M. E. Gardner, & M. Szabo (Eds.), *The constructivist leader* (2nd ed.). New York: Teachers College Press.

Leithwood, K., Louis, K., Anderson, S., & Wahlstrom, K. (2004). *How leadership influences student learning* (Review of Research). New York: The Wallace Foundation. Retrieved from http://www.wallacefoundation.org/knowledge-center/school-leadership/key-research/Documents/How-Leadership-Influences-Student-Learning.pdf

Marshall, K. (2009). *Rethinking teacher supervision and evaluation: How to work smart, build collaboration, and close the achievement gap*. San Francisco, CA: Jossey-Bass.

Matthews, L. J., & Crow, G. M. (2003). *Being and becoming a principal: Role conceptions for contemporary principals and assistant principals*. Boston: Pearson Education, Inc.

Marzano, R. J. (1998). *A theory-based meta-analysis of research on instruction*. Aurora, CO: Mid-continent Research for Education and Learning.

Marzano, R. J., Gaddy, B. B., & Dean, C. (2000). *What works in classroom instruction*. Aurora, CO: Mid-continent Research for Education and Learning.

Maxwell, J. C. (2011). *The 5 levels of leadership: Proven steps to maximize your potential*. Center Street Hachette Book Group. New York: NY.

Mendels, P. (2012). The effective principal. *Leadership, 33*(1) 54–58. Retrieved from http://www.wallacefoundation.org/knowledge-center/school-leadership/effective-principal-leadership/Documents/The-Effective-Principal.pdf

Osborne, C. (2012, July). *The Texas report: Educator preparation programs' influence on student achievement*. Project on Educator Effectiveness & Quality.

Pierce, P. R. (1935). *The origin and development of the public school principalship*. Chicago: The University of Chicago Press. Retrieved from https://archive.org/details/origindevelopmen00pier

Sergiovanni, T. J. & Green, R. L. (2015). *The principalship: A reflective practice perspective*. Boston, Massachusetts: Pearson Education, Inc.

Shelton, S. (2011). *Strong leaders strong schools: 2010 school leadership laws*. Denver, CO: National Conference of State Legislatures. Retrieved from http://www.wallacefoundation.org/knowledge-center/school-leadership/state-policy/Documents/2010-Strong-Leaders-Strong-Schools.pdf

Sorenson, R. (2014). Texas public school organization and administration: A project of Texas council of professors of educational administration. In J. A. Vornberg & W. D. Hickey (Eds.), *Campus leadership in Texas: The effective principal* (pp. 165–187). Hendall Hunt Publishing Company: Dubuque, IA.

Springer, M. G., Podgursky, M. J., Lewis, J. L., Guthrie, J. W., Ehlert, M. W., Springer, J. A., . . . Taylor, L. L. (2007). *Governor's Educator Excellence Award Program: Governor's Educator Excellence Grants: Year One Interim Report: Campus plans and teacher experiences*. A report for the Texas Education Agency. National Center on Performance Incentives at Vanderbilt University's Peabody College.

State Board for Educator Certification/Texas Education Agency. (2010). *Preparation Manual:068 Principal*. Retrieved from http://cms.texes-ets.org/files/5314/3220/6652/068_principal.pdf

Texas Administrative Code. (2009). Title 19, Part 7, Chapter 241, Rule 241.1. Retrieved from http://texreg.sos.state.tx.us/public/readtac$ext.TacPage?sl=R&app=9&p_dir=&p_rloc=&p_tloc=&p_ploc=&pg=1&p_tac=&ti=19&pt=7&ch=241&rl=1

Texas Association of School Administrators. (2015, June). *Bill tracker: 84th legislature*. Retrieved from http://billtracker.tasanet.org/

Texas Association of School Boards (TASB). (2015, July). https://www.tasb.org/legislative/legislativereport/2015/week-3/usde-denies-texas%E2%80%99-nclb-waiver.aspx

Texas Education Agency. (2004). *Texas public schools*. Retrieved from http://tea.texas.gov/About_TEA/Welcome_and_Overview/An_Overview_of_the_Historyof_Public_Education_in_Texas/.pdf

Texas Education Agency. (2009). *Principal standards*. Retrieved from http://tea.texas.gov/Texas_Educators/Preparation_and_Continuing_Education/Approved_

Texas Education Agency. (2013). *Principal standards and appraisal*. Retrieved from http://tea.texas.gov/index2.aspx?id=25769817488

Texas Education Agency (TEA). (2014). *Texas teacher evaluation and support* system. Retrieved from http://tea.texas.gov/Texas_Educators/Educator_Evaluation_and_Support_System/Texas_Teacher_Evaluation_and_Support_System/

Texas Education Agency. (2015). *Texas principal evaluation and appraisal system*. Retrieved from http://tea.texas.gov/Texas_Educators/Educator_Evaluation_and_Support_System/Texas_Principal_Evaluation_and_Support_System/

Texas Education Code, §21.3541. (2014). *Commissioner's rules concerning educator standards, Subchapter BB. Administrator Standards*. Retrieved from http://ritter.tea.state.tx.us/rules/tac/chapter149/ch149bb.html

Texas Education Code, 11:202. (1995). *Principals*. Retrieved from http://www.statutes.legis.state.tx.us/Docs/ED/htm/ED.11.htm

Texas Education Code, 21.046. (1995). *Qualifications for certification as superintendent or principal*. Retrieved from http://www.weblaws.org/texas/laws/tex._educ._code_section_21.046_qualifications_for_certification_as_superintendent_or_principal

The Wallace Foundation. (2008). *Becoming a leader: Preparing school principals for today's schools*. Retrieved from http://www.wallacefoundation.org/knowledge-center/school-leadership/principal-training/Pages/Becoming-a-Leader-Preparing-Principals-for-Todays-Schools.aspx

The Wallace Foundation. (2013). *The school principal as leader: Guiding schools to better teaching and learning*. Retrieved from http://www.wallacefoundation.org/knowledge-center/school-leadership/effective-principal-leadership/Documents/The-School-Principal-as-Leader-Guiding-Schools-to-Better-Teaching-and-Learning-2nd-Ed.pdf

Walker, D. (2002). Constructivist leadership: Standards, equity, and learning—weaving whole cloth from multiple strands. In L. Lambert, D. Walker, D. Zimmerman, J. Cooper, M. Lambert, M. Gardner, & M. Szabo (Eds.), *The constructivist leader* (2nd ed.) (pp. 1–33). New York: Teachers College Press.

Waters, T., & Cameron, G. (2007). *The balanced leadership framework: Connecting vision with action*. Denver, CO: Mid-continent Research for Education and Learning.

Waters, J. T., Marzano, R. J., & McNulty, B. (2003). *Balanced leadership: What 30 years of research tells us about the effect of leadership on student achievement*. Aurora, CO: Mid-continent Research for Education and Learning.

CURRICULUM AND INSTRUCTION

Ross Sherman ◆ *Timothy Jones*

In the business world, corporations are divided into two divisions: financial and operations. Public schools are similarly organized. While the financial operations of a school district are comparable to that of business with the addition of noninstructional programs such as transportation, food service, etc., curriculum and instruction is how we refer to the operations side of the school district. This is the essence of what we do in schools and comprises heart and soul of the educational process. Curriculum defines "what we teach" and instruction relates to "how we teach." Curriculum articulates the intended learning outcomes, whereas instruction is pedagogy of how teachers go about facilitating the learning outcomes.

According to the Texas Administrative Code (TAC, 2015, 149.001), teachers are expected to demonstrate the following behaviors as related to curriculum and instruction:

- Instructional Planning and Delivery—Providing standards based, data driven, differentiated instruction that engages students
- Knowledge of Students and Student Learning—Ensuring high levels of learning, social-emotional development, and achievement outcomes for all students
- Content Knowledge and Expertise—Exhibiting a comprehensive understanding of their content, discipline, and pedagogy
- Learning Environment—Maintaining a physically and emotionally safe, supportive learning environment
- Data Driven Practice—Using formal and informal methods to assess student growth aligned to instructional goals and course objectives

Research supports that a student's teacher is the most important in-school factor in improving student learning (McCaffrey, Lockwood, Koretz, & Hamilton, 2003; Rivkin, Hanushek, & Kain, 2005).

◆ CURRICULUM

Despite the critical importance of curriculum to a quality education, prior to the 1980s what students were taught was primarily left to the local school district. Statewide accountability for specific learning was nonexistent during this time, making a formal statewide curriculum unnecessary. While the state of Texas had always had broad discretionary powers in establishing high school graduation requirements, courses that could be taught, and textbook selection, legislators seldom got involved in specific learning outcomes of the local school district.

In 1981, the 67th Texas legislature changed the curriculum landscape for all Texas public schools by passing legislation for the first statewide curriculum. The results of this legislation culminated in the publication entitled, *State Board of Education Rules for Curriculum*, known as Chapter 75 of the TAC. This curriculum, known as "essential elements" (EEs), was adopted by the Texas State Board of Education and was implemented in Texas public schools during the 1985–1986 school year. By specifying both the courses and the content to be taught, the legislature dictated to every school the intended learning outcomes for each student in every classroom. This curriculum was described by the Texas Education Agency (TEA) as an attempt to standardize and provide a minimum set of learning outcomes. The EEs became the basis for state-adopted textbooks, state accountability assessment, and staff development for teachers and administrators.

The next evolution of curriculum came a decade later when the Texas Legislature, in Chapter 28 of the Texas Education Code, directed the State Board of Education to adopt "essential knowledge and skills" for the state-mandated curriculum. The Texas Essential Knowledge and Skills (TEKS) were more rigorous then the EEs and focused on higher order thinking skills.

Texas Essential Knowledge and Skills (TEKS)

The Texas Essential Knowledge and Skills (TEKS) for each academic discipline can be found in the TAC Title 19, Part II, Chapter 110 through Chapter 130. The required TEKS curriculum consists of two parts. The first part is a "foundation curriculum" where the "essential knowledge and skills" must be taught in each of the following four disciplines:

- English language arts;
- Mathematics;
- Science; and
- Social science.

The second component of the curriculum encompasses the "enrichment curriculum." This "enrichment curriculum" consists of the following areas:

- Languages other than English (LOTE);
- Health Education;
- Physical Education (PE);
- Fine Arts;
- Economics with Emphasis on the Free Enterprise System and Its Benefits;
- Technology Applications;
- Career Development;
- Spanish Language Arts and English as a Second Language; and
- Career and Technical Education.

The TEKS serve as the basis for instructional materials, state accountability assessments, and teacher and administrator staff development. The TEKS are composed of three parts: (1) basic understandings that identify concepts from each of the academic disciplines;

(2) knowledge and skills informing students of what they need to know and be able to do; and (3) performance indicators outlining how students will demonstrate understanding of the acquired knowledge and skills (TAC Title 19, Part II, Chapter 74).

TAC Chapter 74 directs local boards of school trustees to adopt policies and procedures ensuring all students will have the opportunity to participate in a well-balanced curriculum. The TEKS allow each district the flexibility to develop a local focus and to modify the intended learning outcomes, thus a local curriculum. The TEKS are not instructionally listed in hierarchical order, nor do they represent a course outline. However, the TEKS do represent most of the important concepts for each grade level or course, since the state accountability system is aligned to the TEKS.

Curriculum Alignment

The key to success in implementing the Texas Essential Knowledge and Skills (TEKS) is the presence of curriculum alignment. When most educators refer to curriculum alignment, it is a reference to a correlation within and between grade levels regarding content. However, in reality, there are different types of curriculum that must be aligned to promote the attainment of the instructional outcomes (TEKS). These types, listed in order to alignment, are the recommended, written, taught, supported, tested, and learned curriculums.

The "Recommended Curriculum" is the curriculum that is recommended by scholars and professionals with expertise in the discipline. The recommended curriculum in the State of Texas, which was developed with broad-based input from teachers, administrators, and university personnel is the TEKS.

The next type of curriculum is the "Written Curriculum" and comprises the official curricular documents of the school district. For most districts, this involves the development of curriculum guides, scope and sequence charts, or simply providing teachers a copy of the TEKS for a particular course or area. The school district's written curriculum should include all of the TEKS for that course or area. The third type of curriculum is the "Taught Curriculum" and is what the teacher actually teaches in the classroom. The taught curriculum is documented in the teacher's lesson plans and identifies the TEKS to be covered during that lesson. The next type of curriculum is the "Supported Curriculum," which is the materials and training provided for teachers. The supported curriculum includes textbooks, instructional materials, and staff development to facilitate the teaching of the TEKS.

The fifth type of curriculum is the "Tested Curriculum." This consists of state-mandated assessment system entitled the State of Texas Assessments of Academic Readiness (STAAR), as well as teacher-made assessments such as exams, tests, and projects. The tested curriculum addresses the degree to which the student has mastered the TEKS. The final type of curriculum is the "Learned Curriculum," which encompasses what the student actually learns as a result of the educational process. However, for students in the state of Texas to master the TEKS, all of the different types of curriculum—recommended, written, taught, supported, and tested—must be aligned.

Standards-Based Curriculum Model

Texas uses a standards-based model for curriculum and assessment, founded on the idea that standards are created because they improve the students' ability to function in a free society. According to Ravitch (1995), "standards can improve achievement by clearly defining what is to be taught and what kind of performance is expected" (p. 25).

Standards come from many places, but the primary source for standards comes from national academic societies. In considering these national standards, Marzano and Kendall (1996) describe three types of standards that include: (1) subject-area standards; (2) thinking and reasoning standards; and (3) lifelong learning standards. A standards-based curriculum includes content knowledge and skills. In addition, it defines courses and subjects, how student achievement is depicted, and how student products are assessed and reported (Marzano & Kendall, 1996). The most compelling argument for a standards-based curriculum model is the current emphasis on educational "outputs" as opposed to educational "inputs." Texas embraces the "output" view of accountability. Making sure students achieve academically is more important than any other single issue, and a standards-based curriculum helps accomplish this task. Therefore, the state of Texas identifies the curricular requirements for each level of education.

Elementary Curriculum

Chapter 74.2 of the TAC specifies that the elementary curriculum, kindergarten through grade 5, consist of a series of knowledge and skills in each of the following areas:

- Health;
- Fine Arts;
- Social Studies;
- English Language Arts and Reading;
- Mathematics;
- Science;
- Physical Education;
- Technology Applications; and
- To the extent possible, languages other than English (TAC Title 19, Part II, Chapter 74).

Originally, Chapter 75 dictated the disciplines, content, and amount of time each area must be taught on a daily and/or weekly basis. Legislation was passed that prohibited the State Board of Education from dictating instructional methodology and time requirements for each discipline. Chapter 74 ensures the instructional integrity of school districts by stating that instruction may be provided in a variety of settings and time frames. Mixed-age classes intended to provide flexible learning environments for appropriate instruction and attainment of course and grade-level standards is allowed for kindergarten through grade 6 (TAC Title 19, Part II, Chapter 74).

Middle School Curriculum

Middle schools, as defined in TAC Title 19, Part II, Chapter 74, include grades 6 through 8. The curricular requirements for middle schools are the same as the elementary curriculum for kindergarten through grade 5. While the curriculum may be the same, the TEKS are significantly different. The curriculum consists of the following disciplines:

- English Language Arts;
- Mathematics;
- Science;
- Social Studies;

- Health;
- Physical Education;
- Fine Arts;
- Technology Applications; and
- Languages other than English (TAC Title 19, Part II, Chapter 74).

High School Curriculum

A school district that houses grades 9 through 12 must offer the Foundation School Program. The high school program consists of the following courses:

- English Language Arts (English I, II, III, IV, and advanced ELA)
- Mathematics (Algebra I, II, Geometry, Precalculus, and Mathematics Models with applications)
- Science (Biology, IPC, Chemistry, Physics, and two additional science courses from the advanced science credit list)
- Social Studies (U.S. History since 1877, World History, U.S. Government, World Geography Studies, Economicswith an emphasis on free enterprise)
- Languages other than English Levels I, II, and III or higher of the same language
- Fine Arts—Art I, II, III, IV, Music I, II, III, IV, Theater I, II, III, IV, Dance I, II, III, IV
- P.E. Foundations of Personal Fitness, Adventure/Outdoor Education, Aerobic Activities or team or individual sport
- Career and Technical—Coherent sequence of courses selected from 16 career clusters
- Technology Applications
- Speech—Communication Applications

In addition, the State Board of Education must identify a variety of advanced courses that can be taken to comply with the foundation school program.

Graduation Requirements

The Foundation School Program requires 22 credits for graduation. The graduation requirements consists of the following courses:

- 4 credits in English language arts (English I, II, III, and advanced ELA)
- 3 credits in mathematics (Algebra I, geometry, and advanced math credit)
- 3 credits in science (Biology, IPC or advanced science credit, and another advanced science credit)
- 3 credits in social studies (U.S. History, 0.5 economics, 0.5 government, and either world history or world geography, or a new course combining world history and world geography)
- 2 credits in languages other than English (computer programming languages may substitute per SBOE rule, other flexibility for second LOTE credit for students due to a disability who are unlikely to complete two courses in the same language)
- 1 credit in fine arts (can be community based program with appropriate TEKS coverage)
- 1 credit in P.E. (including approved off campus programming)
- 1 credit Fine Arts
- 5 credits in electives (may include career and technology or certification courses)

A student may elect to pursue an endorsement in one of five categories that can be achieved by earning 26 credits including four in mathematics and science and two additional elective credits. The endorsement areas, which will be noted on the student's diploma and transcripts, include:

- Science, Technology, Engineering and Mathematics (STEM)
- Business and Industry
- Public Service
- Arts and Humanities
- Multidisciplinary

High School Curriculum Scheduling and Organization

In terms of courses taught, the high school curriculum is dependent on the number of students and teachers and the type of scheduling model used on the campus. Increasing graduation requirements have impacted the high school curriculum by requiring more courses and allowing fewer electives. More courses in English language arts, science, mathematics, and social studies dictate fewer courses in homemaking, physical education, and the fine arts.

Perhaps the biggest influence on the curriculum was the increased graduation requirements,which place a significant strain on class schedules. Historically, the traditional class schedule in Texas was composed of six or seven 55-minute periods per day. Beginning with the 1994–1995 academic year, Texas high school graduation requirements were raised to 21 credits for students entering the ninth grade. With graduation requirements increasing and limited financial resources available, principals and superintendents began to lobby the Texas State Board of Education to allow flexible course schedules. The National Association of Secondary School Principals released *Breaking Ranks*, its commissioned study on changing the American high school (1996). One of the major tenets of this study was the use of flexible scheduling as a way to provide students with a broader academic experience and as an answer to teacher staffing problems. High schools needed to create more flexible schedules, compatible with learning objectives, to facilitate the ability of each student to meet the requirements of the curriculum. *Breaking Ranks* (1996) stated, "The time available in a uniform six-hour, 180-day school year is the unacknowledged design flaw in American education" (p. 47). The Texas State Board of Education moved to allow flexible time schedules, and school districts have taken advantage of this opportunity.

Several school districts in the state moved from the traditional six-period day to the four-by-four accelerated block schedule that utilizes 90-minute class periods. Using this model, the academic year is divided into fall and spring terms of 18 weeks each. Students enroll in four courses that meet 5 days per week for a total of 90 days during the fall term. In the spring term, students enroll for four more courses, allowing them to earn a total of eight credits per year. This four-by-four accelerated block schedule allowed students to meet the growing demand for graduation requirements and helped staffing problems by having instructors teach one additional section per year.

An alternative to the four-by-four accelerated block schedule is the A-B block schedule. This scheduling model requires students to take eight 90-minute courses on alternating days for the entire 36 weeks of the academic school year. The weeks are divided into "A" days and "B" days, and students attend their "A" scheduled courses 3 days in 1 week and 2days in the next week. The same applies for the "B" scheduled classes, meeting 3 days the next week and

2 days the week after. The A-B block schedule was created over the concern that students were not getting enough instructional continuity in courses that had spiraling content. Recently, Texas schools have seen a significant decrease in the use of block schedules and have instead replaced them with the formerly used six- and seven-period day schedule. Some schools concede that teachers have not been effectively trained in the use of the block schedule and have therefore reverted back to a more traditional schedule. Still, the block schedule is being effectively used in many Texas schools.

The trimester scheduling plan is utilized by some high schools across the state. This model divides the academic year into three semesters of 12 weeks each. Students enroll in four courses that meet 90 minutes each day during the 12 weeks of the trimester. They earn eight units of credit over the three trimesters. It is possible to operate an additional 12-week session during the summer if the financial resources will allow.

Detractors of flexible scheduling have attempted to demonstrate that learning has not been achieved to a sufficiently high level using the flexible time schedule models. To date, no definitive research has surfaced that indicates flexible time schedules are any better or worse than the traditional six-period day. Research has informed practice that the scheduling model utilized by a campus has little to do with the academic success of students. The real issue in the flexible scheduling debate is: "What instructional strategies does the teacher utilize during the time he or she has the students in class?" Instruction is the key to learning, not the type of scheduling model or time frame implemented.

◆ INSTRUCTION

Accountability and the advent of brain research have dramatically changed instruction in Texas over the past two decades. Teaching theory has given way to learning theory. In 2005, for example, the Texas legislature, in passing HB 3468, authorized the Commissioner of Education to establish a comprehensive reading intervention program requiring neuroscience-based and scientifically validated instructional methods in order to accelerate learning and cognitive ability. This legislation was the first statute that mandated brain-based strategies.

Over the past decade, the appraisal of teachers has focused less on their activity and more on the behavior of learners. New and innovative instructional models requiring students to take a more active role in learning have replaced traditional "sit and get" practices. The development of these instructional models over the past 30 years has done more than just expand the instructional toolbox for teachers; in many cases, it has replaced some of the traditional methods. It is clear that the emphasis on instruction no longer requires the teacher to be an expert giver of information to students; instead, instruction requires the teacher to act as facilitator or coach by creating innovative and engaging learning environments and authentic tasks to foster critical and higher-order thinking. This teaching model requires the teacher to provide more individual attention to each student's learning needs.

Instructional Models

All instruction can be classified as either inductive or deductive, depending on who or how content is delivered. In deductive teaching, the database is delivered by the teacher and is commonly referred to as teacher-directed instruction. In inductive teaching, the database is gathered in by the students and is referred to as teacher-guided instruction.

The direct instruction modelis primarily based on stimulus-response research. This model is most useful in teaching skills that can be broken into small tasks, building one upon another. Limited time frames for instruction followed by practice until learning is achieved is the strategy used in this model (Gunter, Estes, & Schwab, 1999). Perhaps the most well known of the direct instruction practitioners was Madeline Hunter. Hunter (1984) proposed a seven-step instructional process: (1) anticipatory set; (2) objectives and purpose; (3) instructional input; (4) modeling; (5) checking for understanding; (6) guided practice; and (7) independent practice. These seven steps became the template for using the direct instruction model in Texas.

A new direction for instructional supervision was recommended by the Instructional Leadership Development Model (TEA, 2005) and called for a reduction in teacher-directed instruction in lieu of more teacher-guided models. One example of inductive, or teacher-guided, instruction is inquiry-based teaching models. A version of inquiry-based teaching that is used in many Texas school districts is the 5E Model consisting of the following stages:

- Engage—The teacher presents a problem or event that raises questions and motivates students to discover more about the concept.
- Explore—The students are provided an opportunity to actively explore the concept in a hands-on activity.
- Explain—The teacher uses questioning strategies to lead students' discussion of the information discovered during the explore stage.
- Elaborate—The students are encouraged to apply, extend and enhance the new concept and related terms during interaction with the teacher and other students.
- Evaluate—The students demonstrate their understanding of the concept.

The focus of the inquiry process is on attaining the content but also having students reflect on the thought processes that they engaged in to resolve the problem.

Another prominent inductive model is the cooperative learning model. Most teachers discover early on the power of having students teaching other students. Using this concept as a point of departure, several educators have created what has become known as the cooperative learning model. This model is not new to society or to the education arena as evidenced by the students participating in team sports, drama productions, and other cooperative activities found in most schools. Johnson and Johnson (1984) identified five elements of successful cooperative learning models, which include:

- Positive Interdependence—The students must believe they need each other in order to complete the group's task.
- Face-to-Face Interaction—The students must learn to interact verbally and make their case within the group.
- Individual Accountability—Each student must be held accountable for learning the material.
- Interpersonal and Small Group Skills—Each student must be taught and then demonstrate effective social skills.
- Group Processing—The group must periodically assess how they work together.

Of these five elements perhaps the most important is the development of social skills when considering the workplace, the family, and social activities. Gunter et al. (1999) reinforced this concept when they wrote that learning to cooperate is so important that it must be part of the learning experience in schools.

Recently, project-based instruction has become more prevalent in Texas schools. The central tenet of project-based learning is that real-world problems foster students' interest and stimulate thinking as the students acquire and apply new knowledge in a problem-solving context. The teacher's role is that of facilitator, working with students to frame relevant questions, structure meaningful tasks, and coach students in the acquisition of knowledge and the development of social skills. Typical projects present a problem to solve or a phenomenon to investigate. Project-based instruction:

- Is organized around an open-ended driving question or challenge.
- Creates a need to know essential content and skills.
- Requires inquiry to learn and/or create something new.
- Requires critical thinking, problem solving, collaboration, and various forms of communication, often known as "Twenty-first Century Skills."
- Allows some degree of student voice and choice.
- Incorporates feedback and revision.
- Results in a publicly presented product or performance (Association for Supervision and Curriculum Development (ASCD), 2013).

Constructivist learning models have also been introduced to the landscape in schools over the past decade. This approach to learning often includes methods developed with the advent of brain-mind learning principles and other progressive education strategies (Jones, 2009). Constructivism often incorporates all four of the prior models outlined above (direct teaching, inquiry based, cooperative learning, and project based) but with greater value placed on self-guided learning through constructed knowledge, analysis, and synthesis. One such model, Multitiered Brain-Enriched Learning (MBEL), (Jones, 1998) builds learning engagement around three tiers of activities:

- Exposure—An overt activity on the part of the teacher and could include direct or small group instruction. In this tier, teachers insure that the requisite skills for the new learning are present and then "whet the appetite" of the learner.
- Exploration—An overt activity on the part of the learner and could include discovery learning, inquiry or independent research. Most any line of questions or inquiry of the topic by the learner (motivated by their own curiosity) is valued during exploration.
- Experience—An active assignment in an authentic environment that provides the class an opportunity to report back information and data gathered during the exploration tier and whereby the teacher provides clarification where needed. This tier culminates in an activity that "lives the learning," insuring transfer from the short- to the long-term memory and provides the assessment of student understanding.

The five instructional models outlined in this section are the sampling of the inductive and deductive possibilities that are available to teachers in the instructional arena. Good instruction is the heart of the student-learning process. Constructivism is becoming more prevalent in Texas schools and provides a new lens through which knowledge is attained and examined. The curriculum may contain the most thorough and thoughtfully developed intended learning outcomes, but without instructional models that provide students the opportunity to learn and apply this information, instruction will fail, and so will students.

The final component of the triad is appraisal. The appraisal of instruction is designed to contribute to the attainment of the educational objectives by adhering to the adage that you should "inspect what you expect."

Appraisal of Instruction

A major feature impacting the instructional process for the past two decades in Texas has been in the appraisal of teachers or the appraisal of instruction. In 1984, the Texas legislature, in passing HB 72, created the Texas Teacher Appraisal System (TTAS), the first mandated statewide teacher appraisal system. The TTAS, based on the lesson cycle of Madeline Hunter, prescribed 54 teacher behaviors consistent with good instruction and pedagogy. Consequently, this system influenced the instruction that was taking place in each and every classroom in the state. By the very prescriptive nature of the TTAS instrument, it was inevitable that instruction would be influenced. Administrators seeking certification in appraising teachers first had to take a state-mandated course in Instructional Leadership Training (ILT) and then a course in the appraisal system itself. ILT helped appraisers identify quality teaching and methods for improving poor teaching. The flaw in the TTAS, many suggested, was that it concentrated on teacher behavior with little emphasis on the behaviors of learners or the learning in the classroom. Opponents of the TTAS suggested that a teacher could prepare a "dog and pony" show that would hit all 54 indicators without a student in the class, and thus earn a perfect evaluation.

In 1998, a new instructional supervision model entitled Professional Development Appraisal System (PDAS) was introduced. Structurally, PDAS was similar to TTAS with the exception of eight domains in the PDAS as compared to five domains on the TTAS. The major difference between the two systems was that PDAS primarily focused on student learning as opposed to the teacher behaviors. Instructional Leadership Development replaced ILT as the prerequisite to earning PDAS Appraiser certification.

The latest iteration in teacher appraisal will be introduced during the 2016-2017 academic year. The Texas Teacher Evaluation and Support System (T-TESS) is being piloted in 200 school districts during 2015-2016. T-TESS has three measures of teacher effectiveness: (1) observation, (2) teacher self-assessment, and (3) student growth. Currently, the observation component will constitute 70% of the overall rating with teacher assessment comprising 10% and student growth 20%. The evaluation rubric used in the new system will have four domains: (1) Planning, (2) Instruction, (3) Learning Environment, and (4) Professional Practice and Responsibilities. Within the four domains, there are 16 dimensions, five in instruction, four in both planning and professional practice and responsibilities, and three in learning environments (TEA, 2015).

As the curriculum has increased in complexity from the EEs to the Texas Essential Knowledge and Skills (TEKS), so has the requirement for excellent instruction evolved in the State from ILT to Instructional Leadership Development. Improvements in curriculum parallel improvements and expectations for quality instruction. To assist in this process, the State of Texas makes a sizeable investment in providing textbooks as one resource available to teach the curriculum.

Textbooks

Texas uses a statewide system for the adoption, purchase, distribution, and use of textbooks. The state statutes that address textbooks are found in the Texas Education Code, Chapter 31. Textbooks are adopted by the State Board of Education and are provided without cost to pupils.

The term *textbook* includes: books, supplementary materials, a combination of a book, workbook, and supplementary materials, computer software, magnetic media, DVD, CD-ROM, computer courseware, on-line services, or an electronic medium, or other means of conveying information to the student or otherwise contributing to the learning process through electronic means, including open-source instructional material. A special provision of the law authorizes that textbooks be provided for blind and visually impaired public school students and teachers. In this instance, textbooks include Braille and large-type books.

State Adoption, Purchase, Acquisition, and Custody

The State Board of Education (SBOE) is charged with establishing an adoption cycle based on anticipated funding for the school year as determined by the SBOE, Legislative Budget Board, and Governor's Office for subjects in the foundation curriculum, with no more than one-fourth of the books reviewed each biennium. Reviews and adoptions for subjects in the enrichment courses are on an as-needed basis. The SBOE issues proclamations advertising for textbooks to be used in a particular school year. These are designed to articulate the following:

- Texas Essential Knowledge and Skills (TEKS) in each subject;
- Maximum cost to the state per student; and
- Estimated number of units.

The proclamations also specify the timeline for the adoption of the materials. Typically, the process from the issuance of the proclamation to the utilization of the materials in the classroom is ~24 months. For instance, a proclamation that was issued in 2015 advertised for Mathematics 9–12 books to be used in schools beginning with the 2017–2018 school year.

The Commissioner of Education establishes State Textbook Committee Review Panels. The appointments are for 1 year, and each person selected is experienced and possesses expertise in the fields for which adoptions are to be made for that year. The textbook committee's charge is to evaluate each textbook to determine the coverage of the Texas Essential Knowledge and Skills (TEKS), to identify factual errors, and to report their findings to the Commissioner of Education. The commissioner then recommends textbooks be placed on the adopted list or rejected.

Selection Process

The local board of education must adopt a policy for the selection of instructional materials. Most districts appoint a textbook committee to evaluate prospective textbooks and to gather input from all teachers and other personnel who will be using the book.

During this process, it is important that teachers keep in mind the following criteria:

- Does the text complement the district's philosophy for that subject area?
- Does the text meet the ability level and needs of the students?

Finally, the district's textbook committee recommends to the board its selections.

District Procedures

Legislation from the 82nd Texas Legislature (2011) created an Instructional Materials Allotment for the purchase of instructional materials, technology equipment and technology-related services. A school district receives abiennial allotment from the state instructional materials fund for each student enrolled in the district. The commissioner determines the amount of the allotment per student based on the amount of money available in the state instructional materials fund. The allotment is transferred from the state instructional materials fund and credited to the district's instructional materials account.

It is important to note that all textbooks remain the property of the State of Texas, and the State Board of Education establishes the rules for the requisition, distribution, care, use, and disposal of books. In addition, the board of trustees of the school district are designated the legal custodians of the books. The school district trustees may delegate the custodial responsibilities of books to district personnel. Each district must employ systematic accounting procedures to maintain accurate records of all books issued. In addition, the district or state may conduct annual audits of textbooks.

At the building level, teachers are required to keep a record of all books issued. Books must be returned at the end of the semester/year or when the student withdraws. Each student or his parent is responsible for returning all books issued or for making financial restitution prior to being issued new books. Books may be sold to parents who request at the state contract price. All money accrued from such sales must be forwarded to the commissioner.

◆ IN RETROSPECT

The heart and soul of education is curriculum and instruction. In education today the traditional "Three R's of reading, writing, and arithmetic" have been replaced with the new "Three R's of rigor, relevance, and relationships" designed to foster results. The new three R's are provided through the curriculum, instruction, and assessment processes, which are designed to assure the future success of the students of Texas.

◆ REFERENCES

ASCD. (2013). Seven essentials for project based learning. Retrieved from http://www.ascd.org/publications/educational_leadership/sept10/vol68/num01/Seven_Essentials_for_Project-Based_Learning.aspx

Gunter, M. A., Estes, T. H., & Schwab, J. H. (1999). *Instruction: A Models Approach* (3rd ed.). Boston: Allyn & Bacon.

House Bill 246, *Texas education code*. (1981).

House Bill 72, *Texas education code*. (1984).

House Bill 3468, *Texas education code*. (2005).

House Bill 5, *Texas education code*. (2013).

Hunter, M. (1984). Knowing, teaching, and supervising. In P. L. Hosford's (Ed.), *Using what we know about teaching* (pp. 175–176). Alexandra, VA: Association for Supervision and Curriculum Development.

Johnson, D. W., & Johnson, R. T. (1984). *Circles of learning*. Alexandra, VA: Association for Supervision and Curriculum Development.

Jones, T. B. (1998). The Silver team: An alternative program for everyone. *Texas mentor school network* (4) 2, 4–5.

Jones, T. B. (2009). John Dewey: Still ahead of histime. In P. M. Jenlink (Ed.), *Dewey's democracy and education revisited: Contemporary discourses for democratic education and leadership.* Lanham, MD: Roman and Littlefield.

Marzano, R. J., & Kendall, J. S. (1996). *Designing standards-based districts, schools, and classrooms.* Alexandra, VA: Association for Supervision and Curriculum Development.

McCaffrey, D. F., Lockwood, J. R., Koretz, D. M., & Hamilton, L. S., (2003). *Evaluating value-added models of teacher accountability.* Retrieved from http://www.rand.org/content/dam/rand/pubs/monographs/2004/RAND_MG158.pdf

National Association of Secondary School Principals. (1996). *Breaking ranks: Changing an American institution.* Reston, VA: Author.

Ravitch, D. (1995). *National standards in American education: A citizen's guide.* Washington, DC: Brookings Institute.

Rivkin, S. G., Hanushek, E. A., & Kain, J. F., (2005, March). Teachers, schools, and academic achievement. *Econometricia, 73*, (2), 417-458.

Texas Administrative Code. (2015). [Online]. Retrieved from http://ritter.tea.state.tx.us/rules/tac/index.html

Texas Education Agency. (2005). *Instructional leadership development manual.* Austin, TX.

Texas Education Agency. (2015). Teacher standards (Texas Administrative Code, title 19). Retrieved from http://txcc.sedl.org/our_work/tx_educator_evaluation/teachers/teacher_standards.php

TEXAS ASSESSMENTS AND SCHOOL ACCOUNTABILITY

Yanira Oliveras-Ortiz

School accountability and high-stakes testing have been an increasingly important part of the realm of school principals and district administrators for the last four decades. The growing attention to student performance on state assessments is the outcome of the No Child Left Behind Act (NCLB) of 2001 and the assessment programs states were required to develop to meet the requirements set by NCLB. The purpose of this chapter is to examine the accountability requirements set forth by the US Department of Education, and the latest actions the Texas legislature and Texas Education Agency (TEA) have taken to meet the set requirements.

◆ HISTORICAL FRAMEWORK: ELEMENTARY AND SECONDARY EDUCATION ACT

The NCLB Act, the reauthorized Elementary and Secondary Act (ESEA), was written with the intent to improve all students' academic performance regardless of their ethnic and economic background (U.S. Department of Education, 2004). NCLB set guidelines for student assessment (U.S. Department of Education, 2002, p. 20) and requirements for highly qualified teachers (U.S. Department of Education, 2002, p. 13) while allowing states to develop student assessments and define how to measure teacher effectiveness. NCLB clearly proclaims that it is the state's responsibility to establish a system to hold schools accountable for lack of student progress and low student achievement (U.S. Department of Education, 2004). Additionally, NCLB requires that parents have choice to transfer to other schools when their neighborhood schools are rated as low performing for two consecutive years (U.S. Department of Education, 2004). While NCLB is well known for the assessment requirements, NCLB also requires schools to implement research-based instructional strategies and requires that federal funds be targeted to support the implementation of research-based programs and instructional methods (U.S. Department of Education, 2004).

The NCLB Act expired on September 30, 2007 (Higham, 2013); however, the failure to reauthorize or revised the law has kept NCLB Act of 2001 in effect. Five years after NCLB expired, the Obama administration understood the need for an updated law and as a result, in 2012, the U.S. Department of Education began issuing waivers that allowed for flexibility regarding the NCLB requirements (U.S. Department of Education, n.d.). Waivers have been granted upon the review of the state's plans to "close achievement gaps, increase equity, improve the quality of instruction, and increase outcomes for all students" (U.S. Department of Education, n.d.). Forty-two states, including Texas, as well as DC, and Puerto Rico have received ESEA waivers.

Texas' NCLB-ESEA Waiver

In February of 2013, the TEA submitted a request for a NCLB waiver "to reduce duplication and unnecessary burden" (TEA, 2013b) on the TEA and local education agencies. The U.S. Department of Education approved Texas' request in September in 2013. The waiver was approved with the condition that TEA would finalize the development of new teacher and principal evaluation systems. Since the Texas' request was approved, TEA has submitted various amendments related to the evaluation systems as well as requests for waiver flexibility and extension requests (TEA, 2015c). In September if 2014, a 1-year extension of flexibility, for the 2014–2015 school year, was granted yet again while keeping in place condition that TEA would continue to work and submit the final guidelines for the principal and teacher evaluation systems (Delisle, 2014). On June 2, 2015, TEA submitted the latest waiver renewal request for flexibility in implementing the provisions of ESEA. In September of 2015, The U.S. Department of Education approved the Texas waiver for the 2015–2016 school year. However, given Texas' failure to meet the 2012 ESEA Flexibility requirements regarding teacher and principal evaluations, Texas has been placed on high-risk status. In order for TEA secure an ESEA waiver beyond 2015–2016, the U.S. Department of Education requires that all Texas local education agencies implement the state's teacher and principal evaluation systems, which has been designed and is being piloted to meet the federal requirements. As of October 2015, Commissioner Williams had stated that he does not plan to mandate the use of the state's evaluation systems. He has said that the choice will be made by each local education agency.

◆ HISTORY OF ASSESSMENT IN THE UNITED STATES

Given the recent events related to NCLB and state assessments, the focus on testing has significantly increased; however, standardized testing is not a new phenomenon. In the United States, the first standardized test was administered in Massachusetts in the mid-1800 with the intent to classify students by ability and determine the effectiveness of the Massachusetts' school system (Parkay, Hass, & Anctil, 2010). While the beginning of the modern state testing in the United States, as known today, is dated to 1971 with the passing of the Florida's Education Accountability Act (Firestone, Schorr, & Monfils, 2004). The testing movement spread reasonably fast, and by 1982, 36 states had some sort of mandated testing program. Eighteen years later, most states required students to take at least one standardized, high-stakes test (Editorial Projects in Education as cited in Firestone et al., 2004). In 2002, with the enactment of NCLB, all states were required to develop assessment programs to measure student achievement and the schools' efforts to close the achievement gap (U.S. Department of Education, 2002).

❖ HISTORY OF TEXAS ASSESSMENTS

In Texas, the use of tests as measures of competencies and schools' success dates back to 1979 when the first assessment program began after the 66th Texas Legislature (TEA, 2012). The Texas assessment program began with basic mathematics, reading, and writing assessments for students in third, fifth, and ninth grade (TEA, 2012). The first administration of the Texas Assessment of Basic Skills (TABS) took place at 1980 (TEA, 2012); since then the Texas assessment program has undergone a number of revisions. In 1986, the TEA implemented the first high-stakes testing; high school students were required to pass the Texas Educational Assessment of Minimum Skills (TEAMS) to receive their high school diploma (TEA, 2012). Four years later, with the implementation of the Texas Assessment of Academic Skills (TAAS), the Agency began to focus on the assessment of academic skills rather than minimum skills (TEA, 2012). TAAS not only shifted the focus to the assessment of academic skills but also increased the number of grade levels in which it was required to administer the tests. All students in third through eighth grade and tenth grade were required to take the reading and mathematics TAAS, while students in fourth, eighth, and tenth grade had to take a writing test. In addition, eighth graders had to take a science and social studies assessments (TEA, 2012). Participation was not the only requirement for tenth graders; beginning in 1993, they were required to pass exit level exams in reading, writing, and mathematics to graduate. Throughout the 1990s, additional end-of-course (EOC) exams at the secondary level were implemented. In 1994, a biology EOC was first administered. Later, in 1998, the English II and US history EOCs were added.

Late in the 1990s, TEA faced claims of discrimination against Hispanic and African American students as a result of the requirement that students had to pass the TAAS tests to obtain their high school diploma. The *GI Forum v. TEA* litigation questioned the assessments' alignment to the curriculum and the students' opportunity to learn what was assessed (Cruse & Twing, 2000). TEA showed how through testing they had identified schools and students in need of improvement and had taken the adequate measures to promote improvement. While the judge ruled in favor of TEA, the case set a road map for the development of graduation tests that would be legally defensible (Pedalino Porter, 2001). Soon after, a new assessment program was developed, the Texas Assessment of Knowledge and Skills (TAKS). In 2003, TAKS was developed and aligned to the state's curriculum, the Texas Essential Knowledge and Skills (TEKS). That same year, the stakes got higher for elementary students with the implementation of the Student Success Initiative (SSI) (TEA, 2012). Third graders were required to pass the reading test to be promoted to fourth grade. When those students reached fifth and eighth grade, they were required to pass the reading and mathematics exams to be promoted (TEA, 2012). There were many changes made to the assessment program throughout the decade TAKS was in place. The changes culminated with the development and implementation of the latest assessment program, the replacement of TAKS, the State of Texas Assessments of Academic Readiness (STAAR), as the result of House Bill 3 enacted in the 81st Texas Legislature (TEA, 2010, p. 7). House Bill 3 changed Texas "assessments in a manner that allows the measurement of performance across grades culminating in college readiness performance standards in Algebra II and English III" (TEA, 2010, p. 7). The STAAR program includes the same tests as TAKS in third through eighth grades but replaced high school grade level specific tests with 15 end-of-course exams (TEA, 2012).

The STAAR tests were first administered in 2012, as required by the Texas Legislature to replace TAKS. Unlike its predecessors, the STAAR is scored on a vertical scale system. The vertical scale allows educators to directly compare students' scores from one grade level to the next within the same content area (TEA, 2013a). The STAAR assessment program was designed with the intent to vertically align the assessment of the Texas Essential Knowledge and Skills standards from high school all the way through elementary with an emphasis on college readiness (TEA, 2013a). Given the vertical alignment, the TEA has identified readiness and supporting standards that are eligible for testing, decreasing the standards tested at each grade level (TEA, 2013a). Based on feedback from educators from across the state, TEA identified readiness standards that are essential for students' success in the content. Readiness standards address significant concepts and content, which are important for readiness for the next grade level or course. Readiness standards are emphasized on STAAR on an annual basis. Supporting standards are also important to the grade level or course. However, the supporting standards are introduced in the current grade level or course while being emphasized in the subsequent or previous year. The supporting standards may not be tested annually.

In 2013, House Bill (HB) 5 of the 83rd Texas Legislative Session amended the assessments requirements and reduced the number of high school exams from 15 to five (House Research Organization, 2015d). High school students are given three testing opportunities each year; however, the number of testing opportunity each student has depends on when they take the corresponding courses. For the first time in 30 years, the STAAR components of the Texas assessment contract to Educational Testing Service (ETS) rather than Pearson. Pearson will continue to be contracted to develop and manage the Texas English Language Proficiency Assessment System (TELPAS) and TAKS.

◆ 2015 ASSESSMENT PROGRAM

Table 11.1 shows the assessments administered to Texas students in 2015.

HB 743 of the 84th Texas Legislative Session establishes changes to the time requirements on the administration of the third through eighth grade assessments. Beginning in 2015–2016,

TABLE 11.1
2015 Texas Assessment Program

Content Areas	Grade Levels Tested
Reading	3rd – 8th
Mathematics	3rd – 8th
Writing	4th & 7th
Science	5th & 8th
Social Studies	8th

End-of-Course Exams Required for Graduation

English I
English II
Algebra I
Biology
US History

the third through fifth grade exams must be designed, so that 85% of students are able to complete the assessments within 2 hours while sixth through eighth grade exams should be designed so that the majority of the students finish within three hours. HB 743 changes the time requirement from the previous four hour limit (TEA, 2015b). Additionally, HB 743 requires the redesign of the fourth and seventh grade writing assessments to be administered in 1 day rather than over 2 days. Given the cost of the revision of the third through eighth grade tests, if the assessments cannot be revised prior to the spring 2016 administration of STAAR, the shortened version of the assessments will be administered for the first time in the spring 2017 (TEA, 2015b).

Student Success Initiative

In 2015, the SSI promotion requirements linked to the fifth and eighth grade graders' performance on the math assessments was put on hold given the administration of a new math assessment that assessed the latest math standards. Nevertheless, the math requirements will be reinstituted for 2015–2016 (TEA, 2015d). Similar to the fifth and eighth grade reading assessments, students will have three opportunities to meet the math standard to meet the SSI requirements.

◆ TEXAS ACCOUNTABILITY SYSTEM

The 73rd Texas Legislature mandated the establishment of a school accountability system in 1993. The first accountability system was created and used from that moment forward until 2001–2002 (TEA, 2015a). In 2009, the Texas Legislature required that the TEA redesign the Texas assessment and accountability system in an effort to meet the Federal requirements and promote postsecondary readiness. The latest accountability system was first used to assign district and campus ratings based on STAAR results in 2012–2013 (TEA, 2015a).

The main goal of the latest Texas accountability system is for Texas to "be among the top ten states in postsecondary readiness by 2020" (TEA, 2015a, p. 4). The subgoals aimed to achieve this goal are

- improving student achievement at all levels in the core subjects of the state curriculum,
- ensuring the progress of all students toward achieving advanced academic performance,
- closing advanced academic performance level gaps among student groups, and
- rewarding excellence based on other indicators in addition to state assessment results. (TEA, 2015a, p. 4)

The accountability system is a four-indexes system in which school ratings are determined based on the schools performance in four areas: (1) all students' performance on all STAAR and high school EOC exams, (2) student yearly progress as measured by reading and mathematics STAAR, (3) progress to closing the performance gap between all students and economically disadvantaged students and other historically underperforming racial/ethnic groups, and (4) postsecondary readiness based on student advanced performance on STAAR and high school completion (TEA, 2015a). Each index looks at different passing standards to determine the school's or district's index scores.

The STAAR and EOC Passing Standards

The passing standards for each content area and grade level STAAR and EOC were recommended by a committee of educators in 2012. Upon TEA's review of the committee's recommendations, the Commissioner of Education's approved the passing standards and plans to reach the committee's final recommended level. The passing standards were set on a phase-in schedule with the plan to increase the passing standard every 2 years until the final recommended passing standards were reached in 2016. Yet, given the controversial results of tests and the implementation of new standards, the phase-in 1 standards remained unchanged from 2012 until 2015. After delaying the progress toward the final recommended standards, the decision was made that the standards would go up to the phase-in 2 in 2015–2016. However, in October 2015, the Commissioner of Education proposed a new standard progression plan to reach the final recommended standard in 2021–2022. The Commissioner proposed a more gradual increase of the passing standards by increasing the standards every year rather than abruptly increasing the standards every 2 years. If adopted, the proposed plan will be effective December 28, 2015.

The Four Indexes

The four indexes measure student achievement, academic progress, the efforts of the districts in closing the achievement gap, as well as postsecondary readiness based on STAAR assessments. In 2015, all math assessments in third through grade as well as STAAR-Alternate for all grades and subjects were excluded from accountability calculations. The math assessments were excluded as the result of the implementation of new math TEKS, and the assessment of those TEKS for the first time in third through eighth grade. The Algebra I EOC results were included. Every year, the target for each index is determined by the commissioner based upon the recommendations of the Accountability Policy Advisory Committee (APAC) and the Accountability Technical Advisory Committee (ATAC). The target for some indexes is set while others require that a district or campus perform above certain statewide percentile in order to meet the index target. The four-index system provides ratings that reflect the campus or district's overall performance unlike the previous accountability system than reflected the weakest performance of a student group or content area. In 2015, the accountability system changed the criteria used to assign the overall district and campus ratings. Unlike previous years, districts and campuses did not have to meet the target scores on the four indexes. In order for a school or district to receive a "Met Standard" rating, the school or district had to meet the target on Index 1 or Index 2 and on Index 3 and Index 4. A district or campus that met the target for Index 1, Index 3, and Index 4 was rated as "Met Standard" even if the Index 2 target was not met. Similarly, if the campus or district met the target for Index 2, Index 3, and Index 4, but did not meet the Index 1 target, the district or campus received a "Met Standard" rating. The four indexes are explained in more depth in the subsequent sections.

Index 1. The focus of Index 1 is student achievement. The first index measures the overall performance of all students on all subjects' tests. The total of index points is calculated by the percentage of students who meet the satisfactory standard (Phase-in Level II) on STAAR, meet or exceed the English Language Learner (ELL) progress measure or meet the equivalency standard on the EOC. Unlike in previous years, in 2015, all ELLs were included on the Index 1 calculations.

Index 1 takes a look at satisfactory performance of all students in all subjects. The index score is calculated by looking at the number of tests that met the Phase-in Level II satisfactory standard divided by the total number of tests administered. The number satisfactory performances is added across all content areas and then divided by all content tests given. The overall percentage of satisfactory performances represents the score for Index 1. Table 11.2 provides an example of Index 1 calculations.

If the district or school received 70 points for Index 1 in 2015 (as in the example), the school met the Index 1 target, which was 60 for school districts, and all K-12 campuses, and 35 for alternative education accountability (AEA) charter districts and campuses. In order for the district or campus to be rated as "Met Standard," the district or campus must meet the Index 1 target as calculated above or meet the Index 2 target.

Index 2. The second index of the Texas accountability system focuses on student growth from year to year. Given the new math TEKS and the redesigned math STAAR, math progress measure was not calculated for 2015. Unlike Index 1 that looks at the overall performance, Index 2 looks at student progress by student demographics including race/ethnicity, special education and current and monitored ELLs. ELL must meet the ELL progress measure rather than the standard progress measure. Each subgroup must meet the minimum size requirement, 25 tests per subject, to be included on the Index 2 calculations. In 2015, math assessments and the STAAR Alternate for all grades and subjects were excluded from Index 2 calculations. As a result of the beforehand exclusions, district or high school Index 2 math measure was only based on the Algebra I EOCs. While elementary and middle school Index 2 was calculated solely based on reading scores.

Index 2 is a weighted score based on student progress. The school or district receives one point for each percentage of results that meets or exceeds the progress measure and additional point for each percentage that exceeds progress. In order to calculate whether a student met or exceeded the progress measure, the student's performance, on the same content area assessment over 2 consecutive years, is compared by calculating the difference between the previous year and the current year's scale scores. Once the difference in the scale score is calculated,

TABLE 11.2
Index 1 Calculations

STAAR/EOC Performance	Reading	Math	Writing	Science	Social Studies	Total	% Met Phase-in Satisfactory Standard
# Phase-in satisfactory	307	299	100	88	120	914	70%
Total # of tests	427	425	161	138	161	1,312	
Index 1 score	70						

Note. Given the exclusion of third through eighth grade math assessments in the 2015 accountability calculations, this example could only be for a high school or school district's Index 1 calculations, which include Algebra I scores.

keeping in mind at which level the student performed in the current school year, Level I, II or III, it's determined if the difference falls within a predetermined rage. A student "exceeds progress" if the difference exceeds a predetermined point value. Exceptions are in place for students who perform at a Level III and scores within a top score range. Students that score at the top score range, generally those who only answered no more than two questions incorrectly, are automatically considered as students that "exceeded progress."

Table 11.3 shows how the Index 2 score is calculated for a school with enough tests for the African American (AA), Hispanic (Hisp), White, Special Education (Sp Ed), and ELLs groups to be included in the calculations. The Index 2 scores are calculated by subject area and then combined to calculate the weighted score for all subjects and all grade levels. The first step to calculate Index 2 points is to figure out the percentages that met or exceed progress and the percentages that exceed progress for each subgroup for each test. The two percentage totals are then added for each subgroup to calculate the weighted progress rate for that subject and

TABLE 11.3
Index 2 Calculations

Reading	*All*	*AA*	*Hisp*	*White*	*Sp Ed*	*ELL*	*Total Points*	*Max Points*
# of Tests	321	30	228	44	27	160		
# Met or exceeded progress	189	17	133	27	14	91		
# Exceeded progress	55	1	45	5	3	34		
% Met or exceed progress	59	57	58	61	52	57		
% Exceeded progress	17	3	20	11	11	21		
Reading weighted progress rate	76	60	78	72	63	78	**427**	**1200**
Math	**All**	**AA**	**Hisp**	**White**	**Sp Ed**	**ELL**	*Total Points*	*Max Points*
# of Tests	319	28	227	44	25	160		
# Met or exceeded progress	228	22	165	28	13	118		
# Exceeded progress	98	7	72	13	4	57		
% Met or exceed progress	71	79	73	64	52	74		
% Exceeded progress	31	25	32	30	16	36		

All subjects weighted progress rate	102	104	105	94	68	110	**583**	**1200**
All subjects weighted progress rate	**All**	**AA**	**Hisp**	**White**	**Sp Ed**	**ELL**	**Total Points**	**Max Points**
Reading	76	60	78	72	63	78	427	1200
Math	102	104	105	94	68	110	583	1200
Total Weighted Progress rate							**1010**	**2400**
Index 2 score								**42**

subgroup. Each of subgroup's weighted progress score is then added for the total weighted progress rate for that content area.

In the reading example in table 11.3, the weighted progress rate for all students, 76, was calculated by adding the 59% points of the tests that met or exceed progress and 17% points of the tests that exceed progress. The total reading points, 427, is the total of the sum of all subgroups, 76+60+78+72+63+78. The maximum possible points for reading is 1,200, 100 points per subgroup for the met or exceed progress calculation and 100 points per subgroup for the exceed progress calculation. In this example, there are six student groups, 200 points per group of total 1,200 for the subject area. It is important to note that the percentage of that exceeded progress is calculated by dividing the number of tests that exceeded the progress measure by the total number of tests and not by the number of met or exceed progress. For example using the data from the reading Index 2 calculations in Table 11.3, 55 divided by 321 is 17% points for "all students" that exceed progress.

The Index 2 target is not a set score but rather a statewide percentile by campus type. In 2015, districts and campus that performed in the fifth percentile for their campus type or lower were considered as not having met the Index 2 target. The fifth percentile was recommended by the ATAC members because of the partial number of student progress measures available in 2015. Given that in 2015, districts and schools had to meet the target for Index 1 or Index 2, districts and schools that performed below the statewide fifth percentile could have been rated Met Standard if they met the remaining three indexes targets.

Index 3. The focus of Index 3 is the progress districts and schools have made on improving the student performance of economically disadvantaged students and the two lowest performing ethnic subgroups. The groups that are included in Index 3 calculations are determined by the sub-groups' Index 1 performance the previous school year. The lowest performing ethnic groups are included. To be included in the Index 3 calculations, the ethnic group has to meet the minimum size requirement, 25. However, the economically disadvantaged group is included in the Index 3 calculations regardless of the size of the group. If the district or campus does not have ethnic groups that meet the minimum size criteria, only the economically disadvantaged group is included in the Index 3 calculations. To calculate the Index 3 score, a point is given for each percentage of tests that meet the satisfactory, Phase-in Level II, standard or above. An additional point is given per percentage of the tests meeting the advanced performance standard, Level III. The total maximum points depend on the number of subgroups that meet the size requirement in addition to the economically disadvantaged group. Similar to Index 2, Index 3 scores are calculated by subject area and then combined to figure out the overall Index 3 weighted performance rates. In Table 11.4, only the calculations for a subject area are shown in addition to the overall Index 3 calculations.

Once the weighted performance rates are calculated for all subject areas, the overall index performance rate is calculated. Table 11.5 provides an example of how Index 3 is calculated.

The targets for Index 3 varied by campus type and district. In 2015, the target score for Index 3 was 28 for school districts and elementary campuses, 27 for middle schools, and 31 for high school and K-12 campuses. The Index 3 target for AEA charter districts and campuses was 11. Hence, if the sample calculations were based on a middle school data, the campus would have met the target for Index 3.

TABLE 11.4
Index 3 Calculations

Reading	Econ Disadv	AA	Hisp	Total Points	Max Points
# of Tests	342	137	313		
# Satisfactory (Level II)	235	89	214		
# Advance (Level III)	26	15	33		
% Satisfactory (Level II)	69	65	68		
& Advance (Level III)	8	11	11		
Reading weighted performance rate	77	76	79	**232**	**600**

TABLE 11.5
Overall Index 3 Calculations

All Subject Areas	Econ Disadv	AA	Hisp	Total Points	Max Points
Reading	77	76	79	232	600
Math	83	82	73	238	600
Writing	63	62	61	186	600
Science	63	63	62	188	600
Social studies	75	74	73	222	600
Index 3 weighted performance rate				1,066	3,000
Index 3 score					36

When setting the target for Index 3, the ATAC members engaged in an in-depth dialogue about Index 3 and the implications of measuring the performance of the lowest performing groups. The committee recommended the targets for 2015 with the understanding that their dialogue about Index 3 will continue and consideration will be given to the redesign of this index for the 2016 accountability system.

Index 4. Postsecondary readiness is the focus of Index 4. The index looks at four areas: (1) STAAR at the postsecondary readiness standard, (2) graduation or dropout rate, (3) graduation diploma plan, and (4) postsecondary component: college and career readiness. Each of the components is equally weighted when calculating the overall Index 4 score. When one of the four components is missing, Index 4 only looks at the STAAR performance at the postsecondary readiness standard. Given that elementary and middle schools do not have all four components, Index 4 at those levels focuses in preparing students for high school and only takes into account STAAR performance at final recommended level II. The STAAR postsecondary readiness standard is calculated based on the percentage of students that meet at the final recommended level II on two or more of the tested subjects. When a student is only tested in one subject, the student must meet the postsecondary readiness standard on the test to meet the Index 4 criteria. To calculate the STAAR postsecondary readiness component of Index 4, the percentage of students that perform at the final recommended level II is calculated by subgroup, including only subgroups that meet the minimum size requirement of 25. The percentage of each subgroup is converted into points, which are then added to figure out the total points. The total number of points is then divided by the maximum points; the quotient is the STAAR postsecondary readiness score. Table 11.6 shows the calculations; it is imperative to keep in mind that for students to be counted as having met this standard, they must score at the final recommended level II on two of their tests or on the test if the students only participated on one STAAR test that year.

The graduation rate score used for Index 4 is the higher graduation rate of the four-year and five-year graduation rates. To calculate the 4-year graduation rates, students are tracked from the time they enter ninth grade through their expected graduation year. Students who leave Texas public schools for reasons other than earning a General Educational Development (GED) certificate, graduation or dropping out are removed from the class cohort. Graduation rates are calculated for all students as well as racial/ethnic subgroups, ELL and special education students. When a graduation rate is not available, the dropout rate is used instead. Similar to the STAAR postsecondary readiness standard score, the graduation rate percentage of each subgroup is added to calculate the graduation rate score. Table 11.7 shows the calculations for Index 4 graduation rate component.

TABLE 11.6
Index 4 STAAR Postsecondary Readiness Calculations

	All	AA	Hisp	White	Asian	Total Points	Max Points
% meeting postsecondary readiness standard	35	34	30	51	65	215	500
STAAR Postsecondary readiness standard score							43

TABLE 11.7
Index 4 Graduation Rate Calculations

	All	AA	Hisp	White	Asian	Sp Ed	ELL	Total Points	Max Points
4-Year Plan % Graduated	98%	93%	99%	97%	100%	97%	97%	681	700
5-Year Plan % graduated	93%	94%	100%	100%	100%	100%	98%	685	700
Highest graduation rate score								685	700
Graduation rate score									**98**

Note. The four-year plan data is removed because only the highest scores of the two plans are used to calculate the overall Index 4 score.

The graduation diploma plan calculations and the postsecondary component: college and career readiness score are calculated comparably to the STAAR postsecondary readiness standard and the graduate rate calculations. Similarly to the graduation rate, the graduation plan score looks at a cohort of students' overtime to calculate the percentage of students that graduate under the Recommended High School Program or the Distinguished Achievement Program. In 2015, the postsecondary indicator was replaced by the postsecondary component: college and career readiness indicator. The score is based on:

> the percent of annual graduates who 1) met or exceeded the Texas Success Initiative (TSI) criteria in both English language arts (ELA) and mathematics on the Texas Assessment of Knowledge and Skills (TAKS) exit-level test, SAT, or ACT; or 2) completed and earned credit on at least two advanced/dual credit enrollment courses; or 3) enrolled in a CTE-Coherent Sequence of courses (including the Tech Prep program). (TEA, 2015a, p. 29)

In May 2016, high schools will have the choice of administering STAAR Algebra II and English II assessments as an optional measure of postsecondary readiness. High schools could use their Algebra II and English III STAAR scores to meet the TSI testing requirements. A district may choose to administer one or both exams. If the district decides to administer one or both tests, all students in the district enrolled in Algebra II and/or English III must take the exam the district has chosen to administer (TEA, 2015d).

Once each of the component scores is calculated, each score represents 25% of the overall Index 4 score. Table 11.8 is an example of high school Index 4 calculations.

The target scores for Index 4 varies by campus type as well as whether all components or only the STAAR component are included. For districts and high schools that have all four data points, the target in 2015 was 57 points, which means that the sample school would have met the Index 4 standard. For districts and schools that have missing components of Index 4, and only the STAAR component is calculated, the target varies by type of campus. The target for districts and middle schools was 13 while the elementary schools' target was 12. High schools or K-12 schools that only had the STAAR component must meet the Index 4 target of 21. For AEA charter districts and schools, the Index 4 looks at STAAR results and graduation rate or

TABLE 11.8
Overall Index 4 Calculations

Overall Performance	Score	Weight	Total Points
STAAR postsecondary readiness	43.0	25%	10.8
Graduation rate	98.1	25%	24.5
Graduation plan	86.5	25%	21.6
Postsecondary indicator	64.2	25%	16.1
Index 4 weighted performance rate			**73**

annual dropout rate or the graduation/dropout rate only. For AEA charter districts and schools that have both components, STAAR and graduation rate, the 2015 target was 33 while the target for those that only had a graduation or dropout rate was 45.

Students Included on the Accountability Calculations

All students enrolled in the school district on the state's snapshot date, the last Friday in October, who are enrolled in the same school district on the days of the STAAR tests are included in the accountability calculations. For the campus accountability calculations, only students who are enrolled in the school where they are tested on snapshot date count for the campus accountability. Students who were enrolled in the school district in October but moved within the district are included on the district's accountability calculation but not for the campuses in which the students were enrolled in October and tested in the spring.

Prior to the 84th Texas Legislative Session, high school students receiving special education services were included in the longitudinal rates for accountability regardless of their status and their individualized education program. However, Senate Bill (SB) 1867 removes certain high school students who receive special education services from the accountability calculations. High school students who meet the following criteria will be excluded from the longitudinal rates:

> (1) are at least 18 years of age as of September 1; (2) have satisfied credit requirements for high school graduation; (3) have not completed their individualized education program (IEP); and (4) are enrolled and receiving IEP services. (TEA, 2015a, p. 89)

A group that has historically and provisionally been excluded from accountability calculations is ELL students. However, under the current accountability system, all ELLs are included in all four indexes given the development of the ELL progress measure. ELL students who currently serve through a language program and those have exited but are being monitored are included in the accountability calculations.

High School Diplomas

Texas students have been required to meet the passing standards on the state assessments to receive a high school diploma since 1986. SB 149 of the 84th Texas Legislative Session provides an alternative method of high school seniors to meet the state graduation requirements if the students have failed to meet the standard on two or fewer EOC exams. An individual graduation committee must be established to review the student's academic records, attendance, and postsecondary readiness. The committee is required to recommend additional remediation and completion of an alternative assessment to evaluate the student's proficiency in the content area corresponding to the EOC the student has failed to pass (House Research Organization, 2015d). Similar to the fifth and eight graders' Grade Placement Committees, the individual graduation committee must include the principal or a designee, the teacher of the corresponding ECO course, the student's parent, or the student if the student is at least 18 years old or an emancipated minor, as well as the school's counselor (House Research Organization, 2015b). The school district must designate an advocate to serve as an alternative committee member in place of members unable to attend. The commissioner is expected to develop guidelines for appointing alternate committee members after September 1, 2015 (House Research Organization, 2015b). Upon review of all documentation and requirements as set by SB 149, the committee must reach a unanimous decisions regarding the students' qualifications to graduate and receive a high school diploma. School districts are required to report the number of students per school year that are awarded a high school diploma based upon the decisions of the district's graduation committees (House Research Organization, 2015b).

Additionally, House Bill 2349 revised the requirements for students eligible to receive a Texas high school diploma. If a student earned credit for a course for which there is an EOC, prior to enrollment in a Texas public school, or if the credit was earned prior to 2011–2012, the student is no longer required to pass that EOC to receive a Texas diploma. Prior to HB 2349, students, regardless of their previous course enrollment or credits earned, had to take and pass all five EOC tests to receive a high school diploma (House Research Organization, 2015e).

Implications of an Improvement Required Ratings

Under the current accountability system, districts and schools that fail to meet the accountability standards and are rated as Improvement Required for 2 consecutive years face reconstitution, alternative management, repurposing or closure (House Research Organization, 2015b). Effective upon the release of accountability ratings for the 2015–2016 school year, new procedures for intervention and sanctions of low-performing schools, including the development and submission of a campus turnaround plan, were established by HB 1842 (House Research Organization, 2015b). The implementation of the campus turnaround plan must take place no later than the year following the third consecutive school year that the school has received an improvement required rating (TEA, 2015b). The bill removes the authority of the campus intervention team to decide which educators should remain at the school and the prevention to retain the school principal unless certain requirements were met (House Research Organization, 2015b). The turnaround plan must include (1) a comprehensive description of the academic programs, (2) written input from stakeholders including teacher and parents, (3) if applicable, the term of a district charter without exceeding 5 years, and (4) a comprehensive explanation of staffing, budget and financial resources needed for the implementation of the plan (House Research Organization, 2015b). Turnaround plans are contingent upon the commissioner's approval after determining if the implementation of the plan has the potential to ensure that student performance will meet the standards no later than the second year of implementation (House Research Organization, 2015b). In the event the commissioner does not approve the school's turnaround plan, the commissioner would be expected to appoint a board of managers to oversee the district, alternative management of the campus or closure (House Research Organization, 2015b).

◆ ACCOUNTABILITY REPORTS AND OTHER ACCOUNTABILITY STANDARDS

The district and campus accountability ratings are released by TEA every August, while the accountability reports with detailed data and calculation charts are released later in the fall. TEA must release district and campus accountability ratings by August 8; however, effective the 2015–2016 school year, the deadline will be August 15 as stipulated by HB 2804 of the 84th Texas Legislative Session. Furthermore, districts that received a rating of D or F for the preceding year must be notified of the subsequent rating by June 15.

In addition to the accountability ratings, TEA releases an accountability summary report, indexes calculations and data tables. The accountability summary provides a graph with an overview of the district or campus performance on the four indexes, including the accountability rating, and chart indicating in which indexes the campus met or did not meet standards. Additionally, the report includes a summary of the indexes performance and whether the campus or district received any distinction designations. A campus demographics overview is included as well as an overview of the campus performance as measured by the system safeguards. The data presented in the accountability overview is presented in depth on various separate TEA reports.

Various distinction designations reports are also available. A campus may receive up to seven distinctions: academic achievement in reading, academic achievement in math, academic achievement in science, academic achievement in social studies, top 25% student progress, top 25% closing performance gaps and postsecondary readiness. The distinction designations reports provide detailed information regarding the campus comparison groups as well as detailed data about each distinction.

In addition, to the accountability summary and numerous data reports, TEA releases the Texas Academic Performance Report (TAPR), which compiles a range of data about each campus and school district. In 2012–2013, the TAPR replaced the Academic Excellence Indicator System (AEIS) reports. The TAPR includes student STAAR performance by test and subgroup. It also presents student demographic information as well as information about the faculty, staff and programs offered at each campus or district.

System Safeguards

While the public generally focuses on the indexes and the overall accountability ratings, school administrators must be well informed regarding their district or campus performance in meeting the state and federal system safeguards. Failure to meet state or federal system safeguards has implications for the district or campus. The federal system safeguards were approved by the U.S. Secretary of Education as an alternative to the AYP calculations mandated by NCLB (TEA, 2015a). Schools that fail to meet the state and federal system safeguards are identified as priority or focus schools and must participate in the Texas Accountability Intervention System (TAIS). Moreover, the system safeguards disaggregate data to ensure that the comprehensive nature of the accountability index system does not disguise a district or campus poor performance on a subject area or student group. The system safeguards report provides STAAR performance, STAAR participation and graduation rates of racial/ethnic groups as well as economically disadvantaged, ELLs and students with disabilities that meet the minimum group size criteria. Similar to the indexes calculations, the system safeguards include ELL students who are currently identified as ELL and those who have met the exit criteria but that are still being monitored. The state system safeguard targets are aligned to the Index 1 targets. For 2015, the performance target was 60%, participation was 95%, and the graduation target was 83%. The federal system safeguards are aligned to the federal annual measurable objectives (AMOs). While the federal STAAR participation and graduation targets for 2015 were the same as the state targets, the STAAR performance federal targets were significantly higher. Whereas the state STAAR performance target was 60%,and the federal system safeguard performance targets are 83%. The federal targets apply to reading and math.

Performance-Based Monitoring Analysis System

Since 2004, districts have received an annual Performance-Based Monitoring Analysis System (PBMAS) report. The PBMAS report is generated for school districts to provide them with data on their performance in bilingual education/English as a second language (ESL), career, and technology education and special education. The PBMAS performance levels are unlike any of the indexes or system safeguards. Although PBMAS looks at STAAR performance as the basis to assign performance levels, PBMAS performance levels range from zero to four. The lower the district's performance, the higher the performance level is. As a result of the PBMAS report, districts may be required to develop intervention to address student performance and program effectiveness. If program effectiveness or student performance concerns are unaddressed, the district could face sanctions, additional interventions or even on-site visits from TEA staff (TEA, n.d.).

◆ LOOKING AHEAD

The Texas assessment program and accountability systems are consistently under review and face changes on yearly basis. While the current STAAR and EOC assessments have only been administered to Texas students for 4 years, broad changes could be in the future of Texas assessment program. The new TEC, §39.0236 requires that TEA conduct a study of the alignment of the TEKS curriculum and the state assessments (TEA, 2015b). The results of the study must be presented to State Board of Education (SBOE) by March 1, 2016. The SBOE must present the report and its recommendations based on the findings of the study to the Texas Legislature (TEA, 2015b).

Writing Assessments

Under the current assessment program, fourth and seventh grade students must take the STAAR writing assessments. House Bill 1164 requires that a new writing assessment be developed in 2015–2016 and pilot the program starting in 2016–2017 (TEA, 2015b). The new fourth and seventh grade writing exams and the writing component of the high school EOCs will be replaced by locally designed writing assessments that could include writing portfolios. The results of the writing assessments would not be reported to TEA but will have to be reported in writing to the student's parents or guardians (House Research Organization, 2015a). Additionally, districts will be required to file the overall report of the results of the district and campus writing assessments with the school board and post the report on the district's Website (House Research Organization, 2015a).

While the results of the writing assessments will not have to be reported to TEA once the new assessment program is in place, HB 1164 requires that TEA coordinate a pilot program and work with district to collect the results of the pilot program. Districts participating in the writing assessment pilot program will be required to work in collaboration with TEA to jointly score the writing assessments and report the results to the agency. The results of the pilot assessments will not be reported on the district or agency's websites (TEA, 2015b).

House Bill 1164 has left certain outstanding issues unaddressed. High school students enrolled in the pilot schools are not exempt from the EOC exams required for graduation. Hence, the students participating in the pilot writing assessments will also have to take the English EOCs. The funds allotted for the pilot program will not cover the cost of the implementation of HB 1164.

Future School Ratings

The current district and school ratings, Met Standard and Improvement Required, will be replaced by overall ratings of A, B, C, D, or F as mandated by HB 2804 effective the 2017–2018 school year (TEA, 2015b). The performance of a district or school that receives an A will be considered as exemplary. Recognized performance by a district or school will be recognized by a B rating. A district or school will receive a C rating if the performance is acceptable while schools with unacceptable performance will receive D or F (TEA, 2015b). A district cannot receive an overall or domain rating of A if any campus within the district has received a D or F on the corresponding domain or overall rating (House Research Organization, 2015c).

Not only does HB 2804 change the ratings, it institutes a modification of the current four index system by establishing five domains that will be used to evaluate districts and campuses for accountability purposes (TEA, 2015b). In addition to an overall rating, districts and schools will also receive a letter rating on each of the five domains as well as the community and student engagement indicators. Domain 1, similarly to the current Index 1, will calculate ratings based on the STAAR and EOC assessments combined across grade levels by subject area including the percentage of students who achieved at the satisfactory and college readiness standards (TEA, 2015b). Index 2 will become Domain 2 with a continuous focus on student annual growth regardless of whether the students meet the satisfactory or college readiness standards (TEA, 2015b). Domain 3, as Index 3, will calculate the academic achievement gap among students from different socioeconomic and racial and ethnic backgrounds (TEA, 2015b). HB 2804 establishes Domain 4, which similarly to Index 4, evaluates various indicators depending on whether the school is an elementary, middle, or high school. However, unlike the current system, Domain 4 will use nontest measures of academic attainment (House Research Organization, 2015c). Domain 4 will include attendance as an indicator for elementary, middle and high schools, and a variety of indicators for high schools and other possible indicators of student achievement not associated with STAAR scores as determined by the commissioner (TEA, 2015b). Domain 5 will focus on community and student engagement and gives districts the freedom to choose which three indicators to use and report Domain 5 data to TEA (TEA, 2015b).

The established domains will have varied weight when calculating a district or school's overall rating. Fifty-five percent of the overall rating will be attributed to the first three domains. Thirty-five percent of the overall performance rating of elementary and middle schools will be linked to domain 4. High school graduation rates will account for 10% of their overall ratings and 25% will be attribute to domain 4. The last 10% of all district and campus performance ratings will be based on domain 5 (TEA, 2015b).

◆ REFERENCES

Cruse, K., & Twing, J. (2000). The history of statewide achievement testing in Texas. *Applied Measurement in Education, 13*(4), 327–331.

Delisle, D. (2014, September). *Request for a one-year extension of flexibility.* [Letter to Commissioner Williams]. Retrieved from http://tea.texas.gov/Texas_Schools/Waivers/NCLB-ESEA_Waiver_Information/

Firestone, W., Schorr, R., & Monfils, L. (Eds.). (2004). *The ambiguity of teaching to the test: Standards, assessment, and educational reform.* Mahwah, New Jersey: Lawrence Erlbaum Associates.

Higham, M. (2013, February 12). *No Child Left Behind revisions not expected until 2015. IVN.* Retrieved from http://ivn.us/2013/02/12/no-child-left-behind-revisions-not-expected-until-2015/

House Research Organization. (2015a). *Bill Analysis HB 1164.* Retrieved from http://www.hro.house.state.tx.us/publications.aspx

House Research Organization. (2015b). *Bill Analysis HB 1842.* Retrieved from http://www.hro.house.state.tx.us/publications.aspx

House Research Organization. (2015c). *Bill Analysis HB 2804.* Retrieved from http://www.hro.house.state.tx.us/publications.aspx

House Research Organization. (2015d). *Bill Analysis SB 149.* Retrieved from http://www.hro.house.state.tx.us/publications.aspx

House Research Organization. (2015e). *Bill DigestHB2349.* Retrieved from http://www.hro.house.state.tx.us/publications.aspx

Parkay, F., Hass, G. & Anctil, E. (2010). *Curriculum leadership: Readings for developing quality educational programs.* Boston: Pearson.

Pedalino Porter, R. (2001). *Written statement of testimony.* Washington DC: The Institute for Research in English Acquisition and Development. Retrieved from http://archives.republicans.edlabor.house.gov/archive/hearings/107th/edr/account3801/porter.htm

Texas Education Agency. (n.d.). *Performance-based monitoring analysis system (PBMAS) Overview.* Austin, TX: Texas Education Agency. Retrieved from http://tea.texas.gov/Student_Testing_and_Accountability/PBMAS/

Texas Education Agency. (2010). *Historical overview of assessment in Texas* Austin, TX: Texas Education Agency. Retrieved from http://www.tea.state.tx.us/WorkArea/linkit.aspx?LinkIdentifier=id&ItemID=2147506146&libID=2147506139

Texas Education Agency. (2012). *Historical overview of assessment in Texas.* Austin, TX: Texas Education Agency. Retrieved from http://www.tea.state.tx.us/WorkArea/linkit.aspx?LinkIdentifier=id&ItemID=25769805242&libID=25769805242

Texas Education Agency. (2013a). *State of Texas assessments of academic readiness (STAAR): Vertical scale technical report.* Austin, TX: Texas Education Agency. Retrieved from http://www.tea.state.tx.us/WorkArea/linkit.aspx?LinkIdentifier=id&ItemID=25769806053&libID=25769806056

Texas Education Agency. (2013b). *Texas request for waiver.* Austin, TX: Texas Education Agency. Retrieved from http://tea.texas.gov/Texas_Schools/Waivers/NCLB-ESEA_Waiver_Information/

Texas Education Agency. (2015a). *2015 Accountability manual.* Austin, TX: Texas Education Agency. Retrieved from http://ritter.tea.state.tx.us/perfreport/account/2015/manual/Chapter%2001_Final.pdf

Texas Education Agency. (2015b). *Briefing book on public education legislation*. Austin, TX: Texas Education Agency.

Texas Education Agency. (2015c). *NCLB-ESEA waiver information*. Austin, TX: Texas Education Agency. Retrieved from http://tea.texas.gov/Texas_Schools/Waivers/NCLB-ESEA_Waiver_Information/

Texas Education Agency. (2015d). *News release: Important changes to the Texas assessment program for the 2015–2015 school year*. Austin, TX: Texas Education Agency. Retrieved from http://tea.texas.gov/interiorpage_wide.aspx?id=25769822898

U.S. Department of Education. (n.d.). *Elementary and Secondary Education Act*. Retrieved from http://www.ed.gov/esea

U.S. Department of Education. (2002). *No child left behind: A desktop reference*. Washington, DC: Education Publications Center. Retrieved from http://www2.ed.gov/admins/lead/account/nclbreference/reference.pdf

U.S. Department of Education. (2004). *Four pillars of NCLB*. Washington DC: ED.gov.

12

THE PRINCIPAL AND HUMAN RESOURCES, BUDGETING AND FACILITIES

Gary D. Bigham

Integral to effective instruction and improved student performance are the human resources (HRs), the budgeting, and the facilities functions, all of which fall under the authority and responsibility of the campus principal. Faculty and staff are essential to the teaching and learning process in schools and collectively comprise the HR function. While resources may be inclusive of such things as time, personnel, supplies and materials, and space, all have direct ties to money. Hence, budgeting plays an equally important role in the teaching and learning process. Lastly, instruction must be delivered through a medium, and while technology is currently changing that dynamic, facilities are still central to instructional delivery. In addition to offering class-rooms, facilities also provide office space, storage for supplies and materials, and containment of the technology required for effective instruction. The efficiency and effectiveness with which these three major functions work together are largely reflective of the principal's leadership. Consequently, a thorough understanding of each of these major areas is significant.

This chapter is organized into the following three major functions: (1) HR administration, (2) budgeting, and (3) facilities. Emphasis is placed on campus-level issues important to the principal and other campus leaders. Issues specific to Texas are highlighted, such as applicable Texas statutes, and rules and guidelines set forth by the Texas Education Agency (TEA) and State Board of Education (SBOE). This information is integrated throughout the chapter as appropriate.

◆ HUMAN RESOURCES ADMINISTRATION

The conceptual framework selected for the construction of the human resources (HR) portion of this chapter is patterned after Webb and Norton's (2009) organizational model of HR processes and relationships. The model divides the HR function into the three major categories of HR environment, HR utilization, and HR development. This framework addresses targeted Texas Examinations of Educator Standards (TExES) competencies for Texas principals and their respective descriptive statements, deemed important by the Texas State Board of Educator Certification (SBEC).

HRs Environment

Key to the success of any campus is the shaping of an organizational environment that facilitates student learning and professional growth of the faculty and staff, as highlighted in TExESCompetency 005 for Texas principals. Such an environment does not just happen by chance. Planned change through extensive efforts and involvement of the campus leadership, under the direction of the principal, is required to develop and sustain a desired environment. The two major components of the HR environment are environmental planning and organizational culture and climate, in alignment with TExESCompetency 001 for Texas principals.

Environmental Planning

Environmental planning involves the development and deliberate practice of philosophy, vision, mission, goals, and objectives. Personal values provide the foundation for the entire structure. Guided by values, philosophy must be recognized and articulated prior to vision and mission development as it articulates core beliefs; vision serves as the guiding light for the campus; and mission serves as the standard for setting goals and objectives in educational planning.

Philosophy, Vision, and Mission. Philosophy is present at both personal and professional levels, and it is anchored in values. Ashby and Krug (1998) asserted that the development of a clear understanding of personal and professional values is "essential to leading others through a journey to a place that even you, the leader, may have never seen" (p. 54). The establishment of the leader's values clearly delineates how decisions will be made and where lines will be drawn.

These values inform the school leader's educational philosophy and the values of the stakeholders shape the campus philosophy. The philosophy (what we believe) must be clearly articulated before developing or restructuring the vision or mission. Ramsey (2006) contended, "No vision or mission statement is complete unless it is backed up by a well-defined set of commonly held beliefs. All organizations (including schools) become what they believe. It's always important that everyone involved know what these beliefs are" (p. 20). This is critical for connection and commitment by the educational community.

Once educators on the campus have openly discussed values to develop a clearly articulated philosophy, vision must be considered. According to Hoyle, Bjork, Collier, and Glass (2005), "a clear compelling district vision is the sine qua non of school improvement and character development of students and staff alike" (p. 21). Consequently, the campus vision, in alignment with the district vision, should describe that perfect and ideal campus in accordance with the philosophy of the stakeholders. A compelling vision should serve as the North Star for the campus to sight its compass on and use as a means of getting back on track when it tends to stray (Dimock, 2010). When educators can articulate perfection as seen in the campus vision, they can then truly make strides toward real improvement.

Mission intervenes between philosophy and vision as the action step by which the gap is bridged between the world as it is and the world as seen in the vision, thus connecting reality to an ideal (Bigham, 2010). Mission should serve as the standard against which decisions are made about how to use precious resources of time, energy, money, intellect, and wisdom (Ashby & Krug, 1998). While engaging in mission development activities, campus leaders should remain mindful of the need for the campus mission to align with both the mission of the district, as articulated in Texas Association of School Board (TASB) policy AE(LOCAL), and the mission of Texas public education as codified in TEC § 4.001(a).

Campus Planning

Guided by the campus mission, the planning of goals and objectives can begin. The more concrete process of planning educational goals and objectives is one that involves stakeholders, primarily through the site-based decision-making committee, in developing the campus improvement plan. As codified in statute, the Texas Legislature requires the board of trustees of each independent school district to ensure that campus improvement plans focused on improving the performance of all students are developed, reviewed, and revised annually (TEC § 11.251(a)). The principal, with the assistance of the site-based decision-making committee, is charged with this task (TEC § 11.253(c)). Pursuant to TEC § 11.253(d), the campus improvement plan must assess student achievement, set campus performance objectives, establish strategies for meeting campus goals for each student, assign resources and identify staff for implementation of the plan, set timelines for goal attainment, measure progress of the plan, encourage parental involvement, and include a coordinated health program at the campus. Furthermore, the campus plan must be compliant with the district plan and supportive of the state goals and objectives for public education as outlined in TEC § 4.002 and TEC § 4.001(b) (TEC § 11.251(a)(1–2)).

These environmental planning components serve not only as organizational tools but also as instruments for unifying stakeholders. The environmental planning components create stakeholder buy in and ownership through their involvement in various developmental processes. Moreover, the documents constructed articulate the values and beliefs of the campus, as well as its educational plan for improved student performance.

Organizational Culture and Climate. Environmental planning serves an important role in setting the stage for a strong organizational culture nurtured through a healthy, positive climate. An understanding of the concepts of culture and climate are vitally important to campus leaders because the behavior of people in the school organization "is not elicited by an interaction with proximate events alone, but is also influenced by interactions with intangible forces in the organization's environment" (Owens & Valesky, 2007, p. 192). While interrelated, culture and climate are different concepts with different meanings that warrant individual explanations.

Organizational Culture. Organizational culture may be described as "the unwritten code of conduct that governs the behavior, attitudes, relationships, and style of the organization" (Ortiz & Arnborg, 2005, p. 35). Webb and Norton (2009) described four manifestation levels of increasing abstraction of culture. Beginning at the most concrete level, culture is reflected through language, symbols, and artifacts, including such things as dialects, sayings, stories, myths, legends, art, heroes, and rituals. Norms, making up the second level of culture, define acceptable and unacceptable behavior in the organization. At the third level of increased abstraction, values and beliefs may be observed through recognitions and rewards, levels of student achievement and quality of teaching, as well as in written mission statements and school goals. Lastly, assumptions, which are fundamental to all organizational actions and decisions, represent the most abstract level of culture.

Culture distinguishes one campus from another by providing each with its own sense of identity. Culture facilitates group commitment; enhances social system stability; defines appropriate standards for behavior; and ultimately binds the campus together (Hoy & Miskel, 2005). Glickman, Gordon, and Ross-Gordon (2010) conveyed, "The concept of culture helps us reexamine schools as places of human community with peculiar histories and stories" (p. 20) and articulated the importance of understanding school culture as follows:

> When we grasp the underlying values of our particular school as a work environment, we can consciously act to reshape the organization into a purposeful collection of individuals who believe that schools are for students, for learning, and for improvement rather than for insularity, self-protection, and complacency. (p. 20)

Organizational Climate. Organizational climate reflects a school's personality (Webb & Norton, 2009), and may be defined as:

> the set of internal characteristics that distinguish one school from another and influences the behavior of its members . . . the relative stable property of the school environment that is experienced by participants, affects their behaviors and is based on their collective perceptions of behavior in schools. (Hoy & Hannum, 1997, p. 291)

The atmosphere resulting from the social and professional interactions within a school largely characterizes its climate (Webb & Norton, 2009).

School climates have been described as healthy, unhealthy, open, and closed. The school leader should become adept at gauging the climate and using it as a tool for school improvement. School climate sets the stage for growth and renewal; is important in maintaining effective communication throughout the campus; and serves as a means of conditioning the environment for change (Webb & Norton, 2009). Additionally, the healthy school climate "serves to stimulate the best efforts of people through providing meaningful work, motivating challenges, and continuous opportunities for personal growth and development" (Webb & Norton, 2009, p. 53). Sergiovanni and Starratt (2007) emphasized the importance of educational leaders' understanding and navigation of climate as follows:

> Climate provides a reading of how things are going in the school and a basis for predicting school consequences and outcomes. Such a barometer represents an important tool for evaluating present conditions, planning new directions, and monitoring progress toward new directions. (p. 333)

Creating and sustaining a healthy school environment, through extensive environmental planning and shaping and nurturing a desirable culture and climate, is critical to the success of HR administration. Such an environment has the ability to attract quality applicants to the campus, engage employees in a meaningful way, reduce teacher turnover rates, and ultimately improve student performance. Being more abstract in nature than HR utilization and HR development, it is easy for the school leader's attention to be diverted away from the HR environment. However, the school leader who consistently allows this to happen will find that other areas of HR administration and student performance will ultimately suffer as a result.

HRs Utilization

A review of the information in one particular descriptive statement in Competency 006 of the TExES principal framework is highly reflective of the HR utilization category. In addition to Webb and Norton's (2009) suggestion that the process begin with effective planning, the identified TExESCompetency 006 descriptive statement emphasizes recruitment, screening, selection, assignment, induction, promotion, discipline, and dismissal of campus staff. The HR utilization subsection of this chapter is organized accordingly. Additionally, applications of federal and state law are intertwined into the discussions—a reflection of TExESCompetency 003 for Texas principals.

Planning

Planning is a basic function of management, whereas purposing more resembles a function of leadership (Sergiovanni, 1990). While all of the identified HR utilization processes are obvious functions of management, for true school improvement to occur, from a leadership perspective, purposeful planning is essential. If the environmental planning process has produced a viable mission statement, it should be the guidepost upon which all HR utilization decisions are made.

At its root level, planning assists campus leaders in anticipating and responding to problems and changes that occur by enabling them to focus the energies and resources of the campus on the attainment of desired results (Webb & Norton, 2013). With the desired results being reflected in the mission statement and specifically spelled out in the campus improvement plan, strategic plans can be formulated. Without strategic planning, "the school cannot marshal the physical, financial, and HRs needed to fulfill its mission" (Boone, 2010, p. 352). Tools of strategic planning include student enrollment forecasts (Webb & Norton, 2009), HR inventories, a review of campus goals in relation to future needs, and a forecast of HR requirements (Boone, 2010).

In the end, all planning processes should culminate into a strategic HR plan. Strategic HR planning places appropriate personnel into key places to advance the school's mission and move toward achievement of goals and objectives (Webb & Norton, 2009). Strategic HR planning is far more than a management function. Strategic HR planning requires thoughtful reflection of past practices, the current situation, and future needs. As phrased by Webb and Norton (2009):

> Strategic human resources planning is not necessarily the making of future decisions; it also focuses upon current decisions and their future implications. Strategic human resources planning produces current decisions about what should be done now to realize desired outcomes in the future. (p. 27)

Recruitment.   Although the primary purpose of the recruitment process is to create a pool of qualified applicants for open positions, there is much more to it than simply placing an ad in the local newspaper. While vacancies in current positions or the creation of new positions are commonly viewed as the beginning of the recruitment process, in most cases, the recruitment process actually begins at an even earlier stage. Webb and Norton (2013) described a six-step recruitment process beginning with the establishment of goals, followed by a needs assessment, a job analysis, the preparation of a job description, internal and external recruiting, and ending with the final step which is the establishment of an applicant pool.

Establishing Goals.   Long- and short-term campus goals, in alignment with the goals of the district, are integral to the campus recruitment process. Goals may include, but are certainly not limited to finding personnel with specialized knowledge and skills such as technology or, in the case of a magnet school, discipline specific knowledge related to the magnet focus. Goals may center on alignment with state or federal requirements, or even professional standards. Other goals may encompass a more diverse faculty, adjustments to the economy, and population changes.

Needs Assessment.   A vacated position does not always necessitate a replacement. In the case of a declining enrollment or internal restructuring, the need for the position may no longer be warranted. Based on the established goals and strategic objectives, enrollment forecasts, campus-specific needs, and future issues, the HR structure may need to change; thus warranting a thorough needs assessment prior to posting any position.

Job Analysis.   The process of gathering, organizing, and evaluating job-related information culminates into the official job analysis (TASB, 2006). Upon confirming the need for a position, key to the job analysis process is the establishment of knowledge, skills, abilities, and other characteristics (KSAOs) (Webb & Norton, 2013). Chen, Carsten, and Krauss (2003) noted:

> A comprehensive, high-quality job analysis provides descriptive (i.e., how a job is done), prescriptive (i.e., how a job should be done), and predictive (i.e., how a job will be done) information about the critical tasks of a job and the KSAOs required to perform these tasks. (p. 28)

The steps in the job analysis process include the following:

- Identifying what information needs to be collected;
- Determining the sources of information and who will facilitate the data collection;
- Communicating to employees and supervisors what is being done and why;
- Collecting information from incumbent employees;
- Verifying information with management;
- Incorporating information into job descriptions. (TASB, 2006, p. 1)

Bolton (1997) suggested that a job analysis should be prepared to clarify details of the position, provide information for the creation of the job description, establish a basis for the creation performance evaluation criteria, and identify the job's location within the organization's structure.

TASB (2006) clarified, "A thorough job analysis will identify important and relevant information, such as the qualifications needed for successful job performance, the specific tasks of a job, and the equipment used" (p. 1). The development of a thorough job analysis serves as the precursor for developing a job description.

Job Description.   Informed by the job analysis, a properly constructed job description outlines the requirements of the job. According to TASB (2004c):

> Job descriptions are narrative statements detailing the duties and responsibilities of the specific jobs within an organization. Job descriptions identify, define, and describe the most important features of the jobs and provide districts with documentation of job requirements to support personnel decisions. (p. 1)

As De Cenzo and Robbings (1996) explained, the job description is useful in describing the job to be performed, providing guidance to new employees regarding what is expected in the job, and providing a rational basis upon which to evaluate the employee's performance.

While different approaches may be taken in formatting job descriptions, in addition to the title section, TASB (2004b) suggested the inclusion of the following components:

- a general summary of role and purpose;
- qualifications required;
- major responsibilities and duties performed;
- a description of significant mental and physical demands and environmental factors;
- a disclaimer clause indicating that other related duties may be assigned; and
- a signature section to indicate date reviewed and approved and by whom. (p. 1)

For member districts with a subscription to HR services, TASB provides editable model job descriptions for virtually every position in a school district.

Recruiting.   Once the need for a position has been established in alignment with the goals of the school and a job description has been prepared for the position, a pool of qualified applicants should be assembled. Webb and Norton (2013) mentioned several factors to consider when approaching the recruitment process, beginning with establishing whether the need for the position is short-term, long-term, or ongoing. Second, attention should be given to the desired size of the applicant pool in relation to sources and strategies to use in contacting candidates. Third, the type of job will influence the choice of recruitment methods. Fourth, cost of recruiting and funds allotted for that purpose will certainly enter into the equation. Fifth, determining whether the search will be internal, external, or both will also influence the recruiting approach taken.

Webb and Norton (2013) suggested several advantages of internal recruiting including an inherent cost savings as well as a motivational factor for current employees who may desire to move within the organization. Moreover, evaluating internal candidates' strengths and weaknesses is easier based on past evaluations. Lastly, internal applicants typically require less orientation than external applicants. However, paired with the advantages are the disadvantages of limiting the number of candidates from which to choose, limiting the introduction of new ideas and perspectives that can be gained from external candidates, the potential contribution to complacency within the organization, and the realization that filling one position leaves another position unfilled.

If external recruiting is deemed appropriate, several options avail themselves as avenues for advertising. However, prior to posting a vacant position for which a certificate or license is required as prescribed in TEC § 21.003, principals should be cognizant of the state statute requiring school district policy to provide that no later than the 10th school day before the date on which such position is filled, each current employee must be notified by bulletin board and/or district Website Internet posting of the position to be filled and be afforded a reasonable opportunity to apply for the position (TEC § 11.1513(d)(1–2)). This requirement applies to all TEC § 21.003 positions except those affecting the safety and security of students as defined by the school board (TEC § 11.1513(d)). If a teaching position is vacated during the school year, the district must still provide notice of the position as soon as possible as outlined in TEC § 11.1513(d)(1), however, the ten-day rule does not apply, nor does TEC § 11.1513(d)(2) regarding a reasonable opportunity for insiders to apply for the position.

Once compliance with the "ten day" posting notice has been met, external advertising may commence. External advertising may be conducted through the avenues of professional contacts, media advertisements, employment agencies, educational institutions, professional organizations, and Internet recruiting (Webb & Norton, 2013). Referrals from current and previous employees may serve the recruiting need well and have no associated expense. Media advertising may take the form of newspaper ads, professional journals, radio broadcasts, and television broadcasts, but the cost can sometimes be quite high. Depending on the type of position needing filled, employment agencies may lend themselves to the process. Obviously, colleges and universities that prepare teachers and administrators for certification supply a pool of candidates for various positions. With the widespread use of the Internet, recruiting can be done through the campus or district Website, as well as Education Service Center (ESC) Websites, and Websites of professional organizations.

In addition to the statutory internal posting requirement, attention to other recruiting-related compliance issues in connection with federal and state laws must also be observed. The major employment enforcement agencies are the Equal Employment Opportunity Commission (EEOC) at the federal level and the Texas Workforce Commission (TWC) at the state level. A summary of major Equal Employment Opportunity (EEO) laws associated with recruitment is displayed in Table 12. 1.

While the information contained in Table 12.1 should not be considered an exhaustive list, it highlights the major EEO employment-related laws. Principals should be aware of all employment-related laws and vigilantly guard against any level of non-compliance.

TABLE 12.1
Summary of Major EEO Laws

Law	*Description*
Equal Pay Act of 1963	Prohibits gender discrimination in pay; requires equal pay for males and females in jobs requiring equal skills and responsibilities.
Title VII of the Civil Rights Act of 1964, as amended	Prohibits discrimination in hiring, compensation, and terms and conditions of employment on the basis of race, color, religion, national origin, or sex.
Age Discrimination in Employment Act of 1967, as amended	Prohibits discrimination in employment against persons aged 40 and older.
Equal Employment Opportunity Act of 1972	Extends race coverage of Title VII to include employees of state and local governments and educational institutions. Created the EEO Commission with authority to prohibit discrimination and file suits against organizations believed to be discriminatory.
Title IX of the Education Amendments of 1972	Prohibits discrimination on the basis of gender in programs receiving federal funds.
Section 504 of the Vocational Rehabilitation Act of 1973	Requires federal agencies and organizations receiving federal funds to take affirmative action to recruit, hire, and promote qualified disabled persons.

Vietnam Era Veterans Readjustment Assistance Act of 1974	Requires federal contractors and subcontractors to take affirmative action to hire and promote veterans and disabled veterans.
Pregnancy Discrimination Act of 1978	Provides EEO protection to pregnant workers and requires pregnancy to be treated like any other disability.
Americans With Disabilities Act of 1990	Extends the antidiscrimination provisions of Section 504 to organizations not receiving federal funds. Prohibits employment discrimination against individuals with physical or mental handicaps or the chronically ill.
Civil Rights Act of 1991	Amended Title VII and strengthened it and other civil rights laws that had been weakened by Supreme Court decisions.

Note. Adapted from *Human Resources Administration: Personnel Issues and Needs in Education* (p. 106), by L. D. Webb and M. S. Norton, 2009, Upper Saddle River, NJ: Pearson. Copyright 2009 by Pearson Education Inc.

Screening

When the applicant pool has reached the desired level, the applicant screening process begins. Screening involves reviewing applications and associated materials, a preliminary interview, background checks, the official interview, and an evaluation of candidates remaining at the conclusion of all screening processes. Similar to recruiting, the screening process is multifaceted and meticulous. Slighting any step presents the potential of making a bad hire.

Initial Screening. The initial screening phase engages HR personnel in reviewing application materials against selection criteria for the vacant position. Depending on the position being filled and campus or district requirements, the primary documents to be reviewed will include one or more of the following: (1) the official application, (2) the candidates' resumes and cover letters, (3) academic transcripts, and (4) specialized certifications/licensures. Screening at this level is limited strictly to a review of the documentation provided by the candidate. A thorough review typically eliminates some of the candidate pool. This results in the conservation of time and efforts later in the screening process.

Preliminary Interview. Depending on common hiring practices in the campus or district, and the size of the applicant pool after the initial screening process, a preliminary interview may be used as a screening tool. The obvious disadvantage of the preliminary interview is the time required to conduct each interview. However, the information gained, may prevent a costly mistake in the hiring process. Keep in mind that the preliminary interview is a tool that may or may not be used. Often, this step is skipped and only the official job interview is conducted.

Background Checks. There cannot be enough emphasis placed on the importance of background checks. Because of their failure to conduct adequate background checks, many schools have been found liable for negligent hiring (Webb & Norton, 2013). Background checks should begin with credentials checks, followed by criminal background and reference checks.

Credentials checks, depending on the position being filled, include application of scrutiny to such documents as diplomas, academic transcripts, professional licensure, and professional development records. Different positions require varying levels of credentials. For example, licensure varies among teaching faculty, nurses, counselors, and administrators. Moreover, some positions may require bachelor's degrees whereas others may only require a high school diploma or GED. The nature of the position dictates the credentials required.

From a statutory perspective, the state of Texas is emphatic that all professionals be appropriately certificated or permitted. TEC § 21.003(a) explicitly states "a person may not be employed as a teacher, teacher intern or teacher trainee, librarian, educational aide, administrator, educational diagnostician, or counselor by a school district unless the person holds an appropriate certificate or permit." Moreover, the highly qualified provision of the No Child Left Behind (NCLB) Act requires that any teacher hired in a school receiving federal Title I funds be "highly qualified." To meet the highly qualified federal definition, a teacher must hold at least a bachelor's degree, be fully certified, and demonstrate subject matter competency in each of the academic subjects (s)he teaches (TEA, 2015).

The principal of a Texas campus receiving Title I federal funds, who is attempting to fill the vacated position of a certified teacher, must seek a candidate with credentials that meet state certification requirements as well as NCLB highly qualified requirements. Both require at least a bachelor's degree, which can be verified with college/university transcripts. Both require teacher certification, with Texas requiring specified areas of certification in accordance with SBEC rules. Texas educators' certificates can be verified fairly quickly online at https://secure.sbec.state.tx.us/SBECONLINE/virtcert.asp. Lastly, to meet the definition of "highly qualified," teachers must demonstrate subject matter competency in each of the academic subjects in which the teacher teaches. Depending on when the teacher was certified and his or her years of experience, this may be verified through the passage of state certification exams or through an examination of the professional development certificates provided by the teacher. If, through this credential check process, a candidate for a given position fails to meet either state or federal requirements described, the candidate should be excluded from the pool.

Once the applicant pool has been adjusted following the credentials verification process, criminal background checks should be conducted. In Texas, SBEC is required to review the national criminal history record information of applicants for or holders of educator certificates (TEC § 22.0831(c)). All noncertified school employees (not holding SBEC certification), are also subject to reviews of national criminal history record information, governed by TEA and the school district. The reviews are conducted by the Texas Department of Public Safety through fingerprinting and/or photographs. The school district is responsible for submitting the name of the applicant to TEA, who in turn notifies the school district if the person may not be hired or whose employment must be terminated (TEC § 22.085). In essence, everyone employed in a Texas public school will undergo a national criminal history record information review.

Although reference checks may be conducted before or after the interview, completing this process before the interview equips the interviewers with as much job-related information about the applicant as possible and serves as one more screening tool that may eliminate more applicants from the pool (Gomez & Craycraft, 2002), resulting in a time savings when the interviews begin. Reference checks serve as objective evaluations of applicants' past job performance through conversations with individuals who have worked with applicants in the past (Barada & Mclaughlin, 2004). Ideally, those involved in the interview process should be the ones conducting the reference checks, typically by telephone, and/or reference letter reviews (Webb & Norton, 2009).

From a legal standpoint, strict scrutiny must be applied to the questions asked. Nothing may be asked of an applicant's references that may not be asked directly of the applicant (Gomez & Craycraft, 2002). When checking references by telephone, the interviewer must limit questioning strictly to job-related issues and must guard against asking questions that extend beyond the scope of the position being sought by the applicant. Moreover, the reference check process must never be used as a means of illegally discriminating against any applicants (Gomez & Craycraft, 2002). Similar questions should be asked of references for all applicants. In so doing, the same rules that apply to interview questions also apply here. While reference checking is a time consuming process, it adds useful information about the applicants and should result in a more accurate decision in the final employment steps (Bliss, 2000).

Employment Interview.   The interview process, similar to other pre-employment activities, is a detailed, thought-provoking process, deserving of as much, if not more, time and effort as all processes leading up to this point. Extensive planning and preparation is critical to successful interviews. In preparing for the interview process, the interview team must be assembled and interview training, if needed, must be completed prior to the first interview. Additionally, the number of interviews to be conducted, as well as the desired length of each interview should be determined at this time (TASB, 2003b).

Legitimate selection criteria aligned with the job must be determined and corresponding questions should be formulated. Attention to question formulation at this level of detail ensures that the information gained will pertain directly to the job at hand, while simultaneously reducing the risk of asking unlawful, discriminatory questions (TASB, 2009).

Common types of questions asked in employment interviews may be categorized as closed, open-ended, probing, self-assessment, and situational questions. The closed question requires only a single word response from the applicant (TASB, 2009) for purposes of revealing factual information (Webb & Norton, 2013). According to TASB (2009), the open-ended questions are instrumental in engaging the applicant in thoughtful and reflective cognition. Probing questions are often used to follow up on responses to open-ended questions. Probing questions elicit more information about particular points of interest to the interviewer. Self-assessment questions require applicants to share "their opinions of their own actions, knowledge, or style" (p. 1). Finally, situational questions present a problem or situation for the applicant to devise a solution. The situation may be real or hypothetical and the applicant's answer reveals information about knowledge, experience, and problem-solving skills.

It should be reiterated that interview questions must pertain directly to the job for which the applicant has applied. Unlawful discrimination must be avoided. The two primary types of unlawful discrimination delineated by TASB (2010c) include, "discrimination by specific intent, where employment practices are knowingly and deliberately designed to exclude a protected class of individuals," and "discrimination by adverse impact, whereby employment practices result in unequal treatment of one or more of the protected groups, regardless of intent" (p. 2). A review of the federal laws, in Table 12.1, would be a most worthy undertaking in preparing questions for the employment interview. Fundamental practices for use in avoiding unlawful discrimination include asking only job-related questions, consistently asking the same questions of each interviewee, and documenting all phases of the hiring process (TASB, 2010c).

In addition to formulating interview questions, the interview procedures should be predetermined. This process involves such things as assigning questions to various team members and sequencing the order questions are asked. If notes will be taken or interview forms completed by the interviewers, this is the time to make those decisions (TASB, 2010c).

The interview team members should acquaint themselves with each applicant to be interviewed through a thorough review of all documentation gathered (TASB, 2010c). This includes the application, resume, cover letter, reference letters, and information obtained from reference checks. If any discrepancies or contradictions surface in the document review, the interview is the time to probe deeper for answers and resolutions to any issues identified by the interviewers.

Prior to the arrival of the applicant, the interview room should be prepared to "build a receptive and comfortable environment that will enhance effective listening and elicit more open, honest responses" (TASB, 2003, p. 2). Furthermore, attention should be given to issues of privacy, interruptions, temperature, lighting, and the physical needs of the applicants and interview team (TASB, 2003).

Upon the arrival of the applicant to the scheduled interview, the lead interviewer should set the tone. This involves starting on time, appropriate introductions of everyone involved, and asking a few neutral questions to assist the applicant in becoming comfortable before proceeding (TASB, 2003). The interview structure should be described to orient the applicant to the predetermined process, followed by engagement into the structured interview (TASB, 2003).

Typically, the applicant should be afforded the opportunity to talk about himself/herself. Weller and Weller (2000) suggested this promotes confidence. While following the pre-established interview plan, interviewers should be cognizant of their interpersonal skills including tone of voice, body language, facial expressions, and eye contact. Interviewer interpersonal behaviors have the ability to directly impact the responses received from the interviewee (Webb & Norton, 2013).

The importance of listening cannot be overemphasized. While this is perhaps one of the most difficult tasks for many interviewers, it is also one of the most important (Webb & Norton, 2013).TASB (2003) suggested that 80% of the talking in an interview should be done by the applicant. It is only through active listening that discriminate evaluations may be made among the candidates. To enhance listening skills, Cunningham and Cordeiro (2006) suggested that interviewers:

- get the respondent to clarify, elaborate, and reflect;
- summarize or restate key points;
- look at the person;
- get the main points and test for understanding;
- control desire to mentally agree;
- avoid making assumptions;
- recognize prejudices;
- do very little of the talking; and
- be accepting. (pp. 286–287)

As the interview draws to an end, the applicant should be afforded the chance to ask questions. Once all questions have been addressed, the applicant should be informed about remaining steps in the hiring process, notification methods and time lines, and any other issues or information pertinent to the applicant. Of course, the applicant should always be thanked for his or her time and interest in the vacant position (TASB, 2003).

At the conclusion of each interview, the interview team should document the interview just completed. Notes should be expanded upon if needed and rating forms filled out, if used (TASB, 2003). All documentation should be kept in a secure location to ensure confidentiality.

Common mistakes of interviewers that should be avoided include prejudging the candidate, relying on first impressions, allowing the halo effect to influence a decision, comparing candidates with each other, relying on intuition, allowing personal biases or preferences to influence a decision, and feeling pressured to make a decision (TASB, 2003). With the importance of every position in a school, interviewers should guard against these mistakes and make every effort to make the most objective hiring decisions possible.

Evaluation of Candidates.   At the conclusion of the last interview, an evaluation of all remaining candidates is in order. This is the point in the process that reveals the dire importance of maintaining a detailed set of notes during the interviews. While methods may vary from highly detailed evaluation forms and rating scales to less formalized practices, objectivity must be maintained in reviewing all documentation of each candidate—the application, resume, cover letter, reference checks, and interview notes. Ultimately, the final selection should reflect the candidate who best matches the predetermined criteria for the position.

Selection

Some argue that the selection process may be the single most important step in making substantive organizational change. Every new hire requires a deliberate time investment. Devoting the time on the front side of the process is a far better investment than making a bad hire, likely resulting in remediation, or discipline and potential dismissal of the employee from employment. The odds are that time will be spent on one side or the other of the employment process. Investing that time on the front side is not only less stressful and challenging for the principal, but it is also the wisest choice in addressing the educational needs of the students in the school.

So, who are the key players in making final selections in Texas schools? Potentially, the most key player is the superintendent of the district. TEC § 11.1513(a)(2) states, "The superintendent has sole authority to make recommendations to the board regarding the selection of all personnel other than the superintendent, except that the board may delegate final authority for those decisions to the superintendent." Thus, the board may elect to retain final hiring authority, or it may elect to delegate that authority to the superintendent. Either way, the superintendent is a key player, because even if the board opts to retain the final hiring authority, it may only act on the superintendent's recommendations.

This does not, however, exclude the principal from the process. TEC § 11.1513(a)(3) indicates, "each principal must approve each teacher or staff appointment to the principal's campus as provided by Section 11.202." TEC § 11.202(b)(1) states, "Each principal shall, except as provided by Subsection (d), approve all teacher and staff appointments for that principal's campus from a pool of applicants selected by the district or of applicants who meet the hiring requirements established by the district, based on criteria developed by the principal after informal consultation with the faculty." Thus, while the superintendent is integral in the hiring of all personnel in the district, the principal is a key player in the hiring of all personnel on a given campus. While ultimately, either the board or the superintendent, depending on board policy, makes the actual final hiring selection, it is not without the approval of the principal. The selection is not complete until the school offers the position and the candidate accepts it. Due to this fact, no candidates should be notified of any decision until that offer and acceptance is complete.

The Employment Contract. The formal and legal avenue by which this is accomplished is through the employment contract. Alexander and Alexander (2012) defined a contract as "an agreement between two or more competent persons for legal consideration concerning legal subject matter in a form required by law" (p. 772). Alexander and Alexander described the basic elements essential for an employment contract to be legally binding as: (1) offer and acceptance, (2) competent persons, (3) consideration, (4) legal subject matter, and (5) proper form. Webb and Norton (2013) added that the contract must also meet all additional requirements that may be spelled out in state law. Employment contracts are legally binding and as such may be broken only under the most strict terms and conditions. The school district may end an employment contract during its term only with good cause and due process. Further, if an employee abandons a contract prior to its end, (s)he does so with the risk of having his or her teaching contract suspended (TASB, 2010a).

Texas school employees entitled to employment contracts include classroom teachers, counselors, nurses (RN), principals, and librarians (TEC § 21.002). Employment contracts for Texas educators fall under three main categories in Chapter 21 of the Texas Education Code (TEC). Those are the probationary, term, and continuing contracts (TEC § 21.002).

Probationary Contract. Essentially, all certified teachers new to a school district "shall" be employed under a probationary contract (TEC § 21.002). The probationary term may not exceed one year, but may be less than one year. However, it may be renewed for two additional one-year periods for a total of three years (TEC § 21.002; Walsh, Kemerer, & Maniotis, 2014). The probationary contract may be extended to a fourth year if "the board of trustees determines that it is doubtful whether the teacher should be given a continuing or a term contract" (TEC § 21.002(c)). The exception, which applies to teachers who have been employed in public education for at least five of the eight years preceding employment by the school, is that the probationary period may not exceed one year (TEC § 21.002(b)). Note that for purposes of a probationary contract, 1 year was defined by the commissioner of education as one full school year (*Young v. Lipan ISD*). At the end of the probationary period, for employment to continue, the teacher must receive either a term or a continuing contract (Walsh et al., 2014).

Term Contract. The term contract is non-probationary for a fixed term (TEC § 21.201(3)) not to exceed a statutory maximum of five years (TEC § 21.205). Teacher contracts are typically 1 year in length, whereas administrators will more likely receive multiyear contracts. For employment to continue the term contract should be renewed at the end of each term, however, the board's failure to give the required notice regarding proposed renewal or nonrenewal (TEC § 21.206(a)) "constitutes an election to employ the teacher in the same professional capacity for the following year" (TEC § 21.206(b)).

Continuing Contract. The continuing contract automatically rolls over from 1 year to the next without board action (Walsh et al., 2014). In other words, renewal is not required. Continuing contracts do not specify lengths of employment time, nor do they have an expiration date. This makes the continuing contract similar to tenure rights (TASB, 2010a). The continuing contract literally continues until the employee resigns or retires and "good cause" serves as the only grounds for termination of the employment (TASB, 2010a). Texas statutes regarding the continuing contract are located in the Texas Education Code §§21.151 etseq.

Other Employment Arrangements. In addition to the Chapter 21 employment contracts, other employment arrangements may be made, depending on the position needed by the school and the credentials of the individuals applying for the positions. Other employment categories include at-will employees, non-Chapter 21 professionals, and third-party independent contractors.

Assignment

Personnel assignment may take the form of initial assignment immediately after the hiring process or reassignment at a later point during employment. TEC § 11.201(d)(2) grants full administrative authority and responsibility for the assignment of all personnel in the district to the superintendent with the approval of the campus principals where the assignments or reas- signments are made (TEC § 11.202(b)(1)). Once personnel have been assigned to a campus in accordance with TEC § 11.201(d)(2) and TEC § 11.202(b)(1), the responsibility then falls on the principal for specific assignment of campus-level personnel (TEC § 11.202(b)(5)).

According to TASB (2004a), in the case of reassignment, in the absence of legal restrictions preventing it, the superintendent has full authority to assign, reassign, or transfer teachers and administrators. However, because the U.S. Constitution protects contractual property rights, "The power of the superintendent to reassign personnel is not absolute" (p. 1). Furthermore, "If the reassignment constitutes a demotion, the employee must be afforded due process of law before being deprived of his or her property right in the employment position" (p. 1).

Aside from the legal implications of personnel assignment, the ultimate desire is to place employees such that their talents and skills maximize the educational benefit of the students while simultaneously meeting the needs and goals of the employee. Such placement has a multiplicative effect in areas of student learning, employee motivation, organizational climate, and professional development. Proper selection and assignment of employees may be the single most important activity in meeting the goals and objectives of the school.

Induction. Retention of "highly qualified" teachers is required by the No Child Left Behind Act of 2001 and should be desired by every campus and district. Induction is a useful tool in this quest. By definition, "induction is a comprehensive, coherent, and sustained multiyear process designed to train, acculturate, support, and retain new teachers and seamlessly progress them into a lifelong professional development program" (Wong, 2004 as cited by Webb & Norton, 2009).

Numerous studies addressing effective induction programs (AFT, 2001; Center for Teaching Quality, 2006; Schlecty, 2005; Wayne, Youngs, & Fleischman, 2005; Wong, 2004; Wong, Britton, & Ganser, 2005) have yielded several common characteristics. As compiled and reported by Webb and Norton (2013), effective induction programs:

- articulate organizational values
- require participation from all newly contracted employees
- offer a continuum of professional development
- are supported by the administration
- align with professional, state, and local standards
- assign a qualified mentor to each inductee
- afford ample opportunities for observing and modeling effective practice
- are designed with input from new and veteran teachers
- plan for frequent mentor-mentee interactions through reduced course loads
- provide release time for collaborative interactions with other teachers
- use a standards-based evaluation system to promote learning.

While few would question the importance of pairing a new teacher with a strong mentor, Wong (2005) revealed that mentorship programs alone are not enough. Although well intentioned, many principals may be doing an injustice to new teachers by simply arranging for a mentorship in place of a true induction program. Mentoring, is the pairing of an experienced employee with a new employee (Webb & Norton, 2013), whereas induction is a much more comprehensive process. The comprehensive induction process is inclusive of pre-employment activities, where the initial contact is made between the potential employee and the school; pre-orientation activities such as providing orientation packets to new employees and assessing their needs; orientation, which is the formal process of providing information to the new employees about the school and community; post-orientation induction focused on the efficient transition of personnel into their new roles in the school; and mentoring (Webb & Norton, 2013).

Promotion

Little attention is given to the promotion of personnel in the Texas Education Code. TEC § 11.202(b)(5) states that the principal shall "assign, evaluate, and promote personnel assigned to the campus." With this limited guidance in statute, the issue of promotion must be addressed in school district policies and campus rules and regulations.

Discipline

One of the unfortunate realities of HR administration is that occasionally, employee discipline is required for various reasons. Several factors affect discipline methods including the employment relationship, (i.e., contracted versus at will employee, and the action of the employee that created the need for disciplinary action). For example, at will employees may be terminated at any time for any legal reason without any form of due process (TASB, 2003a; Walsh et al., 2014), whereas termination of a Chapter 21 contracted employee is more complicated. Moreover, the types of discipline vary according to severity of the problem and repetition of the undesired behavior. Listed in increasing punitive levels, employee discipline measures include informal counseling, oral warnings, written warnings, suspension, and termination (TASB, 2003a).

Regardless of the type of disciplinary action taken by a supervisor, documentation is of utmost importance in the case of lawsuits, discrimination charges, unemployment compensation claims, and workers' compensation retaliation claims (TASB, 2003a). Supervisors should also be mindful of federal and state employment laws, and ensure that any disciplinary actions taken against employees are based solely on job-related matters (TASB, 2003a).

Dismissal

The ending of the employment relationship may take one of many forms, depending on the reason for the dismissal and, in some cases, the type of employment relationship held between the employee and the school. The employment relationship may be ended through the processes of resignation, contract non-renewal, termination, or reduction in force (RIF).

Resignation

Most administrators would agree that the least stressful method of ending an employment relationship is by voluntary resignation of the employee. In accordance with TEC §§ 21.105(a),

21.160(a), and 21.210(a), educators employed under probationary, term, or continuing contracts may "relinquish the teaching position and leave the employment of the district at the end of a school year without penalty by filing a written resignation with the board of trustees or the board's designee not later than the 45th day before the first day of instruction of the following school year." With the consent of the school board, however, a teacher employed under any of these three types of contracts may resign at any time (TEC §§ 21.105(b); 21.160(b); 21.210(b)). The at will employee, who enjoys all of the protections afforded by federal and state employment laws, does not benefit from the Chapter 21 laws in the Texas Education Code (Walsh et al., 2014), thus no formal procedures govern at will employee resignations (TASB, 2010b). Regardless of the employment relationship, a written resignation should always be sought by the school. In the absence of a written resignation, non-renewal or termination proceedings must be implemented to officially end the employment relationship (TASB, 2010b).

Contract Non-Renewal

From a statutory perspective, only term contracts may be non-renewed. The actions a school board may take on term contracts include renewing the contract, non-renewing the contract, or terminating the contract. By definition, a term contract expires at the end of its term, and an official contract non-renewal by action of the school board constitutes the decision to let the contract expire, thus ending the employment relationship (Walsh et al., 2014). Contract non-renewal requirements include written notice from the board of trustees informing each term contract employee of its proposed action no later than the tenth day prior to the last day of instruction in a school year (TEC § 21.206(a)), a school board policy containing a statement of all the reasons why a teacher's contract might be non-renewed (TEC § 21.203(b)), and consideration of the teacher's most recent evaluations by the board before making the decision to non-renew the contract (TEC § 21.203(a)). Failure of the board to provide notice to a term contract employee, within the specified timelines, about its intentions of contract non-renewal "constitutes an election to employ the teacher in the same professional capacity for the following school year" (TEC § 21.206(b)). From an employee perspective, contract non-renewal rights include entitlement to a hearing prior to non-renewal, and the right to appeal to the commissioner of education (TEC § 21.207; TEC § 21.209).

Termination

In addition to non-renewal, the board has the option of terminating a term contract. The major difference is that a non-renewal effectively allows the contract to expire at the end of its term. A contract termination, on the other hand, occurs prior to the end of the contract term. While a term-contract employee has no property interest beyond that contract's term (TEC § 21.204(e)), termination of employment deprives the individual of a property interest (Walsh et al., 2014). As such, termination requires "good cause" (TEC § 21.211(a)(1)) and due process.

Continuing contracts, by their nature, cannot be non-renewed. Consequently, to end the employment relationship, either the employee must resign or retire or the contract must be terminated. Reasons for terminating a continuing contract included good cause or a RIF (TEC § 21.154). Any continuing contract employee who is terminated is entitled to notice of the decision to terminate, a hearing before an independent hearing examiner, and the right to appeal the decision to the board (TEC §§ 21.158–21.159). It should be noted that the continuing contract teacher can be returned to probationary status, provided that the teacher consents to the move (TEC § 21.154(6)).

The probationary contract was created by the Texas Legislature to afford to schools the opportunity to evaluate first-time contractual employees and end their employment in the absence of the legal rigors and expense required of other contracts. The probationary contract enables the school to terminate employment without good cause, a due process hearing, or the right to appeal (TASB, 2010a). Specifically, TEC § 21.103(a) states the following:

> The board of trustees of a school district may terminate the employment of a teacher employed under a probationary contract at the end of the contract period if in the board's judgment the best interests of the district will be served by terminating the employment.

It is appropriate to point out the wording "termination" and "end of the teacher's contract." Termination at the end of the probationary contract parallels with non-renewal of the term contract in that it requires the same ten-day notice (TEC § 21.103(a)) that is required for non-renewal of the term contract. Failure of the board to provide notice of its decision to terminate the teacher's employment no later than ten days prior to the last day of instruction requires that the teacher be employed the following school year under a probationary contract if the teacher's previous employment in the school was less than 3 consecutive years, or under a term or continuing contract if previous employment equaled three consecutive years (TEC § 21.103(b)). The probationary contract can be terminated at the end of its term without good cause and with no specific reason for the termination. Furthermore, the use of the wording "the best interests of the district will be served by terminating the employment" will suffice (TEC § 21.103(a)). The law does not require that a due process hearing be afforded to the employee, and there is no right to appeal (TEC § 21.103(a)). However, as Walsh et al (2014) pointed out, "This statement of finality does not prevent the terminated teacher from filing suit alleging a wrongful discharge" (p. 155).

If the probationary contract is prematurely terminated, the school must provide the teacher with formal due process and demonstrate good reasons for ending the employment early (TEC § 21.105; Walsh et al., 2014). While termination of the probationary contract at the end of its term parallels with non-renewal of the term contract, termination before the end of its term is identical to the termination of both the term and the continuing contracts.

In the case of at will employees, with no contract, termination is really the only avenue by which the school may officially end the employment relationship. Walsh et al. (2014) contended, "An employee who serves at will can be terminated at any time, and is not entitled to any pre-termination form of due process. Moreover, the reason for termination does not need to amount to 'good cause'" (p. 153).

Reduction in Force (RIF).   Reduction in force (RIF) is a method of discharging employees through non-renewal or termination during or at the end of the contract term, depending on the employment relationship with the school. A RIF must be in response to financial circumstances requiring cut backs. For a RIF to occur, the school board must do the following:

- Determine that a financial exigency or program change requires the discharge or non-renewal of one or more employees
- Determine which program areas will be proposed for discharge or nonrenewal
- Determine which individuals will be terminated. (TASB, 2007, p. 1)

Due process must be afforded to term- and continuing-contract employees and the school must demonstrate financial necessity for the RIF (TASB, 2007).

HRs Development

The third major category of the framework selected to organize the HR portion of this chapter is referred to as HR development. Within this category, performance evaluation and professional development are obvious subsections worthy of discussion. The topic of human motivation is equally deserving of attention as it impacts not only HRs development but also HRs environment and HRs utilization. These topics are all reflected in TExESCompetency 006 for Texas principals.

Performance Evaluation

In justifying the time, effort, and resources devoted to performance evaluation, Tucker, Stronge, Gareis, and Beers (2003) suggested that for significant improvement in schools and in student learning to occur, the teacher must be the centerpiece. The primary method by which the teacher is held accountable is through the performance evaluation. In the past, performance evaluations of Texas teachers have served both as a tool to improve teaching effectiveness, and in the unfortunate incidents where teachers need to be reassigned, non-renewed, or terminated, they have provided the legal documentation to support such action. However, the new statewide performance evaluation process in Texas was designed to provide meaningful feedback and support to teachers contributing to their continuous professional growth while eliminating the punitive and compliance emphasis of previous evaluation methods.

A brief historical overview of teacher evaluation in Texas revealed that prior to 1981, no state law was in place requiring the formal evaluation of teachers. The Term Contract Nonrenewal Act (TCNA) passed by the Texas Legislature in 1981 required annual written evaluations of term-contract teachers. However, with no state-level guidance regarding the methods employed in these evaluations, any decisions about the instrument used and results yielded were at the complete discretion of the school district. In 1984, HB 72 imposed the Texas Teacher Appraisal System (TTAS), which was the first effort to adopt a uniform system of teacher evaluation across Texas (Walsh et al., 2014). Then in 1995, SB 1 of the Texas Legislature required the Commissioner of Education to develop a recommended appraisal system for teachers with input from teachers and other professionals, from which the Professional Development and Appraisal System (PDAS) evolved (ESC 13, 2015; TEC §21.352). The PDAS was used as the statewide appraisal system from 1997 to 2016 when the Texas Teacher Evaluation and Support System (T-TESS) was implemented. T-TESS became the TEA approved system for evaluating teacher performance in the 2016–2017 school year.

In its development, TEA assembled the Teacher Effectiveness Workgroup in 2011, whose membership was comprised of individuals from the TEA Educator Initiatives department, the Texas Comprehensive Center—funded by the U.S. Department of Education (USDE), Educate Texas, and the Region XIII ESC. Guided by the work of the Teacher Effectiveness Workgroup, in the spring of 2014, a teacher steering committee redesigned a teacher evaluation system directly linked to the revised teaching standards prescribed in 19 TAC §149.1001. The new state evaluation system emphasizes continuous professional growth through feedback and support while de-emphasizing the focus on compliance (TEA, 2014).

The Texas Teacher Standards, issued under TEC §21.351 and articulated in 19 TAC §149.1001 became effective on June 30, 2014. These are "performance standards to be used to inform the training, appraisal, and professional development of teachers" (19 TAC §149.1001(a)). The six standards include: (1) instructional planning and delivery,

(2) knowledge of students and student learning, (3) content knowledge and expertise, (4) learning environment, (5) data driven practice, and (6) professional practices and responsibilities (19 TAC §149.1001(b)(1–6)). Within 19 TAC §149.1001(b)), each standard has a descriptor followed by subsections designed to clearly delineate each component of the respective standards. Although not designated as such in 19 TAC §149.1001(b)), for ease of understanding, the sections will be described in this text's narrative by whole number and its corresponding subsection will be written in the form of a tenths place decimal. For Example 1.3 will represent subsection three of Texas Teacher Standard one.

T-TESS was designed to "provide for actionable, timely feedback, allowing teachers to make efficient and contextual professional development choices that will lead to an improvement in their teaching" (TEA, 2014, p. 5). Cornerstones of T-TESS include (1) a five performance level rubric used in assessing four T-TESS domains in relation to classroom performance, as observed by a trained appraiser in a minimum of one 45 minute observation, (2) a teacher self-assessment, (3) a post-conference, and (4) a student growth measure (TEA, 2014). In addition to these requirements, the state evaluation system strongly encourages (1) multiple formal and informal announced and unannounced classroom observations, (2) pre-conferences for all announced observations, and (3) an in person post conference within 48 hours of each formal observation (TEA, 2014). T-TESS will be phased in over a two year period. In the 2016–2017 school year, evaluation will be comprised of the observation and teacher self-assessment. Then, in 2017–2018, the student growth component will be added. At this full implementation stage, the observation and teacher self-assessment will comprise 80% of the evaluation with the student growth component comprising the remaining 20% (Franklin, 2015; TEA, 2014).

The four *domains* of T-TESS—planning, instruction, learning environment, and professional practices and responsibilities (each weighted at 25% in the summative evaluation)—are scored on performance levels comprised of a five-point ordinal scale, ranging from lowest to highest, in correlation with the instructional focus moving from teacher-centered to student-centered actions, of (1) improvement needed, (2) developing, (3) proficient, (4) accomplished, and (5) distinguished. The summative evaluation scores are derived from the scored *dimensions* of each *domain* (TEA, 2014). The T-TESS domains, dimensions, and correlations to the Texas Teacher Standards are organized in Table 12.2.

Following the formal classroom observation, the T-TESS required post-conference should occur within 48 hours, but must occur no later than 10 days after the formal classroom observation (TEA, 2014). TEA (2014) revealed, "The purpose of the post-conference is to provide teachers opportunities to self-reflect on their lessons with guidance and support from the administrators or teacher leaders who conducted the evaluation" (p. 89). Furthermore, TEA (2014) prescribed a two part post-conference structure inclusive of a reinforcement plan followed by a refinement plan. Informed by multiple data sources including goals and lesson plans formulated by the teacher, information obtained in a pre-conference, copious scripted notes from the formal classroom observation used in scoring the rubrics, and any informal walk through data obtained prior to the formal observation, the appraiser must select an area of reinforcement (strength of the lesson) and an area of refinement (area in need of improvement) on only two dimensions or descriptors from the rubric. Every post-conference must include a reinforcement and refinement discussion "to ensure that a teacher's professional growth will have the maximum impact on the achievement of his/her own students" (TEA, 2014, p. 89).

TABLE 12.2

T-TESS Domains, Dimensions, and Correlations to Texas Teacher Standards

Domains	Dimensions	Texas Teacher Standards
1. Planning	1.1. Standards and Alignment	1.1, 1.2, 3.1, 3.2, 3.3
	1.2. Data and Assessment	1.2, 1.6, 2.2, 2.3, 5.1, 5.3, 5.4
	1.3. Knowledge of Students	1.1, 1.2, 1.3, 2.1, 2.2, 2.3
	1.4. Activities	1.2, 1.3, 1.4, 1.5
2. Instruction	2.1. Achieving Expectations	1.2, 1.4, 1.5, 2.1, 2.3, 3.2, 4.1, 4.4, 5.2
	2.2. Content Knowledge and Expertise	1.1, 1.3, 1.5, 1.6, 2.3, 3.1, 3.2, 3.3
	2.3. Communication	1.4, 1.5, 2.1, 3.1, 4.4
	2.4. Differentiation	1.3, 1.6, 2.1, 2.2, 2.3, 3.3, 4.1, 5.1, 5.4
	2.5. Monitor and Adjust	1.4, 4.1, 4.2, 4.3, 4.4
3. Managing student behavior	3.1. Classroom Environment, Routines and Procedures	1.4, 4.1, 4.2, 4.3, 4.4
	3.2. Managing Student Behavior	4.1, 4.2, 4.3, 4.4
	3.3. Classroom Culture	1.5, 1.6, 3.2, 4.3, 4.4, 5.1, 5.2, 5.4
4. Professional practices and responsibilities	4.1. Professional Demeanor and Ethics	6.2, 6.3, 6.4
	4.2. Goal Setting	5.4, 6.1, 6.2
	4.3. Professional Practices and Responsibilities	6.1, 6.2, 6.3
	4.4. School Community Involvement	2.1, 2.2, 4.1, 4.4, 5.2, 6.2, 6.3, 6.4

Professional Development

Properly planned and implemented, professional development potentially may be the single most important component in improving student performance with an existing faculty. While the synergistic power of effective professional development is astonishing, the unfortunate reality is that, due in part to insufficient planning and implementation, many educators often view professional development in a negative light.

The terms staff development and professional development are often used interchangeably. In prior years, in-service training was commonly used, but it is important to note that the shift from in-service training to professional development was much more than a change in terminology. In-service training was directed at imparting information or specific skills, whereas professional development takes a much broader approach than only skill enhancement (Webb & Norton, 2009). In-service training is directed at imparting information or specific skills, it assumes a deficit in knowledge or skill, and it requires only a passive role by participants. In-service training may be part of a comprehensive professional development program, but standing alone, in-service training is far from a professional development program. With the differentiation between professional development and in-service training noted, a definition that more fully captures the robustness of professional development is in order. Where in-service training is a single event, professional development is an ongoing process that:

> focuses on improving the learning of all students, deepens understanding of what is taught and of the powerful ways of teaching it, affects educators' beliefs about teaching and learning, and produces a coherent stream of actions that continuously improve teaching, learning, and leadership. (Sparks, 2005, p. 88)

Hence, professional development is broader in scope than skill enhancement. Professional development is an ongoing process that is proactive rather than reactive. Professional development is truly developmental, placing greater emphasis on the extension of personal strengths and creative talents than on remediation of personal weaknesses. In reality, professional development is truly self-development (Webb & Norton, 2009).

A comprehensive professional development program is far broader in scope than the traditional one-day workshop. Professional development should be specifically addressed in board adopted policies. A comprehensive professional development program aligns with and is reflective of the vision and mission of the campus. Professional development should be extensively interwoven into discussions about goals and objectives related to school improvement and should be reflected as an integral component of the campus improvement plan. Professional development should be planned in accordance with the T-TESS evaluation process. Obviously, a comprehensive professional development program is carefully and methodically thought out and is a continuous process as opposed to a single event.

Methods and strategies for conducting professional development activities are many. While the traditional lecture format is one method, Webb and Norton (2009) pointed out several other approaches including mentoring, peer coaching, assessment centers, learning walks, study groups, clinical supervision, lesson study, action research, individual professional development plans, teacher centers, job rotation, and peer-assisted leadership. To address each of these individually would exceed the scope of this chapter, but principals should remain mindful of the multiple approaches to professional development and the comprehensiveness of the program.

Motivation

Although the topic of human motivation was reserved for the end of the HR section of the chapter, in reality, motivation is threaded throughout each and every phase of the HR function. Motivation consists of three dimensions—direction (choices selected by the individual among alternatives), effort (how hard the individual works on a given task), and persistence (how long the individual pursues a course of action) (Webb & Norton, 2013).

Principals and other campus leaders may rely on one or more of the motivational theories to understand phenomena they witness, or to more effectively plan professional development or organizational change. Numerous motivational theories are in existence. Webb and Norton (2013) identified three broad categories of motivational theories including needs theories, reinforcement theories, and cognitive theories. With the number of theories that exist, only the highlights of the more common ones are addressed.

Needs Theories. Maslow's hierarchy of basic needs probably tops the needs theories list. Maslow (1970) identified five human needs, typically presented in the literature in a five sectioned pyramid model. The needs, beginning at the bottom of the pyramid and in hierarchical order are physiological, security, social, esteem, and self-actualization needs. Physiological needs include such things as oxygen, food, water, shelter, and clothing. Security needs include safety and the need for order. Belonging and acceptance are represented in social needs. Esteem needs include respect, both of self and from others; and self-actualization represents one's maximum potential including self-direction and self-fulfillment. According to Maslow, each level of need represented in the model can only be fulfilled once the need just below it has been met.

The ERG theory identified the three human needs of existence, relatedness, and growth (Alderfer, 1972). Existence needs are composed of the basic biological needs and the need for safety. The relatedness needs are social in nature, and the growth needs parallel with Maslow's esteem and self-actualization needs. Alderfer's model suggested that individuals might seek higher-level needs even when lower-level needs have not been met.

Herzberg, Mausner, and Snyderman's (1959) two-factor theory of motivation argued that humans have two types of needs—hygiene and motivators. The hygiene factors, otherwise known as maintenance factors, are reflective of physiological, security, and esteem needs. Hygiene factors provide little or no motivation in the workplace, however, when lacking, hygiene factors may not only inhibit motivators, but may actually serve as de-motivators. Motivators, which associate closely with Maslow's self-actualization needs, actually motivate individuals. According to Herzberg, Mausner, and Snyderman, satisfaction and dissatisfaction are not direct opposites, but distinct conditions. In a simplified workplace example, salary may be viewed as a hygiene, whereas involvement of the employee in decision-making processes may be considered a motivator. In accordance with the model, while salary is required for employee motivation to be enabled, salary alone is a hygiene factor that does little to nothing for motivation. However, the lowering or removal of the salary will serve as a de-motivator. With an acceptable salary in place, involvement of the employee in decision-making and job enrichment activities will serve as a motivator.

McGregor (1960) developed Theory X and Theory Y, where he argued that humans by nature fall into one of two categories as employees, each of which requires a very different managerial and leadership approach. Theory X assumes that the average employee dislikes work, will avoid it at all cost, and must be tightly directed and controlled by an authority figure for any level of quality work to be accomplished. Theory Y, on the other hand, recognizes that work, to some is as normal as rest and play, and individuals can be very self-directed, given the proper work environment and the opportunity to excel.

Reinforcement Theories. The major tenet of reinforcement theories lies in behavior modification. In other words, desired behavior can be obtained through behavior modification strategies such as providing rewards and punishments. Pavlov and Skinner were the leaders in behavioral learning theory with the introduction of classical and operant conditioning respectively. Although Pavlov's work in classical conditioning was quite intriguing, it was B.F. Skinner who successfully evolved the work into operant conditioning that included human applications (Biehler & Snowman, 1986). Skinner's reinforcement theory suggested the use of rewards, praise, and recognition to elicit desired behavior and the absence of any form of response to eliminate undesired behavior.

Cognitive Theories.   Cognitive theories of motivation integrate beliefs and values of individuals with their decision-making processes and the meaning they give to consequences (Webb & Norton, 2013). Three better known cognitive theories, as mentioned in this section, include expectancy theory, goal-setting theory, and equity theory.

Expectancy theory incorporates the concepts of valence, instrumentality, and expectancy (Vroom, 1964). Valence may be defined as the value of the perceived outcome to the individual. It is at this point that the individual must decide whether the outcome is desired. Instrumentality relates to the individual's belief that a prescribed set of actions will lead to a defined outcome. Next, the individual must determine if the effort that must be exerted will lead to the reward desired. Furthermore, the individual must determine whether or not one believes one can complete the required task and that the completion of the task will lead to the reward. Expectancy, then, ties to the belief that the individual is able to complete the action that will lead to the desired outcome. When all three concepts align, motivation is high because the reward is at the end of the model. However, misalignment at any level results in the lack or absence of motivation.

Goal-setting theory relies on the setting and accomplishment of goals to motivate individuals. Goals have a content and intensity dimension where content is the outcome sought and intensity is the importance of the goal to the individual (Locke & Latham, 1990). Goals increase attention to the task at hand, increase the effort expended on the task, increase persistence, and increase motivation and performance (Locke & Latham, 1990).

Equity theory asserts that motivation and job satisfaction are directly related to employees' perceptions about how they are treated in comparison to others (Adams, 1965). Additionally, employees' effort in comparison to others also serves as a motivator (Adams, 1965). In other words, employees desire fair and just treatment and the perceived favoring of one employee over another may serve as a de-motivator.

Motivation Summary.   Human motivation is key to the HR function. Wise principals will be attuned to the climate of the building and the personalities within, as they select various models of human motivation to implement in accomplishing campus goals. For additional information on the theories discussed and for access to additional motivational theories, visit http://changingminds.org/explanations/theories/a_motivation.htm.

◆ BUDGETING

TExESCompetency 008 for Texas principals emphasizes financial leadership, which should be reflected in the campus budget. Brimley, Verstegen, and Garfield (2016) described the budget as "a financial plan that involves at least four elements: (1) planning, (2) receiving funds, (3) spending funds, and (4) evaluating results—all performed within the limits of a predetermined time" (p. 284). School budgets are three-dimensional, inclusive of the education plan, the spending plan, and the finance plan. These dimensions are commonly explained diagrammatically in the literature by means of an equilateral triangle with each side representing a major dimension (Brimley et al., 2016; Guthrie, Hart, Ray, Candoli, & Hack, 2008; Odden & Picus, 2008).The education plan is located at the base of the triangle, the spending plan is on the left-hand side of the triangle, and the finance plan is on the right-hand side of the triangle. While there is no doubt that budgeting is a district-level activity, it is also a campus-level activity under the direction of the principal as mandated in Texas statute (TEC 11.202(b)(3)). Interestingly, Caldwell and Spinks (1986) claimed that campus-level budgeting is more complex than district-level budgeting.

In the big picture, principals should understand that at the campus level, ~90% of the total budget is expended on salaries and benefits, 4% on utilities, 3% on supplies, and a final 3% on other expenses such as contracted services, travel, and conference and workshop expenses (Norton & Kelly, 1997). With ~94% of the budget consumed by personnel and utilities costs, little discretion remains for supplies and materials, office supplies, clerical and office expenses, books, etc. Consequently, the budgeting process must be deliberately planned to accomplish the stated goals and objectives of the campus, hence an educational plan is in order.

Educational Plan

A common mistake made in the school budgeting process is to begin with the finance or revenue plan and then develop a spending plan accordingly. In so doing, "many school administrators use the previous year's budget as the sole basis for creating the budget for the next year" (Brimley et al., 2016, p. 292). This temptation should be resisted because "inequities and imbalances tend to become perpetuated" (Brimley et al., 2016, p. 292). Guthrie et al. (2008) asserted, "the school budget is the educational plan translated into dollars" (p. 176), thus the starting point of the budgeting process is the educational plan. In fact, congruent with the equilateral triangle model, the finance plan should be the very last component addressed in the budgeting process and the education plan, at the base, should serve as the foundation upon which the entire budget is built.

Comprehensive Needs Assessment

Any educational plan should begin with a thorough needs assessment. The needs assessment should review multiple forms of student performance data, but should not stop there. Other sources of data to examine include student discipline data, student enrollment information, student retention data, community data, alcohol and drug use data, school safety data, and teacher turnover rate to name a few. The Texas Education Code requires that certain data may be included in the formal comprehensive needs assessment. Additionally, if federal funding is applied for, certain data in addition to that required by the state is also required. The eGrants application for federal funding, accessible by Texas schools on the Texas Education Agency Website, listed 47 areas that could be included in the comprehensive needs assessment (TEA, 2013). Of the 47 listed, nine were required pursuant to the Texas Education Code and eight more were required by various titles of the federal program. While everything listed in the federal application is not required per se, every Texas school would be well advised to review the data sources recommended on the application as being worthy of inclusion in the comprehensive needs assessment. A complied list of the federally recommended data sources is provided in Table 12.3 with TEC and Title program requirements being noted parenthetically on the line by line items.

TABLE 12.3
Comprehensive Needs Assessment

1. Number of Students in a Class, K-4 **(TEC requires 22 to 1 in K-4)**

2. Analysis of Student Academic Assessments **(Title I, Part A; Title I, Part C)**

3. Evaluation of Parental Involvement Activities to Determine Whether Level of Participation Has Increased and if Activities Meet the Needs of Parents **(Title I, Part A)**

4. Analysis of Academic Records, Priority for Service (PFS), Disaggregated by All Migrant Students, as Well as by Students in Order to Target Services **(Title I, Part C)**

5. Analysis of Multiple Sources of Migrant Student Data to Determine Progress Toward On-Time Graduation **(Title I, Part C)**

6. Analysis of Building Bridges or Other Early Childhood Inventories **(Title I, Part C)**

7. Participation Data Disaggregated by Student Groups, Gender, and Age **(Title I, Part D, Subpart 1)**

8. Involvement from Teachers, Especially Those on Title I, Part A, Campuses, in Determining LEA and Campus Needs for Staff Development and Hiring **(Title II, Part A)**

9. Prevalence of Risk and Protective Factors **(Title IV, Part A)**

10. Attendance Rates Disaggregated by Student Groups and Gender **(TEC)**

11. Dropout Rates Disaggregated by Student Groups and Gender **(TEC)**

12. Evaluation of Policies and Procedures to Ensure a Positive Impact on Student Performance **(TEC)**

13. Evaluations of Professional Development Activities to Ensure a Positive Impact on Student Performance **(TEC)**

14. School Violence Incident Data **(TEC)**

15. Student Performance Data Disaggregated by Student Groups and Gender **(TEC)**

16. Tobacco, Alcohol, and Other Drug-Use Incident Data **(TEC)**

17. Multihazard Emergency Operations Plan; Security Audit **(TEC)**

18. Administrator Surveys/Interviews

19. Analysis of Homeless Population

20. Analysis of Screening, Diagnostic, and Classroom-Based Instructional Reading Assessments

21. Community Data on Crime

22. Community Demographics

23. Community Surveys/Interviews

24. Community Surveys on the Use of Tobacco, Alcohol, and Other Drugs

25. Diagnostic Pre-Tests

26. Discipline Referrals

27. Individual Student Pre-Test and Post-Test Scores for TABE

28. Language Proficiency Tests

29. Mastery Tests

30. Parent Surveys/Interviews

31. PEIMS 425 Record Incident Data

32. Health Risk of Drug Use

33. Social Disapproval of Drug Use and Violence

34. Placement Tests

35. Psychological Profiles

36. Results of GED Exam

37. Results of TABE

38. School Violence Incident Data Disaggregated by Student Groups and Gender

39. Staff Surveys/Interviews

40. Student Retention Records

41. Student Surveys/Interviews

42. Teacher Retention

43. Technology to Collect, Manage, and Analyze Data to Inform and Enhance Teaching and School Improvement Efforts

44. Tobacco, Alcohol, and Other Drug-Use Incident Data Disaggregated by Student Groups and Gender

45. Truancy

46. School Safety Choice Option Policy

47. Other

Note. Adapted from PS3221–Comprehensive Needs Assessment, Texas Education Agency eGrants Application, 2011.

Campus Improvement Plan

The comprehensive needs assessment provides the data necessary for effective educational planning. In Texas, the campus-level educational plan is known as the campus improvement plan. Statutory requirements for the campus improvement plan were outlined in the *Campus Planning* subsection of the HR Environment section. Keep in mind that the campus planning process must include the campus planning committee, often referred to as the site-based management (SBM) committee. Statutory guidance regarding the development of the campus improvement plan is contained in TEC § 11.253.

Spending Plan

Glickman (1993) argued, "For a school to decide what it wants for students is the first step. The second step is to allocate its resources accordingly" (p. 74). That appropriate allocation is highly dependent on a sound plan for expenditures in alignment with the goals and objectives in the campus improvement plan. As stated by Guthrie, Garms, and Pierce (1988), "Budgets are the financial crystallization of an organization's intentions. It is through budgeting that decisions are made about how to allocate resources to achieve goals" (p. 216).

The budgeting process begins with a budget planning calendar. While this calendar is initiated at the district-level, there are several campus-specific activities on it. The size of the campus, the organizational structure of the faculty, the level of involvement of faculty and the site-based management team in the budget planning process, and the school district's fiscal year all impact when and how various activities are scheduled on the budget calendar. In Texas, school districts have the choice of operating on either a September 1 through August 31 fiscal year or a July 1 through June 30 fiscal year.

Items to be scheduled on the budget calendar and completed at the campus level include a needs assessment and educational plan to accomplish the goals and objectives of the campus, and formulation of a list of purchases required to address the identified strategies. The fiscal year of the school district and the bureaucracy of the campus dictate when activities must be scheduled on the calendar for completion.

Norton and Kelly (1997) described a logical flow of procedures that should occur in campus-level budgeting. Each department, division, or individual will begin by reviewing formative and summative data to determine student performance strengths, weaknesses, gaps, etc. This will lead to the formulation of strategies, in alignment with the goals and objectives, to maintain areas of strength and address areas of weakness. Many instructional strategies will require resources of time, materials, personnel, equipment, professional development, or facilities-related components. At the department level, this should be summarized, and ideally categorized pursuant to budgeting and accounting guidelines for presentation and submission to the principal. Upon receiving all departmental budget requests, the principal then consolidates them into a single campus-wide request for presentation to and discussion by the site-based management committee. It is at this level that discussions may be held for the campus-wide financial picture. This is also the level at which budgetary needs of the campus should be addressed—that is, those needs that no departmental budget request would likely cover, such as polishing the floors in the hallways and repairing lockers.

This budget, before any real modifications are made to it, is what Guthrie et al. (2008) referred to as the needs budget, which is more idealistic in that it will likely be lacking any realistic parameters associated with the working budget. Once the campus-level needs budget has been compiled and presented to the site-based management committee for deliberation, the working budget starts taking shape.

Guthrie et al. (2008) argued that for budgeting to be most effective, the conditions of annularity, comprehensiveness, and balance should exist. Annularity is self-explanatory. In essence, the budgeting process should occur each year in alignment with the school's fiscal year. From the standpoint of comprehensiveness, the school budget must include all fiscal activities inclusive of a variety of funds and accounts—on both the expenditure and the revenue sides. Lastly, balance simply means that in the end, expenditures cannot exceed revenues.

In addition to the common budget-related areas of instruction, supplies and materials, utilities, and so forth, at the campus-level, another level of fund accounting, mostly related to student activities, comes into play. These activities that require revenues and expenses include such things as admissions collected for participation at extra-curricular events, student class fund raising projects, student organizational activities, concession stands, and vending machine sales. Suffice it to say, "It is essential that all funds be recorded and deposited into one school account" (Brimley et al., 2012, p. 287) under the strictest level of accounting procedures.

Approaches to budgeting vary. Some of the most recognized methods of school budgeting include line-item budgeting, performance budgeting, program and planning budgeting systems (PPBS), zero-based budgeting (ZBB), and site-based budgeting.

First, line-item budgeting, a common approach due to simplicity, utilizes historical data upon which to build the new budget (Guthrie, Springer, Rolle, & Houck, 2007). This method requires a literal comparison of each individual line item listed in the budget. Guthrie et al. (2007) noted that each line item from the previous year becomes the base for expenditure in the budgeted year. The major disadvantage to this approach is that, "Little attention is given to how the line-item object fits into the educational objectives. Thus, the focus of the budget is on the status quo and inputs rather than outputs" (p. 233).

Second, performance budgeting is a rigid approach, centered on outcomes that focus on programs rather than the broader organizational goals whereby budgeted expenditures are based on:

> a standard cost of inputs, multiplied by the number of units of an activity to be supplied in a time period. The sum of all the standard unit costs multiplied by the number of units expected to be provided make up the total operating budget for the organization. (Brimley et al., 2016, p. 287)

A third approach to budgeting is commonly referred to as the Program and Planning Budgeting System (PPBS). This system focuses on long-range planning and de-emphasizes control and evaluation (Brimley et al., 2016). Brimley and Garfield (2008) contended:

> A planning/programming/budgeting system is an integrated system devised to provide administrators and other school staff members with better and more objective information for planning educational programs and making choices among the alternative ways for spending funds to achieve the school's educational objectives. (p. 312)

The fourth approach, Zero-Based Budgeting (ZBB), eliminates historical biases and holds nothing sacred. "Rather than conducting endless revisions of existing budgets" (Guthrie et al., 2008, pp. 181–182), zero-based budgeting literally starts the budgeting process each year at ground zero. Guthrie et al. (2007) noted, "Zero-based budgeting forces careful consideration of priorities and goals, with the highest priority programs receiving funding" (p. 234).

Fifth, site-based budgeting "is a concept of developing a district budget through the involvement of teachers, community, and administrators at the school level" (Brimley et al., 2016, p. 288). With the involvement of stakeholders at the campus level, decentralization of the budgeting process is highlighted. Brimley et al., (2016) argued that "the employees in the building must be a part of the planning process and must recognize cultural, ethnic, and socioeconomic factors that may influence student needs – and then establish priorities and a budget to meet those needs" (p. 288). In summing up this subsection, Norton and Kelly (1997) emphasized, "Effective school leaders today and in the future must become proficient in all aspects of allocating, monitoring the use of, and evaluating the return on the investment of financial resources in the school" (p. 85).

Finance Plan

The final part of the budget development process, which comprises the right side of the equilateral triangle model, is the finance, or revenue plan. This step in the budgeting process identifies all sources of revenue required to finance the expenditures ascertained in the spending plan. At the school district level, this discussion would typically lead into a lengthy and quite complex description of taxation, state revenue funding formulas, and federal title programs. However, since all of that is handled at the district level where it is then allocated to its respective campuses, the complexity of the discussion is reduced.

A perusal through the revenue section of any Texas school district's Public Education Information Management System (PEIMS) financial standard report (accessible at http://tea. texas.gov/financialstandardreports/) reveals that school district revenue is separated into four categories—local tax, other local and intermediate, state, and federal. The majority of Texas school districts receive their largest portion of funding from local taxes and state funding. In Texas, the state's equalized funding formula combines local tax receipts and state funding into a single dollar figure that, in theory, equalizes funding on a weighted average daily attendance (WADA) calculation for every public school district. This process results in some districts receiving funds in addition to taxes collected, whereas others send a portion of tax collections to the state for distribution to lower wealth districts. While lengthy discussions may be held with regard to equality, equity, and adequacy, suffice it to say that upon settling on a given amount of funding, the district then allocates percentages of those funds to the campuses, most of which is consumed by salaries and benefits.

For those campuses receiving federal funds, from a budgeting perspective, emphasis must be placed on the proper expending of those funds. For a school identified as a school-wide Title I campus, the flexibility in the use of those funds is much greater than for the school identified as a targeted assisted Title I campus. Title I, Part C migrant funds may only be expended on migrant students. Rural Education Achievement Program (REAP) funding procedures may be utilized by rural districts, but not by larger urban districts. Then, some schools do not even qualify for federal funding at all. Case in point—different rules apply to different campuses when it comes to federal funding. The prudent principal will be abreast of all strings attached to funds received, expend them appropriately, and track expenditures in accordance with accounting procedures required by the federal government and local school district.

The category of other local and intermediate funds may include a plethora of sources. Included in these funds may be something as complex as public and private grant revenue, to something as simple as vending machine receipts. Norton and Kelley (1997) identified major categories of this type of funding inclusive of foundation funds, school business partnerships, student activity funds, and facility rental funds. The sources of these funds will vary greatly from campus to campus within any district across the state. Sound accounting procedures and strict adherence to any and all requirements associated with the funding sources is critical.

Planning and monitoring the revenue portion of the budget can be every bit as taxing on the principal as the planning and monitoring the expenditures portion. However, in reality, only a small percentage of the principal's overall time is devoted to the budgeting process. Nonetheless, this does not diminish its importance to the educational process.

Evaluating Results

At the beginning of the budgeting section of this chapter, Brimley et al. (2016) were cited as suggesting that a budget is "a financial plan that involves at least four elements: (1) planning,

(2) receiving funds, (3) spending funds, and (4) evaluating results" (p. 284). The equilateral triangle model addresses three of the four elements, but fails to address the evaluative element. In the absence of an effective evaluation at the budget's end, the need for changes in the next budget may be missed. Norton and Kelly (1997) asserted that "The purpose of evaluating the utilization of financial resources is to determine the degree and direction of change in the condition, status, or performance in the specific goal areas identified by the school planning team" (p. 85). Moreover, Norton and Kelly (1997) contended that the assessment must also evaluate "the extent to which the financial resources allocated to that goal were efficiently and effectively utilized" (p. 85).

◆ FACILITIES

Despite the reality that attention regarding teaching and learning is usually focused on curriculum, pedagogy, and school leadership, the fact still remains that the school facility is integral to the overall educational process. From an educational leadership perspective, the facility itself should be viewed as a teaching tool. Whether or not the option of designing a new facility ever avails itself, methods of enhancing the effectiveness of the building as a teaching tool are present in all facilities. Similar to other areas of educational leadership, the facilities leadership function requires numerous management components that are grouped together in this chapter under the major heading of basic operations and maintenance. Finally, school should be a place where students, faculty, and staff feel safe and numerous aspects of the facility lend themselves to the creation of that safe environment. These topics align with TExESCompetency 009 for Texas principals.

School Facility as a Teaching Tool

The significant role the school building plays in the enhancement of education is often overlooked. In reality, the school facility is not only a tool for teachers to use in educating students, but it is also a tool for school leaders to use in promoting a positive climate. Seifert and Vornberg (2002) recognized this fact when they noted that as the first thing encountered at the beginning of the school day and the last thing experienced at the end of the school day, the physical building is a contributor to climate. Consequently, Seifert and Vornberg contended that:

> If the building offers an attractive and helpful environment, then the educational climate tends to be satisfying and inviting. If the building is cold in appearance and unattractive to the psyche, then the climate of the school has a negative component. (p. 486)

School leaders must understand the power of the facility, not only in setting the stage for climate, but also in communicating aspects of the school's culture. Something as simple as the upkeep of the grounds and exterior building attractiveness provides hints to the expectations held for students. Even more important may be what is seen upon initial entry into the building. The signage, decorative pieces, and methods of monitoring safety provide that first impression about what is considered important and valued—a component of the school culture. Moreover, what is displayed on the walls and heard in the halls speaks volumes about culture and climate. Ideally, any visitor entering the building should have a sense of the school's vision and mission, should understand the value placed on students and their education, and should feel that he or she is in a safe environment.

As an instructional tool, the classrooms should be arranged to maximize learning opportunities and safety while minimizing potential interruptions and student discipline-related issues. Classrooms should lend themselves to the use of instructional tools such as white boards and other audio/visual equipment, as well as other forms of technology. Additionally, classrooms should be designed to accommodate variations in teaching methodologies (i.e., direct teach vs. cooperative learning groups, which require rearranging furniture). Specialty learning areas should be designed to accommodate the area of specialty (i.e., science laboratories, computer laboratories, ITV instructional capabilities, and vocational facilities). Lastly, classroom design should be conducive to student learning needs as reflected in brain research, learning styles research, and other forms of improved student performance noted in the literature (Funderstanding, 2015).

Beyond the classroom level, the facility can still aid in the enhancement of teaching and learning. These methods may range from traffic flow patterns that minimize classroom disruptions, to the placement of displays that may encompass educational materials, posting of student work, and technologically generated messaging and bulletin boards. Every dimension of the facility can and should be viewed from the standpoint of assisting educators and students in the teaching and learning process.

Basic Operations and Maintenance

Basic operations and maintenance of the facility are largely a management function, that when managed appropriately, go essentially unnoticed. However, a glitch in the basic operations has the ability to adversely affect the educational process. For example, a heating system failure in the dead of winter wreaks havoc on teaching and learning. With the advanced use of technology, the loss of electricity or Internet connectivity virtually stops many educational processes. Hence, recognition of the elements of basic facilities operations and maintenance is important.

Basic Operations

Basic facility operations are just that—the basics. For the facility to operate properly, electrical power, running water, heating and cooling, etc. are required. More specifically, Seifert and Vornberg (2002) suggested that basic facility operations typically include the following:

- housekeeping services;
- grounds upkeep;
- security of the building;
- safety monitoring;
- HVAC operations;
- equipment servicing;
- electrical plant operations (including utilities);
- simple repairs; and
- assistance to the staff. (p. 494)

Technology has increasingly infiltrated the educational environment, making not only electrical power, but also reliable Internet accessibility a must. While Internet accessibility varies in type, it is becoming more common for schools to have both wired and wireless accessibility. Moreover, with online and hybrid courses becoming more commonplace, continuous accessibility to the campus servers from remote locations has become absolutely essential.

Basic building facilities operations require both equipment and staff. The equipment needs are fairly obvious—ranging from water fountains to heating and cooling units. Staffing needs will include, at a minimum, janitorial and maintenance staff. Regardless of the structure of the staff, or the range of equipment, ultimately, the principal is responsible for the effective and efficient operation of the basic operation of the facility.

A final consideration for principals under the topic of basic operations is compliance with state and federal laws. As a public entity, various laws apply to the facility for reasons of safety, health, and accessibility. Issues related to health and safety are addressed in the safety subsection later in the chapter. From the standpoint of accessibility, all schools must be in compliance with the Americans with Disabilities Act (ADA). ADA compliance applies to issues such as wheelchair ramps and their slopes, guardrails, parking, door widths, restroom stalls, and laboratory table heights (United States Access Board, 2015). While addressing ADA non-compliant areas may be expensive, individuals with disabilities are better served, and enduring the burden of the expense will be far better than battling litigation for non-compliance.

Maintenance

Maintenance is the key to longevity of facilities and equipment. "Maintenance refers to the upkeep or repair of facilities within the site, building, or equipment that keeps these accommodations restored, as nearly as possible, to their original condition or efficiency" (Seifert & Vornberg, 2002, p. 496). The effective and efficient operation of the facility is completely dependent on routine maintenance. The facilities leadership literature recognizes at least five different types of maintenance.

Guthrie et al. (2008) differentiated types of facilities maintenance as preventive, periodic, predictive, recurring, and emergency. Preventive maintenance is an ongoing process of regularly inspecting and servicing facilities components inclusive of structural and mechanical operations, in an effort to prevent a total system breakdown. Periodic maintenance is a regularly scheduled function such as replacing HVAC filters, or cleaning computers (beyond simply wiping dust off of the monitors). Similarly, painting may be on a rotational and regularly scheduled basis. Guthrie et al. noted, "Predictive maintenance can be defined as the ability to estimate the likelihood of an equipment failure over some future time interval so that problems can be identified and maintenance performed before the failure occurs" (p. 310). Recurring maintenance is associated with the daily use of facilities or equipment, usually connected to the need for a quick repair. Lastly, emergency maintenance, similar to recurring maintenance, is typically used on equipment that must be operational, but also when time is of the essence. For example, if a sewer line is plugged, it must be unclogged in a timely manner, but could probably be managed by rerouting traffic to another restroom. This would represent recurring maintenance. On the other hand, in the case of a server malfunction, responsible for hosting the campus Website or online instruction, or anything that must be available 24 hours a day, emergency maintenance is in order. Although other authors may address maintenance in other ways, the bottom line is that maintenance of the facility is a necessary part of facilities leadership.

Safety

Ideally, everyone on the campus should feel safe at all times. The role safety plays in motivation and education was highlighted by Maslow (1970) and the effective schools research

(Lezotte, 1991). The facility is a major contributor to safety. While it is far beyond the scope of this chapter to detail every aspect of facilities-related safety, the principal should have an awareness of the many areas of safety to be considered in relation to the facility. For purposes of discussion in this chapter, safety topics are categorized as fire safety, environmental hazards, and personal and plant security.

Fire Safety

Probably the two most critical considerations regarding fire safety are fire prevention and a sound plan to quickly evacuate every individual from the building. State and local fire codes should be strictly observed. Typically, these will included such things as reducing the number of flammable materials affixed to the walls, proper storage of combustible materials, adequate exits from the building based on occupancy, and well lit exit signs.

Of course, evacuation drills should be practiced on a regular basis so that every student, faculty, and staff member will be enabled to act proactively in the case of an emergency. Inspections should be routine to prevent a fire emergency from ever occurring in the first place.

Environmental Hazards

Guthrie et al. (2008) identified a lengthy list of environmental hazards related to the facility. Their list included radon, mold, asbestos, HIV/AIDS, lead, and pests. Radon is:

> a colorless, odorless, tasteless gas that occurs as a result of the natural breakdown of uranium found in almost all soils. Radon seeps into buildings through holes and cracks in foundations and is generally a threat only in an enclosed space, where concentrations can soar to unacceptably high levels. (p. 323)

Indoor air quality is an area of concern that prompted greater involvement from the Environmental Protection Agency (EPA) in public schools (Guthrie et al., 2008). While indoor air quality is not necessarily limited strictly to mold, it often tops the list. The key to mold prevention is to eliminate concentrated areas of moisture accumulation. Due to environmental conditions in various geographic areas across the state, mold affects some schools worse than others. However, any school is subject to mold build-ups, regardless of environmental humidity levels.

Asbestos, which was used as a building material in many older school buildings, is potentially extremely harmful when its fibers are released into the air and inhaled. Pursuant to the Asbestos Hazard Emergency Response Act (AHERA), school districts must identify and manage asbestos in all facilities (40 CFR 763.80). All Texas schools must develop and maintain a comprehensive asbestos management plan compliant with federal regulations, submit it to the Texas Department of State Health Services, and maintain a copy in the district's administrative office. The Environmental Services division of TASB provides services and training to schools to assist them in all aspects of asbestos management (TASB, 2015).

Although Guthrie et al. (2008) identified HIV/AIDS as a topical area, in reality, this topic should be expanded to that of blood borne pathogens and other bodily fluids. Texas schools with employees responsible for health-care related services or who have a risk of exposure to blood in connection with sharps must maintain a Blood Borne Pathogens Exposure Control Plan in accordance with guidelines enforced by the Texas Department of State Health Services.

Blood borne pathogens are inclusive of diseases such as HIV and hepatitis. From a facilities standpoint, reduction of potential exposure risks and proper placement of bodily fluid clean-up kits comes into play.

Guthrie et al. (2008) suggested that lead poisoning in most children results from the ingestion of lead dust from normal hand-to-mouth activity. Moreover, they claimed that common sources of lead exposure include lead-based paint and lead-contaminated drinking water. The prudent principal will be mindful of lead-containing products used in the school and take preventive measures to eliminate use or reduce potential exposure to students.

Pests may include insects, rodents, weeds, and other unwanted organisms and are sometimes controlled with pesticides, which are potentially harmful to humans. To address this issue, every Texas school district must have an appointed Integrated Pest Management (IPM) coordinator to implement the district-wide IPM program (4 TAC §7.150). While the IPM program may not completely eliminate the use of pesticides in the school, it is designed to seek alternative methods for pest control when possible. The Texas Department of Agriculture (TDA) is responsible for policing schools for compliance with all state and federal laws related to IPM.

Lastly, a final environmental hazard most worthy of inclusion is severe weather. Obviously, the geographic location of the school will dictate the type of severe weather most likely to be encountered, but in Texas, tornadoes and hurricanes probably rise to the top of the list. Pursuant to TEC §37.108, every school district must have a multi-hazard emergency operations plan. As a part of that plan, environmental hazards related to severe weather must be included. Again, the facility is integral to protection from these environmental hazards.

Personal and Plant Security

Personal security typically includes such topics as bullying, bomb threats, and weapons on campus. Preventive measures for these personal security concerns may range from enforcement of policies by administrators to metal detectors at the school's entrance. Likewise, monitoring systems may be as advanced as surveillance cameras in the hallways and congregation areas, to emergency communication systems between each classroom and the main office. Regardless of the level of sophistication employed, all potential hazards must be addressed in the school's multi-hazard emergency operations plan.

Plant security efforts focus on preventing damage to the facility via criminal activity such as vandalism, theft, property destruction, and arson. The options available for security range in type and price depending on the level of security desired. It may start at a locked door and end with burglar and fire alarms and surveillance equipment. A final area of plant security that is becoming increasingly more necessary is in the area of technology. Hackers, viruses, and other forms of malware have forced schools to become vigilant in their efforts to develop firewalls and employ various anti-virus software packages to detect malware and prevent infections.

Facilities Summary

Without a doubt, the facility plays a vital role in multiple aspects of the total educational process. While each area addressed in this section of the chapter deserves discussion in much greater detail, at a minimum, the vast importance of the many facility leadership areas were mentioned. These were broadly grouped as the facility as a teaching tool, basic operations and maintenance, and safety.

◆ SUMMARY

On the topic of the principal and HRs, budgeting, and facilities, this chapter clearly demonstrates the leadership expansiveness in each of these three major areas required for effective public school education. As discussed in the first major section of the chapter, HRs may be categorized into the three major components of HR environment, HR resources, and HR utilization. Secondly, the budgeting function may be visualized on an equilateral triangle model where educational needs serve as the foundation at the base of the triangle, with a spending plan and a finance plan making up the two sides. Lastly, the facility, though often overlooked, is central to so many processes required in education. As important as each of these major areas is, school leaders must never lose sight of the primary purpose for which engagement in such activities is needed. Larry Shumway, as cited by Brimley and Garfield (2008), emphasized that in the end:

> it is teaching and learning that are the reasons for having schools. All our efforts to gather resources, to organize policy, to collect and expend revenue, to recruit, train and retain staff, are wasted if the result is not high quality teaching and learning for each child. (p. 367)

◆ REFERENCES

Adams, J. S. (1965). Inequity in social exchange. *Advances in Experimental Social Psychology, 2*, 267–299.

Alderfer, C. P. (1972). *Existence, relatedness, and growth: Human needs in organizational settings.* New York, NY: Free Press.

Alexander, K., & Alexander, M. D. (2012). *American public school law* (8th ed.). Belmont, CA: Wadsworth.

American Federation of Teachers (AFT). (2001). *Beginning teacher induction: The essential bridge.* Washington, DC: AFT.

Ashby, D., & Krug, S. E. (1998). *Thinking through the principalship.* Larchmont, NY: Eye on Education.

Barada, P. W., & McLaughlin, J. M. (2004). *Reference checking for everyone.* New York, NY: McGraw-Hill.

Biehler, R. F., & Snowman, J. (1986). *Psychology applied to teaching* (5th ed.). Boston, MA: Houghton-Mifflin.

Bigham, G. (2010). Understanding philosophy, vision, and mission and their respective roles in school improvement. *Texas Study of Secondary Education, XX* (1), 9–11.

Bliss, W. (2000). Avoiding 'truth or dare' in reference.*HR Focus, 77*(5), 5–6.

Bolton, T. (1997). *Human resource management: An introduction.* Cambridge, MA: Blackwell.

Boone, M. (2010). The principal and human resources. In J. A. Vornberg & L. M. Garrett (Eds.), *Texas Public school organization and administration: 2010* (12th ed., pp. 351–371). Dubuque, IA: Kendall Hunt.

Brimley, V., & Garfield, R. R. (2008). *Financing education in a climate of change* (10th ed.). Boston, MA: Allyn and Bacon.

Brimley, V., Verstegen, D. A., & Garfield, R. R. (2012). *Financing education in a climate of change* (11th ed.). Boston, MA: Pearson.

Brimley, V., Verstegen, D. A., & Garfield, R. R. (2016).*Financing education in a climate of change* (12th ed.). Boston, MA: Pearson.

Caldwell, B., & Spinks, J. (1986). *Policy formation and resource allocation.* Victoria, Australia: Deakin University. (ERIC Document Reproduction Service ED 283 264).

Center for Teaching Quality. (2006). Why mentoring and induction matters and what must be done for new teachers. *Teaching Quality Across the Nation: Best Practices &Policies, 5*(2), 1–5.

Chen, P. Y., Carsten, J. M., & Krauss, A. D. (2003). Job analysis-The basis for developing criteria for all human relations programs. In J. E. Edwards, J. C. Scott, & N. S. Raju (Eds.). *The human resources program-evaluation handbook* (pp. 27–48). Thousand Oaks, CA: Sage.

Cunningham, W. G., & Cordeivo, P. A. (2006). *Educational leadership: A problem-based approach.* Boston, MA: Pearson.

De Cenzo, D. A., & Robbings, S. P. (1996). *Human resource management: Concepts and practice* (5th ed.). New York, NY: John Wiley & Sons.

Dimock, M. (2010). *Quotes about changing your life.* Retrieved from http://www. manifestyourpotential.com/self_discovery/7_make_dreams_come_true/quotes_about_changing_your_life_inspiring.htm

Educational Service Center (ESC) 13. (2015). Professional Development and Appraisal System. Retrieved from http://www4.esc13.net/pdas/

Franklin, R. (2015). *TEA update.* Texas Education Agency initiatives update presented by members of the TEA leadership team in the second general session of the 67th Annual UT/TASA Summer Conference on Education.

Funderstanding. (2015). Retrieved from http://www.funderstanding.com

Glickman, C. D. (1993). *Renewing America's schools.* San Francisco, CA: Jossey-Bass.

Glickman, C. D., Gordon, S. P., & Ross-Gordon, J. M. (2010). *Supervision and instructional leadership: A developmental approach* (8th ed.). San Francisco, CA: Allyn & Bacon.

Gomez, F. C., & Craycraft, K. R. (2002). *The legal handbook for Texas administrators.* Bulverde, TX: Omni.

Guthrie, J. W., Hart, C. C., Ray, J. R., Candoli, C., & Hack, W. G. (2008). *Modern school business administration: A planning approach* (9th ed.). Boston, MA: Pearson.

Guthrie, J. W., Garms, W. Il, & Pierce, L. C. (1988). *School finance and education policy: Enhancing educational efficiency, equality, and choice.* Englewood Cliffs, NJ: Prentice-Hall.

Guthrie, J. W., Springer, M. G., Rolle, R. A., & Houck, E. A. (2007). *Modern education finance and policy.* Boston, MA: Pearson.

Herzberg, F., Mausner, B., & Snyderman, B. (1959). *The motivation to work* (2nd ed.). New York, NY: Wiley.

Hoy, W. K., & Hannum, J. W. (1997). Middle school climate: An empirical assessment of organizational health and student achievement. *Educational Administration Quarterly, 33*, 290–311.

Hoy, W. K., & Miskel, C. G. (2005). *Educational administration: Theory, research & practice* (7th ed.). New York, NY: McGraw-Hill.

Hoyle, J. R., Bjork, L. G., Collier, V., and Glass, T. (2005). *The superintendent as CEO: Standards-based performance*. Thousand Oaks, CA: Corwin.

Lezotte, L. W. (1991). *Correlates of effective schools: The first and second generation*. Effective Schools Products, Ltd., Okemos, MI. Retrieved from http://www.a2community.org/skyline.home/files/correlates.pdf

Locke, E. A., & Latham, G. D. (1990). *A theory of goal setting and task performance*. Englewood Cliffs, NJ: Prentice Hall.

Maslow, A. H. (1970). *Motivation and personality*. New York, NY: HarperCollins.

McGregor, D. (1960). *The human side of enterprise*. New York, NY: McGraw-Hill.

Norton, M. S., & Kelly, L. K. (1997). *Resource allocation: Managing money and people*. Larchmont, NY: Eye on Education.

Odden, A. R., & Picus, L. O. (2008). *School finance: A policy perspective* (4th ed.). New York, NY: McGraw-Hill.

Ortiz, J. Pl, & Arnborg, L. (2005). Making high performance last: Reflections on involvement, culture, and power in organizations. *Performance Improvement, 44*(6), 31–37.

Owens, R. G., & Valesky, T. C. (2007). *Organizational behavior in education: Instructional leadership and school reform* (9th ed.). San Francisco, CA: Allyn & Bacon.

Ramsey, R. D. (2006). *Lead, follow, or get out of the way: How to be a more effective leader in today's schools* (2nd ed.). Thousand Oaks, CA: Corwin.

Schlecty, P. C. (2005). *Creating great schools: Six critical systems at the heart of educational innovations*. New York, NY: Jossey-Bass.

Sergiovanni, T. J. (1990). *Value-added leadership*. New York, NY: Harcourt Brace Jovanovich.

Sergiovanni, T. J., & Starratt, R. J. (2007). *Supervision: A redefinition* (8th ed.). Boston, MA: McGraw-Hill.

Seifert, E. H., & Vornberg, J. A. (2002). The new school leader for the 21st century: The principal. Lanham, MD: Scarecrow Press.

Sparks, D. (2005). *Leading for results: Transforming teaching, learning, and relationships in school*. Thousand Oaks, CA: Corwin

Texas Association of School Boards (TASB). (2003a). *Employee discipline*. (Employee Performance. HR Library). Retrieved from https://www.tasb.org/serviced/hr_services/mytasb/jobs/documents/ed_discipline.pdf

Texas Association of School Boards (TASB). (2003b). *Structuring the interview*. (Recruiting and Hiring. HR Library). Retrieved from https://www.tasb.org/serviced/hr_services/mytasb/jobs/documents/i_structure.pdf

Texas Association of School Boards (TASB). (2004a). *Assigning and reassigning personnel*. (Contracts and Assignments. HR Library). Retrieved from https://www.tasb.org/serviced/hr_services/mytasb/jobs/documents/ca_assign.pdf

Texas Association of School Boards (TASB). (2004b). *Job description format*. (Model job descriptions. HR Services). Retrieved from https://www.tasb.org/serviced/hr_services/mytasb/jobs/documents/_format.pdf

Texas Association of School Boards (TASB). (2004c). *Purpose of job descriptions*. (Model job descriptions. HR Services). Retrieved from https://www.tasb.org/serviced/hr_services/mytasb/jobs/documents/_purpose.pdf

Texas Association of School Boards (TASB). (2006). *Job analysis.*(Model job descriptions. HR services). Retrieved from https://www.tasb.org/serviced/hr_services/mytasb/jobs/documents/_jobanalysis.pdf

Texas Association of School Boards (TASB). (2007). *Reduction in force.* (Termination. HR Library). Retrieved from https://www.tasb.org/serviced/hr_services/mytasb/jobs/documents/t_rif.pdf

Texas Association of School Boards (TASB). (2009). *Sample interview questions.* (Recruiting and Hiring. HR Library). Retrieved from https://www.tasb.org/serviced/hr_services/mytasb/jobs/documents/i_quest.pdf

Texas Association of School Boards (TASB). (2010a). *Employment contracts.* (Contracts and Assignments. HR Library). Retrieved from https://www.tasb.org/serviced/hr_services/mytasb/jobs/documents/c_contracts.pdf

Texas Association of School Boards (TASB). (2010b). *Resignations.* (Termination. HR Library). Retrieved from https://www.tasb.org/serviced/hr_services/mytasb/jobs/documents/t_resign.pdf

Texas Association of School Boards (TASB). (2010c). *Unlawful discrimination.* (Recruiting and Hiring. HR Library). Retrieved from https://www.tasb.org/serviced/hr_services/mytasb/jobs/documents/i_discrim.pdf

Texas Association of School Boards (TASB). (2015). *Environmental Services.* Retrieved from https://www.tasb.org/Services/Facility-Services/Environmental-Services.aspx

Texas Education Agency (TEA). (2013). *eGrants application, 2010–11.* (NCLB Consolidated Application for Federal Funding). Retrieved from http://maverick.tea.state.tx.us:8080/Guidelines/NCLB/NCLBAA11/NCLB_Sample_Application.pdf

Texas Education Agency (TEA). (2014). *Texas teacher evaluation and support system (T-TESS) appraiser training handbook.*

Texas Education Agency (TEA). (2015). *Highly qualified teachers.* Retrieved from http://tea.texas.gov/About_TEA/Laws_and_Rules/NCLB_and_ESEA/Highly_Qualified_Teachers/Highly_Qualified_Teachers/

Texas Examinations of Educator Standards (TExES). (2010). *Preparation manual.* (State Board for Educator Certification/Texas Education Agency)(068 Principal). Retrieved from http://www.texes.ets.org/assets/pdf/testprep_manuals/068_principal_82762_web.pdf

Tucker, P. D., Stronge, J. H., Gareis, C. R., & Beers, C. S. (2003). The efficacy of portfolios for teacher evaluation and professional development: Do they make a difference? *Educational Administration Quarterly, 39*(5) 572–602.

United States Access Board. (2015). *Guide to the ADA Standards.* Retrieved from http://www.access-board.gov/guidelines-and-standards/buildings-and-sites/about-the-ada-standards/guide-to-the-ada-standards

Vroom, V. H. (1964). *Work and motivation.* New York, NY: Wiley.

Walsh, J., Kemerer, F., & Maniotis, L. (2014).*The educator's guide to Texas school law* (8[th]ed.). Austin, TX: University of Texas Press.

Wayne, A. J., Youngs, P., & Fleischman, S. (2005). Improving teacher induction. *Educational Leadership, 62*(8), 76–77.

Webb, L. D., & Norton, M. S. (2009). *Human resources administration: Personnel issues and needs in education* (5th ed.).Upper Saddle River, NJ: Pearson.

Webb, L. D., & Norton, M. S. (2013). *Human resources administration: Personnel issues and needs in education* (6th ed.).Upper Saddle River, NJ: Pearson.

Weller, L. D., Jr., & Weller, S. (2000). *Quality human resources leadership: A principal's handbook.* Lanham, MD: Scarecrow Press.

Wong, H. K. (2004). Induction programs that keep new teachers teaching and learning. *NASSP Bulletin, 88*(638), 41–58.

Wong, H. K. (2005). *New teacher induction.* Retrieved from www.newteacher.com/pdf/corwingallery

Wong, H. K., Britton, T., & Ganser, T. (2005). What the world can teach us about teacher induction. *Phi Delta Kappan, 86*(5), 378–384.

Young v. Lipan I.S.D., Dkt. No. 102-RI-496 (Commissioner of Education, 1996): 139.

SCHOOL DISTRICT PUBLIC RELATIONS AND COMMUNICATION

Casey Graham Brown ◆ *Shelley Garrett*

Whether a superintendent is working to eradicate a community rumor, a parent is attempting to find out information about his or her child, or a taxpayer is inquiring about a potential bond election, effective communication between and among school personnel and community stakeholders is essential. When an important issue requires a response or resolution, a crisis is at hand, or simply common, everyday information needs to be disseminated, school leaders make communication choices. The leaders select the amount of information they desire to distribute, the audience they wish to reach, and the mode of communication they wish to employ. Each decision depends on the audience, urgency, and importance of the conversation at hand. Choices that school leaders make impact schools, districts, and communities with regard to the trust, or lack thereof, that is established or maintained during the communication processes.

Communication in schools cannot be a one-way street, with school leaders choosing what to tell parents. It is necessary for communication to run back-and-forth between school and stakeholder (Fiore, 2002). School leaders not only administer campuses; they must also do much more than run their schools; they must also "sell themselves aggressively" (Pawlas, 2005, p. 26). With school choice affecting enrollment of once overflowing facilities, school leaders find themselves in competition for student enrollment. School leaders can choose to allow student-related discussions to happen without them, or work to help drive the agendas to inform parents and community members about instructional opportunities and strive to market their schools.

◆ SCHOOL-COMMUNITY RELATIONS

Schools must identify and represent the culture of their communities. Not doing so is disadvantageous. "Failure to develop a school culture respectful and representative of the community's culture can doom a school to failure" (Fiore, 2002, p. 35). Information from stakeholders allows school leaders to take the pulse of the community, thus allowing the leaders to better direct the district (Gallagher, Bagin, & Moore, 2005). Carr (2007b) recommended that district officials consistently communicate with school stakeholders:

> When you speak with one voice, the public hears consensus rather than controversy . . . having a clear, concise, and cohesive message and actively engaging parents and the community in district decision-making processes will keep public support for public schools strong. (p. 47)

The question, "What are the local schools like?" is one that is often asked. In many cases, the people being asked this question are not the superintendents, principals, or teachers of the local schools but area realtors asked by their prospective clients. Gone are the days when schools used newsletters or marquees as the main way to transmit information. Current and potential stakeholders consult a multitude of resources, including official and unofficial school district Webpages, Internet rating sites, blogs, and clips from news media. Public school leaders are challenged to go beyond traditional approaches, become aware of the informal flow of information about their schools, and implement creative, innovative techniques and methods to provide stakeholders with up-to-date, reliable information.

Regardless of whether the public relations (PR) effort is organized or by happenstance, information about the school district is being disseminated, and in a climate of school choice, overburdened taxpayers, and education critics, the need for face-to-face, meaningful, two-way communication between the school and the community is vital (Banach, 2003). This two-way communication between the home and the school must be more than publicity for the next project or program to be implemented—it must be purposeful, intentional two-way communication that is central to the culture of every school, every teacher, and every school leader. Lundblad and Stewart (2005) stated, "public relations is not a tool to manipulate and manufacture favorable images but is a process of managing communication between the school and the public" (p. 7).

Whether a comment page on a school's Website, a response to a blog, or a return e-mail, stakeholders expect to have opportunities to provide feedback. When stakeholders ask for increased communication, they are asking for a "closer connection to school leaders and more involvement in the district's decision-making processes . . . School board members and superintendents need to make parents and other taxpayers feel that their children—and their opinions and tax dollars—matter" (Carr, 2006c, p. 66).

◆ SCHOOL PUBLIC RELATIONS

Used interchangeably with school-community relations, home-school communications, and parent–teacher communication, PR is a planned process of two-way communication between a school and its publics, directed toward school improvement and student achievement (Lundblad & Stewart, 2005). School communication and PR involves two-way communication between school district employees, parents, and other community citizen stakeholders. A written PR plan is absolutely essential if a district's public image is to be managed effectively. A school PR plan provides stakeholders with functional, rather than simply cursory, or even slanted, information (Carlsmith & Railsback, 2001). The school leaders responsible for school PR are challenged to plan to be successful, to direct their message at a specific audience, to "create a quality product or service for it, determine how the product or service will be communicated, and evaluate the marketing effort, all to be done with schools often working with limited budgets, staff, and time" (Padgett, 2007, p. 38). Although there may not be a specific PR department in smaller schools, the role still needs to be addressed, especially in smaller, nonurban communities where what is occurring in the local schools is a dominant conversation topic and citizens are all acquainted (Brennan, Miller, & Brennan, 2000).

More and more districts are evaluating the effectiveness of their communication and PR techniques through the utilization of customer service audits (Carr, 2007a). The reviews investigate diverse issues, from school structures to how acknowledged parents feel when communicating with school staff. No matter how good a school is at conducting PR duties, the PR is simply the introduction to, rather than the totality of, a relationship. According to Carr (2007a), "better public relations may bring parents to the schoolhouse door, but only strong teachers, high expectations, and a caring environment will keep them there" (p. 41).

Schools and districts can also survey stakeholders to ascertain their concerns about school issues. More important than surveys and other data collection efforts is the attempt to "open up new conversations and begin exploring in less formal ways what people think about what's happening in schools" (Johnson, 2013, p. 19).

Padgett (2007) recommended utilizing volunteers to spread positive information about school and being creative with marketing methods. Schools and districts should single out what makes a district or campus the most distinguishable, "then build a campaign around that core benefit using language and experiences that resonate with parents—not fellow educators" (Carr, 2006d, p. 38).

The ultra-rapid transmission of information has affected countless institutions, including schools. Schools have often depended mainly on the media to direct the school-related news that will be circulated, but the schools themselves must examine their own capacity to influence information dissemination (Carr, 2007b). According to Carr (2009a), "with the lines blurring between news and entertainment, fact and fiction, truth and opinion, public officials can no longer rely on news outlets to help set the record straight" (p. 34). Even when challenges exist, stakeholders want facts, not spin. "When times are hard, open, honest, and forthright communication is the only strategy that works" (Carr, 2008, p. 40).

Martinson (1998) stressed, "a desire to communicate truthful information must be at the core of every school public relations effort, even when the information that is communicated might not place the school in the best possible light" (p. 87). District officials should host media briefings about public interest items in order to "set the public agenda on public schools rather than react to it" (Carr, 2007b, p. 47).

◆ BUILDING RELATIONSHIPS WITH PARENTS

Effective communication that leads to increased family participation in the education of children can lead to an increase in student knowledge attainment (Nagro, 2015). A main element of parental involvement is communication between a student's school and home (Hughes & Greenhough, 2006). Kosaretskii and Chernyshova (2013) wrote, "where parents are very involved, there are fewer behavior problems in school, better attendance and preparation for classes, and lower dropout rates" (p. 82). Schools that are successful have the duty to ensure that parents are informed about curricula, instructional methods, and their children's academic development.

According to Murray et al. (2014), "For schools, building strong parent–school partnerships requires practical steps that aim to enhance general school invitations and teacher invitations for involvement" (p. 9). Relationships between families and schools are improved by quality communication (Nagro, 2015). Parents and school personnel should work together to supervise students' behavior and instructional goal attainment (Korkmaz, 2007). The Texas Education Code, §4.001(a) states, in part, that the mission of Texas's public education system is "further grounded on the conviction that a successful public education system is directly related to a strong, dedicated, and supportive family and that parental involvement in the school is essential for the maximum educational achievement of a child."

Effective communication with parents is a well-touted theory that can be overlooked in practice. Effective communication "builds trust between families and schools, which then creates the conditions for better communication in the future" (Mclaren & Schweizer, 2009, para. 41). In their study of communication in early childhood programs, Bridgemohan, van Wyk, and van Staden (2005) found that close, consistent communication with students' families helps to augment how school personnel and students' parents assist students in their development; this leads to an increase in involvement in parent associations and boosts both the accomplishments of students and the approval of their parents. According to Bridgemohan et al. (2005), "effective two-way communication is the most important but least measurable factor in developing successful home-school relationships" (p. 60).

Written communication is important but stands as no substitute for critical face-to-face interactions and group forums between students' parents, teachers, and school leaders (Maclaren & Schweizer, 2009). Spoken communication between parents and school personnel develops rapport and, even more so than written communication, provides the chance to listen to the insights of parents (Bridgemohan et al., 2005). Communication frequency also can impact the level of involvement of parents (Kosaretskii & Chernyshova, 2013).

The e-publication *Choosing a School for Your Child* is part of the U.S. Department of Education Website. The publication's authors encouraged parents to collect information about schools, including answers to questions about school communications, such as "How does the school notify parents about emergency closings? How does the school communicate with parents in other languages? Are there school and student publications? and Are publications for parents available in other languages?" (U.S. Department of Education, Office of Innovation and Improvement, 2007, p. 16). When parents receive recommendations from the federal government to consider these communication areas when choosing schools for their children, we as educators must ensure that our schools are effectively addressing them.

Teachers have identified improved parental support, interest, and communication as the most-mentioned changes necessary to improve student success (Strom & Strom, 2003). Parental support was seen as the most important reason why some schools outperform other schools (Rose & Gallup, 2007). In addition to student achievement and increased test scores, parent involvement was identified as the single most important thing that could be done to reduce school violence and bullying (Strom & Strom, 2003). Research (NSPRA, 2008a) also showed that family participation in education was twice as predictive of students' academic success as family socioeconomic status. It is important to note that the right kinds of communication and parental involvement are critical to student success (Wherry, 2005), and the only way to know what is the right kind is to ask parents what they want to know from the school and how they want to receive that information.

◆ COMMUNICATION AND STUDENT ACHIEVEMENT

There is a positive and convincing relationship between family involvement and student success, regardless of ethnicity, socioeconomic class, or parents' level of education (Henderson & Mapp, 2002). When parents get involved in their children's education, teachers, parents, and students all benefit. The National Parent Teacher Association (2008) suggested that parents decide with their child's teacher at the beginning of the relationship what is the best way to communicate, whether it is by phone, e-mail, home notes, or face-to-face conferences. Research has supported the link between active, involved parents and student success (Education Policy Research Unit, 2008; Mills, 2008), suggesting that parents partner with teachers by joining the parent–teacher team; opening the lines of communication early and often; deciding how to best communicate; being an active parent; and following up (Rice, 2006).

Opening lines of communication between the school and students' homes is critical in ensuring that curricula and student achievement are understood (Ramirez, 2001). Effective communication amid students' teachers and parents can help bridge students' achievement as they advance from middle school to high school and help to minimize language barriers (Crosnoe, 2009).

Since research has consistently demonstrated that student success is contingent upon effective parent–teacher communication (Epstein, 2001; Swick, 2003), teachers must make, find, or insist on the time needed to nurture parent relationships for the success of the students. Teachers must be easily accessible to parents for conferences and use the telephone readily at the beginning of each school year to introduce themselves and discuss student progress. Early and frequent contact builds confidence in the parent–teacher relationship (Banach, 2007).

◆ LEADERSHIP IN COMMUNICATION

Leadership in school communications must occur between all levels of personnel. Effective communication must flow between and among the levels of school personnel and from school personnel to parents and other community citizen stakeholders. Such communication shines light on the mission of the campus and district. The way that information is shared within a school can directly affect the culture of a school (Cox, 2014). Information must flow amid the superintendent, central office staff, principals, teachers, and support staff.

Successful school leadership is dependent upon effective communication. The push for open, reliable communication must begin with district leaders. Not surprisingly, an aptitude for communication is one of the leading characteristics of superintendents who are sought by school boards (Carr, 2009b). Superintendents understand that community support is connected to voting power, which determines the level of resources that superintendents have available to meet their goals (NSPRA, 2008a). Without the support of community members and parents, superintendents cannot succeed. Communication often plays as much a factor in a superintendent's departure as it does in his/her success (NSPRA, 2008a).

Another study (NSPRA, 2005) clearly identified lack of communication expertise as the main reason superintendents lose their jobs, and student achievement played heavily into the communication equation. Increased student achievement depends on superintendents increasing the lines of communication between the home and the school. From the district level to the schoolhouse and then to the individual classrooms and homes, good communication does not randomly occur; it is carefully planned and executed (Gallagher et al., 2005).

"The effectiveness of this planning and execution depends on the expectations of the superintendent" (NSPRA, 2008a, p. 3). Effective communication that engages the student's home with the school is essential in turning a superintendent's vision of student achievement into a reality.

The educational organization is teeming with opportunities for leaders to improve relationships with stakeholders, parents, teachers, and students (Banach, 2007). Leaders must make it a priority to advance education through meaningful communication between the teacher and the parent (NSPRA, 2008b). In an educational climate of school choice and high-stakes testing, it is crucial for staff members on all levels to assume roles and responsibilities that were previously delegated to the district's PR person or the superintendent (Kowalski, 2008). School leaders, principals specifically, are the primary initiators of a culture and climate of effective communication in schools. Bagin (2005) wrote that effective communication becomes the status quo "when principals serve as role models, provide resources and training, and hold staff members accountable for their communication efforts and results" (p. 61).

Teachers depend upon the support of school leaders and need administrators to mediate when parents are unnecessarily difficult by facilitating the development of their parent–teacher communication skills (Tingley, 2007). Teachers need to be secure in their belief that their school leaders will champion their efforts, provide leadership, and step in to assist when dealings with parents become difficult (Tingley, 2007). The teachers who leave the education profession frequently fault school leaders for not providing assistance when the teachers had disputes with parents. Tingley also recommended that, "to keep energetic, enthusiastic new (or even veteran) teachers on board, administrators need to be proactive rather than reactive in working with difficult parents—or any parents at all" (para. 11).

Principals bear a profound responsibility in home-school communication in that they set the tone for the teacher's role in PR and define the communication expectations for their campus (Seifert & Vornberg, 2002). In schools where PR and home-school communication are part of the school culture, the leaders have conveyed its importance in no uncertain terms (Epstein, 2001). These administrators have trained their staff to be simplifiers, communicators, and connectors. In some school districts, PR is briefly mentioned during the induction process in the way of expectations with regard to public behavior, standard of dress, and student confidentiality; however, communication between the home and the school must be a systemic, systematic, and whole systems process (Duffy & Chance, 2007)—it cannot be unplanned or accidental.

Leaders are responsible for informing the staff of their communication expectations. If principals expect teachers to personally contact every parent at the beginning of the school year before any need arise, they must let them know. If school leaders expect teachers to answer e-mails and phone calls within 24 hours, they must let the teachers know. If they expect teachers to create and maintain individualized teacher Web pages, they must communicate this expectation as well. Expectations must be articulated; they cannot be understood or left to chance.

Effective communication creates a two-way connection between the home and the school (Fiore, 2002; Lundblad & Stewart, 2005). This two-way communication must be modeled to teachers by administrators and clearly explained as an expectation set by the school's leadership. Successful principals will set the example and hold their staff accountable on the communication effort (NSPRA, 2008a). Each school and each teacher should find the best ways to reach their parents and then refine that process until it connects with them (Lundblad & Stewart, 2005). It is not an easy or simple task, but research has demonstrated that involved parents make a substantial difference in the academic lives of their children (Fiore, 2002).

◆ DISTRICT COMMUNICATION PLAN

Whether purposeful or unintentional, every school district has a communication plan. It is in the best interest of the school district to make communication meaningful and intentional. A culture of open communication and true partnership must be woven throughout a communication plan that is created and implemented with fidelity by teachers, principals, chief communication officers, and superintendents. Every school district would do well to have a comprehensive communication plan that accomplishes the following:

- Implements a communication program that directly helps achieve the district's strategic goals
- Fosters strong relationships with district stakeholders
- Provides focus and direction for messages and methods in support of the district's goals
- Enables the district to present itself accurately to audiences

The District Communication Plan should include a written document that outlines expectations and procedures for effective communication in order to build relationships toward strengthening the school system. The plan will state the district's strategic plan and communication goals, such as the following:

1. Develop and maintain positive, collaborative relationships with all school community members to strengthen support for the Rockwall Independent School District.
2. Use a variety of media to maximize awareness and support of the District's goals, objectives, and programs.
3. Establish an effective employee communication plan to improve internal communication and employee engagement.
4. Establish strong, positive connections between individual schools and their communities.
5. Establish a clear brand identity for the District and build on that image and reputation.
6. Maintain a proactive media relations program to enhance the District's image at the local, state and national levels.
7. Achieve coordinated communication, both internally and externally, regarding safety issues and crisis management.
8. Use effective operational practices to provide good customer service, increased efficiency and quality printed materials.

The plan should also include a Communications Planning Worksheet, so that various planning components are addressed for every district initiative and project. The worksheet will include the following:

- Goals
- Objectives
- Strategy
- Audiences
- Messages
- Time Line
- Tactics/Activities

- Communication Channels
- Budget Considerations
- Evaluation

The Communication plan will align with the district vision and help all staff members relay key messages that communicate what the district does, what the district stands for, and what value the school district brings to the community. Communication cannot always be controlled, but key messages can. Key messages help a school district prioritize and crystallize information; ensure consistency, continuity, and accuracy; measure and track success; and stay focused when speaking with media or the school community.

◆ UTILIZING TECHNOLOGY IN SCHOOL COMMUNICATION

The integration of technological tools can improve the speed and accessibility of school communications. Parents' expectation for electronic communication from schools is increasing (Kosaretskii & Chernyshova, 2013); messages can be sent to hundreds of parents with the touch of a button. Through the use of technology, teachers, principals, and other school personnel can rapidly communicate with students' families. A possible limitation occurs when parents must have access to forms of technology to access the information. For those with access, however, information can be relayed and received in an efficient manner.

Ramirez (2001) asserted, "teachers often indicate that they do not have enough time to effectively communicate with all parents, but by creating a distribution list of parents with e-mail addresses, for example, teachers can easily notify them of upcoming events" (p. 30). Although e-mail can assist with efficiency, "it is also a medium that makes it easy to be abusive first and think later. For that reason, each school needs a clear protocol for email, agreed upon and enforced" (Mclaren & Schweizer, 2009, para. 52). Although the

> earliest major Web resource educators used was e-mail . . . the last decade has seen an explosion of options: notification systems, Google tools, wikis for collaboration, and Web resources for communicating with parents and students on homework assignments and other activities. (Weil, 2010, para. 5)

Kenney (2011) proposed the following recommendations to encourage stakeholders to participate in social networking:

- Don't try and be everywhere and everything: Identify your target audience, where they go for information (Twitter, Facebook, blogs, etc.) and what information they are interested in, and focus on that.
- Build trust and be present: Your audience needs to know that there is someone at the other end of the online community. They need to know someone is listening and is there to respond and engage with them. Therefore, it is important to appoint an administrator (or administrators) who can monitor the social media accounts on a daily basis.
- Let their community develop its own personality: Pay attention to what your audience is interested in, then facilitate the conversation, don't direct it.
- Bring value to the conversation and ask questions: Ask questions, comment on hot button topics and trends in education, follow other like-minded organizations and engage in dialogue with them, make a point (but keep it short) and comment out of interest.[*]

---

*From http://www.getfreshpr.com. Reprinted by permission.

Gordon (2012) wrote that school districts are becoming more aware that,

in an era of constrained budgets, communicating in a clear and engaging way with stakeholders about everything from the district's overall education vision to scholastic and extracurricular success stories can go a long way toward enlisting broad community support, financial and otherwise. And although face-to-face communications are as important as ever, technology provides a vehicle for reaching more people, more often. (p. 32)

◆ BLOGS

Blogs are another tool school leaders are utilizing to provide information to parents. The word blog was created by merging the words Web (World Wide Web) and log (entry log). According to School Webmasters (n.d.), blogging is "journaling online, with one person posting the main information on a Website and they can be public or private (open to commentary or not)—and about any topic under the sun" (para. 3). The blogs "[humanize] school leaders" as they,

offer parents, teachers, and other key community leaders a glimpse into how superintendents' minds work and what their values are. It's hard to view school leaders as bureaucratic, out of touch, and aloof when they show their humanity week after week online by sharing their fears, dreams, hopes, frustrations, and plans. (Carr, 2007c, p. 30)

Blogs can also serve as ways to publish information quickly and provide opportunities for stakeholders to comment and respond. "The successful blogs all have one thing in common—they post content on a regular basis. One of the common features (and most popular) is that blogs often allow people to leave comments about the articles that are posted" (School Webmasters, n.d., para. 3). These exchanges are important as "it is often these interactions between the blogger and visitors that create a vibrant online community that can attract more visitors and encourage more frequent visits" (School Webmasters, n.d., para. 3).

According to Leedy (2011), sustaining a blog is assistive to school districts:

- they are search engine friendly (adds content and information to your website)
- you can control your message (instead of someone else like the media or disgruntled gossipers controlling it)
- it builds a sense of community (where like-minded folks can share information and ideas or at least find justification for their ideas),
- and you can educate your publics while keeping it human. (para. 2)

◆ FACEBOOK

Facebook is a forum in which information can be relayed, items (photos, videos, articles) can be linked, and individuals can exchange information. "Facebook is not about page content; it is about social interactions between individuals and groups. These exchanges can take many forms, depending on the applications a particular user chooses to use" (McClard & Anderson, 2008, p. 10). "Most people are time-pressed, with few extra minutes to spare during the day for relationship maintenance, and Facebook offers a lightweight way to keep in touch with people" (McClard & Anderson, 2008, p. 10).

"A school district's Facebook page is a prime location for sharing timely, relevant, and interesting content with the community of parents, students, staff and even some random people that have decided to 'Like' the page along the way" (Escovedo, 2011, para. 4). Escovedo cited the convenience of Facebook: "The strategy behind the school district using Facebook could be summed up as fish where the fish are. With so many people on the social utility, it just makes sense for school districts to engage their community there" (para. 5). Communication via Facebook can be transmitted rapidly to inform and update stakeholders.[*]

◆ TWITTER

Twitter is a type of microblogging in which participants post, or tweet, using 140 characters or less (Kwak, Lee, Park, & Moon, 2010):

> Twitter users follow others or are followed. Unlike most online social networking sites, such as Facebook or MySpace, the relationship of following and being followed requires no reciproca-tion. A user can follow any other user, and the user being followed need not follow back. Being a follower on Twitter means that the user receives all the messages (called tweets) from those the user follows. (Kwak et al., 2010, para. 4)

Twitter is used to disseminate information quickly. In the event of an emergency school closing or when a message needs to be relayed to parents or other community members, infor-mation can be tweeted via a district or campus page.

◆ PODCASTS

A podcast is a multimedia file that can be transmitted via the Internet and downloaded to a computer or another portable device. According to Kaplan-Leiserson (2005), podcasting:

> is an amalgamation of two other words: iPod, the popular digital music player from Apple, and broadcasting. But the pod is a bit of a misnomer. Podcasts, digital audio programs that can be subscribed to and downloaded by listeners via RSS (Really Simple Syndication), can be accessed on a variety of digital audio devices, including a desktop computer. (para. 2)

Casting "encompasses a diverse set of terms and specific uses, such as autocasting, blogcast-ing, learncasting, MMS podcasting, mobilecast, narrowcast, peercasting, podstreaming, pho-tofeed, soundseeing tour, vodcasting, voicecast, audio wikinews and phone casting" (Tynan & Colbran, 2006, p. 826). Districts can utilize podcasting "to share upcoming deadlines, special events, and general announcements with their local community, faculty, and student body" (Robin, 2010, para. 2).

◆ WEBSITES

Websites are the norm for campuses and districts. The types of information presented on the sites often differ substantially. School districts are encouraged to post minutes of meetings and other public notice information on the district's website and allow parents a forum in which to respond (Carr, 2008). Some districts include general enrollment and calendar information. Others include extracurricular information, links to teachers' Webpages, and YouTube videos. YouTube is a social networking Website through which individuals can share and comment on

---

*Copyright © by Richie Escovedo. Reprinted by permission.

videos. School districts can post orientations for volunteers on YouTube or upload videos to orient parents to special services that school districts offer.

Websites are often visited during times of inclement weather, as some districts post school closing information to the district sites. Technology has proven especially useful in times of crisis when information can be sent immediately and inexpensively to those who need it (Carr, 2009b).

◆ SHARING OF INFORMATION

Chat rooms, blogs, teacher Web pages, and e-mail have been greatly expanded as means of communicating with students' families. Although technology appears to be limitless, some students, particularly students from low socioeconomic households, may lack home Internet access (Baek & Freehling, 2007, p. 34). In light of the helpful technologies available to provide a near instant exchange of information, Carr (2006b) reminded school leaders that "an email exchange will never replace the discussion you can have over a cup of coffee at the donut shop" (p. 40). Wherry (2006) concurred that mass media has its place in school communications, "but when we must develop supportive attitudes among parents about our school, our goals, and the importance of working together, interpersonal communication is the only game in town" (p. 6). Whichever method is chosen, effective communication signifies developing good lines of communication both to and from the parents (Marzano, Waters, & McNulty, 2005).

◆ COMMUNICATING WITH DIVERSE POPULATIONS

Effective communication is essential in helping meet the needs of public schools' diverse populations. School districts must navigate ways to communicate with the families of students who are homeless, who are being raised by grandparents, who have no family members speaking English at home, and who are in low-income homes with no access to technology.

Swick and Battle Bailey (2004) studied homeless children and found that successful communication between a student's family and school during the early developmental school years is fundamental for the interest of the student and his or her family. The authors encouraged teachers to work together with parents because,

> interactive communication with families in continuous ways enhances this process of meeting needs and empowering families to take ownership of their lives . . . Establishing meaningful communication with families who are homeless begins with the attitudes and behaviors early childhood professionals demonstrate in their ongoing interactions. (pp. 212, 214)

An obstacle often lies in ensuring the accuracy of students' current phone numbers and addresses, especially for students who are homeless or who are children of migrant workers. Carr (2009b) recommended that schools help to resolve the issues of inaccurate and rapidly changing contact information by communicating often and via a variety of methods.

More and more students in the twenty-first century are growing up in homes run by someone other than their parents (Dominus, 2008). In addition to mother-only family groups, more grandparents are taking on the role of primary caregiver, provider, and legal custodian of their grandchildren (Johnston, 2008). This family demographic may present possible challenges to home-school communications: homes led and maintained by grandparents may or may not be technologically savvy and tuned in to online grading access, teacher website information, and teacher-initiated communication via e-mail. Mother-only family groups may be forced to work more than one job, creating time constraints that make parent–teacher conferences and other forms of communication unmanageable and unlikely. Homes where people are living in poverty are less likely to have access to technology, such as teacher e-mails, and more likely to be working shifts that do not enable them to attend parent–teacher meetings and school open house programs.

Opportune communications with parents in schools with large non-English-speaking populations present another challenge to overcome (Flanigan, 2007). School leaders and faculty must address language barriers to ensure information is distributed in a timely manner, regardless of the languages spoken in students' homes. Although still an issue, schools are seeing an improvement in translation services for non-English speakers (Carr, 2009b).

◆ COMMUNICATION OBSTACLES AND BARRIERS

Communication is a tool that is often used poorly or thoughtlessly (Gallagher et al., 2005). According to Vaillancourt and Amador (2014/2015), creating successful partnerships between the school and the community "requires recognition of barriers along with time and commitment from both the school district and community agencies to overcome those barriers" (p. 57). Useful communication is strategic; it is organized and implemented as a system "rather than as a collection of fragmented communication programs and PR messages that compete for attention and leave your faculty and staff struggling to make sense of it all" (Duffy & Chance, 2007, p. 5). There are many recognized barriers to communication between the home and the school—some parent-imposed and some teacher-imposed (Wherry, 2007).

According to Poynton, Makela, and Haddad (2014), "Central to public participation is the idea that individuals or groups affected by a particular decision should be given an opportunity to be engaged in making that decision" (pp. 52–53). Björk, Kowalski, and Browne-Ferrigno (2014) posited, "superintendents' communicator role is shaped by two conditions—the need to restructure school cultures and the need to access and use information in a timely manner to identify and solve problems of practice" (p. 13). In the literature in the field of educational leadership, according to Johnson (2014),"boundary-spanning educational leaders have been portrayed as levers of bureaucratic change, who build new and nontraditional partnership relationships between the school district and community sites" (pp. 169–170).

School personnel and school stakeholders face obstacles to effective communication including language, culture, time, and those related to physical disabilities (Fiore, 2002). School leaders must ensure that language barriers do not stand in the way of effective school communications by securing translators as needed and making certain that materials are interpreted into all represented languages. Administrators must be aware of the effect of space and body language since a great deal of communication occurs nonverbally (Fiore, 2002). Although it is precious, school officials must devote the time required to communicate effectively, with necessary in-person discussions and lengthier messages and responses. Leaders must also be responsive to persons with physical disabilities with regard to providing information to those with hearing, sight, and other impairments. When school leaders are aware of and acknowledge possible barriers to communication, they can work to overcome them.

Language barriers have long been an issue in home-school communication, even before the 21st century brought its wealth of diversity and multiculturalism into public school settings (Seifert & Vornberg, 2002). Language barriers are not exclusive to the native tongue of students' homes not matching up with the native tongue of teachers. Another language barrier is the disconnect parents feel when educators speak in educational jargon, or education-ese (Gallagher et al., 2005). There is also an overriding cultural barrier between the home and the school that some parents and teachers have expressed—a them and us mentality that sets parents and teachers in opposition, rather than working as a team.

For parents who lack English language proficiency, there is often great discomfort in trying to communicate verbally with teachers and administrators. Parents of English language learners face daunting barriers to becoming engaged with their children's schools (Center for the Education and Study of Diverse Populations, 2008). Not understanding the language of notices, progress reports, and other communication sent home compounds the barriers that all parents face, for example, time restrictions and ineffective methods of communication. Teachers can be on the frontline of assuaging these parents' fears.

Ineffective methods of communication are a major barrier to communication. All methods of communication become ineffective when they are not two-way (Banach, 2007). If the message is not received, it is ineffective. If the message is not understood, it is not effective. If a teacher crafts and sends an individualized, well-written, informative e-mail to a parent, but that parent does not have e-mail access, the message is not received, constituting ineffective communication. The same holds true for all forms of communication: phone messages left in English on the home answering machines of Spanish-speaking families are ineffective; information posted on teacher Webpages are of little consequence in homes without Internet access; and teacher notes that never make it home to parents are futile. The challenge of ensuring effective two-way communication efforts between the home and the school lies on both sides of the communications equation, with the teacher and with the parent.

A major challenge facing principals with regard to parent–teacher communication is the fear, uncertainty, and doubt that some parents experience when contacting the school. Some parents fear the condescension and failure they themselves experienced when they were in school (Seifert & Vornberg, 2002), while other parents have an aversion to the professional language and acronyms often used by educators that present a confusing array of language barriers—not to mention non-English speakers, often not supplied with translators, who may not understand the conversation at all. For school leaders to reduce the fear experienced by parents, Seifert and Vornberg (2002) posited,

> The key for principals in reducing the fear factor of parents is grounded in mutual trust, respect, and communication. When principals regard their relationship with families as a collaborative venture where the school and home work together to improve student achievement, then and only then will parents feel comfortable and noncombative with the school. This implies a shared responsibility for children's learning among the school, home, and the community. (p. 258)

Another barrier is the long struggle teachers and administrators have had with viewing parents as equal partners in a student's success, surrendering academic terminology, and speaking in plain language that everyone can understand (Education Policy Research Unit, 2008). Language is a complex system not to be taken lightly, and it is a system that most educators are not formally trained to perform, which leads to another crucial communication barrier—lack of teacher training (Fiore, 2002). The majority of teacher preparation programs in Texas do not have coursework dedicated solely to training teachers how to communicate with parents, how to properly use different methods of communication, and how to conduct a successful parent–teacher conference. Other barriers to effective communication between the home and the school include lack of parental involvement; lack of time, resources, and technology; and ineffective methods of communication (Wherry, 2007).

Some school leaders are concerned with lack of feedback; others are concerned with the type of interaction and feedback from stakeholders, particularly in technological formats. Some districts embrace social networking (Todoric, 2011); others ban it in fear of "inappropriate use and/or goofing off among students" (Schachter, 2011, p. 27), while some "are puzzling over what to do about the brave new world of social media, and weighing its potential use by students and teachers inside and outside of the classroom" (p. 27).

In regard to the social networking site Facebook, Escovedo (2011) suggested that districts "set . . . rules of engagement, prepare and gather content from all over the district to share. Post, listen, engage and promote . . . and repeat" (para. 9). Although leaders may feel a loss of control of information when allowing stakeholders to comment, "The magic is in the feedback. When we post items to Facebook like updates, questions, links, photos, videos, student/staff recognitions, explanations, news, events, etc. it's done with the audience in mind" (Escovedo, para. 10). People may comment negatively or positively, but regardless, communication can be fostered and school leaders can be more informed of the views of community members, thus increasing their awareness of informational needs of stakeholders.

Social media has affected relationships between teachers and students. "Old barriers defining student-teacher relationships are breaking down" (Puzio, 2013, p. 1100) as students interact with and friend their teachers on social media sites. Consequently, legislatures and schools are "faced with the challenge of determining whether these student-teacher online communications are appropriate and just how far they can and should go in restricting them" (p. 1100). Social media and the Internet have also impacted student speech. Blacher and Weaver (2013) posited

> Much of student communication through electronic social media is harmless, but a steady flow of it comes with deliberately hard, sharp, and, most of all, permanent edges. Even spontaneous diatribes frequently propagate in their original form well beyond their intended or imagined audiences. The targets of online vilification and bullying now find that an eternal record documenting their humiliation could reach an enormously wide audience. (p. 82)

Blacher and Weaver (2013) wrote that courts and school stakeholders should consider the effects of such disruptions.

School PR experts agree that in order to combat ineffective methods of communication, schools must focus on effective methods, such as one-on-one contact with parents, which remains the most effective and efficient method of communicating with parents. Carr (2008) recommended applying the theory of multiple intelligences to school communications. "Just as there are seven ways of knowing for students, there are at least seven—if not more—ways of knowing for the adults that school district communications hope to inform, influence, or move to action" (p. 41). School districts' open door policies and commitment to clear, nonconvoluted processes requires consistent, open communication via a variety of methods. Astute school leaders realize that, just like students, stakeholders utilize a variety of learning styles and communication modalities (Carr, 2008).

◆ COMMUNICATING IN TIMES OF CRISES

During a time of crisis, the need to know often reaches a larger population, expanding to state, national, and even international audiences. According to Carr (2006a), "bringing polarized communities together, anticipating issues, and successfully managing 'if it bleeds it leads' reporters require a new kind of public relations executive" (p. 40). School officials must be diligent in not only preparing to respond to crisis situations, but also informing parents what communications to expect if a crisis should occur at the school (Flanigan, 2007).

In the event of a crisis, school personnel should react quickly and communicate openly. "Clear lines of communication are crucial to a successful response to a crisis" (U.S. Department of Education, Office of Safe and Drug-Free Schools, 2007, pp. 6–10). Meetings should be hosted to share with parents the school's response to the event in order to face, rather than hide from, difficult situations. Mclaren and Schweizer (2009) asserted, "without open communication, issues remain submerged and end up contributing to greater anxiety for all involved" (para. 51).

The first hour after a school crisis is the "time when school leaders have their best—and often only—opportunity to take control and frame the issues from their perspective" (Carr, 2009b, p. 58). When school leaders fail, however, "others will gladly jump in to fill the communication void" (Carr, 2009b, p. 58).

The district PR office should act in a proactive manner to manage controversial issues. Carr (2009b) contended that, during a crisis, disclosing even a small amount of information indicates to stakeholders that school employees are properly responding to the situation. An example she provided was: "We are aware of the situation, have administrators at the scene, and are working closely with emergency responders" (Carr, 2009b, p. 58). How school personnel communicate during the crisis is essential; effective communication during emergencies can affect stakeholders' future relationships with schools and school personnel (Howard, 2015).

The U.S. Department of Education, Office of Safe and Drug-Free Schools (2007) recommended that districts and campuses, open the channels of communication well before a crisis. Murray et al. (2014) agreed: "offering opportunities to inform school safety promotion programs and policies may be a good approach to engaging parents in school improvement efforts" (p. 10). According to the U.S. Department of Education, Office of Safe and Drug-Free Schools (2007)

> Relationships need to be built in advance so that emergency responders are familiar with your school. Cultivate a relationship with city emergency managers, public works officials, and health and mental health professionals now, and do not overlook local media. It is important that they understand how the district and schools will respond in a crisis. (pp. 1–10)

◆ CONCLUSION

Effective community relations and PR are important to the success of school leadership (Marzano, 2003). School leaders have a myriad of messages that they need to relay to help facilitate their effectiveness with students, parents, teachers, and other school stakeholders. Poynton et al. (2014): wrote,

> in response to declining citizen engagement and trust in public schools, education leaders must reevaluate their district's internal and external (outreach) problem solving and decision making processes and redouble their efforts to raise their district's capacity for effective public participation. (p. 62)

Regardless of audience, school leaders must ensure that they or the people they empower provide information that is reliable and ethical. It is especially important to apply ethical principles to school district communication with much incorrect information circulating about schools and frequent news stories about less-than-model educator behavior.

Educators must involve all stakeholders in the pursuit of educational excellence. In preparing to do so, they must actively seek input from the community and strive to build relationships. It is important that "school officials . . . spend time cultivating relationships with key employees and community members and keeping them informed if they want to accomplish understanding and acceptance of their school programs" (Oregon School Boards Association, n.d., para. 7).

All parties concerned with decreasing student failure will take interest in effective communication, which is taking place when educators and community stakeholders are giving and receiving the information they want and need to increase student success. All school district employees must support school PR by making parent communication a top priority; working to understand class and cultural differences; and recognizing and removing barriers to communication (Garrett, 2008).

◆ REFERENCES

Baek, E., & Freehling, S. (2007). Using Internet communication technologies by low-income high school students in completing educational tasks inside and outside the school setting. *Computers in the Schools, 24*(1/2), 33–55.

Bagin, R. (2005). *Making parent communication effective and easy*. Rockville, MD: National School Public Relations Association.

Banach, W. J. (2003). What students, parents, and staff are saying about schools. *Journal of School Public Relations, 24*, 187–198.

Banach, W. J. (2007). *The ABCs of teacher-parent communication*. Lanham, MD: Rowman & Littlefield Education.

Björk, L. G. Kowalski, T. J., & Browne-Ferrigno, T. (2014). The school district superintendent in the United States of America. *Educational Leadership Faculty Publications*. Paper 13. Retrieved from http://ecommons.udayton.edu/eda_fac_pub/13

Blacher, M., & Weaver, R. (2013, Winter). The Internet, free speech, and schools. *Independent School, 72*(2), 80–85.

Brennan, K. B., Miller, A. D., & Brennan, II, J. P. (2000). Promoting a positive image: Public relations strategies for special educators. *Rural Special Education Quarterly, 19*(1), 26–30.

Bridgemohan, R., van Wyk, N., & van Staden, C. (2005). Home-school communication in the early childhood development phase. *Education, 126*(1), 60–7.

Carlsmith, L., & Railsback, J. (2001). *The power of public relations in schools*. Portland, OR: Northwest Regional Educational Laboratory. Retrieved from http://www.nwrel.org/request/feb01

Carr, N. (2006a). Hiring the right PR pro. *American School Board Journal, 193*(5), 40–42.

Carr, N. (2006b). Keys to effective communications. *American School Board Journal, 193*(8), 40–41.

Carr, N. (2006c). New rules of engagement. *American School Board Journal, 193*(4), 66–68.

Carr, N. (2006d). The search for the right school. *American School Board Journal, 193*(2), 36–38.

Carr, N. (2007a). Courting middle-class parents to use public schools. *Education Digest, 72*(6), 35–41.

Carr, N. (2007b). Setting the community agenda. *American School Board Journal, 194*(5), 46–47.

Carr, N. (2007c). Using blogs to humanize our school leaders. *Education Digest, 72*(7), 29–32.

Carr, N. (2008). Don't spin hard times. *American School Board Journal, 195*(7), 40–41.

Carr, N. (2009a). Planning in a media sea change. *American School Board Journal, 196*(6), 34–35.

Carr, N. (2009b). Times have changed. *American School Board Journal, 196*(4), 57–58.

Center for the Education and Study of Diverse Populations. (2008). *Improving communication.* Albuquerque, NM: Author.

Cox, A. (2014). Increasing purposeful communication in the workplace: Two school-district models. *Delta Kappa Gamma Bulletin, 80*(3), 34–38.

Crosnoe, R. (2009). Family–school connections and the transitions of low-income youths and English language learners from middle school to high school. *Developmental Psychology, 45*(4), 1061–1076.

Dominus, S. (2008, May 16). A school succeeds with extra study and little homework. *New York Times.* Retrieved from http://www.nytimes.com/2008/05/16/nyregion/16bigcity.html

Duffy, F. M., & Chance, P. L. (2007). *Strategic communication during whole system change: Advice and guidance for school district leaders and PR specialists.* Lanham, MD: Rowman & Littlefield Education.

Education Policy Research Unit. (2008, January 28). *Parental involvement can and should cross language barriers.* Tempe, AZ: Arizona State University.

Epstein, J. L. (2001). *School, family, and community partnerships: Preparing educators and improving schools.* Boulder, CO: Westview Press.

Escovedo, R. (2011, March 31). *Facebook as a school district's newsroom.* Retrieved from http://nextcommunications.blogspot.com/2011/03/facebook-as-school-districts-newsroom.html

Fiore, D. J. (2002). *School-community relations.* Larchmont, NY: Eye on Education.

Flanigan, R. L. (2007). Calming fears, creating partners. *American School Board Journal, 194*(6), 33–36.

Gallagher, D. R., Bagin, D., & Moore, E. H. (2005). *The school and community relations.* Boston: Allyn & Bacon.

Garrett, L. M. (2008). *The public relations role of the public school teacher as perceived by parents and teachers in Texas schools.* Doctoral dissertation, Texas A&M University-Commerce, Commerce, TX).

Gordon, D. (2012). Creating connections. *The Journal, 39*(5), 32–34.

Henderson, A. T., & Mapp, K. L. (2002). *A new wave of evidence: The impact of school, family, and community connections on student achievement.* Austin, TX: National Center for Family & Community Connections with Schools.

Howard, T. (2015). Cramming for a crisis. *American School & University, 87*(9), 12.

Hughes, M., & Greenhough, P. (2006). Boxes, bags and videotape: Enhancing home-school communication through knowledge exchange activities. *Educational Review, 58*(4), 471–487.

Johnson, J. (2013). The human factor. *Educational Leadership, 70*(7), 16–21.

Johnson, L. (2014). Culturally responsive leadership for community empowerment. *Multicultural Education Review, 6*(2), 145–170.

Johnston, A. L. (2008, January). *Grandparents raising their grandchildren: Considerations for the field*. Paper presented at the annual meeting of the Texas Association of School Administrators Midwinter Conference, Austin, TX.

Kaplan-Leiserson, E. (2005, June). *Trend: Podcasting in academic and corporate learning. Learning Circuits*. Retrieved from http://trainingthetrainers2010.pbworks.com/f/Podcasting+in+Academic+Learning.pdf

Kenney, J. (2011, April 26). *How school districts use social media to strengthen community*. Retrieved from http://www.getfreshpr.com/2011/04/how-%09school-districts-can-use-social-media-to-build-community/

Korkmaz, I. (2007). Teachers' opinions about the responsibilities of parents, schools, and teachers in enhancing student learning. *Education, 127*(3), 389–399.

Kosaretskii, S. G., & Chernyshova, D. V. (2013). Electronic communication between the school and the home. *Russian Education & Society, 55*(10), 81–89. doi: 10.2753/RES1060-9393551006

Kowalski, T. J. (2008). *Public relations in schools* (4th ed.). Upper Saddle River, NJ: Pearson Education.

Kwak, H., Lee, C., Park, H., & Moon, S. (2010). *What is Twitter, a social network of a news media?* Presented at WWW 2010, April 26–30, 2010, Raleigh, NC. Retrieved from http://an.kaist.ac.kr/~sbmoon/paper/intl-conf/2010-www-twitter.pdf

Leedy, B. (2011, January 11). *Joining the blogging ranks*. Retrieved from http://www.schoolwebmasters.com/index.cfm?pID=3799&blog=21

Lundblad, S. S., & Stewart, G. K. (2005). *Public relations for schools: A resource guide for principals*. Greenwich, CT: IAP Information Age Publishing.

Martinson, D. L. (1998). School communication to outside publics: Truthfulness must be the bottom line. National Association of Secondary School Principals. *NASSP Bulletin, 82*(594), 81–88. Retrieved from ProQuest Education Journals. (Document ID:25224841)

Marzano, R. J. (2003). *What works in schools: Translating research into action*. Alexandria, VA: Association for Supervision and Curriculum Development.

Marzano, R. J., Waters, T., & McNulty, B. A. (2005). *School leadership that works: From research to results*. Alexandria, VA: Association for Supervision and Curriculum Development.

McClard, A., & Anderson, K. (2008). Focus on Facebook: Who are we anyway? *Anthropology News, 49*(3).

Mclaren, A., & Schweizer, L. (2009). Navigating the Bermuda Triangle of school communication. *Independent School, 68*(3), 106–113.

Mills, J. (2008, January 13). Parental involvement and the at-risk child. *The Daily Sentinel*.

Murray, K. W., Finigan-Carr, N., Jones, V., Copeland-Linder, N., Haynie, D. L., & Cheng, T. L. (2014). Barriers and facilitators to school-based parent involvement for parents of urban public middle school students. *SAGE Open*. doi: 10.1177/2158244014558030 sgo.sagepub.com

Nagro, S. (2015). PROSE Checklist: Strategies for improving school-to-home written communication. *Teaching Exceptional Children, 47*(5), 256–263. doi: 10.1177/0040059915580031

National Parent Teacher Association (NPTA). (2008). *Making parent-teacher conferences work for your child*. Chicago: Author.

National School Public Relations Association (NSPRA). (2005). *How strong communication helps superintendents get and keep their jobs*. Rockville, MD: Author.

National School Public Relations Association (NSPRA). (2008a). *Principal communicator.* Rockville, MD: Author.

National School Public Relations Association (NSPRA). (2008b). *Public relations.* Rockville, MD: Author.

Oregon School Boards Association. (n.d.). *Key communicator network: Building support for your schools: Personal face-to-face contact is the most effective communication method when building support for your schools.*

Padgett, R. (2007). Marketing schools for survival. *Education Digest, 72*(9), 37–38.

Pawlas, G. E. (2005). *The administrator's guide to school-community relations* (4th ed.). Larchmont, NY: Eye on Education, Inc.

Poynton, J., Makela, C., & Haddad, D. (2014). Organizational training and relationship building for increasing public participation in a public school district. *Administrative Issues Journal: Education, Practice, and Research, 4*(1), 50–63. doi: 10.5929/2014.4.1.5

Puzio, E. (2013). Why can't we be friends? How far can the state go in restricting social networking communications between secondary school teachers and their students? *Cardozo Law Review, 34*(3), 1099–1127.

Ramirez, F. (2001). Technology and parental involvement. *Clearing House, 75*(1), 30–31.

Rice, M. (2006). The parent teacher team: Establishing communication between home and school. *The Exceptional Parent, 36*(6), 49.

Robin, J. (2010, June 18). *Podcasts: Potential uses in today's learning environment.* Retrieved from http://k12techsters.blogspot.com/2010/06/podcasts-potential-uses-in-todays.html

Rose, L. C., & Gallup, A. M. (2007). The 39th annual Phi Delta Kappa/Gallup poll of the public's attitudes toward the public schools. *Phi Delta Kappan, 89*, 33–48.

Schachter, R. (2011). The school media dilemma. *District Administration, 47*(7), 27–33.

School Webmasters. (n.d.). *To blog or not to blog.*

School Webmasters.(n.d.). Retrieved from http://www.schoolwebmasters.com/#ad-image-4

Seifert, E. H., & Vornberg, J. A. (2002). *The new school leader for the 21st century: The principal.* Lanham, MD: Scarecrow Education.

Strom, P. S., & Strom, R. D. (2003). Teacher-parent communication reform. *The High School Journal, 86*(2), 14–21.

Swick, K. J. (2003). Communication concepts for strengthening family-school-community partnerships. *Early Childhood Education Journal, 30*, 275–280.

Swick, K., & Battle Bailey, L. (2004). Communicating effectively with parents and families who are homeless. *Early Childhood Education Journal, 32*(3), 211–215.

Texas Education Code. (2003). *Texas statutes: Education code.* Retrieved from http://www.statutes.legis.state.tx.us/Docs/ED/htm/ED.4.htm

Tingley, S. (2007). Working with difficult parents. *School Administrator, 64*(1), 34.

Todoric, M. E. (2011). Guidelines for acceptable electronic communication with students. *Education Digest: Readings Condensed for Quick Review, 77*(3), 47–49.

Tynan, B., & Colbran, S. (2006). *Podcasting, student learning and expectations.* Proceedings of the 23rd Annual Ascilite Conference: Who's learning? Whose technology? Retrieved from http://www.ascilite.org.au/conferences/sydney06/proceeding/pdf_papers/p132.pdf

U.S. Department of Education, Office of Innovation and Improvement. (2007). *Choosing a school for your child.* (Publication ID EU 0121P).

U.S. Department of Education, Office of Safe and Drug-Free Schools. (2007). *Practical information on crisis planning: A guide for schools and communities.* Washington, DC, Author. Retrieved from http://rems.ed.gov/docs/PracticalInformationonCrisisPlanning.pdf

Vaillancourt, K., & Amador, A. (2014/2015). School-community alliances enhance mental health services. *Phi Delta Kappan, 96*(4), 57–62. doi: 10.1177/0031721714561448

Weil, M. (2010, Fall). Develop a strong school district communication strategy. *Scholastic Administrator.* Retrieved from http://www2.scholastic.com/browse/article.jsp?id=3754978

Wherry, J. H. (2005). Do you have a parent involvement disconnect? *Principal, 84*(4), 6.

Wherry, J. H. (2006). Using the right communication tool. *Principal, 88*(3), 6.

Wherry, J. H. (2007). *Barriers to parent involvement.* Fairfax Station, VA: The Parent Institute.

PART III

THE SUPERINTENDENT

DISTRICT LEADERSHIP IN TEXAS

The Effective Superintendent

Wesley D. Hickey ◆ *Pauline M. Sampson* ◆ *Jennifer Jones*

As the top executive officer of the school district, the superintendent is an essential ingredient in effective district-wide organizational improvement and transformation. The superintendent must have both the determination and wherewithal to face the intricacies of the political, instructional, and relational duties of the position. The contemporary view of effective superintendent leadership includes maintaining a fine balance between leadership of the people (culture, vision, climate, and supervision); of instruction (pedagogy, curriculum, and professional development); and management (facilities, financial, resources, systematic processes, and policies). The district leader must be elastic; both flexible and resilient as they are pulled in many directions in response to demands of the position and by constituents of the school community. The superintendent sets the tone, direction, builds human capacity, and with impetus develops a collective purpose for organizational change.

The superintendency is multifaceted, complex, and dynamic. The superintendent shapes the organization's direction, develops a collective purpose, and fosters a culture of success. To shape the direction, the successful leader must establish trust in order to have influence over others to lead them to accomplish the educational goals of the district. To do this, the superintendent must build the capacity of the district by making great use of the strengths of administrators, teachers, staff, and the school community for the improvement of the student learning outcomes. According to Sergiovanni (2005), a significant responsibility of the leader is to "cultivate and amass the intellectual capital" of others to elevate the intelligence of the organization (p. 122). Through building on the capacity of others, the leader can create a collective purpose for increased student and organizational achievement. Fullan and Quinn (2010) describe the latter as collective capacity building by increasing the abilities of the system's human capital for whole school reform. Fullan (2012) further points out the importance of building and developing the talents of both individuals and groups while motivating them for sustained improvement of the whole system. The superintendent can employ several strategies to achieve a collective purpose for systemic reform, such as building trusting relationships, encouraging shared decision-making, along with advocating, and promoting high expectations for student learning.

The superintendent must have a strategic plan of action for change. In his book *Leading Change*, Kotter (2012) describes collective purpose as a "guiding coalition" (p. 53). The guiding coalition shares in the overall reform, giving the team an opportunity for shared ownership and commitment to the change. In leading organization transformation, Kotter suggests an eight-stage change process: (1) establishing a sense of urgency; (2) creating the guiding coalition; (3) developing a vision and strategy; (4) communicating the change vision; (5) empowering employees for broad-based action; (6) generating short-term wins; (7) consolidating gains and producing more change; and (8) anchoring new approaches in the culture. Each stage promotes collaboration, empowerment, and deliberate action.

The effective superintendent strategically approaches organizational transformation and change through aligning and shaping the culture by means of building human capacity for the collective purpose. Successful leaders are adept at cultivating relationships and influential in leading others to reach a higher state of achievement while recognizing the accomplishments of the team along the way. Through effective leadership, the superintendent establishes direction, communicates the vision, and inspires others by building a collective purpose that in turn gives rise to change.

◆ VISIONARY LEADERSHIP AND COMMUNICATION

The ability to take the unique circumstances of a district and incorporate it into a successful strategic plan is an important part of a superintendent's job. As Chief Executive Officer of the district, the superintendent needs to synthesize data in such a way that guides the vision to address important factors related to student achievement. Additionally, superintendents must have an ethical foundation for fairness and equitable decisions. The improvement of the district is about creating an environment for student success, and the superintendent must accomplish the mission with a focus on all students, legal parameters, and community values (Harris, 2009). The guiding leadership of the superintendent is a vital cog to a focused organization.

The superintendent may create a common and focused action toward the advancement of the schools' mission and vision (Weiss, Templeton, Thompson, & Tremont, 2015) through effective communication. Communication can be as simple as an attitude of concern and honesty in normal interactions, or a plan that includes formal and informal methods of giving and receiving information. One component of good communication is public speaking. A superintendent should take whatever speaking opportunities are available to reinforce the mission, inform stakeholders, and celebrate successes.

Public speaking is one of those skills that many people do not have, and fear of it may keep some from getting better. Surveys suggest that public speaking is one of our greatest fears (Pull, 2012). Speaking before a group of people creates a possibility of looking bad or being rejected. This is something a superintendent needs to overcome in order to help the district achieve its mission. Superintendents speak publicly for several reasons, including the need to inform, educate, and sometimes entertain stakeholders. Board meetings, civic organizations, and parent/teacher organizations, among others, often ask the superintendent to share information about the district, which provides excellent venues for sharing important information.

The classic statement that public speaking is a shortcut to success is often correct (Carnegie, 1936). Effective public speakers come across as credible and are able to develop significant support quickly, whereas a poor public speaker is often seen as incompetent, even when that may not be true. The first step in any presentation is preparation. Superintendents must know what they are discussing. This will be the body of the speech—information that you want people to know (Kurtus, 2013). The organization of the speech is wrapped around this pertinent information. Although this information is the backbone of the speech, a successful speaker will often introduce it through a story that reaches the audience on an emotional level. This emotional appeal will relate to the core information, and this should be easy for superintendents since most educators have great stories that address student success despite overwhelming odds. A story about the financially poor family who made sacrifices for their children; the student who overcame serious illness; the organization that donated toys for underprivileged children and similar stories make great emotional introductions.

These stories about the school district engage the audience in the fundamental resilience and goodness of humankind, and they segue into the more technical discussion of the presentation. This technical component includes the purpose for the speech, including any data that lends support to the main point. A superintendent engages the audience through an emotional story and connects this introduction to the speech's purpose. Finally, the conclusion of the speech reiterates the previously addressed components and challenges the audience in some way.

Other forms of communication are also important, such as newsletters, emails, and memos, but there is nothing that takes the place of face-to-face interaction. A superintendent increases effectiveness by being socially adept in their communication. Social competence, or lack thereof, is often the tool that the public uses to evaluate their leaders (Goleman, 1998). Brief interactions with the community are important, and since these individuals talk to school board members, a superintendent's skill in handling the public in emotionally intelligent ways (Goleman, 1995) is often an important factor in the board's perception of his/her success. A superintendent who reads public sentiment effectively, and then is able to motivate others, is often well liked and successful in leading a school district. This does not mean that a superintendent is always smiling and spreading good cheer. Emotional intelligence is about recognizing the correct response to the situation, both personally and publically. To paraphrase Aristotle: It is easy for a superintendent to be angry, but to be angry with the right person in the right way takes skill.

◆ POLITICS AND SCHOOL GOVERNANCE

There are some decisions that require political and emotional capital, regardless of who is involved, that moving forward must be done with caution. Each district has issues that may seem minor, but the history behind them creates an emotional attachment that is hard to understand out of context. A superintendent must pick his/her battles, and there must be a balance between change and the political/emotional capital that will be expended in the process.

The official governance of a school district occurs within the Team of Eight, which is the seven members of the school board elected by the public and the superintendent. School boards in Texas have the responsibility of district oversight and policy adoption (Texas Education Code Chapter 11, 2009). Well-meaning trustees may find it difficult to stay within the boundaries of which are legally permissible, but the power of a school board only exists as a group (or at least a majority of the board, known as a quorum) in a lawfully called meeting. Individual board members do not have formal authority but are responsible for policy adoption. The superintendent is to administer the policies.

There is much discussion regarding the building of effective professional relationships between the school board and superintendent. In fact, the school board/superintendent team is required to have annual team building (Texas Education Code Chapter 11, 2009). This need for a team recognizes that a problem with the superintendent and the school board impacts all of the campuses in a district. A board/superintendent team that focuses on overall student needs will be more effective than one that is concerned about personal agendas. This type of team does not occur by accident and requires communication and training. Continued training of board members is an expectation, and this is reflected in the rules adopted by the State Board of Education, which may be found at http://tea.texas.gov/Texas_Schools/School_Boards/School_Board_Member_Training/. New board members are supposed to attend ten hours of training per year (five of these hours may be in an online format), and experienced trustees are to have five hours (all of these hours may be online). Documentation of these hours is to be kept by the district, and the board president is to announce how much training each board member completed during the December board meeting, and these are to be recorded in the minutes. This public announcement of hours provides information to the ultimate evaluators of the trustees, which are the voters of the district.

There are other requirements for board members based upon experience and position. New board members must receive an orientation related to district policies and goals within 60 days before or after the election. All sitting board members are to receive training in Texas Education Code from the Education Service Center. In addition, Texas Education Code Chapter 26, related to parent rights and responsibilities, and Chapter 28, related to health education, are required topics (Texas Education Code Chapter 11, 2009).

A good professional relationship between the school board and superintendent is important for the overall well being of the district. Any feeling of distrust tends to flow downward; thus, a superintendent needs to consistently work on this relationship. There are several strategies that a superintendent may use to build this relationship, but none of these ideas are radical. They represent characteristics required of any effective leader.

- Honesty—There is nothing that kills a relationship more quickly than the perception that the superintendent is being less than honest. Mike Moses, former superintendent of Dallas ISD and Texas Education Agency commissioner, stated that "if there is bad news to tell, I want to be the one to tell it." A school board that feels ambushed with bad news develops a level of distrust with their superintendent.
- Communication—A superintendent should have several different methods of communicating with their school board. Some examples are: (1) Send out a weekly newsletter (remember, this will be subject to Texas Public Information Act, so you may as well give it to all faculty members and post it in a public area) that discusses the previous week's news and upcoming events. (2) Take a different board member to lunch each week. Board members ran for a trustee position for a reason. Ask them to talk about issues they perceive to be important. This does not guarantee their issues will be addressed, but being heard does wonders for a relationship, and the superintendent is able to get a perspective that may be valuable. (3) Personally deliver board agendas to the members. This is an act that lets you touch base with them, but it also sets the tone that signals a need for the board member to do his/her homework on agenda items. (4) Call board members if something happens in the district that may be of public concern. A board member does not want to appear uninformed when something sensational has happened. A quick call is not trying to discuss policy or request support, only to inform. There is time enough later (in a lawfully called board meeting) to discuss specifics.

- Recognition—January is Board Member recognition month, so this is a formal time to praise your board, but there are many other opportunities throughout the year. Take a moment to recognize and express your appreciation at banquets, public assemblies, etc. This praise needs to be sincere, but that is not difficult. The superintendent may disagree with a board member, but no one runs for the board to make the school a worse place. They run for the board because they want to make it a better place, even if you disagree with their approach.

◆ SCHOOL BOARD ELECTIONS

A position on the school board is not a lucrative one. Board members receive no compensation (Texas Education Code Chapter 11, 2009), and they are asked for a portion of their time at least once a month, and usually much more often. There is little praise associated with the position. They are rarely noticed if the school district is functioning properly, but they are criticized harshly (and sometimes unfairly) if there is the perception of problems. This does not seem to be a position that many people would want, and in many districts, that is true. However, there is usually enough interested individuals to have annual elections.

An individual wanting to run for the school board must file no later than 5 p.m. 62 days before the election. Even write-in candidates must declare within 5 days of this deadline to have his/her votes considered. Candidates in districts that have at-large elections can live anywhere in the district. Candidates in single-member districts must live within the geographic "place" designated. Single-member districts are designed to get representatives from the different areas in the district and prevent unequal representation (Texas Education Code Chapter 11, 2009). There are times when a school board vacancy becomes available due to death or resignation. During these times, the board has two options: Appoint someone for the remainder of the term, or hold a special election to fill the position. The position should not be left vacant for over 180 days (Texas Education Code Chapter 11, 2009).

◆ SCHOOL BOARD FUNCTIONING UNDER THE OPEN MEETINGS ACT

Texas law (Texas Government Code Chapter 551, 2011) outlines the requirements for meetings of governmental agencies. This includes a public posting of an agenda at least 72 hours in advance, and this information should be sent to any media who has previously requested it. Agenda items must provide enough information that a concerned citizen will be aware of the topics being discussed. For example, having an item for "hiring personnel" is not enough if the school board is hiring an athletic director. An athletic director is a position of public concern, so a clear posting is required. The Attorney General has ruled that knowledge of the item being discussed is required for general reports given by administrators (Attorney General of Texas, 2008). Having a line on the agenda that says "Superintendent's Report" does not convey any information about the discussion; thus, there should be enough description to make a citizen aware of the topic. Transparency is important in government. A superintendent should be as open as possible with district information while protecting students, employees, and the district as required by law.

There are several parts to an agenda; each having different purposes. Most school board agendas will have the following components:

- Action items: These are agenda items that require a vote by the board of trustees. For example, "The board will consider a bid for indoor pest control for the 2015–2016 school year."
- Informational items: These are agenda items for discussion. For example, "The board will discuss the curriculum software package being considered for Algebra classes." The superintendent's report (and those of anyone else given time, such as principals) are also informational.
- Consent agenda: This is an agenda item where several routine and noncontroversial items may be added and voted on in one motion. This is a time saver for school boards. Items like previous board minutes, check register, investment report, and many others do not have to be considered and voted upon separately. However, a board member may take exception to an item in the consent agenda. If that is the case, that item may be voted upon separately so that a no vote intended for one part of the consent agenda is not considered for all items.

Transparency exists to provide the public with knowledge of the considerations of their elected officials, but this does not mean that they can get involved in the process of board meetings. Board meetings are public meetings, not meetings of the public. There are policies that guide behavior in board meetings, and they should be followed. For example, most districts have a policy for a "public forum" before the regular board meetings. Outlined in this policy will be the number of people who can be heard from, and for how long (up to six people for up to 5 minutes each is common). The board president should make sure this is being followed. The public forum is to inform the board of trustees of stakeholder perceptions (good or bad), but the board may not act on them or make biased comments. They can ask for clarification, if needed, but that is the extent of their role. This is not a time for extended venting by an unhappy individual, and the school board must follow policies, even in emotionally difficult moments.

The board president is not only responsible for handling public forum issues, he/she is responsible for the efficient operation of the board meetings and ensuring that proper protocol is being followed in these sessions (Texas Education Code Chapter 11, 2009). Officially, the superintendent is a guest at these meetings who is able to educate the trustees on agenda items and make recommendations. Although a guest at the meetings, many superintendents have in their contracts that the board is not to go into executive session without them unless the matter to be discussed is the superintendent's evaluation or contract. The superintendent should be a reliable and trusted source of information.

◆ SCHOOL BOARD FUNCTIONING IN CLOSED MEETINGS

School board meetings are assumed open unless there is a specific reason for the session to be closed within the exceptions outlined in the Texas Government Code Chapter 551 (2011). All meetings must be formally opened before going into closed session. The presiding officer (usually the board president) must announce that the school board will be going into closed session, provide the exception by section number, and announce the time of transition away from open session. Possible exceptions to open meetings that school boards may face are as follows:

1. Consultation with the school's attorney for discussion of pending or contemplating litigation, or to discuss a settlement (Texas Government Code 551.071);
2. Deliberation about the purchase, sale, or lease of property if discussion in open session would be detrimental to the process (Texas Government Code 551.072);

3. Deliberation regarding a prospective gift if discussion in open session would be detrimental to the process (Texas Government Code 551.073);

4. Discussion of personnel issues, although this may be in open session if the employee being discussed prefers (Texas Government Code 551.074);

5. Deliberation regarding security devices or audit (Texas Government Code 551.076);

6. Discussion of student discipline issues, although this may be in open session if the parents of the student prefer (Texas Government Code 551.082);

7. Deliberation of data that could personally identify students. This could include directory information if the parents have requested that this be kept private (Texas Government Code 551.0821);

8. Discussion of standards for a representative in working with an employee group (Texas Government Code 551.083);

9. Discussion of an investigation where the school board wishes to keep witnesses separate (Texas Government Code 551.084);

10. Deliberation of economic development negotiations (Texas Government Code 551.087); or

11. Deliberation regarding a test item that the governmental body believes may be used as a question for a license or certificate (Texas Government Code 551.088).

The discussion in the closed session must be either recorded in a certified agenda or tape recording. The tape recording/certified agenda are not a part of public record, but may be subpoenaed in the event of a lawsuit. The district is to maintain these records for as long as there are legal concerns or for 2 years, whichever is longest. The board president must bring the board out of closed session when finished and record the time of this exit. Any action on the closed session item must be done in open session. There is not supposed to be even an informal vote (straw vote) in closed session.

◆ TEXAS PUBLIC INFORMATION ACT

The legal cousin of the Open Meetings Act is the Texas Public Information Act. Its purpose is to provide interested stakeholders with information about their public institutions. There are many documents that are considered public and must be provided to anyone who asks. A public information request is triggered by a written request. The district should not ask for the purpose of the inquiry but may ask clarifying questions to better understand what is being requested. This becomes important if there is a large amount of data being requested that is redundant (Texas Government Code 552, 2011).

The district should provide the information requested as soon as possible. If the data is easily found and known to be public, the request should be promptly fulfilled. The district has up to 10 days to get information to the requester, but if more time is needed, the district must document this and send it to the person requesting the information. Note that the district does not have to do research or create data. The request may only apply to existing information. If the data in question may not be public then the district must file an exemption request with the Attorney General. This must be filed within 30 days of the original request. The Attorney General has 45 days to rule as to whether the information is to be released to the public.

◆ NEPOTISM

Nepotism law forbids school board members from hiring family members. The law states that no one can be hired who is related by blood within the third degree, or through marriage to the second degree. The Attorney General has ruled that this law pertains to the superintendent, as well, if he is given authority to approve hiring. This does not change the school board's responsibility regarding nepotism; they cannot get around the hiring restriction by giving the superintendent responsibility (Attorney General of Texas, 2010).

Be aware that this law is for the original hire. For example, a board member's wife who was hired before he was elected may continue her employment. Her contract may be renewed each year without triggering the nepotism provision. In addition, there are two exceptions in the nepotism law: (1) an appointment as a substitute teacher and (2) employment as a bus driver if all or the majority of the district is located in a county of 35,000 residents or less (Attorney General of Texas, 2010).

◆ ORGANIZATIONAL LEADERSHIP

The foundation for a good superintendent is knowing the legal policies, synthesizing information in the district, and finding solutions (often creative) to the problems. Finding the best place to start school district improvements may be difficult. First year superintendents are usually great administrators who are given the opportunity to advance. This is expected, but too often, these individuals get into their new office and think, "what now?" The occasional crisis that occurs will demand the attention of the superintendent because these situations will make clear the "what now" situations. However, there are two important points to make regarding the daily improvement of operations: (1) no decision is so small that no one will care about it and (2) since someone is going to be concerned with the changes being made, pick your battles and get others involved in the decision making.

Recognizing that someone will be concerned, and likely take exception, to even seemingly small decisions, is often overlooked by new superintendents. Unilaterally change the purchase order requisition process, members of a committee, or anything else, and there will be unhappy people throughout the district. Improvement is not the issue here; the new procedure could be much better, but humans inherently hate change. This is why it is important to get input from anyone who will be impacted by the decision. Allow others to come to the best decision according to specific guidelines. The resulting decision or procedure will be as good if not better than the one unilaterally made. The superintendent may then be an advocate for the decision of the stakeholders.

This point needs to be repeated: A superintendent should always take responsibility for any problem in the district (this may often seem unfair because many of these problems will be unknown to the superintendent until the last minute), and he/she should not glow in the accolades of successes. A superintendent takes responsibility for problems and gives credit to everyone else for successes. Taking responsibility for problems requires a superintendent to have a strong sense of self-awareness. This is evident in the need for a superintendent to stay calm while those around him/her are not. Many times these moments seem like a crisis, and there are often emotions involved. A deep awareness of personal feelings, and often, separating them from the decision, is important. Making decisions based upon the emotions of the moment often lead to poor decision-making.

A superintendent must not only address the crises of the district but also the day-to-day mundane tasks. Superintendents may not do everything, but they are responsible for all of it. Skills in self-motivation increase the effectiveness of the district by ensuring that the leader is able to work well during both the mundane and difficult times that are inevitable. No one is overseeing the superintendent on a daily basis, so self-motivation is essential.

Organizational initiatives may occur through the district site-based decision making committee. Texas Education Code Chapter 11 (2009) requires that the school board ensure that a district plan be created and revised annually. The school board is to approve this plan and make sure it is aligned with the campus plans. The district and campus level committees aid in the superintendent's communication. These committees can provide an environment of increased transparency, and even more importantly, allow for planning and decision making that takes into account the feedback from varied stakeholders. The stakeholders on the district committee must include professional staff, parents of district students, community members, and business representatives. There are a few caveats to the different committee roles: (1) the parent stakeholder cannot also be the community member; (2) the professional staff cannot be the parent even if they have children in the school; and (3) the business representative does not have to live in the district (Texas Education Code Chapter 11, 2009). This committee provides important input for the district to help align initiatives with local needs.

◆ CURRENT ISSUES FOR TEXAS SUPERINTENDENTS

Superintendents are the Chief Executive Officers of the district, and as such, have ultimate responsibility in all areas. The big issues related to school finance, facilities, and human resources are addressed in other chapters within this book. This section looks at a few of current issues getting attention: religion, bullying, extracurricular activities, and safety.

Religion in Public Schools

Religious issues tend to be important in Texas schools, but they have had legal ramifications in the past few years, likely due to the increasing heterogeneity of the state. The Lemon test, which are guidelines that resulted from the Lemon v. Kurtzman (1971) court case, still provide guidance in reflecting upon a religious issues in public schools, but there continues to be confusion. The Lemon test looks at the relationship between government policy and religion, and if any of these three measures are not met than the action is unconstitutional. The Lemon test requires the following: (1) the public school's policy is secular in nature; (2) the public school's policy neither promotes nor inhibits religion; and (3) the public school's policy does not encourage an excessive entanglement with the government to ensure religion is not being promoted. Basically, the law (and constitution) states that public institutions should not be in the business of religion, but there is often confusion between the right of the individual (such as a student) in a public institution and the responsibility of government representatives (such as teachers, principals, and superintendents) in their role in both protecting religious rights without promoting them.

Creating this separation is becoming more important as our communities become less homogenous. Many towns are beginning to have diverse populations with different religions, or none at all. The city council of the small East Texas town of Hawkins voted in 2011 to have a large sign posted at the city limits that said "Jesus Welcomes You to Hawkins." The Freedom from Religion foundation, and organization whose mission is to protect the constitutional separation of church and state, sent a letter asking for the removal of the sign because of its entanglement with the city government (Shadwick, 2015).

Other Freedom from Religion Foundation letters have been sent to other districts. White Oak ISD had to change the morning announcements at the high school because the reading of Bible verses by the principal was common (Ortiga, 2015). In a complaint that has potential reverberations among most political bodies, the Killeen School Board was contacted regarding the prayers that take place before meetings (Wilen, 2015).

Texas has a history of actions, both administratively and legislatively, that enter the gray area of the establishment clause of the First Amendment of the United States Constitution. These new court cases and legislation are important for a superintendent to be aware, but the bottom line is the same. Students can proselytize in a nondisruptive way, but teachers and other school personnel cannot. This is often difficult for teachers to understand, but public school employees are government representatives who are not to promote faith. There likely will be more lawsuits in this area over the next few years.

Bullying

Texas Education Code (2015) Chapter 37.0832 defines bullying as behavior that creates or threatens to create harm to a student to such an extent that a meaningful education is hindered. There are a number of requirements related to bullying that impact the superintendent, such as the need for the school board to develop a prevention policy, teachers to be trained in recognition and avoidance, and parents to be provided options in the event of bullying (Texas Education Code, 2015).

These requirements occur because schools should be thought of as a safe haven for students to pursue academic and athletic endeavors, and educators can expect more lawsuits to occur when bullying is ignored. Simply put, administrators must take appropriate action when a student is being bullied. Indifference to a student who is experiencing this type of behavior may not only cause emotional and physical harm, taking action to prevent it is the right thing to do. The media has reported on students who have committed suicide because of bullying.

The issue of suicide has led to new legislation from the eighty-fourth Legislature. This law requires that the academic curriculum for a student getting teacher or administrator certified include training in mental health, youth suicide, and substance abuse (LegisScan, 2015). Administrators are not mental health professionals, but they must look for and recognize the signs of students who are exhibiting signs of psychological illness.

Extra-Curricular Activities

Extra-curricular teams are often the "face" of the district. This is unfair in many ways, but these public performances are often the only activities witnessed by those outside of the local community. Stories like the one in which two John Jay High School players hit a referee (Sadeghi, 2015) paint an ugly picture that suggests unruly teens and renegade coaches. As of this writing, we do not know the whole story, but we do know it is not going to make the school look good. However, there are more good stories from school activities than bad ones. Many schools are using activities to reach out to the community in other ways, such as the football team in Massachusetts who set up the game to allow a student in a wheelchair to score (Searles, 2015).

Extracurricular activities are often seen as a strong motivational factor for student engagement in schools. A poor teacher can often stay under the radar for long periods of time unless the principal is diligent in his/her duties to ensure quality classroom teaching. A coach or cheerleader sponsor cannot. Extracurricular activities take the performance of students outside the classroom and present it to the public. Parents and community members alike take pride in the performance of students; after all, school districts are the main attraction of many towns. A superintendent will likely receive more complaints about extracurricular activities than any other component of the district. Lack of knowledge or experience regarding these activities can be difficult on a superintendent. The University Interscholastic League (UIL), which provides rules for sports and academic contests, has information on their Website. This information should be studied. In addition, there are a few key points that will be made here.

The superintendent (or administrative designee) will be a member of the District UIL Executive Committee (UIL, n.d.). This group meets periodically to discuss general issues regarding competitive UIL events in the district. Occasionally, there will be a meeting to discuss a more sensitive matter. This can include student transfers, or what to recommend regarding the punishment of a team for playing an ineligible player. Familiarity with the rules is important.

The no pass no play rule is almost self-explanatory, but there are timelines and exceptions that need to be known. For example, a student who fails a class during a grading period (usually each 6 or 9 weeks) becomes ineligible to play extracurricular activities starting the next Friday after school. Thus, there is a 1-week grace period before ineligibility occurs. The student may regain eligibility if they are passing all courses (not just the one failed) after 3 weeks. The ineligible student may regain eligibility on the Friday 3 weeks into the grading period, but this eligibility actually takes place 1 week later at the end of the school day.

This seems fairly straightforward, but there will be a few schools each year who violate this UIL rule, and as a result, must forfeit the games in which the ineligible student played. No superintendent wants to have to meet with a District UIL Executive Committee to discuss this type of oversight. The athletic director should be directed to create the communication networks needed to ensure that these types of issues do not occur.

Fair athletic participation in public schools requires rules forbidding the recruitment of students. UIL assists with this issue by having students with previous athletic participation at one school complete a form designed to determine if the student is moving for athletic purposes. A student who transfers to another district for non-athletic purposes, stays with his/her family, physically changes houses to one in the district, does not have part of the family continuing to live in the previous district, and a few other criteria will likely be eligible after 15 days of enrollment. A student who moves for athletic reasons, or fails to meet guidelines that UIL has found suggests this type of behavior, may not be eligible to play varsity athletics for a calendar year.

School Safety

The incident in Newtown, CT, has set off a debate throughout the nation in regard to both federal gun laws and the role guns should have in schools. The 83rd Legislative Session passed The Protection of Texas Children Act, which allows a school to arm one employee for every 400 students in the school. This person will be highly trained and remain anonymous to the students and general public. Considering whether to arm employees can be difficult for a superintendent or school board.

Statistics on gun violence are hard to find, and many of the ones online provide different numbers, but it looks like there have been around 325 deaths due to guns in public schools and universities over the past 15 years, resulting in ~21 deaths per year. Taking into account that there are 65 million students in these institutions, the odds of a person being shot is 1 in 3,000,000. However, this may not be the right statistic, since invasions with the intent to harm are more relevant. During the years of 2010–2012, there were 23 school shootings, or 7.7 per year among 140,000 educational institutions. This means the actual odds of having a shooting incident at any particular school is 1 in 18,000. For perspective, the odds of dying in a car wreck are 1 in 6,550.

Statistically, schools are among the safest places for a student. Supervision of students and monitoring of visitors provides a baseline of safety. The passing of policies that allow for armed employees is indicative of the trust communities place in their administrators and teachers, choosing to support a policy that provides them a means to protect children from an armed invader. The idea of employees being helpless in the event of an intruder with guns is unthinkable, and many board members wonder if the school in Newtown would have had fewer casualties if the principal had been armed.

No one outside of the community and board of trustees can adequately determine what course of action is best for their district, but there are considerations that should be examined. A superintendent who recommends a policy allowing select employees to carry guns is wanting the end result to be a school that is safer from firearm attacks, thus decreasing the odds that currently exist. Any possible decrease in school shootings must be considered in relation to the possibility of accidents that occur when people handle guns. Stories of highly trained people accidentally firing a weapon, having emotional breakdowns that compromise safety, making poor decisions regarding the nature of a threat, or losing their weapon in a struggle, can be found throughout the Internet. To be clear, these incidents are uncommon but should be considered. The major question in adopting a school employee firearm policy is whether it decreases the odds of a school shooting enough to offset the unintended consequences of increasing the probability of a gun accident. This is something every superintendent and school board should ponder as policies are adopted.

◆ CONCLUSION

In summary, the Texas Education Code Chapter 11 (2009) defines the role of the superintendent as the leader who is responsible for

1. Planning, operation, supervision, and evaluation of the entire district;
2. Assignment and evaluation of all personnel of the district;
3. Make recommendations regarding the selection of personnel;
4. Initiate the termination or suspension of an employee or nonrenewal of an employee's term contract;
5. Managing the day-to-day operations of the district;
6. Prepare and submit a proposed budget;
7. Prepare recommendations for policies and oversee policy implementation;
8. Develop administrative regulations to implement policies;
9. Provide leadership for the attainment of student performance; and
10. Organize the district's central administration.

This chapter covers some of the basic skills and responsibilities that are integral to a successful superintendent. This is a brief overview, since the role of a superintendent transcends other job positions. Other chapters in this book cover important topics that are left out of this chapter. This all-encompassing role is why the superintendent position is unique. Success in the role involves being held accountable by an elected board of trustees while developing subordinate employees, often as a servant-leader with a focus on the vision and mission of the school district. There is nothing easy about being a superintendent, but it has within its role the moral purpose that is the development of our next generation of leaders.

◆ REFERENCES

Attorney General of Texas. (2008). *Opinion No. GA-0668*. Retrieved from www.oag.state.tx.us/opinions/opinions/50abbott/op/2008/htm/ga-0668.htm

Attorney General of Texas. (2010). *Opinion No. GA-0494*. Retrieved from www.oag.state.tx.us/opinions/opinions/50abbott/op/2010/htm/ga-0794.htm

Carnegie, D. (1936). *How to win friends and influence people* (Revised ed.). Garden City, New York: Dale Carnegie & Associates, Inc.

Fullan, M. (2012). *Transforming schools an entire system at a time*. Retrieved from http://www.mckinsey.com/insights/public_sector/transforming_schools_an_entire_system_at_a_time

Fullan, M., & Quinn, J. (2010). *Capacity building for whole system reform*. Retrieved from: http://www.michaelfullan.ca/media/13435862150.html

Goleman, D. (1995). *Emotional intelligence: Why it can matter more than IQ*. New York: Bantam Books.

Goleman, D. (1998). *Working with emotional intelligence*. New York: Bantam Books.

Greenleaf, R. K., & Spears, R. C. (2002). *Servant leadership: A journey into the nature of legitimate power and greatness 25th anniversary edition*. Mahwah, NJ: Paulist Press.

Harris, S. (2009). *Learning from the best: Lessons from award-winning superintendents*. Thousand Oaks, CA: Corwin.

Kotter, J. P. (2012). *Leading change*. Boston: Harvard Business Press.

Kurtus, R. (2013). *Three parts of speech*. Retrieved from www.school-for-champions.com/speechwriting/three_parts_of_a_speech.htm

LegisScan. (2015). *TX SB674*. Retrieved from https://legiscan.com/TX/bill/SB674/2015.

Lemon v. Kurtzman, 403 U.S. 602 (1971).

Ortiga, B. (2015). *White Oak ISD: No more 'chapter and verse' from Bible*. Retrieved from http://www.news-journal.com/news/2015/mar/15/white-oak-isd-no-more-chapter-and-verse-from-bible/

Pull, C. B. (2012). Current status of knowledge on public-speaking anxiety. *Personality Disorders and Neurosis, 25*(1), 32–38.

Sadeghi, C. (2015). *Players in ref attack tell their story on national TV*. Retrieved from http://kxan.com/2015/09/18/players-in-ref-attack-tell-their-story-on-national-tv/

Searles, K. E. (2015). *Boy in wheelchair scores game winning touchdown*. Retrieved from http://www.wchstv.com/news/features/eyewitness-news/stories/Boy-In-Wheelchair-Scores-Game-Winning-Touchdown-205139.shtml#.VgBw2WTBzRY

Sergiovanni, T. J. (2005). The virtues of leadership. *The Educational Forum, 69*(2), 112–123. Retrieved from http://files.eric.ed.gov/fulltext/EJ683737.pdf

Shadwick, L. (2015). *'Jesus welcomes you to Hawkins' sign in East Texas scheduled for removal.* Retrieved from http://www.breitbart.com/texas/2015/09/22/jesus-welcomes-you-to-hawkins-sign-in-east-texas-scheduled-for-removal/

Texas Education Code. (2015). *Texas constitution and statutes.* Retrieved from http://www.statutes .legis.state.tx.us/?link=ED

Texas Education Code Chapter 11. (2009). *School districts.* Retrieved from www.statutes.legis.state .tx.us/docs/ed/htm/ed.11.htm

Texas Government Code 552. (2011). *Public information.* Retrieved from http://www.statutes.legis .state.tx.us/docs/GV/htm/GV.552.htm

Texas Government Code Chapter 551. (2011). *Open meetings.* Retrieved from law.onecle.com/texas/ government/551.001.00.html

University Interscholastic League. (n.d.). *League governance.* Retrieved from www.uiltexas.org/ policy/league-governance

Weiss, G., Templeton, N. R., Thompson, R., & Tremont, J. W. (2015). Superintendent and school board relations: Impacting achievement through collaborative understanding of roles and responsibilities. *National Forum of Educational Administration & Supervision Journal, 32*(2), 4–16.

Wilen, H. (2015). *Killeen ISD receives complaint about board prayer.* Retrieved from http://kdhnews. com/news/education/killeen-isd-receives-complaint-about-board-prayer/article_c0d4d904-4ec5 -11e5-a9de-f7e1eb828616.html

FINANCING TEXAS PUBLIC SCHOOLS

Chuck Holt

The volatile nature of twenty-first century economics has made it increasingly important for administrators in public schools to have a clear understanding of the way that schools are funded. This knowledge provides an understanding of the nature of the variables and factors that drive funding in the state system. All state funding systems have intricacies and nuances that greatly impact the amount and kinds of funding that a school district will receive. The ability to understand and manipulate these nuances is a critical skill for school administrators. Those involved in school governance need a thorough understanding of school finance, not only to deal with current fiscal concerns but also to make accurate projections to avoid future crises.

This chapter will provide the reader with a general overview of the school finance system in Texas. The sections will provide information about the relevance of money in education, the history of school funding in Texas, the property tax system and its relationship with the state's school funding system, state formula options for financing public schools, and some detail about the sources of revenue available to Texas public schools.

◆ THE SIGNIFICANCE OF MONEY IN EDUCATION

The discussion of the amounts and kinds of funding that school districts receive has little importance unless one develops a philosophy in regard to the relative importance of money in the educational process. It would seem obvious that there are levels of funding or lack thereof that would make this discussion moot. No funds or very small amounts would, obviously, have a deleterious effect on the educational process and, conversely, there would be a point at which more funds would make no difference. This issue must be considered within parameters in the mid-range area where districts find themselves dealing with a situation where they have sufficient funds to make an adequate effort but lack access to additional monies for activities that they believe would make a difference in academic achievement.

Scholars on each side of the debate make convincing arguments in regard to the question, "Does money matter in education?" Hanushek (1989) contends that there is no strong or systematic relationship between school expenditures and student performance. Greenwald, Hedges, and Laine (1994) suggest that reviewing the same data on resources and achievement would lead to the conclusion that money does matter after all.

The statistical evidence of any strong relationship between per-pupil spending and student achievement has been difficult to document (Picus, 1997). Even though this quantitative tie has been hard to find, administrators believe that they have sufficient expertise to allocate resources in such a way as to make a difference in the educational opportunities that they are able to offer to students in their purview. Funding discussions may seem trivial if one does not embrace a philosophical position in regard to this issue.

◆ A BRIEF HISTORY OF PUBLIC SCHOOL FUNDING IN TEXAS

Texas has a long and rich tradition in the administration of property taxes as the basis for school funding. History shows that both Galveston and Corpus Christi levied property taxes for support of public schools as early as 1846. Following the Civil War and during the Reconstruction days, the state adopted a new constitution in 1869. The constitution mandated property taxes in all school districts. This directive was repealed by the Constitution of 1876. This was amended in 1883, giving local districts the authority to levy property taxes for support of public schools. Property taxes were very unpopular and very few districts levied them in the early days of Texas public schools. As economic conditions changed and state funding lagged, the property tax became more acceptable.

Historically, the development of a funding system for Texas public schools has been characterized by a series of starts and stops primarily driven by economic conditions and political considerations. Though this has been an evolutionary process, it became more revolutionary with the 1971 filing of *Rodriquez v. San Antonio ISD* in the federal court system, which challenged the constitutionality of the Texas public school funding system. This effort was unsuccessful and was followed by *Edgewood v. Bynum* in 1984, which challenged the Texas system in state court. This case was refiled in 1985 as *Edgewood v. Kirby*. In 1989, the Texas Supreme Court reversed the appeals court decision and affirmed the trial court's decision that found the Texas system of public school finance unconstitutional (Walker & Casey, 1996). The basis of the ruling was that the constitution calls for an "efficient system" and the court found "an implicit link between efficiency and equality" (*Edgewood v. Kirby,* 1989). Not unlike other states, this ruling was followed by a series of legislative attempts to remedy the problems and subsequent, successful legal challenges to those legislative proposals. In 1993, with the passage of Senate Bill 7, the legislature was able to pass a funding bill that met constitutional muster. Senate Bill 7 provided the framework for the Texas system, called the Foundation School Program (FSP), which has many elements remaining in effect today.

This version of the FSP was a large step forward in the equalization of funding for public school students in Texas. However, areas of contention continued to surface. The most divisive feature was the concept of recapture. Local districts that had property wealth above a predetermined level of wealth per student, referred to as "the cap," were sending large amounts of local revenue back into the system to be accessed by districts with less local property wealth per student. The existence and degree of contention in regard to this matter was largely a matter of perspective. The less contentious, but more pervasive, area was that of capacity or the ability of local boards to raise adequate revenue. The maximum tax rate for Texas school districts for funding operations was $1.50 per $100 valuation. For fiscal year 2004, 60% of the districts had M&O tax rates of $1.46–$1.50 (Thompson, 2004). There was no place to go to deal with inflation or other uncontrollable increases in costs. Many school officials viewed the system as lacking both adequacy and equity. In other words, many believed that the current system no longer provided a mechanism for local school boards to raise enough funds to meet the mission of schools and/or funding was not equitable between schools as measured in funding per penny of tax effort.

The response to these conditions was the filing of what has become known as the West-Orange Cove case. The West-Orange Cove Consolidated Independent School District and various plaintiff intervenors filed suit against the State of Texas in which they challenged the constitutionality of the funding system created by Senate Bill 7. This case was heard by Judge John Dietz in the District Court of Travis County, Texas (250th Judicial District), and his ruling was delivered on September 15, 2004. The judge issued a far-reaching ruling encompassing 125 pages in which he determined (among other things):

1. That Texas school districts lacked sufficient discretion in setting their tax rates to satisfy the constitutional requirement of providing a sufficient diffusion of knowledge. Much expert testimony was employed in resolving this issue, which focused mainly on the issue of adequacy.
2. That facility funding was inadequate.
3. That many of the weights assigned to categories of pupils were inadequate.
4. That the state must be enjoined from distributing any money under the current Chapters 41 and 42 of the Education Code after October 1, 2005.

The state appealed in response to Judge Dietz's ruling. The appellate case, *Neeley et al. v. West-Orange Cove et al.*, was heard and the court issued its ruling on November 22, 2005. The basic determinations were:

1. The court struck down the state's school finance system because it had evolved into an unconstitutional state property tax.
2. The court reversed the trial court's ruling that the system was inadequate.
3. However, the court ruled that the issue of adequacy was "justiciable," i.e., subject to review by the court.

The state responded to the ruling in *Neeley et al. v. West-Orange Cove et al.* in the third-called session of the 79th Texas Legislature during which they passed House Bill 1 (HB 1), which changed the tax rate structure and some funding elements of the FSP. HB 3646, passed in 2009, provided the structure of the FSP by which Texas public schools were funded for only 2 years. In a called session in June of 2011, the 82nd Legislature, facing a daunting shortfall of state revenue, passed Senate Bill 1 (SB 1). SB 1 continued to utilize a target revenue mechanism for individual districts but reduced funding to the FSP by approximately $4 billion, as well as reducing grant programs by $1.5 billion in the 2011–2013 biennium.

In 2012, five disparate groups filed suit against the State of Texas arguing that the finance system was both inadequate and inequitable. This suit was unusual in that the plaintiff groups had very different interests as property-rich schools, property-poor schools, charter schools, and others. In February 2013, State District Judge John Dietz issued an oral ruling from the bench, finding the school finance system unconstitutional, both because of inadequate school funding and flaws in the way the state distributes money to districts. Following action by the 83rd legislature that restored $3.4 billion to the finance system, Judge Dietz reopened the case and heard another round of arguments in January 2014. Judge Dietz stated that in light of the bills passed by the 83rd Legislature, justice is served to re-examine the effects of the recent legislation on the case. The District Court's ruling came in August of 2014. As expected, the state filed an appeal and the Texas Supreme Court agreed to hear the case named the *Texas Taxpayer & Student Fairness Coalition v. Michael Williams*. Legal briefs are scheduled to be filed in the summer of 2015 with arguments to be heard possibly late in the year. A ruling is not likely until the summer of 2016. In an interesting twist, the 84th Legislature also passed Senate Bill 455, which directs statewide cases such as school finance to be heard in a "Special Three-Judge District Court." This bill moves some important cases out of the Travis County District Court where some critics believed a more liberal atmosphere existed for such cases. This three-judge panel is to be appointed by the State Supreme Court. Weber (2015) suggested that this is a Republican effort to move these cases out of Travis County District Court and "pluck the liberal thorn out of its side."

◆ THE PROPERTY TAX SYSTEM

State systems for funding public schools are somewhat unique in their basic structures but, almost universally, share the concept that funding should be a partnership between local and state governing bodies. The essence of a funding system is the nature of that partnership. This partnership determines what factors are used to determine the respective shares of the total cost that each of the entities will provide.

The Texas system for financing its public schools describes a complex relationship between the local district and the state. The nature of this partnership is such that the amount of revenue that the local district can access directly affects the amount of funds that the state will provide. Since the only source of revenue that local districts have available is the local property tax, a strong relationship is created between the local property taxation and the state's funding system. Simply put, as the ability of the district to raise local revenue increases, the access to state revenue decreases and vice versa.

State funding systems during the early history of Texas tended to be of the *per capita* variety and there was no direct link between local revenue and state financial assistance. The lack of a relationship between the two revenue sources allowed appraisal, levying, and collecting of property taxes to be strictly a local matter. As a result, administration of the property tax ranged from haphazard to overzealous and was not subject to oversight by state authorities.

The situation changed dramatically in 1949 with the passage of the first of the Gilmer–Aiken Bills. This represents for the first time that there was a direct link between property tax administration and state funding. The dramatic differences in local property tax administration continued to be a problem for the next 30 years. The state school funding system was troubled by a property tax system that routinely under-appraised property, used fractional assessments, and was guilty of a multitude of sins of omission and commission. Some changes were initiated during the period but reform was completed by the passage of Senate Bill 621 (also known as the Peveto Bill) in 1979. The purpose of the Peveto Bill was to standardize the administration of the property tax system in the state. The primary results of this standardization are as follows:

- Established 253 Central Appraisal Districts (CADs) throughout the state;
- Abolished fractional appraisals and required that all property be appraised at 100% of fair market value every January 1;

- Set out a Texas Property Tax Code that standardized all operations of the property tax system; and
- Provided for the publication of a bulletin entitled *Truth-In-Taxation* that established guidelines and rules that every taxing entity had to adhere in setting tax rates.

The administration of the tax system involves several functions that fall into chronological order. Those functions are assessing the value of property, setting local tax rates, and collecting the taxes levied.

Assessing Property Values

Assessing property values, sometimes called appraisal, is the act of determining the fair market value of taxable property. If the property is deemed to be permanently in the district as of January 1, it is considered to be taxable property. The CAD in which the school district is located is charged with responsibility of determining the market value of all property within the geographical boundaries of the district.

Appraisal districts use a comparative sales and/or a cost approach to determine market value of property. A comparative sales approach is used for determining market value of properties, such as single family homes, that frequently change hands. The process involves taking actual sale prices from comparable properties and using this value to place value on other properties. The cost approach is used to value property that does not change hands often enough to offer comparison. In this method, the appraiser simply determines the cost of replacing the property minus any deduction due to factors such as depreciation.

The Texas Property Tax Code (2013) sets out clearly defined procedures to allow property owners to contest the assigned value of their property. CADs are required to provide property owners with their appraised values by May 15. The property owners are then entitled to protest the appraised value of their property directly to the CAD.

The CAD is charged with the responsibility of providing each taxing entity within its boundaries with a net property value by July 25. This net property value is the critical component of the appraisal process to school districts. This value is the number that local districts use to determine tax rates and local revenue. The term, net district property value, means the value of all taxable property in the district after exemptions and protests.

An understanding of the totality of the kinds and number of exemptions granted is not necessarily instructive in understanding Texas public school finance. However, a brief discussion and a partial listing of exemptions are offered. Simply stated, some property is exempted from taxation and certain properties are granted partial exemptions based on the nature of either the property or the owner of the property. The more prominent of the exemptions are:

- Government property
- Tax ceilings placed on homeowners over the age of 65
- Percentage deductions for certain persons categorized as disabled
- Property used for charitable, educational, or religious purposes
- All homesteads, which are granted a $15,000 exemption

The use of the term "district property value" can sometimes be confusing to one who uses it in conjunction with school finance. There are actually two district property values that are of significance in the Texas funding system. The value that is determined by the CAD is commonly called the District Property Value and is used by local districts in determining tax rates and projecting local tax revenues. The other tax value that is of importance is the Comptrollers Property Tax Division (CPTD) determination of the district's net taxable value. This taxable property value is used in all calculations that involve the state's funding system (FSP).

Tax Collection

The collection of taxes levied by school districts was, historically, accomplished by the districts through the work of collection departments created and funded by the districts themselves. However, a more common method now is for districts to contract that function out to another entity on a per-parcel basis. Many Texas school districts have used the CAD to collect their taxes. Since the CAD is required to appraise the property for all taxing entities within its boundaries, the amount of taxes levied by each entity is readily available and the CAD is able to deliver tax bills for all on a single invoice. This is more economical for the taxing institutions and more convenient for the taxpayer. The collection of delinquent taxes is most frequently contracted out to a legal firm that specializes in this area. The fees for such collection would normally be based on a percentage of delinquent taxes collected.

Setting Tax Rates

The setting of local school district tax rates is a function reserved for the Board of Trustees of the district. The setting of tax rates is more appropriately referred to as adopting a tax rate.

It would be instructive to consider a few basics in order to understand the tax rate structure used by school districts in Texas. Tax rates are levied on each $100 of value rather than on the actual value. That is, if a school had a total tax rate of $1.10, then each $100 of value would be assessed $1.10. For example, consider a piece of property valued at $100,000:

- The amount actually taxed would be the number of $100 value increments in the property or 1,000
- The amount of tax levied would be $1.10 multiplied by 1,000 or $1,100

School district tax rates in Texas are comprised of two components: Maintenance and Operations (M&O) rate and Interest and Sinking Fund (I&S) rate. The M&O rate is the tax rate that the district sets to fund the local share of current year operating costs, and the I&S rate is the rate necessary to fund the district's debt service obligations.

There are two additional tax rate calculations, which all Texas school districts must address. In order to protect the rights of taxpayers and to assure that taxpayers are adequately informed, the Truth-In-Taxation bulletin mandates that all districts calculate both an effective M&O rate and a rollback rate.

The effective M&O rate has been the rate that will yield the same amount of combined state and local revenue per student as the preceding year while using the currents year's taxable values, but that changed in 2009. The current definition of effective tax rate is calculated rates generally equal to the last year's taxes divided by the current taxable value of properties that were also on the tax roll last year.

These rates are used as determiners to calculate a district's maximum tax rate or rollback rate. According to the Texas Comptroller of Public Accounts (2015), a rollback tax rate is a calculated maximum rate that a school district may adopt without voter approval. Districts may increase the levied tax rate beyond the rollback rate only through the use of a Tax Ratification Election (TRE) and only up to the maximum M&O rate allowed by law.

School district tax rates in Texas have traditionally been legislatively limited to certain maximums. Prior to the passage of HB 1 in 2006, the limit on M&O tax rates was $1.50 per $100 valuation and I&S rates were limited to $0.50 for new debt plus a rate for old debt. New debt is any debt authorized after April 1, 1991, and issued after September 1, 1992, old debt is debt issued prior to those dates.

HB 1 did not affect the limit on I&S rates, but did change the cap on M&O rates in an effort to reduce the property tax burden. The setting of tax rates and determination of tax rate limitations are clearly delineated by the legislation in HB 1. Current maximum M&O rates are dependent upon the 2005 base rate for calculations as expressed below. The following concepts and calculation outlines are necessary in order to understand the tax rate calculations mandated by HB 3646:

1. Compressed Rate—A district's 2005 M&O tax rate multiplied by 0.6667
2. Rollback Rates—A calculated maximum rate that a school district may adopt without voter approval
   - Rollback rate for 2011–2012 will be the lesser of:
   - ($1.50 multiplied by 0.6667) + $0.04 + pennies previously approved by a rollback election + debt service rate *or*
   - Effective M&O rate + $0.04 + debt service rate
3. Maximum M&O rates are the compressed rate + $0.17

Under SB 1 passed by the 82nd Legislature, tax calculations remained similar but target revenue was decreased based upon both a percentage cut and reduced funding per Weighted Average Daily Attendance (WADA). However, the 83rd and 84th Texas Legislatures have restored some of those reductions through formula changes. Essentially, the target revenue model has remained in place with some adjustments for certain conditions. Some legislators have expressed a desire to wait for a Supreme Court ruling on the matter before taking up any substantial changes to the law.

There are many calculations, notices, and other requirements that a Texas school district is responsible for in the setting of a tax rate. The most current publication of the Truth-in-Taxation Document, published by the Texas Comptroller of Public Accounts, contains the necessary steps for setting school district tax rates and is a necessary guide for school districts involved in this process.

◆ STATE FORMULA OPTIONS FOR FINANCING PUBLIC SCHOOLS

State formulas for financing public schools, sometimes called methods of intergovernmental transfer, define the variables that drive funds from the state level to the local level and determine the amount and kinds of funds that individual schools receive. All of the states use either one or a combination of the funding methods that are described in this section. The universal acceptance of these theoretical models makes their presentation not only simple but very instructive in terms of understanding school finance.

The development of models of school finance has mirrored the social and economic changes that have occurred in this nation. Education in the early years of our nation's development was limited to some private and local efforts and was generally limited to the more affluent. Over the course of years, some states began to assume some responsibility for education and this resulted in the allocation of some flat grants to local authorities for the purpose of educating those students. The realization that an educated populace was important to sustaining a free, democratic society led to more sophisticated methods of financing public education such as foundation program concepts. The natural progression of the development of funding models led to more complex models that featured equalization concepts and theories.

It would appear that some consideration is necessary in regard to issues that impact the types of models that are appropriate to fund public schools. If there were no issues in regard to differentiation of models, then simple flat-grant funding by giving a set amount for every pupil in attendance would eliminate the need for discussion and thus alleviate confusion. However, further inspection would indicate that there are several factors that should be considered in determining how to fund schools in a way that provides somewhat equal opportunity to avail oneself of an adequate education. Such considerations might include:

- Differences in Educational Need—Not all students have the same degree of need in regard to instructional strategies or methods. The most universally accepted method for dealing with this matter is through the weighted-pupil approach, whereby students who are considered most difficult to teach are weighted most heavily.
- Ability to Pay—Districts vary greatly in their ability to raise funds locally to pay for educational services. The best determinant of ability to pay is local property wealth per pupil. This ratio would enable authorities to measure the relative ability of a local district to fund educational activities.
- Differences in Costs—The cost of providing educational services can vary considerably according to the location of the district. That is, cost of living figures may be dramatically different in one locale as compared to another.

Formula Options

It has been noted earlier that the primary motivating force in the development of funding formulas for financing public schools was an attempt to provide funds on a fairer or more equitable manner. This effort required formulas to be constructed in such a way as to reduce the disparity in access to funds due to differences in local ability to raise revenue. State systems of school finance evolved into formulas that provided state financial assistance in inverse relationship to the local ability to raise funds. The illustration below demonstrates an equity model of state finance represented in many states (Figure 15.1).

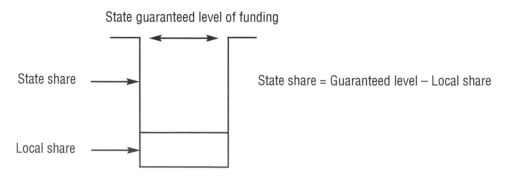

Figure 15.1 Equity Model for State Funding

The degree of equity achieved through this type of formulaic appropriation is a function of the structure of system as established by legislative action. However, it should be noted that virtually all state systems of finance for public schools contain some resemblance of the illustrated model.

Flat Grants

Flat grants are the oldest type of state education aid. The basic characteristics of this type of financial aid are that they distribute funds on a per-pupil or per-classroom basis and provide equal distribution per unit for all school districts.

Flat grants provided the first indication of the states' recognition of an obligation to provide financial assistance to local school districts. However, there are obvious problems with this type of distribution of funds. First, it does not take into consideration the local capacity to access revenue. Second, it does not take into consideration the difference in instructional needs for students of varying characteristics.

Foundation Programs

The evolution of state finance programs continued with the development of the concept of foundation programs by George Strayer and Roger Haig, professors at Columbia University in the 1920s (Odden & Picus, 2008). The principles of foundation programs have been the dominant influence in school finance from that time to the current era. Currently, 45 states use foundation programs either as the system of public school finance or in a combination with some other method (Thompson & Wood, 2005).

Foundation programs are most commonly referred to as minimum foundation programs. The phrase comes from the nature of the formulaic structure in which the state determines a minimum expenditure per pupil necessary to provide an adequate or minimum educational program. The state then guarantees each local district that it will have at its disposal the prescribed number of dollars per pupil.

This task is accomplished by requiring the local district to levy a mandated tax rate to provide the local share of the minimum expenditure per pupil. The state then provides the difference between the guaranteed level and the local share. The nature of the partnership required in a minimum foundation programs is illustrated below (Figure 15.2).

Foundation programs represented a major step forward in the development of equitable means for financing public schools. However, Odden and Picus (2008) suggest three major shortcomings of foundation programs. The first is that most foundation programs allow

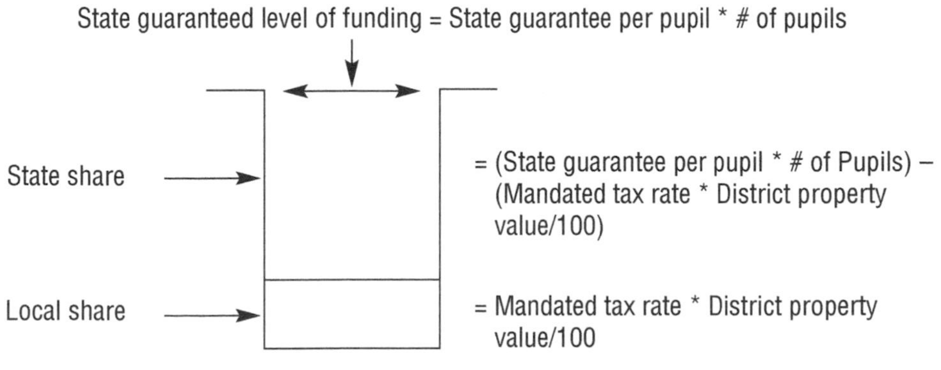

State guaranteed level of funding = State guarantee per pupil * # of pupils

State share

= (State guarantee per pupil * # of Pupils) – (Mandated tax rate * District property value/100)

Local share

= Mandated tax rate * District property value/100

Figure 15.2 Model of a Minimum Foundation Program

spending above the foundation level. If this allowance for funding expenditures above the foundation level is not equalized by other programs, then the access to revenue becomes a function of local ability and, therefore, becomes dramatically disequalizing.

Second, giving the authority to determine minimum expenditure levels for program adequacy to legislative bodies is a considerable weakness. Legislatures may lack the ability to determine adequate spending levels as well as the willingness to fund schools at the prescribed level.

Third, the calculation of the state's share of a foundation program can result in a negative number for wealthier districts. This means that the district can raise revenues above the foundation level expenditure per pupil at the mandated tax rate. This introduces the problem of dealing with the fact that these districts have access to revenue other districts do not have. A foundation program must deny these districts access to this revenue or inequities will exist.

Resource Accessibility Plans

Resource accessibility plans use a different approach to the task of equalizing revenues available to school districts. Foundation programs feature a mandated local tax rate and guaranteed per-pupil revenue from this required tax rate. Resource accessibility plans attempt to give districts the option to determine their own level of funding based on a local decision regarding tax effort.

The defining characteristic of resource accessibility plans is that they attempt to balance wealth, or ability to access revenue, in each district through formulas that adjust for tax base differences. Additionally, tax effort is a local decision and variations in programs and expenditures are allowable as long as access to funds is not the reason for such differences (Thompson & Wood, 2005).

There are four generally accepted resource accessibility plans. These programs are percentage equalization plans, guaranteed tax base, guaranteed tax yield (GTY), and district power equalization. Percentage equalization plans allow local control over costs and programs and the state provides a percentage of the total cost. This percentage is based on calculations relating to the district's ability to raise local revenues. Both guaranteed tax base and GTY programs seek to equalize access to revenue by assuring tax yields that are equivalent for all districts. District power equalization plans introduce the concept of recapture. Recapture involves the state claiming all local revenue that is acquired above a predetermined level.

All resource accessibility plans share the basic characteristics. Therefore, it is not necessary to illustrate each plan individually and the following figure is used to illustrate a GTY program (Figure 15.3).

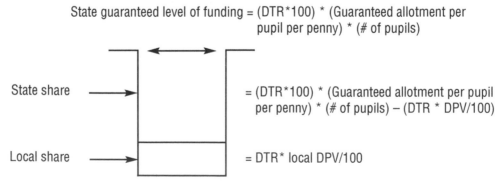

State guaranteed level of funding = (DTR*100) * (Guaranteed allotment per pupil per penny) * (# of pupils)

State share ⟶ = (DTR*100) * (Guaranteed allotment per pupil per penny) * (# of pupils) – (DTR * DPV/100)

Local share ⟶ = DTR* local DPV/100

Where, DTR is district tax rate and DPV is district property value.

Figure 15.3 Model of a Guaranteed Tax Yield Program

◆ FUNDING FOR TEXAS PUBLIC SCHOOLS

This section will examine the primary sources of revenue for Texas public schools. State, federal, and other local and intermediate sources provide the school districts with their basic access to funds. State funds are distributed through the state system of finance, called the FSP. Federal funds are normally provided to districts through categorical block grants and the expenditure of these funds is legally restricted to specific use. Other local and intermediate sources refer to the districts' ability to raise funds from various miscellaneous activities.

A consideration of funds for schools must take into account the fact that school districts access funds for two distinct purposes. First, schools need funds to finance current year operations (usually called M&O funds). This refers to day-to-day expenditures such as employee compensation and purchase of supplies and materials. Second, funds are needed to construct new facilities and/or to meet annual long-term debt obligations. These are often referred to as I&S.

The Foundation School Program

The system that the state of Texas uses to finance its public schools is called the FSP. The FSP is a partnership program between the state and the local district. It has been defined by a long series of legal battles and is characterized as an equity model. Equity models are typically defined as those models in which an inverse relationship exists between local ability to raise funds and state financial assistance. The basic structure of the FSP was established by Senate Bill 7 and has been adjusted by each subsequent legislative session, most recently, by HB 1 passed by the 84th Legislature.

The FSP utilizes flat grants, a foundation program, a guaranteed yield component, and a facilities program. It also features recapture of local funds generated above a legislatively determined cap.

The system has four funding components:

- Flat Grants
- Tier 1—A minimum foundation program
- Tier 2—A guaranteed yield component
- Chapter 46—An Instructional Facilities Allotment (IFA) and an Existing Debt Allotment program

The flat grants, Tier 1, and Tier 2 monies are used to fund current year operations, and Chapter 46 is designed to assist districts with funds to build instructional facilities and to meet their long-term debt obligations.

The FSP provides access to funds through flat grants, Tier1, and Tier 2 to assist districts in financing current year operations. This section will provide some measure of detail in regard to the basic structure of these components.

Flat Grants

The FSP contains some flat grant allotments including the *per capita* allotment and the high school allotment. In 2011, SB 6 eliminated the technology allotment and created the Instructional Materials Fund to provide textbook and technology funding to schools.

The *per capita* allotment is a flat grant given to Texas school districts that is funded from the earnings from the Permanent School Fund. This grant is provided on an Average Daily

Attendance (ADA) basis and the amount varies by year depending on the performance of the Fund.

The high school allotment was new to Texas in 2006 (HB 1, 79th legislative session, 3rd called session). This allotment is based on a rate of $275 and is multiplied by the district's ADA in grades 9 through 12. The high school allotment calculation has been moved and the fund code changed, but it was retained in HB 3646.

Tier 1

Tier 1 of the FSP is a prototypical minimum foundation program. That is, a basic allotment is determined (cost of the basic program for a general education pupil) and a minimum tax rate that each district must set in order to fund its share of the minimum program (local share). The state assistance is the difference between the cost of the basic program and the local share.

The basic components of Tier 1 of the FSP are as follows:

1. Basic Allotment—The legislatively determined cost per student to fund a basic program. Currently set at $5,140.
2. Mandated Tax Rate—The legislatively determined tax rate to provide local share of Tier 1 costs. Currently set at the compressed rate which is defined as the district's 2005 adopted M&O rate multiplied by 0.6667. For example, if a district had a 2005 adopted M&O tax rate of $1.50, the compressed rate would be $1.50 times 0.6667 or $1.00.
3. Cost of Education Index (CEI)—A factor used to adjust for differences in local costs. The factors used in computing the CEI are:
   - Competitive salaries in area
   - County population
   - Independent town
   - Rural district
   - Percentage of low-income students
   - ADA
4. Small and Mid-Sized District Adjustments—A factor used to adjust for small districts (<1,600 students), mid-sized districts (>1,600 students and <5,000) and sparsity (small districts of >300 square miles).
5. Adjusted Allotment—The per-pupil cost of the basic program for a district after adjustments are made for the CEI, size, and sparsity.
6. Weighted Pupils—Weights assigned to pupils according to the nature and characteristics of their educational program. Six programs (categories) are allocated funds using this approach:
   - Regular Program
   - Special Education
   - Career and Technology
   - Compensatory
   - Bilingual/ESL
   - Gifted/Talented
7. Full-Time Equivalents (FTEs)—Because students tend to not to be in some of the programs on a full-day basis, FTEs are used. For example, it would take six special education students in a resource room one period per day (on a six-period day) to represent one full-time student, hence one FTE.

The actual amount and kinds of funding that a school district receives through the FSP is estimated for them by the Texas Education Agency (TEA) through a regularly updated document called a Summary of Finance. Districts may also do their own estimates by using templates available on the agency's Website (www.tea.state.tx.us). The very basic nature of how those calculations are made is presented here as a look at the structure of Tier 1.

The revenue available to a district through Tier 1 (TEA refers to this as the cost of Tier 1) is driven primarily by the district's adjusted allotment and by its categorical pupil count. The total cost of Tier 1 is calculated by multiplying each categorical pupil count by its weight, multiplying by the district's adjusted allotment, and then adding the cost of transportation. The number obtained represents the total amount of revenue available to schools through Tier 1. This total is the sum of local revenue and state assistance.

The amount of state assistance is found by subtracting the local share of the cost of Tier 1 from the total cost of Tier 1. The local share is determined by multiplying the mandated local tax rate (compressed rate per $100 valuation) times the district's property value (CPTD) divided by 100.

Tier 2

Tier 2 of the FSP is referred to as an enrichment program and is a straightforward application of a GTY model of state funding. That is, the state guarantees a specific yield per pupil, per penny of local tax effort. The amount of state financial assistance is the difference between the state guarantee at the local tax effort and the amount of revenue the local district raises at its local tax rate (local enrichment revenue). A significant feature of Tier 2 is its reliance on local option. Tier 2 offers districts the local option of establishing a tax rate at any level between the required compressed rate for Tier 1 and the maximum allowable tax rate for maintenance and operations.

The principle of partnership between the state and local authorities is also a feature of Tier 2. The state guarantees a specific tax yield regardless of the district's property wealth. The district is then required to levy its stated tax rate and collect local taxes equal to that amount. The state assistance is equal to the difference between the guaranteed yield and the amount that the district is able to raise.

The GTY is the legislatively determined guaranteed yield per pupil (WADA), per penny of local tax effort. The tax yield set by the HB 1 of the 84th Legislature is $74.28 for 2016 and $77.53 in 2017 per WADA.

The tax effort is the number of pennies in the local district tax rate above the local fund assignment for Tier 1 (compressed rate). This tax rate (tax effort) actually becomes an effective type of rate calculated by dividing the local tax collections by the CPTD values. If a district wants to raise the tax rate above $1.04, it must hold a TRE to get voter approval for the proposed increase. Tax effort is limited to 17 cents above the compressed rate. In other words local property taxes for maintenance and operations are generally capped at $1.17.

WADA is a student count that adjusts for student and district characteristics and is approximately the same number as the number of regular program students that would be required to generate the total Tier 1 cost as the district's actual student population. The calculation of a district's WADA requires the application of an additional formula. The revenue available to a Texas school district in Tier 2 can be expressed as follows: Tier 2 Revenue = GTY * WADA * Tax Effort (in pennies). The amount of state financial assistance in Tier 2 would be:

State Assistance = Tier 2 Revenue − (District Tax Effort * (District PTAD Value/100))

Recapture

The principle of recapture is a feature of the FSP. The details of recapture are contained in Chapter 41 of the Texas Education Code and the districts that fall into this category are referred to as "Chapter 41 Districts." Recapture in the FSP applies only to M&O; I&S revenues are not subject to recapture.

Recapture, in school finance, is the act of taking revenue that districts access above a property wealth per student (WADA) cap and redistributing it in the system. The FSP currently sets the cap at 3 levels of tax effort.

1. The cap for the compressed rate (2005 M&O tax rate multiplied by 0.6667) is $476,500 property wealth per WADA.
2. There is no cap and, hence, no recapture for the first $0.06 of tax effort above the compressed rate.
3. The cap on tax effort above the compressed rate + $0.06 is set at $319,500 property wealth per WADA. Under SB 1 the cap on districts at the $1.17 tax rate is now $319,500.

The property wealthy districts are offered five options for sharing the wealth. However, only two of those options have ever been utilized. They are:

1. Purchase ADA credits from the state.
2. Contract for the education of non-resident students in a partnership with a poorer district.

The application of recapture in the FSP does not represent a clear application of the mathematics implied in the principle. Wealthy districts are allowed to retain access to revenue above the cap through various discounts and hold-harmless clauses in Chapter 41. Hold-harmless clauses allow wealthy districts to protect sufficient property value to assure access to revenue per student equal to that realized in 1993. Discounts to the amount of recapture are also offered for such things as early determination of the method by which the district will meet the Equalized Wealth Level.

Target Revenue Funding

The FSP and its refinements, including HB 3646 and SB 1, continue to create the illusion that public school funding in Texas is based on formula funding. The reality is that the system is currently a "hold harmless" or "target revenue" program. The current system creates target revenue per WADA for Texas school districts based on "greater of" revenue per WADA. In 2006, the State created the target revenue system funded by a margins tax and reduced local property taxes, shifting more of the burden of funding schools to the State. It is interesting to note that this system was created as a temporary fix but current legislation carries some elements of target revenue several years into the future. Across Texas per-student revenue targets ranged from a low of $3,600 to over $12,000 with the average at about $5,075 per student in 2013. The margins tax never brought in enough revenue to help the State fulfill its responsibility to schools. The shortfall was obscured by a booming economy one biennium and federal stimulus dollars the next. When tax revenue became tight in 2011, the 82nd legislature simply underfunded schools by $4 billion in the FSP and by $1.5 billion in grants. The 83rd and 84th Legislature restored much of those cuts but the basic funding mechanism remains.

In 2009, House Bill 3646 required a district to calculate the largest revenue per WADA available to it by selecting the "greater of" revenue per WADA from the following:

1. 2005–2006 combined state/local revenue per WADA
2. 2006–2007 combined state/local revenue per WADA under old law and using 2005–2006 M&O tax rate
3. 2006–2007 combined state/local revenue per WADA under old law and using 2005–2006 effective M&O tax rate

The district would use the most advantageous of the three numbers generated above and multiply that by the projected 2009–2010 WADA to produce a fair projection of their revenue. HB 3646 guaranteed that each district would receive a maximum increase of $120 per WADA above the target revenue, but mandated that no district would receive more than $350 per WADA above their target.

Recent Legislation

SB 1 passed in 2011 again modified the target revenue system created in 2006. The reductions to the Regular Program Allotment under SB 1 had the effect of reducing the district's WADA funding, so SB 1 WADA was less than HB 3646 WADA. This lower WADA was the trigger for the funding reductions contained in SB 1 for the 2011–2012 and 2012–2013 school years. The 83rd Legislature restored about $3.4 billion of the cuts through formula changes but the structure of the finance system remains the same.

According to a Texas Association of School Administrators (TASA) legislative summary (Texas Association of School Administrators, 2015), HB 1 from the 84th Legislature contained the following provisions:

- $1.2 billion for the basic allotment per ADA ($5,140 both years)
- $200 million for fractional funding (districts with compressed tax rates)
- Guaranteed yield increases to $74.28 (2016) and $77.53 (2017)
- $55.5 million for IFA (FY 2017)
- $47.5 million for the New Instructional Facilities Allotment (NIFA)

Other items not included are $3.8 billion in business and property tax relief measures.

At this point the reader may wonder if the current target revenue is simply a "magic number" pulled from the air. In reality, it is still the hold harmless system created in 2006 with new provisions layered upon it a number of times by the legislature to adjust for economic conditions. The 82nd Legislature's stated goal was to move away from the target revenue system over time. According to SB 1, it is the intent of the legislature, between fiscal year 2014 and fiscal year 2018, to continue to reduce the amount of Additional State Aid for Tax Reduction to which a school district is entitled and to increase the basic allotment to which a school district is entitled. There is little doubt the 83rd Legislature acted to restore some of the cuts based upon the 2013 ruling from State District Judge John Dietz. The 84th Legislature also enjoyed a vibrant economy to generate tax funding and was also able to increase school funding. Some in the legislature hope that these increases may influence the ruling set for next year by the State Supreme Court. The school finance equity/adequacy fight will to continue to the State Supreme Court this year.

Financing Facilities and Long-Term Debt Obligations

Texas public school districts are faced with the problem of building new facilities, renovating existing facilities due to student population growth, or replacing aging facilities that are either unsafe or unsuitable to meet modern educational needs. Decisions in regard to facility needs and actions taken to address those needs are local decisions. The construction of new facilities and/or the renovation of existing structures are expensive undertakings, and very few districts have sufficient capital to enter into this type of program without incurring debt and the resulting annual debt payment on that obligation. In the absence of sufficient funds to finance a building program, Texas public school districts have several options for financing facilities. Only two of those options are currently selected with any regularity. Those options are issuing bonds or entering lease-purchase programs. Almost universally, Texas school districts have chosen the route of issuing bonds for the borrowing of funds to build school facilities.

A school district is empowered to issue bonds only with the permission of its constituency as established through a bond election. The successful passage of a bond proposal entitles the district to borrow, through the sale of bonds, an amount of money as prescribed on the ballot in the election. The preparation of bonds, the bidding and sale of bonds, and the incumbent legal implications are complex and, in most cases, require that districts avail themselves of the services of bond attorneys and financial advisors.

The selling of bonds is equivalent to the issuance of promissory notes to the bond holders to repay the lender both principal and interest over a prescribed time frame. The result of this transaction is that a district amortizes its debt over a specified period of time. The nature of the amortization is a function of the amount of the debt incurred and the district's financial capability. Once the bonds have been sold and the amortization details determined, the district will establish an annual payment or yearly debt service obligation.

Debt service obligations are met by levying an I&S tax rate as discussed in a previous section. Taxes collected on I&S tax rates are required to be used for the retirement of long-term debt incurred through the sale of bonds authorized through a bond election. I&S tax rates levied on local property values can be prohibitively high in low-property wealth districts. The 75th Texas legislature made an attempt to deal with this problem with the passage of HB 4 in 1997 which resulted in Chapter 46 of the Texas Education Code. Chapter 46 details that section of the FSP that deals with the financing of instructional facilities.

Chapter 46 is commonly called the IFA. The original provision of the IFA was designed to assist districts with debt service obligations incurred as a result of successful bond elections. IFA required districts to make application for assistance after the passage of the bond election and districts were provided with this assistance, up to the limit of the appropriated amount, based on the applications, with the applicants prioritized by lowest per-pupil property wealth to highest per-pupil property wealth. The allotment under IFA is a GTY and is established by the legislature as ADA per penny on the debt service tax rate. The state implemented an addition to the IFA beginning in 1999, the Existing Debt Allotment, which provided the same GTY on all debt on which the district made a yearly payment during the immediately preceding year. This provision had the effect of equalizing funding on long term debt in much the same way that other provisions of the FSP equalized funding for current year operations.

Other Local and Intermediate Sources

Texas public school districts are limited to taxes on local property as the only source of tax revenue. However, they are not prohibited from producing revenue through other venues such as sales, fees and dues, ticket revenue from school-sponsored activities, and interest on investment of funds not immediately needed to meet district obligations.

Some revenues realized by sales and activities are fiduciary in nature and are not available for school district operations. Activity funds raised by student groups are an example of fiduciary funds. The district's role in the administration of such funds is to provide stewardship of the funds, not to participate in the expenditure.

Monies assessed through fees and dues and ticket revenues from school sponsored activities are usually a part of the general operating fund and subject to district discretion. Fees and dues, ticket revenues, and sales of various types represent a significant source of revenue for school districts and may represent up to 2% of total operating budget.

Public schools have an opportunity to avail themselves of a considerable source of revenue through utilization of sound investment strategies. Maximizing investment opportunities requires that districts employ cash management procedures. Good cash management programs allow districts to accomplish three goals:

1. Ensure that the district has funds readily available to meet its obligations.
2. Ensure that all available funds are invested.
3. Protect the district's financial assets.

The rewards of good investment programs have become so obvious that current state regulations require that each district have a person responsible for the cash management program and that the person responsible be certified by state standards.

Federal Funds

The history of the role of the federal government in public education reveals an interesting blend of legal restrictions, justifications, and social agendas. The 10th Amendment to the US Constitution speaks clearly to the federal role in education by stating that the powers not delegated to the US government, nor prohibited to the states, are reserved to the states. Since the US Constitution does not mention education, the rights and responsibilities of public education falls, by default, to the states (Thompson & Wood, 2005).

Thompson and Wood (2005) suggest that the federal government has found intervention authority in two ways. The first has been through the power of Congress from Article 1, Section 8 to provide for a strong national defense. An example of this was the passage in 1958 of the National Defense Education Act that provided for training for teachers in the areas of math, science, and foreign language in response to the Soviet Union's success in satellite research. Second, the General Welfare Clause of Article 1, Section 8 has been interpreted to allow intervention into education in pursuit of various social justice areas.

The most significant increase of the federal role in public education funding was the passage of the Elementary and Secondary Education Act (ESEA) in 1965. ESEA was passed as a complement to the Civil Rights Act of 1964 and was primarily directed toward the education of underprivileged children. The ESEA provided aid to public schools through five titles of funding. In 1972, Title IX was added to ESEA, which prohibited sex discrimination in educational programs.

Changes to ESEA were made in 1981 through the passage of the Education Consolidation and Improvement Act that consolidated the provisions of ESEA and reduced funding. The program was reauthorized in 2001 with the passage of the No Child Left Behind Act (NCLB). Funding was increased by NCLB, but its primary focus was an increase in accountability for local schools. Congress is currently considering reauthorizing NCLB with new bills from both the House and Senate.

The common theme of all the funding elements of these Acts has been the reliance on categorical block grants. The result of this type of funding is that the funds are legally restricted as to their usage and must be used to supplement local or state funds, not to supplant them.

The exact amounts and kinds of federal funds allocated to public education in Texas are difficult to determine with great accuracy. The Legislative Budget Board of the Texas legislature provides figures which are historically representative of federal funds in the state. These numbers show that for the recent years, Texas received approximately 9.5% of total K-12 revenues from federal funding. This percentage of district funding includes federal monies for Education and Welfare (Title 1, special education, drug free programs, etc.), the Federal School Lunch Program (lunches and breakfasts, eligibility based on poverty level), and other federal funds (adult education, teen parenting, and temporary assistance to needy families).

Texas school districts are not required to participate in most of the federal programs that have been described. However, it is important to note that if a district receives federal funds, they must abide by all the federal rules and guidelines. Most Texas school districts have been unable to resist the considerable financial benefits of the federal role. A majority of Texas districts participate in these programs and accept the necessary restrictions. Some provisions of NCLB are required for all Texas school districts due to our state's participation in the program.

◆ SUMMARY

The method by which the state of Texas finances its public schools appears to be beyond understanding. The average school administrator or school board member can easily be overwhelmed by its complexity, particularly for those who do not deal with it on a regular basis. However, when viewed through its component parts, the system is amazingly simple in concept. The difficulty comes in dealing with the exceptions and nuances within the system that are a natural outcome of the political processes that created them. Many organizations, including the Texas Association of School Boards, contend that the current school finance system is inequitable and must be fixed.

Despite the difficulties in quantifying the relationship between access to resources and student achievement, school administrators must intuitively reach the conclusion that such a relationship exists. This conclusion makes assuring maximum access to revenue a crucial component of organizational success. The surest way to guarantee that one is accessing the maximum revenue available is to be knowledgeable about the system that provides the funds.

◆ REFERENCES

Edgewood v. Kirby, 777 S.W.2d 391 (Tex. 1989).

Greenwald, R., Hedges, L. V., & Laine, R. D. (1994). When reinventing the wheel is not necessary: A case study in the use of meta-analysis in education finance. *Journal of Economic Finance, 20*(1), 1–20.

Hanushek, E. A. (1989). The impact of differential expenditures on school performance. *Educational Researcher, 18*(4), 45–65.

Odden, A. R., & Picus, L. O. (2008). *School finance: A policy perspective* (4th ed.). New York, NY: McGraw Hill.

Picus, L. O. (1997). Does money matter in education? A policymakers guide. *National Center for Education Statistics*, pp. 97–536.

Texas Association of School Administrators. (2015). *84th legislative session: What passed, what didn't*. Retrieved from the TASA website: http://www.tasanet.org/cms/lib07/TX01923126/Centricity/Domain/329/84th_session_bills.pdf

Texas Comptroller of Public Accounts. (2015). *Truth-in-taxation: Tax rate adoption*. Retrieved from http://comptroller.texas.gov/taxinfo/proptax/tnt/

Texas Property Tax Code. (2013). Retrieved from the Texas State Comptroller website: http://comptroller.texas.gov/taxinfo/proptax/96-297-13.pdf

Thompson, D. (2004). The financing of Texas public schools: An update on the litigation. *Featured strand on school finance summary: Texas Association of School Administrators.*

Thompson, D., & Wood, R. C. (2005). *Money and schools* (3rd ed.). New York, NY: Larchmont.

Walker, B. D., & Casey, D. T. (1996). *The basics of Texas public school finance* (6th ed.). Austin, TX: Texas Association of School Boards.

Weber, P. (2015, June 11). Texas GOP tries to pluck liberal thorn from its side. *Yahoo News*. Retrieved from http://news.yahoo.com/texas-gop-tries-pluck-liberal-thorn-side-182836892.html

SCHOOL DISTRICT BUSINESS AND FINANCIAL OPERATIONS

Timothy B. Jones

Most companies in corporate America are divided between operations and finance, each with a chief officer, called the Chief Operating Officer and the Chief Financial Officer. These two officers, often equals on the organizational chart, report to the Chief Executive Officer or President. In the public school business, the functions are similar although the titles are different. The Chief Executive Officer is called the Superintendent of Schools, an Assistant Superintendent of Curriculum & Instruction replaces the Chief Operations Officer, and the Chief Financial Officer is often the Assistant Superintendent of Administration or Business Services.

In smaller districts, business operations may be the responsibility of a Business Manager or even the Superintendent of Schools. In larger districts, these functions may be delegated to numerous positions rather than just one. Regardless, the financial operations of the school district are the same. Larger districts may have more transactions, dollars, or employees than the smaller ones, but all districts perform the same financial functions. These financial operations include the controlling function, budget development and administration function, and the purchasing and supply management function.

◆ CONTROLLING FUNCTION

The first major function of school district business and financial operations, and perhaps the largest one, is the controlling function. The controlling function is responsible for controlling and protecting the assets of the organization. The financial health of an organization, in this case a school district, is dependent on the protection and maximization of the district assets. Large districts often employ Controllers or Chief Accountants who focus their time on the controlling functions of the districts. Anything that threatens the mission of the organization is potentially part of the controlling function, which includes accounting, investments, cash management, internal controls, internal and external audit, inventory, risk management, and compliance.

Accounting

At the heart of the controlling function is the accounting system. Since a public school district is not-for-profit, fund accounting, also known as governmental accounting, is utilized instead of traditional corporate accounting. In fund accounting, each primary funding source of the school district is a funding source in and of itself and, therefore, has its own set of books or fund, hence the term fund accounting. Funds are divided into two groups: (1) Maintenance and Operations and (2) Interest and Sinking.

Maintenance and Operations

The Maintenance and Operations funds of a school district include General Operating, Special Purpose, Enterprise, and Trust and Agency. Examples of General Operating Funds include all funds that do not fit into the other categories and could include utilities, maintenance, nondesignated purpose instructional services and salaries, supplies, administration, and travel.

Any funds that come to the district earmarked for a designated purpose are considered a Special Purpose Fund, such as special education, gifted and talented education, a grant of any kind, and an endowment. A teacher whose salary is paid from federal or state funds designated for special education would be paid out of a Special Purpose Fund. A teacher who is expensed out of local district funds would not be paid out of an earmarked fund and would be paid from the General Operating Fund.

An Enterprise Fund is an operation that is expected to break-even or make a profit. Although the school business does not normally function this way, often smaller functions are expected to break even or make a profit. For example, a district print shop or school store is expected to be accountable for the bottom line. The accounting of these functions would be dealt with in an Enterprise Fund. District-owned and -operated vending machines would be another possible Enterprise Fund. Food Services could be a Special Purpose Fund and an Enterprise Fund if the school district participates in the National School Lunch Program. If not, Food Service would be a regular Enterprise Fund.

Trust and Agency Funds are held by a school district but do not belong to it. For example, when a district withholds federal income taxes or teacher retirement from an employee's check, those funds do not belong to the school district but rather are held in "trust" until the district pays those funds to the appropriate entity. This would be true for all of the deductions made from payroll checks. An Agency Fund is similar to a Trust Fund except that an Agency Fund is held for the benefit of something else. School Activity Funds are the main source for Agency Funds in the school district. For example, if the drill team has a bake sale, those funds can be deposited into an Agency Fund for later use by the drill team. The money does not belong to the school district or an individual but rather the school district is an Agent of those funds, and in this instance, an agent for the drill team.

Anything that is not long-term debt in the school district is accounted for in the Maintenance and Operations portion of the financial system. Short-term debt (loans to be repaid within the current fiscal year) is accounted for in the Maintenance and Operations category. Long-term debt is facilitated through the selling or floating of bonds. Bonded indebtedness is accounted for in the Interest and Sinking category.

Interest and Sinking

Public school districts are not generally allowed to go into debt. Most school debt is for the building and construction of schools. These projects can involve millions of dollars and the buildings used over many years. Consequently, the State of Texas allows a school district, with voter approval, to sell long-term bonds (called School House Bonds) for the purpose of building and construction projects, as well as capital equipment like computers and furnishings. When a bond is sold (referred to as floating a bond) the districts enters into a long-term financial arrangement with the bondholders to repay the debt (called sinking the bond) along with interest for the use of the money. Hence, bonded indebtedness is part of the Interest and Sinking Funds. As the district makes bond payments (normally semiannually usually in February and August), the interest is paid and the principal of the loan then "sinks" the once-floated bond. The State of Texas allows school districts to levy an ad-valorem tax on district real-property holders for the purpose of repaying the bond. This tax is in addition to the Maintenance and Operation tax also levied on district real property.

One additional way a school district in Texas can incur debt is with an instrument known as a Bus Warrant. Bus Warrants may be issued with an up to 5-year payback for the purpose of purchasing school buses. These warrants, which do not require voter approval, provide intermediate-length funding for a school district for a specific purpose.

Accounting Code Structure

Public school districts in Texas are required to use the 20-digit account code structure that is documented in the Texas Education Agency (*TEA*) *Financial Accountability System Resource Guide* (FASRG) (TEA, 2015). All revenues received and expenditures incurred must be documented by this required code. Figure 16.1 outlines the basic array of this coding system.

Each of the digit groupings serves to provide the detail necessary to understand the nature of the expenditure or source of revenue. There are eight groupings of digits. The first six digits are required by the State of Texas, and the last two are an option for local use.

The first three digits are the Fund Code and are mandatory for reporting. The purpose of the fund code is to identify which of the school district funds will be used to pay for this expenditure. The second grouping of digits is a mandatory two-digit code to describe the purpose of the expenditure. This Function Code provides information about which function is to benefit from this expenditure.

The Object Code is a mandatory four-digit code used to describe what kind or type of goods or services are being purchased. The use of this code allows one to see if supplies and materials, contracted services, or other identifiable goods or services are being purchased. The next two digits are Local Option (sometimes called Sub-Object) and can be used at local discretion. They can be used to further identify the expenditure. For example, these two digits might give additional detail to the type of supplies and materials that one identified in the Object Code.

Fund–Function–Object–Local Option–Organization–Fiscal Year–Program–Local Option

XXX -   XX -   XXXX -   XX -   XXX -   X -   XX -   X-XX

Figure 16.1 Texas Accounting Code Structure

The next three-digit code is a mandatory code used to identify the organization that will benefit from the expenditure. This code normally refers to campuses or other operational centers but does not necessarily mean a location. The Fiscal Year Code is a mandatory one-digit code used to identify the fiscal year of the transaction or the initial year of a project. This code is simply the last digit in the fiscal year. The Program Intent Code is a mandatory two-digit code and is intended to identify the student group that is the beneficiary of the expenditure. The last three digits in the 20-digit accounting code structure may be used at Local Option. An example of local usage might be to provide additional information about the student group identified in the Program Intent Code.

Accounting for increases in a school district's revenue requires identifying the fund (same as expenditure fund code system) and the Object Code that specifically identifies the source. For example, the code 199-5711 would identify an increase in the district's General Fund from Current Year Local Property Tax levy. The accounting code system does not require that all 20 digits be used to identify increases in revenue, thus the other digits would indicate a zero.

Investments

Even with the smallest of school districts, the school business involves millions of dollars. In order to maximize school district funds, investments are important. Although the school district may earn interest in the Depository Bank through the negotiated contract, most districts participate in other investment vehicles that produce a higher rate-of-return. In many states, like Texas, investment pools like Tex Pool are available to give public funds options for investments.

Collections

The revenue, and hence the collections, of a school district is vast. While the monthly payment earned from the state through the funding formulas is a major source of revenue, it is merely one of the monthly collections that a school district conducts. Tax collections are another major source of revenue and often involve thousands upon thousands of taxpayers and property. Collections may include taxes from a previous year levy, foreclosure, interest and penalties, as well as typical current year tax collections.

Other collections may be from the cafeteria, vending machines, athletic gates, and other fee-based events, and generally any other endeavor that involves the collection of money or revenue. All monies collected by the school district are deposited into the appropriate fund as previously discussed in this section. The Board of Trustees, through the adopted budget, estimates the collections of revenue of the school district.

Disbursements

A major part of the controlling function is the disbursement of funds. School district funds are disbursed either through payroll or accounts payable. The majority of school district funds, often 80% or more, are disbursed through the district payroll. This includes the salaries and wages of employees as well as employee benefits. The complexity of the district payroll and employee compensation plan is beyond the scope of this chapter but is a major part of payroll disbursement.

The second method of disbursement is accounts payable. Accounts payable is paying the expenses or bills of the school district. School district bills include debt payments, utility bills, purchase orders, and other bills associated with the Maintenance and Operations or Interest and Sinking of the organization. Texas law requires that districts encumber funds before disbursing them in order to assure their availability. Like collections, all disbursements must be made out of the appropriate fund in accordance to the district budget that has been adopted by the Board of Trustees.

Cash Management

The Cash Management task deals with assuring that funds in the school district are available when needed. The funding sources of the district are vast and funds flow into the school district at differing times. In Texas, for example, state aid payments are made monthly on the twenty-fifth between the months of September and August. Most local tax money is collected during the months of December and January. Federal money is received generally from a different fiscal year of July through June. While money flows into a school district at different times of the year, it normally flows out more consistently. Good cash management will provide funds as needed while maintaining the reserve money in investments.

For example, a district that has a $15 million payroll each month does not want to move that money from an investment that earns money to a disbursement account until those funds are needed. If the state sends state-aid money on the twenty-fifth of the month, then it would make good investment sense to have a payroll date that maximizes investment dollars. Payment of payroll on the fifteenth of the month, for example, may require the district to borrow money for 10 days to cover the disbursement, or require the district to sell out of an investment.

Risk Management

School districts are the trustees of many valuable assets including real property but also other not so obvious assets that have to be managed from a risk perspective. The more obvious assets include things, such as buildings, vehicles, equipment, and land. The less obvious assets include school district cash, valuable documents, financial papers, and the often forgotten school district electronic data (an enormous asset). Imagine if a school district, due to any circumstance, lost the entire cadre of electronic student and financial data records. Extensive student history, grades, and transcripts would be lost, financial accountability and records gone, and hence, the district would be unable to pay its bills or disburse its payroll. The number of human resources required to recreate the records would be astronomical, if the data could be recreated at all. Perhaps even worse, without this data, the district cannot submit Public Education Information Management System (PEIMS) data that is required to earn state funding. These systems (PEIMS, payroll, accounts payable, etc.) must operate on a "zero-failure" basis since so many people, and the organizations very existence, are dependent on being able to do these things. Consequently, extensive risk management is required, as well as a good system of internal controls, that will help assure that the lost never occurs.

Risk implies exposure to loss, damage, or injury. Risk management is a human activity that involves recognition, assessing, and developing strategies to manage the risk. This means that the school district administrator realizes that the risk exists, predicts the type and severity (assessing) of the risk, and then invokes a process to limit the negative effects.

Identification of Risks

There are some commonalities among school districts in regard to risk. Identification infers that each district must address risks that may be unique to them. Some possible risk situations that all districts might face would include:

- Liability, such as
  - That which results from operation of motor vehicles,
  - That which results from ownership of physical facilities, and
  - That which results from acts of commission or omission of employees.
- Financial risk resulting from
  - Damage to or loss of physical facilities,
  - Workman's Compensation Claims,
  - Health/hospitalization,
  - Theft,
  - Incompetence/omission.

Assessing the Risk

This is a management function that involves determining the possibility of the risk event occurring and making a decision in regard to the relative damage to the organization. That is, the administrator would consider and need to answer two questions. One, what is the probability of the risk event occurring? Second, what is the severity of the damage if the risk event occurs? For example, if the probability of the event occurring is very low and the damage incurred as a result is minimal, then the risk is probably not something of which one must address. The process of assessing risk will give the administrator good information in determining how to deal with a potential risk.

Managing the Risk

The management of risk is the process of limiting the organization's exposure to the risk. Ray, Hack, and Candoli (2001) suggested four techniques for limiting exposure to risk: avoidance, reduction, assumption, and transfer. The school administrator can take these four techniques and tailor them to the district's unique situation.

Avoidance and reduction of risk means that one must assess hazards and put together programs to eliminate or minimize exposure to risk. This would include both human and physical programs. On the human side, one could provide training in recognizing hazardous situations and strategies for avoiding them. On the physical aspect, simply recognizing and eliminating potential hazards, such as chemical exposure and dimly lighted stairwells, could be beneficial. The goal would be to avoid risk, but if that is not possible, to reduce the probability that exposure will occur.

Assumption of risk infers that the administrator recognizes the risk involved, has assessed the severity, and determined that if the risk cannot be avoided, it is manageable by the district. Transfer of risk is the technique that school districts are most familiar with. This technique involves purchasing the right to transfer the risk to another entity. An example is the purchase of insurance. Insurance is available in many forms and is complex beyond the scope of this discussion. It is sufficient to say that school districts need knowledgeable staff or contracted consultants to lead them through the insurance maze.

Audit, Compliance, and Internal Controls

School districts and its resources belong to the public and not to the people in their employ. Hence, the public has a reasonable expectation that their resources, their money, is being safeguarded and in the good stewardship to the people they elect to represent them and ultimately the people they employ. To that end, administrators are expected to employ a system of internal controls to insure such stewardship. The law and numerous accounting standards (which will be discussed in the compliance section on this chapter) require a system of internal controls.

As part of the controlling function, internal audits should be periodically and methodically conducted. The internal controls and audits are designed to protect the administrators as well as the public. Good controls not only minimize the risk to loss of resources or the trust of the public, but they will also minimize any appearance of impropriety. Public confidence in the stewardship of the district is paramount in producing good schools. In Texas, the law requires that a school district conduct an external audit anually. Among many things, the external auditor will examine and test the system of internal controls. For example, while it is not illegal for a teacher to have $500 of picture money in his or her pocket, it is indicative of poor internal controls and creates the appearance of impropriety. Poor internal controls that an external auditor discovers and deems material must be reported to the Board of Trustees and the TEA in the audit report.

◆ BUDGET DEVELOPMENT AND ADMINISTRATION FUNCTION

The budgeting function is designed to allow a school district to allocate its resources effectively enough to accomplish the goals of the district. Discussions about whether money can make a difference in the quality of the educational opportunities that a district may offer most often agree that money (resources) can make a difference only if it is allocated appropriately. Planning and prioritizing of needs are at the heart of sound budgeting practices.

Budgeting allows a school district to present its estimate of the two parameters of revenues and expenditures. The school district budget will detail and code all sources and amounts of revenues and expenditures. It is important to note that budget development relies on estimates of both revenues and expenditures. This feature places additional emphasis on administrators' ability to plan and forecast. FASRG (TEA, 2015) suggested that in order to meet the Governmental Accounting Standards Board's objectives for budgeting, the following requirements should be met:

- Revenues should be sufficient to pay for budgeted expenditures.
- The budget should be prepared in accordance with all applicable federal, state, and local mandates.
- The budget should serve as an evaluative instrument for cost-effectiveness and program outcomes.

FASRG (TEA, 2015) stated that the budgeting process consists of three major components: planning, preparation, and evaluating. This analysis of the process is consistent with other authorities and will be followed in this approach to budget development and administration.

Budget Planning

Planning for budgeting requires that campuses and districts determine what they intend to accomplish by setting goals and objectives. The next step in this process is to decide on the programs, goods, and services that are required to meet these goals. It is important to consider that current Texas school mandates contain a provision requiring the use of school and campus based committees throughout the budgeting process. This requires that teachers, staff, parents, and community members have a voice in all matters relating to programs and budgets.

The planning process necessarily includes decisions in regard to budgeting model to be used, forms to be required, who is to be involved when and to what degree, and persons responsible for each step of the process. There are several theoretical budget models that are consistently included in any discussion about how to conduct the budgeting process. Few of these models are incorporated intact by school districts and a discussion of those models would not be instructive at this point. Combinations of the various models have been the most popular approach used by Texas school districts. However, most current usage focuses on an accountability approach that links expenditures to outcomes.

Budget Preparation

Budget preparation is the process by which the district translates its educational program into costs. Once the cost of the proposed program is determined, its affordability is determined by comparing it with the district's estimated revenues. This seemingly simple process is complicated enormously by the logistics of gathering projected costs from all the operational centers (campuses, maintenance centers, custodial departments, food service organizations, etc.), combining them into a single, coherent document, and then negotiating differences in perceived needs and available revenues. The task of preparing a budget begins with an understanding of the legal requirements and mandates imposed by state and local authorities.

Legal Requirements for Budgets

The legal basis for the development of school district budgets is found in Sections 44.002–44.006 of the Texas Education Code. FASRG (TEA, 2015) provides the following summary:

- The superintendent is responsible for development of the budget and is the designated budget officer.
- The State Board of Education is responsible for setting a date by which the budget must be prepared. That date is currently August 20 or June 19 if the district has adopted a June 30–July 1 fiscal year.
- The board is required to call a meeting for the purpose of adopting the budget. The board must give a 10-day public notice in a newspaper and taxpayers have the right to attend and participate in the meeting.
- Districts may not expend funds in any manner except that which is prescribed in the adopted budget.
- The budget must be done in accordance with generally accepted accounting principles.
- The board must adopt the budget before setting a local property tax rate.

In addition to the requirements of state law, the TEA has mandated additional requirements for school district budgets. FASRG (TEA, 2015) listed the following requirements:

- The board must adopt the budget no later than August 31 or June 30 if the district uses a July 1–June 30 fiscal year.
- TEA will use minutes of the board meetings to record adoption of the budget.
- Budgets must be prepared and approved, at least, to the fund and function level and budgets for the General Fund, the Food Service Fund, and the Debt Service must be included.
- The official budget must be filed with TEA through PEIMS. Greater detail is required for this filing.
- A school district may not exceed the budgeted amount for a functional expenditure category except as amended by the board.

School districts may establish additional requirements for the preparation of budgets that go beyond those established by state law and TEA. The nature and scope of such requirements is a function of local policy and practice.

Budget Process

Budget preparation is the actual process of determining the limit of the district's resources and deciding how to allocate them in order to reach its goals. The process of determining the amounts and types of revenues is comparatively simple and consists of identifying and properly coding all funds according to TEA regulations. The more complex issue is how to allocate these funds in the most efficient and effective way. The function of the allocation of funds is the basis of this discussion.

The manner in which funds are distributed in school districts are as unique as the districts themselves. The process is basically a function of determining who makes the decisions in regard to the amount of funds that will be available to each suborganization and for what purposes the funds are to be used. The distribution of power throughout the district is the major determinant of how the funds will be distributed. It should be noted that the state of Texas strongly supports the concept of Site-Based Management, which proposes the decentralization of authority.

It appears obvious that some of the functions of the budget preparation process must be performed at a centralized location. An example of this is employee compensation. In budget preparation, the primary issue for any district is which of the functions is to be performed by central administration and which will be reserved for the management team at the operational level.

The approach most commonly used in Texas school districts is for the central administration to determine the funds allocated to each function or location for those functions that tend to be common to all. For example, central administration would determine the allocation of funds for such things as personnel allocation and costs, utility costs, and costs of maintenance and custodial services. Other revenues available to the operational centers would be allocated by a consolidated allocation formula. Utilizing a consolidated formula allows both central administrators and operational level managers to calculate their allocations based on programmatic issues and projected enrollments. A critical item in this approach is the issue of non-allocated funds. The district must make a decision as to whether a process is developed that allows management teams at the operational level to make special requests for additional resources for new programs or special needs. The inclusion of such a process would seem necessary as a tool to promote innovation and efforts for improvement.

Another approach that has proven popular in Texas school districts is the "wish-book" method. In this approach to budget preparation, each operational center is encouraged to use their personnel (site-based teams, grade-level teams, subject-matter groups, heating, ventilating, and air conditioning technicians, etc.) to prepare expenditure requests that represent what they believe would allow them to reach their individual goals. This type of approach is more labor intensive and creates a cyclic process where mediation is required between available resources and expenditure requests. An obvious advantage to this approach is that when adjustments to expenditures must be made, they are made by those most affected by them.

Regardless of the budgeting model that is used, it is imperative that budget calendars be prepared. A budget calendar, done properly, will clarify and solidify the budget preparation process. Budget calendars should include due dates, person(s) responsible, documentation required, and functions to be performed. Once a district calendar has been developed, budget calendars should be developed at the operational level. The operational level budget calendar must be developed to support all the requirements of the district calendar.

The culminating activity of the budget preparation process is to take all the individual budget drafts and combine them into the district budget. The final draft of the district budget infers that all mediations with individual budgets have been successfully implemented and a balance between revenues and expenditures has been achieved.

The final draft of the budget must be submitted to the board for approval according to all legal, TEA, and local guidelines. The role of the board of education has not been discussed in detail in this discussion. However, it is important to note that the board is a critical component in the cyclic process of mediation between requests and resource limitations. It is the job of the central administration team to inform and communicate with the board at every point in the process of budget preparation.

Monitoring the Budget

An important issue in budget preparation is determining how the budget is to be administered and monitored. The responsibility for monitoring spending patterns will be commensurate with the authority granted in allocations. Those with spending authority must assume the responsibility for assuring that funds are expended for the purposes for which they were budgeted. Most site-based managers have access to the district's computerized accounting system and those who do not should be provided with periodic budget status reports. Most district budget reporting formats include columnar headings for goods or services to be purchases, amount budgeted, amount expended, amount encumbered (purchase order approved, but vendor not paid), and the balance remaining in the account. Site-based and district-level administrators have the responsibility of monitoring the budget in such a way as to keep some fidelity between budgeted amounts and actual expenditures. Budgeting is a dynamic process and there will always be some discrepancies between budgeted amounts and expenditures. Object Code categories may be over-expended, but function categories may not, except by amendment approved by the board. Budget amendments are a necessity because of the dynamic nature of budgets, and it is important to eventually clean up the expenditure budget with amendments so that it may provide critical intelligence for the preparation of future budgets.

Budget Evaluation

The method by which a budget is evaluated is a function of the philosophy of the district in regard to budgeting. Those things that are evaluated will reflect the position of the organization as to the relationship of the budget to accuracy, efficiency, effectiveness, and its priorities. Some possible criterion might be

- The degree of fidelity between budgeted amounts and actual expenditures.
- The number of preferred outcomes realized by the planned expenditures.
- The cost-effectiveness of the outcomes.
- The relative degree of difficulty in preparing the budget.
- The complexity involved in administering and monitoring the budget.

Few people fully understand the complexities of the budget process for a school district. It obviously involves many people, constituencies, and processes and thus is a year-round endeavor. Typically, only a few short months after a new budget is passed and the new fiscal year begins, the budget development process begins again for the following fiscal year. Hence, business office officials are almost always working in a minimum of two different fiscal year periods.

◆ PURCHASING AND SUPPLY MANAGEMENT FUNCTION

Any organization that is committed to efficiency and effectiveness in its operation requires a system for delivery of goods and services in a timely manner. School districts are not exempt from this requirement. The wide variance in the types of goods and services needed to provide support services and delivery of instruction dictates that an orderly system of requests, approval, timely delivery, and prompt payment to vendors be put in place. A comprehensive program for purchasing and supply management would include policy statements of the district's philosophy, relevant legal requirements, and an efficient system for requisitioning and purchasing supplies and services.

Purchasing Policy

School districts must have policies in place that supports the district's objective of providing the highest quality of goods and services at the best price. The term "best price," as it is used here, implies that the price is in the best interest of the school district and does not always mean the absolute lowest price. Policy design should take into account the nature of the purchase, its usage, and the ability of the vendor to provide the request in a timely manner. A school district's policy for purchasing should include the appropriate level of documentation for each type of purchase. Every purchase made by a school district is subject to audit, and an appropriate purchasing policy will dictate the type of documentation required for the various purchases that a district might make. FASRG (TEA, 2015) suggested that each district should have a purchasing procedures manual, which should contain the district's policy.

Legal Requirements for Purchasing

Legal requirements for purchasing by Texas public school districts can be found in Texas Education Code 44.031. This section of the TEC sets out the following stipulations in regard to purchasing:

1. Competitive procurement or bidding is required when a school district makes purchases of similar items in the amount of $25,000 or more, in the aggregate for each 12-month period. Several options for meeting this legal requirement are offered in FASRG (TEA, 2015) under the title of purchasing.
2. Formal quotes from at least three vendors are required when the purchase of like materials/equipment is at least $10,000, but less than $25,000, in the aggregate for the 12-month period.
3. Some selected purchases may be exempt from competitive procurement requirements if they meet established criteria for sole source purchase.

The TEA offers some alternatives to the process of requiring sealed bids and formal quotes through catalogue purchases through the General Services Commission. School districts also simplify this process through forming consortiums or through Regional Education Centers where commonly used items are submitted for bid collectively and then the items are offered for direct purchase through a catalogue of the items listed at the bid price.

Districts must maintain detailed files of competitive procurement of supplies, equipment, and property. The files should contain all documentation in regard to requests for proposals, advertisements, vendors contacted and responding, tabulation of responses, and board action.

System for Requisitioning and Purchasing

An orderly system for requesting goods and services, purchasing, and timely delivery of these items is critical to school district success. Communication about this system to all who have purchasing or requesting authority is as important as the development of the system. Communication that is structured to assure understanding will eliminate many potential errors and should help to eliminate questions about the time lag between requests and delivery.

The size, sophistication, and electronic capability of a district will play an important part in determining the system of purchasing that is adopted. The suggested steps listed below will distinguish between a purchase requisition and a purchase order. In reality, some personnel may have access to actual purchase orders. It should also be noted that no distinction is made between paper and electronic requisitions and orders. The following steps will illustrate a model for requisition and purchasing of teaching supplies by a teacher. The same process can be applied to a person making a purchase request from any of the operational centers.

1. A teacher prepares a purchase requisition and submits it to the principal for review and approval.
2. The principal (or designee) determines if the expenditure is within the budgetary limits of this category and, if so, approves the requisition.
3. The purchase requisition is forwarded to the business office where it is again verified against the account and, if approved, prepares a purchase order which is forwarded to the vendor. This encumbrance is posted to the general ledger and will appear on the next budget status report.

4. The vendor receives the purchase order and delivers the goods to the district. The place of delivery is a function of the district's policies. In some districts, it would be delivered to the location of the person making the request and, in some, it would be delivered to the central warehouse.

5. The teacher making the request receives the supplies and verifies the shipment as specified on his/her copy of the purchase order. If all is in order, this information is relayed to accounts payable.

6. The accounts payable department will make payment to the vendor and when this is posted to the general ledger, the encumbrance will be changed to reflect an expenditure.

The implementation of a good system of purchasing and supply management can be greatly enhanced by a centralized warehousing, shipping, and receiving function. This may be prove to be inappropriate for some small districts but can prove to be an asset to any district that is committed to timely delivery of goods and services.

◆ SUMMARY

In this chapter, the three major functions of the financial and business operations of the school district were discussed. These operations include the controlling function, budget development and administration function, and the purchasing and supply management function. While the major aspects of each function were outlined, the FASRG (TEA, 2015) is the primary guide for greater depth into these functions and an understanding of school business operations in Texas.

◆ REFERENCES

Ray, J. R., Hack, W. G., & Candoli, I. C. (2001). *School business administration: A planning approach* (7th ed.). Needham Heights, MA: Allyn & Bacon.

Texas Education Agency. (2015). *A Financial Accountability System Resource Guide, Version 15 (FASRG)*. Austin, TX: Texas Education Agency. Retrieved from http://tea.texas.gov/Finance_and_Grants/Financial_Accountability/Financial__Accountability_System_Resource_Guide/

THE SUPERINTENDENT AND HUMAN RESOURCES

Chuck Holt

One of the most important responsibilities of the superintendent is to guide the district in providing a high-quality workforce to accomplish its mission. This task not only has increased in complexity over the years but also has become increasingly important to the success of the district. Schools are essentially a people business, and organized learning is a uniquely human endeavor. While other components of the school system are necessary, none is more important than the human resources available to realize the school's goals. In most schools, personnel costs are 80% or more of the district's annual operating budget (Brimley & Garfield, 2008). Predictably, the majority of the staff associated with a school is teachers or personnel who directly support teaching, such as instructional aides. Research emphasizes the importance of the instructional staff to the success of the organization. In Texas schools, the function of human resources is typically a shared responsibility between both the central office and district campuses. To assure success of the district, the superintendent must develop systems to recruit, employ, develop, motivate, and retain a high-quality staff.

◆ THE HUMAN RESOURCE FUNCTION

Schools are unique social organizations responsible to society through the democratic process. The issues, goals, problems, and ultimate successes of schools are linked to people. The term *personnel* evolved into *human resources* as an indication of the importance of this function. The superintendent is responsible for administrative components that include instructional program and support service administration. While both of these are necessary for the school organization, none is more important than the human resource function in determining the school's success. Marzano (2003) demonstrated that teachers' actions in their classrooms have twice the impact on student learning as do school policies regarding curriculum, assessment, staff collegiality, and community involvement. Norton (2008) posits that the human resources' function in education is increasingly viewed as vital only to the extent that it supports the guiding goals and objectives of the organization as a whole. "In this sense, the issues, problems, challenges, and trends facing a school system become those of its human resources function as well" (Norton, 2008, p. 3). It becomes obvious that all facets of the human resource function are necessary to meet the high standards required by both the *State Accountability* system [Texas Education Agency (TEA), 2015a] and the federal No Child Left Behind (NCLB) Act of 2001 and updated in 2011.

There are important components of the human resource function beyond just the hiring of teachers. Planning, recruitment, selection, induction, evaluation, professional development, and compensation are all elements of the human resource function. According to Young (2008), the human resource function plays a role in helping the system operate within legal mandates, honor contracts, adapt to emerging technologies, and uphold ethical standards while maintaining the centrality of purpose. Many of these tasks are decentralized and usually fall under the direction of other administrators. The superintendent is ultimately responsible, however, for their implementation to assure a stable, effective workforce.

Human Resource Planning

Rebore (2011) states that through the process of planning, a school may insure that it has the right number of people, with the right skills, in the right place, and at the right time to carry out its mission. A school needs financial resources, physical resources, and people. Too often planning for staff is taken for granted, and yet they are the force that directly affects the primary objective of the school—to educate children. Young (2008) describes planning as a methodological mechanism for projecting intentions and actions rather than reacting to events affecting the schooling process. The goals of human resource planning are for both budgeting and employment. It is a broad and continuous process that should respond to district changes and staffing needs.

Human resource planning in large part is a central office function. Campuses can be allotted a determined number of personnel units based upon student enrollments and program projections. Campuses often participate in the process by prioritizing programs through site-based management and making requests to human resources for certain staff. The superintendent or designated administrator must prepare for staffing due to changes in instructional programs or enrollments. Planning should be both short term and long term.

Districts should begin planning by developing a human resource inventory. This inventory allows analysis of the number and type of teachers and staff available for assignment. Another important task is enrollment projections. While many districts maintain a stable student population, some rapid growth districts employ demographers to assist in long-term planning for staff and facilities. A review of district objectives adopted by the board of trustees is also necessary. These objectives, often prepared as a cooperative effort of the board, administration, and site-based planning groups, will determine the number and mix of staff required for the school's mission. It should be noted that staffing for elementary schools versus secondary schools is also quite different. Factors precipitating change at the secondary level are often different than those of elementary schools that tend to be more stable. The final step in forecasting is to match the future staff needs with the current supply. This will highlight shortages or potential overstaffing and identifies how the district must recruit to meet future needswhile considering the 70-plus different teaching certifications that exist in Texas. All of these steps help to create a human resource forecast that allows a district to develop a targeted strategy for recruitment and selection.

The supply of teacher and staff candidates is affected by a number of factors. While an increase in staff can be planned for more easily, a decrease in existing staff is not as predictable since resignations, retirements, and dismissals are harder to forecast. Increased alternative certification programs have changed the path to certification for many teachers and have impacted the recruiting process for schools. The economic downturn that began in 2008 had a dramatic impact on employment for many schools. The decrease in state funding per pupil by the 82nd Legislature precipitated staff downsizing in many schools that led to higher teacher–student–classroom ratios. While the 83rd and 84th Legislatures have restored some of the lost funding, a reduction in overall per pupil spending continues to impact staffing. In the meantime, shortages of teachers in some fields, including math, science, and foreign language, have led districts to create "grow-your-own" style programs to assure a pool of certified candidates for open positions. In light of the current political and economic changes, human resource planning has probably never been more difficult, and yet it should remain a high priority for superintendents.

Recruitment and Selection

According to Norton (2008), personnel recruitment is the human resources' process that informs candidates of positions available and assesses their interest and qualifications. It is a systematic method of identifying and attracting personnel in order to create an applicant pool for vacant positions in the school system. While schools were once dependent upon walk-in applicants to create an employment pool, this strategy no longer fulfills the need for a diverse and talented cadre to carry out the mission of the school. Common methods of recruiting include university placement centers, job fairs, advertisements on the Internet, internal searches, and referrals. In recent years, school and professional organization Websites have become the primary place applicants look for position announcements. The policies of most school boards require notices of vacancies to be posted on the district Website or bulletin board for positions requiring a certification.

Traditional recruitment methods for teachers are changing. Technology has had an impact on the way schools recruit and select candidates through advertising on the Internet and the use of online application systems. Alternative certification programs now provide as many new teachers in Texas as traditional university teacher preparation programs. Schools with high needs students often form school–university partnerships for early recruiting. Another facet of recruiting is the need for an ethnically diverse staff. Texas public schools serve a high population of minority children. This trend will continue, as Hispanic children from birth to 11 years of age currently represent the majority ethnicity in Texas (Eschbach, 2009). It is important to have staff members that are ethnically representative of the school's students. Recruiting minority applicants has become commonplace for most districts.

With Texas public school enrollment growing by ~80,000 students per year, the need for certified teachers will certainly continue to rise in the future. According to a National Center for Education Statistics report the number of teachers needed in the United States by 2017 will increase in 28% nationally (National Center for Education Statistics, 2008). Furthermore, Rebore (2011) states that the primary implication of this demographic for the recruitment process is that competition for the best teaching candidates will be fierce. Because many smaller-sized school districts do not have a designated human resource administrator, the increasingly important job of recruiting will fall to other central office and campus staff. Superintendents and other administrators are professionally obligated to find and hire the best-qualified people for the position.

The term re-recruitment has come into the vernacular due to the importance of retaining valuable employees. One of the goals of the human resource function is to create stability in the workforce. Research indicates that teachers change jobs or leave the profession for three primary reasons: (1) teaching is not satisfying, (2) teaching is devoid of opportunities for success, career advancement, and recognition, and (3) teachers find better paying jobs (Norton, 2008). To increase the staff retention rate, superintendents should implement a system of examining high-value employees and assuring that their professional needs are being met. Insuring that principals have mentor programs and relevant staff development for new teachers in place may reduce turnover and help create stability, particularly in hard-to-staff campuses.

The central office usually handles initial screening to narrow the pool to qualified applicants. This task involves both determining a person–job fit as well as a person–organization fit (Villanova & Muchinsky, 1997). Campus principals and/or interview teams most often review the pool and select candidates for further screening. This decentralized selection process requires coordination by the central office to be efficient and effective. The goal of the selection process is to identify individuals that will be successful in their job role and contribute to the organization as measured by a formal evaluation process. Selection is typically a multistep process that begins with writing a job description and ends with notifying all candidates of the final selection. In the middle, are many small steps that control the application process, including checking credentials, doing reference and background checks, and managing interviews.

Interviews are often the final step in making hiring decisions. It is important to have a human resource administrator or other qualified individual to guide the interview particularly in light of the number of schools that depend upon group interviews to select staff. Tests of aptitude and ability may be used for most jobs in the school setting. Assessment centers may test the aptitude of candidates in simulated teaching environments, and some candidates are asked to complete a writing sample or problem solving exercise. Performance- or behavior-based interviews are also more common in schools now for many positions. Based on the premise that past behavior is the best predictor of future performance, behavior-based interviewing uses specific questions based on the candidates' skills, backgrounds, and experiences to determine if they can do the job (Clement, 2008). One current beliefconcerning teacher effectiveness contends that good teachers share a common set of values about education, such as caring, commitment, and persistence. To translate affective beliefs, attitudes, and values into practicable teacher selection, many schools have turned to commercial teacher hiring instruments, such as Gallup's Teacher Perceiver Interview (Metzger & Wu, 2008). While larger districts often utilize behavior, performance, or ability tests, smaller school districts usually do not have the specialized personnel or resources to implement them.

The selection of individuals can be an expensive process and is one of the most important tasks in the human resource function. Harris (2004) points out that one of the duties superintendents assume in order to meet the challenges of federal and state school accountability systems is to ensure quality instruction. No single factor will influence instruction more than selecting the right individuals for the job. It is difficult at best to select the best candidate even when using interview teams and the most current selection instruments available. Hiring mistakes are costly not only in terms of lost time and effort but, most importantly, to the reduced achievement of the district's students. To complicate matters, recent findings in Florida by Harvard researchers demonstrate only a modest relationship between teacher certification, advanced degrees, or experience to student achievement (Chingos & Peterson, 2010). Since a sound selection process may decrease administrative problems, improve the learning environment, and support positive change in the district, it behooves the superintendent to evaluate the recruiting and selection process against employee performance evaluations to measure success (Norton, 2008).

Induction and Assignment

Teaching has been a career in which the greatest challenges and most difficult responsibilities are faced by those with the least experience (Glickman, Gordon, & Ross-Gordon, 2010). These authors also point out that beginning teachers in many schools are faced with a number of difficulties, including tough assignments, unclear expectations, and a sink-or-swim mentality (Glickman et al., 2010). The reality of the classroom soon sets in and can overwhelm the novice teacher. The purpose of the induction process is to get new staff members acquainted with their coworkers, the school, and the community. It is designed to get employees comfortable with the environment and help them become effective teachers. An effective induction can also help set district expectations and encourage team building. Norton (2008) indicates that an effective induction program can be instrumental in fostering staff morale and reducing staff turnover. For beginning teachers, this process reduces isolation and anxiety. Research emphasizes that addressing the needs of novice teachers may improve retention, since teachers with high levels of job satisfaction are more likely to remain in the profession (Norton, 2001).

Studies of teacher loss in education indicate that over 25% of new teachers leave the profession after 1 year and this loss increases to 50% by the fifth year. Industry has long recognized the value of an induction effort to retaining employees. It is difficult for any organization to maintain a stable workforce with high turnover rates. Recent studies by Wang, Odell, and Schwille (2008) point out that in the last 20 years induction has moved from emotional and social support for the teachers to supporting learning. The change was accelerated by NCLB and its efforts toward teacher quality and beginning teachers' learning. An extensive review of literature concerning induction found numerous other factors affecting new teacher effectiveness and cautions against assumptions that induction programs are adequate to assist teachers (Wang etal., 2008).

Mentoring programs are common in schools but rarely get the resources or priority they deserve. Mentoring is often a part of school policy but in reality lacks the support to be effective. Mentoring can be described as a method of support from a more experienced colleague who serves as a role model, advisor, and tutor to a beginning teacher. According to Sorenson and Goldsmith (2009), mentoring can build effective communications, provide personal support, extend insight into the campus vision and mission, provide professional growth, and ensure a working relationship with a master teacher/mentor who can serve as a role model for appropriate educational practices. Effective mentoring can provide the new teacher with much more than just an understanding of procedures and policies. These authors emphasize that successful mentoring programs should go beyond the technical and instructional skill development of a new employee (Sorenson & Goldsmith, 2009). It can also serve to give guidance in the areas of student discipline, classroom management, lesson planning, and parental communication. Mentoring programs should be part of the professional development plan of all new teachers, and the superintendent should insure that resources are available to provide effective mentoring on all campuses.

Staff assignment is essentially getting the right person into the right position. Human resource authors believe that appropriate assignments are one of the best ways to help an organization reach its goals. While the recruitment and selection process build a pool and employ capable people, assignment takes the next logical step in maximizing an employee's potential to meet the goals of the campus or district. Teachers that are well matched to their assignment will be more satisfied professionally and are more likely to be retained in the school. Campus assignments generally begin at the central office through the superintendent or human resource administrator. The principal usually makes specific assignments so again this process becomes a shared responsibility. Norton (2008) emphasizes that position assignments require several essential considerations: the specific nature of the position, the professional competencies and interest of the employee the extent to which the assignment provides motivation, and the characteristics of the school's structure and culture. Providing a positive work experience that meets the personal and professional needs of the employee may reduce other personnel problems in the long term. Staff assignments can have a significant impact on school effectiveness and teacher retention. The superintendent should use employee performance appraisals to review assignment effectiveness and should be prepared to consider assignment changes to improve the organization.

Compensation and Benefits

Compensation in education cannot be separated from the wider issue of school finance. Superintendent and school board surveys have consistently identified school finance as the number one problem-facing education today. Financing education is mostly a human resource cost with Texas schools spending ~80% of their maintenance and operations budget on compensation each year. The current economic environment was only exacerbated when the eighty-second Texas Legislature reduced funding to Texas schools by ~$5.4 billion in the 2012–2013 biennium. This reduction had an impact on salaries, benefits, and positions. Many schools froze salaries and hiring to meet the mandated cuts. Other impacts included increased student–teacher ratios and elimination of many programs and positions. The 83rd Legislature restored about $3.4 billion of that funding through formula changes. Most recently the 84th Legislature added back another $1.5 billion for the Foundation School Program abovethe $2.3 billion for enrollment growth (Texas Association of School Administrators, 2015).

Texas has long followed the national norm of having a single salary schedule as a basis for teacher pay. The minimum salary schedule has been the method of allocating salaries in Texas since 1949 and has provided a guarantee to employees of an established number of days of work per year and a minimum salary. A minimum salary schedule based upon years of teaching experience is spelled out in the Texas Education Code (TEC) for teachers, librarians, counselors, and nurses. The single salary schedule traditionally provides compensation based upon degrees earned and/or years of experience. This has evolved over the years due to competition between districts to local salary schedules based on pay above the mandated minimum. Some schools are initiating pay for performance schemes where teachers are rewarded primarily for student achievement gains. Dallas ISD has rolled out its Teacher Excellence Initiative in which exemplary teachers may earn up to $90,000/year (The Hub, 2015).

Schools sometimes contract for market studies to find a competitive price point for salaries in a specific geographic region. Schools in suburban or urban areas often pay more than their rural counterparts due to both the cost of living and competition for quality teachers. Negotiating salaries for teachers is not common in Texas. Most schools do pay teachers more than the state minimum salary, but the use of signing bonuses is rather infrequent (Kelly, Tejeda-Delgado, & Slate, 2008).

Ina special session, the 82nd Legislature passed legislation that allows some districts to alter or reduce existing salaries. Senate Bill 8 (SB 8), also called the spending flexibility/mandate relief bill, repealed a section of the TEC that requires a salary increase for charter schools and one that requires maintenance of salaries for teachers, counselors, nurses, librarians, and speech pathologists at 2010–2011 levels in public schools. SB 8 also provided for furloughs — reductions of workdays without pay—of up to six noninstructional days. To be eligible for district furlough days, the commissioner must certify that current funding is below 2010–2011 levels. The furlough process must involve district professional staff and must give employees the opportunity to express opinions. It also requires a public meeting to discuss a furlough and to consider other options, including use of the fund balance and/or a tax increase. All contract staff are subjected to the same number of furlough days, and a furlough may not result in an increased number of teacher workdays. This bill does allow resignations without penalty subsequent to a furlough decision by the board. A furlough decision is final, may not be appealed, and does not require collective bargaining or create a cause of action.

Administrator salaries were also affected by this legislation. SB 8 requires that a widespread reduction in salaries bebased on financial conditions rather than teacher performance, and the district must reduce administrator salaries by a percent or fraction of a percent that is the same as the reduction to teacher salaries. SB 8 also allows the board of trustees to modify a superintendent's contract on the basis of financial exigency that requires a reduction in personnel. With reasonable notice, a superintendent can resign without penalty if this occurs.

There does exist legal issues related to compensation involving reductions of pay during a contract term. Contract law requires that salaries spelled out in a contract are a property right and must be honored. Most salaries in Texas, however, are listed in salary schedules adopted by the board annually, not in the contract itself, and that may change from year to year. Another consideration for superintendents is the penalty-free resignation date of 45 days prior to instruction for teachers. A board cannot reduce compensation, including any benefits, following the penalty-free resignation date since that essentially changes the terms of employment. Texas also has a mandated healthcare provision in which schools must provide a local group health plan at least equal to the benefits in the Teacher Retirement System (TRS)-Active Care Program available to all districts in the state. Many schools offer other benefits, including life insurance, group dental plans, and the like through a third party provider.

The superintendent is responsible for recommending all salary schedules and benefit programs to the board of trustees for adoption. While teachers and professional staff are a major piece of the puzzle, other worker salaries in the district, including maintenance, food service, and transportation departments, also must be considered. There is a significant legislation that governs hourly worker pay, including the Fair Labor Standards Act (FLSA), the Equal Pay Act of 1963, and the Individuals with Disabilities Education Act, which all have an impact on local district compensation. Just as teacher, salaries have progressed from a statewide minimum salary schedule, the competition for skilled workers in specific job markets can impact what a district must pay to find qualified support staff. Supply and demand is just as important in education hiring as in the private sector. Compensation for some jobs not listed under the minimum salary schedule or regulated by FLSA may be more closely tied to comparable private sector salaries. Administrators, technology personnel and other professional's salaries are often determined by wage structure decisions instead of comparative wage-level decisions. Instead of comparing salaries to other organizations, this method attempts to link the value of the position to job responsibilities, education, skills, and physical requirements. These jobs are often structured differently depending upon the size of the district or department in which the position resides. Competency-based pay is now receiving more attention in Texas. Merit pay, currently the most popular version, is discussed in the motivation section of this chapter.

The budget shortfall of 2011 greatly impacted school human resource law. The Legislature adopted a number of changes to long-standing regulations as mentioned earlier. With a better economy in recent years, little legislation was passed by the 83rd or 84thLegislature that directly affected educator or employee policy as found in TEC (2015, Chapter 21).

Professional Development

In this age of information as opposed to the former industrial age, professional development is more broadly based than in the past. Society accumulates knowledge at a much faster rate; therefore, no static skill set remains effective. In addition, the mandate to educate all children regardless of race, socioeconomic status, language barrier, or disability has compounded the skills required for teacher effectiveness. Rebore (2011) cites three trends that have contributed to the changes in professional development: result-driven education, the systems approach to school, and school district organization.

Professional development is defined as training staff members for both present and future positions. It is the responsibility of the superintendent to help all staff members to fulfill their potential by enhancing skills and developing new abilities. There are three components to a professional development program. A need assessment first determines the needs of faculty and staff before initiating training. This step identifies the needs of the entire district or campus as well as small group and individual needs. For years, professional development was typically presented through in-service workshops that grouped most teachers into a common annual training program for a few days. The increasingly specialized fields in which teachers work coupled with specific campus goals have made staff development a much more individualized effort. Beyond orientation and induction, staff development should be prescriptive for administrators and teachers to meet the goals of the district. Implementation techniques for training can include simulation, action research, conferences, on-the-job training, and many others depending upon the strategy best suited for the particular program. Evaluation remains an important, yet often overlooked, component of the professional development program, primarily because effective evaluation is a challenging process.

Another consideration for professional development should include adult learning theories, such as andragogy (Knowles, 1984). Adults learn differently than children and have different motivations. The accessibility to technology, including instructional tools, in the past decade has also changed the classroom forever. Students coming to school now grew up in a digital world and see learning differently (Prenksy, 2001). The impact of these "digital learners" on the schoolhouse will become more pronounced in the future, and teachers must be prepared.

For a superintendent, a special concern exists for the principals' professional development. These front-line school leaders, including assistant principals, exert direct influence on the quality of instruction and hence a campus's accountability rating. Since campuses receive ratings individually and usually very publicly, campus leaders often feel the pressure to achieve results as much as anyone in the school organization. Identifying professional growth for these employees is becoming very individualized in schools. Regarded more as instructional leaders than managers as in years before, principals must know how to evaluate teaching and learning. Providing professional training on curriculum leadership to principals should be a top priority.

Leadership training can also be valuable, as principals are required to make so many daily decisions that affect the success of the school. Traditional management training that includes budgeting, resource acquisition, and building management is certainly paramount. In most cases, given the number of staff supervised and their varying attributes, human relation training must also be considered as a vital component of leadership development. Rebore (2011) highlights a number of staff development opportunities for principals that are necessary due to societal changes in the previous 10 years. Topics, such as cultural pluralism, community involvement, program assessment, technology-assisted instruction, and inclusion, are relatively new trends that must be addressed in today's schools. Response to intervention is one of the trends requiring extensive training.

Performance Evaluation

For the superintendent, appraisals cover a wide swath of jobs and individuals that contribute to all facets of the school's operation. Superintendents must develop a system to appraise all instructional staff, auxiliary staff, central office staff, and other professionals that work at the district level. This system will require different types of instruments and different supervisors to carry out the evaluations. There are several reasons for performance evaluations, including decisions about compensation, promotions, and terminations; follow-up on hiring decisions; and as feedback for professional development activities. Evaluating principal will be one of the superintendent's most important evaluation tasks and is covered in a separate section of this chapter.

Organizations utilize a number of methods to evaluate performance. Lunenburg and Ornstein (2012) group these methods into three categories: a judgmental approach, an absolute standards approach, and the results-oriented approach. The judgmental method requires the school administrator to compare an employee with other employees and rate the individual traits. The absolute standards method uses a job analysis and compares the employee to an established standard of behavior. The results-oriented approach has gained favor in recent years and is typified by goal-setting measures. This is common in leadership and administrator appraisals with mutually agreed upon goals measured at the end of the appraisal period. As mentioned earlier, the approach the superintendent chooses for any group of employees will depend upon the nature of the work and the leadership required in the position.

Principals are generally responsible for direct teacher evaluations. For more than 20 years, most districts adopted the Professional Development and Appraisal System model as provided by TEA. A new system of teacher appraisal named the Texas Teacher Evaluation and Support System (T-TESS) is currently being piloted by 60 school districts across the state. It will be implemented in about 200 districts in 2015–2016 and will become statewide in 2016–2017 (TEA, 2015b).

Research has provided a clearer idea of how to recognize effective teaching. The challenge is to connect accurate teacher appraisals with campus goals, teacher professional development, and contract renewals. Wong and Wong (2004) defined the effective teacher as the teacher capable of having a positive effect on student lives. That teacher can change the behaviors of students to develop the characteristics of a lifelong learner. They also identified three overarching characteristics of effective teachers. First, the effective teacher has positive expectations for student success. Second, the effective teacher is an extremely good classroom manager. Finally, these authors stipulated that the effective teacher knows how to design lessons to help students reach mastery.

Challenges and Trends

The NCLB Act of 2001 as updated in 2011 is the latest federal version of school reform. Texas has been on a much longer path of educational transformation. In 1984, the Texas Legislature passed what is commonly known as House Bill 72, enacting sweeping reforms of the public school system. Changes to NCLB in 2011 have more recently added other requirements to states. Other state reforms have followed at an even more frequent pace. According to Rebore (2011), reform is always present in education because change and improvement are embedded in the education profession. Maximizing the potential of every child is the goal of education, and society will always have an influence on change. House Bill 5 from the 83rd Texas Legislature brought sweeping changes in the accountability system, testing and high school course offerings that impacted the need for teachers certified in the Career and Technology fields. The 84th Legislature recently redesigned the accountability system with elements on school turnaround and alternative management for underperforming schools that will also likely impact school human resources (TEA, 2015d). Reform efforts will continue to occupy the efforts of administrators, particularly human resource administrators, since people are the initiators and implementers of reform. The superintendent must insure that the human resource function supports school reform efforts and any district initiatives and/or campus goals.

Any teacher that has been in the classroom more than a few years has witnessed the change in students coming to today's classrooms. Prenksy (2001) observed that students have changed radically; today's students are no longer the people that our educational system was designed to teach. This has tremendous implications for human resource administrators as they staff schools for a generation of children who learn differently from any preceding generation. Human resource administrators must recruit and train individuals with the capacity and inclination to function in a classroom that is evolving with the technology available and with students who expect a digital classroom environment.

While staffing schools has been a shared responsibility in schools, it also is becoming even more decentralized. Today principals are often responsible for more of the recruitment and selection tasks as well as assignment and professional development. Schools are often the largest employers in the community while at the same time the state's schools face shortages of teachers in particular fields. Accountability standards now present very different needs for different campuses in the same district. The correct assignment of staff suitable to the climate or particular needs of a campus is more important than ever for the school's academic success and for its image. The school superintendent must understand the human resource needs of not only the district but also for each campus and must create systems that provide this most important resource.

◆ LEGAL ISSUES AFFECTING PERSONNEL ADMINISTRATION

According to Walsh, Kemerer, and Maniotis (2010, p. 186), "no other area of school law generates more legal disputes than personnel. This is not surprising, since school districts employ so many people and have to comply with so many federal and state mandates." Public schools are governed by a myriad of laws and regulations enacted by federal, state, and local governments. Agency regulations and court decisions add to this body of rules. Laws relating to human resources have flourished over the past three decades complicating this function even more. Superintendents and human resource administrators cannot use ignorance of the law as a defense and essentially must be experts in this area of the law to effectively serve their districts.

Federal Law

Public education is not mentioned in the Unites States Constitution, but federal laws have had a significant impact on school human resources (La Morte, 2008). Federal law requires that employment decisions be based on qualifications, performance, and merit rather than factors, such as race, sex, religion, age, and disability. Federal regulations are extensive, complex, and at times confounding (Thomas, Cambron-McCabe, & McCarthy, 2009).

Much federal law related to school employment is based on the rights of individuals. The Equal Protection Clause of the Fourteenth Amendment prohibits actions by state governments that "draw lines" favor or disfavor a particular class of persons based on impermissible criteria. Equal protection is based on the theory of justice that each person has the right to the same advantages as any other person similarly situated. This amendment provides for antidiscrimination laws as well as the due process associated with some employment contracts.

Certain employment contracts are considered property, and the Fourteenth Amendment prohibits states from depriving citizens of life, liberty, or property without due process. Due process is a flexible concept—the more serious the consequences, the more intense the process that is due. For example, due process is more formal for dismissing a tenured (property right) teacher than for a reprimand or short suspension.

The federal judiciary has addressed issues, such as teacher searches, discriminatory employment practices, and teacher freedom of expression. Public educators do not shed their constitutional rights as a condition of public employment. However, freedom of speech of a government employee may not be as open and unrestrained as other persons not in public employment. According to the fundamental maxims of free speech, the government cannot restrain the exercise of free speech in open debate by the public even if it is offensive or discordant. Such a right, however, is not absolute, and there are exceptions in the school setting where freedom of speech has limitations.

Title VI of the Civil Rights Act of 1964 states that no person in the United States shall, on the ground of race, color, or national origin, be excluded from participation in, be denied benefits of, or be subjected to discrimination under any program or activity receiving federal financial assistance. Title VII deals with equal employment opportunities and was amended in 1972 specifically to address educational institutions. It has been used most often to challenge discrimination in teacher and administrative employment. Affirmative action is a voluntary program that institutions and organizations may use in hiring and should not be confused with law. The courts look it upon favorably as long as it is not too broadly applied. Title IX of the Education Amendments of 1972 prohibits any agency receiving federal funds from discriminating on the basis of gender. Under this law, sexual harassment is the basis for most of the recent school liability litigation. School districts now commonly provide training for all employees, including substitute teachers on the topic of sexual harassment. The district and school administrators may be held liable for "deliberate indifference" if appropriate actions are not taken when sexual harassment is reported.

The Rehabilitation Act of 1973 protects qualified persons with disabilities and the Age Discrimination Act of 1975 bars age discrimination in federally assisted programs. The Family and Medical Leave Act of 1993 allows employees to take reasonable leave for medical reasons, birth or adoption, and care of a child or parent with a serious ailment. The Act includes a special section concerning schools and staff members principally in instructional positions. It states that if the time missed will exceed 20% of the instructional period, the employer may require either that the leave be taken for a specific duration not to exceed the treatment, or that the employee transfer to a temporary alternative position.

The NCLB Act of 2001 had an impact on several areas of education, including human resources. The requirements related to "highly qualified" teachers may not align with certain certification rules already in place in Texas. All teachers in core academic areas must be deemed highly qualified by special certification testing, subject area degree attainment or, for experienced teachers, meeting special guidelines of high, objective, uniform state standard of evaluation rules. The confusion for districts lies in verifying the highly qualified status for certain teachers, such as special education teachers, and notifying parents of teachers that are inappropriately certified.

State Law

State law may have several sources, including statutory law, that is enacted by the Legislature, judicial law resulting from federal or court decisions, and administrative law, such as local school board policies and state agency regulations. While much of the foundation of rules governing human resources is statutory, judicial law attempts to interpret legislative intent and to settle conflicts. Certification and employee contracts are a significant body of statutory law and are covered in separate section.

The superintendent has the right to assign and reassign employees under most school employment contracts. That right is limited by the concept of *same professional capacity*, which only allows administrators to reassign employees to positions at the same professional level. Reassignments have led to litigation related to the property right concept discussed earlier. Position changes through reassignment are not usually a sound basis for litigation except when used as in a retaliatory manner and as long as the test of same professional capacity is met.

Compensation reduction may also be viewed as a loss of property right unless done in a manner not to conflict with the language of the contract. For example, a reassignment may only reasonably reduce salary if it complies with district salary schedules for the new position and does not violate any specific financial compensation listed in the contract. Most Texas school employment contracts do not list a dollar amount but refer to board adopted salary schedule. A superintendent or other school executive contract is likely an exception to that rule and will often spell out compensation and benefits. Any change of compensation for an employee during the term of a contract requires careful consideration.

An employee's work schedule or duties may also be points of litigation even when position or salary is unaffected. Most teacher contracts contain a clause specifying that the supervisor may assign or reassign staff to such duties as appropriate. This provision has been challenged especially in cases where an employee was assigned to additional duties or to extended hours of work. It should be noted that hourly employees, such as instructional aides and secretaries, are regulated by other labor and wage laws and different considerations may apply.

◆ CERTIFICATION AND CONTRACTS

Certification

Credentialing in Texas is approaching a completely online enterprise. The current and official database of professional certificates is listed online at the State Board for Educator Certification (SBEC) Website (SBEC, 2015). Teachers and other professionals now apply for, renew, and maintain their certificates on the SBEC Website. Schools verify teacher certifications officially through this Website. SBEC regulates all areas of teacher certification, including continuing education and standards of conduct. It can establish training requirements for teachers but must have its rules approved by the State Board of Education. This agency also has the responsibility of monitoring and approving teacher preparation programs in colleges and universities. SBEC also regulates all aspects of nontraditional employment, including alternative teacher certification and district teaching permits.

Current Texas law also provides that all employees undergo criminal background checks, including fingerprinting prior to certification or employment. TEA houses a Division of Fingerprinting (TEA, 2015c) to facilitate the submission of fingerprints. Based on fingerprints, photos, and other identification, this entity enables the employing school district and TEA and/or SBEC to have positive identification and to have access to the employee's current national criminal history. It also provides updates of the employee's subsequent criminal history.

◆ EMPLOYEE CLASSIFICATION AND CONTRACTS

Employees in Texas public schools belong to one of the six employment classifications. The superintendent must understand the particular legal ramifications of each of these employment arrangements since he or she is likely to encounter all six groups within a typical school district. Two considerations for each of these classifications are (1) what if any property right is granted by the employment arrangement and (2) how much due process is required to terminate the relationship. A teacher contract must satisfy the same legal requirements as contracts in general. These are offer and acceptance, competent persons, consideration, legal subject matter, and proper form. A teacher contract establishes a property right that is protected by the Fourteenth Amendment. The type of contract determines the scope of that property right. Chapter 21 of the TEC provides that teachers, principals, librarians, nurses, and counselors shall receive a probationary, term, or continuing contract. Other employees in the school have other employment arrangements as discussed below. A wise personnel attorney once quipped that a superintendent should understand how one might end any particular employment relationship before offering the position.

All first-year educator contracts in Texas are probationary by statute. This contract allows the district 1 year to evaluate the employee. The district may renew the probationary contract or move it to either a term contract or a continuing contract. For beginning teachers, the district has this option for at least 3 years and may opt for a fourth year in some circumstances. Typically a successful beginning teacher will be on a probationary contract for 3 years before moving to a term or continuing contract. If a teacher has prior experience at another district, the rule is different. If the teacher has been employed in other districts for five of the previous 8 years, the district may only maintain the probationary contract for 1 year. A probationary contract may be nonrenewed without a formal hearing, and there is no appeal for the employee beyond the local board of trustees.

Term contracts for educators differ in both length and due process requirements. Following the probationary contract period, an educator may be offered a term contract. As the name implies, this contract has a beginning and ending date. Following evaluations and recommendations by the administration, the board may renew, take no action, or propose nonrenewal of the contract. The length of the contract may be up to 5 years, but teachers typically have 1-year contracts and administrators have multiyear contracts. The other key difference in a term contract is the property right associated with the arrangement for the term specified in the contract.

Termination of a term contract denotes ending the contract prior to its ending date for "good cause." Termination for good cause requires procedural due process and a substantial burden of proof. Term contracts are typically extended 1 year at a time; the contract ending date may be a year or more from the current school year. If the board "nonextends" a contract, it is simply allowing the time to run out until the end of the contract when a nonrenewal process will be required. If at the end of a term contract a term contract is nonrenewed, the educator is entitled to a hearing. The board may conduct the hearing themselves or appoint a hearing officer. If a decision for nonrenewal is determined, the educator may appeal to the commissioner. This level is only a review of substantial evidence and allows the commissioner to overturn the board decision only if its decision was arbitrary, capricious, unlawful, or not supported by substantial evidence. The procedural and notification timelines are strict in a nonrenewal process, and decisions may be overturned on any violation of these rules.

Continuing contracts differ from term contracts in that they are allowed to "roll over" from year to year and require no action from the board. Continuing contracts do not end unless a teacher retires, resigns, is terminated, or returns to a probationary contract. Texas continuing educator contracts are something akin to tenure in other states. The due process for teachers on continuing contracts is similar to term contracts, but there is some distinction in the law about who is eligible for a continuing contract. These contracts are not as common in schools today compared to the term contracts offered by most districts.

Non-Chapter 21 contracts were created for school employees falling outside the definition of teacher, principal, counselor, librarian, or nurse. The rights granted to TEC Chapter 21 employees are not connected to other employees, such as business managers, athletic trainers, maintenance directors, and technology directors. Other professionals, such as educational diagnosticians and physical therapists, are also included in this contract category. School boards may determine how and when these contracts are terminated. While non-Chapter 21 contracts are not subjected to the Texas statutory nonrenewal hearing process, they must meet constitutional due process for termination.

At-will employees at public schools are most often the hourly jobs not related to certified instructors. Most supported jobs, such as maintenance, custodial, food service, and bus drivers, are at-will jobs that have no contractual agreements and, therefore, no property interest. At-will positions in schools closely resemble jobs in the private sector. The FLSA also regulates these positions to some extentin terms of hours and wages. While not credentialed by SBEC, these positions may require certain certifications and training by agencies, such as Texas Department of Public Safety, Texas Commission on Environmental Quality, Structural Pest Control Board, and others. The courts have upheld the Texas concept of at-will employment on numerous occasions in both schools and other governmental institutions. While employment is not "contracted" in these positions and no property right exists, employees are still due a nondiscriminatory workplace. Employee claims of retaliation often have a background in earlier discrimination complaints.

Third party independent contract educators are a recent development in Texas. Private companies began providing retired teachers to school districts on an annual contract basis. This contractual arrangement has existed for services, such as transportation and food service successfully for some time. The advantage for the educator was to collect TRS benefits and continue working. These practices lost some advantage when TRS changed its rules regarding the TRS annuity penalties for retire/rehire workers. While these contracts have assisted many districts in filling positions, there remain questions about these contract arrangements regarding due process and liability. Districts should understand the implications for these contracts before entering into them.

SB 8 from the 82nd Legislature provides significant changes in the provisions of educator contracts, including nonrenewal notifications. It moves the 45-day notice of nonrenewal to the 10th day before the last day of instruction for term and probationary contracts. Notice must be by hand-delivery unless the teacher is not present on the campus on the date that the hand-delivery is attempted. Then the notice must be by prepaid certified mail or express delivery service, postmarked by the 10th day before the last day of instruction.

SB 8 also created an alternative contract termination hearing process in districts with an enrollment of at least 5,000 students. It allows the board to designate an attorney to hold hearings on behalf of the board, create a hearing record for the board's consideration and action, and recommend an action to the board. At a hearing, the board shall consider the hearing record and the designee's recommendation as well as oral argument. The board may accept, reject, or modify the designee's recommendation.

Schools have long had the authority to conduct a reduction in force if the board declares financial exigency. A reduction in force allows schools to void contracts but must be carried out under certain legal parameters. SB 8 required the commissioner to adopt minimum standards for financial exigency declarations and provide for expiration of financial exigency declarations at the end of a fiscal year unless the board adopts a resolution extending the declaration for another year. It also permits an alternative hearing process for mid-term contract nonrenewals or for termination of probationary contracts in cases of financial exigency reductions in personnel. In addition, the legislation changes the method for reductions in force of teachers employed under continuing contracts from reverse order of seniority to primarily based on teacher appraisals. It was not supported by some teacher organizations.

◆ PRINCIPAL EVALUATION

For the superintendent, insuring a fair and developmental method of appraising principals is a top priority. Superintendents have the responsibility to appraise principals on job-related performance each year by statute. SBEC has identified nine competencies in three domains for the Texas Principal, including school-community leadership, instructional leadership, and administrative leadership. These competencies are the basis for the Texas Examination of Educator Standards exam used to certify principals. The board and superintendent are responsible for ensuring that theirappraisal documents and procedures meet all requirements of statute, including those that explicitly link student performance with theappraisal of principals.

Texas schools may use either a locally developed system of principal appraisal or the commissioner-recommended system. If a local system is developed, it must be created in consultation with the site-based decision-making committee and must be approved by the board of trustees. Documents relating to administrator appraisals are also considered confidential. According to TEC 21.354, the principal appraisal instrument shall include consideration of the performance of a principal's campus on the student achievement indicators established and the campus's objectives established, including performance gains of the campus and the maintenance of those gains. Most districts use a locally developed principal appraisal containing the commissioner-recommended student performance measure. Reeves (2009) described how educational leadership evaluation is broken in our country. His research revealed a significant knowing–doing gap in which school leaders often know what effective practices are but fail to implement them. After a study of appraisal documents from across the country, this author also finds them incoherent and unsuitable for the task. He also posits that improving leadership evaluation will prove difficult in this climate characterized by high stakes testing and a shortage of educational leaders. Texas is currently piloting a new principal appraisal system that includes a behavior rubric to address this phenomenon of the knowing-doing gap.

The evaluation of most teachers was done for years utilizing the Professional Development and Appraisal System by most districts. Similar to teachers, principals may be evaluated on a locally developed system or the commissioner-recommended system. SB 1833 of the eighty-second Legislature ultimately lead to the creationof the Texas Evaluation and Support System (T-PESS) to parallel the development of the T-TESS for teachers. T-PESS was developed by a statewide principal advisory committee and utilizes three measures of principal effectiveness (TEA, 2015e). This appraisal system will assure that the mandated elements of principal appraisal are utilized and that the instrument is both reliable and valid. T-PESS will likely create a much more uniform method of evaluating principals in Texas. According to TEA, the intended purpose of T-PESS is to assess the principal's performance in relation to the Texas Principal Standards. This new system uses a behavior rubric, a goal-setting process, and student growth measurements to create a more complete picture of principal effectiveness. Like T-TESS, the initiative was piloted in 2014–2015 and will expand in 2015–2016. The following year will bring a full implementation of the system across the state. Commissioner's rules for administrator appraisal are found in the Texas Administrative Code §150.1021 and §150.1022.

The job of principal has become ever more complex and demanding in the past two decades. In years past, school administrators were viewed as managers concerned with efficiently running a school (Shipman, Queen, & Peel, 2007). Principals ran schools with a top-down bureaucratic style to be efficient. Today the principal's primary role is to improve teaching and learning, and the standards-based movement heavily defines this new role. Instructional leadership is now at the forefront of what we expect from principals. Daresh (2001) points out that a simple comparison of managers versus leaders is oversimplified. An effective principal requires skills of leadership and management. According to Hanson (2009), a career in school administration is particularly difficult at the current time because of a multitude of influences affecting student and teachers. This author points out how intensely scrutinized school leaders are today by individuals from all walks of life who claim to have the remedy for what ails education.

◆ EMPLOYEE GRIEVANCES

Schooling is essentially a human endeavor involving teachers, children, parents, administrators, board members, and the community. With so many elements of society involved in such an effort, conflict is inevitable. In Texas, the rights to have the government hear a complaint begins with Article 1 of the State Constitution. The right of public employees to file grievances is found at Government Code 617.005. The TEC provides that each district must have a grievance policy in which concerns can be heard by the district's board of trustees. During the 1980s, an attorney general opinion and rulings by the Commissioner of Education broadened the scope of what might be included in a school employee grievance.

While principals need to have a working understanding of the grievance process, the superintendent and human resource administrator should be experts regarding state law and local policy. Serious grievances from employees often involve attorneys on both sides and potentially expensive proceedings. While Texas is a right to work state and there is no union representation for employees, professional associations may provide an attorney for the employee while school districts usually utilize law firms specializing in school law.

Schools have numerous statutory requirements related to grievances, including timeliness, record keeping, and responses. Employee grievances proceed through a series of steps toward resolution. The goal of any grievance process is to resolve the issue at its lowest administrative level if possible. Districts are required to hear the employee grievance at the first level with a principal. Board policy will usually direct an administrator to meet with the employee within a set timeline and offer a written response. If the employee is not satisfied, grievances move up by level to the superintendent's office and finally to the board of trustees. The law is very clear concerning the required opportunity for a grievance to be heard by the board. Schools also bear the burden of keeping an accurate and detailed record of the grievance for review by the commissioner if needed. This includes a written or electronic transcript of all testimony and arguments. A grievance proceeding, however, is not as formal as a nonrenewal hearing, and the rules of evidence outlined in the Texas Rules of Civil Evidence do not apply. Timelines are critical for both the employee filing the grievance and the district's response at each level. A grievance may be denied if it is deemed untimely as delineated in the local district board policy. Administrators at each level must be careful to meet with the complainant, hear the grievance, and respond in a timely matter. An employee seeking relief beyond the school district can appeal the decision of the local board of trustees to the Commissioner of Education. An employee may ultimately file suit in court but must exhaust all administrative remedies first. Most school districts in Texas utilize the Texas Association of School Board policy service. The district's local policy manual includes the Texas Association of School Board section DGBA that spells out the employee grievance process in detail.

◆ MOTIVATING PROFESSIONAL EMPLOYEES

Superintendents now serve in much broader roles than 20 years ago. From the traditional CEO and organizational manager, add to the list of duties educational statesman, social scientist, activist, and communicator (Kowalski, 2005). The culture of any organization is in great part in the responsibility of its leaders. One measure of the culture is how motivated the employees are who carry out the mission. Daresh (2001) points out that motivation is one of the most important and challenging supervisory responsibilities undertaken in schools. As the chief educational leader of the district, the superintendent should make sure that all district leaders understand the implications of employee motivation and its impact on the school culture.

Traditionally difficult to define, motivation is most simply the effort individuals who are willing to expend toward a goal. Some authors also add persistence and direction of the effort to the definition. A little like great teaching, motivation is hard to define but easier to recognize when we see it. The literature is replete with motivational theories; a study of these numerous theories is beyond the scope of this chapter, but a simple review is certainly in order.

Lunenburg and Ornstein (2012) have grouped the traditional motivational theories into two broad categories. The first group, described as the content theories of motivation, focuses on what energizes human behavior. These theories are concerned with identifying specific factors that motivate people. All teachers are familiar with Maslow's Hierarchy of Basic Needs theory, which is used extensively to study organizations. Others in this category are Herzberg's motivation-hygiene theory and McClelland's learned needs theory. Each of these theories attempts to categorize and prioritize human needs in some measurable units. These authors emphasize that each of these theories is an attempt to provide a clear, meaningful explanation of the factors that motivate people (Lunenburg & Ornstein, 2012).

A second category described by Lunenburg and Ornstein (2012) includes the process theories of motivation. These theories are concerned with the process by which motivational factors interact to produce motivation. Examples of these are the self-efficacy theory, the expectancy theory, and the goal-setting theory. In the current environment of standards and accountability systems, it is easy to find examples of goal-setting theory. In Texas schools, site-based decision-making bodies and the inherent goal setting that accompanies their annual plans are a perfect example of this theory in practice. These theories attempt to clarify people's perception of work inputs, performance requirements, and rewards. Again, all of these theories have value and relevance to administrators in understanding individual and group motivation.

It seems one of the hottest topics recently in the United States related to teacher and administrator motivation is merit pay. Schools across Texas and the nation have instituted various schemes of paying educators for performance, including merit pay, that is a usually a onetime reward for meeting a specified goal. A business model of reward and a taxpayer concern for teacher quality drive much of this effort. Indeed, pay for performance is a primary motivation particularly in sales or marketing positions. Governmental bodies have encouraged this movement through legislation and financial support programs for competency-based compensation. Critics argue that teachers are motivated by the work itself, while proponents believe that teachers are not recognized appropriately and extra pay would reward and motivate superior work. Rebore (2011) posits that, consistent with the outcry for accountability, performance-based pay may be the only realistic approach to improve the quality of education.

The difficulty is developing a fair system of performance pay. The controversial and failed Texas career ladder of the 1980s is an example. Others believe that cooperation is a hallmark of good teaching, and competitive environments do not align with this cooperative model of work. Proponents of merit pay point to how well competition works for much of our society, including students, so therefore it must work for teachers. Compensation ranks low as a motivator for teachers as compared to professional growth, achievement, and recognition, which fall much higher on the scale of satisfaction. The political bodies that create educational policy ultimately will settle this argument. A superintendent, however, will likely be highly influential in a board's decision if and how to implement a performance pay system in the district.

Lehman (1989) outlined some important practical strategies for motivating school staff. While these seem obvious to many, administrators must remind themselves of these approaches and create routines that emphasize them. Showing genuine regard for employee concerns is vital to the health of an organization. Clear and consistent goals coupled with good communication characterized by active listening are also critical to success. Recognition of effort and appreciation is obvious but often overlooked by busy administrators. Finally, staff participation in decisionmaking and faculty voice in professional development planning create a team mentality that is also important (Lehman, 1989). The TEC states that decisions about professional development are the only area that is not "advisory only" in the site-based decision making committee. The faculty has the final vote in what professional development will be provided.

It has been said that no one ever truly motivates another person. Whichever motivational theories to which the administrator subscribes, each staff member decides how hardhe/she will work. Daresh (2001) points out that a supervisor's motivational effectiveness depends not on the specific tactic used but on the extent to which the staff believes in the supervisor and the consistency of the supervisor's performance. This consistency is related to develop one's own educational philosophy as a leader, how one views the role of staff, and therefore how the instructional leader motivates staff members.

◆ SUMMARY

Darling-Hammond (1996) points out that the educational challenge facing the United States is not that its schools are not as good as they once were. It is that schools must help the vast majority of young people reach levels of skill and competence that were once thought to be within the reach of only a few. The accountability movement is a societal demand to educate all children and eliminate the gaps of learning that have plagued certain groups of children for decades. Profound shifts in demographics have increased both the number and diversity of public school students in Texas. Human resource administrators need to recruit, employ, and train effective teachers that represent the diversity in our classrooms. The explosion of technology, including social media and networking, has broadened the boundaries of learning but also threatens to widen the digital divide that separates the poor from mainstream society. This technology shift will affect both instruction and professional development. People are the school's most important asset. Either directly or by proxy, the superintendent is ultimately responsible for the district's personnel. This task has grown increasingly more decentralized, requiring all school leaders be knowledgeable regarding the human resource function. Education is a human endeavor; a superintendent must be skilled in human resources to be an effective leader of the district.

◆ REFERENCES

Brimley, V., & Garfield, R. R. (2008). *Financing education in a climate of change* (10thed.). Boston: Allyn & Bacon.

Chingos, M. M., & Peterson, P. E. (2010, June). *Do school districts get what they pay for? Predicting teacher effectiveness by college selectivity, experience, etc.* Paper presented at PEPG conference merit pay: Will it work? Is it politically viable? Cambridge, MA. Abstract retrieved from http://eric.ed.gov/PDFS/ED510249.pdf

Clement, M. C. (2008). Improving teacher selection with behavior-based interviewing. *Principal, 87*(3), 44–47. Retrieved from http://www.naesp.org/resources/2/Principal/2008/J-Fp44.pdf

Daresh, J. C. (2001). *Supervision as proactive leadership* (3rd ed.). Prospect Heights, IL: Waveland Press.

Darling-Hammond, L. (1996). What matters most: A competent teacher. *Phi Delta Kappan, 78*(3), 193–200.

Eschbach, K. (2009). *The changing demography of Texas children: Current trends and future patterns.* Retrieved from http://txsdc.utsa.edu/presentations/superintendents_conf_2009.php

Glickman, C. D., Gordon, S. P., & Ross-Gordon, J. M. (2010). *Supervision and administration: A developmental approach.* Boston, MA: Allyn & Bacon.

Hanson, K. L. (2009). *A casebook for school leaders: Linking the ISSLC standards to effective practice.* Upper Saddle River, NJ: Pearson Prentice Hall.

Harris, S. (2004). Strategies to meet the age of accountability. *Insight, 18*(3), 25–28.

Kelly, P., Tejeda-Delgado, C., & Slate, J. (2008). *Superintendents' views on financial and non-financial incentives on teacher recruitment and retention.* Retrieved from http://cnx.org/content/m16989/1.1/

Knowles, M. S. (1984). *Andragogy in action.* San Francisco, CA: Jossey-Bass.

Kowalski, T. J. (2005). Evolution of the school district superintendent position. In L. G. Bjork & T. J. Kowalski (Eds.), *The contemporary superintendent: Preparation, practice, and development* (pp. 1–18). Thousand Oaks, CA: Corwin.

La Morte, M. W. (2008). *School law, cases and concepts.* Boston, MA: Allyn & Bacon.

Lehman, L. E. (1989). Practical motivational strategies for teacher performance and growth. *NASSP Bulletin, 73,* 76–80.

Lunenburg, F.C., & Ornstein, A.C. (2012). *Educational administration.* Belmont, CA: Wadsworth.

Marzano, R. J. (2003). *What works in schools: Translating research into action.* Alexandria, VA: Association for Supervision and Curriculum Development.

Metzger, S. A., & Wu, M. (2008). Commercial teacher selection instruments: The validity of selecting teachers through beliefs, attitudes and values. *Review of Educational Research, 78*(4), 921–940. doi:10.3102/0034654308323035.

National Center for Educational Statistics. (2008). *Projections of education statistics to 2017.* Retrieved from the NCES website: http://nces.ed.gov/programs/projections/projections2017/index.asp

Norton, M.S. (2001). *The school superintendency in Arizona: A research study.* Tempe: Division of Educational Leadership and Policy Studies, Arizona State University.

Norton, M.S. (2008). *Human resources administration for educational leaders.* Thousand Oaks, CA: Sage Publications.

Prenksy, M. (2001). Digital natives, digital immigrants. *On the Horizon, 9*(5), 1–6. Retrieved from http://www.albertomattiacci.it/docs/did/Digital_Natives_Digital_Immigrants.pdf

Rebore, R. W. (2011). *Human resources administration in education: A management approach* (9th ed.). Upper Saddle River, NJ: Pearson.

Reeves, D. B. (2009). *Assessing educational leaders.* Thousand Oaks, CA: Sage Publications.

The Hub. (2015, April 20). Salary Range for Dallas ISD Teachers Increases to $50,000–$90,000. Retrieved from https://thehub.dallasisd.org/2015/04/20/salary-range-for-dallas-isd-teachers-increases-to-50000-90000/

Shipman, J. J., Queen, J. A., & Peel, H. A. (2007). *Transforming school leadership with ISLLC and ELCC.* Larchmont, NY: Eye on Education.

Sorenson, R. D., & Goldsmith, L. D. (2009). *The principal's guide to managing personnel.* Thousand Oaks, CA: Corwin.

State Board for Educator Certification. (2015). *Official record of educator certificates.* Retrieved from https://secure.sbec.state.tx.us/SBECONLINE/virtcert.asp

Texas Association of School Administrators. (2015). *84th legislative session: What passed, what didn't.* Retrieved from http://www.tasanet.org/cms/lib07/TX01923126/Centricity/Domain/329/84th_session_bills.pdf

Texas Education Agency. (2015a). *State accountability.* Retrieved from http://tea.texas.gov/Student_Testing_and_Accountability/Accountability/State_Accountability/

Texas Education Agency. (2015b). *Texas teacher evaluation and support system.* Retrieved from http://tea.texas.gov/Texas_Educators/Educator_Evaluation_and_Support_System/Texas_Teacher_Evaluation_and_Support_System/

Texas Education Agency. (2015c). *Briefing book on public education.* Retrieved from http://tea.texas.gov/Reports_and_Data/Legislative_Reports/Legislative_Briefing_Book/

Texas Education Agency. (2015d). *Fingerprinting for Texas educators and school district personnel.* Retrieved from http://tea.texas.gov/Texas_Educators/Certification/Fingerprinting/

Texas Education Agency. (2015e). *Texas principal evaluation and support system.* Retrieved from TEA website: http://tea.texas.gov/Texas_Educators/Educator_Evaluation_and_Support_System/Texas_Principal_Evaluation_and_Support_System/

Texas Education Code. (2015). Retrieved from http://www.statutes.legis.state.tx.us/Docs/ED/htm/ED.21.htm

Thomas, S. B., Cambron-McCabe, N.H., & McCarthy, M. M. (2009). *Public school law, teachers' and students' rights.* Boston, MA: Allyn & Bacon.

Villanova, P., & Muchinsky, P. M. (1997). Person-job fit. In L. H. Peters, C.R. Green, & S. A. Youngblood (Eds.), *The Blackwell encyclopedic dictionary of human resource management* (pp.257–258). Oxford, England: Blackwell.

Walsh, J., Kemerer, F., & Maniotis, L. (2010). *The educator's guide to Texas school law.* Austin, TX: University of Texas Press.

Wang, J., Odell, S. J., & Schwille, S. A. (2008). Effects of teacher induction on beginning teachers' teaching: A critical review of literature. *Journal of Teacher Education, 59*(2), 132–152. doi: 10.1177/0022487107314002.

Wong, H. K., & Wong, R. T. (2004). *The first days of school: How to be an effective teacher.* Mountain View, CA: Harry K. Wong Publications, Inc.

Young, I. P. (2008). *The human resource function in educational administration* (9th ed.). Upper Saddle River, NJ: Pearson Merrill Prentice Hall.

THE SUPERINTENDENT AND DISTRICT FACILITIES

Vance Vaughn

The educational system has grown from a little red, one-room schoolhouse that was occupied by a single race of children to a metropolis of major urban, major suburban, central city, independent town, rural, and charter schools. The need for quality teachers has also grown, and concomitantly, the need for better facilities that meet the demands of this technological age are increasingly warranted.

The short story *Rip Van Winkle* by the American author Washington Irving, published in 1819, is a vivid example of how one might view our school facilities. Mr Van Winkle might find current facilities recognizable with the students' desks in rows and the teacher's desk formally positioned out in middle-front, separating the students' desks from the black or green chalkboards. Little has changed in modern schools, and there are facilities that have failed to maintain pace with the exponentially increasing demands that technology has consigned tosociety. Schneider (2002, p.1) concluded, "the average age of our schools is close to fifty years, and studies by the U.S. General Accounting Office have documented widespread physical deficiencies in many of them." These deficiencies exist due to aging, deterioration, overcrowding, major disasters, and neglect. In many schools, students and teachers find themselves in a physical environment that adversely affects their morale and health (Schneider, 2002). In addition, technology is changing the way school leaders design and construct infrastructures.

Technology is changing the way people educate, socialize, and live in this world. Prensky (2001) suggested schools be designed for the "digital natives" who have never known a world without technology as opposed to the "digital immigrants" who did not grow up with technology. The question then is, how can school administrators design, erect, and sustain school facilities in such a way that they serve students for 50–100 years? How can school administrators protect and maintain the substantial investment their taxpayers have constructed? And, will these administrators use the taxpayer's finances wisely for the cost of operating and maintaining these facilities? These are three of the fundamental questions that should linger in the minds of those administrators who have been given the privilege and responsibility of educating children of the community.

According to Schneider (2002, p. 1), "on any given school day, about 20% of Americans spend time in a school building." The majority of these attendees are children. Children are sent to school to learn, and the physical environment is a resource for supporting this mission (Schneider, 2002). People are influenced and affected by their environment (Connolly, Svendsen, Fisher, & Campbell, 2013). Children exposed to the environmental conditions in school facilities are no exception. Although hard evidence is scarce, Schneider (2002) indicates that when a school building is in disrepair, student achievement suffers. Since learning is a priority for school administrators, it is common place that school administrators spend quality time reflecting and negotiating their time, energy, and resources to assure students are educated in the most comfortable and safe environments.

In order for school leaders to effectively and strategically plan for short- or long-term facilities' needs, he/she must engage in conscientious reflection. Figure 18.1 displays a grid in which school administrators can often find themselves operating subconsciously in each hour of the day. The first block (I) represents those situations that administrators handle that are urgent and simultaneously very important. An example of such a situation could be an injured child who just fell from playground equipment. This unfortunate incident is urgent and certainly very important. In this case, the administrator will operate in block (I). The remaining blocks are reserved for school leaders to insert their own examples. However, school administrators should focus their attention to school facilities in block (III). In block (III), these administrators can evaluate their facilities' needs, determine their action plan, and execute their plan to maximize their facilities for student achievement.

During the school administrator's conscientious reflection, what thoughts, ideas, and questions should he/she be analyzing, especially if he/she is facing school facility issues for the first time? This discussion focuses on providing the school administrator with the knowledge of understanding the correlational relationship between clean, safe, and updated school facilities and student achievement, the importance of inspecting those facilities, designing and erecting new facilities, maintaining current and newly designed facilities, and finally, financing these

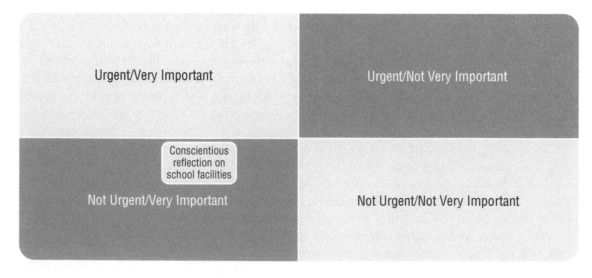

Figure 18.1 Administrator Reflection Grid

operations in a statewide budget crunch that highlights a $10 billion shortfall. Those communities and schools able to provide quality facilities, maintain the courage, and fortitude to press forward. This chapter will provide information to schools on improving facilities.

◆ INSPECTING AND EVALUATING FACILITIES

Developing the Facilities Planning Committee

The superintendent or designee should constantly monitor the school facilities. Of course the size of the district is a contributing variable in determining the level of participation in which the superintendent can and might be involved. Superintendents in smaller more centralized schools and districts might be more able to personally inspect the facilities. Irrespective of the size of the district, when analyzing the facility needs, the superintendent is wise to develop a facilities planning committee. Developing a facilities planning committee involves selecting a group of people in the district who are concerned about the structure and are willing to devote time and energy into improving the facilities.

The superintendent should carefully select the planning committee. The planning committee might include the superintendent or designee, campus level administration, teachers, staff, students, community members, business partners, and interested community constituents who have a vested interest and commitment in improving the facilities of the campus. The purpose of the planning committee would be to outline and develop a needs assessment, complete internal and external reviews, and use the results of the findings to design facilities that are safe, secure, and comfortable enough to aid in continuous student achievement

Needs Assessment

Once the planning committee is formed, a facility needs assessment would be completedby the planning committee. These members are citizens and employees who may not be the experts on designing facilities, but their perspectives can be valuable. The planning committee walks, inspects, and monitors the facilities to determine facility needs and improvements.After careful review and monitoring of facilities, the planning committee conducts the needs assessment, which is inclusive of internal and external reviews. Internal and external reviews can be conducted in several ways. For example, self-designed surveys can be developed by the committee so that each individual can analyze and evaluate what he or she inspects. When completed, the results of each evaluation can be combined and reviewed collectively to create a comprehensive list of needs. Narratives, checklists, and surveys are other examples of data collection tools that could be used to collect necessary data on facility needs. The committee could divide the facility into sections, and certain individuals could inspect their own sections for improvements. The needs assessment is critical and should be developed in a written, formal, and comprehensive manner. The completion of the needs assessment should involve key players in the district who have authority to begin the process, conduct the assessment, and finalize the plan.

Internal Review

The internal review might consist of spacing for students, classroom size, compliance with the educational specifications outlined in the Texas Education Code (TEC), Chapter 61, technology concerns, lighting, asbestos concerns, pest management, indoor air quality, ventilation, and thermal comfort. After these concerns have been addressed attention should be focused on interior design, cosmetics, and decor. The internal review could include a physical design that showcases an innovative and creative approach to address the needs of students, faculty, and the community, not only to satisfy immediate needs but also to address the needs of the internal publics and external publics for years to come. However, the members of the committee that might have the most impact on these decisions are the internal committee members most closely associated with the finished product. This approach to design school facilities considers the financial responsibility of the taxpayers who voted on this tax when they approved the bond.

External Review

The external review should consist of designs that satisfy the structure, appearance, quality, landscaping, and transportation necessities that are needed to route students in and out of buildings and control the flow of traffic. Included in this review consideration should be given to the leveling of grounds and runoff patterns needed to protect the property from wash outs and erosion. The external reviews beyond the structural designs are normally conducted and designed by architects and their professional staff and/or the construction managers. In other words, the external review, although just as important as the internal review, does not require as much attention to instructional needs and educational specifications. The external reviews are cosmetic, focused on property protection and centered on routing of students.

◆ FINANCING SCHOOL FACILITIES

Topics of conversation concerning financial position of public schools in Texas have been serious, controversial, and ongoing. The federal government, in the tenth Amendment to the Constitution, has left the states responsible for educating their own children. Although the federal government does participate, funding education is basically a state responsibility. Historically, court cases (see the chapter titled "Financing Texas Public Schools" in this edition) have resulted in many changes in the way our schools are financed. States have difference ways in which they finance education for the students they serve. However, many agree on one question—where should the money come from?

Financing school facilities is primarily a local function with some participation from the state. The school districts shoulder a large percentage of the funding. Moreover, some school districts receive very little facilities funding. Charter schools receive no facilities funding. Long term planning should be essential when developing a financial plan for building facilities. A demographic report determines how the population settles in the district. The report also produces a picture of where families settle, where property owners and taxpayers are located, and where anticipated growth will occur.

The local school district uses bond proceeds to aid in the funding of facilities. The Maintenance and Operations (M&O) part of the tax rate is used for operations and maintenance of facilities while the Interest and Sinking (I&S) tax rate is set by the Board of Trustees with voter approval to issue bonds. The state's participation in the financing of public school facilities includes providing funds through competitive grants and noncompetitive allotments, which come with qualification measures and deadlines. The grants and programs include the following:

- Bond Guarantee Program (BGP),
- Existing Debt Allotment (EDA), and
- New Instructional Facilities Allotment.

The BGP

The BGP is a Texas state program that uses the Permanent School Fund to protect bonds that have been properly handled and sold by public school districts. This bond protection guarantee must be approved by the commissioner of education. Currently, the guarantee receives "AAA" ratings from the major bond rating services and replaces the need for private bond insurance [Texas Education Agency(TEA), 2011].

> To participate in the BGP, districts must apply to the Texas Education Agency (TEA) and be approved by the commissioner of education. The TEA reviews each application according to statutory requirements and State Board of Education (SBOE) rules. This review includes making sure the application is complete and accurate and the district is financially sound. The TEA reviews the district's School FIRST [Financial Integrity Rating System of Texas is a financial report card created by the TEA from district financial data on revenue spending in the district] rating, its annual financial audit report, its accreditation status, and complaints. (TEA, 2011)

EDA

The EDA provides state assistance for bonded debt that is paid through I&S local tax effort. It provides tax rate equalization for local debt service taxes. By providing a guaranteed yield on I&S taxes levied by school districts to pay the principal of and interest on eligible bonds, the program guarantees a specific amount of state and local funds per student for each cent of tax effort up to $0.29 per $100 of assessed valuation. Currently, the guaranteed yield for EDA provides $35 per student in average daily attendance (ADA) per penny of tax effort. To receive EDA, districts must have issued bonds and paid on them as of August 31, 2005. In addition, districts must have had sufficient tax effort in 2004–2005 that currently must not exceed $0.50 per $100 of assessed valuation. Created by the Texas Legislature in 1999, the program operates without applications and has no award cycles (TEA, 2011). The EDA is adjusted and calculated for each district through the Foundation School Program.

New Instructional Facilities Allotment (NIFA)

The NIFA, birth from the IFA, is designed and introduced to help school districts finance instructional facilities that were going to be new to the district. Therefore, existing newly constructed instructional buildings would not qualify for participation in the NIFA application process. The purpose of the NIFA is to assist schools with the cost of constructing *new* instructional campuses. The buildings must be new structures. The funds may not be used for renovations or for the purchase of portable buildings. The TEC, §42.158, enacted by Senate Bill 4 of the 76th Texas Legislature in 1999, created the NIFA to assist public school districts and open-enrollment charter schools (TEA, 2011). The NIFA is provided for operational expenses associated with the opening of a new instructional facility and is available to all public school districts and open-enrollment charter schools that construct new instructional facilities that meet the requirements of the statute and rules(TEA, 2011). The 84th Legislative session ended in 2015 appropriating an additional $47.5 million for continuation of the NIFA. The IFA and the NIFA are formularized in the Foundation School Program.

Fund Balance to Finance Facilities

When districts are struggling to pass a bond election, having a healthy Fund Balance can aid in the plan of building school facilities. According to the School First ratings, schools are allowed to maintain a certain percentage of funds in Fund Balance, unless those funds have been designated for certain purposes. One of the purposes is capital improvements. When designated as capital improvements schools may use the available funds to construct facilities.

When districts are struggling financially to maintain a healthy Fund Balance, they might rely on passing a school bond to cover their facilities need. A school bond is a popular and appropriate avenue by which superintendents and school boards can finance a building project. Since passing a bond requires voter approval, the following section discusses the bond process.

Appropriations for facilities are constantly changing in Texas. For example, the eighty-second Legislature removed the Instructional Facilities Allotment and the Science Laboratory Grant Program. These funding programs are no longer available as of the 2011–2012 school year. However, preexisting applications are still being funded. The eighty-fourth Legislative session ended with an appropriation of $55.5 million through 2017 to aid schools with these applications.

◆ THE SCHOOL BOND

Since funding school facilities is a major issue for school districts as they struggle to balance budgets each school year, selling school bonds is one way that school districts can meet their capital project needs. This sectionis intended for those superintendents who are new to the office or for those who may want to refresh their memories on school bonds. The intent of this section is not to make the reader an expert in the field of school bonds. It is intended to become a source of knowledge and guidance for those who have the need to improve education for students and community members in schools they serve.

What Is a School Bond?

A school bond is a contract to repay borrowed money on a given date and to pay interest at an agreed rate. This contract is an agreement between a public school district and the lending institution. If the money were loaned to an individual, it would be a promissory note. Home mortgages are paid monthly while the bond is paid by the school district semiannually, usually in February and August. The school district may use the bond to cover the following costs:

- Construction projects,
- Other capital projects,
- Purchase of classroom furnishings,
- Technology,
- Purchase of land,
- In exchange for bonds (refunding), and
- Purchase of school buses.

A school district can issue bonds for almost any sort of permanent improvement or facility required for an educational program below college level.

How Does the Bond Work?

The bond issue is made up of individual bonds, which are usually in denominations of $5,000 each, which matures in installments, which is a mark of a "serial" bond issue. For example, a $5,000,000 bond could be in installments of ($5,000 × 1,000), which matures, say, 25 or 50 years, however, most school bonds mature in 20 years or less. Superintendents should seek advice from their bond adviser. No mortgage on property is given in the issuance of school bonds as such bonds are secured solely by a pledge of the ad valorem (property tax) taxing power of the district. The bonds are sometimes classified as tax bonds or "general obligation bonds," and sometime "municipal bonds." The TEC Chapter 20 outlines the information and uses of the bond.

A limited tax bond is limited to 10% of assessed valuation of taxable property. Unlimited tax bonds usually carry a lower interest rate. Total bonded debt is limited by the amount of the district's I&S tax rate, again with a maximum of $0.50 per $100.00 valuation. Constant consultation with architects, financial consultants, and bond attorneys cannot be stressed enough as they are the experts who deal with bond referendums as part of their professions.

Some bonds are Capital Appreciation Bonds. Capital Appreciation Bonds are defined as follows:

> A municipal security on which the investment return on an initial principal amount is reinvested at a stated compounded rate until maturity. At maturity the investor receives a single payment (the "maturity value") representing both the initial principal amount and the total investment return. CABs typically are sold at a deeply discounted price with maturity values in multiples of $5,000. CABs are distinct from traditional zero coupon bonds because the investment return is considered to be in the form of compounded interest rather than accreted original issue discount. For this reason only the initial principal amount of a CAB would be counted against a municipal issuer's statutory debt limit, rather than the total par value, as in the case of a traditional zero coupon bond. (Municipal Securities Rulemaking Board, 2015)

The 84th Legislative session concluded in 2015 with limitations on Capital Appreciation Bonds, which included the bonds must mature within 20 years of their issuance, districts must hold a written estimate of issuance costs, including principal and interest, outside vendor fees, the tax impact, and the amounts paid to financing team members, school boards must report to the Texas Ethics Commission any relationship that exist between a board member and bond underwriter, financial counselor or bond counselor, and finally, districts must post on websites a project financed with bond proceeds, the total amount of bond indebtedness, the total amount of the bond proceeds, the length of the maturity of the bonds, and the projects to be funded by the bond (Texas Association of School Administrators, 2015).

After the successful bond election, the district must adopt a plan of procedures for administration of the bond. This plan of procedures should include the sale of the bond. The sale can be conducted all at one time or over a period of time. In the sale of the bond, legal statutes call for competitive bidding. The bids are received from dealers who underwrite bonds, and the bids are submitted made on the basis of lowest "net interest cost."

After the bond sale and award to the best bidder, there is a great deal of work to be done, and it may be as long as 60 days before the bonds can be delivered and their cash proceeds received. At this juncture, it becomes necessary as a requirement of law to submit to the Attorney General of Texas for his examination and approval a complete transcript of all legal proceedings up to this point. The Constitution and laws must be followed, and the Comptroller of Public Accounts gets involved at this point. To this end, the bonds are stamped with a registration number, manually signed by the Comptroller, and are then ready to be delivered to the underwriters.

For small amounts, for example $5,000,000, delivery to the underwriters is usually accomplished at a bank in Austin. For large amounts, underwriters have specific delivery at a bank located in a Federal Reserve Center outside of Austin—usually in New York City. The bonds become "live" when the Comptroller signs them. At this point, the expense of shipping becomes high and includes insurance. After delivery, proceeds are paid to the district. The institutions who usually purchase the bonds are banks, trust fund handlers, Savings and Loan Associations, Insurance Companies, and in some cases wealthy individuals.

Superintendents and school districts should work diligently year to year to establish and maintain a strong financial position so that their chances of receiving high ratings on their bond sale are illuminated. This includes maintaining an exceptional tax collection history that reflects a consistently high percentage of collections from year to year, collecting delinquents, and filing legal claims against delinquents who refuse to pay. A reasonable surplus of funds should be maintained at all times in debt service funds to show strong financial position for repaying bonds. Finally, financial reporting should be adequate, and broad dissemination of financial information and financial position should be practiced.

Bond Election Processes

A bond election is a process that initiates with the local school board setting a date based on legal statues that require voter approval in November or May. Citizens participate in an election where a simple majority of the voters who expressed their right to vote can pass a bond election. Voters approve tax increases through the formal approval of specific referenda at the polls. The referenda must be designed for capital projects in the district (Agron, 2006). There are many timelines and technical requirements associated with bond elections; therefore, most superintendents use lawyers and bond agents to keep the district in compliance.

Importance of the Bond to School and Superintendent

Hickey and Vaughn (2010) professed "bond elections are often important to superintendents and school districts" (p. 91). Bond elections are important to superintendents and school districts because the bond monies represent a major avenue for paying debt, and passing a bond election adds merit to the superintendent's capabilities. The bond represents a major facility-building finance issue, which is without the bond, and the district might be incapable of producing the funds needed to construct district facilities. Bordelon (2005) also suggests that having the ability to hold a successful bond election is a vital part of the superintendent's skills.

Aging facilities, increasing student enrollments, and technological needs exacerbate the need to gain community support for capital improvement projects. Appropriate facilities are needed not only for the physical space they provide, but also because well maintained,appropriate buildings improve student achievement (Schneider, 2002).

How to Pass a School Bond

"The development of effective strategies for [passing] community school bond elections is becoming increasingly important" (Hickey, 2006, p. 146). Schools throughout the state are aging, and combined with increasing enrollment, having the money for capital improvements is important for providing a quality education. Hickey, Vaughn, Dunn, and Evans (2006, p. 26) offer three general steps in passing a bond election. Those steps include,

1. Getting the community involved,
2. Creating a shared vision of the capital improvement plan, and
3. Sharing that plan to all constituents.

Approximately 75% of the schools who hold bond elections are successful in gaining the community support needed for passage, and the strategies of these districts provide an outline for small schools that are planning their own referenda (Agron, 2006). Trust becomes one of the foremost factors in the ability to plan a successful bond election after prior failures (Hickey et al., 2006).

Research suggests that the most important factor in school bond success is trust in the leadership and good communication (Faltys, 2006; Hickey, 2006; Schrom, 2004). If the teachers lack confidence in the capital improvement plans, their impact extends beyond a personal vote (Hickey et al., 2006).

Successful Bond Planning in a Texas School District

Successful bond planning always starts with community involvement. The leadership of the school district should reach out to the community stakeholders and the Board of Trustees to inform them and involve them in the gathering of necessary data to determine the district needs. These needs will in turn establish the bond plan. The following steps represent a guideline that has proven to be successful for school districts across the state:

- Establish task force teams to assess existing facilities and growth potential in the school district,
- Establish mandates and timelines for these task force teams,
- Establish the final bond plan components,
- Establish an outline of necessary bond referendum events, and
- Promote the school bond referendum,

The responsibilities of the existing facility task force team will include initiating the following:

- Existing facilities review;
- Evaluating principal and maintenance questionnaires;
- Reviewing facilities assessments, which include a basic list of average daily attendance improvements, code corrections, and maintenance needs with corresponding construction costs;
- Prioritizing items and making recommendations on timelines; and
- Making recommendations on all new instructional and support space, including new building and additions to existing buildings.

Based on student growth, introduction of new facilities, additions, and portables, this committee establishes a 5-year staffing plan to support the new facilities and produces probable timeline for construction and staffing based on the velocity of enrollment growth.

The task force team is charged with identifying all needed improvements to existing elementary schools, junior high schools, high schools, and all district support facilities. The committee shall base its recommendations on a familiarity with basic curriculum and instructional delivery. The final report shall be a prioritized list of corrective work items with associated costs. The work items shall address all current needs and anticipated needs for the next 5 years. Specific facility issues that shall be addressed include:

- Compliance with federal, state and local building codes;
- Compliance with Americans with Disabilities Act;
- Identification of needed campus renovations to enhance the learning environment and ensure compliance with state and federal facility guidelines;
- Identification of major repairs needed and material replacements (i.e., roofing, carpet, and air conditioning systems); and
- Automated categorization of work items with recommendations for execution with bond proceeds or maintenance and operations funds.

The demographic and new facilities task force team is charged with the accurate interpretation and refinement of existing district demographic information followed by the development of a 5-year plan for new facility introduction. The final report shall include the following:

- Demographic information and ratios;
- Recommended start time for design;
- Start time for construction and date of completion of each new facility;
- An analysis of all currently owned district sites with recommendations for suitability for future use;
- Recommendation of geographic location of each new facility; and
- Best estimate for each new facility that is recommended including land acquisition and development costs.

The next step in finalizing the bond plan includes the following:

- Submit a final prioritized existing facilities improvement plan showing bond referendum work items with associated costs and recommended time frame for execution;
- Submit a final existing facilities document showing prioritized maintenance and operations expenditures during the next 5 years;
- Submit a final document showing the recommended bond referendum(s) during the next 10–12 years;
- Submit a property "Facility Plan" document showing size and general location of needed land acquisitions;
- Submit a new campus document showing schools needed with associated projected costs, location and start dates for design and construction, as well as final completion date;
- Submit a district-wide infrastructure expansion document showing any and all expansions to existing support facilities with associated costs and time frames; and
- Submit a financial proposal including implications with the "Facility Plan" showing recommended bond referendums, bond sales, and projected effects on tax rate.

After the bond plan has been finalized, the bond referendum is outlined so that communication can be made sharing the events of the bond process. The bond referendum outline would include the following steps.

STEP 1:   Time period—at least 100 days prior to the bond election. Citizen's Bond Committee transmits final bond referendum to Board of Trustees.

STEP 2: Time period—at least 100 days prior to the bond lection. Board of Trustees conducts workshop with architects and financial advisors to determine the final plan and most advantageous financing arrangements.

STEP 3: Time period—at least 90–100 days prior to the bond referendum.

At this juncture, the district contacts its bond attorney who furnishes the district with the proper board motion wording. Generally, the bond attorney will write out the entire motion.

STEP 4: Time period—at least 90 days prior to the bond election. The Board of Trustees "calls" the referendum in open session by having one of the trustees to make a motion, which ultimately is seconded and voted upon. Hopefully, it is a unanimous decision to proceed. The board member who makes the motion states it in the exact wording furnished to him/her by the bond attorney.

STEP 5: Time period—at least 80–90 days prior to the bond election the bond referendum committee reorganizes and becomes the bond promotion committee.

STEP 6: Time period—day 0. Bond Election Day.

STEP 7: Time period—7 days after bond referendum. Board of Trustees meet in open session to canvas the votes.

STEP 8: Time period—8 days after bond referendum. District's financial advisor is contacted and prepares bidding documents for the first bond sale.

STEP 9: Time period—60 days after bond referendum. Proceeds from first bond sale are available to district.

In promoting the school bond referendum, the following steps are offered as a plan of action for a successful venture.

Planning

STEP 1: Form a Citizens Committee to oversee the entire effort:
A. The group should consist of ~10–30 people and should include the following:
1. Influential community leaders;
2. City council member(s), mayor(s), etc.;
3. Chamber of commerce official(s);
4. County official(s);
5. CEO's of corporations or institutions in the district;
6. Reporter(s) from the local newspaper(s);
7. Former respected school board members;
8. Parent/teacher association presidents or representatives from several campuses (preferably all campuses);
9. Interested and motivated citizens from the community;
10. Consider placing an advertisement in the local paper inviting any interested citizen to participate;
11. The group should be given a name (i.e., Citizens for Quality Education).

STEP 2: Schedule a general "kick-off" meeting:

A. Assemble the list of names from Step 1, schedule a "kick-off meeting" and construct a personal invitation letter signed by the President of the Board of Trustees inviting each person to the first meeting.

STEP 3: Call a Citizens Committee meetings:
A. Coordinate and schedule ~3–4 planning meetings with the Citizens Committee.

Promotion

Bond promotion must come from the community, and this is why community involvement is especially critical. School employees, including superintendents and school board members, are vital for support, but they cannot and must not advocate the passing of the bond. They can, however, promote the facts of the bond.

STEP 4: Conduct the first meeting of the group. At this meeting, the following should be accomplished:
A. As the first order of business, a chairperson should be selected, or elected. (Ideally, the chairperson should be selected prior to the meeting by the administration and board. Arrange for the chairperson to be nominated at the first meeting.)
B. Immediately after election of the chairperson, the meeting should be "turned over" to the new chair.
C. The goals of the Citizens Group should be communicated to the group by the new chairperson.
D. The chairperson should then form the following subcommittees:
1. Speakers Bureau:
The Speakers Bureau should be formed to arrange for speakers to present the bond election information to local civic groups, such as the Rotary Club, Lions Club, church groups, and other similar organizations.
2. Publicity subcommittee:
Responsible for placing ads in local newspapers, football programs, etc.
3. Finance subcommittee:
A finance subcommittee should be formed to secure donations from local area businesses and individuals. These proceeds will be used to fund bond promotion literature, brochures, local newspaper ads, etc.
4. Telephone Committee:
A Telephone Committee should be formed to make telephone contact with as many voters as possible during the 3 days prior to the election. This committee is extremely important in that it would be the last opportunity to explain the proposed bond election to the voters prior to election day.

STEP 5: Conduct the first meeting of the group. The following should be accomplished:
A. A chairperson for each subcommittee should be elected.

STEP 6: Set goals and objectives. Each subcommittee should set goals and objectives and meet weekly for 4–6 weeks prior to the bond election.

◆ THE ARCHITECT'S ROLL IN A TEXAS SCHOOL DISTRICT

Any building that houses students should be designed to resist an immense amount of daily wear and tear while retaining its functional integrity for many years. To assure this type of functional integrity, the best architects should be a part of the district's long-range facility planning team. Every school district superintendent and/or assistant superintendent at some time in their tenure with a school district will realize the need to hire an architect design professional. School district personnel should be constantly studying district growth trends, curriculum trends, and stakeholders' philosophies. Every construction project that arises, whether triggered by a demographic study, a long range facilities master plan, or a new mandate from the State Legislature or from the TEA all planning should be centered around curriculum as the primary concern.

Locating a design professional who understands the curriculum project principle and places that principle above all else can be quite a daunting task. It is imperative that the school district seeks and employs a competent school designer, based on his or her educational experience, quality, and standards. Developing a strong, positive relationship early in the building process is paramount. The superintendent and school board would be wise to take full advantage of the services offered by the professional architect. The architect needs to be involved in the construction process early in the designing, buildings, and assessing stages.

District knowledge is paramount for a designer. The more knowledge of the district the architect as designer possesses the closer the relationship could be with the district. To this end, the architect would be wise to concentrate on the issues of equity in the building process and across the district with students and employees and also engage stakeholders while completing the building process. The architect should be examining the school district's demographics, student enrollment, boundaries, and growth trends. He/she should be familiar with each facility in the school district and understand the functioning of the grade level alignments, as well as district, curriculum and capacity of each school.

Equity/Parity

One of the most stringent needs across any school district is equity among similar facility types. It is of utmost importance that each student in the school district be afforded the same opportunities and that those opportunities are facilitated in similar physical environments. TEA updated and published a system of educational specifications and guidelines in 2004 that serve as standards for school districts to use in regards to space sizes and planning (see Appendix).

Again research supports that the buildings in which students learn and teachers teach have an incredibly huge influence on success (Schneider, 2002). There are many factors that come into play other than space planning that effect educational equity. For example, if a new elementary school opens in the school district, it will have to meet the criteria set forth in the TEA guidelines. There may be some older facilities that have smaller classrooms that do not meet TEA guidelines. This type of difference from campus to campus may not be the priority for equity as long as the buildings have the same number of teaching spaces. If that same elementary school opens and it has new science labs with the most up to date technology integrated into the facility, and the older facilities do not, the stakeholders whose children attend the older school might voice an opinion about denying equitable access to educational opportunities as compared to the children who attend the newer facility. Consequently, it is paramount for superintendents and school boards to give consideration to these issues across the board when planning building projects. Moreover, an architect who does not possess the knowledge of how curriculum shapes the district facilities plan would not be a good fit in the district's short- or long-term facilities plan.

Engaging the Stakeholders

A school district superintendent needs to remain abreast and informed about the community's desires. Community members' concerns are also key to the success of any facility planning project. Having an architect who understands the importance of connecting to the community and who portrays the professionalism and discretion it involves should be considered when selecting the architect. Planning a new school facility project or renovations to an existing one should involve the community. Promoting transparency is extremely important, and without it the project suffers. The more involved the stakeholders of the school district feel, the more likely they are to support future efforts to facilitate the need of changes, growth, and modifications to district facilities. More important, the more community members are involved in the building project, the more they are ready to support future bond elections.

Employing architects based on their qualifications, past performance, character, honesty, and knowledge is the fundamental step in facilities planning. Such a proactive approach to heading off problems set the stage for a professional relationship with the architect. This relationship will afford a school district the opportunity to evaluate several architects, their references, and even interview them before contracting with them. An open selection process is advisable because this will also provide a process of diligence that can be reported to concerned stakeholders and members of the Board of Trustees in a public forum.

◆ TRANSPARENCY

Some school districts are large enough to maintain many projects simultaneously. Some may be able to employ more than one architect. This strategy is not a bad idea if a school district has an administrative person whose job is to manage the facility projects with different architects. In either scenario, the architects hired should be evaluated for more that their ability to create architectural masterpieces that shows the latest design trends for any type of building. The architect should be curriculum and student driven in all design principals and be willing to go the extra mile for the school district and the community. However, a school district establishes criteria the selection for an architect, the relationship should be one of a teaming spirit, open lines of communication, and the intent to last. Understanding the importance of the relationship and how they impact the school district community is critical for the architect. Once the architect has been selected, a school district can now focus on the basic architectural services required to move forward with any building project.

When superintendents and school boards employ architects, they must hold these architects to high standards. Architects are trained and are responsible to the school and the school's project. Therefore, they must be held accountable for the huge part they play in making the joint venture as successful and faultless as possible. Architectural professional services include but are not limited to the following:

- Master planning,
- Programming,
- Schematic design,

- Design development,
- Construction document production,
- Management of the procurement process (commonly known as bidding),
- Construction administration, and
- Project closeout (refer to the section on how to successfully turn a completed building project over to the end user).

Master Planning

Master planning of a school district begins with facility assessments of each facility owned by the school district. The existing district information is a starting point to assess district needs. This process involves a lot of time and coordination of district facility personnel as well as the architect's time. Every school building will need to be analyzed for its building and systems condition. Every school building will also need to be analyzed for its educational condition. School capacity is critical in a master plan. Each school is able to house a maximum number of students.

TEA has set forth in the 2004 educational specifications of TEC Chapter 61 the number of students that should be taught at one time in a single classroom. For example, in the fifth grade the TEA sets a 700 ft^2 classroom as a minimum and recommends a teacher-to-student ratio of 22 students per teacher in classroom. If one is confirming student capacity of the entire facility, simply multiply the number of classrooms for that grade level in the facility by 22. Table 18.1 outlines the required educational specifications.

For example, the facility may have 36 classrooms total so the capacity would be 792 if the facility functioned at 100% capacity in 100% of the rooms for 100% of the time. Take the 792 and multiply it by 0.85 just to give the students some breathing room. So the final result in this example is 673.

This information is critical because it needs to be compared to the current district enrollment and also to the current district demographic study for growth trends over the next 10 years or 20 years and so on. Master planning truly takes place when a complete facility assessment of every building is conducted, and a working student capacity study is completed and compared to the district enrollment numbers over a working period of time. For example, in an elementary school with a student capacity of 673, the current working demographic study for the school district may indicate that same boundary area for the elementary school will increase by 5% per year over the next 6 years, then dwindles to 2% per year for the next 14 years (and these trends can change before any of it comes to fruition).

After the increase of 5% per year for 6 years, the capacity of that elementary school facility will need to be 900 students. That will have significant results for the school district because the information dictates some form of action plan. An increase in student volume of these 227 students cannot be ignored. Some things a school district can consider is a adding to the existing facility the 11 classrooms and support rooms necessary by TEA and local codes to facilitate the growth. Another option is more global to the entire district. If there are some facilities that the master plan reveals to be underutilized, a new boundary plan can be drawn up and approved so the student population can shift into classroom spaces across the district without building, or a combination of both.

The scenarios are endless, but it should be obvious to a school district administrator how important it is to evaluate school facility capacity and compare it to the current working demographic study for the district. It is paramount that the architect selected understands this

TABLE 18.1
TEA School Facility Space Planning Guideline Based on the Texas Administrative Code, Title 19, Part 2, Chapter 61, Subchapter CC, Rule 61.10316

(Elementary School–Pre-K Through Grade 5 or Grade 6)

Space Type	Grade Level	Minimum Square Footage Required	Square Footage Per Student	Comments
General classroom	PK–1	800	36	22 student capacity
General classroom	2–6	700	32	22 student capacity
Dedicated computer classroom	PK–6	900	36	25 student capacity
Supporting computer lab	PK–6		25	Per work station or 20 ft² per laptop
Special education classroom	PK–6	400	40	10 student capacity
Gymnasium	PK–6	3,000		
Combination science lab/classroom	2–6	900	41	22 student capacity
Small science class	2–6	700	41	17 student capacity
Science classrooms w/ no science lab	2–6	700	32	22 student capacity
Science lab w/ no general classroom instruction	2–6	800	36	22 student capacity
Small science classroom w/ no science lab	2–6		32	
Small science lab	2–6	600	36	17 student capacity

process and be able to perform it and presents it in a way that is effective and transparent. School districts are not required to utilize the services of an architect to master plan their school district facility needs, but architects working for a school client in any capacity should have the expertise.

A district may choose to perform this study with their own resources and staff or hire a different type of planning consultant. Although no state agency of Texas requires that a licensed architect perform master planning for a school district, the law does require districts to hire a licensed architect to design and manage any building projects that result from such a study.

Programming

Once the district master plan is in place, the architect can take that information and begin to organize crews to perform the work. In the earlier example of the elementary school with a student capacity of 673 students, we determined a need for 11 classrooms in just 5 years. The architect will need to determine what spatial needs are required and what the district standards are to create this program. A building program is a list of all of the spaces in a building and what the Additional Spaces should be. District-wide equity will come into play here for the architect as the program evolves.

One has to consider the district philosophy of curriculum, the use of each teaching space, and the adequacy of support facilities, i.e., restrooms and storage rooms. It is the architect's responsibility to seek out each item that will affect building needs and what the individual spaces could be. All of these components are listed and evaluated according to the educational specifications required by the statutes. TEA requires this documentation as a check and balance that new facilities are designed to meet and satisfy their guidelines and standards. Those standards are illustrated in Tables 18.1–18.3. The programming phase also affords the district with an opportunity to reach out to the end users of the facility for input creating another layer of transparency and trust.

TABLE 18.1
TEA School Facility Space Planning Guideline Based on the Texas Administrative Code, Title 19, Part 2, Chapter 61, Subchapter CC, Rule 61.10316
(High School–Grade 9 or 10 Through Grade 12, or Only Grade 9)

Space Type	Grade Level	Minimum Square Footage Required	Square Footage Per Student	Comments
General classroom	9–12	700	28	25 student capacity
Dedicated computer classroom	9–12	900	36	25 student capacity
Supporting computer lab	9–12		25	Per work station or 20 ft² per laptop
Special education classroom	9–12	400	40	10 student capacity
Gymnasium	9–12	7,500		
Combination science lab/classroom	9–12	1,400	58	24 student capacity
Small science class	9–12	1,100	58	19 student capacity
Science classrooms w/ no science lab	9–12	700		24 student capacity
Science lab w/ no general classroom instruction	9–12	1,000	42	24 student capacity
Small science classroom w/ no Science Lab	9–12		32	
Small Science Lab	9–12	800	42	17 student capacity

TABLE 18.2
TEA School Facility Space Planning Guideline Based on the Texas Administrative Code, Title 19, Part 2, Chapter 61, Subchapter CC, Rule 61.10316
(Middle School–Grade 6 Through Grade 8 or 9, or Only Grade 6)

Space Type	Grade Level	Minimum Square Footage Required	Square Footage Per Student	Comments
General classroom	6–8 or 9	700	28	25 student capacity
Dedicated computer classroom	6–8 or 9	900	36	25 student capacity
Supporting computer lab	6–8 or 9		25	Per work station or 20 ft² per laptop
Special education classroom	6–8 or 9	400	40	10 student capacity
Gymnasium	6–8 or 9	4,800		
Combination science lab/classroom	6–8 or 9	1,200	41	24 student capacity
Small science class	6–8 or 9	950	50	19 student capacity
Science classrooms w/ no science lab	6–8 or 9	700		24 student capacity
Science lab w/ no general classroom instruction	6–8 or 9	900	36	24 student capacity
Small science classroom w/ no Science Lab	6–8 or 9		32	
Small science lab	6–8 or 9	700	38	17 student capacity

Schematic Design

The American Institute of Architects document B101 Standard form of Agreement Between Owner and Architect defines the required *Schematic Design Process* as the stage in the project where the architect prepares a preliminary evaluation of the school district's program, schedule budget for the cost of the work, project site, and the proposed procurement or delivery method for the construction phase of the project (refer to the section "Construction Delivery Methods for Texas Schools").

The architect must begin to produce preliminary floor plans and site studies at this point to begin demonstrating to the owner how the building should work and how the site will function as a result of the program needs. Parking requirements, driveways, deliveries, security, and visitor circulation are but a few major needs to be studied on a school site during this phase. Important questions to ask are

TABLE 18.3
TEA School Facility Space Planning Guideline Based on the Texas Administrative Code, Title 19, Part 2, Chapter 61, Subchapter CC, Rule 61.10316
(Libraries for All Grade Levels)

Library will include the following minimum requirements

- Reading/instructional area
- Reference/independent study area
- Stack area
- Circulation desk and/or area
- Computer/online reference area
- Necessary ancillary areas, such as offices, workstations, and head-end room

Space size requirements are based on student enrollment and are as follows

- 100 students: 1,400 ft²
- 101–500 students: 1,400 ft² plus 4 ft² per student in access of 100
- 501–2,000 students: 3,000 ft² plus 3 ft² per student in access of 500

  2,001 plus students: 7,500 ft² plus 2 ft² per student in access of 2,000

Notes: If library contains >12 computers, add 25 ft² per computer in access of 12. The percentage of space types in a library shall be as follows: 30% for reading/instructional area and reference/independent study area; 45% for stack area, circulation desk/area, and computer/online reference areas; and 25% for necessary ancillary spaces.

1. Does the site mix parent traffic with bus traffic?
2. What about the delivery of food products to the kitchen area?
3. Where are the playgrounds located . . . in a safe area away from the traffic?

Site lighting needs will need to be discussed also. A clear concept plan with a cost estimate is the goal. During this phase, the architect is likely to ask a school district for an approval, which will actually be required by the contract language before the architect can then move on to the next phase of the project.

Design Development

The drawings and plans being produced by the architect will begin to take shape in this phase. It is the responsibility of the architect in the *design development phase* of the work to demonstrate, illustrate, and describe the completed development of the approved *schematic design phase*. The documents deliverable to the owner shall contain but not be limited to the following:

1. Drawings of floor plans to scale with dimensions;
2. Drawings of elevations and building sections to scale;
3. Typical wall section drawings and construction details to scale;
4. An outline of all of the specified building materials and operational systems;
5. Complete plans showing those building system concepts, such as structural drawing concepts;

6. Mechanical and electrical system concepts; and
7. Technology system concepts and civil engineering concepts that are required for a complete project.

The architect will also be required to update a cost estimate for the project and compare it to the budget. School districts are struggling financially. Revenues are decreasing, and expenditures are increasing rapidly. This inverse relationship is making it difficult for districts to maintain a workable budget. Therefore, it is critical that a district holds the architect designing a project accountable to the budget that was proposed at the beginning of the project. Nothing will destroy trust more than violating the transparency established in the master planning stages than cost overruns on a project. The more information the architect can produce for the owner in this phase, the better the planning and results will be in the end. It will be very important for the architect to sit down with the school district at this point also and go over project schedule in a very detailed format.

Again, school districts are very unique in many ways, and project schedules are one of the most critical concepts for a project team to understand. Facilities are needed on time for the start of school. The school district will need a team in place (architect and contractor) that understands the project schedule concept and has built the project schedule around this very urgency. Once all of these items are reviewed with the owner and the owner has given the architect approval, it will be time to advance to the next phase.

Construction Documents Phase

In the *construction documents phase*, the architect has to prepare all of the technical drawings and specifications by which the bidding and the construction of the project are realized. These documents must be very accurate and represent every trade of work required to complete the construction. For example, if the project requires cabinets, then each cabinet required must be drawn and detailed. This phase of the architect's design will take the longest period of time on the schedule. It should take about 3 months for an architect to produce a good set of construction documents for an average elementary school. That will depend largely on the procurement method that is being utilized as well.

Construction documents referred to in the simplest vernacular are nothing more than a complete set of instructions by which a contractor constructs a complete building. Getting to the completed result, however, takes an extreme amount of coordination, review, and old fashioned hard work on the part of the architect and design team. An architect will have to hire certain consultants as part of the scope of work, such as a mechanical engineer, an electrical engineer, a civil engineer, and a structural engineer. Typically, the architect will proceed with this hiring when his/her services are retained. The National Council of Architectural Registration Board defines construction documents as follows: "construction documents are the written and graphic instructions used for construction the project. These documents must be accurate, consistent, complete and understandable." These documents will also contain the bidding requirements that must be carried out by the contractors, inclusive of general condition, bonding, and insurance requirements.

Once the construction documents are completed, the architect will need to review them with the owner for quality assurance reasons and scope compliance. The owner is responsible to confirm the required scope of the project prior to the project being released for bids. The owner is not responsible for the technical accuracy of how that scope is demonstrated in the architect's specifications and drawings. Neither is the owner responsible if the contractor covers this issue in his bid. Once the owner acknowledges that the architect understands the scope of the project and has reviewed the drawings, he can then approve the release of the construction documents for the bidding phase.

Bidding

During the course of architect's preparation of the construction documents, the architect will ask for review sets to be printed and reviewed with the owner. This typically occurs at 25%, 50%, and 75% and just before the drawings are released for bidding, about completion. The architect is responsible to update the cost estimate at these phases also. This should eliminate the "fear of the unknown" prior to the bidding of the project. The way the bidding phase unfolds is highly dependent on the procurement method selected for the project. Refer to the section "Construction Delivery Methods for Texas Schools." Basically, the architect's responsibilities are to assist the owner in the following:

1. Obtaining competitive bids or proposals,
2. Confirming responsiveness and completeness of bids or proposals,
3. Evaluating to determine the successful proposer, and
4. Awarding and preparing contracts for construction.

Once all of the bidding process is complete, no matter what construction delivery method is used (except for design/build), the architect is responsible to evaluate the bidding process and compare the drafted bid pricing to the original budget and the current approved cost estimate. If the total pricing for the complete cost of the work as represented in the construction documents does not exceed the cost estimate and budget, the project is normally a go at that point. If the total pricing works out for more than the budget, the owner has a few options to allow some adjustment in the scope or in the budget depending on which is appropriate. With an understanding of prices being evaluated, the project can move forward into the construction phase.

Construction Administration Phase

Once the project is "bid" and a contract price is approved by the school district, the two parties must enter into a contract. A notice to proceed is then issued by the architect on behalf of the owner to the contractor giving notification that the clock is ticking on the agreed construction schedule. A new elementary school may take up to 14 months to build, depending on geographic location, but in recent years, the trend has been faster paced construction schedule requirements. The construction administration phase involves the architect's participation almost as much as the contractor. In this phase, the architect's responsibilities are numerous in that they must constantly check the work that is being constructed as planned. Although the architect is not directly responsible for the contractor's construction means, methods, techniques, sequences, or procedures he is responsible to visit the site at intervals appropriate to the stage of construction and be familiar with the progress and quality of the portion of the work completed. The architect shall be responsible to determine that the work observed does conform to the construction documents that were produced.

There are several procedural things that take place by the architect to accomplish this. It is critical that the architect and the contractor have a good working relationship throughout the process. A teaming collaborative environment will result in a successful project. Construction excites the community, and stakeholders of the school district will be interested in how things are progressing on the job site. The community will be interested in the answers to the following three questions:

- Will the job be finished on time?
- Are we in budget?
- Did we get everything we are supposed to get?

School districts keep the community actively informed by regularly posting reports and construction photos on their websites. Since the community will be very aware of the construction phase, it is important to hire a contractor that is a "good neighbor." It helps a great deal when the neighborhoods surrounding the school or construction zone are informed about deliveries that may block the street from time to time, or the occasional extreme noise that is associated with certain phases of construction. Information on the continuing development of the project will be appreciated by your stakeholders. The architect should also be willing to assist in presentations and reports that help the school district relay information to the public as they manage each sequence of the construction administration phase.

Owner Occupancy

Before the architect agrees that the contractor should be released from responsibilities certain things need to take place. The architect will help coordinate training of new systems with the appropriate school district personnel. For example, kitchen equipment should be tested well before operational training is even considered. A school kitchen has several components, and just like every industry, technological advances make them more efficient and safer, but always with differences in operation that need to be explained. Every system in the building must undergo the same type of process. Every lockable door, every cabinet, or storage system requires sequencing for keying, keeping in mind that not everyone in the building will need access to the same rooms or supplies. Once the school district takes over the facility and agrees it is complete, there is a 1-year warranty period on everything in the building for which the contractor is responsible. This will give the owner time to test the building while it is in operation. For example, the heating systems in a Texas school building may not need to be operational in August. By contrast, the air-conditioning system will certainly need to be tested, and if someone's classroom is not cooling properly the architect should be notified immediately. The architect will issue a warranty request to the contractor to take immediate action to correct any minor problems that occur. In the cold months when the heating system is usually maximized, the warranty is still active. At this point in the project, the main goal should be to ensure student and teacher comfort so the educational process can be realized in the most pleasant environment.

◆ CONSTRUCTION DELIVERY METHODS FOR TEXAS SCHOOLS

Modern school systems face special issues with the need for economical, adaptable, and efficient accommodations. The majority of public and private schools around the country face a student population that is growing faster than ever, leading to overflowing classrooms in spite of dwindling construction budgets. What is the best school construction method to choose when the district is struggling with passing bond elections, busting at the seams with increasing student populations, and financial constraints that are forcing dismissal of instructional staff?

This section emphasizes the existing trends within the facilities project delivery systems in Texas for public schools and illuminates the debate concerning advantages and disadvantages of these construction procurement methods. Project delivery methods and more generally the procurement policies that currently drive the management of the Texas infrastructure system are examined. Historically, these methods have ranged from combined procurement of the design, construction, operation, and maintenance of a facility to the separate procurement of these services (Pietroforte & Miller, 2010). According to Pietroforte and Miller (2010), the last 50 years have experienced a shift toward the exclusive reliance on separate procurement, such as *Design Build* and the use of public funding. However, the increasing needs of the existing infrastructure system make it practically impossible to sustain this approach. In Texas, a combination of construction procurement mixed with public funding is usually necessary.

There are five approved methods for school facility project contractor selection and construction procurement. Each method offers a unique frame of reference by which to develop a public funded construction project in the state of Texas. The five construction procurement methods are as follows:

- DesignBuild,
- Construction Manager at Risk (CMR) (or Construction Manager as Contractor),
- Construction Manager as Agent,
- Competitive Bidding (also known as Design/Bid/Build), and
- Competitive Sealed Proposals (CSPs).

Each of the five methods has an appropriate application and mandatory framework required by Texas statues. The method for the owner to choose depends on (1) the type of project under consideration, (2) the means by which the project will be funded, and (3) the required schedule that drives completion of the project.

Design Build

When a facility project is predominately schedule driven, the district has arrived at a point to begin negotiating costs, phased construction prior to completion of design drawings from their Architect have concluded, and a final cost agreement has been reached, the *Design Build* method is appropriate. The *Design Build* method of construction procurement allows the owner to award a single contract to a design/build company, usually a general contractor, to hire a design professional directly under their contract and begin work almost immediately. This arrangement requires the *Design Build* company to assume all responsibility for the design, bidding, and construction of the project. The *Design Build* method promotes a team concept and provides the owner with selection flexibility based on the qualifications of *Design Build* companies rather than wait to hire a contractor based on a proposal amount for the cost of the work.

A company selected under this arrangement will develop the cost of the work with the owner's approval based on the project scope requirements. This "early" formulation of the cost of the work, known as a guaranteed maximum price (GMP), will allow the owner to evaluate the scopeof the project and decide to add scope or deduct scope as needed. In addition, the owner escapes worrying about cost overruns. The contractor is responsible for the design, bidding, and schedule; therefore, the GMP is an absolute. A major advantage of this type of procurement model is the peaceful arrangement and agreement shared by the architect and contractor. Another advantage to this method is the schedule. *Design Build* is a fast-track delivery method that saves time, and saving time means saving money.

There are some disadvantages of selecting *Design Build* as a construction procurement. The disadvantages include having no quality control checks and reviews between the architect and builder. This lack of quality control could means the standard on quality of design might not be met. Under these conditions, it is highly possible that the final design may not be achieved or approved by the owner before the GMP is formulated. To this end, there are some important questions superintendents and school boards must ponder when deciding to accept and approve *Design Build* construction procurements. The questions include:

1. Can a succinct, informal review of a *Design Build* schematic plan provide enough accurate information for the superintendent and school board to make an intelligent decision about the building project?
2. Have the owner controlled the quality of the final product since the GMP will be based on a "minimum criteria standard" set forth in the contract between the owner and design builder?

The question for the novice superintendent and the superintendent who has practiced for many years is, When does a district chose the *Design Build* process? A *Design Build* project should be chosen when a project does not demand a large amount of professional design capability, the schedule is extremely crunched, and a construction manager in which the district has paramount confidence and impeccable trust can by employed.

CMR

The CMR delivery method is arguably the most popular method of constructing school facility projects across the state of Texas. The contract term for a CMR is Construction Manager as Contractor. This delivery method requires the construction manager to assume all risk for the construction of each trade while meeting the GMP.

A school district may select a construction manager based on qualifications rather than a low bid. Under this arrangement, the owner is allowed to hire the construction manager before the design drawings are completed requiring them to give cost estimates and constructability reviews to the architect's and engineer's construction documents before they are released for bids. This process is called preconstruction services. Preconstruction services include completing the drawings before the building process begins, allowing the construction manager to consult the design professionals, and creating a team approach among the owner, architect, and contractor. The architect does not work directly for the contractor in CMR; therefore, he or she should be held accountable to the owner for quality control and program scope. Perhaps this level of accountability is why CMR has gained so much popularity among owners.

Constructing projects with public funding demands accountability and transparency to the stakeholders. An advantage for CMR is that it offers accountability to the owner during design and construction. In selecting the CMR method, the owner is required to utilize the CSP procurement method for all trade contracts. It is the construction manager's responsibility to manage all advertising and solicitation of trade and subcontractors to implement the CSPs. Once the proposals are submitted and opened, they are reviewed openly with the owner and the architect to review pricing and quality of service they wish to provide. Each trade contractor should relay their understanding of the scope of the work required in the proposal. Upon completion of the initial process, the construction manager is required to produce the GMP.

The CMR construction procurement method is well suited for large, complex construction projects when the owner hires an architect to program the scope of the project around a fixed budget. CMR works well for tricky renovation and addition projects because the construction manager can help solve phasing issues during the design phase. Historically, these projects have substantiated a slight premium to pay due to a more selective bidding process for trade contractors, and also for the construction manager of having prior knowledge about phasing-budget and responsibility for constructability reviews of the construction documents. Results support that fewer change orders will be necessary.

Competitive Bidding (Design-Bid-Build, DBB)

The DBB method is the most traditional method of construction procurement for public school districts in the state of Texas. The DBB was operable before Texas Senate Bill 583 opened the door for other procurement methods. Using the DBB process, a school district can establish criteria for best value selection of a contractor. In the early stages of the building process, the owner hires an architect to program and design a project. Next, the architect manages the procurement process for a general contractor. Once the architect completes the design process and all contract documents, including the project manual, technical specifications, and construction drawings, advertisements are published to the general contractor community to ignite the bidding process.

The DBB is highly competitive in that general contractors are required to submit their qualifications and a complete insured bid price. The bid price from each general contractor is ranked, and qualifications are compared. The bids are graded against the criteria set forth by the school district, and the best value for the school district is then awarded the contract for construction of the project. Prior to Senate Bill 583, the general contractor with the lowest bid price had to be selected. This selection limited the owner's option for selecting the most qualified general contractor.

It is important to note that the contract must be awarded at the bid price. The owner cannot negotiate the contract price or does the owner have the right to review any of the subcontractors or trade contractor contracts or bids. Subcontractor bids and contracts are private information and documents privy only to the general contractor. An advantage of the DBB delivery method is that it has a history of being the most economical. This method is best utilized when an owner has a lengthy schedule that allows the architect and his design team to produce complete, accurate drawings and specifications. Any omissions form the architect's plans could result in change orders (extra costs) at the end of the project. The DBB carries no GMP.

CSP

CSP is similar to the *Competitive Bidding Process*. An architect is selected initially to program and design the school project. The architect then prepares a complete set of contract documents and again, accuracy is paramount. Once the documents are prepared and reviewed, the owner then publishes a Request for Proposalsfor the general contractor community to solicit price and qualifications. The school district should establish a set criteria so the general contractor can be selected based on "best value" for the school district construction project. It is important to note that in this process the owner can note in the contract documents that they have the right to reject any or all proposals based on the established criteria. Announcing this right allows some flexibility in contractor selection.

Once the pricing and qualifications are evaluated and a general contractor is selected, a post proposal negotiation is allowed. The owner may modifyscope, or value engineer scope to reduce the contract cost, or have discussions about schedule. If an agreement cannot be reached between the contractor and the owner, the owner has the right to terminate those negotiations for due cause and move on to the next most qualified, best value proposer/general contractor. This entire process can be managed by the owner's architect, or the owner's representative and the architect.

CSP has proven to be a very cost-effective way to produce new projects for simple additions that do not require a lot of construction evaluation prior to the drawings being completed. This process does in some cases require more time on the production schedule for drawings, and there is no cost estimating or constructability reviews from a construction manager. The architect is responsible for cost estimates, and the owner may hire third-party reviewers in the form of a cost estimator or constructability quality control plans reviewer.

Construction Manager Agent (CMA)

Although the title construction manager is still utilized for this process, CMA is quite different than CMR. CMA is intended to represent the owner as agent; basically, the owner's purchasing agent. The distinguishing component is fairly simple: a CMA may not perform any construction work. CMAs can manage all phases of the design completely through the construction process as long as there is no engaging in construction. The CMA facilitates the owner's hiring of each of the trade contractor's and manages the trade contractors on the project site. Duties of a CMA are typically outlined in the contract to provide the following:

- Cost estimating,
- Constructability reviews during the design process,
- On-site construction management,
- Administrative personnel,
- Payment and performance bonds of each contractor,
- Equipment, and
- Utilities.

They may also include minor field labor noninclusive of any required trade contractor work. If a school district decides to utilize a CMA for the construction delivery method, the school district will be required to hire a full-time general contractor. In addition, all of the trade contractors are contracted directly with the owner. Each of these contractors required to complete the construction project must be procured by method in accordance with state law, such as the aforementioned processes. The CMA does give the owner the ability to hire everyone working on the project directly and allows for fast-track delivery. It allows for flexibility in bidding packages of certain pieces of scope. Some trades can be procured by the design-build method, by the design-bid build method, by direct CSPs, etc. If a school district has a general contractor-minded person to manage these processes simultaneously with the CMA, it proves to be an extremely effective method, both in terms of cost and schedule.

◆ MAINTAINING SCHOOL FACILITIES

The local school board has the authority to set two different tax rates per $100.00 valuation on property values within the school district zone. The I&S tax rate is calculated and set for debt service. The M&O tax rate is set for maintaining and operating the school district, and this revenue collection can be used for almost any expenses occurred within the district. Maintenance of the school district encompasses cleaning, painting, repairing, protecting, and maintaining the facilities in the best condition possible. Operations include the activities, processes, procedures, and day-to-day necessities of running a school district. The M&O tax rate is used to collect local funds to cover the cost of maintaining and operating school facilities. This discussion concerns maintaining school facilities.

Maintaining school facilities is a major chore. A dedicated, energetic, and hardworking custodial staff would be perfect for daily cleaning and routinely painting and maintaining buildings. Of course maintenance planning is funded from the M&O side of the school district's budget. This is actually what separates maintenance planning from capital improvements. Districts usually have a maintenance reserve fund for unexpected expenses, and they depend on risk management funds to cover major disasters.

Deferred Maintenance

Deferred maintenance includes a maintenance project needed to be completed but cannot be completed within the current budget year. Deferred projects are put on hold until the following school year. One reason for the deferment could be lack of funds to accomplish the task. Another reason could be lack of a commitment from administration of the school board. Although there could be reasons specific to the district, deferred maintenance does not remove the facilities problem. It pushes the problem further in the future.

Preventative Maintenance

Preventative maintenance slows the wear and tear on a piece of equipment. Preventative maintenance is an excellent way to maintain facilities. For example, waxing and polishing floors and walls could not only improve the appearance of the facilities but can improve the life of the buildings. A new coat of paint each year on the building would help to preserve the wood and stretch the life. Preventative maintenance on a routine basis is an ideal strategy for postponing major building projects. Conceptually, implementing a preventative maintenance plan defers the need for bond elections and capital improvement projects.

◆ SAFETY AND SECURITY

The challenge to keep school buildings safe is ever increasing. The purpose of this section is to discuss safety and security measures that keep our children safe. Likewise, it is essential to understand how building codes will dictate many required building elements, such as heat detectors, smoke and fire detection, alarm systems, and other building components,that make a building safe in case of an emergency. This section is intended to focus on the elements that can be built in to the architecture that maximize safety in regards to human behavior. There are specific building design elements that should be considered in every school facility, both new and existing. A school building designer must consider safety principles that can be translated into various planning and design strategies as follows:

- Secured vestibule at building entry,
- Clear lines of sight,
- Minimize isolation,
- Safe bus traffic and visitor traffic patterns,
- Good site and building lighting,
- Technology, and
- A well maintained home away from home environment.

Secured Vestibule at Building Entry

It is vital to have a specific and safe traffic route for visitors coming to the school campus. The visitor must have specific signage on the site directing them to the appropriate parking area. That in turn should grant them direct access to the main entry. A specific entry point on a school building can be not only an aesthetically pleasing building element but also a focal point that directs visitors to a single entry point of the school building that should function as a controlled check point. A visitor walks into the secured vestibule entry and is immediately directed into the reception area of the administrative offices, where they have to check in with the secretary and state their business. They should register, sign in and even be given an identification badge that clearly shows their name and lets the school personnel recognize that they have entered the building appropriately. They can then be directed to the room the meeting is to take place. A well designed administration area should have a conference room to facilitate such meetings to keep visitors out of the school proper as much as possible. The system is more accommodating for parents too. They understand where they should go and what the protocol is. A safe school environment begins from the moment someone enters the building.

Clear Lines of Sight

A sight line is defined by a visual distance of depth, length and width. The further and clearer one can see, the better the line of sight. The inability to see what is ahead or around the next corner can reduce the feeling of safety in any environment. This is as applicable to the interior and exterior building elements. Large barricades, walls, tall fences, bushes, and trees adjacent to any path of travel can be elements on a site or in a building that shield an attacker. Lines of sight are a part of every space inside a school but are more commonly associated with travel paths from one space to another typically known as a corridor or hallway. Corridors can be a tricky building element in a school. Schools are typically large buildings with a number of teachers and a mass of student population. Students must travel from one classroom to the next in merely a matter of minutes and corridors are the required path of travel. The safest solutions are always the most simple. Designing straight corridors with no or few offsets will promote the safest feeling. Teachers can see more students, and students that have an awareness of a more direct path to their next required location are more likely to go directly to that location. Something as simple as leaving window shades open can promote awareness on a campus and help create lines of sight for teachers during the day also.

Minimize Isolation

Isolation areas can be defined as those areas in a school building that are not easy to see or monitor not commonly used and offer the opportunity for attackers to hide. Isolated areas can exist inside the building and outside the building on the school site. A single piece of playground equipment that is located in an obscure location could provide an opportunity for an attacker to hide. It can even be that the location is easy for students to create mischief or even promote bullying opportunities. It must be understood that promoting good choices starts with the teacher and staff, but a well-built, well-monitored environment eliminates many potential bad choices that can escalate over time. Isolated areas need to be quickly identified on the school campus by the administration so they can take care to have teachers monitor those areas during lunch periods and passing periods. There is no substitute for a student being aware that they are being monitored. When a student or students discover a place on campus that is not being monitored that area of isolation will become a potential safety breach. Isolation areas should be locked if possible.

Safe Bus Traffic and Visitor Traffic Patterns

Traffic is heavy in school zones with school buses picking up and dropping off students, visitors entering and leaving campus and parents making quick drop-offs. Food and other deliveries are necessities for campuses. For example, textbooks, office supplies, band uniforms, athletic equipment, and other instructional and noninstructional activities contribute to the vehicle traffic on a school campus. It is extremely important to have separate and safe traffic flow for as many of these conditions as possible. Easy to read directional signage can assist in directing traffic. Separating the parent and visitor traffic from the bus loop is a must on any campus. Making sure that students do not have to walk over driveways during the school day to access outdoor learning areas or playgrounds is important. Keeping the traffic patterns well managed can be a challenge when school dismisses for the day. The administration on campus needs a plan of action where staff can help direct traffic flow and make sure parents are being safe in their vehicles and children are not walking in front of traffic. Designated drop off and pick up points that are clearly marked with signage will aide in this effort also. Training by attrition takes place within the community when these strategies are implemented daily. Local police should be made of aware of any incidents or traffic challenges that cannot be handled by the staff. Local policemen can assist in the direction of traffic. A presence of authority goes a long way to create safety awareness. Pedestrian traffic to and from the site is important. Sidewalks adjacent to the street should be wide enough to accommodate the amount of students and parents at peak times safely so no one has to walk in a driveway or the street.

Good Site and Building Lighting

Vision and monitoring capability is a key factor to every layer of safe building. Lighting is a must for people to see or be seen. Appropriate exterior lighting at night can encourage natural surveillance. If neighbors can observe inappropriate behavior taking place on the campus after hours, they can report it to the authorities. Lighted pathways, such as sidewalks and tracks, that are used by the community after school hours not only provide an element of security but also promote a positive sense of joint ownership. How much lighting will be the next challenge? School districts are constantly having unfunded mandates handed down by state legislature that require energy cost reduction. The exterior lighting is an easy target. If the district can adopt a policy to keep a minimum amount of site lighting available to each campus to promote safety. Districts should consider certain lighting philosophies, such as adequate lighting to observe face recognition for up to 10 m away. Does the lighting provide a uniform spread and reduce contrast between shadow and illuminated areas? Consider the opposite effect, such as too much glare. Lighting should be planned in conjunction with security camera operation. If a light is located to close to a security camera, all that will be detected is a glare of light. If the light source is too far away, the images being detected are blurred. It is always better to plan on where the person is likely to be, such as at corridor intersections inside the building and light that area. The camera can be pointed to that area from a reasonable distance for the optimum detection. Any isolated areas inside or around the campus should be well lit and well monitored (again it is always best to avoid isolated areas totally). Traffic areas and parking lots can be lit effectively from wall mounted fixtures on the building. Outdoor wall mounted light fixtures (known as wall packs) can provide a dual source of night time security lighting. A single fixture can cast enough light to illuminate shrubs and planter beds adjacent to a building (where an attacker could hid easily if not lit) and also cast enough light in a distance to illuminate driveways, portions of parking lots and sidewalks. Visibility removes all doubt when investigating negative and unfortunate incidents, and vision over the campus is bright and within recognizable distances.

Technology Integration in Safety and Security

With today's complex educational facilities and the integration of many different building systems, security design in schools has taken on a whole new appearance. Owners are looking to combine intrusion detection, access control, and security cameras into a seamless, reliable, and powerful system. Integrating these systems and still provide an effective tool becomes extremely important. Understanding the importance of security system design and integration of devices, such as security cameras, screen monitors, digital video recording systems, visitor data recognition used at the registration desk, motion sensors, and other systems, is vital. A school district should hire or appoint a key staff member to research these systems and consult with experts to design and implement systems that fit the need of each building. Security cameras are beneficial for a number of reasons. They can capture inappropriate activity among students. When used in conjunction with monitors and digital video recording devices, it can help a school principal determine the cause and effect of that event. Cameras can also capture after school hour activities, such as break-ins, or custodial operations. Cameras can also be set up in specific areas, such as nooks and corners, that are known isolated areas that are hard to monitor. If a student knows there is a camera watching them, the chance for inappropriate behavior choices will radically decrease. Visitor data recognition is a simple way to register visitors at the registration desk. Typically, a desk computer can be utilized with the correct software. Many systems require a visitor to hand their driver's license to the school clerk or secretary, they in turn scan the license at the computer and the information quickly goes into a data base for a background check. The system can even store the visitor's information in the school district data base so it will recognize a friendly visitor or unfriendly visitor. Electronic access is becoming more popular at key exterior door locations around a school building. Districts are keeping doors locked to avoid some of the aforementioned scenarios of visitors being able to walk in the building undetected. This does create a burden for teachers and students who have to exit the building for play time or outdoor learning activities needing to have quick access into the building. The integration of an electronic locking system, which can open at the swipe of a key card is very helpful in functioning with the proper access clearance. Electronic systems aid in the lock down of schools in case of emergencies. It can be overwhelming to think of the issue that can arise and all of the things that could have been done to prevent each one. Ultimately, the leader of a school district must decide on a philosophy to implement safety and security throughout the district. It should be discussed with the Board of Trustees openly and even adopted as resolution for the school district standards of practice. Transparency in the community about the district safety and security plan should be a priority also. Get the local police and fire department involved. Meet with them often and have them come to school to meet the students and advise them on security issues. Involve the local Neighborhood watch program. They can be a great surveillance resource for the school district. Give the local authorities floor plans of the buildings so they are familiar with them. It will help them respond quicker to any issue. With today's complex educational facilities and the integration of many different building systems, security design in schools has taken on a whole new appearance. Owners are looking to combine intrusion detection and access control and security cameras into a seamless, reliable, and powerful system. Integrating these systems and still provide an effective tool becomes extremely important. Plan and practice emergency response routines with the local authorities and make the public aware you are doing so. A community should know the school district is serious about the safety and security of the students. It should be a part of the community culture. In summary, a checklist of items for each school is helpful. Campus safety must ultimately be managed at the campus level. Consider the following items a guideline:

1. Provide an safe distribution and separation of bus and automobile traffic with clearly marked signage.
2. Visitor parking having excellent sight lines from the main entrance and administrative offices.
3. Main entrance is protected from vehicular assault by a parking circle.
4. Direct and logical line of pedestrian movement from the main parking areas to the athletic fields and to assembly occupancies,
5. Main hallway kiosks (work stations) having direct sight lines to all major movement spaces.
6. Student restrooms are located on both floors in convenient areas that are easy to monitor and that away from stairs and exits that would provide escape routes for potential offenders.
7. Staff reception areas on all floors strategically located to provide natural surveillance and access monitoring for all classroom areas.
8. Restroom locations for the gymnasium and auditorium are placed in areas where there will be constant movement and excellent opportunities for monitoring.
9. Leave window shades open.
10. Use passing vehicular traffic as a surveillance asset.
11. Create landscape designs that provide surveillance, especially in proximity of designated & opportunistic points-of entry.
12. Use the shortest, least sight-limiting fence appropriate for the situation.
13. Use transparent weather vestibules at building entrances.
14. Use a single, clearly identifiable point-of-entry.
15. Use low, thorny bushes beneath ground level windows.
16. Eliminate design features that provide access to roofs or upper levels.
17. Security cameras in key locations.
18. Appropriate exterior lighting to allow visibility. No dark hiding spaces.

◆ THE FEDERAL GOVERNMENT'S ROLE

Qualified Zone Academy Bond (QZAB) Program

QZABs reduce the burden of interest payments for a district by giving financial institutions holding the bonds or other debt mechanism a tax credit in lieu of interest. The school district or charter school remains obligated to the initial principal amount but is freed from interest payments. Texas, as with other states, is limited in the amount of QZABs that may be offered. Capital projects funded under these bonds can be repair or renovation projects. The QZAB program is a federal program designed to provide to bond holders tax credits that are approximately equal to the interest that states and communities would ordinarily pay the holders of taxable bonds. The program does not grant funding. No monetary payments or awards are issued from the state to the school district or charter school. This program allows the state to grant program authorization to a limited number of qualifying school districts and charter schools. This authorization allows those school districts and charter schools to issue QZABs that benefit qualifying projects.

For a school district or charter school to gain QZAB program authorization, it must submit a program application that satisfies all requirements of the application process. Additional requirements may have to be met after receipt of an authorization to comply with federal tax law regarding the authorization. Superintendents and school boards have local bond attorneys who are available when more information and direction are needed when building under this federal program. An application must be filed and an authorization must be approved before the school district or charter school issues its QZAB debt.

Qualified School Construction Bond (QSCB)

QSCBs are a United States debt instrument created by Section 1521 of the American Recovery and Reinvestment Act of 2009. QSCBs allow school districts to borrow money at 0% interest for the rehabilitation, repair, and equipping of schools for instructional purposes. In addition, QSCB funds can be used to purchase land on which a public school will be built. The QSCB lender receives a Federal tax credit in lieu of receiving an interest payment. The tax credit rate is set by the Internal Revenue Service (IRS) and is positioned with the United States Treasury Qualified Tax Credit Bond Rates. Each school year an allocation is approved for the state. The US Treasury and the IRS allocate the authority to issue QSCBs to all 50 states and United States territories. The 50 states and US territories are allocated 60% of the allocation, and 40% is allocated among "large local educational agencies."

The funds from QSCBs may also be used for equipment purchases and land acquisition. All state and local laws applicable to bonds also apply to QSCBs, including Section 148 and Section 54 of the IRS Code.

◆ CONCLUSION

The conversation about "closing the achievement gap" among students is becoming more prevalent in our communities and schools, and even among those in legislative positions to write and interpret the laws that govern strategies to close these gaps. Closing the disparity gap in school building quality should be an integral part of closing the achievement gap and should be an explicit objective of state and federal education law, including No Child Left Behind and other funding sources. In Texas, the state makes no effort to "recapture" funds from the TEC Chapter 41 school district's I&S tax collections on the district's I&S tax collection rate per $100.00 valuation. No changes from the eighty-thirdLegislative session were made to alter this process of revenue collections.

How do schools make a conscious effort to deliver rigorous, personal, and relevant instructional and facilities environments capable of preparing all students for bright futures? This is the fundamental question that school superintendents and school boards must not only ponder but also find an answer to in the next decade. Facility improvements help to attract and retain qualified and capable teachers, and strong, stable families that become proponents of those who manage the schools. While superintendents and school boards should be engaged in facilities studies in their districts, these studies should be nested in the philosophy of continued student achievement for all students. Facility improvements, with no consideration of student achievement, destroy the entire concept of educating all for the benefit and sake of all.

When leading Texas schools, build your schools upon a strong foundation. A foundation made of not only wood, brick, and martyr but also a foundation of trust, respect, and high expectations for all.

◆ REFERENCES

Agron, J. (2006). Betting on bonds. *American School & University, 78*(5), 6.

Bordelon, J. (2005). *School bond failure.* Retrieved from www.news8austin.com/content/top_story/default.asp?ArID=138063

Connolly, J. J., Svendsen, E. S., Fisher, D. R., & Campbell, L. K. (2013). Organizing urban ecosystem services through environmental stewardship governance in New York City. *Landscape and Urban Planning. 109*, 76–84.

Faltys, D. J. (2006). *Factors influencing the successful passage of a school bond referendum asidentified by selected voters in the Navasota Independent School District in Texas* (Unpublished doctoral dissertation). Texas A&M University, College Station, Texas.

Municipal Securities Rulemaking Board. (2015). *Glossary of municipality terms.* Retrieved from http://www.msrb.org/glossary/definition/capital-appreciation-bond-_cab_.aspx

Hickey, W.D., & Vaughn, V. (2010). Legislation, financial self-interest, and bond electionsuccess. *Education Leadership Review, 2*(11), 91–99.

Hickey, W. D., Vaughn, V., Dunn, D., & Evans, G. (2006). Planning your community school bond election. *TACS Today*, 28–29.

Hickey, W. D. (2006). Overcoming negative sentiment in bond elections: An analysisof three case studies. *Educational Leadership Review, 2*(7), 146–158.

Pietroforte, R., & Miller, J. (2010). Procurement methods for US infrastructure: Historicalperspectives and recent trends. *Building Research& Information, 30*(6), 425–434.

Prenksy, M. (2001). Digital natives, digital immigrants. *On the Horizon, 9*(5), 1–6. Retrieved from http://www.albertomattiacci.it/docs/did/Digital_Natives_Digital_Immigrants.pdf

Schneider, M. (2002). Do school facilities affect academic outcomes? Retrieved from http://www.ncef.org/pubs/outcomes.pdf

Schrom, J. W. (2004). *School community interaction and communication during a general obligation bond election* (Unpublished doctoral dissertation). University of California, Riverside.

TEA. (2011). *Bond guarantee program.* Texas Education Agency. Retrieved from http://tea.texas.gov/Finance_and_Grants/State_Funding/Facilities_Funding_and_Standards/Bond__Guarantee_Program/

Texas Association of School Administrators. (2015). *Finance.* Retrieved from http://www.tasanet.org/Page/716

PART IV

PROGRAMS

STUDENTS OF DIVERSITY

Challenges and Opportunities for School Leadership

Art Borgemenke ◆ *Melissa Arrambide*

As the general public school population becomes increasingly diverse, school administrators must ensure that students, who are also members of educational subpopulations, reflect that diversity. Students who are secondlanguage learners, students who are in need of special education services, students with disabilities not covered by special education, and students who qualify for gifted and talented (GT) programs must appropriately reflect the greater school demographics in meaningful ways. School leaders are charged with providing appropriate services for students that may be members of one, two, or more of these groups.

◆ ENGLISH LANGUAGE LEARNERS (ELLS) AND TEXAS PUBLIC SCHOOLS

According to the Migration Policy Institute, there are 4,851,527 ELLs in the United States. With a student enrollment of 49,474,030, this represents 9.8% of the overall student population. Texas has 5,077,507 students, and the ELL student population is at 773,732, which comprises 15.2% of the student population in Texas (Zong, Batalova, & Migration Policy Institute, 2015). Texas ranks in the top five among the states servicing ELL student populations in the United States. Educators are faced with providing rigorous, grade-level content to struggling students whose first language is not English, and as a result, have unique learning needs. According to the Texas Education Code (TEC) (2012) Section 29.052, the definition of an ELL is "student of limited English proficiency whose primary language is other than English and whose English language skills are such that the student has difficulty performing ordinary classwork in English." The terms limited English proficiency and ELL are used interchangeably (Texas Administrative Code, 2012).

◆ Legislation and the Education of Second Language Learners

The Elementary and Secondary Education Act (ESEA) is arguably the one act that has had the greatest direct impact on American education. As with many other special programs, the education of ELLs falls under the ESEA. This act was first signed into law on April 11, 1965, and since its inception, has undergone several revisions and amendments. The most commonly referred to reauthorization of this act was signed by President Bush on April 11, 2002 and is known as the No Child Left Behind Act (NCLB). The overall purpose of the ESEA is to provide equal educational opportunity to underprivileged and underperforming students (USDepartment of Education, 2015).

Federal funding has been made available to schools and districts through Title grant programs under NCLB. Specifically, Title I is available to assist underprivileged struggling learners. Title III is available to assist ELLs and immigrant students with language instruction. Title funds are expected to supplement a learner's education, through providing additional resources and services. Title funds are not intended to supplant educational services that are typically provided to all students [Texas Education Agency (TEA), 2015].

Along with federal legislation, bilingual and English as a second language (ESL) programs are largely governed by state statues. TEC Sections 29.051–29.064 outline all requirements for bilingual education and ESL programs in Texas. Texas Administrative Code, Chapter 89. Subchapter BB contains the Commissioner's Rules Concerning State Plan for educating ELLs. Schools and districts use both federal and state legislative guidelines to develop and implement specialized programming to meet the unique needs of ELLs.

The TEA defines an ELL as "a person who is in the process of acquiring English and has another language as the first native language" (Texas Administrative Code, 2012). Identification of language status begins at enrollment, where districts require all students to complete a home language survey in both English and Spanish. Questions must include "What language is spoken in your home most of the time?"and "What language does your child speak most of the time?" (Texas Administrative Code, 2012). Districts may choose to seek additional student information from the home language survey if so desired.

Language Proficiency Assessment Committee

The Language Proficiency Assessment Committee (LPAC) oversees ELLs at the campus. Much like the admission, review, and dismissal committees in special education, LPACs are responsible for making educational decisions for students qualifying as ELLs. The LPAC is responsible for initial classification of ELL status, program placement, instructional and assessment accommodations, as well as any changes in program placement. Texas has delineated specific criteria a student must achieve before eligibility of "exit status" (Texas Administrative Code, 2012).

Administrator Need to Knows

- Identification is key. If a student's home language is other than English, schools must begin the testing process to determine the student's oral language proficiency in English.
- Academic programming for ELLs, including program placement and educational accommodations, are governed by the LPAC.

- Decisions made by the LPAC committee are to be upheld by all parties involved in educating the ELL student.
- A student may not be reclassified as a non-ELL until he/she meets all exit criteria as delineated by the TEA. Upon meeting this criteria, he/she is eligible for exit; however, the ultimate decision is made by the LPAC.

Theories of Second Language Acquisition

The learning process for acquiring a second language can look different than that for a monolingual learner. As with all theories, the literature reveals some debate regarding the accuracy and efficacy of the second language acquisition process. The theories presented below are widely accepted among educators with deep involvement in the language literacy community.

Stephen D. Krashen

Dr Stephen Krashen is a professor at the University of Southern California who is widely known for his research regarding second language acquisition. Schutz (2014) provides a summary of Krashen's theory of second language acquisition, which is based on the following five hypotheses:

- Acquisition-learning hypothesis—language is acquired through natural communicative experiences.
- Monitor hypothesis—language is acquired through conscious and deliberate learning experiences.
- Input hypothesis—language development occurs when a child receives comprehensible input that is one step beyond his/her current linguistic stage.
- Natural order hypothesis—acquisition of grammatical structures follows a "natural order" which is predictable.
- Affective filter hypothesis—affective factors such as "motivation, self-confidence, and anxiety" affect the language development process.

Krashen's theory embodies the concept that language acquisition is a subconscious process, while language learning is conscious (Krashen, 1982). Both are essential for bilingual fluency and literacy.

Dr James Cummins

Dr Jim Cummins, professor at the University of Toronto, is another prominent leader in the research of second language acquisition and literacy development. His most noted-work includes Basic Interpersonal Communication Skills, Cognitive Academic Language Proficiency Skills, and Common Underlying Proficiency theories. These terms were introduced to provide a distinction between communicative fluency in one's second language and grade appropriate academic language (Cummins, 2003). In other words, the Basic Interpersonal Communication Skills refer to common social language, and the Cognitive Academic Language Proficiency Skills refer to academic language acquired through intentional learning experiences. Further research indicated, "despite teacher observation that peer-appropriate conversational fluency in English developed rapidly, a period of 5–7 years was required, on average, for immigrant students to approach grade norms in academic aspects of English" (Cummins, 1981).

The Common Underlying Proficiency refers to the notion that everyone has a central location in the brain whereby skills and knowledge are housed. This location is not necessarily language specific, and information acquired in one's first language is also beneficial in the second language. As Cummins (2000) stated "Conceptual knowledge developed in one language helps to make input in the other language comprehensible."

Administrator Need to Knows

- Administrators should have a basic knowledge of second language acquisition processes, including local policies and procedures, state codes and federal statues, and legislation.
- Administrators should be keenly aware that ELLs need language acquisition to take place meaningfully.
- Administrators should understand that ELLs need specialized programming designed to meet their educational needs.

◆ SERVING ELLs

Bilingual Programming

According the Texas Administrative Code (2012)

> each school district that has an enrollment of 20 or more English language learners in any language classification in the same grade level district-wide shall offer bilingual education . . . for the English language learners in prekindergarten through the elementary grades who speak that language.

Furthermore, Texas has delineated four acceptable models from which districts can choose to implement.

1. Transitional bilingual/early exit. This is a bilingual program model that serves a student identified as limited English proficient in both English and Spanish, or another language, and transfers the student to English-only instruction. This model provides instruction in literacy and academic content areas through the medium of the student's first language, along with instruction in English. Nonacademic subjects, such as art, music, and physical education, may also be taught in English. Exiting of a student to an all-English program of instruction will occur no earlier than the end of Grade 1 or, if the student enrolls in school during or after Grade 1, no earlier than 2 years or later than 5 years after the student enrolls in school.

2. Transitional bilingual/late exit. This is a bilingual program model that serves a student identified as limited English proficient in both English and Spanish, or another language, and transfers the student to English-only instruction. This model provides instruction in literacy and academic content areas through the medium of the student's first language, along with instruction in English. Nonacademic subjects, such as art, music, and physical education, may also be taught in English. A student enrolled in a transitional bilingual/late exit program is eligible to exit the program no earlier than 6 years or later than 7 years after the student enrolls in school.

3. Dual language immersion/two-way. This is a biliteracy program model that integrates students' proficient in English and students identified as limited English proficient. This model provides instruction in both English and Spanish, or another language, and transfers a student identified as limited English proficient to English-only instruction. Instruction is provided to both native English speakers and native speakers of another language in an instructional setting where language learning is integrated with content instruction. Academic subjects are taught to all students through both English and the other language. Program exit will occur no earlier than 6 years or later than 7 years after the student enrolls in school. A student who has met exit criteria in accordance with Texas Administrative Code (2012) §89.1225(h), (j), and (k) of this title may continue receiving services, but the school district will not receive the bilingual education allotment for that student.

4. Dual language immersion/one-way. This is a biliteracy program model that serves only students identified as limited English proficient. This model provides instruction in both English and Spanish, or another language, and transfers a student to English-only instruction. Instruction is provided to ELLs in an instructional setting where language learning is integrated with content instruction. Academic subjects are taught to all students through both English and the other language. Program exit will occur no earlier than 6 years or later than 7 years after the student enrolls in school. A student who has met exit criteria in accordance with Texas Administrative Code (2012) §89.1225(h), (j), and (k) of this title may continue receiving services, but the school district will not receive the bilingual education allotment for that student (Texas Administrative Code, 2012, Chapter 89).

ESL Programming

For years, educators have sought to find the most effective means of educating ELLs. Gaining popularity over the past 15 years is the concept of sheltered instruction. "Sheltered instruction is an approach for teaching content to ELLs in strategic ways that make the subject matter concepts comprehensible while promoting the students' English language development" (Echevarria, Vogt, & Short, 2012, p. 1). Sheltered instruction is a widely implemented methodology designed to provide second language learners access to mainstream curriculum while building language. In contrast to the older style ESL strategies, sheltered instruction focuses less on basic language acquisition and more on providing scaffolding techniques to make grade level content and academic English more comprehensible. It is important to note that while a sheltered instruction approach is beneficial to struggling students who are also identified as second language learners, it is a widely used approach for second language learners and general education students who may or may not be presenting learning difficulties. The Sheltered Instruction Observation Protocol (SIOP) model developed over 15 years ago by Echevarria et al. (2012) is among the most popular approaches to providing second language learners a sheltered instruction approach to learning grade level content. The SIOP model consists of eight overarching components and 30 features. The first component of SIOP centers on key components of lesson preparation, such as well-written and clear content and language objectives. The content objective is directly aligned to the specific local or state standard being taught. The language objective is designed to provide a description of activities to support a student's language development. Language objectives will contain one or more of the four language domains of listening, speaking, reading, and writing (Echevarria et al., 2012).

Texas Administrative Code (2012), Chapter 89 requires that "all ELLs for whom a school district is not required to offer a bilingual education program shall be provided an ESL program as described in subsection (e) of this section, regardless of the students' grade levels and home language, and regardless of the number of such students." Texas has delineated two acceptable program models from which districts can choose to implement ESL programs.

1. ESL/content-based program. This model is an English program that serves only students identified as ELLs by providing a full-time teacher certified under the TEC (2012), §29.061(c), to provide supplementary instruction for all content area instruction. The program integrates ESL instruction with subject matter instruction that focuses not only on learning a second language, but using that language as a medium to learn mathematics, science, social studies, or other academic subjects. Exiting of a student to an all-English program of instruction without ESL support will occur no earlier than the end of Grade 1 or, if the student enrolls in school during or after Grade 1, no earlier than 2 years or later than 5 years after the student enrolls in school. At the high school level, the ELL receives sheltered instruction in all content areas.

2. ESL/pull-out program. This is an English program that serves only students identified as ELLs by providing a part-time teacher certified under the TEC, §29.061(c), to provide English language arts instruction exclusively, while the student remains in a mainstream instructional arrangement. Instruction may be provided by the ESL teacher in a pull-out or inclusionary delivery model. Exiting of a student to an all-English program of instruction without ESL support will occur no earlier than the end of Grade 1 or, if the student enrolls in school during or after Grade 1, no earlier than 2 years or later than 5 years after the student enrolls in school. At the high school level, the ELL receives sheltered instruction in all content areas (Texas Administrative Code, 2012).

Administrator Need to Knows

- There are four bilingual program options for districts to choose from, each with different design and intent.
- The State of Texas has provided two ESL program options for district implementation.
- Much research has been conducted to determine the most effective program models for instructing ELLs. While the results of the research are beyond the scope of this text, students are encouraged to seek a greater understanding of the various bilingual programs models and their respective strengths and weaknesses.

◆ SECTION 504 OF THE REHABILITATION ACT 1973

In the realm of education, Section 504 prohibits the discrimination of students with disabilities based on their identified handicapping condition. "Under Section 504, students with disabilities may receive accommodations and modifications as well as supplementary aids and services to ensure that their individual educational needs are met as adequately as those of non-disabled students" (Texas Project First, n.d.).

Some student service requirements and protections exist both in Section 504 regulations and special education legislation, but many important distinctions remain. Students qualifying for special education services are protected under the Individuals with Disabilities Act

(IDEA). Section 504 of The Rehabilitation Act of 1973 is a broad umbrella legislation and also covers students who qualify for services under IDEA. However, students who are protected under Section 504 are not necessarily covered under special education services of IDEA. The definition of a student with special needs ". . . is broader than the IDEA's definition and not limited to specific disability categories" (Texas Project First, n.d.). Section 504 is a civil rights law and is therefore overseen by the Office of Civil Rights. In contrast, all IDEA-related issues are overseen by the state education agency (Texas Project First, n.d.).

Administrator Need to Knows

- Section 504 is broad and includes services for employees as well as students.
- Adherence to Section 504 is not optional.
- Parents often seek protection for their children under Section 504 when the child presents with "chronic medical conditions such as asthma or diabetes" which are not covered under IDEA (Texas Project First, n.d.).
- Unlike, IDEA, Section 504 does not require an Individual Educational Plan (IEP).

◆ STUDENTS WITH DISABILITIES AND SPECIAL EDUCATION

The TEA estimates that nearly one in eight public school students in the state are in need of special education services (TEA, 2014). Latest reporting data indicates that over 5.1 million students are enrolled in Texas schools and nearly 650,000 of those enrollees may indeed qualify for and be in need of special education services (TEA, 2014).The effective school leader is tasked with ensuring that all students are provided with appropriate educational opportunities, including students with disabilities.

The knowledge, skills, and abilities a school administrator must possess are many, broad, and varied. Appropriately addressing the needs of students who are members of special populations, specifically special education, is of great emphasis in an era of increasedschool accountability. McLaughlin (2009) lists five critical areas that the educational leader must be keenly aware of to effectuate a special education program with appropriate student outcomes.

The school administrator should:

1. Thoroughly understand the state and federal legal framework supporting the special education system.
2. Ensure that special education instruction closely matches the learning modalities of students in special education.
3. Understandthat special education does not reside in a single place nor exist in a specific program but rather in a broad continuum of services provided in the most appropriate location to facilitate a free and appropriate public education (FAPE).
4. Know that it is imperative to include students with disabilities in accountability systems.
5. Be able to initiate and perpetuate a school climate and culture that supports effective special education with appropriate student outcomes.

These are not the totality of areas that administrators must address when engaging with the complexities of the special education system, but solid starting points that are experienced in multiple situations.

◆ THE BASIC LEGISLATION THAT SUPPORTS SPECIAL EDUCATION

The legislation and educational policies that impact and address students with special needs have evolved over time. An examination of the specific laws and regulations regarding special education reveals that the modern era of special education legislation can be seen to have begun in the second half of the twentieth century. Beginning with the sweeping Rehabilitation Act of 1973 (P.L. 93–112, Section 504), federal lawmakers began the first steps in the evolutionary chain of laws, codes and policies that guide and safeguard students with disabilities today.

Table 19.1 includes descriptions of legislation that has had great impact on special education. Understanding the basic intent of these laws is vital to the school administrator who is responsible for serving the students this legislation is meant to serve. These examples are not an exhaustive list, but core to properly understanding special education leadership.

TABLE 19.1
Special Education Legislation

Legislation	*Intent*
Rehabilitation Act of 1973 (P.L. 93–112), Section 504	"Section 504 covers qualified students with disabilities who attend schools receiving Federal financial assistance. To be protected under Section 504, a student must be determined to: (1) have a physical or mental impairment that substantially limits one or more major life activities; or (2) have a record of such an impairment; or (3) be regarded as having such an impairment. Section 504 requires that school districts provide a free appropriate public education (FAPE) to qualified students in their jurisdictions who have a physical or mental impairment that substantially limits one or more major life activities."
	This Act can be seen as the beginning of modern special education initiatives requiring reasonable accommodations in schools for those with special needs.
	Notable highlights:
	Free and Appropriate Public Education (FAPE),
Education of all Handicapped Children Act 1975 (P.L. 94–142)	"to assure that all children with disabilities have available to them . . . a free appropriate public education which emphasizes special education and related services designed to meet their unique needs to assure that the rights of children with disabilities and their parents . . . are protected to assist States and localities to provide for the education of all children with disabilities to assess and assure the effectiveness of efforts to educate all children with disabilities"
	Notable highlights:
	Due Process reinforced for students and parents before schools exercise specific actions and Parental Participation Rights,
	Individual Education Plans (IEP),
	Least Restrictive Requirements (LRE)

Individuals with Disabilities Education Act 1990 (P.L. 101–476)	A reaffirmation of the EHEA; Extended LRE requirements and included broadened transition services
Individuals with Disabilities Education Act: Reauthorization of IDEA 1997 (P.L. 105–17)	Maintained IDEA 1990 provisions and strengthens LRE toinclude more emphasis on access to general curriculum as appropriate for students in special education. Notable highlights: Over identification of disabled students in disciplinary placements. The creation of the Behavior Intervention Plan and disciplinary regulations began. Independent Educational Evaluations (IEE) may be requested by parent caregivers at the expense of the school district.
Individuals with Disabilities Education Improvement Act IDEIA 2004 (P.L. 108–446)	"(A) to ensure that all children with disabilities have available to them a free appropriate public education that emphasizes special education and related services designed to meet their unique needs and prepare them for further education, employment and independent living USC 1400 (d)(1)(A)." Notable highlights: This reauthorization addresses the fast growing population of minority and second language learners in special education classes. Over-representation of these students is a concern that school administrators need to be aware of. Proper assessment and instruction in the general education classroom must be the first options.

◆ THE INDIVIDUALS WITH DISABILITIES EDUCATION IMPROVEMENT ACT (IDEIA) 2004 (P.L. 108–446)

IDEIA has evolved through several reauthorizations, to become a powerful amalgam of federal regulations for special education that ensures a FAPE for students with disabilities who attend public schools. IDEIA requires that each public school provide services to eligible special education students in the least restrictive environment (LRE) and in accordance with each student's individualized education plan (IEP). The Act also requires schools to actively pursue identification and evaluation of children with disabilities regardless of the severity of their disability through the "child find" section of the legislation. This requirement needs to be followed whether the student is the active beneficiary of special education services or not.

The IDEIA lists categories of specific disabilities for special education qualification, each with its own detailed requirements. Special education pertains to students aged 3–22 (with few exceptions) who attend a public school. To qualify, a child must be diagnosed as having one of the identified disabilities, and it must adversely affect their educational performance. Beyond that, school districts have the legal responsibility to locate, identify, evaluate, and provide a FAPE to children who are in need of special education services, identified in this legislation as "child find."

The special education qualifying categories include:

- Auditory impairment,
- Autism,
- Deaf-blindness,
- Developmental delay,
- Emotional disturbance,
- Intellectual disabilities,
- Noncategorical early childhood,
- Multiple disabilities,
- Orthopedic impairment,
- Other health impairment,
- Specific learning disability,
- Speech or language impairment,
- Traumatic brain injury,
- Visual impairment.

◆ INSTRUCTING STUDENTS IN SPECIAL EDUCATION

The IDEIA legislation provides guidance in many areas of special education to include curriculum and instruction. The law provides for various incentives for schools and teachers to utilize research-based or scientifically based reading programs for students in special education. Early instructional intervention for students who are struggling in general education is also a focus of IDEIA. Administrators are encouraged to use a whole-school approach when designing curriculum for students who qualify for special education beginning with the consideration of regular classroom placement using the general educational curriculum before more restrictive placements are recommended. While all students in special education are to have individual education plans, school administrators would do well to understand the emphasis that the 2004 reauthorization has put upon students access to the general educational curriculum even if they receive special education services. That coupled with the emphasis on rigorous evaluation and an increased accountability for students in special education should have the educational leader engaged in the continuing evolution of state and local policies and procedural implementation of IDEIA.

In order to address student needs in the general education classroom, IDEIA has put special focus on interventions that are performed before students are tested for a specific learning disability. Response to Intervention is a term that refers to a well-organized, data-driven program of attempts to academically or behaviorally "catch" a student up while remaining in the general education classroom. Administrators might view the Response to Intervention thrust as a shift to proactive student assistance while they "stay in class."

◆ THE CONTINUUM OF PLACEMENTS

Students with special needs must first and always be considered for placement in the general education classroom. A LRE is the recommended best practices model and required legislative mode of student program placement. Section 101: Amendments to the IDEIA provides this latest description and guidance on LRE:

> To the maximum extent appropriate, children with disabilities, including children in public or private institutions or other care facilities, are educated with children who are not disabled, and special classes, separate schooling, or other removal of children with disabilities from the regular educational environment occurs only when the nature or severity of the disability of a child is such that education in regular classes with the use of supplementary aids and services cannot be achieved satisfactorily.

IDEIA also specifically addresses the need for a broad spectrum of alternative placement options to be available for students in need of special education services:

> Each public agency must ensure that a continuum of alternative placements is available to meet the needs of children with disabilities for special education and related services.
>
> These must include the alternative placements listed in the definition of special education under Sec. 300.38 (instruction in regular classes, special classes, special schools, home instruction, and instruction in hospitals and institutions); and make provision for supplementary services (such as resource room or itinerant instruction) to be provided in conjunction with regular class placement.

School administrators must also insure that all appropriate placement options are made available for students with special needs. The discredited notion of the "one size fits all" education model applies equally to any school placement. The LRE intent of IDEIA can be just as easily violated by inappropriately placing students in a self-contained classrooms or putting all students in special education solely in general education classrooms.

◆ ACCOUNTABILITY/EVALUATION AND STUDENTS IN SPECIAL EDUCATION

How to appropriately evaluate and assess educational progress of students with disabilities is a contentious issue. The NCLB and IDEIA require that all students be tested at least yearly for educational progress. Students in special education programs are not exempt from participation in statewide testing programs.

Students in special education have traditionally been assessed using goals and objectives from their IEPs. IEPs are still the main "governing" documents that spell out the specific curriculum plans for each and every student in special education. Requirements for addressing how and to what extent each student will participate in statewide assessments are to be in each IEP. While these procedures can and do vary by state education agency, the common theme is to ensure that all students (to include those in special education) are rigorously evaluated to the maximum extent appropriate by the same assessment system used for general education students.

The TEA has continuously developed and refined the methods, frequency, and rigor with which it assesses students. The current testing system, State of Texas Assessment of Academic Readiness (STAAR), has specific procedures in place to ensure that students in special education are included in the state assessment.

For the purposes of STAAR testing:

"A student with a disability can be a student:

- With an identified disability who receives special education services;
- With an identified disability who receives services under Section 504 of the Rehabilitation Act of 1973; or
- With a disabling condition who does not receive special education or Section 504 services."

Most students in special education take the statewide STAAR assessment with few accommodations and modifications, but there are alternative choices provided. Alternative tests include:

- STAAR—test given to all students in general education. Accommodations for some student specific needs are available.

- STAARA—"an accommodated version of STAAR©, is offered as an online assessment in the same grades and subjects as STAAR. The passing standards for STAAR A are the same as any STAAR test. STAAR A will provide embedded supports designed to help students with disabilities access the content being assessed. These embedded supports include visual aids, graphic organizers, clarifications of construct-irrelevant terms, and text-to-speech functionality" (http://tea.texas.gov/student.assessment/STAARA/).
- STAAR—Alternate 2—" TEA has developed the STAAR Alternate 2 assessment to meet the federal requirements mandated under the ESEA, a federal education law previously known as No Child Left Behind. TEA designed the STAAR Alternate 2 to assess students in Grades 3–8 and high school who have significant cognitive disabilities and are receiving special education services" (http://tea.texas.gov/student.assessment/STAARA/).

These state assessments are meant to hold each school district accountable for the educational progress of all special education students. The scores from these assessments are used to calculate campus ratings and do help ensure that education of students with special needs get appropriate levels of support to achieve student goals and objectives.

◆ SUPPORTING A CULTURE OF INCLUSIVENESS FOR STUDENTS IN SPECIAL EDUCATION

The Association for Supervision and Curriculum Developmentpresents a powerful argument for the inclusion of students with special needs in the general education classroom. In the Association for Supervision and Curriculum Development published text, *Creating an Inclusive School*, Falvey and Givner (2005) give a rigorous account of the philosophy and reality of inclusive education:

> Inclusive education is about embracing everyone and making a commitment to provide each student in the community, with the inalienable right to belong. Inclusion assumes that living and learning together benefits everyone, not just children who are labeled as having a difference . . . inclusion is a belief system.

A school culture that supports inclusive education has many hallmarks that differentiate it from nonsupportive environments. Some practices and beliefs extant in inclusive schools may include the notions that:

- Each student can and will learn and succeed.
- Diversity enriches us all, and students at risk can overcome the risk for failure through involvement in a thoughtful and caring community of learners.
- Each student has unique contributions to offer to other learners.
- Each student has strengths and needs.
- Services and supports should not be relegated to one setting (e.g., special classes or schools).
- Effective learning results from the collaborative efforts of everyone working to ensure each student's success.

Developing a campus culture that supports diversity including all students starts with a vision of solidarity. The belief that all students can achieve and have contributions to make to the greater benefit of all members of the school community. The proactive educational leader foresees all educational stakeholders working in concert build a stronger and more tolerant system that bridges divisions and fortifies student outcomes can result.

Administrator Need to Knows

- The administrator should have a useful understanding of state policies and procedures and the framework of federal laws supporting the special education system.
- The administrator should ensure that how students in special education are taught (the curriculum) closely matches their ability to understand (learning modality).
- The administrator should understand that special education does not reside in a single place nor exist in a specific program but rather in a broad continuum of services provided in the most appropriate location to facilitate a FAPE.
- The administrator should know that it is imperative to include students with disabilities in accountability systems (statewide testing programs).
- The administrator understands that they must initiate, articulate, and maintain a school climate and culture that supports a broad inclusive vision for all students to promote effective special education with appropriate student outcomes.

◆ STUDENTS WITH GT ABILITIES

The latest reporting data from the TEA indicates that 7.6% of the students enrolled in Texas schools are identified as GT (TEA, 2014). Furthermore, just over 5% of the teachers in Texas are actively teaching in GT programs. The Texas Legislature requires that a plan for students with gifted and talent abilities be developed, implemented, and revised on a regular basis. The current state plan was revised most recently in 2009.

The overarching State goals for students who are GT remains:

> Students who participate in services designed for gifted/talented students will demonstrate skills in self-directed learning, thinking, research, and communication as evidenced by the development of innovative products and performances that reflect individuality and creativity and are advanced in relation to students of similar age, experience, or environment. High school graduates who have participated in services for gifted/talented students will have produced products and performances of professional quality as part of their program services.

The TEA (2014) describes a gifted/talented student as a child or youth who performs at or shows the potential for performing at a remarkably high level of accomplishment when compared to others of the same age, experience, or environment and who:

- Exhibits high performance capability in an intellectual, creative, or artistic area;
- Possesses an unusual capacity for leadership; or
- Excels in a specific academic field (TEC, 2012).

The National Association for Gifted Children provides a different perspective but still useful-definition—"the gifted individual are those who demonstrate outstanding levels of aptitude (defined as exceptional ability to reason and learn) or competence (documented performance or achievement in top 10% or rarer) in one or more domains."

◆ A Brief History and an Examination of Basic Legislation that Supports GT Education

Education changed on October 4, 1957, when the Soviet Union successfully launched Sputnik I (National Aeronautics and Space Administration, 2014). The satellite's otherworldly tones emanating from space announced a new age dawning for the world at large and a perceived threat for the United States in particular. The challenge to keep pace was taken up by lawmakers at the national level and resulted in the National Defense Act of 1958. This multifaceted legislation had broad ranging impact on many parts of our society, education chiefly among them. Title V of the National Defense Act 1958 has specific language that targets identification and instructional support for students who are academically gifted.

A quarter century later the landmark report *A Nation at Risk* authored by the National Commission on Excellence in Education alerted educators to yet another crisis in education for GT students (National Commission on Excellence in Education, 1983). The research commissioned by the US Department of Education revealed that over half the population of gifted students did not match their tested ability with comparable achievement in school. That discrepancy between probable student capability and actual school achievement was a call to action for many educators. National and state efforts to provide increased emphasis on quality curricular programming resulted from this study. Table 19.2 describes some of the seminal legislation and state educational policies that school administrators should be aware of to appropriately address the needs of students who are academically GT.

TABLE 19.2
Legislation Supporting GT Education

Legislation	Intent
The National Defense Education Act (1958)	The initial sizeable legislation to address and support gifted education enacted by the federal government. Spurred by successful Russian efforts in space engineering, this Act charges schools to improve educational outcomes specifically for students who show gifted abilities.
Jacob K. Javitz Gifted and Talented Students Education Act of 2001	The purpose of the Jacob K. Javitz Gifted and Talented Students Education Program is to carry out a coordinated program of scientifically based research, demonstration projects, innovative strategies, and similar activities designed to build and enhance the ability of elementary schools and secondary schools nationwide to meet the special educational needs of gifted and talented students.
Texas Education Code. Subchapter D. Educational programs for gifted and talented students, Sections 29.121, 29.122, and 29.123	State Goal for Services for Gifted/Talented Students. Students who participate in services designed for gifted/talented students will demonstrate skills in self-directed learning, thinking, research, and communication as evidenced by the development of innovative products and performances that reflect individuality and creativity and are advanced in relation to students of similar age, experience, or environment. High school graduates who have participated in services for gifted/talented students will have produced products and performances of professional quality as part of their program services.

Texas Administrative Code Title 19, Part 2, Chapter 89. Adaptations for Special Populations. Subchapter A. Gifted/Talented Education

§89.1. Student Assessment.

School districts shall develop written policies on student identification that are approved by the local board of trustees and disseminated to parents.

§89.2. Professional Development.

School districts shall ensure that:

(1) prior to assignment in the program, teachers who provide instruction and services that are a part of the program for gifted students have a minimum of 30 hours of staff development that includes nature and needs of gifted/talented students, assessing student needs, and curriculum and instruction for gifted students;

(2) teachers without training required in paragraph (1) of this section who provide instruction and services that are part of the gifted/talented program must complete the 30-hour training requirement within one semester;

(3) teachers who provide instruction and services that are a part of the program for gifted students receive a minimum of six hours annually of professional development in gifted education; and

(4) administrators and counselors who have authority for program decisions have a minimum of six hours of professional development that includes nature and needs of gifted/talented students and program options.

§89.3. Student Services.

School districts shall provide an array of learning opportunities for gifted/talented students in kindergarten through Grade 12 and shall inform parents of the opportunities.

§89.5. Program Accountability.

School districts shall ensure that student assessment and services for gifted/talented students comply with accountability standards defined in the Texas State Plan for the Education of the Gifted/Talented.

The TEA targets the following areas that educational leaders need to be aware of when addressing GT education in Texas.

The school leader who meets the intent of the state plan:

- Provides information on best practices, developments, and achievements in the field of GT education to all interested parties.
- Develops materials designed to assist districts in the development and implementation of model assessment procedures and services.
- Facilitates partnerships among parents, institutions of higher education, communities, and school districts to design comprehensive GT services.
- Sponsors demonstration projects and develops materials that support the implementation of Advanced Placement and International Baccalaureate programs that are differentiated for the GT students.

- Collaborates with business and industry to provide additional opportunities for GT students.
- Monitors and implements any state and/or federal legislation designed to provide educational opportunities for GT students.

TEA is charged by the Texas Legislature with maintaining and monitoring the state plan for educating students who are GT. The Education Service Centers serving the 20 regions across the state also provide a primary resource for schools and administrators in addressing the needs of students who are GT. All Education Service Centers have personnel that are ready to assist with the many facets of GT programming in each school district.

◆ IDENTIFICATION OF STUDENTS WHO ARE GT

The Texas Administrative Code requires that all school districts develop written plans to properly identify students with GT abilities. These plans must be approved by local school boards and made available to parents of all students.

The policies must:

1. Include provisions for ongoing screening and selection of students who perform or show potential for performing at remarkably high levels of accomplishment in the areas defined in the TEC, §29.121;
2. Include assessment measures collected from multiple sources according to eacharea defined in The Texas State Plan for the Education of Gifted/Talented Students;
3. Include data and procedures designed to ensure that students from all populations inthe district have access to assessment and, if identified, services for the gifted/talented program;
4. Provide for final selection of students to be made by a committee of at least three local district educators who have received training in the nature and needs of gifted-students; and
5. Include provisions regarding furloughs, reassessment, exiting of students fromprogram services, transfer students, and appeals of district decisions regarding program placement.

◆ INSTRUCTION AND STUDENTS IN GT PROGRAMS

The state plan for GT students spells out clearly defined curriculum guidelines. The concept of a "continuum of learning experiences" is introduced. The continuum refers to a curriculum that provides intellectual activities that scaffold upon each other and provide opportunities to address areas of artistic, creative, and leadership abilities for students who have GT abilities. The curriculum and instruction should be vertically aligned and consistent from grade-level to grade-level. The state goal is to ensure that a rigorous instructional curriculum will produce increased student outcomes.

The curriculum should also address all four of the foundation areas (English language arts, mathematics, science, and social studies) using rigorous learning activities. These "appropriately challenging learning experiences" should be designed to appeal to the unique abilities and interests of GT students. These learning opportunities must be made available in all four core curricular areas but students in GT programs are not required to access each.

◆ ACCOUNTABILITY/EVALUATION AND STUDENTS IN GT EDUCATION

School administrators remain accountable for serving students who are GT on each individual school campus. Students who may qualify for GT services must be actively sought out and identified by various staff members tasked by the school district. The district also has the responsibility to monitor the GT program to see that all portions follow guidelines in the state plan.

Administrator Need to Knows

- Administrators must use multiple data sources when assessing students for admittance into a GT program. Single test procedures will not meet the intent of the state plan.
- Administrators must include students in special education for possible participation in GT programs.
- Administrators must implement all 504 and special education accommodations and IEP modifications when instructing and assessing a student that is in a GT program.
- Administrators must insure students have multiple placement options available to them for access to GT programming. For example; GT curriculum programming may be offered in a separate GT classroom, in the regular education classroom, or in advanced placement and dual credit classes.

School districts across the State of Texas are responsible for implementing thepolicies and procedures contained in the State Plan for Education of Students who are GT. All five aspects of GT programs (assessment, design, curriculum and instruction, professional development, and family/community involvement) in the plan state must be addressed by administrators to ensure compliance. The intent of the policies and procedures included in the GT plan are to increase opportunity for students across the state to participate in advances learning activities and thereby raise educational outcomes.

◆ SUMMARY

This chapter is devoted to assisting school administrators in understanding some of the myriad complexities encountered when serving students of diversity. Students entering school are often members of multiple subpopulations, all with varying special needs. This is a large and growing demographic that requires proactive leadership. These student populations are accompanied by specific federal, state and local rules, policies, and procedures that require the savvy school administrator to plan early and often to ensure increasingly better student outcomes.

Involving all levels of educational stakeholders in the process of educating students of diversity is important for school leaders. Data collection about student strengths and areas of need from all sources available yield better planning and implementation. The swelling ranks of these students in schools provide the educational administrator with unique challenges and opportunities to impact lives of children in our school systems.

◆ REFERENCES

Cummins, J. (1981). Age on arrival and immigrant second language learning in Canada: A reassessment. *Applied Linguistics, 2*, 132–149.

Cummins, J. (2000). *Language, power and pedagogy: Bilingual children in the crossfire*. Clevedon: Multilingual Matters.

Cummins, J. (2003). *BICS and CALPS*. Retrieved from http://iteachilearn.org/cummins/bicscalp.html

Echevarria, J., Vogt, M., & Short, D. J. (2012). *Making content comprehensible for English learners: The SIOP model* (4th ed.). Boston: Pearson.

Education for All Handicapped Children Act of 1975 (P.L. 94–142) 20 USC §1401.

Falvey, M. A., & Givner, C. C. (2005). What is an inclusive school? In R. A. Villa & J. S. Thousand (Eds.), *Creating an inclusive school* (2nd ed., pp. 1–11). Los Angeles: ASCD.

Individuals with Disabilities Education Act of 1990 (P.L. 101–476).

Individuals with Disabilities Education Act of 1997 (P.L. 105–17).

Individuals with Disabilities Education Improvement Act of 2004 (P.L. 108–446).

Jacob K. Javitz Gifted Education Act 2001. Retrieved from http://www2.ed.gov/programs/javits/index.html

Krashen, S. D. (1982). *Principles and practice in second language acquisition.* Oxford: Pergamon. Retrieved from http://www.sdkrashen.com/Principles_and_Practice/Principles_and_Practice.pdf

McLaughlin, M. J.(2009). *What every principal needs to know about special education.* Thousand Oaks, CA: Corwin Press.

National Aeronautics and Space Administration. (2014). *NASA history homepage.* Retrieved from http://history.nasa.gov/sputnik/

National Defense Education Act. (1958). (P. L 101–476). Retrieved from http://www.gpo.gov/fdsys/pkg/STATUTE-104/pdf/STATUTE-104-Pg1103.pdf

Rehabilitation Act of 1973 Section 504 Reasonable Accommodations in Schools (P.L. 93–112). Retrieved from http://www.gpo.gov/fdsys/pkg/STATUTE-87/pdf/STATUTE-87-Pg355.pdf

Schutz, R. (2014, June). *Stephen Krashen's theory of second language acquisition.* Retrieved from http://www.sk.com.br/sk-krash.html

Texas Administrative Code. (1996). *Title 19, Part II, Chapter 89. Adaptations for Special Populations. Subchapter A. Gifted/Talented Education.* Retrieved from http://ritter.tea.state.tx.us/rules/tac/chapter089/ch089bb.html

Texas Administrative Code. (2012). *Chapter 89. Adaptations for Special Populations Subchapter BB. Commissioner's Rules Concerning State Plan for educating English language learners.* Retrieved from http://ritter.tea.state.tx.us/rules/tac/chapter089/ch089bb.html

Texas Education Agency. (2014). *Snapshot 2014.* Retrieved from http://ritter.tea.state.tx.us/perfreport/snapshot/2014/state.html

Texas Education Agency. (2015). *Title III, Part A—English Language Acquisition, Language Enhancement, and Academic Achievement Act*. Retrieved from http://tea.texas.gov/TitleIII/PartA/

Texas Education Code. (2012). *Chapter 29. Educational Programs Subchapter B. Bilingual Education and Special Language Programs*. Retrieved from http://www.statutes.legis.state.tx.us/SOTWDocs/ED/htm/ED.29.htm

Texas Project First. (n.d.). *Section 504 of the Rehabilitation Act of 1973*. Retrieved from http://www.texasprojectfirst.org/Sect504.html

US Department of Education. (2015). *Elementary and Secondary Education Act*. Retrieved from http://www.ed.gov/esea

US Department of Education. (1983). *A nation at risk: The imperative for educational reform*. The National Commission on Excellence in Education.

Zong, J., Batalova, J.,& Migration Policy Institute. (2015, July). *The limited English proficient population in the United States*. Retrieved from http://www.migrationpolicy.org/article/limited-english-proficient-population-united-states

Partnering with Professional School Counselors to Promote Student Success

Karl J. Witt ◈ *Christine McNichols* ◈ *Charles Barké*
◈ *Rosemary Barké*

Counseling is "a professional relationship that empowers diverse individuals, families, and groups to accomplish mental health, wellness, education, and career goals" [American Counseling Association (ACA), 2014, p. 20]. Counselors are master's-level mental health practitioners who work in a variety of settings, such as community mental health agencies, behavioral health hospitals, nonprofit organizations, prisons, private practices, and schools. They provide services to individuals, groups, families, and couples and address mental health concerns ranging from depression and anxiety to workplace adjustment. Numerically, they constitute the second-largest group of mental health workers after all social workers [Texas Department of State Health Services (DSHS), 2014]. Counselors also serve in a variety of roles within their organizations, including administration and management, often making the provision of mental health services possible. One of the most widespread and potentially impactful settings for their work is in PreK-12 schools, where professional school counselors practice. To practice in schools, professional school counselors must be certified by the state education agency, which in Texas is Texas Education Agency (TEA).

This chapter focuses on understanding the role of the professional school counselor, empirically based best practices, and how partnerships between counselors and administrators can lead to better, stronger outcomes for students and schools. It begins with an overview and some history to provide context, followed by a summary of the national and Texas models for school counseling, insight into effective administrator–counselor relationships, recent Texas legislative actions that affect school counseling, and ends with a discussion of research evidence and best practices that we recommend to administrators.

To become a professional school counselor in Texas, a person must complete a master's degree in counseling or a related field. This includes a practicum or internship where counselors-in-training work with clients (e.g., students, parents, and faculty members) under the dual clinical supervision of a university faculty member and an experienced practitioner. The internship must be a minimum of 160 clock-hours over a single semester by law, though others last as long as 700 hours over a four-semester period. Counselors must also take a specific combination of courses and achieve a passing score on the state certification exam (Requirements for the Issuance of the Standard School Counselor Certificate, 2009). These requirements ensure that school counselors are properly trained and prepared for their unique and important role. In Texas, aspiring school counselors must also have 2 years of teaching experience or, if from another state, 2 years of counseling experience in a school setting to be eligible for certification. Some school counselors also choose to seek Licensed Professional Counselor status, which requires at least a 48–60-hour master's degree, passage of the national licensure and Texas jurisprudence exams, and an additional 3,000 clock-hours of postmaster's counseling work under the supervision of a Licensed Professional Counselor Supervisor. Regardless of specification or setting, core counselor training focuses on prevention, empowerment, wellness, diversity and multiculturalism, and social justice and advocacy. In addition, professional school counselors receive specialized training to develop and deliver a comprehensive school counseling program (CSCP) in schools.

◆ GENERAL HISTORY

A Myriad of Important People and Events that Shape Counseling Background and Identity

Modern counseling in school settings has its roots in both psychotherapy and guidance. Psychotherapy helps a person or persons gain insight into their thoughts, emotions, and behaviors to live in healthier, more effective ways. Guidance focuses on helping people make choices. In modern counseling, these come together to help people understand themselves, others, and options in a developmentally appropriate way to lead healthier, more fulfilling lives.

Different authors (e.g., Gladding, 2012; Hoyt, 2001; Peterson & Nisenholz, 1999; Pope, 2000; Thompson, 2012; Zunker, 2006) describe the history of the profession. Each emphasizes different elements, while providing a consistent overview. Counseling has been in school settings in the United States from its inception. In the early 1900s, leaders like Jesse B. Davis and Frank Parsons recognized the need for vocational guidance and character development in teens and young adults. Massive migrations from agricultural communities to urban ones meant individuals needed help identifying skills and finding employment (Herr, 2013; Pope, 2000). Davis, a high school principal, recognized that students' academic success, social–emotional development, and workplace skills were all intertwined. In 1907, he started the first systemic guidance program in Grand Rapids, Michigan. The program was designed to proactively address growth of character, career, and suitable behavior in a developmentally appropriate way (Cinotti, 2014; Pope, 2009).

A year later, Parsons, often considered the father of guidance, started the first vocational bureau in Boston. The bureau assisted high school graduates with job placement through school-to-work programs. His revolutionary book *Choosing a Vocation* was published posthumously in 1909. Parsons, who had worked in a number of fields, including education, engineering, and law, helped individuals use "simple common sense" to choose their vocations (Herr, 2013).

He emphasized understanding the self (one's skills and aptitudes), gaining knowledge of the work requirements, and "true reasoning" (understanding how one's traits and potential job factors may or may not work together; Herr, 2013; Pope, 2000).

As Parsons and Davis were addressing adolescents' vocational and character development needs, others were highlighting the need for mental health reform. In 1908, Clifford Beers wrote *A Mind that Found Itself* chronicling his time in a mental intuition (Peterson & Nisenholz, 1999). For the first time, the public became aware of the maltreatment of institutionalized patients and called for reform. Beers himself founded Mental Health America, an organization to support mental health, in 1909 and created the first outpatient mental health clinic in 1913 (Mental Health America, n.d.; Peterson & Nisenholz, 1999). This emphasis on social and emotional interventions increased as schools and communities recognized the benefits and the profession became more established.

Initially, classroom teachers were assigned to incorporate counseling duties into their regular roles. Davis, for instance, initially included them as part of the English curriculum (Pope, 2000). With time, these duties became the responsibility of specially trained personnel (Cinotti, 2014; Herr, 2013), and training became available at an extraordinarily rapid rate. Harvard began offering master's-level classes in 1911, less than 4 years after Parsons, Beers, and Davis formally implemented their programs (Zunker, 2006).

Throughout the rest of the early 1900s, the nation's political and social events helped further propel the counseling field forward. During World War I, the Alpha and Beta systems devised for the US Army efficiently matched service personnel to tasks based on personal attributes and skills in a strengths-based way. Before the war's end, the influential Smith-Hughes Act of 1917 gave schools money for vocational training (Herr, 2013; Pope, 2000).

In the 1920s and 1930s, educational guidance was extended to younger grades to enhance appropriate peer interactions, character development, and career exploration. With the beginning of the Great Depression, helping individuals find and keep employment again became a major goal of guidance counseling. During this time, the Department of Education formed the Civilian Conservation Corps to provide training and employment for young adults (Pope, 2000). This provided jobs for counselors and worked to solidify the need for counselors in society.

With the outbreak of World War II, counselors were again used to recruit servicemen and women and match them with appropriate military roles. The passage of the G.I. Bill right before the war's end led to a massive increase in college attendance and expanded college counseling (Pope, 2000). The influx also strengthened formal counselor training and the profession as a whole, leading to the creation of the ACA in 1951. ACA sought to unify the various counseling groups and support the overall work of counselors. A year later, it created its first new division, the American School Counselor Association (ASCA), for practitioners working in school settings.

By the late 1950s, the United States was deep in a cold war with the Soviet Union, and the first successful orbit of the Soviet satellite Sputnik launched the space race. The US government responded by funding school counseling positions in an effort to encourage people into math and science related careers (Herr, 2013; Lambie & Williamson, 2004; Pope, 2000). By the 1960s, counselors were acknowledged as specialists in human nature and the world of work as younger generations sought more personal satisfaction in the workplace (Pope, 2000). The deinstitutionalization that took place under the Mental Health Act of 1963 re-emphasized mental health in schools. Psychiatric hospitals were replaced with community mental health centers to provide outpatient care; school-aged patients began to be reintegrated into educational settings

(Peterson & Nisenholz, 1999). Although counseling primarily began with vocational guidance and character development, as the profession grew, the emphasis on social and emotional interventions increased.

With societal changes in the 1970s and 1980s, the idea of seeking a counselor for personal concerns became more popular and less stigmatizing. In the 1980s, many states implemented counselor licensure laws to protect consumers from poor training and predatory practices. The Carl D. Perkins Act funded more counseling positions in schools and again stressed the career component of counseling (Pope, 2000). Meanwhile the War on Drugs introduced Red Ribbon Week and awareness of substance use and abuse.

Counseling continued to grow and expand in the 1990s and early 2000s. Updated best-practice standards and ethical codes called for counselors to work towards multicultural competencies and be advocates for social justice. Internationalization pressed researchers to re-examine premises about what works for whom. These decades also brought increased interest in accountability. Practitioners began using technology to provide services, consult, and connect with colleagues (Pope, 2000). Incidents like the Columbine High School shootings reinforced the importance of the counselor's role as the school mental health expert and the need for proactive prevention.

◆ COMPREHENSIVE MODELS

Through its history in schools, counseling has had three foci: academic, career, and personal/social–emotional development. To help counselors balance these strands and clarify counselors' roles, ACA created a systematic plan and description of appropriate counseling tasks in schools through ASCA (ASCA, 2012; Cinotti, 2014). Rather than simply listing tasks, the resulting ASCA National Model created a comprehensive approach to programming for counselors based on best practices (Cinotti, 2014). While it contains its own shortcomings, it is an effort to ensure comprehensive services for every student to the greatest extent possible.

Several states, including Texas, adapted the National Model to local conditions. The Texas version, *A Model Comprehensive, Developmental Guidance and Counseling Program for Texas Public Schools: A Guide for Program Development Pre-K-12th Grade*, was last revised in 2004 (Henderson, 2004). It was codeveloped by the TEA and the Texas Counseling Association (TCA) to more explicitly address the responsibilities for counselors outlined in the Texas Education Code. While changes in the counseling profession and law highlight the need for revision, it remains the model endorsed by TEA.

The Texas Education Code outlines the components of a counseling program for a school. Section 33.005. Developmental Guidance and Counseling Programs. A school counselor shall work with the school faculty and staff, students, parents, and the community to plan, implement, and evaluate a Developmental Guidance and Counseling Program. The school counselor shall design the program to include:

(1) A guidance curriculum to help students develop their full educational potential, including the student's interests and career objectives;

(2) A responsive services component to intervene on behalf of any student whose immediate personal concerns or problems put the student's continued educational, career, personal, or social development at risk;

(3) An individual planning system to guide a student as the student plans, monitors, and manages the student's own educational, career, personal, and social development; and

(4) System support to support the efforts of teachers, staff, parents, and other members of the community in promoting the educational, career, personal, and social development of students(Developmental Guidance and Counseling Programs, 2013).

ASCA (2012) and Henderson (2004) describe each of these elements. The guidance curriculum consists of lessons delivered to all students. Topics include character development, effective communication with peers, tobacco awareness, high school graduation plans, career exploration, and bullying to name a few. These lessons may also be viewed as preventive mental health and wellness interventions. Lessons are designed to complement academic material being taught in the classroom when possible (Henderson, 2004). Individual planning helps individual students explore, consider, and clarify needs and goals in the academic, career, personal, and social domains as an extension and application of the guidance curriculum. Describing the 16 career clusters is part of the guidance curriculum; a tailored conversation about course selections toward a specific post-secondary outcome in individual planning. Responsive services meet immediate individual needs and may be either preventive or remedial. These include crisis intervention, individual and group counseling, and addressing high priority topics, such as substance abuse. Leading a group for students impacted by divorce, checking on the emotional well-being of a student whose parent died, or investigating an individual's sudden decline in grades are some examples. Attempted self-harm, pregnancy, and child abuse are others. Responsive services are generally time-limited and referrals to external mental health providers are appropriate when students need more extensive counseling interventions. Finally, system support consists of program management activities to establish, maintain, and enhance the counseling program, including professional development, consultative services to other professionals and parents, and community outreach.

The Texas model recommends approximate percentages of time for each function. These remain fairly consistent for responsive services and system support across grade levels, while needs for guidance and individual planning shift as students age (Henderson, 2004). Table 20.1 breaks down the percentage of time that should be dedicated to each function based upon age.

Because data-driven decision-making is a core premise of the ASCA National Model, there is ongoing research on its implementation and effectiveness. Carey and Dimmitt (2012) looked at the results of six statewide implementations of the ASCA National Model. They found that the most successful schools in those states were the ones where counselors spent most of their time

TABLE 20.1
Recommended Percentages of Time by Function

Level	Function (%)				
	Guidance Curriculum	Responsive Services	Individual Planning	System Support	Nonguidance
Elementary	35 – 45	30 – 40	5 – 10	10 – 15	0
Middle	35 – 40	30 – 40	15 – 25	10 – 15	0
High	15 – 25	25 – 35	25 – 35	15 – 20	0

Based on data in Henderson (2004).

providing direct services to students and where a coordinated program was in place. They also found significant correlations between positive student outcomes and lower student to counselor ratios. Finally, they observed that counselors must keep current with developments in the profession and may need additional training in some areas, including the use of data.

◆ THE ROLE OF THE COUNSELOR

Because counselors are involved in so many elements of students' lives, it is helpful to outline elements of their role in the academic, career, and personal/social–emotional strands. In addition, practical considerations, such as identifying students in need, ethical practice, and crisis planning, are addressed.

Academic Development

The counselor's role in academic development is perhaps the most familiar. While counselors are often perceived as exclusively addressing the needs of the highest and lowest students (Dahir & Stone, 2012; Dollarhide & Saginak, 2012), in reality, the counselor is responsible for meeting the academic needs of all students (Henderson, 2004). Counselors should have systems in place to monitor both the products and process of students' academic progress. Counselor training provides insight into motivation, achievement, typical development, and formal assessment, and counselors should be proficient in interpreting everything from SAT scores to reports from psychologists and educational diagnosticians. This knowledge, combined with in-depth student contact and regular consultation, makes counselors a valuable resource in creating age- and developmentally appropriate Individualized Education Plans and placement in programs like Advancement Via Individual Determination (AVID), gifted and talented (GT), or peer tutoring. It is also important to recognize that counselors are typically not trained in administration; indeed, there is very little overlap between core counselor and principal training other than serving student populations (Cinotti, 2014). It therefore follows that an administrator is more appropriately in charge of the organization, administration, and meetings for special education, Section 504, GT, and Response to Intervention, while the counselor functions as a knowledgeable expert, team member, and student advocate, each in line with their specialized training.

Career Development

Counselors in schools are also responsible for facilitating students' career development. At a minimum, they help orient students and parents to postsecondary and workplace expectations; select, administer, and interpret career, interest, and aptitude inventories; encourage the exploration and development of interests and skills; and connect school performance to earning potential, life choices, and other post-secondary outcomes (Thompson, 2012). Districts often recognize the importance of administering career-related inventories, but interpreting the results is one of the oft-neglected components of the career counselor role. Students become upset or discount important information when the results do not match self-image or self-expectations. A student seeing "accountant," for instance, may initially reject the result based on the perception "I am not good at math," while failing to recognize the reflection of his excellent organizational skills and desire to engage in detail-oriented work.

In school settings, counselors facilitate the progression of career exploration from the initial "who am I" and "what is out there" in kindergarten and again in adolescence to preparation, entry, and re-evaluation as students hold jobs in their mid- and late-teens. Indeed, with the increased national emphasis on employability, Career and Technical Education, the States' Career Cluster Initiative, dual credit, and early college high schools, outcomes of this process have become increasingly important to student and school success.

At the elementary level, career development is often included as part of classroom guidance activities and primarily consists of exposing students to the broadest possible array of careers. Researchers have demonstrated that broad exposure during the elementary years more often correlates to a greater number of advanced degrees, higher levels of professional attainment, better incomes, and enhanced quality of life. Conversely, prematurely limiting options reduces the number of women and minorities in the sciences, medicine, and other high-earning professions. In secondary settings, college and career fairs are often used in conjunction with classroom guidance and individualized attention during the course selection and personal graduation plan processes.

Informational and exposure elements can often be conducted via a classroom guidance model or even through school- or district-wide activities. Collaboration with teachers can lead to effective delivery as part of academic lessons in the classroom. It is also apparent, however, that more individualized career counseling requires either small groups or even one-on-one time with the counselor. Authors (e.g., Oliver, Ricard, Witt, Alvarado, & Hill, 2010; Thompson, 2012) have highlighted that first-generation college students need more support and "college knowledge" from grade school personnel and are more likely to rely on other significant non-familial relationships. The "new" three R's in education, rigor, relevance, and relationship (International Center for Leadership in Education, n.d.) are crucial in career counseling just as they are in the classroom.

Personal and Social–Emotional Development

While other school personnel, such as deans of students and counseling center staff, can assist with components of the academic and career roles, the personal and social–emotional development role calls for the unique combination of knowledge and skills developed through school counselor training. According to DSHS (2014), there are significant student needs in this area. Summarizing data from the Center for Health Statistics, DSHS (2014) reported that 36.8% of high school female students and 20.2% of high school males in Texas reported feeling sad or hopeless for at least a 2-week period in the year prior to the survey. This means that roughly one in five males and two in five females meet the length criteria for a major depressive disorder diagnosis (American Psychiatric Association, 2013). The suicide statistics compiled by DSHS (2014) were even more sobering: 16.7% of Texan adolescents had seriously contemplated suicide, 15.1% had a plan for suicide, and 10.1% had attempted suicide in the prior year. More holistically, one quarter of adolescents reported "negative emotional states" in the prior year (DSHS, 2014).

A participant in a recent study (McNichols & Witt, 2015) described the personal and social–emotional role of a counselor in this way:

> School counselors [need to be free to perform] more of a counseling role versus testing [coordinator] versus 'You're really the Vice Principal.' [. . .] You can't be the bad guy and the school friend. I tell the elementary kids: 'I'm the school friend; that's my job. If you need a friend, that's me. I'm the school friend, and I'm the one that helps you with grownup problems. [. . .] When you hit a grownup problem or even a problem [. . .] that's not a grown up problem, if it's too big for *you*, you come see me. I'm the school friend.' And counselors need to be able to do that.

In this role, counselors work with students on the development of identity, character, and decision-making processes. They also help students learn effective communication with peers, parents, and school personnel through more appropriate word choice, timing, goal clarification, and perspective taking. Examples of personal and social–emotional development include teaching elementary students to recognize emotions, to make friends, to take turns, or about stranger danger. Middle school topics might involve bullying, getting along with others, recognizing personal and social interests, and tobacco awareness, while high school counselors might discuss dating violence, changing roles within the family unit, and healthy involvement in and differentiation from peer groups. Coping with divorce, death, self-harm, pregnancy, and crisis counseling often appear across grades. In a broader sense, the personal and social–emotional role requires counselors to connect to students, parents, and school personnel regularly on a meaningful level.

Other Elements

Other elements of the counseling role do not neatly fall into academic, career, and personal/social–emotional development categories. In the last decade, crisis intervention, consultation, advocacy, and leadership have become increasingly prominent. To effectively perform all these functions, counselors must also be able to identify students in need and, most importantly, engage in ethical practice.

Crisis Counseling

A crisis is "a perception or experiencing of an event or situation as an intolerable difficulty that exceeds the person's current resources and coping mechanisms" (James, 2008, p. 3). Left unattended, a person who experiences a crisis and does not receive some sort of help or intervention can experience significant impairment and malfunctioning. Although crises are often thought of as events such as mass school shootings that affect multiple people, individuals and small groups also experience crises, such as a student who threatens or completes a suicide. School settings and personnel are not exempt from crisis situations. The death of a beloved teacher or student, personal threat of suicide and/or homicide, a natural or manmade disaster event during school hours, gang violence, hostage situations, and mass shootings are all crisis events that can have lasting effects on all involved.

School counselors are trained for crisis response. They are trained to work with bereavement, assess a client for potential suicide and/or homicide, and deescalate a volatile situation, Counselor also provides psychological first aid, conducts triage assessments, and makes appropriate referrals when outside resources are needed. Though specialized law enforcement should negotiate hostage situations, counselors can assist by providing important information about the students involved. After a crisis, school counselors can provide individual and group support to help students and faculty process the experience and adjust to postcrisis life.

School counselors should also be involved and included when developing school-wide crisis plans. James (2008) covers the topic in depth. Crisis plans should be comprehensive and include specified roles to be held by preappointed faculty and staff. Roles are often held by administrators or select trained teachers and include the crisis response coordinator, who is usually a senior administrator, media liaison, security liaison, community/medical liaison, and parent liaison. Counselors, however, are crisis interveners. Depending on the size of the school and resources, some teachers may also be trained in psychological first-aid. These teachers may function as secondary crisis interveners. Crisis plans should also include a detailed system comprised logistics for onsite communications, procedural checklists, and building plans and clear physical requirements, such as counseling locations, a communication center, a first-aid room, and a break room (James, 2008).

Consultation and Advocacy

School counselors are expected to serve as consultants to parents, teachers, and administrators. By providing information pertaining to behaviors and processes tied to normal and atypical human growth and development in children and adolescents, school counselors can help consultees address situations independently. This has the dual benefits of teaching others to proverbially fish on their own while expanding the scope of services counselors are able to provide (Dahir & Stone, 2012).

A second crucial role of counselors is that of student advocate (ACA, 2014). This requires school counselors to not only work on behalf of individual students but also to work on a systemic scale. Addressing policies that may inadvertently create inequity with the school and proposing well-conceived suggestions to better serve all students in collaboration with other members of the school and community are part of this particular function.

Leadership

Counselors are also often expected to serve as members of the school's leadership team, since their skill sets and training frequently complement those of teachers and administrators. In 2009, the National Association of Secondary School Principals, the College Board, and ASCA collaborated to examine the perceptions and experiences of principals and school counselors to create effective teams for improved student achievement (Finkelstein, 2009). A foundational belief shared among these entities is that the principal–school counselor relationship is an important resource for creating educational reform.

As in most effective relationships, principals and counselors agreed that communication, mutual trust and respect, a shared vision, and shared decision-making are essential in the development and maintenance of an effective principal–counselor relationship. When the relationship was less than ideal, principals often felt that there was not enough time for effective communication, and school counselors often felt that principals did not respect the counselor's training and expertise, and that the school structure required the counselor to spend more time doing supportive administrative tasks, such as record keeping and clerical tasks, coordinating and facilitating the standardized tests given to students, and managing scheduling tasks. Although principals and school counselors agreed that "helping to promote student personal and social development' and 'helping students with career planning" were the most important counselor activities, often the existing structure did not allow a school counselor to spend adequate time on these valuable goals (Finkelstein, 2009).

The study also identified ten characteristics of an effective principal–counselor relationship:

- Open communication that provides multiple opportunities for input to decision making,
- Opportunities to share ideas on teaching, learning and school-wide educational initiatives,
- Sharing information about needs within the school and community,
- School counselors' participation on school leadership teams,
- Joint responsibility in the development of goals and metrics that indicate success,
- Mutual trust between the principal and school counselors,

- A shared vision of what is meant by student success,
- Mutual respect between the principal and school counselors,
- Shared decision making on initiatives that impact student success, and
- A collective commitment to equity and opportunity.

Identifying Students in Need

Since current state law mandates an approximate maximum ratio of 500 students per counselor (Certified School Counselor, 2013), and counselors have a wide array of responsibilities, one of the major challenges is identifying students in need. There are several actions that counselors can take to address this need. Identification might come through self-referral, other school personnel, parents and significant others in the student's life, and counselor observation.

First, counselors need a sign-in system for students who are referring themselves for services. These lists can be checked periodically throughout the day so needs can be addressed. Some schools have also begun to implement electronic versions of a sign-in system. Counselors should generally avoid social media, however, except perhaps to help students and parents become aware of services.

Counselors also need a referral process in place for teachers and administrators. Some choose to handle this informally through open-door policies, while others develop standardized forms that are distributed among the staff at the beginning of the year. Either way, the process must be clearly communicated to all with periodic reminders. It should also be emphasized that the counselor's role is not that of disciplinarian. Indeed, acting as a disciplinarian undermines the fundamental concept of the counseling role: a listening ear and support, even in times of last resort. Often, the counselor can have a conversation with a student to brainstorm or practice skills to effectively avoid future trouble while helping the student understand that others may be administering disciplinary consequences for past actions.

Counselors must also be available to respond to parent concerns. Email, telephone, drop-in visits, and scheduled appointments are all ways parents seek to communicate. Timely intervention on a student's behalf with teachers, staff, and other students can sometimes prevent situations from becoming headaches for administrators. Similarly, counselors are sometimes in a position to perceive different patterns than administrators due to the types of interactions they have.

Finally, counselors need to maintain a feel for the "pulse" of the school. This requires being present with students and listening for common threads regarding other students, teachers, and school-wide morale. Informally visiting with faculty members during their conference periods or after school to establish a rapport can help counselors better understand and address concerns expressed by students, parents, and teachers. Discreet observations of classrooms and students and simply spending time in the halls can greatly enhance counseling services.

Practicing Ethically

According to the ACA Code of Ethics (2014), "Counselors recognize that trust is a cornerstone of the counseling relationship. Counselors aspire to earn the trust of clients by creating an ongoing partnership, establishing and upholding appropriate boundaries, and maintaining confidentiality" (p. 6). Confidentiality is essential to building trust between counselor and client/student and is a promise to never reveal anything about clients without their consent. There are, however, some limitations to confidentiality that counselors must communicate to their clients. These limits include a threat to harm oneself or someone else (as in the case of suicide or homicide), disclosure of abuse of a child, elder, or vulnerable person, communications with third parties only with client consent (e.g., communicating with a student's doctor), and if counseling records are subpoenaed by a court of law. Because students are typically minors, the rules of confidentially vary slightly in terms of consent and information sharing with parents. Again, exceptions exist. For instance, parental consent is not required for suicide prevention, substance abuse, or sexual, physical, or emotional abuse (Henderson, 2004). Rather than creating potentially adversarial relationships, however, counselors explain to parents the importance of confidentiality and how it builds trust between the counselor and the student. Counselors also "work to establish, as appropriate, collaborative relationships with parents/ guardians to best serve clients" (ACA, 2014, p. 7). Counselors should also be well acquainted with the Family Educational Rights and Privacy Act (FERPA), Health Insurance Portability and Accountability Act (HIPAA), and other laws pertaining to appropriate disclosure. These dictate who may be privy to student counseling information and the circumstances under which such disclosure may occur. For instance, counselors in Texas are explicitly forbidden from disclosing a student's participation in a substance abuse recovery program, even to parents of a minor.

◆ RECENT CHANGES IN THE PROFESSION

Like other human service fields, counseling has become increasingly focused on concrete accountability to its stakeholders and the public at large. This often feels unnatural for counselors, who have traditionally focused directly on the welfare of clients. In the past then, success was measured directly by the improvement of client conditions.

Accountability

When the accountability movement began, counselors in schools first approached the issue by documenting time on task. By demonstrating time spent with students, planning components, and conducting other job-related responsibilities, counselors showed that they were indeed contributing to the school rather than fulfilling the "roaming the halls with a cup of coffee" stereotype (Dahir & Stone, 2012).

Accountability in counseling programs has taken on a new dimension (Dahir & Stone, 2012). While researchers (e.g., Carey & Dimmitt, 2012) have repeatedly demonstrated the effectiveness and necessity of counseling services provided by fully trained professionals, parents, administrators, and counselors themselves understandably want to know that counseling is making a difference in their schools (Dahir & Stone, 2012; Henderson, 2004). Documenting increased attendance, improved grades, reduced office referrals, and scholarship awards can help stakeholders realize that *their* counselors are contributing to students' academic, career, personal, and social–emotional success, especially after prolonged, intensive interventions.

Of course, counseling interventions alone are not a magic bullet. Nor can counselors' crucial roles be reduced to a few numbers. Fewer countable instances of bullying are certainly a positive sign, but it is more difficult to quantify the intrapersonal change for the aggressor and the aggrieved than results from time invested. Similarly, as with the small moments of care and compassion demonstrated by many educators, the efforts may not bear visible fruit for years.

Texas Legislature 2015 Changes Pertaining to Counselors in PK-12 Schools

A large number of bills related to counseling in schools were proposed during the 2015 session of the Texas Legislature [TCA, 2015; Texas Legislature Online (TLO), 2015]. Some pertained to a need for additional training. Others impacted information shared with students. Still others include potential extensions to existing counselor responsibilities.

Legislation altered some student opportunities, and the information that counselors share with those students (TCA, 2015; TLO, 2015). House Bills 18 and 505 removed the possibility of limiting enrollment in dual credit courses. Students can no longer be limited to a set number of dual credit courses or college hours taken in a single semester, by grade level, or in their entire secondary academic career. House Bill 1,430 explicitly incorporated the mental health professions into the health sciences career cluster, another change affecting course choices. In a related vein, Senate Bill 239 added new state loan repayment programs for those providing mental health services in a high need area, again encouraging students to consider a health sciences career cluster. House Bill 1,559 required that information be posted on the school Website pertaining to programs and services locally available for homeless students. House Bill 2,472 removed the expiration of certain provisions of the current admissions process to The University of Texas at Austin tied to graduating from a Texas public high school with a particular class rank, and several bills enhanced benefits for military service.

The eighty-fourth session also increased school counselor responsibilities (TCA, 2015; TLO, 2015). Extended counselor responsibilities include increased testing responsibilities to determine Pre-K eligibility and the development and implementation of a family engagement plan for Pre-K students as described in House Bill 4. House Bill 18 formally extended the requirement for personal graduation plans/high school graduation plans down to grade 7 for all students. House Bill 1,613 created another measure for counselors to track for graduation purposes by exempting students who satisfy Texas Success Initiative college readiness benchmarks in mathematics and English from the corresponding end-of-course exams. Likewise, Senate Bill 149 established a method of graduating from high school for those that do not pass end-of-course exams. House Bill 1,993 allowed parents to electronically sign grade and performance notices in districts using electronic platforms, and House Bill 3,748 was designed in part to enhance the academic, personal, and social–emotional services in schools for students in the foster care system. Finally, House Bills 2,628 and 2,804 made modifications regarding college and career alignment and readiness and measures thereof.

House Bill 18 authorized the creation of an advanced training academy in college and career readiness for school counselors and related personnel at The University of Texas at Austin. Suicide prevention training became mandatory for all district educators under House Bill 2,186. Senate Bill 133 incentivized training in mental health first aid training for school district employees. This complements Senate Bill 460 from the 2013 legislative session requiring educators to receive training in signs of suicide and mental or emotional disorders and their inclusion in coordinated school health efforts, and 2015's Senate Bill 674 extends these into standard educator training.

A combination of three senate bills (200, 202, and 219) significantly altered the landscape of the state's health professions and social services (TCA, 2015; TLO, 2015). This impacts the work counselors do in schools by changing referrals and the nature of the agencies with whom they work. A host of agencies were abolished by these bills and absorbed into other organizations. Senate Bill 200 also created a division within DSHS for prevention and early intervention. Because much of prevention and early intervention takes place in school settings, this will doubtless affect the provision of counseling services in schools.

◆ WHAT WORKS: TOWARD THE EFFECTIVE EVIDENCE-BASED PRACTICE OF SCHOOL COUNSELING

Evidence-based practice (Leff, 2002) is the gold standard for many professions, including medicine, where it first appeared, nursing and other health care affiliates, psychotherapy and all forms of counseling, as well as education (Coe, 1999). This standard promotes the use of practices, interventions, and programs that have been empirically demonstrated to be effective and have positive outcomes for people served by the profession. School counseling has been the focus of an extensive empirical research process for many years, from which has developed a strong set of empirically based practice guidelines that are reflected in the national school counseling model (ASCA, 2012), and in the model developed by the state of Texas. There are journals devoted specifically to the school counseling profession, as well as broader counseling publications that frequently include school counseling articles. Within school counseling, there has been a significant increase in attention to this standard of evidence-based practice, including projects funded by the Institute of Educational Sciences (IES), a division of the US Department of Education. IES is the research arm of the US Department of Education, whose mission is to provide rigorous and relevant evidence on which to ground education practice and policy and to share this information broadly.

In this section, we offer a summary review of some of the most salient and potentially impactful research results that school administrators might find helpful in guiding the best practices of school counseling programs at their campuses. Because there have been hundreds of research articles on the effectiveness of school counseling programs, we sought to examine and share meta-analyses that organized and integrated those results into comprehensive outcome results across the several program dimensions that have been studied, as well as some representative individual studies. Dimmit and Holt (2011), at The Center for School Counseling Outcome Research and Evaluation at the University of Massachusetts (recent IES grant recipients), undertook a collation of this entire body of school outcome research evidence and published a report available from the ACA:(http://www.counseling.org/PublicPolicy/PDF/Research_Support_School_Counseling-ACA-CSCORE_02-11.pdf). Subsequently, Carey and Dimmit (2012) added another compilation of school counseling effectiveness studies, this one published by ASCA: (https://www.school-counselor.org/asca/media/asca/Careers-Roles/Effectiveness.pdf).These reports include empirical results across several distinguishable domains of school counseling outcome evidence documented by research on school counseling programs. Within each of these outcome domains, we will cite several studies from these reports and provide additional details about one or more example outcome studies.

Overall Effectiveness of School Counseling Programs in Schools

There have been some meta-analyses examining the overall effectiveness of school counseling program across many studies. An early review of more than 50 studies (Whiston & Sexton, 1998) found that guidance curriculum, individual and career planning, responsive services, and system support aspects of CSCPs all have positive influences on students. More recently, Whiston, Tai, Rahardja, and Eder (2011) conducted a meta-analysis of school counseling outcome research systematically analyzing and synthesizing the results from 117 studies, in which 153 school counseling interventions were done with a total of more than 16,000 students. They reported that across all of those studies, when comparing treatment and control group means, there was an overall effect size of 0.30. Students who received counseling improved almost a third of a standard deviation more than those who did not receive the treatment. These results were found in multiple areas, including academic achievement, problem solving, and career knowledge.

In terms of overall effectiveness, in a recent study reporting on a federally funded project (Duarte& Hatch, 2014), a school district implemented a CSCP in three elementary schools, based on the ASCA National Model. In their study, Duarte and Hatch provided prevention education for all students and more targeted and specific interventions for subgroups of students with specific needs. There were substantial improvements in attendance, behavior, and achievement in the schools using this approach. Based on this and other studies they reviewed, Whiston and Quinby (2009) conclude that, "in addition to overall effectiveness and positive impact, school counseling programs have evidence for positive outcomes with students' experience of school, college/career readiness, academic achievement and retention, promoting positive behaviors, and improving mental health of students, in both crisis and non-crisis contexts" (p. 267).

Students' Experience of School

Dimmit and Holt (2011) identified a number of studies that have provided empirical evidence about the positive effects of school counseling programs on how students experience school. For example, Lapan, Gysbers, and Sun (1997) conducted a large scale (n = 22,000+) statewide survey in Missouri about the perceived effects of CSCPs on students' school experiences. The research concluded that counseling services improved student grades and career preparation through better information and a better school climate.

In a more recent, similar study, Lapan, Gysbers, and Petroski (2001) conducted the most rigorous program evaluation study on school counseling programs to date. They used hierarchical linear modeling with another large sample of more than 22,000 students and nearly 5,000 teachers in 184 middle schools across a Midwestern state. They found that counseling services increased the students' feeling of safety and allowed them to develop better relationships with teachers. These students were more optimistic and better behaved. These are notable positive effects of fully implemented school counseling programs.

College and Career Readiness

Dimmit and Holt (2011) describe another important school outcome domain that has accumulated evidence from school counseling researchers, namely college and career readiness. Their analysis indicates that counseling services are effective in increasing college preparation for secondary students. For example, Whiston et al. (2003) did a meta-analysis of treatment modalities used in career interventions comparing individual career counseling, group career counseling, career workshops and classes, and computerized career systems. The study showed that the use of school counselors was much more effective than other methods of disseminating information.

Academic Achievement and Retention

There are many, varied studies empirically demonstrating the positive effects of CSCPs on academic achievement across the K-12 spectrum. In a compendium of recent school counseling research studies published by ASCA (2012), a large number of studies are presented providing strong empirical evidence for the positive impact of school counseling on academics. This includes a meta-analysis of six statewide studies (Carey & Dimmitt, 2012) in which they found consistent evidence that school counseling programs enhance academic achievement along with other valuable results. In an early study, Lapan et al. (1997) found that students in high schools with CSCPs were more successful academically, based on grade point average (GPA) than those without comprehensive programs. Sink and Stroh (2003) used a causal comparative method to determine whether counseling programs produced higher achievement scores among elementary students. Data from 150 public elementary schools were randomly included and identified as either CSCP schools or non-CSCP schools. This sample included achievement data from more than 20,000 elementary school students. They found that students did better on both national tests of academic knowledge and on state tests of academic achievement in the CSCP schools.

Improving Mental Health Functioning

Responsive services and counseling interventions within school counseling program have consistently been shown to have positive effects on student behavioral, emotional and mental health (Prout & Demartino, 1986; Prout & Prout, 1998; Whiston & Quinby, 2009). These studies show that that effective counseling services are capable of improving the school climate through decreasing aggression among students.

Research Implications for the Practice of School Counseling

In their white paper for ASCA, Carey and Dimmit (2012) report on a summary of six statewide studies on student outcomes related to school counseling. They end their summary with a set of practice implications that we believe are worth including here (ACA, 2015).

School counselor level of practice:

- Use data.
- Prioritize college and career-readiness counseling, Career and Technical Education, promoting academic success, parent involvement.
- Spend time on responsive services, guidance curriculum and individual planning, as well as program evaluation and system support.

Program/school level of practice:

- Implement a differentiated school counseling program delivery system if one is not in place. Implement the ASCA National Model if not already in place.
- When implementing the ASCA model, begin with the management system and add in foundation and evaluation components later.

District level of practice:

- Implement the national ASCA model if not already in place.
- Decrease student-to-counselor ratios to improve student attendance, improve student discipline rates, improve student graduation rates, and improve student technical proficiency.
- Provide district-level professional development for school counselors in relevant areas with other peers.
- Create district policies that ensure equitable school counseling program access for all students.

State level of practice:

- Mandate ASCA National Model use.
- Mandate student-to-school counselor ratios to improve student outcomes.
- Provide state-level professional development for school counselors at statewide and regional events.
- Create policies that ensure equitable school counseling program access for all students.

Evidence-Based Best Practices

From the body of empirical work that has been done to evaluate and document the effectiveness of school counseling programs, there are a number of best practices that we offer to help administrators collaborate with their school counselors to positively impact the education, development, and well-being of all students in their schools.

- Adopt and implement the ASCA National Model for School Counseling to the fullest extent possible.
- Collect, analyze, and share data to determine the needs of students and then use those data to create programs and specific interventions to address the identified needs.
- Collect outcome data on programs and interventions above to determined their effectiveness and provide results-based accountability to administrators, boards, and parents.
- Provide college and career education so that all students can make informed choices.
- Establish accessible responsive services, both individual and group, to provide brief interventions for a variety of student issues, concerns and behavioral problems, with appropriate referrals outside of school for more extensive treatments.
- Be available to meet with parents about their concerns related to their children's progress in school or identified issues at home that can affect school.
- Consult with teachers to help them learn and use effective responses to classroom behavior and academic concerns they have about their students.
- Collaborate with other professional staff, including LSSPs, nurses, and administrators to address a variety of academic, behavioral, and health-related needs.
- Maximize school counselors' time and effort on school counseling roles and activities and limit their involvement in nonschool counseling roles and activities.

Our recommendations and hopes are that administrators will take full advantage of the opportunity to promote and collaborate in the development and ongoing growth and improvement of CSCPs. If you are already engaged in the best practices cited above, congratulations and well done! If not, we encourage you to work toward them. We have no doubt at all that this will return your investment of time, energy and resources many times over, and reflect positively on your leadership.

In closing, the world of counseling in schools is constantly evolving. Professional school counselors, by virtue of their education, training, unique professional prospective, and roles, support and enhance students' success in their academics, careers, and personal, social, and emotional development. School counselors can play an important part in the organization of successful schools. Those who are free to fulfill the role for which they were trained can meet stakeholders' expectations and collaboratively contribute to the school's mission.

◆ REFERENCES

American Counseling Association. (2014). *ACA code of ethics*. Retrieved from http://www.counseling .org/ethics/

American Counseling Association. (2015). *FAQs: Licensure policies*. Retrieved from http://www. counseling.org/knowledge-center/faqs-licensure-policies

American Psychiatric Association. (2013). *Diagnostic and statistical manual of mental disorders* (5th ed.). Arlington, VA: American Psychiatric Publishing.

American School Counselor Association. (2012). *The ASCA National Model: A framework for school counseling programs* (3rd ed.). Alexandria, VA: Author.

Carey, J., & Dimmitt, C. (2012). School counseling and student outcomes: Summary of six statewide studies. *Professional School Counseling, 16*(2), 146–153.

Certified School Counselor, Tex. Educ. Code Ann. §33.002 (Vernon 1995 & Supp. 2003, 2009, 2013).

Cinotti, D. (2014). School counseling: A historical perspective and commentary. *The Professional Counselor, 4*(5), 417–425. doi:10.15241/dc.4.5.417

Coe, R. (1999). *A manifesto for evidence-based education*. Retrieved from http://www.cemcentre.org/ evidence-based-education/manifesto-for-evidence-based-education

Dahir, C. A., & Stone, C. B. (2012). *The transformed school counselor* (2nd ed.). Belmont, CA: Brooks/ Cole, Cengage Learning.

Developmental Guidance and Counseling Programs, Tex. Educ. Code Ann. §33.005 (Vernon 1995 & Supp. 2001, 2013).

Dimmit, C., & Holt, D. (2011). *Research support for school counseling*. Retrieved from http://www. counseling.org/PublicPolicy/PDF/Research_Support_School_Counseling-ACA-CSCORE_02-11 .pdf

Dollarhide, C.T., & Saginak, K. A. (2012). *Comprehensive school counseling programs: K-12 delivery systems in action* (2nd ed.). Upper Saddle River, NJ: Pearson.

Duarte, D., & Hatch, T. (*2014*) Successful Implementation of a Federally Funded Violence Prevention Elementary School Counseling Program: Results Bring Sustainability. *Professional School Counseling*, 18, (1), 71–81. doi: http://dx.doi.org/10.5330/prsc.18.1.vtl5g6343m4130v7

Finkelstein, D. (2009). *A closer look at the principal-counselor relationship: A survey of principals and counselors*. Retrieved from https://www.schoolcounselor.org/asca/media/asca/home/CloserLook.pdf

Gladding, S. T. (2012). *Counseling: A comprehensive profession* (7th ed.). Upper Saddle River, NJ: Pearson.

Henderson, P. (2004). *A model comprehensive, developmental guidance and counseling program for Texas public schools: A guide for program development Pre-K-12th grade* (Revised 2004). Austin, Texas: Texas Education Agency.

Herr, E. L. (2013). Trends in the history of vocational guidance. *The Career Development Quarterly, 61*, 277–282. doi:10.1002/j.2161-0045.2013.00056.x

Hoyt, K. B. (2001). A reaction to Mark Pope's (2000) "A brief history of career counseling in the United States". *The Career Development Quarterly, 49*, 374–379.

International Center for Leadership in Education. (n.d.). *Rigor/relevance framework*. Retrieved from http://www.leadered.com/our-philosophy/rigor-relevance-framework.php

James, R. K. (2008). *Crisis intervention strategies* (6th ed.).Belmont, CA: Brooks/Cole.

Lambie, G. W., & Williamson, L. L. (2004). The challenge to change from guidance counseling to professional school counseling: A historical proposition. *Professional School Counseling, 8*(2), 124–131.

Lapan, R., Gysbers, N., & Petroski, G.F. (2001). Helping seventh graders be safe and successful: A statewide study of the impact of comprehensive guidance and counseling programs. *Journal of Counseling and Development*, 79, 320–330.

Lapan, R., Gysbers, N., & Sun, Y. (1997). The impact of more fully implemented guidance programs on the school experiences of high school students: A statewide evaluation study. *Journal of Counseling & Development*, 75, 292–302.

Leff, H. S. (2002). Section V: Insurance for Mental Health Care: Chapter 17. A Brief History of Evidence-Based Practice and a Vision for the Future. SAMHSA's National Mental Health Information Center. Retrieved from http://mentalhealth.samhsa.gov/publications/allpubs/SMA04-3938/Chapter17.asp

McNichols, C., & Witt, K. J. (2015). *The wisdom of experience: The success of seasoned rural counselor supervisors and their ideas for change.* Manuscript in preparation.

Mental Health America. (n.d.). *Mental Health America: Our history.* Retrieved from http://www.mentalhealthamerica.net/our-history

Oliver, M., Ricard, R. J., Witt, K. J., Alvarado, M., & Hill, P. (2010). Creating college advising connections: Comparing motivational beliefs of early college high school students to traditional first-year university students. *NACADA Journal, 30*(1), 14–22. doi: http://dx.doi.org/10.12930/0271-9517-30.1.14

Peterson, J. V., & Nisenholz, B. (1999). *Orientation to counseling* (4th ed.). Boston: Allyn & Bacon.

Pope, M. (2000). A brief history of career counseling in the United States. *Career Development Quarterly, 48*(3), 194–211.

Pope, M. (2009). Jesse Buttrick Davis (1871–1955): Pioneer of vocational guidance in the schools. *The Career Development Quarterly, 57*, 248–258.

Prout, H. T. & DeMartino, R. (1986). A meta-analysis of school-based studies of psychotherapy. *Journal of School Psychology*, 24, 285–292.

Prout, H.T., & Prout, S.M. (1998). A meta-analysis of school-based studies of counseling and psychotherapy: An update. *Journal of School Psychology*, 36, 121–136.

Requirements for the Issuance of the Standard School Counselor Certificate, 34 Tex. Reg. 9201. (2009).

School Counselors, General Duties, Tex. Educ. Code Ann. §33.006 (Vernon 1995 & Supp. 2001, 2013).

Sink, C.A., & Stroh, H.R. (2003). Raising achievement test scores of early elementary school students through comprehensive school counseling programs. *Professional School Counseling*, 6(5), 350–364.

Texas Counseling Association. (2015). *84th legislative session—Bill tracking final report.* Retrieved from http://www.txca.org/images/Legislative/84R_FinalBillTrackingReport_06.02.2015.docx

Texas Department of State Health Services. (2014). *The mental health workforce shortage in Texas.* Retrieved from https://www.dshs.state.tx.us/mhsa/announcements/HB1023_Final.doc

Texas Legislature Online. (2015). Retrieved from http://www.capitol.state.tx.us/Home.aspx

Thompson, R. A. (2012). *Professional school counseling: Best practices for working in the schools* (3rd ed.). New York, NY: Routledge, Taylor and Francis.

Whiston, S.C., & Quinby, R.F. (2009). Review of school counseling outcome research. *Psychology in the Schools*, 46(3), 267–272.

Whiston, S.C., & Sexton, T.L. (1998). A review of school counseling outcome research: Implications for practice. *Journal of Counseling and Development*, 76, 412–426.

Whiston, S. C., Tai, W.L., Rahardja, D., & Eder, K. (2011). School Counseling Outcome: A Meta-Analytic Examination of Interventions. *Journal of Counseling and Development, 89*(1), 37–55.

Zunker, V. G. (2006). *Career counseling: A holistic approach* (7th ed.). Belmont, CA: Brooks/Cole, Cengage Learning.

than just the basics. Entry-level employees must have mastery of the skills required by the job openings, including technical skills and teamwork know-how. Today's employee is expected to think and to problem-solve. Understanding the changes occurring in the workplace is essential to the success of today's job training professional. Effective CTE training programs should be measured by their relevance to students and employer needs and employer willingness to become involved and to hire participants. Millions of dollars are being spent annually on training and retraining. That amount is expected to increase significantly in the years to come. One of the major resources companies look at when selecting location sites is the availability of a trained workforce in the area. One of Texas most known partners is Texas Business & Education Coalition (TBEC). Its mission statement is "To secure the future of Texas by bringing business and education leaders together to affect improved performance of Texas Public Education." Today one of its focuses is "Support the development and establishment of articulated CTE programs in high schools, 2-year and 4-year higher education institutions that meet current employer needs and the anticipated needs associated with regional and state economic development goals." (Texas Business & Education Coalition, http://www.tbec.org/)

◆ POPULATION CHANGE IN TEXAS

Dr Steve Murdock, former Director of the US Census, State Demographer of Texas, and Professor at Texas A&M University, states in *Population Change in Texas: Implications for Human and Socioeconomic Resource—The 21st Century*:

> Planning for growth in Texas is very important. In the future three out of four workers will be Non-Anglo. The existing Anglo population will be older. The new immigrants are entrepreneurs and the cities must address these needs. The future is tied to the success of the Non-Anglo population in Texas. Planning in and for the years to come must seriously consider the changing demographics of Texas. These changes have major implications for the economic ventures of our state as well as the educational goals for educating all children and the preparation of a trained and educated workforce. (Murdock et al., 2003)

According to the growth in Texas, Dr Murdock's projections for our state are coming true. Those changes and growth according to some are taking place much faster than anticipated.

◆ RELEVANCE TO EMPLOYERS AND STUDENTS

CTE programs in public secondary schools have the unique opportunity to fill the growing gap between the shortage of skilled entry-level workers and the available workforce. CTE can become "The Hub of Relevance," the catalyst for relevance for the entire high school curriculum (Dean, 1997). By focusing efforts to meet the needs of employers and students, CTE can prepare students to fill the high-wage, high-skilled career openings. To meet these ongoing needs, supporters and those that are responsible for the implementation of CTE in Texas are responsible for:

- Developing a delivery system that is flexible, user-friendly, rapidly responsive to students and credible to employers
- Overcoming resistance to preparing US students for careers other than those requiring a 4-year college degree (Charp, 1997)

CAREER AND TECHNICAL EDUCATION IN TEXAS

Phillip Gilbreath

Virtually, all students will enter the workforce at some point in their lives. Career and technical education (CTE) programs in public schools link public education to the workforce and economic growth of Texas. The economy of Texas is dependent upon the state's ability to prepare and maintain a quality workforce. Today, very few careers exist in the workforce that do not or will not require continuing education beyond high school. While preparing students either to enter the workforce or to continue their education after high school, CTE courses must offer students an opportunity to prepare for high-skilled careers with the highest number of job openings and comparable wages. State and national leaders are recognizing the importance of CTE in helping to develop the state's workforce. Texas employers say "they want employees that possess good communication skills, critical thinking skills, technical knowledge, can-do attitude/pleasant attitude, and people who can work with people of a different age, race, gender, and education level than you" (Froeschle, 2011).

◆ CAREERS AND POSTSECONDARY EDUCATION

Long-term high demand for employees in an industry sector should be the basis for developing a sequence of CTE courses in any school district. New and expanding technologies are predicted to create 80% of the new careers in the next 10 years. Most of these careers will require specialized preparation, but not necessarily a college degree. Although 68% of all students do not obtain a postsecondary degree, all students must be prepared for continuing their education beyond high school. CTE plays a critical role in preparing students for the workforce and postsecondary education as well as in improving the academic achievement of students in Texas schools. Recent state standardized test scores reveal that students in a coherent sequence of CTE courses passed all tests at a higher rate than the rate of students not enrolled in CTE courses.

GLOBAL COMPETITION

High schools are entrusted with the task of preparing our young citizens for the future. Today's schools face the complex challenge of assuring that all students, including those from diverse backgrounds and circumstances, graduate from high school with the intellectual, practical, and interpersonal skills they need to be successful in an increasingly global and technology-driven workforce.

The level of competition encountered today by most businesses has greatly changed from the markets of recent years, and the pace of the change is rapidly accelerating. The pressure of global competition, the impact of technology, deregulation, shortened product life cycles, and new standards of quality and customer satisfaction are changing the way business is done in Texas, in the United States, and in the global marketplace. The way CTE courses prepare students for further education and the workforce is changing to meet that need. A lack of CTE opportunities can lead to higher dropout rates, which can lead to fewer students taking post-secondary CTE courses thus further reducing the Texas technically skilled workforce.

TEXAS ECONOMICS

Texas is a major producer of electronic components and the second largest US employer in the industry. The state ranks second in the nation in overall manufacturing and related employment. High tech has challenged the place of oil, just as oil once supplanted agriculture. Nonagricultural employment in the state, the most widely used indicator of economic growth, is projected to grow considerably for the next 5 years. Changes in the energy industry and in manufacturing are impacting the state's economy. Texas is projected to have strong employment gains for the near future. According to US Congressman Pete Sessions (2009), "Texas had more new jobs produced in 2008 than all 49 states combined. Even in today's economic crisis times, the outlook for Texas looks good." Former Governor Rick Perry (2010) is quoted as saying "since 2005, 80% of all the private sector jobs in America were created right here in Texas." Low-skilled jobs are those that take less than 12 months to learn. They have equally low wages. To serve the needs of students and employers, CTE must be focused on careers that require more than 12 months to learn. The careers that require academic, technical, and personal skills will pay a salary that can support the worker and his/her family. CTE programs in Texas must be positioned to match the unprecedented need for high-skill employees with the needs of learners for high-salaried careers. Today there is increased emphasis on students obtaining certifications and licensures upon their completion of CTE classes. According to Candy Slocum, Executive Director for Interlink, "Career and Technology in Texas results in jobs for our students. A review of Texas labor statistics shows that the fastest growing occupations in highest demand, and highest paying occupations all lead through CTE pathways. One could accurately say that CTE is economic development!" (C. Slocum, personal communication, 2011). Governor Greg Abbott stated (2015) "Technologies not yet invented will drive continuing innovation. We are making college more affordable and ensuring the path to career and technical training is cleared of obstacles. We are aiming to be the No. 1 education system in America."

PARTNERING WITH INDUSTRY

Industry is becoming more and more committed to helping improve public education, but industry needs a payback on its investment. Industry expects employees to arrive with more

- Listening to business and industry to connect curriculum to work
- Involving parents and students in planning educational and career goals that are realistic
- Providing avenues for continual renewal of the skills of teachers, including internships in industry
- Offering the needed skills and knowledge in a format that addresses the student's learning styles
- Using technology-based delivery systems

HISTORY AND LEGISLATION

Early Background

In colonial times, academic and vocational instruction was offered separately. Early apprenticeship agreements of colonial America charged the master with teaching literacy in addition to civic and moral responsibilities. The apprentices were generally sent to evening schools for the nonvocational learning. There was little connection between academic and vocational instruction, which is a big change from today's career requirements of academic, technical, and people skills.

In the early nineteenth century, the decline of apprenticeships ended vocational instruction for most American youth, as most schools' occupational instruction was limited to the professions and available only to the wealthy. By the 1850s, however, a few visionaries were calling for education that combined academic learning with mechanical and agricultural instruction. In 1862, President Lincoln signed the First Morrill Act, making possible the establishment of state land-grant colleges of agriculture and engineering.

The extension of vocational education into the common schools was far more difficult because of economic considerations and the opposition of academicians. In 1876, Victor Della Vos, Moscow's Imperial Technical School, introduced his system of instruction shops. Featured at the 1876 Centennial Exposition in Philadelphia, the Victor Della Vos trade education program was based on four precepts:

1. Analysis of the elements of the trade to be taught
2. Ordering of those elements from simple to complex
3. Use of a craftsman as teacher for group instruction
4. The shop as part of the formal school facility

As individual apprenticeships were gradually disappearing because of the high demand for skilled workers brought about by the Industrial Revolution, the Victor Della Vos method seemed to be exactly what was needed and public schools the place to provide the training. The Victor Della Vos system quickly became the basis for many secondary school manual training programs, but did not satisfy all the needs for employment training.

The next major changes in the system involved moving to a more specific curriculum. In the late 1800s and early 1900s, technical institutes, trade schools, commercial and business schools, and agricultural high schools grew and were finally combined with comprehensive high schools designed to serve all youth. The comprehensive high school was actually implemented in very few communities, and most secondary schools gradually drifted in the direction of emphasis on the college-bound youth.

This drift prevailed until the late 1930s, when the threat posed by the Civilian Conservation Corps and the National Youth Administration awoke the leaders of comprehensive schools to the danger of a separate school system outside their control. World War II offered an opportunity to offer highly effective programs that responded to a need. Following World War II, the drift away from vocational education began again, only to be reversed by the Vocational Education Acts of 1963 and 1968.

The 1960s

The Vocational Education Act of 1963 reflected a change in attitude toward vocational education. Until this point, vocational education had served the purpose of providing job skills that would afford individuals job opportunities. The Vocational Education Act of 1963 stressed that this training should provide an enrichment of the lives of people throughout their work. This attitude stemmed from a report filed by a committee designated by John F. Kennedy in 1961 to review and evaluate existing Vocational Education Acts. The panel issued a report entitled "Education for the Changing World of Work."

While the Vocational Education Act of 1963 dramatically changed the purposes and scope of vocational education, the power over programs was still controlled, primarily, at a federal level. During the next 5 years, the states showed some independence in program development and implementation, but it was not until the 1970s that they accepted virtually full authority for programming. The Vocational Education Amendments of 1968 continued to focus on people and their needs. The amendments drew attention to and gave priority to people with special needs, the handicapped, and the disadvantaged.

In the early 1970s, a nationwide "career education" movement encouraged districts to provide students with introductory, exploratory, and preparatory experiences that would prepare them with information and opportunities to make wise career decisions as well as to prepare them with career skills. This movement attempted to make career education the responsibility of all teachers instead of a few. The actual implementation of career education nationwide and in each state, though mandated, was stifled due to very limited funding support.

The Perkins Era

In 1984, the Carl D. Perkins Vocational Act (P.L. 98-524) was passed. The Perkins Act as it was known had two interrelated goals. The economic goal was to improve the skills of the labor force and prepare adults for job opportunities. The social goal was to provide equal opportunities for adults in Vocational Education (Scott & Sarkees-Wircenski, 1996). The Carl D. Perkins Vocational and Applied Technology Education Act of 1990 (P.L. 101-392) amended and extended the Act of 1984. The new act provided funds to assist in teaching skills and competencies necessary to work in a technological society and to provide greater opportunity for disadvantaged persons (Scott & Sarkees-Wircenski, 1996).

By 1998, Perkins III was passed by the House and Senate and signed into law. The previous Carl D. Perkins Vocational and Applied Technology Education Act was renamed the Carl D. Perkins Vocational and Technical Education Act of 1998, P.L. 105-322. The purposes of the 1998 act were as follows:

- To assure that students taking CTE courses meet the same rigorous academic standards as all other students
- To work toward integration of academic and career and technology instruction into both programs

- To link secondary and postsecondary education
- To provide technical assistance, professional development, and dissemination of national research

Perkins III Core Student Performance Indicators were as follows:

- High achievement
- Attainment of a diploma
- Postsecondary education or employment
- Preparation for nontraditional careers

Two areas of emphasis, accountability and flexibility, stood out in this newest version of the act. States were allowed much more flexibility in how to accomplish the goals of the act, but were required to report yearly on the results of implementation. States were required to submit a 5-year state plan on how the act would be implemented and results reported.

In 2006, the Perkins Act was reauthorized again as the Carl D. Perkins Career and Technical Education Act, P.L. 109-270. This version of the Act continued to expand accountability, requiring new negotiations and reporting for local recipients, and included a new requirement for every school district and postsecondary institution to offer at least one CTE "program of study." A program of study is defined in the law as

- Incorporating secondary education and postsecondary education elements
- Including coherent and rigorous content aligned with challenging academic standards and relevant career and technical content in a coordinated, nonduplicative progression of courses that align secondary education with postsecondary education to adequately prepare students to succeed in postsecondary education
- Possibly including the opportunity for secondary education students to participate in dual or concurrent enrollment programs or other ways to acquire postsecondary education credits
- Leading to an industry-recognized credential or certificate at the postsecondary level, or an associate or baccalaureate degree

Federal funds provided by the Perkins Act generally amount to less than 10% of the local budget of a CTE department, but are an important source of capital expenditures and program improvement funding. These funds came under repeated attack during the early 2000s with attempts to totally eliminate funding. The Act fell victim to budget cuts in 2011 due to the economy and pressure to reduce federal spending overall. For fiscal year 2015, a total of $1,117,598,000 was appropriated. Texas' allocation of these funds was $92,114,336. Funding amounts are considered annually. Re-authorization is considered approximately every 6 years (Hyslop, personal communication—E-mail to the author, 2015).

No Child Left Behind P.L. 107-110

No Child Left Behind legislation amended the Elementary and Secondary Education Act of 1965. According to Alisha Hyslop, the legislation, though not directly addressing career and technology education, directly affected raising the achievement standards for all children; addressed the reading, science, and math instruction for the children that are taught; appropriated more funds for staff development; and presented new qualifications and certification for all teachers (Hyslop, personal telephone interview, 2003). The No Child Left Behind Act, now often referred to by its general name of the Elementary and Secondary Education Act, is scheduled for re-authorization and has been under consideration by Congress for the past several years. Dramatic changes are expected when legislation to renew the law is approved. According to the Texas Education Agency (TEA), the primary function of NCLB was to close the achievement gap between groups of students by requiring greater accountability and offering increased flexibility and choice (Texas Education Agency, 2015a–c).

Workforce Development Boards

Other federal legislation that impacts CTE in Texas includes H.R. 1385. Approved by the US House in April 1997, H.R. 1385 requires state governors to establish local Workforce Development Boards (H.R. 1385, Sec. 112). The act closely resembles legislation previously passed in Texas, with the boards providing guidance and oversight, rather than directly running programs.

The 74th Legislative Session in Texas passed House Bill 1863 requiring state agencies to consolidate workforce education and training programs under a new state agency, the Texas Workforce Commission (TWC). Twenty-eight regional local workforce boards serve the state of Texas. The federally funded network gives services to customers, employers, and job seekers at local Texas Workforce Centers. Each board has its own board of directors and develops a strategic plan for their service area (C. Slocum, personal communication, 1997).

Tech Prep and Course Sequencing

Within comprehensive high schools and magnet schools, Tech Prep programs were established and expanded as students became aware of the advantages of completing courses offered through this system. Tech Prep far-reaching reform model linked secondary and postsecondary school programs. Tech Prep joined the teaching of academic and occupational skills to promote continued education and acquisition of advanced technical skills. To receive college credit for the course, students usually were required to enroll in the respective college within a year to 18 months. However, recent federal legislation, followed by the Texas state legislation in 2011, eliminated future funding for Tech Prep.

There is much positive data that supported the success of Tech Prep in Texas. However, it was the lack of continuing state financial support that lead to the "chopping block."

College Credits Through Dual Credit Opportunities

With Tech Prep a popular trend of the past, the focus program in its place is Dual Credit. Dual Credit or similar programs are articulated credits that often are at no cost to the student or the school district.

Dual Credit agreements grant college credit for the high school CTE course that is articulated with a college course. Although agreements vary, to receive credit, generally the students must have received a required grade in the high school course.

Dual Credit courses have been available for several years. It must be pointed out that Dual Credit courses may be those from the areas of academics or electives including CTE. Recent legislation requires districts to develop plans with postsecondary institutions thus structuring secondary courses which allow students to earn a minimum of 12 semester hours of college credit by the time they graduate from high school. Dual Credits are awarded immediately on both transcripts (high school and college) once the course is completed in high school.

Articulating the Content

School districts wishing to articulate a course for Dual Credit with a community college can generally contact the Dual Credit coordinator for the college. Courses are articulated through a process established by the colleges and agreed upon by the local education agency. This may include exchanging course outlines and syllabi between college and high school staff and reaching agreement on course content and textbooks to be used. A written articulation agreement is then signed by the college and school district. Local school district staff must also meet certain qualifications and credential requirements established by the post secondary institution and the Southern Association of Colleges and Schools. The agreement outlines how students can obtain college credit for the high school courses. Statewide articulation agreements have been established in a number of courses and more are planned. This will give students more opportunity to receive credit in more geographically diverse settings.

Program Areas and New Development

For decades, Vocational Education, now known as CTE, was made up of eight program areas including Career Investigation/Occupational Orientation. Within the eight major program areas, a comprehensive array of CTE courses and sequences are available to Texas school districts students. Those program areas include the following:

- Agricultural Science
- Business
- Family and Consumer Science
- Health Science
- Marketing
- Technology Education
- Trade and Industry

The sequence of courses offered within the program areas depended on the number of students enrolling, geographic location, proximity to a related business and industry, available space, community support, available finances, qualified/certified staff, employment opportunities for students, as well as other factors. When existing courses are no longer meeting district needs, a course can be closed or redirected. Redirection, for example, could mean changing the focus from Sales and Marketing to E-Commerce or Sports and Entertainment Marketing. With staff development and curriculum revision, many times current teachers can help revitalize or redirect a course.

Career Clusters

The US Department of Education has identified 16 career clusters. The career clusters are groupings of related occupations. National standards for each career cluster are being developed. The standards outline the technical and academic skills and knowledge needed to succeed in both secondary and postsecondary education for the career and in employment within the cluster of careers. The standards are portable across state lines and recognized as value added to the prospective employee.

Texas adopted and implemented the career clusters through the "Achieve Texas" model. All districts in Texas were to have implemented all clusters by 2012. It is very important to recognize that this is not a CTE initiative. This is an initiative for all areas of instruction to include core and electives. The "Achieve Texas" model enhances greatly the new efforts of College and Career Readiness.

Career Clusters Frameworks

The standards for each career cluster are developed around a framework that includes:

- Foundations—which define all of the skills and knowledge needed in the cluster, regardless of the career chosen.
- Pathways—which define the scope and sequence of courses required for various jobs within a cluster. The pathways lead to postsecondary as well as the chosen career.
- Career specialties—which define the full range of careers within a cluster. For example, within the retail/wholesale sales and services career cluster, jobs such as fashion marketing or chemical account executive would be included.

As early as the 1970s, Career Clusters existed. At that time they may have been better known as occupational clusters. In the more recent years, Texas, along with many other states, has aligned its CTE program areas with the 16 Career Clusters.

"Achieve Texas"

"Achieve Texas" is an education initiative sponsored and funded by the TEA. Designed to prepare all students for a lifetime of success, it states:

> *"Achieve Texas"* is a system designed to help students (and their parents) make wise education choices. It is based on the belief that the curriculum of the twenty-first century should combine rigorous academics with relevant career education. (Achieve Texas, 2015)

This initiative uses the 16 federally defined Career Clusters of the States' Career Clusters initiative (www.careerclusters.org) as the foundation for restructuring how schools arrange their instructional programs. A Career Cluster is a grouping of occupations and broad industries based on commonalities. The 16 Career Clusters provide an organizing tool for schools, small learning communities, academies, and magnet schools. Career Pathway Programs of Study (POS) have been developed for each of the Career Clusters. The POS represents a recommended sequence of coursework based on a "student's interest or career goal." (Achieve Texas, 2015). Local school districts across the state have and are transitioning to "Achieve Texas." This process has and is taking several years for full implementation. Some districts chose to implement several clusters at a time. Others chose to implement the total 16 clusters at one time.

Developing New Courses

The following steps will help to develop new courses and redirect/revitalize the sequence of courses in a career area:

1. Research labor market information on sites such as *www.cdr.state.tx.us*. The labor market information should indicate a long-term need for a large number of employees in related fields.

2. Set up a business-industry parent advisory group to make recommendations for the career area. Building community support early in the process assures assistance for the completers of the program when they seek employment. Advisory committees may visit other districts having similar programs; talk with TEA staff members; and even work with companies or vendors representing furniture, equipment, materials, supplies, and curriculum as resources in planning new or postsecondary institution, redirected programs. The local Chamber of Commerce, a job-specific affiliation or association, and TWC are also good resources.

3. Develop a public information plan to inform the community, school district, students, and others about the plans for a new or revitalized career area.

4. Identify a teacher for the course and involve him/her in the planning. The teacher should become a member of the advisory committee and eventually take a leadership role. The earlier the teacher for the new course can be hired, the sooner the teacher can "buy-in" to the new course being developed.

5. Identify the sequence of courses that will lead to postsecondary education and the career being addressed.

6. Develop the broad curriculum content based on the TEKS.

7. Develop the equipment, supplies, and materials list for the courses.

8. Plan for the space needed. When planning the program or new facility involves an architect, a close working relationship with that company or individual is essential. The space allocated for a course should be based on the maximum number of students to be served by the course at one time.

Planning for Safety

Safety of the students when using equipment is a major factor to be considered. The number of students should never exceed the number of workstations provided in the lab. Square footage recommendations for CTE are available from program specialists in the Curriculum Department at the TEA. Other information may be available from the state CTE curriculum centers. By following these steps and utilizing available resources, a new course sequence will have a greater opportunity for long-term support and success.

◆ CURRICULUM

The curriculum in CTE courses is a combination of academic knowledge and skills critical to all work and standards specific to a business and/or industry area. Locally adopted curriculum should address the Texas Essential Knowledge and Skills (TEKS) and locally added enhancements. Changes to the curriculum are driven by the needs of business, industry, society, and other decisions by local and state boards of education as well as the state legislature. Changes in technology are increasing the level of knowledge and skill required for earning a livable wage. Outstanding CTE courses are addressing the increased level of technology training required for today's careers. The newest TEKS approved by the State Board of Education also allow for the offering of some CTE courses for math, science, and fine arts credit. HB5 passed by the 83rd Legislature provides flexibility with student schedules, courses, and revised the state graduation requirements thus allowing students to enroll in more CTE classes. The newest legislation allows for more CTE classes to count toward the core courses.

TEKS–The Enrichment Cluster

In 1995–1996, teams of teachers from around the state met to develop the outline of the content for courses taught in Texas public schools. The results were the TEKS. The state board adopted the TEKS for CTE courses in July 1997. The CTE TEKS included input from business and industry sources to assure that what was to be taught was relevant to the employment opportunities related to each course. The CTE TEKS became effective for the 1998–1999 school year.

The 80th Texas Legislature in May 2007 passed HB 3485, requiring the State Board of Education by rule to revise the TEKS. Implementation was to be completed beginning with the 2010–2011 school year. The process eliminated approximately 400 courses from the list of TEA-approved courses. Course crosswalks comparing existing courses with the new courses were also developed. The process of the development of the new TEKS (with the exception of certification of CTE teachers) actually restructured CTE into the 16 clusters. The most recent 84th Legislature mandated the TEA to reconsider the addition of new courses.

As with all Texas teachers, CTE teachers need to use the TEKS as the basis for content in addition to locally developed course goals, standards, and outlines. Excellent materials, including course outlines, are also available from the instructional materials centers located across the state and at other curriculum centers across the nation. With approval of the new TEKS comes the need for the development of new materials and textbooks for each course. Curriculum centers are funded with both state and federal Carl D. Perkins funds. Due to the nature of the ever-changing curriculum for CTE, change and adoption of the newest TEKS being adopted are scheduled for implementation in the fall of 2017. Even with a well-developed curriculum, CTE teachers need time to plan lessons. Setting up hands-on labs used by most CTE teachers is a time-consuming process when done effectively. The development by specialists of CTE Curricula and materials provides great resources for CTE teachers.

One of the most positive documents written in support of CTE addresses "Protecting the Student Interest, A Broader Vision: CTE, and The Future of Career and Technical Education" (Laitsch, 2005). Written by Dan Laitsch and published by the Association for Supervision and Curriculum Development, the publication describes an extensive view of the importance and relevance of CTE in the educational process.

Sequenced Courses

Within the program areas, now transitioned into 16 career clusters, are the course names listed and the knowledge and skills to be taught. Within each program area/career cluster, the courses are sequenced into categories by progression from a broad area to more specific courses. A district should offer sequences of CTE courses in a selection of program areas to address the needs of many students. With the newest TEKS, career clusters, and career pathways/programs of work, comes the need to report student enrollment by cluster.

What students should know and be able to do are spelled out for every course in each cluster. The knowledge and skills for each course are intended to allow each school district the freedom to teach the content in the most effective manner for the students involved. Local business and industry advisors, with approval from school boards and administration, can help determine the extent to which the course must be established. Listed below are some of the assistance that can be offered from the local business and industry community.

- New textbooks
- Teacher training

- Design of the school district's CTE program
- Alignment of course changes
- Teacher certification and credentialing of staff
- Standards for assessing achievement within courses

Grade Point Options

CTE courses can be taught at different levels each with or without grade points. The level of expectations of learning for students in CTE courses can be set to take advantage of grade point credits in districts where grade points impact class rank. Many districts today have chosen to not offer grade points for elective courses such as CTE and Fine Arts.

Planning High School Years and Beyond

The new TEA Graduation Program allows students and parents new options including

- Foundation High School Program
- Distinguished Level of Achievement
- Endorsements in five areas
  - Science, Technology, Engineering and Mathematics (STEM)
  - Business and Industry
  - Public Service
  - Arts and Humanities
  - Multidisciplinary
- Performance Acknowledgments
- Industry Workforce Credential

Given these opportunities all students have the ability to fully customize a graduation plan for themselves that will prepare them for college and career readiness. CTE plays a vital part in the overall plan for all students (Texas Education Agency, 2014). CTE courses can and should become a meaningful sequence of mainstream electives, instead of a series of separate classes.

Double Options

Changes by the Texas State Board of Education in state high school graduation requirements have had a profound impact on the requirements and electives that students are able to take. CTE courses can be set up to offer the double option of an elective and also serving as a graduation requirement. Examples are courses in the area of math, science, and fine arts. Courses can be set up to allow students to take advantage of as many of these options as possible. For students to take full advantage of all options, this takes planning and career guidance several years in advance.

SCANS

Technical skills and knowledge may be quickly outdated but the workplace skills or critical skills are those that are transferable to many high-performance workplaces. In 1990, the

Secretary's Commission on Achieving Necessary Skills (SCANS) worked with business and industry nationwide to determine the skills employees' need. The commission completed its work in 1992. Even though the SCANS were developed in the early 1990s, they are still a valuable source of information for those involved in education and workforce development. These industry-wide skills must be integrated throughout the CTE curriculum if true preparation for the workplace is taking place. The SCANS skills are one of the key components of what every employee should know. In addition, employees need more specific preparation for their career. SCANS is still considered paramount for all students.

◆ INTEGRATION WITH ACADEMICS

Integration of Math and Science with CTE

Alignment of CTE curriculum with district and campus goals requires new and renewed partnerships with other district educators. In school districts across the state, career and technical educators are finding themselves working side-by-side with K–12 curriculum leaders to develop curriculum. The standards and goals for CTE and the core subject areas are rapidly merging to meet the needs of the changing workplace for flexible problem solvers. The integration of CTE and core subjects requires a great deal of change and removal of the traditional barriers among all educators. The results can be improved achievement for all students and district initiatives such as College and Career Readiness. Oftentimes, it is reported that students enrolled in CTE classes are achieving at a more successful rate on state assessments than others not enrolled in those classes.

Schools must be careful not to integrate subjects just to integrate. There must be a valid reason. Integration of career and technical and core subjects frequently centers around the development of projects, thus the new academic trend in Project-Based Learning. The new academic trend is not new to CTE, Project-Based Learning has been around a long time. The projects that have proven to be most beneficial are those centered around problems provided by business and industry. Advisory groups can play a key role in development and assessment of the resulting projects.

An outstanding method of integrating is to identify areas of low achievement for CTE students, for example, the passing rate on the math section on the state assessment. If CTE students are passing at a lower rate than the district as a whole, integration of math concepts into CTE curriculum can be a solution. Staff development time can be scheduled to allow math and CTE teachers to develop lessons together based on the most commonly missed objectives. Districts are also accountable in the Performance-Based Monitoring Analysis System (PBMAS). Here students enrolled in CTE classes are also expected to perform successfully in comparison to the state standards. Performance of these students is reported according to Indicators (CTE, Limited English Proficiency [LEP], Economically Disadvantaged, and Special Education [SPED]). PBMAS reports are usually made available to each district in August. Today's student is being gauged by the newest standardized assessment, STARR/EOC. Here, HB5 has reduced from 15 to 5 the number of standardized tests students must pass to graduate.

In the recent past, many educators have misunderstood the need for mastery of basic skills by students who are enrolling in career and technical courses. The need has always existed, but is even more critical today as low-skill jobs cease to exist. CTE and core subjects are blending in content areas and methods of delivery in increasing relevance and rigor. With this blend, it becomes apparent that more than basic skills are required of everyone who wants to earn a livable wage.

◆ INSTRUCTIONAL METHODOLOGY

Hands-On and Minds-On

In career and technical courses, learning can be fun and relevant. The subject matter taught and the methods used to teach make both teaching and learning relevant. Students apply subject matter to real life, real things, real principles, and real problems, here again, Project-Based Learning. The relevance of the subject matter and the applied instructional methodology combine to increase student learning.

CTE teachers have long been facilitators of learning, guiding the students to discover the answers. By asking the right questions, CTE teachers become discussion leaders and facilitators rather than lecturers. Critical thinking skills are taught, using questioning techniques that allow the students to discover answers and connect knowledge to application. CTE teachers should assist students in acquiring the skills needed to continue learning and synthesizing information to new situations.

Learning in Teams

It is predicted that the average workers of the future will have to prepare for a minimum of two or three careers in their lifetime. Some predictions are that they may also be employed with six to eight different employers. Learning to think and apply technology-based tools to the job is a fundamental requirement for careers paying above minimum wage. The ability to work in teams, problem-solve, make decisions, and plan strategies are also skills in demand by business and industry. Instruction can be organized so that students work in teams while learning skills and knowledge.

In the area of technology education, modular instruction is commonly used in various clusters. In modular instruction, students study a certain area of technology, such as applied physics, engineering, or animation and graphics at a workstation setup for a team of two or more students. The workstation might consist of a computer with related software, peripherals, and the essential curriculum materials needed to study the technology area such as robotics, engineering, desktop publishing, or animation. The period of study might be for 7–15 days at a specific workstation, before the student moves on to a new and different workstation or activity.

◆ ASSESSING STUDENT WORK

Using Portfolios to Assess

Methods for assessing student achievement in CTE courses can vary widely. An assessment method that is significant for future use by students when applying for jobs is the development of a portfolio. Students can develop portfolios using multimedia resources to provide evidence of their skills and knowledge. When a portfolio is to be used for grading, the teacher specifies the contents of the portfolio. Input from business and industry advisors on the content and format of the portfolio could be beneficial to the student's future use of a portfolio during a job search. If the portfolio is to be valuable to the student after the course, the contents should also be of interest to postsecondary educators and/or future employers.

Portfolios can be saved in a digital format and contain evidence of the student's mastery of the specified skills and knowledge. The portfolio can contain samples of products produced or completed research. Simple examples of sample work include computer-aided drafting and graphics. These are the same illustrations that any employee might want to share with prospective employers regarding the type work they have completed or been involved in.

CTE Rubrics

Establishing the standard for products or research can most readily be done with a rubric. A rubric, written by the instructor, should spell out in detail standards for what is expected of the student learner. This information must be given to the student at the beginning of the project and referred to throughout the project or research. When the students understand exactly what is to be done and what is expected, the results will more likely be an excellent product. Rubrics deeply define what is expected and how to get there. Rubrics should be used on projects, processes, or content that is big enough and deep enough to require detailed definition. Business and industry partners can assist the teacher by reviewing rubrics to assure that the resulting products and processes meet industry standards.

◆ STUDENTS: THE PROGRAM FOCUS

A misconception has existed for years, not just in Texas, is that CTE is only for a special population of students. The truth is that CTE courses and programs are beneficial to all students. A look at the demographic makeup of the CTE courses within a district or across the state should dispel this myth. CTE courses generally have students representing a cross-section of the total population served by the district. An example might be that some students enrolled in the CTE Health Science cluster might represent the top percentage of the class. Today, data compiled by the TEA report students enrolled in program areas (CTE, LEP, SPED, Economically Disadvantaged) and the degree of success students experience. Ethnic group representation and respective achievement are now readily available and reported. Students are provided an opportunity to develop basic skills essential for all high school graduates including those who plan to attend college. Students also develop occupational skills that prepare them to enter the job market immediately upon graduation from high school, enter a community college with advanced standing in articulated and Dual Credit courses, or enter a 4-year university.

Meeting Student Needs/Special Populations

For special populations students to benefit from CTE programs, teachers of CTE courses must be included in the development of Individual Education Plans and modifications as necessary. By law, a CTE representative, preferably the CTE teacher, is a voting member during the Admissions, Review and Dismissal (ARD) Committee meeting. The CTE teacher must use the modifications recommended by the committee to develop lessons for the special education student. Modifications might include providing verbal assessments and large print type books.

Developing Character Through Youth Leadership Organizations

CTE has for many years been credited with the leadership training and development of many of today's successful business, civic, industrial, and government leaders. A school district seeking ways to promote student character development would be wise to support youth leadership organizations. Youth leadership and character development are emphasized in the organizations sponsored by the different program areas. The youth leadership organizations or clubs require extra time and effort on the part of the teacher, but are extremely beneficial to students. The clubs serve the student much as a professional organization serves a teacher. The clubs offer opportunities to participate in community service projects, learn parliamentary procedure, and gain personal recognition by competing in career-related activities on the district, area, state, national, and international level.

District and campus administrative and financial support of the youth organizations can reap bountiful returns in improved student achievement, behavior, and loyalty to the school. Potential employers sometimes cite character development as missing from high school graduates. Career and Technical Student Organizations create opportunities to develop the confidence, integrity, leadership and character of students as well as to provide scholarship resources. There is also strong parental support for student involvement in the youth organization activities and competition.

◆ ADMINISTRATION OF CTE

Funding

Funding for public education in Texas including CTE is often being considered and debated. Funding for CTE usually comes from local, state, and federal sources. Currently, CTE state funding is calculated using an average daily membership/contact hour accounting process, which grants local school districts funds at a rate of 1.35 for all courses. This means school districts' CTE programs qualify for 35% more state funds than regular programs. The greater percent takes into consideration the increased overall cost of CTE programs when compared with the cost of other regular programs. Of the state funds generated by membership and contact hour accounting, a certain percentage must be directly spent on the CTE instructional programs. It is the intent of the Legislature that a minimum percentage of the district's Foundation School Program Career & Technical Education Allotment be expended for indirect cost related to career & technical education programs.

While the weighted state funds constitute the majority of the operating funds for CTE programs in many districts, local district funds may also be used for support. The local funds, generated by local tax revenue, are most frequently used to provide equipment, facilities, maintenance and operations, utilities, salary supplements/benefits, and administrative support such as purchasing and payroll services.

Federal funds for the support of CTE are provided for under Texas Education Code, Chapters 28, 29, and 42 and the Carl D. Perkins CTE Improvement Act, P. L. 109-270. Each spring local school districts receive a posting of planning amounts they may apply for via an annual federal application from the TEA. The application is available on the CTE home page at the TEA website www.tea.state.tx.us/CTE/. The application and guidelines identify those considerations essential in planning for CTE for the following year. Individual districts or a consortium of districts submit the application. The application is used to convey federal funds to districts and outlines the district's plans for expenditure of those funds within the guidelines. The federal funds are to be used to supplement, rather than supplant, local and state funds.

Personnel and Certification

Most teachers of CTE courses must hold a Professional Teacher Certificate in the field or be eligible for certification. A college degree is required for certification in all program areas, except Trade and Industrial Education. Specific trade and industrial (T&I) program area pre-employment laboratory courses such as auto technology, machine shop, and electronics may be taught by a teacher without a college degree who has 5 years related work experience within the last 8 years. Details of work experience requirements for all CTE courses can be found on the CTE page of the TEA website (http://tea.texas.gov) or by reference to the State Board for Educator Certification—19 TAC Chapter 231 (State Board For Educator Certification, 2015).

The critical shortage of certified teachers is becoming chronic in technology education and certain specific skill level jobs in computer and technical areas, electronics, air conditioning and refrigeration, plumbing and pipefitting, auto technology and automotive collision repair and refinishing technology. Special effort can be made to recruit teachers among skilled personnel looking for a second career. Persons retiring from the military or other industries are prime candidates for filling CTE openings. New alternative certification programs exist for those holding a college degree and desiring entry into the teaching profession. Those seeking certification through alternative certification agencies may make contact with alternative education agencies, regional education service centers or colleges and universities regarding their qualifications, costs, and various requirements. Completion of a Statement of Qualifications (SOQ) is required for those teaching positions requiring related work experience (Trade and Industrial Education, Health Science Technology, and Marketing Education). The SOQ must be submitted to the certifying agency prior to approval for entrance into any CTE teacher certification program. In addition, some positions require a license or certification in the field in which they are also seeking teaching certification (Example: Cosmetology). The 84th Texas Legislature modified the law and ruled that beginning September 1, 2015 school districts have the option to approve local permits for teachers who are assigned "non-core academic CTE courses" (Texas Education Agency, 2015a–c).

Staff Development

CTE teachers must receive opportunities to enhance and update their technology skills each year to stay in line with the advances of business and industry in their field. For decades, CTE has been a leader in offerings of professional development at the state and national levels. Business, industry, and technology skills change frequently. As these skills change, teachers must become familiar with the most current changes to provide that information and those related skills to the students. Yearly CTE program improvement conferences are sponsored to meet these needs for all respective teachers, counselors, and administrators.

Professional Improvement Conferences

The state program improvement conferences provide opportunities for teachers of like programs to meet and receive updates on the latest technologies and curriculum. Interpretations of the most current rules and regulations; opportunities to visit exhibits of new software, equipment, materials, and supplies; and presentations from colleagues and the leaders of business and industry are some of the opportunities provided at the conferences. Field trips and tours are often included to allow teachers first-hand knowledge of business and industry.

Needed for Improvement

In most cases, one day of the program improvement conference is dedicated to new teachers. The conferences are a must for new teachers and are required for certain areas of certification. Experienced teachers need to attend at least every 2–3 years. Funds should be made available to pay for the travel expenses of CTE teachers to the state conferences. Attendance to the state conference is also an allowable expense for federal funds. A positive return on the investment is certainly assured.

Local Staff Development

On a local level, CTE teachers should be afforded all of the staff development opportunities provided all district teachers. CTE teachers also need yearly training in the use of new software and improved teaching strategies. The professional development time is an excellent opportunity to have CTE and academic teachers work together to develop lessons that integrate the two areas. Additionally, CTE teachers are encouraged to shadow in business and/ or industry to gain the experience needed to teach the latest technology as well as to promote their own professional growth. Trade and professional associations as well as business and industry advisory councils can be a great source for teacher internships. Staying on top of what is new in business and industry is critical to preparing students for the careers of today.

Business/Industry Advisory Councils

Advisory committees and special interest groups have been utilized in CTE for many years. Where else can better resources be found than in the people who have established their career and earned their living in the areas related to CTE? When utilizing advisory groups, it is essential to plan well; be very selective in the membership; organize meetings for a purpose; utilize time wisely; communicate goals and objectives; carry through with plans; and follow up. Advisory committees and their membership can provide valuable input in beginning new courses/programs; solving problems; enhancing instruction; seeking teachers resources, material, and equipment; planning for renovation of facilities; planning new facilities or buildings; and planning meetings, conferences, or competitive activities. Ideas for use of the advisory groups have been suggested throughout this chapter.

Career Guidance and Counseling

The student/counselor ratio in many public schools in Texas remains above 500 to 1, and yet the needs for students to plan their education and life goals grow. Students need to understand the relationship of education to their life goals. Access to career information can assure that students and parents understand the benefits of taking specific academic and CTE courses in high school.

Career and Technical Counselors

Some school districts value career planning and utilize CTE Counselors. Some of the responsibilities include working and counseling with students to explore needs, interests, aptitudes, and abilities with a career focus and providing interaction with business and industry on field trips or shadowing experiences. Information about coherent sequencing of courses, 4-year and/or 6-year plans, utilization of articulated/Dual Credit programs, planning for postsecondary education, and personal counseling are activities for career counselors. Counseling with teachers in addressing specific CTE needs of students is also a vital role.

The SAS (Standard Application System) for federal funds has defined Career Guidance, Career Counseling, and Placement as those programs that:

1. Pertain to the body of subject matter and related techniques and methods organized for the development of career awareness, career orientation, career planning, career decision making, placement skills, and knowledge, and understanding of local, state, and national occupational, educational, and labor market needs, trends, and opportunities
2. Assist individuals in making and implementing informed educational and career choices (SAS Standard Application System, 2015–2016).

CTE funds may be expended to employ counselors to provide career development, guidance and counseling programs to all students within the SSA. This too is an allowable expenditure of Carl D. Perkins funds (Texas Education Agency, 2015a–c).

Careers Information Online

Information about career options can also be explored using the Internet. Units of study or entire courses can be developed around material available on the Internet. Students can be allowed to develop career plans and relate them to course offerings within and beyond the school district. As students discover their own interests, aptitudes, and abilities, teachers can make opportunities for learning that key on their interests and abilities. Students knowing what they enjoy and do well can lead to future planning. A vision of the future gives purpose to learning. Guiding students to understand the connection between school and work can lead to immediate benefits through gains in academic achievement and improved behavior. In addition to Internet sources for career interest, aptitude, and abilities, new software that may be Internet based is available for purchase.

Evaluation/Accountability

CTE programs show accountability by exceeding the expectations of the program customers, students, parents, and employers. Exceeding the expectations of the customers in the preparation of students for postsecondary education and the world of work is documented through follow-up of former students, annual program evaluation, employer support, student enrollment in the courses, input from representation of business and industry, and accountability determined by State standardized test results. Annual results are reported from TEA revealing how students enrolled in CTE perform in comparison to the state standards. The results are reported in the categories of all CTE students, LEP, Special Education, Economically Disadvantaged, and Nontraditional (Male and Female). Districts using federal Perkins funds are accountable to make programs equitable to all students, to provide academic success, and are responsible fiscally in the use of those funds.

Success Stories

Former students offer excellent sources for gauging program success. When parents believe that the sequence of courses within a program made a significant difference in the success of their child, the program is on track. Quality programs can be traced to excellent teachers with substantial support from the community, campus and district administration, support staff, counseling and guidance team, and an attentive board of trustees. Quality programs continuously improve and exceed the expectations of their customers.

Annual Evaluation

Evaluation for CTE is an ongoing process and is required annually by state law. The systematic review of each program operated by a district helps determine the quality and effectiveness of the courses. The intent of an annual review is to appraise the extent to which instruction is provided through a coherent sequence of courses or program of study that prepares students for gainful employment or further education. The basis for improving, redirecting, or discontinuing each course is also a focus of the review. Evaluation instruments may be obtained from TEA or developed locally. They should include periodic review by business/industry advisory members. Decisions should be data-driven using data such as follow-up of completers of the programs or enrollment history. Another source of evaluation is to contract with an external auditor or evaluator to accomplish the evaluation.

◆ CURRENT ISSUES AND FORECASTS

Work-Based Experiences

In many unique situations, the ideal setting for students to experience first-hand knowledge and exposure to business, industry, technology, and related areas may be through partnerships. Firms willing to work with the public schools to share their facilities, staff, resources, and technology can be sought to develop partnerships. Such strategies will give ownership to all parties involved and provide real settings in which students can learn. These partnerships may be experienced through internships, mentorships, shadowing, or practicums.

Web-Based Experiences

Students in CTE classes benefit from having Internet access to experts in the fields related to their studies. Electronic field trips can offer students inexpensive trips throughout the world to the best location related to their industry area. In an international marketing class, students may study the customs of the regions to which they wish to market. The costs of actual visits to that location may be prohibitive, but electronically they can be there during any class period. Students can conduct a real meeting with international clients, an experience that would be impossible in person.

According to John Naisbitt, "The introduction of new technology has always resulted in social change. There is an increasing gap between technological and social change, and it is that gap that is creating a problem. High Tech is about shortening time, about pushing everything towards real-time. High Tech is about taking time. High Tech is about the demand on the individual to produce more in less time. High Touch is about process, about allowing time for discovery. The underlying theme is to balance technology with human needs" (Naisbitt, 1998). Keeping all things in perspective, education and especially CTE must provide experiences that will balance technology with the needs of our youth and the ever-changing society in which they live.

◆ REFERENCES

Abbott, G. (2015). The Texas 'Economic Miracle' is far from finished. Press Release – Office of the Governor.

Achieve Texas. (2015). Retrieved from www.achievetexas.org

Charp, S. (1997, March 6–7). Enhancing workplace skills. THE Journal, *24*(8), 6.

Dean, H. (1997). Industry Commentary: One Down, Two to Go! Florida Technology Teacher, ITEA 1997 Conference Special Edition, pp. 20–22.

Froeschle, R. (2011). The changing face of the Texas labor market. Labor market & career information. Texas Workforce Commission. Richard.froeschle@twc.state.tx.us

Laitsch, D. (2005, May). Protecting the student interest. INFOBRIEF, Association for Supervision and Curriculum Development.

Murdock, S. H., White, S., Hoque, M. N., Pecotte, B., You, X., & Balkan, J. (2003). *The new Texas challenge: Population change and the future of Texas*. College Station, TX: Texas A&M University Press.

Naisbitt, J. (1998, August). High Tech/High Touch, Culture's New Paradox. Government *Technology, 11* (11): 8–44.

Perry, R. (2010, October 13). *The Texas Tribune*. US Bureau of Labor Statistics.

Scott, J. L., & Sarkees-Wircenski, M. (1996). *Overview of vocational and applied technology education*. Homewood, IL: American Technical Publishers, Inc.

Sessions, P. (2009). US Congressmen. In *North Texas Machinist Association Meeting, Carrollton, TX*.

Texas Education Agency. (2014). *Graduation Toolkit*.

Texas Education Agency. (2015a). *Program Guidelines 2015–2016 Title I, Part C Carl D. Perkins Career and Technical Education Act Grant Application—P.L. 109-270*.

Texas Education Agency. (2015b). Retrieved from http://tea.texas.gov/Curriculum_and_Instructional _Programs/Learning_Support_and_Programs/Career_and_Technical_Education/Career_and _Technical_Education/

Texas Education Agency. (2015c). *Texas Education Code 21.055 (d-1)*.

STUDENT RIGHTS, PARENTAL RIGHTS, AND ATTENDANCE

David P. Thompson ◆ *Elisabeth Krimbill*

Particularly since the 1960s, court cases and policy changes have changed the way schools address stakeholders. School leaders can no longer administer discipline without regard to student and parent concerns because of the increased emphasis on student and parental rights. This means that principals and superintendents must know the law in order to lead their schools in legally justifiable ways.

◆ STUDENT RIGHTS

By 1918, all states had passed compulsory attendance laws predicated on their states' constitutions granting a free public education. It is within this context of compulsory education that states have enacted statutes, and courts have developed common law to describe the rights and responsibilities of those involved with student rights.

Student conduct has traditionally been one of the most consistent concerns in public schools. For most of education's early history, discipline was "punishment to fit the crime" with an almost exclusive focus on "punishment." School officials had unquestioned authority to determine the appropriate penalty. Within the past several decades, however, courts have recognized the legal rights of American school children. Consequently, relationships within the school and with parents regarding the control and discipline of students have changed substantially.

Prior to the United States Supreme Court's decision in *Tinker v. Des Moines Community School District* (1969), the prevailing concept of *in loco parentis* (in the place of the parent) resulted in the courts deferring, except in extreme cases of abuse, to school authorities in all matters involving the control of student behavior. Since *Tinker*, school personnel have had to defend their actions as reasonable and necessary to maintain orderliness and school efficiency.

Additionally, with the 1975 court case *Goss v. Lopez* (1975), the U.S. Supreme Court defined the minimum due process that school officials must afford students under the 14th Amendment to the United States Constitution prior to depriving students of educational services. To meet the minimum due process standard, administrators must, either orally or in writing, notify the student of the rule or law violated. If the student denies the violation, the administrator must share the evidence with the student and allow the student to defend his/her actions. Ideally, a student should be afforded due process prior to the removal of any educational service. However, in some instances, it may be impossible to conduct even this informal hearing before the student is "disciplined." For example, if the situation is so volatile or if the student is incapable of rational thought, such a process can be conducted as soon as feasible and still provide the student with his or her "*Goss* rights."

While the recognition of student rights has occurred primarily through federal court action, until 1984 the Texas Legislature had left student discipline largely to the discretion of local school districts. With the passage of the Education Reform Act of 1984, Senate Bill 1 in 1995, and the more recent, although less substantive, legislative changes, Texas has nearly completely codified procedures to govern student discipline. Common within each rewrite of student discipline legislation is the goal to change disruptive students' behavior and protect the learning environment for nondisruptive students. The removal of misbehaving students from the classroom and placement in in-school suspension or disciplinary alternative education programs (DAEPs), or placement of serious offenders in Juvenile Justice Alternative Education Programs (JJAEP), clearly demonstrates the legislature's desire to keep students in schools and off "the streets."

The Texas Legislature's recognition that student discipline is not the sole responsibility of the school continues to grow, as various laws establish clear expectations regarding parent and community involvement, examples of which are listed below.

1. A school district's code of conduct must address the notification of the parent(s) or guardian(s) of a student who commits a code of conduct violation that results in suspension, removal to a DAEP, or expulsion (Tex. Educ. Code § 37.001 [a][6]).
2. A school district shall provide "notice of and information regarding" the student conduct code annually to parents (Tex. Educ. Code § 37.001 [d]).
3. School officials must notify juvenile justice courts when students are placed in DAEPs or expelled (Tex. Educ. Code §37.010).
4. Parents and guardians are required to supervise their expelled children (Tex. Educ. Code 37.009[h] [2]).
5. School districts and juvenile boards must collaborate to provide services appropriate for students who have been expelled or assigned to DAEPs (Tex. Educ. Code §37.013).
6. Public and private school principals or their designees must report to local or county law enforcement authorities about their reasonable belief that a student has committed certain types of criminal offenses that occur "in school, on school property, or at a school-sponsored or school-related activity on or off school property," irrespective of whether school security officers investigate the conduct (Tex. Educ. Code § 37.015).
7. A superintendent or designee must disclose information in the educational records of a student to a juvenile services provider for that student (Tex. Educ. Code §37.084[a]).

The realm of student discipline in Texas has become almost exclusively defined by state statute, rather than locally determined. Even so, "it [does] not make the lives of campus-based administrators less complex," as recognized by school law attorney Jim Walsh (1995, p. 28). For example, principals need to distinguish assaults from aggravated assaults and misdemeanors from felony drug and alcohol offenses and know the legal standards for, among other things, indecency with a child, indecent exposure, public lewdness, bullying, sexual harassment, and off-campus Internet speech. Accordingly, a summary and discussion of the key provisions of Chapter 37 of the Texas Education Code, titled "Discipline: Law and Order," follows, along with a discussion of implications for school administrators.

Student Codes of Conduct

Prior to the passage of SB 1 in 1995, Texas law required that parental conferences regarding student behavior be held, parent training workshops be offered, and written statements be signed by each parent stating that the parent understood and consented to the responsibilities as outlined by the school. These requirements have since been deleted from the Education Code; however, each school board is required to, with the advice of its district-level planning and decision-making committee, adopt a student code of conduct which must be prominently displayed on each district campus or made available for review in the principal's office (Tex. Educ. Code § 37.001 [a]). The student code of conduct is intended to communicate to students and their parents/guardians the types of, and consequences for, unacceptable conduct. Therefore, the code should comprehensively address the procedures necessary to affect the control and discipline of a district's students.

The student code of conduct developed under the provisions of Chapter 37 must address at a minimum the following issues:

1. The circumstances under which a student may be removed from the classroom, campus, DAEP, or a district-owned or –operated vehicle (Tex. Educ. Code §37.001[a][1]);
2. The conditions allowing or requiring a principal or other appropriate administrator to transfer a student to a DAEP (Tex. Educ. Code §37.001[a][2]);
3. The circumstances authorizing student suspension (Tex. Educ. Code §37.005) or expulsion as provided by statute (Tex. Educ. Code §37.007) (Tex. Educ. Code § 37.001 [a][3]);
4. That school districts will give consideration to the following factors in each decision concerning a student's suspension, expulsion, removal to a DAEP, or placement in a JJAEP, regardless of whether the foregoing placements are mandatory or discretionary:
   a. self-defense;
   b. intent or lack thereof at the time of the alleged misconduct;
   c. the student's disciplinary history; or
   d. a disability that substantially impairs the student's capacity to appreciate the wrongfulness of his/her alleged misconduct (Tex. Educ. Code §37.001[a][4]);
5. The guidelines for setting the lengths of expulsions and removals to DAEPs (Tex. Educ. Code §37.001[a][5]);
6. The notification of parents or guardians whose children have been suspended, expelled, or removed to a DAEP (Tex. Educ. Code §37.001[a][6]);

7. The statutory prohibition and school districts' enforcement of the prohibitions on bullying, harassment, and making hit lists (Tex. Educ. Code §37.001[a][7]); and

8. The provision of grade-level appropriate methods and options to manage student behavior in classrooms, on school grounds, and in district-owned and -operated vehicles; disciplining students; and preventing and intervening in student discipline problems, including, but not limited to, bullying, harassment, and making hit lists (Tex. Educ. Code§37.001 [a][8]).

Additionally, student codes of conduct should also address:

- Attendance
- Class conduct
- Dress codes
- Student expression, including Internet acceptable use policies
- Student search and seizure
- Hazing
- Controlled substance and alcohol use
- Use of school facilities
- Extracurricular activities
- Sexual harassment
- Bullying
- Application of academic penalties
- Permitted and prohibited student organizations
- Use of tobacco products
- Use of pagers and other electronic telecommunications devices
- Conduct on school buses and bus stops
- Discipline of students with disabilities
- Corporal punishment

Due to developing statutory and case law, several of these areas are further elaborated in the following sections.

Student Search and Seizure

This area of school law is governed primarily by the Fourth Amendment to the U.S. Constitution, which states,

> The right of the people to be secure in their persons, houses, papers, and effects, against unreasonable searches and seizures, shall not be violated, and no Warrants shall issue, but upon probable cause, supported by Oath or affirmation, and particularly describing the place to be searched, and the persons or things to be seized.

Whether the Fourth Amendment applied to searches of public school students was in question until 1985, when the U.S. Supreme Court, in *New Jersey v. TLO* (1985), held that the Fourth Amendment does apply; however, school officials need only "reasonable suspicion" in order to search a student. A search of a student is "reasonable" if it satisfies two conditions. First, the search must be "justified at its inception," meaning that school officials have "reasonable grounds for suspecting that the search will turn up evidence that the student has violated or is violating either the law or the rules of the school." Second, the search must be justified in its scope, which means that "the measures adopted are reasonably related to the objectives of the search and not excessively intrusive in light of the age and sex of the student and the nature of the infraction." Thus, the high court held that students do have a legitimate expectation of privacy in their persons and effects, but that school officials need not have probable cause—a higher standard than "reasonable suspicion"—prior to conducting less intrusive searches.

In 1995, the U.S. Supreme Court expanded the authority of school officials to conduct more intrusive searches, particularly to combat increased drug use among student athletes, when it handed down its landmark decision in *Vernonia School District 47J v. Acton* (1995). In *Vernonia*, the Court held that school districts may require secondary school students submit to random urinalysis drug testing as a condition for participating in extracurricular athletics. In its ruling, the court relied heavily on the school district's finding that student athletes were "leaders of the drug culture" and that the disciplinary consequences were related only to participation in extracurricular activities, not regular school discipline. The court rationalized that the expectations of privacy of student athletes, already diminished because of the school's *in loco parentis* standing, was even less in the extracurricular athletic setting since student athletes voluntarily participate. Next, the court held that the nature of the intrusion in collecting the urine samples was "minimal," not unlike the conditions one might encounter in a public restroom. Finally, the court noted that the school's interest was "important-indeed, perhaps compelling" enough to outweigh student athletes' legitimate expectations of privacy, and that the means used to achieve the school's interest was sufficiently efficacious.

Giving public school districts further constitutional leeway to combat drug problems among students, the U.S. Supreme Court in 2002 extended its decision in *Vernonia* to allow school districts to test all secondary students involved in any competitive extracurricular activity. In *Board of Education v. Earls* (2002), the high court upheld the Pottawatomie, Oklahoma, school district's random urinalysis drug testing policy that required all secondary students who participate in competitive extracurricular activities to submit to drug testing prior to participation. The court, relying predominantly on its rationale in *Vernonia*, importantly held that a school district, "given the nationwide epidemic of drug use," need not demonstrate a "constitutional quantum of drug use necessary to show a 'drug problem.'" Thus, public school districts arguably may institute such drug testing regimes on a purely preventative basis.

In 2003, a Texas appellate court rejected a challenge to a school district's drug testing policy on the grounds that the policy, which tested for drugs and alcohol, violated the free worship rights under the Texas Constitution of two Jewish students who consumed wine as part of their religious observances. In *Marble Falls I.S.D. v. Shell* (2003), the Texas appellate court held that the students did not have a right of recovery under the Texas Constitution, as the drug testing policy was a facially neutral law of general applicability with only an incidental burden on the students' religious beliefs.

Motivated by the well-documented deleterious effects of steroids and buoyed by the U.S. Supreme Court decisions referenced above, the 80th Texas Legislature in 2007 passed Senate Bill 8 (codified as Tex. Educ. Code § 33.091), which requires the University Interscholastic League (UIL) to adopt rules that prohibit a student from participating in a high school athletic competition unless the student and his/her parents agree to submit to random testing for steroids. In addition, the statute requires that a "statistically significant number" of students from ~30% of Texas high schools be tested beginning with the 2007–2008 school year. The test results may only be disclosed to the student, the student's parent, the activity directors, principal, and assistant principals of the student's school. In meeting the statute's requirement that the UIL administer penalties for verified positive tests, during the summer of 2007, the UIL established the following penalties for student-athletes who test positive: (1) a 30-day suspension from participation for the first positive test; (2) suspension for 1 year for a second positive test; and (3) a ban on participation for the remainder of the student athlete's high school career for the third positive test (Cantu, 2007). According to Peterson (2009), the $6 million spent on steroid testing since the implementation of the program resulted in only 19 of 45,000 students testing positive.

Perhaps as a result of the low incidence of positive tests, the 81st Texas Legislature appropriated $1 million per year for each of the 2009–2010 and 2010–2011 to continue a reduced testing program. That appropriation was projected to be reduced to $650,000 per year in each of years 2011–2012 and 2012–2013 (Garrett, 2011), perhaps based in part on the University Interscholastic League's most recent report on steroid testing (University Interscholastic League [UIL], 2011), conducted during the fall of 2010, which reported one positive test out of 2,083 students tested. In 2014, the Texas Sunset Advisory Commission recommended that the testing program be dissolved (Smith, 2014). SB 213 (84th Texas Legislature, 2015) was introduced to carry through the Sunset Advisory Commissions' recommendation, but the bill died prior to reaching the Governor's desk, apparently leaving the testing program intact. However, there was no appropriation from the 84th Legislature to support the program, leaving the program's future in doubt. The UIL's 2013–2014 report (University Interscholastic League, 2014) revealed only two positive results out of 2,633 tests conducted, for a percentage of 0.076, or 76/100 of one percent.

The most recent significant United States Supreme Court decision on student searches and seizures was issued in June 2009, and represented the first time that the Court addressed the issue of strip searching students. In *Safford Unified School District #1 v. Redding* (2009), the Court held that the strip search of a 13-year old Arizona middle school female student was unreasonable under the 4th Amendment. The search of the student was directed by the assistant principal and was conducted by the female school nurse and female administrative assistant on the assistant principal's suspicion that the student was involved in distributing prescription-strength pain medication (Ibuprofen 400 mg and Naproxen). At the direction of school officials, the student disrobed to her underclothing, pulled her bra away from and to the side of her body, exposing her breasts, and also pulled her underpants away from her body. Nothing was found in the search. In applying the *T.L.O.* reasonable-at-inception standard (reasonable grounds to believe that the student possesses material that violates the law or school rules), the majority found that the assistant principal was justified in conducting the search of the student's outer clothing and backpack (as there was evidence that a day-planner belonging to the student contained the prohibited contraband). However, the majority at this point drew its first distinction among "*T.L.O.*-type searches," holding that the search of belongings and outer clothing is "categorically distinct" from a strip search (which the majority termed as a fair application of the term to the search of the student) that requires "distinct elements of justification" for school officials to conduct such a search. In applying *T.L.O.*'s reasonable-in-scope requirements that the conducted search be "reasonably related . . . to the circumstances" justifying the search in the first place and not be "excessively intrusive in light of the age and sex of the student and the nature of the infraction," the Court found that the degree of the assistant principal's suspicion did not "match the degree of intrusion." The Court further found that while the assistant principal knew beforehand what the drugs were, his search went too far in light of the nature and the power of the drugs and the limited threat that they posed, as well as the lack of evidence that the drugs were being widely distributed. Furthermore, the assistant principal had no reason to believe that the student was secreting the drugs in her underclothing and that rendered the search unconstitutional in light of the majority's holding that when a school official strip searches a student, the reasonableness of that search requires "suspicion that will pay off." In sum, while the majority (with one exception) made it a point to not criticize the assistant principal, it also made clear that a strip search "requires the support of reasonable suspicion of danger" for it to be reasonable, as the strip search represents a "quantum leap" from a search of outer clothing and belongings. Thus, the search was held to be unconstitutional, but because the law concerning strip searches was not clearly established at the time of the search in 2003, the assistant principal who directed the search was entitled to qualified immunity. Further information on student searches and seizures may be found in Texas Association of School Boards (TASB) Policy FNF (Legal).

Student Expression and Attire

Regulation of student attire falls under the larger umbrella of student speech protected to varying degrees by the First Amendment and is governed by four landmark U.S. Supreme Court First Amendment cases. In the first, *Tinker v. Des Moines Independent Community School District* (1969), the court held that school officials could, with a reasonable forecast of "material and substantial" interference with school operations or the rights of others, suppress private student expression occurring on school grounds. Years later, in *Bethel School District v. Fraser* (1986), the court held that school officials could prohibit private student speech that was "vulgar," "lewd, "indecent," or "offensive" in nature. Next, in *Hazelwood School District v. Kuhlmeier* (1988), the court held that school officials could regulate school-sponsored student expression "as long as their actions are reasonably related to legitimate pedagogical concerns."

The fourth and most recent student expression case was decided in June 2007 and was the first United States Supreme Court decision in nearly 20 years to examine the contours of public school students' First Amendment right to free speech. In this case, the high court held that an Alaskan high school principal did not violate the free speech rights of a high school student who displayed a banner with the words "BONG HiTS 4 JESUS" when she confiscated the banner and suspended the student for 10 days. After the Ninth Circuit upheld the right of the student to display the banner because it did not result in a "material and substantial interference" with school operations, the U.S. Supreme Court reversed the lower court decision, finding in *Morse v. Frederick* that "a principal may, consistent with the First Amendment, restrict student speech at a school event, when that speech is reasonably viewed as promoting illegal drug use" (2007, internal citation omitted).

Shortly after the U.S. Supreme Court rendered its decision in *Morse*, the U.S. Court of Appeals for the Fifth Circuit was faced with the question of the extent to which school officials may go to regulate student expression that could be interpreted as promoting violence. In *Ponce v. Socorro Independent School District.* (2007), a high school student kept a diary which he wrote in the first person, and in which he described creating a "Neo-Nazi" group at his and other district high schools, ordering the group "to brutally injure" gay and minority persons, punishing a classmate by committing arson and murdering his dog, and committing a district-wide "Columbine shooting" attack. In addition, the student acknowledged that his anger had "the best of him," and that he would "lose control" on the day that his classmates were to graduate. When the diary was discovered, the assistant principal suspended the student and recommended a long-term alternative educational placement, believing the student's writings constituted a terroristic threat. The student and his parents sued, alleging that the discipline violated the student's right to free speech under the First Amendment. After the federal district court granted the student's motion for a preliminary injunction on the grounds that the diary did not constitute a material and substantial interference with the operation of the school, the Fifth Circuit reversed, relying on the U.S. Supreme Court's decision in *Morse v. Frederick* noted above. The court paid particular attention to the concurring (and as the court termed, controlling) opinion of Justice Samuel Alito, which limited the court's decision to speech advocating illegal drug use without restricting speech that commented on social and political issues, including issues pertaining to drugs. However, the court also found that Alito's concurrence arguably set out parameters for regulating student expression to prevent "serious and palpable" dangers to students. The court then further analyzed Justice Alito's concurrence to gain insight into the circumstances under which school officials may regulate student expression without having to "evaluate their disruptive potential" under *Tinker* and determined that the concurrence set out the circumstances to be present when there is a "threat to the physical safety of students" in schools, which "Experience shows . . . can be special places of danger". Applying this reasoning, the Fifth Circuit held that "speech advocating a harm that is demonstrably grave and that derives that gravity from the 'special danger' to the physical safety of students arising from the school environment is unprotected." The court further noted that,

> If school administrators are permitted to prohibit student speech that advocates illegal drug use because "illegal drug use presents a grave and in many ways unique threat to the physical safety of students," then it defies logical extrapolation to hold school administrators to a stricter standard with respect to speech that gravely and uniquely threatens violence, including massive deaths, to the school population as a whole.

Finally, the appellate court found

> that when a student threatens violence against a student body, his words are as much beyond the constitutional pale as yelling fire in crowded theater . . . and such specific threatening speech to a school or its population is unprotected by the First Amendment. School administrators must be permitted to react quickly and decisively to address a threat of physical violence against their students, without worrying that they will have to face years of litigation second-guessing their judgment as to whether the threat posed a real risk of substantial disturbance.

Applying this holding to the facts of the case, the Fifth Circuit found that the student's speech was unprotected, and vacated the preliminary injunction.

More recently, the Fifth Circuit upheld the Burleson Independent School District's prohibition against the display of the Confederate flag. In *A.M. v. Cash* (2009), the federal appellate court upheld the district's policy prohibiting the display of the Confederate flag under *Tinker's* material and substantial interference standard. The court found that school officials were justified in prohibiting the symbol, as the well-documented history of racially charged incidents that occurred at the district's high school gave school officials a reasonable forecast that subsequent displays of the Confederate flag would lead to further disruptions of school activities.

In addition to regulating student expression, and thus attire, under the principles elaborated earlier, the Texas Supreme Court has in two cases upheld the right of school officials to regulate student hair length. In *Barber v. Colorado Independent School District* (1995), the state high court refused to intervene in a case where a student claimed that the district's attempt to regulate the hair length of males violated the Texas Equal Rights Amendment, thereby allowing the school district to so regulate hair length. In *Bastrop Independent School District v. Toungate* (1997), the Texas high court held that grooming codes that differentiate on the basis of gender do not violate the Texas Tort Claims Act. Thus, Texas school officials may reasonably regulate student attire (including gender-based regulation) as long as regulations are not unconstitutionally vague and do not unreasonably interfere with students' sincerely held free exercise rights (see, e.g., *Chalifoux v. New Caney Independent School District* [(1997]). However, as illustrated by the *A.A. v. Needville Independent School District* (2010) case, school officials' discretion in regulating hair length is not without limits. *A.A.* was the case of a male Native American elementary school student who refused to cut his hair to conform to the school district's hair code. The Fifth Circuit held that the district's hair length policy violated the Texas Religious Freedom Restoration Act (TEX. CIV. PRAC. & REM. CODE § 110.003 *et seq.*), which prohibits the state from substantially burdening a person's free exercise of religion unless justified by a compelling governmental interest and employing the least restrictive means to further that interest. In this case, the court found that the student, who had never cut his hair based on his and his father's Native American beliefs, had a sincerely-held religious belief that the school district substantially burdened with its policy. Furthermore, the court found that none of district's five asserted interests—teaching hygiene, instilling discipline, preventing disruption, avoiding safety hazards, and asserting authority—were sufficiently compelling to justify the district's policy with regard to the student.

Student attire has also been the subject of Texas laws and court decisions. In 1995, the Texas Legislature gave local school boards the prerogative to require that students wear uniforms "if the board determines that the requirement would improve the learning environment at the school." The statute (Tex. Educ. Code §11.162) requires school districts to earmark funding sources to assist economically disadvantaged students in purchasing uniforms and to allow parents to exempt their children from such a requirement based on "a bona fide religious or philosophical objection." Predictably, litigation surrounding school districts' implementation of uniform policies ensued, and in 2000, the Fifth Circuit upheld the Forney Independent School District's uniform policy (see *Littlefield v. Forney Indep. Sch. Dist.*, [2001]). The court noted that the policy, which contained an opt-out provision, did not violate students' right of free speech under the First Amendment (indeed, the court held that the wearing of individualized clothing did not rise to the level of protected speech under the First Amendment), nor did the policy violate the students' 14th Amendment substantive due process liberty interest to wear the clothing of their choice, the students' parents' right under the 14th Amendment to direct the upbringing of their children, or the parents' free exercise rights under the First Amendment. With regard to the free speech challenge, the court found that the policy furthered the school district's important or substantial interest of improving the educational environment, an interest unrelated to the expression of student expression, and that the restrictions on student expression were "incidental."

Further support for mandatory uniform policies is also found in the Fifth Circuit's decision in *Canady v. Bossier Parish School District* (2001), in which the federal appellate court upheld the school district's uniform policy as not violating the First Amendment speech rights of students. Importantly, the appellate court overturned that part of the federal district court's decision in *Littlefield* which held that the wearing of clothing could not rise to the level of protected speech under the First Amendment, holding instead that the district's asserted interest in improving student behavior and achievement outweighed what limited First Amendment protection students enjoyed in choosing their clothing.

A more recent Fifth Circuit decision gives school officials arguably even greater latitude to regulate student attire. In *Palmer v. Waxahachie Independent School District* (2009), the Texas school district enacted a dress code which in essence prohibited students from displaying any messages on clothing that were not associated with approved curricular organizations or clubs, school sports teams, or school spirit. In addition, the code allowed the display of unspecified logos on shirts as long as the logos were not larger in area than 2 inches by 2 inches. When the school district prohibited a student from wearing three shirts (a t-shirt displaying an "Edwards for President" message, a polo shirt displaying a similar message, and a t-shirt displaying "Freedom of Speech" on the front and the text of the First Amendment on the back), the student and his parents brought a First Amendment claim against the district. In affirming the federal district court's denial of the student's request for a preliminary injunction, the Fifth Circuit (on different grounds than those cited by the district court), held that the dress code did not violate the free speech clause of the First Amendment. The court found that the dress code was a "content-neutral" regulation of student expression (as it sought to prohibit expression without regard to the content of the messages on clothing); as such, the familiar *Tinker* (material and substantial interference), *Bethel* (lewd, vulgar, indecent), *Hazelwood* (school-sponsored), and *Morse* (reasonably viewed as promoting illegal drug use) tests generally targeting individual student expression did not apply to the school's dress code. The court, relying in part on its decision in *Canady* (2001), applied an "intermediate scrutiny" test, which determines whether a content-neutral regulation on expression "furthers an important or substantial government interest; if the interest is unrelated to the suppression of student expression, and if the incidental restrictions on First Amendment activities are no more than is necessary to facilitate that interest." The court found that the district's interests in promoting a safe learning environment, increasing instructional focus, etc., were more than sufficient under the intermediate scrutiny test; that these interests did not relate to a desire to suppress student expression; and—because students could wear buttons displaying messages that could not be displayed on clothing and because the ban on message-displaying clothing did not extend beyond the school day—that the dress code did not suppress any more expression than was necessary to further the school district's interests. Thus, with regard to student attire, the Fifth Circuit is relying less on the traditional free-speech tests, and more on the intermediate scrutiny test as elaborated in *Canady* and *Palmer*.

Three decisions by the Texas Commissioner of Education in religious or philosophical challenges to uniform policies have clarified several issues, including that which constitutes both philosophical and religious objections and that which constitutes bona fide objection. In *Kaytie T. v. Forney Independent School District* (2002), the commissioner granted the petitioner a religious exemption to Forney ISD's mandatory uniform policy. The commissioner held that a bonafide objection is one that is honest, open, and sincere. A religious objection need not be rooted in a specific doctrine or religious denomination to be legitimate; indeed, the objection may be based on one's interpretation of religious literature. The commissioner further held that an objector's refusal to complete a questionnaire articulating the objection is not a determinant of sincerity. In two cases from the Natalia Independent School District

(*Benjamin B. v. Natalia Independent School District*, 2002; *Diane C. v. Natalia Independent School District* 2002), the commissioner acknowledged the legitimacy of philosophical objections based on the arguments that uniforms stifle diversity and intrude on the rights of parents. The commissioner ruled in favor of the parents in the *Benjamin B.* case based on the fact that the district did not challenge the sincerity of the parents objections, but ruled in favor of the district in the *Diane C.* case because the parents' philosophical objections were not sincere, as evidenced by the children's wearing of uniforms in other contexts and the parent's voluntary wearing of a nurse's uniform. Further information on student attire can be found in Texas Association of School Boards Policy FNCA (Legal), while information on student expression can be found in TASB Policy FNA (Legal).

Student Religious Expression

Long a controversial topic, the rights of students to express their religious viewpoints took center stage in 2007 as a result of the 80th Texas Legislature's passage of House Bill 3678, also known as the "Religious Viewpoints Antidiscrimination Act" (RVAA). The RVAA is codified as Subchapter E in Chapter 25 of the Texas Education Code and in general requires a school district to "treat a student's voluntary expression of a religious viewpoint, if any, on an otherwise permissible subject in the same manner the district treats a student's voluntary expression of a secular or other viewpoint on an otherwise permissible subject" (Tex. Educ. Code § 25.151). The legislation is then divided into five sections addressing the following topics: (1) limited public forum, (2) religious expression in classroom assignments, (3) freedom to organize religious groups and activities, (4) the adoption of a policy, and (5) a model policy that, if adopted by local school districts, places the district in compliance with the provisions of the RVAA as deemed by the legislature. Each component of the RVAA is briefly described below.

Limited Public Forum

Tex. Educ. Code § 25.152 requires school districts to adopt "a policy, which must include the establishment of a limited public forum (roughly described as a forum for speech established by the state which limits access to the forum based on subject matter and/or speaker identity; see, e.g., *Perry Education Association. v. Perry Local Educators' Association* [1983]) for student speakers at all events at which a student is to publicly speak." The policy requiring the establishment of this limited public forum must also meet the following four legislative stipulations: (1) it must provide that students cannot be discriminated against based on their "voluntary expression of a religious viewpoint" on a subject that is permitted for discussion in the forum; (2) it must provide for the selection of speakers at graduation ceremonies and other school events based on "neutral criteria;" (3) it must ensure that student speakers refrain from engaging in "obscene, vulgar, offensively lewd, or indecent speech;" and (4) it must state verbally and/or in writing that any views expressed by student speakers do not "reflect the endorsement, sponsorship, position, or expression of the district" [Tex. Educ. Code § 25.152 (a) (1-4)]. In addition, the statute requires that a disclaimer "must be provided at all graduation ceremonies" and for all other activities at which students publicly speak until there is no longer a need to "dispel confusion" that the views expressed by student speakers are considered private speech [Tex. Educ. Code § 25.152(b)]. This provision reiterates that a student's religious viewpoint on an otherwise permissible subject may not be excluded from the limited public forum.

Religious Expression in Classroom Assignments

Codified in Tex. Educ. Code § 25.153, this provision permits students to "express their beliefs about religion in homework, artwork, and other written and oral assignments free from discrimination based on the religious content of their submissions." Furthermore, the provision requires school districts and teachers to judge homework and other assignments "by ordinary academic standards of substance and relevance and against other [district-identified] legitimate pedagogical concerns." School districts are prohibited from penalizing or rewarding students based on the religious content of their schoolwork.

Freedom to Organize Religious Groups and Activities

The third major section of the RVAA (Tex. Educ. Code § 25.154) gives students the right to "organize prayer groups, religious clubs, 'see you at the pole' gatherings, or other religious gatherings" if the same right to organize has been afforded to other noncurricular student groups [for a discussion of one of the legal bases for this provision, see *Board of Education v. Mergens* (1990)]. If this right has been afforded, student religious groups must be given equal "access to school facilities as is given to other non-curricular student groups" and a school district may not discriminate in this regard "based on the religious content of the students' expression." If a school district elects to disclaim sponsorship of non-curricular student groups or events, it must do so "in a manner that does not favor or disfavor groups that meet to engage in prayer or religious speech."

Adoption of Policy

Tex. Educ. Code § 25.155 required school districts to adopt a policy implementing the foregoing by not later than September 1, 2007. The legislature deems a school district to be in compliance with the requirements of the RVAA if it adopts the model policy found in Tex. Educ. Code § 25.156. Local district policies implementing the RVAA can be found in TASB Policy FNA (Local).

In 2009, the Fifth Circuit rejected a challenge to the Texas moment-of-silence statute (codified at Tex. Educ. Code § 25.082), which added the word "pray" as one of the optional activities in which students can participate (along with reflect, meditate, or participate in any other silent activity that is not disruptive). In rejecting the plaintiffs' First Amendment Establishment Clause challenge to the statute, the federal appellate court held that the statute had a secular legislative purpose, did not have the primary effect of advancing or inhibiting religion, and did not excessively entangle religion and the state (*Croft v. Perry*, 2009).

Furthermore, in 2011 the Fifth Circuit, sitting *en banc*, issued a significant decision in Plano Independent School District "Candy Canes" case. This action was brought by a group of then-elementary aged students and their parents and asserted that the district prohibited students from distributing religiously-themed objects (such as candy canes, pencils with religious messages, and tickets to a local church's production of the Passion play) during non-instructional time, thus violating the First Amendment free speech rights of the students. In ruling in favor of the students (but also ruling that the principals at the involved campuses were entitled to qualified immunity, as the law in this area was not clearly established at the time of the incidents in late 2003 and early 2004), the federal appellate court made two holdings: (1) the protections of the free speech clause of the First Amendment extend to elementary schoolchildren, including the right to be free from religious viewpoint discrimination; and (2) two elementary school principals violated those rights when restricting students from privately and non-disruptively distributing religiously themed materials to their classmates in clearly non-curricular settings. This decision places these rights into the "clearly established" category, making it necessary for school officials to review the *Morgan v. Swanson* (2011) case carefully when formulating policies and procedures governing student religious expression.

Finally, in a case that has generated a great deal of publicity in the popular media and which the Texas Supreme Court is considering for review, the Kountze ISD was sued by a high school cheerleader after the district prohibited the cheerleaders from displaying religiously-themed messages on banners that student-athletes "run through" prior to the start of football games (and other events). The superintendent, on advice of legal counsel and after receiving a demand letter from the Freedom from Religion Foundation, prohibited the display of the banners in fall 2012. The plaintiff student and her parents sued, and received a temporary injunction almost immediately permitting the display of the banners. The request for injunctive relief was also accompanied by free speech, free exercise, and equal protection claims. In April 2013, the board by resolution determined "that school personnel are not required to prohibit messages on school banners, including run-through banners that display fleeting expressions of community sentiment solely because the source or origin of such messages is religious." However, the state district court denied the district's plea to the jurisdiction (motion to dismiss). On appeal, the state appellate court reversed, finding that the district's resolution and pledge not to change the policy again rendered the case moot (*Kountze Indep. Sch. Dist. v. Matthews*, 2014). The plaintiffs have appealed, and the Texas Supreme Court is currently considering whether to review the case (for a full elaboration of the docket, please see http://www.search.txcourts.gov/Case.aspx?cn=14-0453&coa=cossup, last accessed September 25, 2015).

Student Internet Expression

It has been roughly two decades since the Internet became a staple in the lives of Americans. With the continued influence of the Internet, and the technology that has enabled Americans (indeed, the World) to access the World Wide Web, it was only a matter of time before students would be able to use the Internet for purposes both admirable and otherwise. As advancements in technology have accelerated, school districts and the courts have struggled to keep up with this acceleration, particularly with regard to student expression that begins off-campus on a personal electronic communication device but is targeted at school officials or students and that somehow reaches the confines of campus. Until August 2015, the Fifth Circuit had not weighed in on the issue of when and under what circumstances school officials can discipline students' speech originating off-campus and involving the use of electronic communication.

This changed in the case of *Bell v. Itawamba County School Board* (2015), where a Mississippi high school student who wrote and produced a rap song to, as the student asserted, bring attention to two coaches whom he believed were sexually harassing female students. The rap identified the coaches specifically, was termed "incredibly vulgar and profane" by the *en banc* majority, and contained four lines about which the court was concerned (emphasis added by court):

http://www.ca5.uscourts.gov/opinions%5Cpub%5C12/12-60264-CV2.pdf

When the school district suspended the student and placed him in a disciplinary alternative program until the end of the grading period (~6 weeks), the student challenged the discipline on free speech grounds. After a federal district court ruled in favor of the student, a three-judge panel of the 5th Circuit reversed, holding that the student's speech was protected by the First Amendment. Sitting *en banc*, the full 5th Circuit affirmed the lower court's ruling in favor of the school district, holding that in these circumstances, *Tinker's* "material and substantial interference" standard applies:

> *Tinker* governs our analysis, as in this instance, when a student intentionally directs at the school community speech reasonably understood by school officials to threaten, harass, and intimidate a teacher, even when such speech originated, and was disseminated, off-campus without the use of school resources. (2015 U.S. App. LEXIS 14630 at 37)

Key to the court's invocation of *Tinker* was that the student intentionally directed the rap at the two coaches and intended that the speech reach the school community. In addition, in finding that the school district could reasonably determine that the speech forecast a material and substantial disruption, the court elaborated 11 factors that school officials can consider, while noting that school officials must be afforded the discretion "to be able to react and quickly and effectively to protect students and faculty from threats, intimidation, and harassment intentionally directed at the school community". . . "before speech leads to violence" (2015 U.S. App. LEXIS 14630 at 30). Texas school officials should be familiar with these 11 factors, as they represent one of the clearest articulations to date of factors school officials can consider in reasonably forecasting when student expression may lead to substantial disruption. Finally, the court acknowledged the challenges that school officials face in balancing school safety and the First Amendment free speech rights of students:

> Over 45 years ago, when Tinker was decided, the Internet, cellphones, smartphones, and digital social media did not exist. The advent of these technologies and their sweeping adoption by students present new and evolving challenges for school administrators, confounding previously delineated boundaries of permissible regulations. (2015 U.S. App. LEXIS 14630 at 27)

Finally, school officials in Texas, while given significant guidance on the circumstances in *Itawamba* that would permit regulation of off-campus student expression, must remain cognizant of off-campus expression that does not meet the requirements of the standard elaborated earlier.

"Sexting"

Another issue that has accompanied the increased use of electronic telecommunication devices is that of "sexting," i.e., the transmission of either verbal or visual sexually explicit messages from one person to another via an electronic communication device, most often cell phones. School administrators address this issue when finding students' cell phones displaying such material, and in 2011 the Texas Legislature responded by passing SB 407 (codified at. PENAL CODE § 43.261), which prohibits minors (i.e., persons younger than 18) from:

1. "by electronic means promot[ing] (defined in Tex. Penal Code § 43.25) to another minor visual material (defined by Tex. Penal Code § 43.26, but for this discussion includes still images or video) depicting a minor, including the actor, engaging in

sexual conduct (defined by Tex. Penal Code § 43.25), if the actor produced the visual material or knows that another minor produced the visual material; or

2. possess[ing] in an electronic format visual material depicting another minor engaging in sexual conduct, if the actor produced the visual material or knows that another minor produced the visual material." (Tex. Penal Code § 43.261 [b]).

Conduct in (1) above is punishable as a Class C misdemeanor, unless the minor has been convicted previously for either types of conduct noted above, or if the minor intentionally promoted the material to "harass, annoy, alarm, abuse, torment, or offend another" (Tex. Penal Code § 43.261 [c]), in which case the conduct is punishable as a Class B misdemeanor. Ultimately, the conduct can be punished as a Class A misdemeanor. Conduct under (2) above is punishable as a Class C misdemeanor, a Class B misdemeanor for the second conviction for either of the two offenses noted above, and a Class A misdemeanor for the third conviction on either offense.

Finally, several categories of individuals may assert a defense to prosecution under the statute: (1) an individual within two years of the minor and with whom the minor had a dating relationship, or spouse and only if the individual and the minor in a dating relationship or the spouse solely promoted or received the visual material (Tex. Penal Code § 43.261 [e]); (2) those individuals who received, but did not promote or solicit, the material; received the material from another minor; and destroyed the material in a "reasonable" amount of time after receiving it (Tex. Penal Code § 43.261 [f]); and (3) school administrators and law enforcement officials who possessed the material in good faith as part of an allegation, displayed it to other law enforcement or school officials appropriately based on an allegation, and reasonably attempted to destroy the material in an "appropriate" amount of time after receiving the allegation (Tex. Penal Code § 43.26 [h]).

Student-to-Student Sexual Harassment

As amended in 2005, Tex. Educ. Code §37.083 requires that a school district's discipline management program "provide for prevention of and education concerning . . . sexual harassment." In light of the U.S. Supreme Court decision in *Davis v. Monroe County Board of Education* (1999), nearly all Texas school districts already address sexual harassment in their codes of conduct (see, e.g., Texas Association of School Boards Policy FFH [Legal]). Student-to-student sexual harassment is a federal issue as a result of Title IX of the Educational Amendments of 1972 (20 U.S.C. § 1681), which prohibits a student from being excluded from participation in, being denied the benefit of, or being subjected to discrimination under any educational program or activity that receives federal financial assistance.

In *Davis*, the Court announced its standard of liability for student-to-student harassment when it found that federally assisted education institutions can be liable under Title IX if: (1) responsible school officials have actual knowledge of the harassment; (2) the school is deliberately indifferent; (3) the deliberate indifference causes a student to experience further harassment or makes them more vulnerable to the harassment; (4) the district exercises substantial control over both the harasser and the context in which the harassment occurred; and (5) the harassment is severe, pervasive, and objectively offensive enough to have the effect of denying educational benefits to the victim. The message is clear: schools need to ensure that all of their employees (i.e., teachers, secretaries, bus drivers, custodians, nurses, aides, etc.) are able to both recognize harassment and know to report it. Obviously, the "boys will be boys" attitude and "turning a blind eye" to certain behaviors can no longer be tolerated if school districts hope to escape liability.

In a recent decision, the U.S. Supreme Court in *Fitzgerald v. Barnstable School Committee* (2009) held that Title IX does not provide the exclusive remedy to students and their families seeking redress for sex discrimination, including sexual harassment. Students and their families seeking such redress may do so through asserting violations of the Equal Protection Clause of the 14th Amendment, which provides for judgments against school officials in their individual capacities.

Finally, in 2005, the Texas Legislature extended substantive rights to students who are the victims of sexual assault while, at the same time, giving school districts additional latitude to remove certain perpetrators of sexually assaultive offenses from the campus to which they are assigned. Codified in Tex. Educ. Code §25.0341, this provision applies to students who are the victims of continuous sexual abuse, sexual assault, or aggravated sexual assault, committed on or off school property, if the perpetrator has been convicted, placed on deferred adjudication, adjudicated delinquent, received deferred prosecution, or been placed on probation for any of these offenses. In addition, both the perpetrator and the victim must have been assigned to the same campus at the time of the conduct described above. If this is the case, the school board must, on request of the parent or other person acting in authority over the victim, transfer (without providing transportation) the victim to another district campus, and one to which the perpetrator is not assigned; or to a neighboring school district if the district only maintains one campus serving the grade level of the victim. If the victim does not wish to transfer, the school board must transfer the perpetrator to another district campus, or to the DAEP or JJAEP if the district has only one campus serving the grade level of the perpetrator. Finally, to the extent permitted by federal law, a school district is required to notify the parent or other person acting in authority over the victim as to the campus to which the perpetrator is assigned, if the perpetrator has been convicted or received deferred adjudication for the misconduct described above.

Of final note is that Tex. Educ. Code § 37.0831 requires school districts to adopt and implement a policy as part of the district improvement plan to help prevent dating violence. The statute requires school districts to define dating violence and to address such issues as "safety planning, enforcement of protective orders, school-based alternatives to protective orders, training for teachers and administrators, counseling for affected students, and awareness education for students and parents."

Sexual Abuse Policies

Since 2009, the Texas Legislature has required school districts to adopt and implement a policy that addresses both sexual abuse and "other maltreatment" of children. This statute is codified at Tex. Educ. Code § 38.0041. This policy must be included in both the school district's improvement plan and in informational handbooks disseminated to parents. In general, the policy must address three areas: (1) methods for increasing parent, staff, and student awareness of sexual abuse and other maltreatment issues as well as awareness of prevention techniques and "likely warning signs" of such abuse/maltreatment; (2) recommended actions a child who is a victim of sexual abuse/maltreatment should take to seek assistance and intervention; and (3) counseling options available to students who have been affected by such abuse or maltreatment (Tex. Educ. Code § 38.0041 [b]). The statute also requires mandatory training of employees new to a school district or open-enrollment charter school and optional training for all other employees on increasing awareness of sexual abuse/other maltreatment.

(Tex. Educ. Code § 38.0041 [c]). This training must include information on risk factors, likely warning signs, procedures for students at-risk of sexual abuse or other methods for seeking assistance, and techniques for decreasing a child's risk of being subjected to sexual abuse/ other maltreatment. School districts and open-enrollment charter schools must keep records of those who take part in the training.

By way of HB 10, the Texas Legislature amended Tex. Educ. Code § 38.004(a), which directs the Texas Education Agency to "develop a policy governing the reports of child abuse and neglect," and expanded this direction to include "reports related to the trafficking of a child" as that term is defined in Chapter 20A of the Texas Penal Code. This policy applies specifically to school districts and open-enrollment charter schools and the employees of each. Mindful of the need for cooperation between public schools and law enforcement agencies, the statute requires school districts, open-enrollment charters, and their respective employees to cooperate with investigations conducted by law enforcement and the Department of Family and Protective Services "without the consent of the child's parents if necessary." TEA's policy, which must be adopted by school districts and open-enrollment charters, requires employees to report child abuse, neglect, and now, trafficking in according with the reporting require-ments of Chapter 261 of the Texas Family Code.

Finally, and importantly, the 84th Texas Legislature enacted HB 1783 to clarify the rights of school district and open-enrollment charter school employees to report crimes (including child abuse) that are "witnessed at the school." Educators may report such crimes "to any peace officer with authority to investigate the crime," and school districts and open-enrollment charters may not enact policies that require such employees to: (1) "refrain from reporting a crime witnessed at school," and (2) "report a crime witnessed at school only to certain persons or peace officers."

Bullying

To no one's surprise, bullying has received a great deal of attention in both research literature (see, e.g., Lee, 2011) and in the popular press (see, e.g., Smith & Draper, 2011). As a result, many state legislatures have taken up this policy issue, and the Texas Legislature is no excep-tion. In 2005, the legislature first required that a school district's code of conduct prohibit bullying (Tex. Educ. Code §37.001[a][7]) and that a school district's discipline management program include prevention of and education concerning bullying. In 2011, the Legislature spoke further, requiring Texas school boards to, by not later than the 2012–2013 school year, adopt policies (Policy FFI for Texas school districts subscribing to the Texas Association of School Boards' Policy Service) and procedures regarding bullying (Tex. Educ. Code § 37.0832 [c]). The Legislature defines bullying as: "engaging in written or verbal expression, expression through electronic means, or physical conduct that occurs on school property, at a school-sponsored or school-related activity, or in a vehicle operated by the district and that:

- has the effect or will have the effect of physically harming a student, damaging a stu-dent's property, or placing a student in reasonable fear of harm to the student's person or of damage to the student's property; or
- is sufficiently severe, persistent, and pervasive enough that the action or threat creates an intimidating, threatening, or abusive educational environment for a student" (Tex. Educ. Code § 37.0832 [a]).

In addition, to be considered bullying, the conduct must exploit a power imbalance between the perpetrator and victim and must either substantially disrupt the school operation or interfere with the victim's education (Tex. Educ. Code § 37.0832 [b]).

Policies and procedures established by Texas school districts must: (1) prohibit bullying; (2) prohibit retaliation against any person "who in good faith provides information" regarding bullying incidents; (3) put in place procedures for the school district to notify the parents and/or guardians of both the victim and perpetrator of bullying in a reasonable amount of time from when an incident has taken place; (4) establish actions that students should take to gain "assistance and intervention in response to" a bullying incident; (5) elaborate counseling options available to victims and perpetrators of and witnesses to bullying; (6) set out procedures for reporting, investigating, and disposing of bullying incidents; (7) prohibit disciplining a victim of bullying who reasonably relies on self-defense in response to being bullied; and (8) ensure that the discipline of students with disabilities who are found to have bullied to comport with the Individuals with Disabilities Education Act (IDEA) and other federal laws impacting student discipline (Tex. Educ. Code § 37.0832 [c]). The district's policy and procedures must be published annually in student and employee handbooks and the reporting procedures must be, "to the extent practicable," posted on the district's website. However, the legislature remained silent on specifying bullying as either an offense requiring removal to a DAEP or expulsion, thereby leaving school districts discretion as to how bullying will be disciplined.

Adding to its previous legislation extending transfer rights to school-district verified victims of bullying on parent/guardian request (Tex. Educ. Code § 25.0342 [b]), the 82th Texas Legislature in 2011 through House Bill 1942 gave districts the discretion to transfer students who have engaged in bullying (Tex. Educ. Code § 25.0342 [b-1]). This legislation permits school districts to transfer the bullying perpetrator to another classroom on the same campus, without parent/legal guardian consultation, or to another campus in the school district "in consultation" with the parent/legal guardian. When identifying a bully, school districts are permitted to consider the alleged aggressor's past behavior; moreover, the determination of the board or its designee as to whether the alleged victim was a victim of bullying is final and not appealable. A school district is not required to provide transportation to another campus in the district for verified victims who have received a transfer.

While the Texas Legislature added both obligations and tools for school districts to address bullying, the United States Department of Education's Office of Civil Rights (OCR) arguably clouded the issue with its release of a "Dear Colleague Letter" in October 2010. In this letter penned by Assistant Secretary for Civil Rights Russlynn Ali, the OCR "reminded" school officials subject to other anti-discrimination laws enforced by the OCR that, to the extent bullying is based on a victim's membership in a class protected by these statutes (e.g., gender protected by Title IX; race, color, or national origin protected by Title VI; disability protected by Section 504), to that extent school officials' responses to bullying are subject to the anti-discrimination (including harassment) provisions of these statutes and any accompanying regulations. To illustrate, citing its own sexual harassment guidance revised in 2001 (United States Department of Education, 2001), the OCR noted that schools subject to these statutes are "responsible for addressing harassment incidents about which [they know] or reasonably should have known," effectively telling school districts that their negligent failure to address bullying with connotations of discrimination or harassment could lead to a finding that the educational institution is in violation of such statutes. This letter generated a great deal of concern, and in December 2010, Charlie Rose (2010), General Counsel for the National School Boards

Association (NSBA), responded to the "Dear Colleague" Letter by arguing, first and foremost, that OCR's stated intent to hold educational institutions to a "knew or should have known" standard expands the scope of liability beyond that which the U.S. Supreme Court articulated with regard to student-to-student sexual harassment under Title IX in *Davis v. Monroe Co. Bd. of Educ.* (1999) (i.e., actual knowledge/deliberate indifference). Mr. Rose also chided the OCR for requiring institutions to take all measures to stop bullying, again expanding Supreme Court guidance that remedial actions must only be "not clearly unreasonable." The NSBA letter expressed concern that OCR has rendered educational institutions more vulnerable to student bullying challenges beyond that which the U.S. Supreme Court envisioned in *Davis*. In its March 2011 response (Ali, 2011) to the NSBA's letter, the OCR took the position that the "actual knowledge-deliberate indifference" standard elaborated in *Davis* only applies in cases where complainants seek monetary damages through the courts, and not to OCR's administrative enforcement of its anti-discrimination statutes and regulations, where OCR argues that the "knew or should have known" standard should apply.

Texas case law regarding bullying has started to accumulate during the past two years, and this brief summary of six cases, including three involving the suicides of bullying victims, may begin to illuminate the important issues. Four of these cases have reached the Fifth Circuit. The first case is styled *Carmichael v. Galbraith* (2014), and involves a suit brought by the estate of a Joshua Independent School District 13-year old middle school student who committed suicide in 2010 after being subjected to relentless bullying by classmates. When the federal district court heard the case, it dismissed all claims against the defendant district and teachers, finding first that the deceased student could not prevail on his 14th Amendment due process claim that the defendants' actions violated his rights to life and liberty, observing that the due process clause protects individuals from the state only, and not from other private actors such as classmates. The court rejected the estate's 14th Amendment equal protection claim, finding that the school district did not treat claims of the student's bullying differently from bullying claims brought by other students, nor did it treat bullying claims differently based the genders of the perpetrators and the victims. Finally, the court dismissed the Title IX claim against the school district, finding no evidence that the district discriminated in its alleged response to the student because he was male, or even that the bullying occurred because the student was male. However, in 2014 the 5th Circuit reinstated the Title IX claim against the school district, finding that the complaint alleged several "incidents of sexual assault," namely the classmates accosting the child on "numerous occasions" and forcibly removing his underwear. Based on this portion of the complaint, the court found that that estate sufficiently alleged that the conduct was sexual harassment that was "severe, pervasive, and objectively" offensive to meet the definition of actionable sexual harassment under Title IX. After the 5th Circuit's opinion, the district court set a trial date for fall 2015, but dismissed the case with prejudice at the request of the estate (www.pacer.gov), last accessed September 24, 2015).

The second case also involves the suicide of a middle school student in the Cypress-Fairbanks Independent School District who allegedly was bullied both verbally and physically, with the bullying carried religious and sexual overtones. When the student committed suicide in September 2010, his estate brought suit against the school district and several school officials, asserting that the defendants' response to the bullying incidents resulted in the death of their son and violated in relevant part his 14th Amendment due process and equal protection rights as well as his rights under Title IX. In two decisions dismissing all but the Title IX claim (*Estate of Brown v. Cypress-Fairbanks Independent School District*, 2012; *Estate of*

Brown v. Ogletree, 2012), the federal district court again dismissed the due process claims against the defendants on the same grounds as noted in the first case, i.e., students cannot claim due process protection when injured/killed by a private actor. With regard to the equal protection claim, the observed that the estate failed to adequately plead (1) that the district followed its bullying policies with regard to the other students while failing to follow them for the deceased student, and (2) that the district enforced its bullying policies differently for male victims than for female victims. Left standing was the Title IX claim, with the district court finding sufficient pleadings that the school district had actual notice (through a complaint made to an assistant principal), that the district was deliberately indifferent to this knowledge (by doing nothing), that the bullying was based on sex (due to it being "overtly sexual or involv[ing] sexual innuendo"), that the sex-based bullying occurred in a context subject to the district's control (on school premises), and that the bullying was sufficiently "severe, persistent, and objectively offensive" to deprive the students of his educational benefits. Key to this ruling was the finding that the bullying was "based on sex," which is necessary to convert a bullying claim into a sexual harassment claim.

The third bullying case involved a claim brought by the estate of a 10-year old student with a disability who hanged himself in the nurse's restroom in the Lewisville Independent School District after being subjected to, for lack of a better term, bullying based on his perceived sexual orientation (ostensibly related to his having a speech impairment). The estate brought claims against the district and several school officials under the due process clause of the 14th Amendment, as well as under Section 504 and the Americans with Disabilities Act (ADA). The federal district court dismissed all claims (*Estate of Lance v. Kyer*, 2012), beginning with the due process claim, again for the reason that the perpetrators of the bullying were private actors (students), and not the district, which does not have a constitutional duty to protect one student from another. The court also dismissed the Section 504 and ADA claims, essentially for the reason that there was no evidence of disability-based discrimination on the part of the defendants. In affirming, the 5th Circuit in *Estate of Lance v. Lewisville Indep. Sch. Dist.* (2014), disposed of the Section 504 claims on the grounds that because the school met its duty to provide a free appropriate public education (FAPE) under the IDEA, by law it also satisfied any duty owed to the child under Section 504. Furthermore, because the school district investigated and, when appropriate, took disciplinary action against the perpetrators of the bullying, the district could not found to be deliberately indifferent to the child's bullying.

The fourth case, *G.M. v. Shelton* (2014), involved an Aledo Independent School District 4th grade student who allegedly had been subjected to bullying over a multi-year period, including being pushed, kicked, shoved, and spit upon. Through his mother, he sued the school district and school officials, claiming violations of the Due Process and Equal Protection Clauses of the 14th Amendment and asserting municipal liability claims against the school district for the alleged constitutional violations of its employees. In affirming a federal district court's motion to dismiss the liability claim against the school district (the court did not address the constitutional claims against the principal), the 5th Circuit held that the plaintiffs could not establish that the school district had a policy, custom, or practice that was the moving force behind any alleged constitutional violations committed by the principal.

The fifth case involved an elementary school student in the Arlington Independent School District diagnosed with attention deficit hyperactivity disorder (ADHD) and a learning disability who claimed that he was verbally bullied by a female classmate. Complaining that the district's only action when notified of the bullying was to move the classmate to another class, the student through his parent filed suit, alleging violations of Section 504, the Americans with Disabilities Act, the Equal Protection Clause, and Title IX. The federal district court dismissed the entire complaint (*Williams-Grant v. Arlington Independent School District*, 2012), finding initially that because there was no evidence that the district treated this student's complaint differently from other "similarly situated" (i.e., other male and/or disabled) students, the student could not prevail on his equal protection claim. The ADA and Section 504 claims failed, again because the plaintiffs did not allege discrimination based on disability. Finally, with regard to the Title IX claim, the court observed that the student did not allege facts that he was bullied because he was male or that the school district's response to the student constituted gender discrimination.

Finally, the last case involves race-based harassment, but is included in this section as illustrative of the analysis that a court might use in evaluating such claims. The case, which has now been argued before the 5th Circuit, concerns three African American students in the Marion Independent School District who alleged that they were subjected to race-based bullying dating back to at least 2008, suffered at the hands of both students and educators. While the facts are too numerous to mention, the federal district court granted summary judgment to the school district on Title VI and equal protection claims, and the high school athletic director and women's softball coach on equal protections. The upshot of the decision was that the individual defendants did not act with deliberate indifference to the students, nor did they display an intent to discriminate (*Fennell v. Marion Indep. Sch. Dist.*, 2014).

In summary, several trends can be gleaned from the bullying cases decided to date. First, students seeking redress under the due process clause of the 14th Amendment have been, and will likely continue to be, unsuccessful due to the general principle that the due process clause does not impose a duty on school officials to protect one student from another (see, e.g., *Doe v. Covington Cty. Bd. of Educ.*, 2012). Second, students seeking to hold school officials liable under the equal protection clause of the 14th Amendment must demonstrate that the school district treated their complaints of bullying differently from other similarly situated students, based on such factors as students' gender, or the student must allege that the bullying was due to their membership in a protected class. Third, students seeking redress under disability-related statutes (e.g., Section 504 or the ADA) must allege disability-based discrimination and that school officials intentionally discriminated in their response to bullied students based on the disability of the students. Finally, students seeking to redress bullying through Title IX must allege that the bullying would not have occurred but for the gender of the student, or that the bullying had a sexual connotation; and that school officials demonstrated deliberate indifference to actual knowledge of bullying occurring in the school context. Based on the cases to date, only two claims have met with limited success (Title IX); at the same time, school officials cannot turn a blind eye toward bullying any more than they can turn a blind eye to student-to-student sexual harassment.

Corporal Punishment

Efforts to improve safety and discipline vary widely across states and school districts. Some schools have implemented programs to teach children how to resolve conflict and build values, while others have installed high-tech security systems and taken a "zero-tolerance" stance. Though specific disciplinary techniques may vary, few techniques remain more controversial than corporal punishment.

Texas remains in the minority of states that permits corporal punishment in public schools. Though allowed, districts within the state vary widely in their decision to use corporal punishment, and for good reason. Tex. Educ. Code §22.0511 provides fairly broad civil immunity for acts within the scope of a professional employee's duties when discretion on the part of the employee is involved. However, this immunity does not extend to the discipline of students.

In the course of imposing discipline, school employees waive their statutory immunity for the use of excessive force or negligence in discipline resulting in bodily injury to a student. However, Tex. Educ. Code §22.0512 shields school district professional employees from disciplinary proceedings (i.e., a school district initiated adverse employment action, or an action by the State Board for Education Certification to enforce the educator's code of ethics) when a professional employee uses physical force to the extent justified by Tex. Penal Code §9.62, which provides that "the use of force, but not deadly force, against a student is justified: (1) if the actor is entrusted with the care, supervision, or administration of the student, and (2) when and to the degree the actor reasonably believes the force is necessary to further the purpose of education or to maintain discipline in a group." However, the same statute permits school districts to take adverse contract or certification actions if an educator violates the district's corporal punishment policy (including by administering such punishment when district policy prohibits it). Tex. Educ. Code §22.0511, taken in conjunction with Tex. Penal Code §9.62 suggests that the use of corporal punishment may be a legally justifiable disciplinary technique, but its application should be extremely judicious and cannot be used if prohibited by district policy.

The Fifth Circuit cited to each of the above statutes when concluding that a student who allegedly sustained serious injuries when required to do 100 squat thrusts in his junior high school physical education class was not entitled to relief under the substantive due process clause of the 14th Amendment. In *Moore v. Willis Independent School District* (2000), the federal appellate court held that the 14th Amendment could not provide a remedy for the injured student as long there were adequate remedies under state law. The court held that Tex. Educ. Code §22.0511 and Tex. Penal Code §9.62 provide such adequate remedies, and refused to hold the case over for trial.

Most recently, the 82nd Texas Legislature weighed in on the issue of corporal punishment, setting out specific guidelines for the use of corporal punishment. Codified in Tex. Educ. Code § 37.0011, the statute first defines corporal punishment as "the deliberate infliction of physical pain by hitting, paddling, spanking, slapping, or any other physical force used as a means of discipline," and excludes from the definition "physical pain caused by reasonable physical activities associated with athletic training, competition, or physical education" or restraint authorized by statute (see later). Next, the legislature permits the use of corporal punishment to the extent that a school district adopts a policy so authorizing it, and permits its use as long as a parent or person exercising lawful control over a schoolchild has not in writing prohibited school officials from using it (Tex. Educ. Code § 37.0011 [b]). To maintain this prohibition, parents/guardians must submit this written, signed statement each school year and may revoke this prohibition in writing at any time (Tex. Educ. Code § 37.0011 [c]).

Related to traditional notions of corporal punishment is the use of "time-out," restraint, seclusion, or confinement. Tex. Educ. Code §37.0021 addresses this issue with the following three major provisions: (1) students with disabilities "may not be confined in a locked box, locked closet, or other specially designed locked space" as a discipline management or behavior management technique; (2) no student (with very limited exceptions (see Tex.

Educ. Code § 37.0021 [c]) may be secluded (i.e., "confined in a locked box, locked closet, or locked room") solely designed for seclusion and containing less than 50 square feet in space; and (3) and the commissioner was to adopt rules governing the use of time-out and restraint, as those terms are defined in statute. These rules are now codified in Title 19 of the Texas Administrative Code, Chapter 89, Section 1053 (19 TEX. ADMIN. CODE § 89.1053). The statute allows school officials to place students in unattended confinement if the student is awaiting the arrival of law enforcement for weapon possession and if the confinement is necessary to prevent the confined student from causing bodily harm to others (Tex. Educ. Code § 37.0021 [f]). Under 19 TEX. ADMIN. CODE § 89.1053 (l), adopted effective January 1, 2015, the restraint rules now apply to peace officers only if the officers are "employed or commissioned by the school district or provide[s], as a school resource officer (SRO), a regular police presence on a school district campus under a memorandum of understanding between the school district and a local law enforcement agency." As such, school leaders are now obligated ensure that peace officers in these categories receive required training on the use of restraint and time out.

Campus Behavior Coordinator

The 84th Texas Legislature, by way of SB 107, added Tex. Educ. Code § 37.0012, and now requires a person at each campus to be designated as the "campus behavior coordinator" (hereafter abbreviated as CBC). The CBC may be the campus principal or an administrator designated the principal. Tasked with the primary responsibility "for maintaining student discipline" (Tex. Educ. Code § 37.0012 [b]) and implementing the student code of conduct, SB 107 lays out specific duties for the CBC that may be supplemented by district or campus policy. The duties are as follows:

- the CBC shall perform those duties otherwise assigned under the student code of conduct "by the campus principal or other campus administrator" (Tex. Educ. Code § 37.0012 [c][1]); and
- the CBC may exercise powers regarding implementation of the student code of conduct that are also granted to the "campus principal or other campus administrator" (Tex. Educ. Code § 37.0012 [c][2]).

In addition, the CBC must "promptly notify a student's parent or guardian . . . if the student is placed" in any of the following disciplinary placements for conduct that violates the student code of conduct (Tex. Educ. Code § 37.0012 [d]):

- in-school suspension;
- out-of-school suspension;
- removal to a DAEP;
- expulsion;
- removal to a JJAEP; or
- placement into the custody of a law enforcement officer.

To comply with the notification requirements, the CBC must "promptly" contact the parent or guardian in person or by telephone (Tex. Educ. Code § 37.002 [d][1]), and must make "a good faith effort to provide written notice of the disciplinary action to the student, on the day the action is taken, for delivery to the student's parent or guardian" (Tex. Educ. Code

§ 37.0012 [d][2]). Furthermore, the CBC must mail written notice to the parents or guardians of a student who have not been contacted by phone or in person by 5:00 pm of the first business day following the day the disciplinary action is taken (Tex. Educ. Code § 37.0012 [e]). Finally, the notification duties must be assumed by the principal if the CBC is either unavailable or unable to provide "prompt" notification (Tex. Educ. Code § 37.0012 [f]).

Student Removal from the Regular Classroom

Tex. Educ. Code § 37.002 recognizes three levels of removal initiated by the teacher based on the specific student behaviors at issue. The first level is that which is traditionally referred to as "being sent to the principal's (now campus behavior coordinator's) office" [Tex. Educ. Code § 37.002(a), amended by SB 107, 84th Texas Legislature, 2015], and the CBC must respond by employing the appropriate discipline management technique(s) as outlined in the code of conduct "that can reasonably be expected to improve the student's behavior before returning the student to the classroom" (SB 107, 2015). Should these techniques not result in the improvement of a student's behavior, SB 107 requires the CBC to "employ alternative discipline managements, including any progressive interventions designated" by the student code of conduct.

The second and third levels of removal [Tex. Educ. Code § 37.002(b) and (d)] give teachers additional control over the management of their classrooms. Also known as "discretionary" teacher removals, Section 37.002 (b) states that a teacher may remove a student from the classroom for: (1) documented and repetitive interference with either the teacher's ability to teach or with the ability of the other students to learn, or (2) a single occurrence of unruly, disruptive, or abusive behavior that seriously interferes with the teacher's ability to instruct or students' ability to learn. The third level of teacher removal is known as a "mandatory" removal (Tex. Educ. Code 37.002 [d])), for which teachers must remove students. The reasons for mandatory removal are the same as for a mandatory administrative placement in a DAEP and for expulsion (Tex. Educ. Code § 37.006 or § 37.007) and will be discussed later in this chapter.

Students who are removed from the classroom (levels two and three teacher removals, plus administrative removals that permit or require placement in a DAEP) must take part in a "conference" or hearing within three class days of the removal that must the student, his/her parent or guardian(s), the teacher (if the teacher initiated the removal), and the CBC or other appropriate administrator (Tex. Educ. Code § 37.009[a]). If, after a "good faith" attempt by the CBC or other appropriate administrator to arrange a conference to which parents do not respond, the CBC must hold the conference without them. The conference also may be held even if the student refuses to attend. After this conference, the principal (or by implication, the CBC) may place the student in another classroom, in in-school suspension, or in a DAEP (Tex. Educ. Code § 37.002[c]). The student, however, may not be returned to the teacher's classroom without the teacher's consent unless the placement review committee determines that it "is the best or only alternative available." Also, a student may not be returned to class while an appeal is pending. There is no limit to the number of times the committee can return a student to the same teacher's classroom. The Legislature strengthened this teacher removal statute in 2005 when it added a provision to Tex. Educ. Code § 37.002 (d) stipulating that a student removed by a teacher for conduct containing the elements of assault, aggravated assault, sexual assault, or aggravated sexual assault against the teacher, may not be returned to the teacher's class without the teacher's consent at any point, and the placement review committee may not override this provision.

The placement review committee established to determine whether a student may be placed back in the classroom of the teacher who removed (particularly for discretionary, but also for mandatory, removals) under Tex. Educ. Code § 37.003 is a three-member committee composed of two teachers chosen by the campus faculty (with one teacher also chosen as an alternate member) and one professional staff member chosen by the principal. The principal may select him/herself as the "professional staff member" to serve on the committee. In 2003, the 78th Texas Legislature mandated (Tex. Educ. Code § 37.004[a]) what was already required under the Individuals with Disabilities Act, namely that any placement decisions of the placement review committee must be made in conformance with the Act.

A campus administrator's authority to place a student in a DAEP is in no way limited by Tex. Educ. Code § 37.002 or § 37.006 regarding "teacher removals." Grounds for such administrative removals to a DAEP, however, should be set out in the student code of conduct. Passed in 2013, Tex. Educ. Code § 37.0181 requires all principals and appropriate administrators to attend updated professional training on Chapter 37, specifically sections 37.002 (a) and 37.002 (b). This training must be completed at least once every three years and is targeted to all public school personnel who deal with student disciplinary procedures.

Two recent Legislative actions are relevant to children who have been convicted of certain misdemeanor offenses. Senate Bills 1114 (codified as Tex. Code of Crim. Proc. § 45.058) and 393 (codified as Tex. Educ. Code § 37.141), both passed in 2013, were signed with important relevance, particularly to secondary administrators. These statutes were further amended by Senate Bill 108 in 2015. The sum total of these legislative actions are as follows. Tex. Educ. Code § 37.143 (a) prohibits peace officers, law enforcement officers, and SROs from issuing a citation to a child (defined as student who is between the ages of 10 and 16, ages inclusive [see Tex. Educ. Code § 37.141 (1)]) who has committed a school offense (i.e., "an offense committed by a child enrolled in a public school that is a Class C misdemeanor" [with the exception of a traffic offense] and "that is committed on property and under the control and jurisdiction of a school district" [Tex. Educ. Code § 37.141 [2]). Under SB 1114, children under the age of 12 may not receive a citation from a law enforcement officer for [any] conduct that is alleged to have occurred on school property or in a school owned vehicle. Children aged 12 or higher may receive a citation for conduct that does not constitute a school offense (i.e., Class B misdemeanors or higher) if the alleged conduct occurred on a campus or on a school owned vehicle. The law enforcement officer must submit to the court the offense report, witness and victim statements prior to any trial taking place. Based on the Student Code of Conduct, the school may then enforce disciplinary actions including removal from the classroom or campus, suspension, assignment to DAEP, expulsion, or placement in JJAEP.

Suspensions

A suspension, as referred to in this chapter, is the complete removal of a student from campus. Principals may suspend a student for up to three days, with no limit to the total number of days a student may be suspended within a term or year (Tex. Educ. Code § 37.005). The reasons for which a student may be suspended must be outlined in the district's student code of conduct. Additionally, a student may be suspended and then later placed in a DAEP after having completed the term of suspension for the same offense. In addition, prior to suspending a student (or placing a student in a DAEP, or recommending a student's expulsion), the campus behavior coordinator must, in addition to offering the student an opportunity to give his/her side of the story,

> . . . consider whether the student acted in self-defense, the intent or lack of intent at the time the student engaged in the conduct, the student's disciplinary history, and whether the student has a disability that substantially impairs the student's capacity to appreciate the wrongfulness of the student's conduct, regardless of whether the decision of the behavior coordinator concerns a mandatory or discretionary action. (Tex. Educ. Code § 37.009 [a], amended by SB 107, 84th Texas Legislature)

Section 37.019 of the Texas Education Code also allows a district to place a student in a DAEP on an "emergency" basis. This section allows for the immediate removal of a student from the classroom, school transportation, or district only if the principal believes that the student's behavior poses a serious disruption to classroom activities, the operation of the school, or a school-sponsored activity. Students who are emergency placed must be given oral notice of the reason for the placement; this reason must be similar to those reasons for placement on a non-emergency basis, and students must be afforded appropriate due process procedures not later than 10 days after the emergency placement (Tex. Educ. Code §37.019 [c]).

In 1995, the Texas legislature removed from law the requirement that a suspended student's absence be considered excused if the student satisfactorily completes the assignments for the period of suspension. Yet, being able to make up work and receive credit for having done so should be considered during a district's development of its code of conduct. A student will naturally have suffered academic loss during the time away from campus. To add further academic penalty seems counterproductive to the overall intent of Chapter 37 (i.e., keeping the student in the educational process and "off the streets"). In fact, Tex. Educ. Code §37.021 requires that students who are removed from the regular classroom and placed in in-school suspension or other non-disciplinary alternative education placements must be afforded the opportunity to complete each course enrolled in which the student is enrolled at the time of the placement prior to the beginning of the following school year.

Disciplinary Alternative Education Programs

The clear intent in Texas regarding law and order in the public schools is to provide a safe environment for all students. Concomitantly, there is a desire for all students to perform at grade level and to ultimately graduate. The legislative solution passed in 1995 to address both concerns (i.e., orderly environment and increased graduation rates) was the requirement for school districts to establish alternative education programs (AEPs).

Mandatory placement of students into AEPs (now termed by the Legislature as disciplinary AEPs, or DAEPs) depends on two primary factors: the conduct itself and where the conduct occurred. Tex. Educ. Code § 37.006 specifies the conditions under which public school students ages 6 years and older must and may be placed into a DAEP. Under Tex. Educ. Code §37.006, students must be placed into a DAEP for the following offenses committed on school property, within 300 feet of the school's real property line, or at any school-sponsored or school-related activity:

- conduct punishable as a felony;
- conduct containing the elements of assault;

- sale, possession, or distribution of marijuana or controlled substances or a dangerous drug;
- sale, possession, distribution, or being under the influence of an alcoholic beverage; or the commission of a serious act while under the influence of alcohol;
- conduct containing the elements of an offense relating to abusable volatile chemicals; and
- conduct containing the elements of indecent exposure or public lewdness.

In addition, Tex. Educ. Code § 37.006 requires that students be removed to a DAEP for the following conduct, irrespective of the location of the conduct and whether the conduct occurred at a school-sponsored or school-related activity:

- conduct involving a public school and containing the elements of a false alarm or terroristic threat;
- conduct containing the elements of retaliation against a school employee; and
- conduct defined as felony conduct under Title 5 (Offenses against the person) of the Texas Penal Code or felony aggravated robbery (see Tex. Penal Code § 29.03) for which the student receives deferred prosecution under the Texas Family Code; delinquent conduct defined as felony conduct under Title 5 of the Texas Penal code or felony aggravated robbery; or conduct that a superintendent or the superintendent's designee reasonably believes is conduct defined as a felony under Title 5 of the Texas Penal Code or felony aggravated robbery.

Furthermore, Tex. Educ. Code § 37.121 (b) requires school districts to recommend a DAEP placement for a student who is a member of, joins, pledges, or solicits membership in a public school fraternity, sorority, secret society, or gang.

Finally, Tex. Educ. Code § 37.006(d) provides that a student may be placed in a DAEP if the superintendent or the superintendent's designee reasonably believes that the student committed felony conduct, irrespective of location and school-sponsorship, other than that defined in Title 5 of the Texas Penal Code or felony aggravated robbery (Tex. Penal Code § 29.03) and if the student's continued presence in the regular classroom threatens the safety of others or would be "detrimental to the educational process."

Not later than the second business day after the decision to remove a student to a DAEP, school district officials are required to notify the juvenile court in the county in which the student placed in a DAEP resides. While placed in a DAEP, the student cannot attend any school-sponsored or school-related activity. Additionally, at the receiving district's discretion, a DAEP removal can transfer with the student if the student was placed in a DAEP and then withdrew from a Texas school district, open-enrollment charter school, or out-of-state district and enrolls in another school district during the term of the punishment, as long as the receiving district obtains a copy of the placement order and, in the case of a student coming from an out-of-state DAEP, that the receiving district has a reason for placement that is similar to the out-of-state sending district (Tex. Educ. Code §37.008[j]).

Tex. Educ. Code §37.008 requires a district to establish a DAEP in a setting other than a student's regular classroom, and that is located on or off of the regular school campus. There are multiple arrangements available to each school district to meet this mandate. For example, the DAEP may provide for a transfer to a different campus, a school-community guidance center, or a community-based alternative center.

Joint AEPs may also be provided among districts. Additionally, juvenile boards in counties with a population greater than 125,000 must establish a juvenile justice AEP (JJAEP) (Tex. Educ. Code § 37.011). These JJAEPs are "subject to the approval of the Texas Juvenile

Justice Department (formerly the Juvenile Probation Commission). In certain circumstances, counties with a population of over 125,000 may be determined to be a county with a population of less than 125,000, and thus not be required to establish a JJAEP (*see*, Tex. Educ. Code § 37.001 [a-1], [a-2], and [a-3]). School districts in the approximately 10% of the counties in Texas with populations of 125,000 or more have the option of removing or expelling a student to these JJAEPs.

By statute, DAEPs must employ only teachers who meet all state certification requirements (Tex. Educ. Code § 37.008 [a] [7]) and the program must provide the minimum amount of instructional time per day as defined in Tex. Educ. Code §25.082[a]). In addition, Tex. Educ. Code § 37.008 (a-1) requires that the Texas Education Agency adopt minimum standards for operating DAEPs, including standards relating to student-teacher ratios; student health and safety; reporting of student abuse, neglect, or exploitation; teacher training in behavior management and safety procedures; and student transition planning for return to a regular campus.

Regardless of the arrangement or number of DAEPs a district chooses to establish, each must accomplish the following (see, in general, Tex. Educ. Code § 37.008 [a]–[m], for an exhaustive list of requirements):

1. provide for the separation of students assigned to the DAEP from those who are not;
2. focus on instruction in the foundation curriculum (i.e., English language arts, mathematics, science, and social studies) and self-discipline;
3. provide for students' educational and behavioral needs;
4. provide supervision and counseling;
5. provide courses necessary for students to fulfill high school graduation requirements by offering students an opportunity to complete coursework prior to the beginning of the next school year, using a method of the district's choosing, but free of charge to the student (Tex. Educ. Code § 37.008[l]); and
6. provide that school districts notify, in writing, parents of students placed in a DAEP of the district's obligation "to provide the student with an opportunity to complete coursework required for graduation" at no cost to students (Tex. Educ. Code § 37.008 [l-1]).

The management and accountability requirements of the DAEPs are also addressed in law. Students placed in DAEPs are counted when computing the average daily attendance (ADA) for the student's assigned campus. To finance the DAEPs, districts allocate the student expenditure amount from the sending campus to the DAEP. In terms of accountability, off-campus DAEPs are not subject to the majority of rules and regulations governing the public schools. However, under Tex. Educ. Code 37.008 (m), the Commissioner of Education is required to develop rules to evaluate DAEPs, including the required assessment scores of students placed in a DAEP and, under Tex. Educ. Code 37.008 (m-1), the Commissioner is required to develop a process to evaluate DAEPs electronically.

Hearing and Review Requirements: Placement in DAEPs

The Fifth Circuit ruled in *Nevares v. San Marcos CISD* (1997) that the transfer to a DAEP does not deprive a student of a 14th Amendment due process property or liberty right. However, by Texas statute, a teacher or administrator-initiated removal to a DAEP requires a scheduled hearing no later than the third class day after the teacher or administrator removed the student [Tex. Educ. Code § 37.009(a)]. The hearing must include the campus behavior coordinator or other appropriate administrator, a parent or guardian, the teacher or administrator removing the student, and the student. "Valid attempts" to solicit the participation of all parties must be documented. As with suspensions, prior to ordering the placement of a student in a DAEP, the campus

> behavior coordinator must consider whether the student acted in self-defense, the intent or lack of intent at the time the student engaged in the conduct, the student's disciplinary history, and whether the student has a disability that substantially impairs the student's capacity to appreciate the wrongfulness of the student's conduct, regardless of whether the decision of the behavior coordinator concerns a mandatory or discretionary action. (Tex. Educ. Code § 37.009 [a], amended by SB 107, 84th Texas Legislature)

In an effort to keep parents informed and pursuant to Tex. Educ. Code §37.009(g), a copy of the written order placing the student in a DAEP must be given to both the student and parent; however, placement in a DAEP can be immediate and is not appealable (Tex. Educ. Code §37.009[b]) (A limited exception to Tex. Educ. Code §37.009(b) exists in the context of discretionary placements in a DAEP for off-campus, non-school sponsored activities punishable as a felony, when the superintendent relies on information obtained from law enforcement; see Tex. Educ. Code §37.006[j]).

If a student's placement in a DAEP is to extend beyond the end of the next grading period or beyond 60 days, whichever occurs earlier, the student's parent or guardian is entitled to "notice of and an opportunity to participate in a proceeding before the board of trustees . . . or the board's designee" (Tex. Educ. Code § 37.009[b]). This decision is final and may not be appealed.

Placement extending beyond the end of the school year requires a finding that either the student's presence represents a physical threat to others or that the student has engaged in serious or persistent misbehavior (Tex. Educ. Code § 37.009[c]). In addition, a placement for more than one year must be accompanied by a district's review and determination that the student threatens the safety of students or employees (Tex. Educ. Code § 37.009[a], amended by SB 107, 84th Texas Legislature). A student's placement in a DAEP must be reviewed at least every 120 days. At this review, the student or the student's parent or guardian may present arguments for the student's return to the regular classroom.

Placement of Registered Sex Offenders

In 2007, the 80th Texas Legislature passed House Bill 2532, which included as one of its two major provisions the addition of a subchapter addressing the placement of public school students who are required to register as sex offenders for offenses that occur on or after September 1, 2007. The legislation, codified in Tex. Educ. Code §§ 37.301–313, requires school districts, after receiving the appropriate notice, to remove registered sex offenders from the regular classroom and place them in a district DAEP or, under certain circumstances, in a JJAEP (Tex. Educ. Code §37.303). The statute then details the placement requirements for student registered sex offenders under the two classifications noted immediately below:

- Student registered sex offenders *under court supervision*, including probation, community service, or parole must be placed in the appropriate AEP for at least one semester. If the student transfers to another school district during the placement, the receiving district may require an additional semester placement without review, or count the time spent in the sending district toward the "at least one semester" requirement (Tex. Educ. Code §37.304).

- Students registered sex offenders *not under court supervision* must be placed in the appropriate AEP for one semester. The placement may not extend beyond one semester unless the school board or its designee determines that placing the student in a regular classroom: (1) threatens other students' or teachers' safety, (2) "will be detrimental to the educational process," or (3) does not serve the district's students' best interests (Tex. Educ. Code §37.305).

Review Requirements

Regardless of the student registered sex offender's court supervision classification, the board or its designee must convene a committee—which must be composed of a regular education teacher at the campus to which the student would be assigned if not in the applicable AEP; the student's parole or probation officer or other representative of the local juvenile probation department; an AEP instructor; a district designee assigned by the board; and a district-employed counselor—to conduct a review of the student's placement. By a majority vote, the committee makes a recommendation to the board or its designee to either continue the AEP placement or place the student into the regular classroom. The board is obligated to return the student to the regular classroom if the committee so recommends, unless the board or its designee determines that placing the student in a regular classroom: (1) threatens other students' or teachers' safety, (2) "will be detrimental to the educational process," or (3) does not serve the district's students' best interests. Conversely, if the committee recommends continued AEP placement, the board may return the student to the regular classroom over the committee's recommendation only if the board finds that the student's placement does *not* affect *all three* of the stipulations noted immediately above. As long as the student registered sex offender remains in the AEP, the board must conduct subsequent reviews of the student placement at the beginning of each school year (Tex. Educ. Code §37.306). In keeping with the requirements of the IDEA, placement of student registered sex offenders must comply with all requirements of IDEA, and the review procedures noted above must be conducted by an admission, review, and dismissal (ARD) committee (Tex. Educ. Code §37.308). As part of this review, the ARD committee may request that the board or its designee convene a committee as described in Tex. Educ. Code §37.306 (and described earlier) to assist in its placement review.

Parental or guardian appeal rights are very limited. Parents/guardians may appeal the decision by the board or the designee to place their child in an AEP by requesting a conference among the board or its designee, the parents/guardians, and the student. However, the only issue on appeal is "the factual question of whether the student is required to so register as a sex offender under Chapter 62, Code of Criminal Procedure." Once it is determined that the student is required to register, the board is obligated to place the student in the AEP, and that decision is final and not subject to appeal (Tex. Educ. Code §37.311).

Expulsion

The 78th Texas Legislature in 2003 limited the length of expulsions to 1 year, unless the school district determines that the student threatens the safety of other students or district employees, or that an extended expulsion is in the student's best interest (Tex. Educ. Code

37.009[h]). However, districts are permitted to continue the expulsion of students expelled by other districts. On readmission of an expelled student, the placement review committee makes recommendations to the district regarding the conditions placed on the student's return.

Texas does not allow a student younger than 10 years of age to be expelled from school (Tex. Educ. Code §37.007[h]). If a student under age 10 engages in expellable conduct, the student must be assigned to a DAEP only with other elementary-aged students (Tex. Educ. Code 37.006[f]). Expulsion is required for the 17 offenses listed below if the student commits offense(s) on school property or at a school-related activity:

- engaging in conduct that contains the elements of the offense of unlawfully carrying weapons (as elaborated in Tex. Penal Code § 46.02) or an offense relating to prohibited weapons (as elaborated in Tex. Penal Code 46.05) (the 81st Texas Legislature in 2009, by means of Tex. Educ. Code § 37.007 (k), provided that students "may not be expelled solely" for possessing, using, or exhibiting a firearm as long as it occurs "at an approved target range facility" not located on a school campus *and* "while participating in or preparing for a school-sponsored shooting sports competition or a shooting sports educational activity that is sponsored or supported by the Parks and Wildlife Department or a shooting sports sanctioning organization working with the department.") This same legislation provides that students are not authorized to bring a firearm "on school property to participate in or prepare for a school-sponsored shooting sports competition or a shooting sports educational activity" (Tex. Educ. Code § 37.007 [l]);
- possession, exhibition, or use of an illegal knife (defined by state law or local policy);
- possession, exhibition, or use of a club;
- possession, exhibition, or use of a prohibited weapon;
- aggravated assault;
- sexual assault;
- aggravated sexual assault;
- arson;
- murder;
- capital murder;
- criminal attempt to commit murder or capital murder;
- indecency with a child;
- aggravated kidnapping;
- conduct involving the use, possession, or sale of drugs or alcohol, if punishable as a felony;
- aggravated robbery;
- manslaughter;
- criminally negligent homicide;
- continuous sexual abuse of a young child or children; or
- bringing a firearm to school (the expulsion period may be modified by the superintendent and the placement may be reduced to one in a DAEP) (Tex. Educ. Code §37.007).

Expulsion is also permitted for the following student misconduct, regardless of whether the conduct occurs on or off school property or at a school-sponsored or school-related activity:

- false alarm or report involving a public school;
- terroristic threat involving a public school;

- aggravated robbery against another student;
- aggravated assault, sexual assault, or aggravated sexual assault directed at another student;
- murder, capital murder, or criminal attempt to commit murder or capital murder against another student; or
- engaging in conduct containing the elements of breach of computer security (defined in Tex. Penal Code § 33.02) where a student knowingly accesses a school district's computer, computer network, or computer system to alter, damage, or delete property or information; or otherwise knowingly breaches a district's computer, network, or system (Tex. Educ. Code § 37.007 [b] [5]).

In addition, school districts may expel students for the following conduct that occurs on or within 300 feet of school property or at a school-sponsored or school-related activity on or off school property:

- retaliation against a volunteer or school employee containing the elements of assault (in Tex. Penal Code §22.01(a)(1), whether the expellable conduct occurred on or off campus);
- intentionally, knowingly, or recklessly causing bodily injury to a school district employee or volunteer;
- engaging in documented serious misbehavior of the student code of conduct while in a DAEP "despite documented behavioral interventions" (see Tex. Educ. Code 37.007 [c] for the list of "serious misbehavior);
- criminal mischief if punishable as a felony (both damage of less than $20,000 due to graffiti on a public school, as well as coercing, soliciting, or inducing a child to join a street gang by threatening the child with imminent bodily injury and causing bodily injury to the child are identified as felony criminal mischief);
- sale, delivery, possession, or under the influence of marijuana, controlled substances, dangerous drugs, and/or alcohol at school or a school-sponsored event regardless of the amounts;
- offenses relating to an abusable volatile chemical at school or a school-sponsored event;
- engaging in deadly conduct;
- possessing a firearm; and
- engaging in most other expellable conduct on the property of another Texas school district.

A school district may, after a hearing, expel a student and place that student into either a DAEP or JJAEP if the student has been charged with, referred to a juvenile court for allegedly committing, received deferred prosecution for, engaged in delinquent conduct resulting from committing, received probation or deferred adjudication for, been convicted of, or arrested or charged with, any felony offense under Title 5 of the Texas Penal Code (i.e., criminal homicide, kidnapping and unlawful restraint, trafficking of persons, sexual offenses, and assaultive offenses) or aggravated robbery (Tex. Penal Code § 29.03). The board or its designee must also find that placing the student in the regular classroom: (1) threatens other students' or teachers' safety, (2) "will be detrimental to the educational process," or (3) does not serve the district's students' best interests. Under this statute (Tex. Educ. Code §37.0081), the decision of the board or its designee to place the student into the DAEP or JJAEP is final, and not subject to appeal.

Before a student is expelled, the board or board's designee must provide the student with a hearing at which the student is afforded constitutionally-guaranteed due process. Due process includes: (1) giving prior notice of the charges and the proposed sanctions in order to afford a reasonable opportunity for preparation of a defense; (2) conducting a hearing before an impartial board; (3) inviting in writing the student's parent or guardian to attend; and (4) allowing the student the opportunity to present testimony, to examine evidence presented by the school administration, and to question witnesses. Prior to ordering a student's expulsion:

> . . . the board of trustees must consider whether the student acted in self-defense, the intent or lack of intent at the time the student engaged in the conduct, the student's disciplinary history, and whether the student has a disability that substantially impairs the student's capacity to appreciate the wrongfulness of the student's conduct, regardless of whether the decision of the board concerns a mandatory or discretionary action. (Tex. Educ. Code § 37.009 [f], amended by SB 107, 84th Texas Legislature)

A decision to expel is appealable to a district court of the county in which the school district's central administration's office is located (Tex. Educ. Code §37.009 [f]). There may be occasions, however, when immediate action is necessary to protect persons or property from imminent harm. Under these circumstances, a principal may order an "emergency expulsion" of a student pursuant to Tex. Educ. Code §37.019.

School district officials are required to notify the juvenile court in the county in which the expelled student resides no later than the second business day after the expulsion decision has been made. Unless the juvenile board and the district's board of trustees have executed a memorandum of understanding regarding support services, a court may not order a student to attend the school as a condition of probation. Students who are expelled and live in counties with less than 125,000 residents (i.e., counties not required to have a JJAEP) may be exempted from compulsory attendance. If the student does reside in a county with a JJAEP, the student must attend that program.

The 79th Texas Legislature in 2005 expanded the responsibilities of school districts to notify educators of the conduct of expelled students. Tex. Educ. Code §37.007(g) requires school districts to notify each educator who is responsible for, or who is under the direction and supervision of an educator responsible for the student's instruction, of a student who has engaged in expellable conduct. Under Chapter 52 of the Family Code, notification must also to be given to all instructional and support staff that has regular contact with a student who has been arrested or detained by the police. In all cases, the information is confidential and any educator who intentionally violates this confidentiality may have his or her certification revoked or suspended by the State Board for Educator Certification. Additionally, districts are required under Tex. Educ. Code §37.020 to annually report information regarding alternative education placements and expulsions to the Commissioner of Education

Discipline of Students with Disabilities

The discipline of students with disabilities covered under the IDEA (20 U.S.C. §1400 et seq.) is regulated by both state and federal law. Notably, Congress reauthorized IDEA in 2004 as Public Law 108-446; this reauthorization brought about several significant changes in the discipline of students with disabilities. Those changes are discussed in this section.

In a nutshell, students with disabilities are afforded two "tracks" of due process: one afforded by state law (see especially Tex. Educ. Code §37.009 for due process procedures applicable to all students for teacher removals, DAEP removals, and expulsions) to determine whether the conduct occurred and one afforded by federal law to determine whether the conduct is a manifestation of the student's disability. TEXAS EDUC. CODE §37.004 requires that placement (including a disciplinary change of placement) of students with disabilities "may be made only by a duly constituted admission, review, and dismissal [ARD] committee." Tex. Educ. Code §37.004 requires that any disciplinary change of placement be effected only after the "student's admission, review, and dismissal committee conducts a manifestation determination review" in accordance with federal law. Federal regulations define a change of placement for discipline as one that: (1) exceeds 10 consecutive school days (34 C.F.R. §300.536 [a][1]); or (2) subjects a child "to a series of removals that constitute a pattern because . . . the series . . . total more than 10 school days in a school year," results from substantially similar conduct, and "because of such additional factors as the length of each removal, the total amount of time the child has been removed, and the proximity of the removals to one another" (34 C.F.R. §300.536 [a][2]).

Under IDEA, students may have their placement changed for disciplinary reasons under generally four scenarios: (1) by school officials when students carry or possess a weapon "to or at school, on school premises, or to or at a school function under" the state or district's jurisdiction [20 U.S.C. §1415(k)(1)(G)(i)]; (2) by school officials when a student" knowingly possesses or uses illegal drugs, or sells or solicits the sale of a controlled substance, while at school, on school premises, or at a school function under" the state's or district's jurisdiction [20 U.S.C. §1415(k)(1)(G)(ii)]; (3) by school officials when a student "has inflicted serious bodily injury upon another person while at school, on school premises, or at a school function under" the state's or district's jurisdiction [20 U.S.C. §1415(k)(1)(G)(iii)]; and (4) by school officials for students who violate a provision of the district's code of conduct that is applicable to all students. Under the first three scenarios noted above, termed "special circumstances" in IDEA, school officials may remove a student to an interim alternative educational setting for not more than 45 school days regardless of whether the conduct is a manifestation of the student's disability. Under the fourth scenario, the term of placement must be consistent with that which would be assigned to non-disabled students, and only after a finding that the behavior is not a manifestation of the student's disability. Importantly, IDEA's implementing regulations also provide that school officials may order multiple disciplinary removals for not more than 10 consecutive school days without these multiple removals constituting a change in placement, as long as the removals are for separate incidents of misbehavior and the incidents of misconduct are not "substantially similar" to one another (34 C.F.R. §300.530 [b]).

Clearly, the term "change of placement" becomes important because of the requirement that school districts conduct "manifestation determination reviews" for students whose placements are changed for disciplinary reasons. These reviews are to be conducted by the ARD committee (called the IEP team under federal law) to determine if the student's misbehavior is a manifestation of his/her disability. When the ARD committee decides to change a student's placement, parents must be informed of this decision no later than the date the decision is made and be provided with a notice of procedural safeguards [20 U.S.C §1415(k)(1)(H)]. Within 10 school days of the decision to change a student's placement, the ARD committee must conduct the manifestation determination review [20 U.S.C. §1415(k)(1)(E)(i)]. Under

IDEA, a student's behavior is considered to be a manifestation of his/her disability only if (1) "the conduct in question was caused by, or had a direct and substantial relationship, to the child's disability" [20 U.S.C. §1415(k)(1)(E)(i)(I)]; or (2) "the conduct in question was the direct result of the local educational agency's failure to implement the IEP" (individualized educational program) [20 U.S.C. §1415(k)(1)(E)(i)(II)]. If a student's behavior is determined not to be a manifestation of his/her disability, then discipline procedures applicable to students without disabilities may be applied in the same manner as they would be applied to students without disabilities, except that students who are "expelled" must still be provided with free appropriate public education [20 U.S.C. §1412(a)(1)(a)]. If the student's behavior is a manifestation of his/her disability, the ARD committee must do the following: (1) "conduct a functional behavioral assessment (FBA), and implement a behavioral intervention plan (BIP)," if these had not been in place prior to the conduct [20 U.S.C. §1415(k)(1)(F)(i)]; (2) review and modify as necessary the BIP if one had been previously developed [20 U.S.C. §1415(k)(1)(F)(ii)]; and (3) "return the child to the placement from which the child was removed, unless the parent and the local educational agency agree to a change of placement as part of the modification of the" BIP [20 U.S.C. §1415(k)(1)(F)(iii)]. However, the requirement that the student be returned to the "then-current" placement does not apply in "special circumstances" cases as noted earlier (i.e., weapons, drugs, and serious bodily injury offenses.). Most importantly, the requirement that a child be returned to the then-current placement during the appeals process (i.e., "stay-put") is not a part of IDEA 2004. In other words, during the pendency of parental or school district appeals in cases involving student discipline under "special circumstances", the student must remain in the interim alternative educational setting until the expiration of the placement term, or the decision of the hearing officer, whichever occurs first (unless the parents and the school district agree otherwise); and the appeal hearing must be expedited [20 U.S.C. §1415(k)(4)(A& B)].

One final note regarding the discipline of students with disabilities. Tex. Educ. Code § 37.001 (b-1) requires that schools must conduct a manifestation determination review for students with disabilities under IDEA prior to administering any discipline to a student who engages in conduct prohibited by Tex. Educ. Code § 37.001 (a) (7), i.e., bullying, harassment, or making hit lists. This requirement is irrespective of the disciplinary option employed by school officials or the length of any proposed change of placement.

Implications for Educators

Former U.S. Secretary of Education Richard Riley, when responding to the findings of the report, "Violence and Discipline Problems in U.S. Public Schools: 1996–97," cautioned schools not to simply discard troublemakers. He urged schools to "do everything possible to make sure that expelled students are sent to alternative schools. These young people need to get their lives turned around." The major objective of schools in addressing student discipline, therefore, should not be simply to find a "punishment to fit the crime;" rather, it should be to move students to the point where they can discipline themselves while preserving the classroom for learning. School administrators and teachers must hold students accountable for both their behavior and academic performance. Students must be taught to deal with normal levels of criticism and conflict. In a free society such as ours, self-discipline must be a part of each person, for when self-control is lost, the individual freedoms we value so highly are surely lost.

Control of student behavior does not begin with a school official's admonition; rather, it begins with the establishment of a school's climate. School climate is a major determinant of how students are going to behave and, hence, a significant factor in determining the number of discipline cases.

Teachers play an integral role in the establishment of positive school climate. Effective teaching practices are positively related to appropriate student behavior (see, e.g., Jennings & DiPrete, 2010). Factors that lead to excellence in teaching are as follows:

- creating an effective room arrangement;
- clearly defining behavioral and academic expectations;
- holding students accountable for their work;
- using well planned, well-paced, individually appropriate lessons; and
- stopping inappropriate behavior quickly and consistently.

Positive school climate will build trust, high morale, and an *esprit de corps* in students, all which translate into student respect for teachers, the school, and each other. Another factor that school administrators must seek to improve is the interpersonal relationships among students and staff. There is an increasing need to emphasize these skills as the environment seemingly becomes more in conflict and our interpersonal actions more adversarial. Modeling productive interpersonal behaviors and teaching students these interpersonal skills are the basis for creating a caring atmosphere. When students believe teachers and administrators care about and value them, the nature and number of discipline problems will decrease.

There is, however, a small portion of any school population that does not positively engage in the educational process. This group, representing only a small fraction of the school population, is alienated from the school and does not respond to normal positive stimuli. This may occur for a variety of reasons, and it is incumbent on the school system to identify and attempt to address the unique needs of these disenfranchised students. These students may come from difficult family situations, need to work to supplement family income; have health issues, do not attend school regularly, have unidentified learning problems, or a variety of other personal situations that put them off track for graduating on time.

It is the disciplining of these students that causes the most concern for teachers and administrators. It is primarily, then, for these students that the AEPs and expulsion procedures have been legislated. HB 1952 established an additional professional development training requirement for all principals or administrators who work with students in the disciplinary system at least one time every three years.

The 84th Legislative Session brought additional requirements for schools and districts specific to discipline and campus safety:

- Implementation of required training for District Peace Officers and School Resource Officers (SRO) for districts with more than 30,000 students (HB 2684, codified in Tex. Educ. Code § 37.0812).
- SB 507 (codified in Tex. Educ. Code § 29.022) will require, effective with the 2016–2017 school year, the placement of video equipment in a special education setting upon request by a parent, trustee, or a staff member. The special education setting is defined a "self-contained classroom or other special education setting in a which a majority of students in regular attendance are: (1) provided special education and related services, and (2) assigned to a self-contained classroom or other special education setting for a

least 50 percent of the instructional day." Further clarification regarding parent access, archiving of the video, and confidentiality is articulated in the bill.

The review of and familiarity with the specific policies of a school district are important, but just as important is the consistency with which these rules and procedures are applied. A successful administrator is one who knows the rules and who applies those rules in such a way as to balance the rights of each individual student with the right of all students to experience a safe, secure, and effective learning environment.

◆ PARENTAL RIGHTS

Parents and schools both have rights and responsibilities regarding the education of Texas children. Thus, the establishment of educational partnerships strengthens our schools, families and communities. There are now over 55 specific parental rights recognized in either Texas or federal statute that support parents' active involvement in the education of their children. The term "parent" includes not only a child's natural parents and adoptive parents, but additionally any person with legal control of the child under a court order (e.g., a guardian).

In collaboration with the Region 18 Education Service Center, the Texas Education Agency has recently updated its documentation for parents of children with disabilities that are covered under the IDEA. Titled *A Guide to the Admission, Review and Dismissal Process*, this guide can be downloaded from the Region 18 website at http://framework.esc18.net/Documents/ARD_Guide _ENG.pdf. The Spanish version of this document is found at http://framework.esc18.net/ Documents/ARD_Guide_SPAN.pdf. The information in the guide contains direct references to the current Texas Education Code. The majority of the "parental rights" are located in Chapter 26 of the Texas Education Code. However, other parental rights are addressed elsewhere in Code. For example, parental rights associated with bilingual students and students with disabilities are located in Chapter 29. Also, Tex. Educ. Code §21.057 requires schools to notify parents when a person not properly certified teaches their child for more than 30 consecutive instructional days. The rights delineated in Chapter 26 of the Texas Education Code are categorized into 10 areas and are as follows. For purposes of Chapter 26, a child is a student who has not yet reached the age of 18.

Rights Concerning Academic Programs

A parent may:

- request a particular school within the district for his/her child to attend;
- request a change in his/her child's class or teacher if such a change would not affect the assignment of another child;
- request the addition of a specific academic class offering that is in keeping with the required curriculum;
- request that the child attend a class above his or her grade level for credit;
- request early graduation from high school and to participate in the graduation ceremonies at the time the child does graduate; and
- request that their child be allowed to enroll in the state's "Virtual School Network," with the expectation that the request not be denied, with certain exceptions (Tex. Educ. Code §26.0031).

Access to Student Records (Tex. Educ. Code §26.004)

A parent must be given access to all written documents concerning his or her child including: attendance records, test scores, grades, disciplinary records, school counseling records, psychological records, applications for admissions, health and immunization information, teacher and counselor evaluations, and reports of behavioral patterns. A district is able to request an Attorney General's opinion if a parent requests to examine any standardized test given by the district under a contract with a company that requires confidentiality.

Access to State Assessments (Tex. Educ. Code §26.005)

A parent is to be given access to a copy of each state assessment after the last time it will be administered for a school year. Other stipulations related to the release of test questions can be found in Tex. Educ. Code §39.023.

Access to Teaching Materials (Tex. Educ. Code §26.006)

A parent is entitled to review all teaching and instructional materials, including textbooks, used in the classroom of the parent's child and review, after administration, each test the child is given. The school district must make these materials available to the parent, but the district may specify reasonable hours for parental review.

Access to Board Meetings (Tex. Educ. Code §26.007)

A parent has complete access to any meeting of the school board except legally closed meetings. All public meetings must be held within the boundaries of the district, except as required by law or to hold a joint meeting with another district. All board meetings must comply with the Open Meetings Act (Chapter 551, Texas Government Code).

Right to Full Information Concerning Student (Tex. Educ. Code §26.008)

A parent has the right to all information regarding his or her child's school activities except regarding child abuse reports. Any attempt by a school district employee to encourage or coerce a student to withhold information from the student's parent(s) is grounds for an adverse employment action against the employee's contract.

Right to Information Concerning Special Education (Tex. Educ. Code §26.0081)

The Texas Education Agency is required to produce and provide to school districts for dissemination to parents a "comprehensive, easily understood document" which outlines parental rights and responsibilities concerning special education programs and which explains the IEP (Individualized Education Plan) development process. This information is generally found at http://ritter.tea.state.tx.us/special.ed/resources/.

Consent Required for Certain Activities (Tex. Educ. Code § 26.009)

Written parental consent must be obtained before:

- A psychological exam, test, or treatment may be given, unless it is a part of a child abuse investigation; or
- Videotaping or recording a child's voice, unless it is needed for safety or discipline purposes in common areas of the school or school buses; is related to co-curricular, extracurricular, or regular classroom activities; or is related to the placement of video cameras in self-contained classrooms (SB 507, 84th Texas Legislature).

Exemption from Instruction (Tex. Educ. Code § 26.010)

A parent may remove his or her child temporarily from a class or activity when the content conflicts with the parent's religious or moral beliefs. To do so, the parent must give the teacher a written statement authorizing the student's removal from the class or activity. Temporary removal may not be used to avoid a test or to prevent the student from taking a subject for an entire semester. This section does not exempt a child from satisfying grade level or graduation requirements.

Student Directory Information (Tex. Educ. Code § 26.013)

School districts must provide to parents at the beginning of each school year or on initial enrollment in the district a written explanation of that portion of the Family Educational Rights and Privacy Act (FERPA, codified at 20 U.S.C. § 1232g) regarding the release of student directory information and the right of the parent to object to the release of directory information.

As the policymakers for the school district, school boards are required to:

- cooperate in the establishment of ongoing operations of at least one parent-teacher organization within the district which focuses on increasing parental involvement in school activities (Tex. Educ. Code §26.001[e]);
- set reasonable fees for copies of requested materials (Tex. Educ. Code §26.012); and
- adopt a procedure for handling complaints or grievances regarding abridgment of parental rights (Tex. Educ. Code §26.011).

Parental rights, however, are not absolute, since a board or its designee has the authority to deny a request dependent on economic feasibility and professional judgment regarding the best interests of the child. Though encouraged to do so, school officials are under no mandatory obligation to give special notice to parents regarding their rights and responsibilities.

◆ STUDENT ATTENDANCE

Who attends Texas' public schools? According to *Snapshot 2014* published by the Texas Education Agency (see http://ritter.tea.state.tx.us/perfreport/snapshot/2014/), over 4.9 million students were enrolled in the state's more than 1,000 public (non-charter) school districts. In addition, nearly 203,000 students were enrolled in the state's 588 charter schools. Of those enrolled in non-charter public schools, 70% were racial/ethnic minorities (non-White). The largest racial/ethnic minority student group in Texas is the Hispanic student population, representing 51.6% of all students. A total of 60% of Texas students are economically disadvantaged, and 17% are English Language Learners.

So, who must attend Texas' public schools?

Compulsory Attendance and Free Admission

Under Texas law, entitlement to the benefits of the available school fund (i.e., free admission to public schools, subject to residency and other pertinent requirements) is available to three classes of individuals: (1) those who, as of September 1 of any school year, are at least 5 years of age and under 21 years of age; (2) those who are at least 21 years of age and not older than 26 years of age and are admitted at the school district's discretion to complete the requirements for a high school diploma (however, the admission of these students may be revoked by the district for conduct calling for DAEP or JJAEP placement and districts are prohibited from placing such students who have not attended school in the previous three school years with students who are 18 or younger in a classroom, cafeteria, or other school activity not open to the public); and (3) those who are in pre-kindergarten as that term is defined in Tex. Educ. Code § 29.153 or Tex, Educ. Code, Chapter 29, Subchapter E-1 (pertaining to the "High Quality Prekindergarten Grant Program") [these three classes of students are found in Tex. Educ. Code §25.001 (a) & (b)].

Texas has had compulsory attendance laws since 1916. Today, a child aged 6–18, or who is younger than 6 and has been previously enrolled in the first grade, or who is or has been enrolled in pre-kindergarten or kindergarten, is required to attend school, unless exempted (Tex. Educ. Code §25.085, amended by HB 2398, 84th Texas Legislature, 2015). Under Tex. Educ. Code §25.085(d), compulsory attendance also applies to certain extended-year programs, tutorial classes, accelerated reading, accelerated instruction, and basic skills programs. Furthermore, a school district may adopt a policy requiring any student under 21 years of age to attend school until the end of the current school year (Tex. Educ. Code §25.085 [f]).

Students attending parochial or other private schools (which include home schooling) and those expelled from schools in counties with populations less than 125,000 are exempted from the law. However, all expelled students from counties with populations at least 125,000 must comply with the compulsory attendance law by attending a JJAEP. Additionally, a student who is 16 or 17 years of age and enrolled in a GED course may also be exempted (see Article 45.954, Code of Criminal Procedures and Tex. Educ. Code §25.086).

A Texas school district, however, is not required to admit a student under 18 years of age who is seeking to establish residency apart from his/her parent or guardian if the student:

1. has engaged in conduct or misbehavior within the preceding year that has resulted in:
   a. removal to an AEP or
   b. expulsion;
2. has engaged in delinquent conduct or conduct in need of supervision and is on probation or other conditional release for that conduct; or
3. has been convicted of a criminal offense and is on other conditional release [Tex. Educ. Code §25.001(d) and Tex. Educ. Code § §25.085].

Additionally, a child under the age of 5 who performs satisfactorily on the third-grade STAAR test will receive the entitlements in districts that endorse the policy of admitting students younger than 5 years. Residency, enrollment, and transfer requirements modify the eligibility rules. These specific requirements can be found in Chapter 25 of the Texas Education Code. Tex. Educ. Code §25.001(b) (9) extends residency to students who do not reside in a school district but whose grandparent(s) "reside in the school district and provide a substantial amount of after-school care" for the student. Finally, SB 206 (84th Texas Legislature, 2015), codified at Tex. Educ. Code §§ 25.001 [(g) and (g-1)], respectively, grants residency status to: (1) primary or secondary public school students to the school they attended *before* being placed in the conservatorship of the Texas Department of Family and Protective Services at a facility outside the attendance area of the school or district until the student completes the highest grade level at the school in which the student resided prior to placement. This residency extends for the duration of the student's enrollment, regardless of whether the student remains placed by the DFPS; and (2) students under DFRS conservatorship who are enrolled in a public primary or secondary school other than the one they were enrolled at the time of placement into conservatorship. These students may continue to attend this school until they complete the highest grade level that the school offers, and may continue to attend regardless of whether they remain in DFPS conservatorship.

The age eligibility for students with disabilities to receive services from the public school system is determined by the specific disability. A student with visual or auditory impairment will be served if the student is not older than 21 years. A student with a physical, learning, or speech disability; mental retardation; emotional disturbance; autism; or traumatic brain injury will be served if at least 3 but not older than 21 years (Tex. Educ. Code §29.003).

As amended by HB 2610 (84th Texas Legislature, 2015) each school must provide at least 75,600 minutes of instruction for students, "including intermissions and recesses" (Tex. Educ. Code § 25.081 (a), unless the school receives approval from the Commissioner of Education" for fewer than [the required 75,600] minutes . . . if disaster, flood, extreme weather conditions, fuel curtailment, or another calamity causes the closing of schools" (Tex. Educ. Code § 25.081 [b]). A school day consists of at least seven hours each day, including intermissions and recesses (Tex. Educ. Code §25.082); concomitantly, a "day of instruction" is equal to 420 minutes of instruction (Tex. Educ. Code § 25.082 [e]) Absences from school *may be excused* for any cause acceptable to the teacher, principal, or superintendent; and for students who serve as an early voting election clerk; and *must be excused (including for travel time)*: (1) to observe religious holy days; (2) to attend a required court appearance; (3) to appear at a governmental office for the purposes of completing paperwork for U.S. citizenship; (4) to participate in an oath ceremony for U.S. naturalization; (5) to serve as an election clerk; (6) for students in the conservatorship of the Texas Department of Protective and Regulatory Services, to participate in a court-ordered activity that is not practicable to attend "outside of school hours," or a service-plan required activity; (7) to keep an appointment with a health care professional (including non-medical "health care practitioner" offering "generally recognized service" for a student diagnosed with autism spectrum disorder [Tex, Educ. Code § 25.087 (b-3)]), so long as the student is an attendance before or after the appointment on that date; and (8) for students who are active duty military dependents to visit (with some restrictions), their parents or guardians who are leaving or returning from deployment (Tex. Educ. Code § 25.087 [b]). In addition, a school district *may* excuse the absence of a student in grades 6 through 12 "for the purpose of sounding 'Taps' at a military honors funeral held in this state for a deceased veteran" (Tex. Educ. Code §25.087 [c]); and for high school junior and senior students who visit accredited institutes of higher education, provided that the district has adopted a policy concerning this type of absence and that students cannot be excused for more than 2 school days in each of their junior and senior years [Tex. Educ. Code §25.087 (b-2)]. For purposes of calculating the ADA, days and/or classes missed for religious purposes, court appearances, and health care appointments are counted as if the student was in attendance. Students are allowed to make up, in a reasonable time, any work missed and doing so allows those days and classes missed to count toward compulsory attendance (Tex. Educ. Code §25.087).

Previously, voluntarily enrolled students age 18 or over with more than five unexcused absences in one semester could have their school enrollment revoked. After the passage of HB 2398 (codified at Tex. Educ. Code § 25.085 [e]), that age is now 19 or older, and the student's enrollment cannot be revoked on a day that the student is physically present at school. Moreover, Tex. Educ. Code §25.085 (f) permits school boards to adopt a policy requiring voluntarily enrolled students who have reached their 19th birthday to complete the school year for which they are enrolled, under the rules of compulsory attendance, until their 21st birthday. In this instance, the provisions of the newly-enacted truancy statutes in Tex. Family Code Chapter 65, as well as the current provisions applicable to parents contributing to the nonattendance of a student and warning notices to the parent (Tex. Educ. Code § 25.093 and § 25.095, respectively), do not apply.

In general, Tex. Educ. Code § 25.092 [a] requires that students may not be given credit for a class unless they attend the class for at least 90% of the days the class is offered. However, Tex. Educ. Code § 25.092 (a-1) permits school districts to give students who attend at least 75% but less than 90% of the days a class is offered an opportunity to gain credit or earn a final grade for the class. In order to be given credit or a final grade, the student must complete a plan approved by the principal that provides for the student to fulfill the instructional requirements. In an effort to ensure flexibility and fairness, each school board must appoint one or more committees that may grant credit due to extenuating circumstances. The board must also establish alternative methods for students to regain credit lost due to excessive absences. Finally, the board must also establish at least one method that is "free" to the student.

Compulsory Attendance Enforcement

The 84th Legislature in 2015 substantially rewrote the compulsory attendance laws by way of HB 2398. First of all, the Legislature defined truant behavior as a student's absence from school on 10 or more days or parts of days within a six-month period in the same school year (TEX. FAM. CODE § 65.003 [c]), and further decreed, "truant conduct may be prosecuted only as a civil case in a truancy court" (TEX. FAM. CODE § 65.003 [d]). Finally, the Legislature designated a class of courts to serve as truancy courts based on the size of the county, and set out the powers and operations of the courts. Noteworthy in this legislation is the right of a child alleged to have committed truant conduct to a jury trial (TEX. FAM. CODE § 65.007 [d]). A school district is required to refer a child to truancy court within 10 school days of a student's 10th unexcused absence for at least a part of a day "within a six month period in the same school year" (Tex. Educ. Code 25.0951 [a]).

Beyond truancy courts for students, school districts and open-enrollment charter schools may take the following actions against parents and students. First, all parents must be notified in writing that if their child is absent "on 10 or more parts of days within a six-month period in the same school year," the parent may be prosecuted for "parent contributing to nonattendance" and the child may be referred to truancy court (Tex. Educ. Code § 25.095 [a]). Second, if a student has unexcused absences on at least a part of three days within a four-week period, the school district must notify the parents of this event, reaffirm to the parent their duty to require their child to attend school, and notify the parent that their child is subject to truancy court referral, and request a parental conference (Tex. Educ. Code § 25.095 [b]). Third, at the same time, the school district must initiate "truancy prevention measures" on the student's behalf (Tex. Educ. Code § 25.0951 [a-4]; the truancy prevention measures are elaborated in Tex. Educ. Code § 25.0951 §§ [a-1 through a-3]). Importantly, a school district must, when referring a child to truancy court, state in writing that it employed truancy prevention measures without meaningful success and that the child is eligible for or receives special education services (Tex. Educ. Code § 25.0915 [b]). Finally, if the child commits truant conduct, the school district must initiate a referral to truancy court, and the school district may file a complaint against the parent for "contributing to nonattendance" if the parent, with criminal negligence, fails to require their child to attend school, and the child has 10 or more unexcused absences within a six month period in the same school year (Tex. Educ. Code § 25.093 [a]). This offense is punishable as a Class C misdemeanor by fines only, and the fine schedule is laid out in Tex. Educ. Code § 25.093 [c]).

The School Attendance Officer

Children residing in Texas not only have the right to attend free public schools, but also are compelled to do so. To ensure that age-eligible students do attend school, attendance officers are appointed. Tex. Educ. Code §§ 25.088 and 25.090 permit the governing body of an independent school district or an open-enrollment charter school to select an attendance officer to enforce the attendance of students enrolled. If the open-enrollment charter school docs not select an attendance officer, § 25.090 requires that the county peace officers perform the duties of attendance officer with respect to students in the open-enrollment charter school.

Tex. Educ. Code §§ 25.091 and 25.095 lists the duties of a school attendance officer. The duties of attendance officers who are peace officers and the duties of those who are not peace officers are listed separately. Each district has the right to select an attendance officer. If no such officer is selected, the duties become the responsibility of the school superintendent and the peace officers of the county. The attendance officer is a paid school position; however, a superintendent or peace officer is excluded from receiving additional compensation for performing these services. Texas statute permits peace officers who function as school attendance officers and have probable cause that a student is in violation of compulsory attendance laws to take that student into custody and return them to school (Tex. Educ. Code §25.091 [b-1]).

The activities of the attendance officer are restricted in that the officer may not enter any private residence without permission of the owner or legal permission from the court, nor may the officer forcibly take custody of any child without the permission of the parent or legal guardian, except when ordered to do so by the court.

The Education Code does not specify any qualifications for the person who serves as an attendance officer; yet, the position is an important one for the school and the community as a whole. Effective school attendance officers have a genuine interest in the welfare of children; the ability to be firm, but fair; the strength to deal with less-than-ideal circumstances without becoming personally overwhelmed; the ability to understand the legal process and to carry out the process in a manner acceptable to the district; and excellent interpersonal skills. The selection of the school's attendance officer should be based on an established set of qualifications determined to specifically meet the needs of the district.

Student Attendance Accounting

The amount of state dollars allocated to finance each public school district in Texas is based on the ADA of that district. Understanding this basis for state funding should clearly suggest the importance of accuracy in the student attendance accounting process.

Accounting procedures are strictly controlled by statutory and administrative law. Provisions within the Texas Education Code address attendance accounting issues (see especially Chapters 25 and 42). Rules and procedures governing attendance records are found in Title 19 of the Texas Administrative Code (T.A.C.), specifically in Chapter 129. The following is a summary of key T.A.C. requirements regarding student attendance accounting for state funding purposes.

1. Superintendents, principals, and teachers are responsible to their school boards for the maintenance of accurate and current attendance records (19 TEX. ADMIN. CODE § 129.21 [a]).
2. School district superintendents are "responsible for the safekeeping of all attendance records and reports" (19 TEX. ADMIN. CODE § 129.21 [d]).
3. TEA provides daily attendance registers for use by school districts. While school districts may choose to use a locally developed record or automated system, it must contain the minimum information required by TEA (19 TEX. ADMIN. CODE § 129.21 [f]).
4. A student must be enrolled for at least two hours to be considered in attendance for half-day, and for at least four hours to be considered in attendance for one full day (19 TEX. ADMIN. CODE § 129.21 [g]).
5. Attendance for all grades is determined by absences recorded in the second or fifth period of the day, though an exception may be granted by TEA (19 TEX. ADMIN. CODE § 129.21 [h]).
6. The conditions for which a student who is not actually in school at the time attendance is taken but is considered in attendance for funding purposes include (19 TEX. ADMIN. CODE § 129.21 [j]):

   - participation in a board-approved off-campus activity if led by either professional or an adjunct staff member holding a bachelor's degree and eligible to participate in the Teacher Retirement System;'
   - participation in a district-approved mentorship for the purposes of attaining advanced measures under the Distinguished Achievement Program; or
   - any other reason deemed as an excused absence under Tex. Educ. Code §§ 25.087 (b), (b-1), (b-2), (b-4), or (c).

Students referred to a juvenile court for delinquent conduct or conduct indicating a need for supervision, as well as students referred to the Texas Department of Human Services or a welfare unit, receive excused absences if the student successfully completes all missed assignments. In contrast, a child who is living in a residential facility is not considered for accountability purposes for the district in which the facility is located (Tex. Educ. Code § 39.055).

From the perspective of the student, recognition of the absence as "excused" allows the student to meet the compulsory attendance laws and, hopefully, meet academic standards. However, those absences that reduce a district's ADA percentage obviously reduce the amount of state funding the district will receive. Many families continue to struggle with understanding the differences between excused and unexcused absences. Parents often feel that if they are excusing the absence with a note the school must excuse the absences based on their statements, but that is not necessarily the case. As noted above there is significant legal guidance to direct schools to assess absences to be in compliance with compulsory attendance laws. Clarity in the message from the schools, consistency throughout the district in implementation, and parent education can help prevent negative interactions with the families regarding attendance concerns.

This overview should not be construed as a legal opinion or legal advice. Rather, the narrative is intended to highlight features within the Texas Education Code affecting student discipline, parental rights, and student attendance. State Board of Education, Commissioner of Education, and State Board for Educator Certification rules, legal opinions, and ensuing litigation will surely clarify and perhaps contravene some of what is presented. The reader should, therefore, stay current through various state and federal educational publications and attendance at educational conferences.

◆ REFERENCES[1]

A.A. v. Needville Indep. Sch. Dist., 611 F.3d 248 (5th Cir. 2010).

A.M. v. Cash, 585 F.3d 214 (5th Cir. 2009).

Ali, R. (2010). *Dear colleague letter: Harassment and bullying.* Retrieved from http://www2.ed.gov/about/offices/list/ocr/letters/colleague-201010.pdf

Ali, R. (2011). *Letter to Francisco Negron.* Retrieved from http://www.nsba.org/SchoolLaw/Issues/Equity/ED-Response-to-NSBA-GCs-Letter-to-ED-on-OCR-Bullying-Guidelines.pdf

Barber v. Colorado ISD, 901 S.W.2d 447 (Tex. 1995).

Bastrop ISD v. Toungate, 958 S.W.2d 365 (Tex. 1997).

Bell v. Itawamba Cty. Sch. Bd., 2015 U.S. App. LEXIS 14630 (5th Cir. 2015)

Benjamin B. v. Natalia Independent School District, Dkt. No. 008-R5-901 (Texas Commissioner 2002).

Bethel Sch. Dist. v. Fraser, 478 U.S. 675 (1986).

Bd. of Educ. v. Mergens, 496 U.S. 226 (1990).

Board of Educ. v. Earls, 536 U.S. 822 (2002).

Canady v. Bossier Parish School District, 240 F.3d 437 (5th Cir. 2001).

Cantu, R. (2007, July 31). UIL: Steroid testing will happen this fall. *Austin American-Statesman.* Retrieved August 18, 2007 from http://www.statesman.com/sports/content/sports/stories/highschool/07/31/0731uil.html

Carmichael v. Galbraith, 574 Fed. Appx. 286 (5th Cir. 2014).

[1]All references to statutory and regulatory law are found in text.

Chalifoux v. New Caney ISD, 976 F.Supp.2d 659 (S.D. Tex. 1997).

Croft v. Perry, 562 F.3d 735 (5th Cir. 2009).

Davis v. Monroe County Board of Education, 526 U.S. 629 (1999).

Diane C. v. Natalia Independent School District, Dkt. No. 019-R5-1001 (Texas Commissioner 2002).

Doe v. Covington Cty. Bd. of Educ., 675 F.3d 849 (5th Cir. 2012).

Estate of Brown v. Cypress-Fairbanks Independent School District, 2012 U.S. Dist. LEXIS 72347 (S.D. Tex. 2012).

Estate of Brown v. Ogletree, 2012 U.S. Dist. LEXIS 21968 (S.D. Tex. 2012).

Estate of Carmichael v. Galbraith, 2012 U.S. Dist. LEXIS 857 (N.D. Tex. 2012).

Estate of Lance v. Kyer, 2012 U.S. Dist. LEXIS 160580 (E.D. Tex. 2012).

Estate of Lance v. Lewisville Indep. Sch. Dist., 743 F.3d 982 (5th Cir. 2014).

Fennell v. Marion Indep. Sch. Dist., No. 5:12-cv-00941-DAE (Document 48) (W.D. Tex. 2014). Retrieved from www.pacer.gov

Fitzgerald v. Barnstable Sch. Comm., 129 S. Ct. 788 (2009).

G.M. v. Shelton, 2014 U.S. App. LEXIS 22512 (5th Cir. 2014), cert. denied, 2014 U.S. App. LEXIS 22512 (2014).Garrett, R.L. (2011, June 2). High school steroid testing is backed with less funds. *Dallas Morning News*. Retrieved September 19, 2011, from www.lexisnexis.com/universe

Goss v. Lopez, 419 U.S. 565 (1975).

Hazelwood Sch. Dist. v. Kuhlmeier, 484 U.S. 260 (1988).

Jennings, J.L., & DiPrete, T.A. (2010). Teacher effects on social and behavioral skills in early elementary school. *Sociology of Education, 83*(2), 135–159.

Kaytie T. v. Forney Independent School District, Dkt. No. 040-R5-101 (Texas Commissioner 2002).

Kountze Indep. Sch. Dist. v. Matthews, 2014 Tex. App. LEXIS 4951 (Tex. App.—Beaumont 2014).

Lee, C. (2011). An ecological systems approach to bullying behaviors among middle school students in the United States. *Journal of Interpersonal Violence, 26*, 1664–1693. DOI: 10.1177/088626051037059

Littlefield v. Forney I.S.D., 268 F.3d 275 (5th Cir. 2001).

Marble Falls I.S.D., 2003 Tex. App. LEXIS 2845 (unpublished opinion) (Tex.App.—Austin 2003).

Moore v. Willis Indep. Sch. Dist., 233 F. 3d 871 (5th Cir. 2000).

Morgan v. Swanson, 659 F.3d 359 (5th Cir. 2011).

Morse v. Frederick, 127 S. Ct. 2618 (2007).

Nevares v. San Marcos CISD, 111 F. 3d 25 (5th Cir. 1997).

New Jersey v. T.L.O., 469 U.S. 325 (1985).

Palmer v. Waxahachie Indep. Sch. Dist., 579 F.3d 502 (5th Cir. 2009).

Perry Educ. Ass'n v. Perry Local Educators' Ass'n, 460 U.S. 37 (1983).

Peterson, M. (2009, August 20). A year later, the effectiveness of mandatory high-school athlete steroid testing under microscope. *Dallas Morning News*. Retrieved from http://www.dallasnews.com/sharedcontent/dws/dn/latestnews/stories/082009dnmetsteroids.fd0f38d8.html

Ponce v. Socorro Indep. Sch. Dist., 508 F.3d 765 (5th Cir. 2007).

Rose, C. (2010). *Re: "Dear colleague letter issued October 26, 2010.* Retrieved from http://www. nsba.org/SchoolLaw/Issues/Safety/NSBA-letter-to-Ed-12-07-10.pdf

Safford Unified Sch. Dist. #1 v. Redding, 129 S. Ct. 2633 (2009).

Smith, C. (2014., August 13). Recommendations to end UIL steroids testing program approved by sunset advisory commission. Dallas Morning News. Retrieved from http://www.dallasnews.com/sports/high-schools/headlines/20140813-uil-s-steroid-testing-following-no-positive-tests-at-172-schools-and-costing-near-10-million-likely-to-end-in-2015.ece

Smith, K., & Draper, N. (2011, March 8). Schools struggle to battle bullies. *Minneapolis Star Tribune*, p. 1A.

Texas Education Agency. (2011). *Snapshot 2010.* Retrieved from http://ritter.tea.state.tx.us/perfreport/snapshot/2010/state.html

Tinker v. Des Moines Independent Community School Dist., 393 U.S. 503 (1969).

United States Department of Education. (2001). *Revised sexual harassment guidance: Harassment of students by school employees, other students, or third parties.* Retrieved from http://www2.ed.gov/about/offices/list/ocr/docs/shguide.pdf

University Interscholastic League. (2009). *UIL anabolic steroid testing auestions and answers.* Retrieved October 15, 2009 from http://www.uil.utexas.edu/ATHLETICS/health/pdf/steroid_testingQ&A.pdf

University Interscholastic League. (2011, April 21). *Fall 2010 UIL anabolic steroid testing report.* Retrieved September 19, 2011 from http://www.uiltexas.org/press-releases/detail/fall-2010-uil-anabolic-steroid-testing-report

University Interscholastic League. (2014). 2013–2014 *UIL anabolic steroid testing report.* Retrieved from https://www.uiltexas.org/health/info/2013-2014-uil-anabolic-steroid-testing-report

Vernonia School District 47J v. Acton, 515 U.S. 646 (1995).

Walsh, J. (1995). A Sure-Fire Recipe. *Texas Association of Administrators INSIGHT. 9*(2), 27–29.

Williams-Grant v. Arlington Indep. Sch. Dist., 2012 U.S. Dist. LEXIS 165277 (N.D. Tex. 2012).

TECHNOLOGY AND EDUCATION IN TEXAS

Brian C. Brown ◆ *Mary P. Winn*

Since the 1980s, technology increasingly has been included among educational resources in public school classrooms. This technology influx has sparked fierce debate among both detractors and supporters using technology for instruction. While technology's supporters have touted its ability to motivate students, encourage creativity, and increase test scores (Butzin, 2000; Mann, Shakeshaft, Becker, & Kottkamp, 1999; Matthewman & Triggs, 2004), critics have noted that educational technology's monetary cost outweighs its benefits and that other instructional methods and tools appear to be more cost-effective (Cuban, 2001; Oppenheimer, 2003; Schmoker, 2006). Technology's rapid pace of change inhibits any study of its effectiveness, but like other instructional tools, technology is most influential when integrated with curriculum and assessment (CEO Forum on Education & Technology, 2001a). Furthermore, educational technology is not a homogeneous intervention and features a wide variety of tools, modalities, and strategies for learning (Ross, Morrison, & Lowther, 2010).

Oppenheimer (1997) provided five primary arguments often used in disputes pertaining to the incorporation of technology in schools:

1. Technology increases student achievement.
2. Younger students adapt to computer skills much quicker than older ones.
3. Understanding technology is an important component of preparation for the job market.
4. Businesses are more likely to support a technology-rich environment in schools.
5. Technology can make the classroom more global by increasing networks.

Combinations of these arguments for inclusion of technology in education continue to be utilized by technology proponents (EdTech Action Network, 2011).

Conversely, Schmoker (2006) wrote, "there may be great possibilities for improving instruction through the judicious, experimental use of technology" (p. 142), but added, "I have yet to see a single technology objective linked tightly to assessment or based on achieved results, in language that requires leaders or practitioners to gauge the actual impact of specific lessons that incorporate technology" (p. 142). Schmoker (2006) contended that the infusion of technology in schools is often linked to training that is nonsustaining and ill-spent money. In other words, the deluge of technology into schools has created environments where teaching and learning are being stifled by technology-related problems rather than enhanced.

Despite opinions from those who oppose the inclusion of technology in schools, noted works by Bickford (2005), Brown (2009), Haystead and Marzano (2010), Ringstaff and Kelley (2002), and Schacter (1999) suggested that technology can impact student learning positively. It has been demonstrated that students with access to a variety of technologies show positive gains in achievement on researcher constructed tests, standardized tests, and national tests (Bickford, 2005; Ringstaff & Kelley, 2002; Schacter, 1999). Students in technology-rich environments experience achievement gains in all major content areas (Prensky, 2010). In a recent multiyear study, student academic performance increased by an average of 16 percentile points when teachers taught their lessons using the ActivClassroom (Haystead & Marzano, 2010). In addition, a second-order metaanalyses of 1,055 primary studies revealed that average students taught using technology-enhanced instruction performed 12 percentile points higher than the average student in classrooms where technology is not used (Tamin, Bernard, Borokhovski, Abrami, & Schmid, 2011).

Often state agencies and local school boards focus upon the amount of technology available to teachers and students. The quantity of accumulated technology is reported using terms such as *students-per-computer*, *percentage of Internet connected classrooms*, and *amount of available network bandwidth* (Texas Education Agency, 2006b). Additionally, the Texas Education Agency (TEA) has begun to collect data in other areas of technology outside of infrastructure like instructional practices and technology leadership (2006b). Too often, school leaders focus upon utilization of classroom technology for administrative tasks like attendance and record keeping (Hodas, 1993; Snoeyink & Ertmer, 2002) or even the number of computers per student instead of the accessibility or functionality of those computers (Mergendoller, 1996; Rogers, 2000).

Researchers have suggested that application and accessibility of technology has the greatest influence on student achievement and success (Baylor & Ritchie, 2003; Brown, 2009; Rogers, 2000). As such, educators should spend more time on investigating how teachers and students can effectively incorporate technology into teaching and learning and less time worrying about quantity of equipment currently present in schools (Baylor & Ritchie, 2003; Glass, 2010; Haystead & Marzano, 2010). Educators must commit to properly incorporating technology in education to benefit engaged student learning and achievement. It is the responsibility of school leaders to balance accessibility of classroom technology with proper training in order to promote authentic teaching and learning (Baylor & Ritchie, 2003). Additionally, careful consideration must be made when planning implementation of new technologies to ensure that schools do not focus entirely on administrative tools. Administrators should emphasize a balance between tools for administrative record keeping and instructional purpose (Becker, 2007; Cohen, 1988; Snoeyink & Ertmer, 2002; Means et al., 1993; Mergendoller, 1996; Prensky, 2010). Regarding student motivation, Prensky (2010) provided five classroom tips that engage and motivate students in the digital age, as well as positively change schools today:

1. Relate to student passions.
2. Reduce the amount of *telling* relative to the amount of classroom activities and partnering.

3. Utilize relaxation tools (videos and software) at the beginning of class to create a learning environment.

4. Facilitate collaboration between students and peers around the world with the use of free tools such as ePals.

5. Permit the use of devices already being utilized by students (cell phones, tablets, laptops).

◆ TECHNOLOGICAL TRENDS IN EDUCATION

Digital Literacy and Information and Communication Technology (ITC)

Digital literacies are the constantly changing practices through which people make traceable meanings using digital technologies (Gillen & Barton, 2009). According to Gilster (1997), digital literacy is the ability to use digital technology, communication tools or networks to locate, evaluate, use, and create information in multiple formats from a wide-ranging sources when presented on the Internet or on a technical device (i.e., smart phone, tablet, laptop). It can be described as the knowledge and skills needed for understanding the meaning and context in an information age. Overall, digital literacy can be interpreted as sets of particular skills to be learned and competencies to be demonstrated (Bawden, 2001). This type of literacy can be subdivided into network, Internet, hyper-, and multimedia literacy (Bawden, 2001). Unfortunately, many students are not regularly using these skills and competencies nor are they being taught by many teachers (Armstrong & Warlick, 2004). This negligence has resulted in a need to address students' literacy of the technological tools available to them. Teachers must assist students to become not only digitally literate but also "use that literacy within their personal information environment in order to succeed now and in the future" (Armstrong & Warlick, 2004, p. 1). Warlick (2007) explained,

> The containers that we once guarded—the libraries, book shelves, reference books, and file drawers—can no longer hold the information that most of us actually use. We can no longer be the gatekeepers. We must, instead, teach children how to be their own gatekeepers, and this is an ethical imperative. (p. 21)

For teachers and students to obtain digital literacy, it is necessary to move beyond ideas of technology integration and focus more on how to find and evaluate content and less on the content itself. Mann (2001) stated that "instructional technology only works for some kids, with some topics, and under some conditions—but that is true of all pedagogy. There is nothing that works for every purpose, for every learner . . . all the time" (p. 241). If this statement implies instructional technology should be integrated into the existing curriculum, it appears that these researchers did not capture the essence of true digital literacy. Digital literacy requires a re-evaluation of yesterday's assumptions and approaches. Rather than teaching the same content using new instructional strategies, digital literacy focuses on skills associated with finding, decoding, evaluating, and organizing information into personal learning networks (Armstrong & Warlick, 2004).

The Partnership for the twenty-first Century Learning identifies information and communication as a key skill needed to prepare students for success in the twenty-first century ensuring that students explore and experiment with new and sophisticated technologies, including:

- using technology to research, organize, evaluate, and communicate information
- using digital technologies (e.g., computers, PDAs, media players, GPS), communication/networking tools, and social networks appropriately to access, manage, integrate, evaluate, and create information to successfully function in a knowledge economy
- applying fundamental understanding of the ethical/legal issues surrounding the access and use of information technologies (Partnership for 21st Century Learning, 2011).

While some debate on the existence of generational characteristics (Bennett & Maton, 2010; Helsper & Eynon, 2009; Trzeniewski & Donnellan, 2010), many have contended that contemporary learners think, behave, and learn differently due to ubiquitous exposure to technology (Prensky, 2001a; Tapscott, 2009; Taylor, 2005). Prensky coined the term *digital natives* to describe the students attending our schools (2001a, p. 1). He claimed that students readily adopt and master new technologies intuitively (Prensky, 2005). Specifically, Prensky (2001a) said that students "think and process information fundamentally differently from their predecessors" (p. 1). Because an environment that is saturated with media surrounds young people in the United States, changes must occur within the classroom to address students' social, emotional, and mental differences (Prensky, 2001a; Roberts, Feohr, & Rideout, 2005). Physical evidence corroborates brain differences resulting from exposure to digital media in terms of how digital learners process, interact, and apply information (Jensen, 2005; Jukes & Dosaj, 2006; Willis, 2008). Digital learners fundamentally think and process information differently than their predecessors by using multitasking and parallel processing; they prefer graphics to text, random access (hyperlinks), networking, instant gratification, frequent rewards, and games rather than *serious* work (Prensky, 2001b).

Teachers are encouraged to *plug-in*, that is, to adopt new technologies, and begin utilizing technology within their classrooms to captivate and motivate their student audiences. These teachers are digital immigrants who are urged to embrace technology, learn it, and use it to address methods of instruction and course content (Prensky, 2005). In more recent works, Prensky (2010) stated that technology is an extension of the brain; it is a new way of thinking. Technology is the solution that humans have created to deal with the difficult new context of variability, uncertainty, complexity, and ambiguity. The human mind, as powerful as it is, is no longer powerful enough for the world; the old *tried and true* human capabilities just are not enough. Technology provides new and enhanced capabilities. Technology is not something that humans need *in addition* to mental activity; technology is now *part* of mental activity, and must be used wisely.

Today's students are fluent in a multitude of technologies, but still need guidance to navigate the Internet for learning. Zuboff (1988) differentiated between automating (applying technology to existing processes and procedures) and informating (the shift in organizational control of information). Automating uses technology as a means to track student attendance, academic progress, and generate reports. Informating involves using technology to create cultural shifts and empower both students and teachers with access to information. November (2009) noted a need for schools to empower students with access to technology in a highly collaborative environment; thus, guiding students through informating processes and changing how students use technology for learning. Part of this process is providing students with the tools for digital literacy and the skills for ITC.

Mobile Learning

Mobile learning, or m-learning, is a subdivision of e-learning that exploded in the early 2000s. Created by the prevalence of mobile technologies, some claim that it has potential to change both teaching and learning (Chinnery, 2006; Evans, 2008; Nyiri, 2002). Nyiri stated,

> we have to re-think Dewey. His argument was that we need schools, artificial educational environments, because the young can no longer learn spontaneously by moving around in the world of adults. I believe this state of affairs is rapidly changing. The medium in which children play, communicate, and learn—the world of networked computing and mobile communications—is increasingly identical with the world in which adults communicate, work, do business, and seek entertainment. The patterns of primary and secondary education are bound to change. (p. 6)

Furthermore, these researchers predicted that e-learning will be replaced as m-learning as Internet access transforms from traditional computing technologies to mobile devices (i.e., smartphones, MP3 players, tablets) (Chinnery, 2006; Nyiri, 2002).

Resulting from the newest consumer technologies, m-learning and its theoretical base is currently being explored (Kearney, Schuck, Burden, & Aubusson, 2012). However, the pedagogical perspective highlights three central features: authenticity, collaboration, and personalization (Kearney et al., 2012). That is to say, m-learning was found to be successful if the activities where authentic, collaborative, and allowed for personalization by the individual learner (Chinnery, 2006; Kearney et al., 2012).

Caution should be utilized when employing m-learning strategies. Researchers have demonstrated that while m-learning can be successful, when introduced into a previously existing e-learning environment, the learners reported the benefit of the m-learning technology was nonexistent (Hewagamage, Wickramasinghe, & Jayatilaka, 2012; Guo, Fu, Yin, Yuan, Zhang, & Gao, 2013). The researchers concluded that m-learning required a new learning service that considered both learning and technical infrastructure together, not as an extension of the existing learning environment (Hewagamage et al., 2012).

Massive Open Online Course

The phenomenon of e-learning, assisted by the subset known as m-learning, has given rise to a unique online learning experience called Massive Open Online Courses (MOOCs) (de Waard et al., 2011). MOOCs integrate "the connectivity of social networking, the facilitation of an acknowledged expert in a field of study, and a collection of freely accessible online resources" (McAuley, Stewart, Siemens, & Cormier, 2010, p. 4). Online courses increase active engagement among the participants.

MOOC online participants utilize various social networking tools (i.e., Twitter, Facebook, Google Groups) to find, decode, evaluate, and organize information. Discussions are held synchronously via videoconferencing and messaging technologies or asynchronously via blogs, forums, or e-mail. Typically, MOOCs are free-of-charge and are announced via social networking sites and e-mail lists (McAuley et al., 2010). Additionally, while facilitators could exist, courses are a-hierarchical with course participants leading one another through the course objectives (McAuley et al., 2010). It has been said that "participation in an MOOC is emergent, fragmented, diffuse, and diverse" (McAuley et al., 2010, p. 11).

MOOCs can serve a purpose in today's schools by providing free and open access to worldwide experts in areas of interest for students. With universities like Stanford and Harvard creating and maintaining MOOCs, the access to high-quality information and thinking is at an unprecedented high. While these courses have not focused on providing K-12 students with engaging activities, they should be considered as a source of learning for our students.

◆ TECHNOLOGICAL STANDARDS FOR ADMINISTRATORS, TEACHERS, AND STUDENTS

Educators are presented with multiple levels of technological standards for administrators, teachers, and students. The International Society for Technology in Education (ISTE) has developed several versions of the National Educational Technology Standards (NETS). There are NETS versions for administrators, teachers, students, technology coaches, and computer science teachers. Additionally, the state of Texas has developed standards for teachers and students. In the following, we will discuss three of the NETS versions as well as the state standards for teachers and students.

National Educational Technology Standards for Administrators

The ISTE has created a set of national standards for administrators. According to the ISTE, the National Educational Technology Standards for Administrators (NETS·A) were written to "enable us to define what administrators need to know and be able to do in order to discharge their responsibility as leaders in the effective use of technology in our schools" (2009a, para. 1). The standards have been arranged into five areas: visionary leadership, digital-age learning culture, excellence in professional practice, systemic improvement, and digital citizenship.

In the area of visionary leadership, administrators "inspire and lead development and implementation of a shared vision for comprehensive integration of technology to promote excellence and support transformation through the organization" (ISTE, 2009b, p. 1). This area includes the facilitation of a shared vision with all stakeholders; development, implementation, and communication of a technology strategic plan aligned with the vision; and advocating of the plan and vision on a local, state, and national level (ISTE, 2009b).

The digital-age learning culture area requires administrators to "create, promote, and sustain a dynamic, digital-age learning culture that provides a rigorous, relevant, and engaging education for all students" (ISTE, 2009b, p. 1). This area is embodied by administrators focusing on continuous improvement of digital-age learning, modeling and promoting technology for learning, providing learner-centered environments, ensuring effective practice in the study of technology, and participating in local, national, and global learning communities (ISTE, 2009b). Most educators "value technology and use the Internet frequently . . . far fewer are exploring the use of digital media for professional development and communication, including interaction with colleagues beyond their schools and districts" (Markow & Cooper, 2008, p. 110).

Excellence in Professional Practice sets the standard that administrators will promote an environment of professional learning and encourage innovation among educators (ISTE, 2009b). Administrators are to perform this standard by allocating time and resources to professional growth in technology, facilitate and participate in learning communities focused upon the use of technology, model effective communication using digital-age tools, and maintain a working knowledge of educational research and emerging trends regarding the use of technology in education (ISTE).

The fourth area, systemic improvement, asks that administrators "provide digital-age leadership and management to continuously improve the organization" (ISTE, 2009b, p. 1). To complete this mission, administrators should leader purposeful change to maximize the achievement of learning goals, collaborate to improve staff performance and student learning, recruit highly competent personnel, establish partnerships to support improvement, and maintain a robust infrastructure for technology.

The fifth and final area within the NETS·A standards is digital citizenship. In this area, administrators are to "model and facilitate understanding of social, ethical, and legal issues and responsibilities related to an evolving digital culture" (ISTE, 2009b, p. 1). Digital citizenship is ensured by maintaining equitable access to appropriate digital tools, promoting safe, legal, and ethical use of technology, model responsible social interactions related to the use of technology, and facilitating the development of a shared cultural understanding of global issues (ISTE, 2009b).

The NETS·A establish a solid foundation for administrators seeking to develop professional learning communities within schools that teach in student-centered learning environments. Along with ISTE's NETS for Students and NETS for Teachers, these standards apply the concepts of digital literacy in a meaningful and applicable manner. By utilizing the foundation presented by ISTE, administrators can ensure that they are appropriating leading technology within the schools and districts.

National Education Technology Standards for Teachers

ISTE has developed a similar set of national technology standards for teachers referred to as NETS-T. These standards, like the administrator standards, focus on five key areas; however, the areas differ slightly. Teachers should facilitate and inspire student learning and creativity, design and develop digital age learning experiences and assessments, model digital age work and learning, promote and model digital citizenship and responsibility, and engage in professional growth and leadership (ISTE, 2008).

By utilizing NETS-T alongside NETS-A, administrators can ensure that teachers and administrators will be working together to create a technologically savvy environment that supports digital age teaching and learning. These standards support student learning and the student standards developed by ISTE, called NETS-S (ISTE, 2007b).

National Education Technology Standards for Students

The National Education Technology Standards for Students (NETS-S) create a system for evaluating the skills and knowledge that students need to live productively in a digital world. Focused on six key areas, the standards concentrate on the students need to be able to use technology to analyze, learn, and explore. The areas are creativity and innovation; communication and collaboration; research and information fluency; critical thinking, problem-solving, and decision-making; digital citizenship; and technology operations and concepts (ISTE, 2007a).

In addition to the standards, ISTE has developed four student profiles to provide a basis for age-appropriate skills that adhere to the standards. The profiles cover grades Pre-K through second, third through fifth, sixth through eighth, and ninth through twelfth (ISTE, 2007b). These profiles are provided to give educators and example of age-appropriate activities and skills that could be used and indicators of achievement (ISTE, 2007b).

the Texas Campus STaR Charts. The Campus STaR Chart had been a state-mandated survey for the entire period of the study.

The Texas Campus STaR Chart is based upon the work of The CEO Forum on Education & Technology. The CEO Forum on Education & Technology developed the original STaR Chart as a teacher preparation tool for colleges and universities to use with preservice teachers (2001b). The CEO Forum on Education & Technology (2001a) original STaR Chart called for four levels, or indicators, of technology implementation: early tech, developing tech, advanced tech, and target tech. Each of these indicators was assigned a method of measurement within five categories: educational benefits, hardware and connectivity, professional development, digital content, and student achievement and assessment (CEO Forum on Education & Technology, 2001a,b).

The key area of teaching and learning is comprised of six focus areas: patterns of classroom use, frequency/design of instructional setting using digital content, content area connections, online learning, TA-TEKS implementation, and student mastery of TA-TEKS. The key area of educator preparation and development addresses the focus areas of content of professional development, models of professional development, capabilities of educators, access to professional development, levels of understanding and patterns of use, and professional development for online learning.

The leadership, administration, and instructional support key area includes the focus areas of leadership and vision, planning, instructional support, communication and collaboration, budget, and leadership and support for online learning. The key area of infrastructure for technology is comprised of the focus area students per computers, internet access connectivity/speed, other classroom technology, technological support, local area network/ wide area network (LAN/WAN), and distance learning capacity. The resulting chart is a matrix-style rubric with sections that list the qualifications for the subcategory and level indicators (TEA, 2006b).

Until 2014, each Texas public school campus administrator is required to complete the STaR Chart on an annual basis (TEA, 2006b, 2008). The STaR chart is accessed utilizing an online interactive website hosted on the TEA Region 12 Education Service Center's website. Each subcategory appears on its own screen and the administrator selects the level of indicator for the campus. Once an indicator is selected, the site automatically forward to the next subcategory. Once the chart is completed, the administrator can review the recorded information and make necessary changes before the report is submitted.

Each response is assigned a number based on the indicator selected by the administrator. Early tech responses earn a one, developing tech receive a two, advanced tech earn a three, and target tech receive a four. The total of each subcategory is then tabulated for a category total that ranges from a minimum of 6 to the target score of 24. Schools are then assessed on the four category totals. The goal of this process is to increase the category totals each year for each individual campus (TEA, 2006b).

Texas Teacher School Technology and Readiness (STaR) Chart

In addition to the Campus STaR Chart, a Teacher STaR Chart was developed in 2004 and updated in 2006 in order to align with the Texas Long-Range Plan for Technology (TEA, 2006c). Like the campus chart, the instrument is arranged around four key areas: teaching and learning; education preparation and development; leader, administration and instructional support; and infrastructure for technology (TEA, 2006c). In the initial first 2 years of utilization, the chart was voluntary but beginning in the 2006–2007 school year, "all Texas teachers are required to complete the online version of the Texas Teacher STaR Chart annually" (TEA, 2006c, p. 1).

Within the Teacher STaR Chart, each of the four key areas is further broken down into six subcategories. Each of the subcategories corresponds with the subcategories found on the campus chart (TEA, 2006b,c). However, the components of the scoring matrix are written in a way to be directed at the behavior of teachers as they interact with technology, administrators, and students. Therefore, the indices of the Teacher STaR Chart are more meaningful to the intended respondents: classroom teachers. For example, in the key area of infrastructure and technology, the fourth subcategory is labeled *technical support*. The indices of the campus chart focuses upon the number of technology support personnel per computer, whereas those of the teacher chart concentrates on the response time of technical personnel to a teacher-reported issue. It should be understood that the campus and teacher charts are closely correlated, but are not exactly the same in content.

No Child Left Behind Technology Reporting System. Beginning in 2008, school districts receiving formula or competitive funding from No Child Left Behind Title II, Part D are required to report additional information annually (Region 12 Education Service Center (ESC), 2008). These additional data requirement are entered into the Texas STaR Chart website under a separate reporting area. This area consists of three sections: the individual campus administrators complete the parts one and three, and the second section is completed by the district STaR Chart contact (Region 12 ESC, 2008).

The data collected under this report include information about Internet connectivity, student proficiencies, and school administrator proficiencies. The school administrator proficiencies are based upon the ISTE's National Educational Technology Standards for Administrators (NETS·A) (Region 12 ESC, 2008). The student proficiencies focus upon technology literacy of 8th grade students while the Internet connectivity section concentrates on computer minimum specifications and Internet connections (Region 12 ESC, 2008). The reporting on Internet connectivity requires the campus administrator to list the quantity, age, and location of student desktop computers and other Internet-connected devices.

◆ STATE OF TEXAS TECHNOLOGY FUNDING

All Texas school districts have an overarching goal to enhance education through the use of technology. Since 1992, the primary goal of the long-range plan for technology in Texas has been to make technology available in every school district in Texas. With the premise that funding for technology facilitates student achievement and implementation of the state's long-range plan for technology, technology in Texas schools is funded through E-Rate, Title II, Part D, and technology allotment. E-Rate provides discounts for telecommunication services to schools and libraries. Title II, Part D of NCLB (Enhancing Education through Technology) has provided the state with a myriad of funding to support professional development of teachers for integration of technology.

Planning, programs, budgets, people, and processes are key factors in the implementation of technology within Texas schools. As stated in the TEA's Technology Plan for 2006–2008 (Southwest Educational Development Laboratory, 2003), "Effective integration of technology within our education system provides schools with the resources necessary to increase student achievement, enhance teacher's knowledge and proficiencies, and provide administrators with the tools to effectively manage their responsibilities" (p. 117). Students as well as their teachers have increasing expectations for anytime, anywhere connectivity to digital content, video, and data. With the goal being development of statewide connectivity, infrastructure is critical in providing equitable access to all learners in the state of Texas.

Federal Technology Funding

The schools and libraries universal service support program, known as E-Rate, was created to provide public schools and libraries with affordable telecommunications and internet access. This program is managed by the Universal Service Administrative Company (USAC), which is overseen by the Federal Communications Commission (FCC) (Federal Communications Commission, 2014b).

In 2014, the FCC made two sweeping modernization orders to the E-Rate program, which greatly impacts public schools. Within the modernization orders were new goals for bandwidth per user, increased support for internal and broadband connections, and decreased support on mobile and landline telephone systems. The orders also set the following three performance goals:

- Ensuring affordable access to high-speed broadband sufficient to support digital learning in schools and robust connectivity for all libraries.
- Maximizing the cost-effectiveness of spending for E-rate supported services.
- Making the E-rate application process and other E-rate processes fast, simple, and efficient.

A new short-term goal of 100 MB per 1,000 users of internet connectivity was established with a long-term goal of 1 GB per 1,000 users. Additionally, the program has a 5-year goal of $150-per-student budget (Federal Communications Commission, 2014a; Foundation for Excellence in Education, 2014).

One of the most significant potential impacts to school districts is the phase out of legacy communication services. For example, voicemail, paging, email, web hosting, and text messaging immediately lose funding under the new modernization order. Local and long distance phone and cellular/mobile phone services will incur a 20% reduction each year over the next 5 years. The phased out support for phone services could greatly impact Texas schools in the immediate future as many schools rely on the E-Rate program to help subsidize phone services (Federal Communications Commission, 2014a; Foundation for Excellence in Education, 2014).

◆ BARRIERS TO IMPLEMENTATION OF INSTRUCTIONAL TECHNOLOGY

In order for the precepts of digital literacy, ICT, and instructional technology to be catalysts for student achievement, schools must remove the barriers that block paths to implementation. School-level barriers include lack of time (BECTA, 2004), lack of effective training (Albirini, 2006) lack of accessibility (BECTA, 2004; Bingimlas, 2009; Clark, 2006; Pelgrum, 2001), lack of technical support (Pelgrum, 2001), and lack of infrastructure. Teacher-level barriers include lack of teacher competence and resistance to change (BECTA, 2004; Bingimlas, 2009; Pelgrum, 2001) and negative attitudes (BECTA, 2004). There is a clear connection between the decision to use technology for instruction and the degree to which teachers experience barriers (Inan & Lowther, 2010). The most common barriers include accessibility, teacher competence and resistance to change, technical and instructional support, and lack of infrastructure. The key to dealing with these barriers is being able to identify them and utilizing strategies for moving beyond them.

Accessibility

The most common obstacle to effective use of classroom technology is not only the accessibility of computers but also connectivity to the Internet. The student-to-computer with internet access ratio altered from 6:1 (2000) to 3:1 in (2008) in US public schools (Institute of Educational Sciences, 2013). As of 2009, 97% of teachers indicated they had one or more computers in classroom every day, and 54% shared they could bring mobile computers into the classroom (Institute of Educational Sciences, 2010). Moreover, Internet access was available to 93% of classroom computers and 96% of mobile computers. Other technologies available in the classroom included LCD (liquid crystal display) or DLP (digital light processing) projectors (36% and 48%, respectively), interactive whiteboards (28% and 23%, respectively), and digital cameras (64% and 14%, respectively) (U.S. Department of Education, National Center for Statistics, 2010). While the presence of technology increases, technological infrastructure remains a barrier. The ability to access the Internet has consistently improved; however, finding enough bandwidth to run more complex applications such as streaming video and audio is still a concern. The FCC noted in 2010, 97% of public schools in the United States had connectivity to the Internet, but many lacked infrastructure to meet the higher speed access (Federal Communications Commission, 2010). With more schools adopting a bring-your-own-device (BYOD) policy enabling students to bring their own smartphones, laptops, and tablets, demand for bandwidth has increased. Some progress has been made noted in the Speak Up research of Project Tomorrow (2010) where students cited their chief concern as restrictive Internet filtering; whereas, 5 years earlier it was connectivity speed.

Teacher Competency and Resistance to Change

The availability of technology has increased in schools, and yet, many teachers struggle utilizing it, and even may be resistant to integrating it into their practice. Lei (2010) attributed this resistance to the unclear benefits of technology and pressures that teachers feel to ensure student achievement. Other issues tied to resistance include lack of time, lack of technology, and lack of training–or teacher competency. Teacher competency using technology for instructional purposes is increasing. While in the early phases of technology implementation teachers may have struggled with loss of authority due to their insufficient technology skills (French & Raven, 1968; Hodas, 1993), data indicate that teachers increasingly use technology for instructional purposes. In 2000, 39% of teachers indicated that they used computers or the Internet to create instructional materials, 34% for administrative recordkeeping, while less than 10% reported to access model lesson plans or to access research and best practices (NCES, 2000). In 2009, 40% teachers reported either they or their students used computers often during instructional time; while 29% reported sometimes (IES, 2009). As teachers feel more competent utilizing technology for instruction purposes, they are more likely to implement into instructional formats.

Technical and Instructional Support

One way to assist teachers in the process of integrating technology into their instruction is to provide ongoing informational support. Teacher integration of technology is connected heavily to the level of support they receive, their own beliefs about using technology for learning, and their skills with using technology for instruction (Ertmer & Ottenbreit-Leftwich, 2010; Inan & Lowther, 2010). Another means of assistance is mentoring that includes sustained workshop and in-classroom training focused on addressing teacher skills and pedagogy (Lowther, Inan, Strahl, & Ross, 2008; Swan & Dixon, 2006). Suggested ways to increase technology integration include: (1) providing professional development workshops, (2) enhancing curriculum with technology-enhanced materials, (3) increasing collaboration between schools, and (4) ensuring teachers more autonomy in the selection and coverage of curriculum materials (Almekhalafi & Almeqdadi, 2010; Bauer & Kenton, 2005; Kotrlik & Redmann, 2005; Zorfass & Rivero, 2005).

◆ PROFESSIONAL DEVELOPMENT

Demand for a better understanding of instructional strategies supportive of today's learners and technologies is driving the need for more professional development for teachers. Although the virtual world of professional development is relatively new, the need for teacher collaboration is not. As schools work to meet the demands of a rapidly changing world, there is much agreement that the teacher will be the key figure ensuring the needed changes occur (Darling-Hammond & Bransford, 2005). Teacher isolation must shift to colleagueship, not only on the campus with implementation on professional learning communities, but also through online avenues such as professional learning communities 2.0 or professional learning networks (Lieberman & Mace, 2010). Cavanagh (2013) reported a significant increase in the percentages of teachers and principals participating in online classes, webinars, and virtual professional learning communities from 2008 through 2013. The number of principals supporting professional growth via some form of social networking more than tripled, from 8% in 2008 to 25% 2013. Successful completion of online professional development courses is tied to self-discipline (Beaudoin, Kutz, & Eden, 2009; Boyd, 2004) and school administrators' expectations of successful completion (Vu, Cao, Vu, & Cepero, 2014).

◆ ADMINISTRATIVE RESPONSIBILITIES

With the continuous emergence of new technologies, school leaders hold key responsibilities for addressing legal and ethical issues and curriculum responsibilities to ensure that students and teachers can make the best use of technology while acting as good digital citizens (Schrum & Levin, 2015). The 2014 proposed Interstate School Leaders Licensure Consortium (ISSLC) Standards for Administrators support this role of school leaders by stating an educational leader holds responsibility of enhancing instructional capacity (Standard 2), promoting instruction that maximizes student learning (Standard 3), and promoting a robust and meaningful curricula and assessment programs (Standard 4) (Council of Chief State School Officers, n.d.).

One key component of administrative responsibility is to ensure the development of a digital citizenship curriculum. The nine elements of digital citizenship include digital access, commerce, communication, literacy, etiquette, law, rights and responsibilities, health and wellness, and security. Since students are already using technologies in school, the nine elements provide leaders with a useful lens and resources to ensure that technologies are being used appropriately and effectively (Ribble & Bailey, 2007). Other resources for assisting school leaders developing a digital citizenship curriculum include Common Sense Media and Internet Keep Safe Coalition (ikeepsafe.org) (Shrum & Levin, 2015).

◆ TEXAS VIRTUAL SCHOOL NETWORK–ONLINE SCHOOL PROGRAM

The TEA recently implemented the Texas Virtual School Network-Online Schools Program (TxVSN), which provides full-time online instruction to Texas public school students in grades 3 through 12. Courses are 100% online and are reviewed to ensure the curriculum standards meet TEKS and national standards (TEA Texas Virtual School Network—Online Schools Program). TEC Chapter 30A.001 defines an electronic course as one in which:

- instruction and content are delivered primarily over the Internet;
- a student and teacher are in different physical locations for a majority of the student's instructional period;
- most instructional activities take place in an online environment;
- the online instructional activities are integral to the academic program;
- extensive communication between a student and a teacher and among students is emphasized; and
- a student is not required to be located on the physical premises of a school district or open-enrollment charter school (Texas Education Code, 2015, Chapter 30A.001).

Furthermore, TEC 30A.002 clarifies student eligibility to enroll in TxVSN if, as of September 1 of the school year, the student is younger than 21 or is younger than 26 years of age and entitled to the benefits of the Foundation School Program under Section 42.003; has not graduated from high school; and is otherwise eligible to enroll in a public school in this state. Additionally, a student is eligible if he/she was enrolled in a public school in this state in the preceding school year; or has been placed in substitute care in this state, regardless of whether the student was enrolled in a public school in this state in the preceding school year.

The TEA website (tea.texas.gov) provides a yearly list of schools meeting the criteria to participate in TxVSN and 19 TAC Chapter 70. Technology-based instruction addresses the Commissioner's Rules concerning TxVSN. According to TEA, enrollment in TxVSN for fall 2013–2014 included 2,198 high school students and 369 dual credit students. Fall 2014–2015 showed an enrollment of 2,439 high school/142 dual credit (TEA, 2015b; TxVSN Reports, 2015a).

TxVSN is fairly new, but emerging trends suggest the potential for continued growth. Data collection on K-12 online completion rates is in the early phases; however, data from higher education revealed in Fall 2012, 32% (6.7 million students) took at least one online course, showing an increase of more than 570,000 students from over the previous year, a 9.3% growth rate for online enrollment (Allen & Seaman, 2013). Concerns regarding online delivery include learning outcomes and student attrition in online courses. A 2012 survey of chief academic officers revealed 77% of academic leaders rated learning outcomes addressed in online education to be the same or superior to those in face-to-face. This finding was an increase to the 57.2% in 2003 (Allen & Seaman, 2013). Another concern is the number of students who fail to complete online courses. This attrition can be attributed to various issues, but Lee and Choi (2011) noted a key factor as insufficient with interaction peers and with the instructor. Other issues included lack of technology orientation, scheduling conflicts, and difficulties completing assignments.

◆ TECHNOLOGICAL TOOLS IN EDUCATION

The Internet evolved from Web 1.0, a read-only web into an interactive Web 2.0, which allowed computer users with minimal technical skills to generate content through a read/write web. In addition, Web 2.0 created an opportunity for a cacophony of voices to collaborate and communicate instantaneously through blogs, videos, photos/images, and discussion forums. In essence, social media exemplifies 2.0 (e.g., YouTube, Facebook, Pinterest, Twitter, Google). Web 3.0, referred to as the Semantic Web, is expected to vastly increase the ability for individuals to share, reuse, and combine information and data through complex queries. The emergence of Web 3.0 is evidenced in virtual reality, seamless internet access, increased open-source software, and natural-language processing (e.g., Siri and "OK, Google"). Web 3.0 technologies include machine-to-machine interaction such as using a smartphone to control the thermostat or alarm system (Schrum & Levin, 2015).

The rapid pace of technological change presents both challenges and opportunities for schools. The benefits include greater availability to courses in rural areas through online classes/distance learning, Internet access, professional development, and more personalized learning. However, the challenges include the constant need to upgrade technological infrastructure and revise instructional strategies and pedagogy. Moreover, the continuing flow of new technologies makes defining *best practices* difficult because some technologies are obsolete before research can be finalized. Another resulting issue of continual change in physical technology products is a parallel need for updated pedagogy to complement the technologies. The intention to have a technology-rich classroom is too often quashed when old models of teaching and learning are applied to learning that features revamped or new technologies (McClure, Jukes, & MacLean, 2011). Puentedura (2008) identified four levels of technology use in class instruction: substitution, augmentation, modification, and redefinition (SAMR). Created to help teachers reflect and refine their use of technology in instruction, the first two levels of the SAMR model focus on instructional enhancement, technology as a tool substitute, but provides no functional change (testing on computer instead of paper). At the next level, technology still substitutes for a conventional tool, but with functional improvement (watching a video versus modeling the process). However, at the transformation level, technology significantly improves instruction. Technology used to redesign or create original tasks result in richer, more engaged and integrated learning at higher levels of thinking. The use of digital tools coordinated with effective research-supported instructional practices can promote collaborative learning environments focused on student engagement and in-depth conceptual investigation (Freidman, Beauchamp, Blain, Lirette-Pitre, & Fournier 2011; Kahveci, 2010; Keser, Uzunboylu, & Ozdamli, 2011; Smeureanu & Isaila, 2011).

Virtual Learning Environments

Virtual learning environments (VLEs), also known as learning management systems, essentially provide students and teachers with an online classroom and assist management and facilitation of students learning activities, including content and resources. There are multiple types of VLEs, both free and subscription-based. Freely available VLEs include Edmodo, Schoology, and Google Classroom while Desire2Learn, Blackboard, and eCollege offer fee-based versions. Additionally, there are free-and-open-source-software (FOSS) versions like Moodle, DrupalEd, and Sakai.

Social Networking

Social networking, mainstreamed with sites such as Facebook, Twitter, LinkedIn, Pinterest, Tumblr, Instagram, Snapchat, and Google+, utilizes Web 2.0 applications and websites to connect users with similar interest. Today's teens are more connected than any generation before them. According to The Pew Research Center, 92% of teenagers acknowledged being online daily while 24% reported being online almost constantly. Facebook was this most popular with 71% of all 13- to 17 year-olds using this site followed by Instagram (52%), Snapchat (41%), Twitter 33%), and Google+ (33%) (Lenhart, 2015). Social networking provides individuals with a broadcast style platform for notifying contacts, usually friends and family, about the events in their lives. Some social networks are focused entirely on a professional level (e.g., LinkedIn), while others are intended to bring together groups of people interested in similar topics (e.g., Ning). Ultimately, social networks allow individuals to be able to keep up with other people without having to have direct social contact.

Wikis

From the Hawaiian word meaning *quick*, wikis are touted as a computer-supported collaborative learning tool (Augar, Raitman, & Zhou, 2004). Wikis are web pages or websites designed for user collaboration. Wikis enable anyone with access to the site to utilize a web browser to edit, create, or share information related to the content. The most extreme example of a wiki is Wikipedia, which has over 3 million articles in the English language. However, due to its open nature, the site has been plagued by accusations of inaccuracies and inconsistencies. Some sites, like WikiSpaces and PBWorks, provide free wikis to educators. Google Docs can also be created and shared as a Wiki. There are multiple uses for wikis in education; they can be especially useful to school leaders in facilitating planning and decision-making. Sample uses could include collaborative meeting agenda, plans for professional development, program development, class scheduling, and handbook development (Schrum & Levin, 2015).

Blogs

Blogs are another form of social media in which an individual or group employs a personal webpage to facilitate an online journal or public diary of sorts that is usually focused on a specific topic. The author of the blog can allow for comments or feedback from visitors to the blog. In addition, blog can be posted to websites dedicated to their creation or posted within social networking sites. Blogs differ from Wikis in that only the author can change the original text. Some of the most popular blog platforms include Wordpress, Tumblr, Blogger, Medium, Svbtle, LiveJoural, and Weebly. While blogging has remained consistently with adults, there has been a decline in its use among teens from 2006 (28%) to 2010 (14%) (Lenhart, Purcell, Smith, & Zickuhr, 2010). Blogs can be excellent networking and professional communication tools for school administrators some popular blogs in this venue include: Connected Principals, A Principal's Reflections, Education Week Blogs, Edutopia, Innovative Educator, Mindshift, The 21st Century Principal, and The Principal Difference.

Content Creation Tools

Increases online delivery in educational forums has generated a need for greater productivity in content creation, which, for this purpose, is the contribution of information to digital media for a specific audience. Tools for content creation can be text-based such as Softchalk or demonstration-based such as presenter or screencast-o-matic.

Another component in this arena is content curation, which currently facilitated with tools like Diigo Education Edition, Evernote, Storify, and Scoop.it. Content curation is the art of collecting and sharing content in an organized format, usually focusing on one area of interest. As educators and students improve their abilities to utilize the Internet's vast resources, content curation will be an excellent tool for research, sharing, and collaboration.

Apps

The development of smartphones and tablets facilitated the emergence of the *app*, short for application, which function as self-contained programs or software created for a targeted purpose. Apps are usually downloaded to a mobile device. As more schools embrace BYOD or a one-to-one initiatives, Apps are not only being used for teaching and learning but are also finding uses in classroom management, parent and student communication, assessment, and note-taking. There are seemingly unlimited applications available; here are a few acknowledged by various associations and educational technology websites:

Learning and Assessment

- *Kahoot* works with all levels of students. It allows teachers to create surveys or quizzes to which students respond using any number of mobile devices.
- *Skitch* is a visual communication tool which allows a shared image to be edited with text, highlight, or stickers. For example, an image of a cell could be shared, and students would then label the parts of the cell.
- *Quizlet* provides an avenue to create virtual flashcards.
- *Socrative* assists teachers in developing formative assessments using quizzes, question polls, exit tickets, and space races.
- *MobyMax* works with ELA and math using a pretest to place students in personalized lessons. Teachers can track progress through a dashboard.
- *Khan Academy* includes over 3,000 videos on a variety of subjects including higher-level classes such as chemistry, physics, and finance.
- *TapQuiz Maps World Edition* provides students with interactive games to teach the counties of the world.
- *TED* shares thousands of inspiring talks from people all over the world.

Organization and Communication and Classroom Management

- *Collaborize Classroom* uses a web-based application to allow students and teachers to interact. This site also has professional development tools and a topic library.
- *Livebinders* uses the web to create virtual 3-ring binders. The workspace allows educators/students to categorize and store information by subject, grade-level, and more.
- *Seesaw* works with all grade levels and allows students to independently create portfolios of pictures and artifacts.
- *Google for Education* supports the teacher to create a class group in which documents, information, progress, reminders, and deadlines can be shared.

- *Remind* allows teacher to text students and parents without displaying their personal phone numbers. It is used to send reminders about assignments, homework, schedule changes, or even motivating or encouraging messages.
- *Class Messenger* provides direct, two-way communication between parents and teachers. Parents can join the class and view results, reminders, photos, and videos.
- *Edmodo* uses the web to provide secure and safe social networking for students and teachers. Edmodo promotes collaboration and shared content/information. It can also provide access to homework, grades and school notices.
- *ClassDojo* provides avenues for positive classroom management including soft skills such as grit, curiosity, and focus.

Presentation

- *Creaza Education* uses a web-based application offering tools to students encouraging them to use their imagination to create, publish, and share digital stories. Creaza also has tools for online mind mapping, cartoon creation, audio editing, and moving editing.
- *Gloster* provides digital tools to create poster or graphic blog using text, music, images, and video. Also includes a safe and private classroom management platform. Free educator accounts available.
- *Animoto* uses a web-based application to turn photos, video clips, and music into video slideshows. Free accounts are available, but have limited features.
- *Kerpoof Studio* is designed for young children and allows them to make a movie, card, drawing, or picture. There is also a story-telling option.
- *Prezi* is presentation software that uses spatial relationships, motion, and zoom.
- *Slideshare* provides users the ability to publically or privately share their PowerPoint, Word documents, and Adobe PDF portfolios.
- *Jing* allows users to capture and share images and videos.

Note-Taking

- *Evernote* allows photos, recordings, and notes to be stored in one place.
- *OneNote* follows the concept of a physical notebook in the digital world accommodating both documents and images.
- *Noteshelf* facilitates the creation of individual files which allow PDFs to be uploaded and marked up or manipulated.
- *Notability* allows for sketching, voice memos, and recordings.

Other Interesting Technologies

- *Google Tools* provides a large number of options for sharing information, collaboration, surveys, etc. The benefit of Google Tools is productivity of collaboration in real time.
- *Office 365* by Microsoft offers access to Microsoft Office applications through cloud services.
- *DropBox* is a cloud-based storage for synced files and documents that can be easily shared or retrieved.

◆ REFERENCES

Albirini, A. (2006). Teachers' attitudes towards information and communication technologies: The case of Syrian EFL teachers. *Computers & Education, 47*(4), 373–398.

Allen, I. E., & Seaman, J. (2013). *Changing course: Ten years of tracking online education in the United States.* Babson Park, MA: Babson Survey Research Group and QuahogResearch Group. Retrieved from http://www.onlinelearningsurvey.com/reports/changingcourse.pdf

Almekhalafi, A. G., & Almeqdadi, F. A. (2010). Teachers' perceptions of technology integration in the United Arab Emirates school classrooms. *Educational Technology & Society, 13*(1), 165–175.

Armstrong, S., & Warlick, D. (2004, September). *The new literacy. Tech-learning: The resource or technology education.* Retrieved from http://www.techlearning.com/showArticle .jhml?articleID=47102021

Augar, N., Raitman, R., & Zhou, W. (2004). Teaching and learning online with wikis. *Proceedings of the 21st ASCILITE Conference.* Retrieved from http://www.ascilite.org.au/conferences/perth04/ procs/augar.html

Bauer, J., & Kenton, J. (2005). Toward technology integration in the schools: Why it isn't happening. *Journal of Technology and Teacher Education, 13*(4), 519–546.

Bawden, D. (2001). Information and digital literacies: A review of concepts. *Journal of Documentation, 57,* 218–259. Retrieved from http://arizona.openrepository.com/arizona/ bitstream/10150/105803/1/bawden.pdf

Baylor, R., & Ritchie, D. (2002). What factors facilitate teacher skill, teacher morale, and perceived student learning in technology-using classrooms? *Computers & Education, 39*(4), 395–414.

Beaudoin, M. F., Kutz, G., & Eden, S. (2009). Experiences and opinions of e-learners: What works, what are the challenges, and what competencies ensure successful online learning. *Interdisciplinary Journal of E-Learning and Learning Objects, 5,* 275–289.

Becker, K. (2007). Digital game-based learning once removed: Teaching teachers. *British Journal of Educational Technology, 38*(3), 478–488.

Bennett, S., & Maton, K. (2010). Beyond the "digital natives" debate: Towards a more nuanced understanding of students' technology experiences. *Journal of Computer Assisted Learning, 26,* 321–331.

Bickford, A. (2005, January). *Analysis of 2004 MAP results for eMINTS students.* Columbia, MO: Office of Social and Economic Data Analysis. Retrieved from http://www.emints.org/evaluation/ reports/map2004.pdf

Bingimlas, K. A. (2009, March). Barriers to the successful integration of ICT in teaching and learning environments: A review of the literature. *Eurasia Journal of Mathematics, Science & Technology Education, 5*(3), 235–245. Retrieved from http://www.ejmste.com/v5n3/eurasia_v5n3_bingimlas .pdf

Boyd, D. (2004). The characteristics of successful online learners. *New Horizons in Adult Education and Human Resource Development, 18*(2), 31–39.

British Educational Communications and Technology Agency (BECTA). (2004). *A review of the research literature on barriers to the uptake of ICT by teachers.* Retrieved from http://dera.ioe .ac.uk/1603/1/becta_2004_barrierstouptake_litrev.pdf

Brown, B. C. (2009). *An examination of the relationship between digital literacy and student achievement in Texas elementary schools.* Norman, OK: University of Oklahoma. Retrieved from http://gradworks.umi.com/3352840.pdf

Butzin, S. M. (2000). Project CHILD: A decade of success for young children. *Technology Horizons in Education Journal, 27*(11), 90. Retrieved from http://www.thejournal.com/articles/14835

Cavanagh, S. (2013). Rapid rise seen in use of digital tools for PD. *Education Week, 6*(3), 10.

CEO Forum on Education & Technology. (2001a). *The CEO forum STaR chart: A tool for accessing school technology and readiness.* Washington, DC: Author.

CEO Forum on Education and Technology. (2001b, June). *The CEO Forum school technology and readiness report: Key building blocks for student achievement in the 21st century.* Retrieved from http://www.ceoforum.org/downloads/report4.pdf

Chinnery, G. M. (2006). Emerging technologies: Going to the MALL (Mobile Assisted Language Learning). *Language Learning & Technology, 10,* 9–16.

Clark, K. (2006). Practices for the use of technology in high schools: A Delphi study. *Journal of Technology and Teacher Education, 14*(3), 481–499.

Cohen, D. (1988). Educational technology and school organization. In R. S. Nickerson & P. P. Zodhiates (Eds.), *Technology in education: Looking toward 2020* (pp. 231–264). Hillsdale, NJ: Erlbaum.

Council of Chief State School Officers. (n.d.). *2014 ISLLC Standards: Draft for public comment.* Retrieved from http://blogs.edweek.org/edweek/District_Dossier/Draft%202014%20ISLLC%20 Standard s%2009102014.pdf

Cuban, L. (2001). *Oversold and underused: Reforming schools through technology, 1980–2000.* Cambridge, MA: Harvard University Press.

Darling-Hammond, L., & Bransford, J. (2005). *Preparing teachers for a changing world: What teachers should learn and be able to do.* San Francisco, CA: Jossey-Bass.

de Waard, I., Koutropoulos, A., Keskin, N., Abajian, S. C., Hogue, R., Rodriguez, C. O., & Gallagher, M. S. (2011). Exploring the MOOC format as a pedagogical approach for mLearning. In *Proceedings of 10th World Conference on Mobile and Contextual Learning* (pp. 138–145). Retrieved from http://mlearn.bnu.edu.cn/source/ten_outstanding_papers/Exploring the MOOC format as a pedagogical approach for mLearning.pdf

EdTech Action Network. (2011). *Why technology in schools?* Retrieved from http://www .edtechactionnetwork.org/why-technology-in-schools.

Ertmer, P., & Ottenbreit-Leftwich, A. T. (2010). Teacher technology change: how knowledge, confidence, beliefs, and culture intersect. *Journal of Research on Technology in Education, 42*(3), 255–284.

Evans, C. (2008). The effectiveness of m-learning in the form of podcast revision lectures in higher education. *Computers & Education, 50*(2008), 491–498.

Federal Communications Commission. (2014a, December 18). *Universal service program for schools and libraries (e-rate).* Retrieved from https://www.fcc.gov/guides/universal-service-program-schools-and-libraries

Federal Communications Commission. (2014b, December 11). *FCC continues e-rate reboot to meet nation's digital learning needs.* Retrieved from https://www.fcc.gov/document/fcc-continues-e-rate-reboot-meet-nations-digital-learning-needs

Federal Communications Commission. (2010). *FCC enables high-speed, affordable broadband for schools and libraries, September 23, 2010.* Retrieved from https://www.fcc.gov/document/ fcc-enables-high-speed-affordable-broadband-schools-and-libraries

Foundation for Excellence in Education. (2014). *Summary of the e-rate modernization order.* Retrieved from http://digitallearningnow.com/site/uploads/2014/09/ExcelinEd-E-rate-Summary. pdf

Freidman, V., Beauchamp, J., Blain, S., Lirett-Pitre, N., & Fournier, H. (2011). Problem-based scenarios with laptops: An effective combination for cross-curricular learning in mathematics, science, and language. *World Journal on Technology Education, 3*(3), 136–152.

French, J. R. P., & Raven, B. H. (1968). Bases of social power. In D. Cartwright and A. F. Zander (Eds.), *Group dynamics: Research and theory* (pp. 259–270). New York, NY: Harper & Row.

Gillen, J., & Barton, D. (2009). *Digital literacies.* London Knowledge Lab, London. Retrieved from http://www.tlrp.org/tel/files/2009/02/digital-literacies-gillen-barton-2009.pdf

Gilster, P. (1997). *Digital literacy.* New York, NY: Wiley.

Glass, G. V. (2010, April). Potholes in the road to virtual schooling. *The School Administrator, 67,* 32–35.

Guo, L., Fu, Y., Yin, X., Yuan, M., Zhang, F., & Gao, J. (2013). Application of mobile learning system in operating system course. *Communications and Network, 5*(2), 157–160. doi: 10.4236/cn.2013.52017

Haystead, M. W., & Marzano, R. J. (2010). *Preliminary report: A second year evaluation study of Promethean ActivClassroom.* Englewood, CO: Marzano Research Laboratory.

Helsper, E. J., & Eynon, R. (2009). Digital natives: Where is the evidence? *British Educational Research Journal, 36*(3), 503–520.

Hewagamage, K. P., Wickramasinghe, W. M. A. S. B., & Jayatilaka, A. DeS. (2012). "M-learning not an extension of e-learning": Based on a case study of Moodle VLE. *International Journal of Mobile and Blended Learning, 4*(4), 21–33.

Hodas, S. (1993). Technology refusal and the organizational culture of schools. *Education Policy Analysis Archives, 1*(10). Retrieved from http://epaa.asu.edu/epaa/v1n10.html

Inan, F. A., & Lowther, D. L. (2010). Laptops in the K-12 classrooms: Exploring factors impacting instructional use. *Computers & Education, 55*(3), 937–944.

Institute of Educational Sciences. (2013). *Fast facts: Number and internet access of instructional computers and rooms in public schools, selected by school characteristics: Selected years, 1995 through 2008.* Washington, DC: National Center for Education Statistics. Retrieved from https://nces.ed.gov/programs/digest/d12/tables/dt12_120.asp

Institute of Educational Sciences. (2010). *Teachers' use of educational technology in U.S. public schools: 2009.* Washington, DC: National Center for Education Statistics. Retrieved from https://nces.ed.gov/pubs2010/2010040.pdf

International Society for Technology in Education. (2009a). *National educational technology standards for administrators (NETS·A).* Arlington, VA: Author. Retrieved from http://www.iste.org/Content/NavigationMenu/NETS/ForAdministrators/NETS_for_Administrators.htm

International Society for Technology in Education. (2009b). *NETS for administrators 2009.* Arlington, VA: Author. Retrieved from http://www.iste.org/Content/NavigationMenu/NETS/ForAdministrators/2009Standards/NETS_for_Administrators_2009.htm

International Society for Technology in Education. (2008). *NETS for teachers 2008.* Arlington, VA: Author. Retrieved from http://www.iste.org/docs/pdfs/nets-t-standards.pdf?sfvrsn=2

International Society for Technology in Education. (2007a). *NETS for students 2007.* Arlington, VA: Author. Retrieved from http://www.iste.org/docs/pdfs/nets-s-standards.pdf?sfvrsn=2

International Society for Technology in Education. (2007b). *Profiles for technology (ICT) literate students.* Arlington, VA: Author. Retrieved from http://www.iste.org/docs/pdfs/nets-s-2007-student-profiles-en.pdf?sfvrsn=4

Jensen, E. (2005). *Teaching with the brain in mind* (2nd ed.). Alexandria, VA: ASCD.

Jukes, I., & Dosaj, A. (2006, September). *Understanding digital children (DKs): Teaching and learning in the new digital landscape.* The InfoSavvy Group lecture prepared for the Singapore Ministry of Education Conference. Retrieved from https://edorigami.wikispaces.com/file/view/Jukes+-+Understanding+Digital+Kids.pdf

Kahveci, M. (2010). Students' perceptions to use technology for learning: Measurement integrity of the modified Efnnema-Sherman Attitude Scales. *Turkish Online Journal of Educational Technology, 9*(1), 185–201.

Kearney, M., Schuck, S., Burden, K., & Aubusson, P. (2012). Viewing mobile learning from a pedagogical perspective. *Research in Learning Technology 20*: 14406—doi: 10.3402/rlt. v20i0.14406

Keser, H., Uzunboylu, H., & Ozdamli, F. (2011). The trends in technology supported collaborative learning studies in 21st century. *World Journal on Educational Technology, 3*(2), 103–119.

Kopcha, T. J. (2012). Teachers' perceptions of the barriers to technology integration and practices with technology under situated professional development. *Computers & Education, 59*, 1109–1121. Retrieved from http://marianrosenberg.wiki.westga.edu/file/view/KopchaTTeachersPerceptions.pdf

Kotrlik, J., & Redmann, D. (2005). Extent of technology integration in instruction by adult basic education teachers. *Adult Education Quarterly: A Journal of Research and Theory, 55*(3), 200–219.

Lee, Y., & Choi, J. (2011). A review of online course dropout research: Implications for practice and future research. *Educational Technology Research and Development, 59*, 593–618.

Lei, J. (2010). Quantity versus quality: A new approach to examine the relationship between technology use and student outcomes. *British Journal of Educational Technology, 41*, 455–472.

Lenhart, A. (2015, April). *Teen, social media, & technology: Overview 2015.* Retrieved from http://www.pewinternet.org/2015/04/09/teens-social-media-technology-2015/

Lenhart, A., Purcell, K., Smith, A., & Zickuhr, K. (2010, February). *Social media and young adults.* Retrieved from http://www.pewinternet.org/2010/02/03/social-media-and-young-adults/

Liberman, A., & Mace, D. P. (2010). Making practice public: Teacher learning in the 21st century. *Journal of Teacher Education, 61*(1–2), 77–88. doi: 10.1177/0022487109347319

Lowther, D. L., Inan, F. A., Strahl, D., & Ross, S. M. (2008). Does technology integration "work" when key barriers are removed? *Educational Media International, 45*(3), 195–213.

Mann, D. (2001). Documenting the effects of instructional technology, a fly-over of policy questions. In W. F. Heineke & L. Blasi (Eds.), *Research methods for educational technology: Methods of evaluating educational technology, Vol. 1* (pp. 239–249). Greenwich, CT: Information Age.

Mann, D., Shakeshaft, C., Becker, J., & Kottkamp, R. (1999). *Achievement gains from a statewide comprehensive instructional technology program.* Santa Monica, CA: Milken Family Foundation.

Markow, D., & Cooper, M. (2008, October). *The MetLife survey of the American teacher: Past, present, and future.* New York, NY: MetLife. Retrieved from http://www.metlife.com/assets/cao/contributions/citizenship/teacher-survey-25th-anniv-2008.pdf

Matthewman, S., & Triggs, P. (2004). "Obsessive compulsive font disorder": the challenge of supporting pupils writing with the computer. *Computers & Education, 43*(1–2), 125–135.

McAuley, A., Stewart, B., Siemens, G., & Cormier, D. (2010). *The MOOC model for digital practice.* Retrieved from http://www.elearnspace.org/Articles/MOOC_Final.pdf

McClure, M., Jukes, I., & MacLean, R. (2011). *Getting it right: Aligning technology initiatives ormeasurable student results.* Thousand Oaks, CA: Corwin Press.

Texas Education Agency. (2011). *Technology applications TEKS*. Austin, TX: Author. Retrieved from http://www.tea.state.tx.us/index2.aspx?id=8192

Texas Education Agency. (2014). *Texas campus and teacher school technology and readiness (STaR) charts*. Austin, TX: Author. Retrievedfrom http://tea.texas.gov/About_TEA/News_and_Multimedia/Correspondence/TAA_Letters/Texas_Campus_and_Teacher_School_Technology_and_Readiness_(STaR)_Charts/

Texas Education Agency. (2015a). *Texas virtual school network—Online schools program*. Austin, TX: Author. Retrieved from http://tea.texas.gov/Curriculum_and_Instructional_Programs/Learning_Support_and_Programs/Texas_Virtual_School_Network/Texas_Virtual_School_Network_-_Online_Schools_Program/

Texas Education Agency. (2015b). *Texas virtual school networks: Reports*. Austin, TX: Author. Retrieved from https://catalog.mytxvsn.org/enrollments

Texas Education Code. (2015). Chapter 30A. *State virtual school network*. Retrieved from http://www.statutes.legis.state.tx.us/Docs/ED/htm/ED.30A.htm

Trzeniewski, K. H., & Donnellan, M. B. (2010). Rethinking "generation me": A study of cohort effects from 1976–2006. *Perspectives on Psychological Science, 5*(2), 58–75.

Vu, P., Cao, V., Vu, L., & Cepero, J. (2014, June). Factors driving learner success in Online Professional Development. *The International Review of Research in Open and Distance Learning, 15*(3), 121–139.

Warlick, D. (2007). Literacy in the new information landscape. *Library Media Connection, 26*(1), 20–21.

Willis, J. (2008). Building a bridge from neuroscience to the classroom. *Phi Delta Kappan, 89*(6).424–427.

Zorfass, J., & Rivero, H. (2005). Collaboration is a key: How a community of practice promotes technology integration. *Journal of Special Education Technology, 20*(3), 51–60.

Zuboff, S. (1988). *In the age of the smart machine: The future of work and power.* New York, NY: Basic Books.

URBAN SCHOOLS

Kriss Kemp-Graham

Urban schools and urban students are faced with numerous challenges; however, these challenges are not unique only to cities and it is important to note that not all urban schools face the same challenges. Albeit, urban schools are quantitatively and qualitatively different than suburban and rural schools. Suburban and rural schools do not operate in densely populated areas such as one would find in urban school districts. Urban schools are also composed of higher concentrations of student poverty, larger percentages of ethnic and linguistic student diversity, higher concentrations of immigrant populations and high rates of student mobility when compared to rural and suburban school districts (Ahram, Stembridge, Fergus, & Noguera, 2013; Jacob, 2007).

Urban schools by definition are located in cities. However descriptors, "city" and "urban" may bring to mind contrasting images. Contingent upon where one lives, works and plays in the nation's cities, divergent experiences and realities of "city" life exist. Imageries of cities may be reminiscent of culture, arts, wealth, theaters, skyscrapers, corporate headquarters and law and order, whereas descriptions of "urban" may evoke images of dilapidated buildings, crime, drugs, poverty, unemployment and lawlessness (Dixson, Royal, & Jr, 2013; Jacob, 2007). One may query the authenticity of two contrasting views of one city thus ascribing the dichotomy of the observations as illogical or counterintuitive. However divergent realisms of the lived experiences of city residents do exist and can result in "two distinct narratives" of the same city. When visually or mentally pondering the possibility of this phenomena, the cleverly penned words found in the opening lines of Charles Dickens' classical novel *A Tale of Two Cities* may provide a more palatable context:

> It was the best of times, it was the worst of times, it was the age of wisdom, it was the age of foolishness, it was the epoch of belief, it was the epoch of incredulity, it was the season of Light, it was the season of Darkness, it was the spring of hope, it was the winter of despair, we had everything before us, we had nothing before us. (Dickens, 2000)

As the imagery and passion found in Dickens' words resonates, let's explore the urbanity of Dallas, TX, the 9th largest city in the United States. There are 1.25 million persons living in

Dallas, TX; 42% Hispanic, 25% Black and 30% White. The city of Dallas accounts for 27% of the economic output in Texas. If the city of Dallas were a Fortune 1000 company it would be ranked #801 (Dallas Office of Economic Development, 2015). Dallas is one of the leading corporate headquarters in the United States where 21 Fortune 500 companies and 656 local business headquarters are located. Of Forbes' largest privately held companies, seven are also located in the Dallas area. Examples of Fortune 500 Companies located in Dallas are listed below:

- Exxon Mobil
- American Airlines Group
- Fluor Corp.
- Kimberly-Clark
- J.C. Penney
- GameStop D.R. Horton, Inc.
- Commercial Metals
- Celanese
- Dr. Pepper Snapple Group
- Alliance Data Systems
- Pioneer Natural Resources

In Dallas, there are thousands of restaurants, more restaurants per capita than any other U.S. city. The Dallas Arts District is home to a diverse mix of museums, performance halls, restaurants, and residences. Dallas is also home to the largest collection of Art Deco architecture in the world and hosts the largest state fair in the country, the State Fair of Texas. Housing types in Dallas consist of high rise apartment buildings with concierge services, mansions, bungalows, ranch homes and low income subsidized housing (Dallas Office of Economic Development, 2015). Home prices in Dallas can range from $53,000 in Park Row to $1.8 million in Bluffview.

Dallas is a city where the rich are very rich, and the poor are very poor. Dallas was ranked number 13 in the US in terms of income inequality. In 2012, the top 5% of households earned about $200,000, ~11 times more than the $17,000 earned by the poorest 20% of households in Dallas, TX (Jean, 2014). Given the inequality of wealth in Dallas, the city has struggled to maintain mixed-income school environments that could produce satisfactory outcomes for low-income kids (Nicholson, 2015). The pervasiveness of the income inequality in Dallas, like most big cities in the US, often results in high concentrations of poor persons residing in the same impoverished under-resourced neighborhoods. Impoverished communities are associated with numerous risk factors that adversely impact children and their academic success. Although students reside in Dallas, a city known for its wealth, culture, art, philanthropy, glamour and glitz, a great majority of students attending public schools in Dallas are not beneficiaries of those accouterments. The demographics of the students attending public schools in the Dallas Independent School District are as follows:

- Approximately 90% of students attending Dallas public schools in DISD are economically challenged
- 61% of children in Dallas live in low income housing
- 38% of children under the age of 18 live in poverty
- 50,000 children live in extreme poverty (incomes less than $12K for a family of 4)
- 111,000 (35%) of children live in areas of high concentrations of poverty (Kids Count, 2015).

The city of Dallas is not an anomaly in terms of its economic inequality and high concentrations of student poverty. A similar socio economic trend exists for large cities throughout the nation such as New York, Los Angeles, Houston and Chicago. Decades of research on urban areas in the US have consistently informed us that where there are large concentrations of poverty, there will also be large concentrations of failing schools.

◆ URBAN SCHOOL DISTRICTS IN TEXAS-MACRO PERSPECTIVE

In Texas, urban school districts are defined as follows:

The largest school districts in the state that serve the six metropolitan areas of Houston, Dallas, San Antonio, Fort Worth, Austin, and El Paso. Major urban districts are the districts with the greatest membership in counties with populations of 870,000 or more, and more than 35% of the students are identified as economically disadvantaged. In some cases, other size threshold criteria may apply (Texas Education Agency, 2015).

In Texas, there are 11 urban school districts which represent less than 1% of all school districts in Texas; however, 19% of the student population in Texas are educated in urban schools; roughly 1 million students. Urban school students in Texas represent 15% of all students enrolled in urban schools in the United States. During the 2014–2015 school year, the characteristics of the students attending schools in urban districts in Texas were as follows:

- 41% of the all economically disadvantaged students in Texas attend urban schools;
- 23% of all African American students enrolled in Texas attend urban schools;
- 25% of all Hispanic students enrolled in Texas attend urban schools;
- 33% of all LEP students in the state of Texas attend urban schools; and
- More than 83% of urban school students in Texas are non-white.

◆ URBAN SCHOOLS IN TEXAS-MICRO PERSPECTIVE

Of all of the school types in Texas (i.e., urban, rural, town) based on locale, urban schools have the highest percentage of non-White students at 83%; highest percentage of economically disadvantaged students at 73.6%; the highest percentage of ELL students at 25.7%; and the highest percentage of bilingual/ESL students at 24.5% (Texas Education Agency, 2015).

According to the Texas Education Agency (2015), urban schools have the highest percentage of teachers with less than 5 years teaching experience (34%), the highest percentage of non-White teachers (54.5%), of and highest student to teacher ratio of 16.3. In terms of academics, 14% of the schools located in urban districts have a school accountability rating of Needs Improvement; the lowest percentage of students scoring at or above criterion for college admissions; lowest average SAT score (1331); the lowest ACT average score (19.3); the highest percentage of annual high school dropout rates (2013–2014 school year) of 2.4% and correspondingly have the lowest graduation rate of 85.7% (Texas Education Agency, 2015).

In terms of finance, on average urban schools in Texas have the third lowest total revenues per pupil of $9,681 compared to the highest amount of $12,346 spent in rural schools statewide, the lowest percentage of the school funding for urban schools comes from the state of about 32% and the highest percentage of school funding for urban schools comes from the federal government of 13.2% (Texas Education Agency, 2015). Demographic information for each of the 11 urban school districts in Texas are reported in Table 24.1.

TABLE 24.1
Texas Urban School District Student Demographics

School District	# of Students	Total Non-White	Black	Hispanic	Econ Dis.	ELL
Houston	210,716	87%	25%	62%	81%	30%
Dallas	159,487	93%	23%	70%	89%	40%
Northwest	101,549	75%	6%	69%	52%	7%
Austin	85,014	68%	8%	60%	61%	27%
Fort Worth	84,360	86%	23%	63%	77%	31%
North East	67,986	64%	7%	57%	47%	10%
Arlington	64,629	68%	8%	60%	61%	27%
El Paso	61,290	87%	4%	83%	70%	25%
San Antonio	53,811	98%	6%	91%	93%	19%
Socorro	44,405	93%	2%	91%	72%	20%
Ysleta	43,007	95%	2%	93%	81%	25%

Poor students throughout the nation have historically had higher rates of academic under-achievement than their non-poor peers, and this same achievement gap exists in schools in Texas. Student scores from the state standardized exams for the last five years are reported in Table 24.2.

◆ URBAN POVERTY AND STUDENT ACADEMIC ACHIEVEMENT

> Making bold assertions that all children can achieve while doing nothing to address the challenges they face is neither fair nor sound public policy.
> —Noguera (2011)

Urban poverty occurs in cities with populations of 50,000 or more. Persons living in urban poverty contend with numerous deprivations. Challenges may include one or more of the following:

- Limited access to employment opportunities and income,
- Inadequate and insecure housing and services,
- Violent and unhealthy environments,
- Little or no social protection mechanisms, and
- Limited access to adequate health and education opportunities (Jensen, 2009; WorldBank, 2011).

Low-income students and English Language Learners in Texas perform lower on state standardized exams for every content area assessed and for all grades that are tested than their-non-low income peers. In every grade, low-income students in Texas are retained at a

TABLE 24.2

Five Year Trend of the Percentage Passing Rate on State Standardized Tests in Texas by Subgroups in Grades 3–12 for the SY2013-14

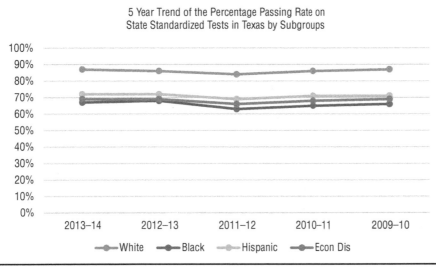

Source: Texas Education Agency Website

rate of 2.4 times their non-low-income peers (Lee & Shea, 2015). Factors associated with poverty have resulted in creating a negative trajectory of academic success for many low-income culturally and linguistically diverse students. The impact of poverty and academic achievement has been well documented in the research literature for decades. Empirical research has informed us that being poor, minority and linguistically diverse does not in and of itself indicate or serve as a predictor of academic failure. However, the juxtaposition of these student characteristics with the ecological contexts of urban communities, school district and school capacities often present unique, and for some schools and districts, insurmountable challenges that result in the lack of opportunity for success among ALL children; thus academic failure of students who are poor, minority and linguistically diverse results.

Researchers present compelling evidence that suggest environmental obstacles exist for poor urban students who reside in neighborhoods with high concentrations of poverty of which can adversely impact their academic achievement (Ahram et al., 2013; Berliner, 2009; Jackson & Feuerstein, 2014; Jackson & McDermott, 2012; Kataoka et al., 2011; Kim, Mazza, Zwanziger, & Henry, 2014; Nikulina, Widom, & Czaja, 2011; Noguera, 2011; Noguera & Williams, 2010; Perkins & Graham-Bermann, 2012).

Environmental obstacles refers to the adverse, "conditions that influence students' health, safety, and well-being which influences learning" (Noguera, 2011, p. 10). Noguera references William Julius Wilson theory of the "concentration effect" when explaining environmental obstacles poor urban children experience. In cities with high concentrations of poverty, communities lack services to adequately address the numerous mental health and medical issues that are present due to high levels of violence and poor health. Children being raised in these communities experience a lower quality of life and overall health when compared to their middle class peers. Children living in low-income neighborhoods have lower quality social, municipal and local services that their families can access for assistance. Additionally, poor children are more frequently exposed to crime, violence, inadequate healthcare, over crowded homes, mobility, mental and physical abuse, poor nutrition and diet resulting in emotional and social challenges, acute and chronic stress, cognitive delays, health and safety issues. These insidious challenges are multifaceted and multilayered—one creating another resulting in an unending cycle of adverse consequences for poor students that are damaging to their physical, socio-emotional and cognitive well-being (Jensen, 2009).

> The opportunity gap is the unconscionable disparity in access to the quality educational resources needed for all children to be academically successful. Students from historically disadvantaged families have just a 51% Opportunity to Learn compared to White, non-Latino students. Closing this opportunity gap is essential to closing the academic achievement gaps that separate most Black and Hispanic students from their White and Asian peers.
> —National Opportunity to Learn Campaign

In order for all children to be successful academically, ALL children must be provided with opportunities to be successful. Decades of school reform have been implemented with the goals of leveling the achievement playing field for poor urban students, beginning with ESEA: Title I Funding, Goals 2000, No Child Left Behind and Race to the Top. Billions of public dollars have been expended to support the improvement of educational opportunities for millions of urban students in the US over several decades. Unfortunately, these efforts have consistently failed to have sustained and replicable results for all urban school students (Heilig, Khalifa, & Tillman, 2013; Jackson & Feuerstein, 2014; Ladd, 2012). A burgeoning empirical research base has begun to emerge which informs us that "within school" reform initiatives cannot be successful without the intentional focus on mediating out of school factors that have been proven to adversely impact the educational success of urban school students (Ahram et al., 2013; Berliner, 2009; Jackson & Feuerstein, 2014; Jackson & Veronica McDermott, 2012; Kataoka et al., 2011; Kim et al., 2014; Nikulina et al., 2011; Noguera, 2011; Noguera & Williams, 2010; Perkins & Graham-Bermann, 2012).

◆ ECOLOGICAL APPROACH: IMPACT OF OUT OF SCHOOL FACTORS ON ACADEMIC ACHIEVEMENT

> The occasional school that overcomes the effects of academically detrimental inputs—high rates of food insecurity, single heads of households, family and neighborhood violence, homelessness and transiency, illnesses and dental needs that are not medically insured, special education needs, language minority populations and so forth—has allowed some advocates to declare that schools, virtually alone, can ensure the high achievement of impoverished youth.
> —Berliner (2009)

In the United States, students spend ~1,150 hours yearly in school and approximately 4,700 waking hours with their family and community (Berliner, 2009). The thought that home and community context for urban students would not be considered when attempting to close the achievement gap is unfathomable. Research informs us that individual and family characteristics may have between four and eight times the impact on student achievement than teachers (Rand Education, 2012).

An ecological approach should be considered when examining academic underachievement of poor students residing in highly disadvantaged neighborhoods. Noted psychologist and seminal child development researcher Bronfenbrenner (1994) argued that in order to understand human development, there must be a consideration of the entire environment from which the person grows which includes community context. The findings from empirical research exploring the ecological theory developed by Bronfenbrenner to understand the impact of community context and urban student academic and social behaviors in schools has been presented in the research (Bowen & Bowen, 1999; Johnson, 1994; Leonard, 2011; Samson & Lesaux, 2015; Strayhorn, 2009). The findings are clear, the influence of community factors such as the lack of access to key resources, exposure to health and safety risks and overall quality of life will have a powerful influence on poor urban student academic and social performance in schools. According to Jensen (2009) children in poverty are more likely to display the following behaviors:

- Acting out
- Impatience and impulsivity
- Gaps in politeness and social graces
- Limited range of behavior responses
- Inappropriate emotional responses
- Less empathy for others' misfortunes. (Jensen, 2009, p. 19)

Teachers will often misinterpret these behaviors as willful defiance or lack of respect which then results in negative consequences for students who may not have developed the appropriate social responses from their homes (Jensen, 2009). As with income and high quality resourced schools, out of school risk factors such as violence, poverty, inadequate healthcare and food insecurity are not equally distributed throughout the nation. In fact these risk factors are more concentrated in poor communities where poor children of color reside and attend school.

There has been an ongoing debate in the research literature on the factors that impact academic achievement. An exhaustive listing of confounding factors exist that contribute to the underachievement of poor minority children, thus no one factor alone can be used to explain this phenomena (i.e., poverty, single parent households, ineffective teachers). A combination of in school and out of school factors is essential to understanding underachievement of poor children. Ladd (2012) proffers that student educational outcomes are a function of both public school quality and community context [f(public school quality, context)]. The researcher defines public school quality as the quality of the school the student attends and context is defined as the socioeconomic background of students, cultural memberships and familial commitments to the education of their children.

The confluence of factors present in low-income communities such as violence, abuse, malnutrition and hunger and inadequate healthcare individually and collectively must be taken into consideration when pondering the ways and means of leveling the academic achievement playing field for children of color. Poor children who are exposed to violence, are food insecure and lack adequate medical insurance often present academic and behavior problems. The problems are often mistaken by teachers and school leaders as indicators of cognitive deficiencies and/or learning disabilities and as result a disproportionate number of poor, minority and linguistically diverse students are referred for special education intervention and services.

Violence

According to the FBI, approximately 80% of crimes in 2013 were committed in the city, compared to 28% in the suburbs and 3% in the non metropolitan areas (The Federal Bureau of Investigations, 2015). In 2014, 1,825 children were abused and neglected per day in the US (Children's Defense Fund, 2014). Children exposed to violence often show higher incidences of aggressive behavior, depression and anxiety which manifests negatively into diminished academic performance (Jackson & Feuerstein, 2014; Jensen, 2009). In fact, stress produced from experiencing violence can change hormonal levels of children which then has a negative impact on a child's brain (Berliner, 2009; Perkins & Graham-Bermann, 2012). Perkins and Graham-Bermann (2012) report that children with a history of violence exposure often withdraw socially and behaviorally, which may result in possible problems with peer relationships especially in school settings. The researchers further state that children who experience violence may exhibit neurological changes that can lead to problems of cognition in memory, executive functioning (i.e., the ability to organize of synthesize information) and learning delays (Perkins & Graham-Bermann, 2012). Perkins and Graham-Bermann (2012) also reported that children who experience child abuse and neglect have twice the rate of referral for special education. Additional research has been reported that children who have prolonged exposure to violence may experience decreased IQ and reading ability, lower grade point averages, more days of absence from school and decreased rates of graduation from high school (Kataoka et al., 2011).

In a study conducted by the United States Department of Justice on children exposed to violence, the following was reported:

- Children exposed to violence are more likely to abuse drugs and alcohol; suffer from depression, anxiety, and post-traumatic disorders; fail or have difficulty in school; and become delinquent and engage in criminal behavior.
- Sixty percent of American children were exposed to violence, crime, or abuse in their homes, schools, and communities.
- Almost 40% of American children were direct victims of two or more violent acts, and one in ten were victims of violence five or more times.
- Children are more likely to be exposed to violence and crime than adults.
- Almost one in ten American children saw one family member assault another family member, and more than 25% had been exposed to family violence during their life.
- A child's exposure to one type of violence increases the likelihood that the child will be exposed to other types of violence and exposed multiple times (Finkelhor, Turner, Ormrod, Hamby, & Krackle, 2009).

Hunger/Food Insecurity/Malnutrition

One in nine children in the United States are food insecure which means that students who reside in homes that are food insecure do not have ongoing access to adequate quantities of food that is nutritious (Children's Defense Fund, 2014). According to the Children's Defense Fund, 2014, Texas ranked 45th in nation in terms of the percentage of children in households that lacked access to adequate food (1 being the least and 50 being the highest). Food insecurity is 3.4 more times likely to occur in homes with incomes below the poverty level; 2.7 times more likely in single female parent households; two times more likely in black and Hispanic homes. Food insecurity is an issue for both urban and rural communities.

Research reported by Wilder Research (2014) and Centers for Disease Control and Prevention (2014) have found that good nutrition can be linked to school behavior and academic achievement. For a child under the age of three, the lack of a nutritional diet can negatively impact their entire school career. The lack of food results in the children not being adequately nourished. They may lack energy, can become apathetic and have impaired cognitive capacity. Malnutrition can adversely impact the architecture of the brain; lessons in prefrontal cortex of the brain can develop which impact high order thinking and problem solving. Further, malnutrition has been found to negatively impact the development of neural systems of children which can stunt the development of language and executive functioning such as paying attention, remembering details and higher level thinking skills (Jackson & Feuerstein, 2014). Poor nutrition can result in students having headaches and stomach aches resulting in missed school days and essential instructional time. Children need balanced healthy diets comprised of protein, carbohydrates and glucose which has been shown to improve students cognition, concentration and energy levels (Wilder Research, 2014). Centers for Disease Control and Prevention (2014) reported the following trends related to diet and student academic achievement.

- Skipping breakfast is associated with decreased cognitive performance (e.g., alertness, attention, memory, processing of complex visual display, problem solving) among students.
- Lack of adequate consumption of specific foods, such as fruits, vegetables, or dairy products, is associated with lower grades among students.
- Deficits of specific nutrients (i.e., vitamins A, B6, B12, C, folate, iron, zinc, and calcium) are associated with lower grades and higher rates of absenteeism and tardiness among students.
- Absenteeism, repeating a grade, and an inability to focus among students.

In a cross-sectional study of the diet quality and weight status in 248 randomly selected low-income urban children, aged 7–13 years, the researchers reported that

- Over 75% of participants in this study failed to meet minimum recommended servings for grains, vegetables, dairy, and fruit group.
- Sixty-nine percent of participants failed to meet the recommended requirement for meat.
- Over 90% of the children surveyed did not meet the recommendations for dairy and vegetable intake.
- 24% of the younger children and 47% of the older children did not meet the recommended Dietary Allowance for folate.
- 100% of the students did not meet the Recommended Dietary Allowance for iron (Langevin et al., 2007).

Food insecurity is not the only factor contributing to malnutrition in poor children, access to healthy fresh fruit and vegetables is limited in many urban communities. There are few full service grocery stores and/or farmers' markets that sell a variety of fruits and vegetables in low income communities, thus residents have limited to access to fresh fruit and dairy products. Full service grocery stores are often located outside of low-income communities so that transportation is required. Low income families located in low income neighborhoods often have to rely on neighborhood convenience stores and corner stores that may not readily stock fresh fruit and vegetables as their main source for groceries. In the instances when healthier food such as fresh fruit and vegetables are available, the food are much more expensive than would be found in middle and upper class neighborhoods (Food Research and Action Center, 2010).

Another important factor to consider in terms of the unhealthy diets of poor children is the easy access and availability of fast food in low-income communities. Fleischhacker, Evenson, Rodriguez, and Ammerman (2011) reviewed forty research studies conducted over a ten-year period that primarily examined fast food access and socioeconomic status. They found that in 76% of the articles, fast food restaurants were more prevalent in low income communities compared to middle and upper income neighborhoods and fast food restaurants are more prevalent in communities with high concentrations of minorities.

HealthCare

Children in poor families in the United States are six times less likely to be in good health, thus they will experience a wide variety illnesses and injuries at six times the rate of children from higher income families (Berliner, 2009). Poor attendance contributes to the achievement gap for students struggling with poverty and from communities of color. Chronic absenteeism is most prevalent among low income students (Balfanz & Byrnes, 2012).

According to the CDC, 4.8 million children do not have health insurance; 81% of the children live in cities. Approximately 89% of all Black children and 90% of Hispanic children who do not have health insurance live in the city (Schiller, Ward, & Freeman, 2014)

Texas is ranked 49th in the nation in terms of the percentage of children that do not have health insurance in 2013; that is approximately 888,000 children do not health coverage (Lee & Shea, 2015). Having medical insurance can provide families with the opportunities to seek medical attention for ill children, which will reduce student absenteeism due to medical issues and thus will positively impact student academic achievement.

Asthma. Children in poverty are disproportionately more likely to have asthma, and also disproportionately more likely to attend schools with lower indoor air quality (Sparks, 2012). Asthma is one of the most common chronic childhood illnesses, and it has been linked to higher rates of school absenteeism, lower grades and test scores. Poor children living in urban areas are also more likely to contract asthma from breathing fumes from low-grade heating oil, diesel trucks, and buses. Additionally, excessive dust and allergic reactions to mold, cockroaches, and secondhand smoke also contribute to the disproportionality of poor students in urban areas who suffer from Asthma. Unmet vision, hearing and dental problems also plague poor urban children which inadvertently impacts their academic achievement.

Vision Problems. Fifty percent of poor children have vision impairment that interferes with academic work, twice the normal rate (Rothstein, 2011). Poor minority children are two to three times more likely than white children to have unmet vision care needs (Hellen Keller International, 2015). Due to the lack of health insurance or access to eye doctors, unrecognized or untreated vision problems may contribute to higher incidences of urban youth with academic and behavioral challenges (Basch, 2010). In some instances, children who have undiagnosed eye problems have been misdiagnosed as having attention deficit disorders (Jackson & Feuerstein, 2014).

Dental Problems. Poor oral health, dental disease, and tooth pain can place poor urban children at a serious disadvantage in school. Untreated tooth decay can cause pain and infection that may lead to difficulty eating, speaking, socializing and sleeping, as well as poor overall health (Seirawan, Faust, & Mulligan, 2012). Inadequate dental care and prevention can lead to tooth pain, dental disease, and poor access to dental care adversely affect how children perform in school and are associated with increased school absences. Children with toothaches pay less attention in class and are more distracted during tests, which will negatively impact academic performance. Seirawan et al. (2012) researched the impact of dental diseases on the academic performance of disadvantaged children from Los Angeles County public schools found that:

- Students with toothaches were almost 4 times more likely to have low grade point averages.
- About 11% of students that did not have access to needed immediate dental care missed more school compared with 4% of those students that had access to dental care.
- Per 100 elementary and high school–aged children, 58 and 80 school hours, respectively, are missed annually due to lack of access to dental care providers to address dental concerns.

Hearing. Poor children also have more hearing difficulties, due to untreated ear infections that occur in children whose overall health is poor and for those who lack regular pediatric care. Poor children experiencing unaddressed hearing difficulty may appear to be less attentive or uninterested in school.

◆ INTERNAL CHALLENGES

Urban schools experience internal challenges that can adversely impact the opportunities for success for poor urban students. Urban schools are often under-resourced lacking both fiscal and human capital resulting in poor children being underfunded and undereducated producing under achievement.

Teacher Quality-Hard to Staff Schools

Teachers in urban schools face great challenges daily and are expected to achieve high stakes accountability measures of improved academic achievement of students with unmet academic and non-academic needs who have been traditionally under-educated, under-served in under resourced schools. Schools that experience high teacher turnover also experience low academic achievement (Boyd, Lankford, Loeb, & Wyckoff, 2005; Guin, 2004).

No other school factor has a greater impact on student achievement than an effective teacher (Darling-Hammond, 2000; Hanushek, 2011; Rand Education, 2012). It is estimated that an effective teacher can have 2 to 3 times the impact of any other school factor in terms of student academic achievement, including leadership, school facilities and available services (Rand Education, 2012). In the US there is an unequal distribution of effective teachers. Poor children of color are disproportionality assigned to classrooms with teachers who received the least preparation and have the weakest academic backgrounds (Murnane & Steele, 2007). Teachers teaching in low income high poverty schools when compared to their contemporaries working in suburban schools are more likely to be inexperienced, lack certification, less likely to have graduated from a competitive college and scored lower on standardized exams (Ahram et al., 2013; Jacob, 2007; Shields, 2009; Simon & Johnson, 2013). Clotfelter, Ladd, and Vigdor (2007) reported on their ten-year longitudinal study of teacher credentials and student achievement of teachers in North Carolina, that teacher credentialing matters especially for improving the academic achievement of disadvantaged students.

Nationally, 30% of teachers leave the profession within 5 years, and the exit of teachers are 50% higher in urban schools (Ronfeldt, Loeb, & Wyckoff, 2013). Several reasons have been cited in the research to explain why urban teachers exit urban schools so abruptly: high concentrations of poverty (Boyd et al., 2005; Rivkin, Hanushek, & Kain, 2005) and organizational [school] context (Jacob, Vidyarthi, & Carroll, 2012; Johnson, Kraft, & Papay, 2012; Shields, 2009).

Low-income high poverty schools experience difficulty in attracting and retaining high quality teachers. These schools are often referred to as "hard to staff" schools. Urban schools are often left with hiring substitutes due to this lack of available supply (Jacob, 2007). The exorbitant rate of "churn" experienced by these hard to staff schools often results in negative impact on academic achievement for students and high financial costs for already financially strapped schools and school districts. Research conducted by Ronfeldt et al. (2013) found that this high turnover rate had a profound adverse impact on low performing Black students than for their higher performing non-Black peers. The revolving door of teachers in urban schools also results in these schools having a higher percentage of replacement teachers who are less experienced.

Nationwide, school districts pay on average 7 billion dollars to replace teachers. For urban districts, this amount translates to ~70,000 dollars per teacher almost twice the amount incurred by non-urban schools (Simon & Johnson, 2013).

Not all urban schools are staffed with inexperienced, uncertified, ineffective teachers. The research indicates that poor urban schools are more likely than suburban schools to have a higher percentage of teachers with those characteristics. With that being said, exemplary teachers dedicated to working in low income high poverty schools do exist and they are not an anomaly but they are outnumbered by less effective teachers. Moreover, approximately 10,000 of these exemplary "hard to replace" teachers leave the 50 largest school districts in the country each year (Jacob et al., 2012). At the same time, approximately 100,000 low performing teachers remain. It is interesting to note that the great majority of the exemplary teachers are new teachers and the less effective teachers who remain are more experienced, thus contributing to the vicious cycle of millions of students learning from ineffective teachers underwriting their continued academic failures.

Jacob et al. (2012) conducted a large study of over 20,000 exemplary teachers in four large urban districts to better understand their decisions to leave their urban schools. The researchers found that when irreplaceable exemplary teachers leave a low performing school, it can take 11 hires to find one a teacher of comparable quality. For 75% of the teachers who left, they indicated that they would had stayed if their concerns had been addressed and they had been valued for their contributions to the academic success of their students.

Funding Challenges

It costs more to educate children who come from low-income families, are English language learners, or who qualify for special education services to the same level as those children who do not have these extra needs (Epstein, 2011). Urban schools have unique characteristics that put them at risk for funding inequalities. First and foremost, urban schools are located in major cities and therefore the cost of living in these areas is much higher than suburban and rural areas. Urban districts that are also "property poor" are faced with eroding tax bases due to a lack of business and low home values that minimize local ability to adequately fund schools via property taxes (Jacob, 2007). In Texas, the greatest percentage of school funding in urban schools is raised locally; that is 54.7% of funding for urban schools is generated from local sources. The communities with the least property wealth are required to generate the highest percentage of funding for schools when compared to rural and suburban communities in Texas. Additionally, urban schools in Texas receive the least percentage of their school funding from the state. Ongoing legal battles to address the inequities in school funding are presently being litigated to address these inadequacies.

School Leadership

District leaders are operating in an environment of ever shifting priorities. During the first half other 20th century, district management could be defined by the four Bs: Bonds, Budgets, Buses and Buildings. By the 1970s it had become the four Rs: Race, Resources, Relationships and Rules—as heretofore mostly ignored groups such as member of minority groups, teachers, students and communities began asserting themselves. Priorities shifted again in the 1980s when the contemporary school reform movement gained traction. Today, district leaders must concern themselves with a host of different concerns: the four As: Academic Standards, Accountability, Autonomy, and Ambiguity and the five Cs: Collaboration, Communication, Connection, Child Advocacy and Community building. (Jackson, 2005, p. 194)

Principal turnover is often cited in the research literature as an impediment to improving schools, especially in high poverty schools (Branch, Hanushek, & Rivkin, 2013; Leithwood, Seashore Louis, Anderson, & Wahlstrom, 2004; Miller, 2013).

There is no specific leadership style that will work with every school; high or low performing, high SES or low SES, urban, rural or suburban. There are certain challenges that urban school principals must successfully mitigate that will require specific skills. Urban school principals must successfully assuage the impact of student homelessness and new immigrants, child abuse, ELL, single parent homes, aging school facilities, teacher turnover, drug use, lack of teacher training, gangs, dropout rate, suspensions (Kimball & Sirotnik, 2000), funding inequities, lack of material and human resources, high student mobility, high levels of poverty and persistent achievement gaps (Jackson, 2005), all the while in attempting to increase academic performance of allstudents.

With increased accountability, demands and expectations of the immediate turnaround of failing schools, an urban school leader has a difficult task. According to a recent study conducted by the School Leaders Network (2014), twenty-five thousand principals, approximately one quarter of the current sitting Principal population in the United States leave the principalship. More alarming is the fact that 50% of new principals quit or leave the principalship after leading schools for just three years. For many new school leaders that do remain, many opt to lead schools in affluent school districts rather than working in low income, struggling schools (School Leaders Network, 2014). Principals leading schools in high poverty, low performing schools leave because of the stress of having to deal with numerous challenges present in low performing schools (Béteille, Kalogrides, & Loeb, 2012; Burkhauser, Gates, Hamilton, & Ikemoto, 2012; Gates et al., 2006). Other research suggests that school leaders leave the urban school principalship because they lacked social justice preparation from their principal preparation programs (Miller & Martin, 2015).

◆ CONCLUSION

Leaders charged with the responsibility of leading urban schools must have an understanding and commitment to social justice, democracy and equity (Brown, 2004; Cambron-McCabe, 2005; Hernandez & Fraynd, 2014; Jean-Marie, Normore, & Brooks, 2009; Miller & Martin, 2015; Theoharis, 2010; Theoharis & Causton-Theoharis, 2008). Social justice leadership will require urban school leaders to demonstrate through ongoing actions, skills and habits of mind that all children regardless of race and class are entitled to a high quality education. Urban schools have unique challenges that will require school leaders who understand the challenges both within and outside of the school. The research is replete with references to urban schools that are successful; however, widespread replicable results have not been achieved nationwide. Urban school leaders will need to lead with the grit and resiliency that urban students are expected to possess to achieve academic success. Urban leaders cannot view students from a deficit perspective and expect change. Leaders must understand the factors that are associated with poverty and make a concerted effort to mitigate those challenges to ensure that poor urban children are successful. This type of commitment will require leaders to lead with a social justice mindset, to defy societal misperceptions of poor children and their ability to achieve academically and to provide authentic high quality opportunities for ALL children to learn.

Leadership will be needed that can facilitate the leveraging of resources to support student success. Leaders must lead by example, expecting and demanding that all children be provided with a high quality education. Ensuring that teachers are provided with on-going relevant professional development that helps them to understand the school community contexts and the corresponding impact on student achievement, behavior and dispositions. Finally, leaders are needed who understand that demography does not determine destiny and with the right supports, urban students can be successful.

◆ REFERENCES

Ahram, R., Stembridge, A., Fergus, E., & Noguera, P. (2013). Framing urban school challenges: The problems to examine when implementing response to intervention. Retrieved from http://www .RTInetwork.org/learn/diversity/urban-school-challenges

Balfanz, R., & Byrnes, V. (2012). *The Importance of in School: A Report on Absenteeism in the Nation's Public Schools*. Baltimore, MD: Johns Hopkins University Center for Social Organization of Schools.

Basch, C. (2010). *Healthier Students Are Better Learners: A Missing Link in School Reforms to Close the Achievement Gap*. New York, NY: Teachers College, Columbia University. Retrieved from http://www.equitycampaign.org/i/a/document/12557_EquityMattersVol6_Web03082010.pdf

Berliner, D. C. (2009). *Poverty and potential: Out-of-school factors and school success*. Boulder and Tempe: Education and the Public Interest Center & Education Policy Research Unit.

Béteille, T., Kalogrides, D., & Loeb, S. (2012). Stepping stones: Principal career paths and school outcomes. *Social Science Research, 41*(4), 904–919.

Bowen, N. K., & Bowen, G. L. (1999). Effects of crime and violence in neighborhoods and schools on the school behavior and performance of adolescents. *Journal of Adolescent Research, 14*(3), 319–342.

Boyd, D., Lankford, H., Loeb, S., & Wyckoff, J. (2005). Explaining the short careers of high-achieving teachers in schools with low-performing students. *American Economic Review, 95*(2), 166–171.

Branch, G., Hanushek, E., & Rivkin, S. (2013). School leaders matter. *Education Next, 13*(2), 62–69.

Bronfenbrenner, U. (1994). Ecological models of human development. *Readings on the Development of Children, 2*, 37–43.

Brown, K. M. (2004). Leadership for social justice and equity: Weaving a transformative framework and pedagogy. *Educational Administration Quarterly, 40*(1), 77–108.

Burkhauser, S., Gates, S. M., Hamilton, L. S., & Ikemoto, G. S. (2012). First-year principals in urban school districts: How actions and working conditions relate to outcomes. Technical Report. *Rand Corporation*.

Cambron-McCabe, N. (2005). Educating school leaders for social justice. *Educational Policy, 19*(1), 201–222. doi:10.1177/0895904804271609

Centers for Disease Control and Prevention. (2014). *Health & Academics*. Retrieved from http://www.cdc.gov/HealthyYouth/health_and_academics/

Children's Defense Fund. (2014). *The state of America's children*. Washington, DC: Children's Defense Fund.

Clotfelter, C. T., Ladd, H. F., & Vigdor, J. L. (2007). Teacher credentials and student achievement: Longitudinal analysis with student fixed effects. *Economics of Education Review, 26*(6), 673–682.

Dallas Office of Economic Development. (2015). *City of Dallas Economic Development Profile 2015*. Dallas, TX: Dallas Office of Economic Development.

Darling-Hammond, L. (2000). Teacher quality and student achievement. *Education Policy Analysis Archives, 8*, 1.

Dickens, C. (2000). *A tale of two cities*. London: Penguin.

Dixson, A., Royal, C., & Jr, K. L. H. (2013). School reform and school choice. In H. R. Milner IV & K. Lomotey (Eds.), *Handbook of Urban Education*. London: Routledge.

Epstein, D. (2011). *Measuring inequity in school funding*. Washington, DC: Center for American Progress.

Finkelhor, D., Turner, H., Ormrod, R., Hamby, S., & Krackle, K. (2009). *Children's exposure to violence: A comprehensive national survey*. Washington, DC: US Department of Justice.

Fleischhacker, S., Evenson, K., Rodriguez, D., & Ammerman, A. (2011). A systematic review of fast food access studies. *Obesity Reviews, 12*(5), e460–e471. Retrieved from http://onlinelibrary.wiley.com/store/10.1111/j.1467-789X.2010.00715.x/asset/j.1467-789X.2010.00715.x.pdf?v=1&t=ics9vxvr&s=d95c5c3872f3e02b2fe7d18f5c357d1e7fcd5bd2

Food Research and Action Center. (2010). Why Low-Income and Food Insecure People are Vulnerable to Overweight and Obesity. Retrieved from http://frac.org

Gates, S. M., Ringel, J. S., Santibanez, L., Guarino, C., Ghosh-Dastidar, B., & Brown, A. (2006). Mobility and turnover among school principals. *Economics of Education Review, 25*(3), 289–302.

Guin, K. (2004). Chronic teacher turnover in urban elementary schools. *Education Policy Analysis Archives, 12*, 42.

Hanushek, E. A. (2011). The economic value of higher teacher quality. *Economics of Education Review, 30*(3), 466–479.

Heilig, J. V., Khalifa, M., & Tillman, L. (2013). High-Stake Reforms and Urban Education. In H. R. Milner IV & K. Lomotey (Eds.), *Handbook of Urban Education*: London: Routledge.

Hellen Keller International. (2015). *Clear Vision for Newark Students*. Retrieved from http://www.marketwired.com/press-release/clear-vision-for-newark-students-2059076.htm

Hernandez, F., & Fraynd, D. J. (2014). Leadership's Role in Inclusive LGBTQ-Supportive Schools. *Theory Into Practice, 53*(2), 115–122.

Jackson, J. (2005). *Leadership for urban public schools.* Paper presented at the The Educational Forum.

Jackson, Y., & Feuerstein, R. (2014). *Pedagogy of confidence*: New York: Teachers College Press.

Jackson, Y., & Veronica McDermott. (2012). *Aim high, achieve more: How to transform urban schools through fearless leadership*: ASCD.

Jacob, A., Vidyarthi, E., & Carroll, K. (2012). The Irreplaceables: Understanding the Real Retention Crisis in America's Urban Schools. *TNTP.*

Jacob, B. A. (2007). The challenges of staffing urban schools with effective teachers. *The Future of Children, 17*(1), 129–153.

Jean, S. (2014, June 20). *Report: U.S. metro economic growth is crucial to national economic health.* Retrieved from http://bizbeatblog.dallasnews.com/2014/06/report-u-s-metro-economic-growth-is-crucial-to-national-economic-health.html/

Jean-Marie, G., Normore, A. H., & Brooks, J. S. (2009). Leadership for social justice: Preparing 21st century school leaders for a new social order. *Journal of Research on Leadership Education, 4*(1), 1–31.

Jensen, E. (2009). *Teaching with poverty in mind: What being poor does to kids' brains and what schools can do about it*: Alexandria, VA: Association for Supervision and Curriculum Development.

Johnson, G. M. (1994). An ecological framework for conceptualizing educational risk. *Urban Education, 29*(1), 34–49.

Johnson, S. M., Kraft, M. A., & Papay, J. P. (2012). How context matters in high-need schools: The effects of teachers' working conditions on their professional satisfaction and their students' achievement. *Teachers College Record, 114*(10), 1–39.

Kataoka, S., Jaycox, L. H., Wong, M., Nadeem, E., Langley, A., Tang, L., & Stein, B. D. (2011). Effects on school outcomes in low-income minority youth: Preliminary findings from a community-partnered study of a school trauma intervention. *Ethnicity & disease, 21*(3 0 1), S1.

Kids Count. (2015). Kids Count data center. *A project of the Annie E. Casey Foundation.* Retrieved from http://datacenter.kidscount.org/data/#TX/3/0

Kim, S., Mazza, J., Zwanziger, J., & Henry, D. (2014). School and behavioral outcomes among inner city children five-year follow-up. *Urban Education, 49*(7), 835–856.

Kimball, K., & Sirotnik, K. A. (2000). The Urban School Principalship: Take This Job and...! *Education and Urban Society, 32*(4), 535–543.

Ladd, H. F. (2012). Education and poverty: Confronting the evidence. *Journal of Policy Analysis and Management, 31*(2), 203–227.

Langevin, D. D., Kwiatkowski, C., McKay, M. G., Maillet, J. O. S., Touger-Decker, R., Smith, J. K., & Perlman, A. (2007). Evaluation of diet quality and weight status of children from a low socioeconomic urban environment supports "at risk" classification. *Journal of the American Dietetic Association, 107*(11), 1973–1977. Retrieved from http://www.andjrnl.org/article/S0002-8223(07)01618-5/pdf

Lee, J., & Shea, C. (2015). *2015 State of Texas Children.* Austin, TX: Center for Public Policy Priorities.

Leithwood, K., Seashore Louis, K., Anderson, S., & Wahlstrom, K. (2004). Review of research: how leadership influences student learning.

Leonard, J. (2011). Using Bronfenbrenner's ecological theory to understand community partnerships: A historical case study of one urban high school. *Urban Education*, 0042085911400337.

Miller, A. (2013). Principal turnover and student achievement. *Economics of Education Review, 36*, 60–72.

Miller, C. M., & Martin, B. N. (2015). Principal preparedness for leading in demographically changing schools: Where is the social justice training? *Educational Management Administration & Leadership, 43*(1), 129–151. doi:10.1177/1741143213513185

Murnane, R. J., & Steele, J. L. (2007). What is the problem? The challenge of providing effective teachers for all children. *The Future of Children, 17*(1), 15–43.

Nicholson, E. (2015, March 19, 2015). Income Inequality in Dallas is Rising Fast. *Dallas Observer*.

Nikulina, V., Widom, C. S., & Czaja, S. (2011). The role of childhood neglect and childhood poverty in predicting mental health, academic achievement and crime in adulthood. *American Journal of Community Psychology, 48*(3–4), 309–321.

Noguera, P. (2011). A broader and bolder approach uses education to break the cycle of poverty: making bold assertions that all children can achieve while doing nothing to address the challenges they face is neither fair nor sound public policy. *Phi Delta Kappan, 93*(3), 8.

Noguera, P., & Williams, J. (2010). Poor schools or poor kids. *Education Next, 10*(1), 44–51.

Perkins, S., & Graham-Bermann, S. (2012). Violence exposure and the development of school-related functioning: Mental health, neurocognition, and learning. *Aggression and violent behavior, 17*(1), 89–98.

Rand Education. (2012). Teachers matter: Understanding teachers' impact on student achievement. Retrieved from www.rand.org

Rivkin, S. G., Hanushek, E. A., & Kain, J. F. (2005). Teachers, schools, and academic achievement. *Econometrica, 73*(2), 417–458.

Ronfeldt, M., Loeb, S., & Wyckoff, J. (2013). How teacher turnover harms student achievement. *American Educational Research Journal, 50*(1), 4–36.

Rothstein, R. (2011). *A look at the health-related causes of low student achievement*. Retrieved from http://www.epi.org/publication/a_look_at_the_health-related_causes_of_low_student_achievement/

Samson, J. F., & Lesaux, N. (2015). Disadvantaged language minority students and their teachers: A national picture. *Teachers College Record, 117*(2).

Schiller, J. S., Ward, B. W., & Freeman, G. (2014). *Early release of selected estimates based on data from the 2013 National Health Interview Survey*. Retrieved from http://www.cdc.gov/nchs/data/nhis/earlyrelease/earlyrelease201406.pdf

School Leaders Network. (2014). *CHURN: The High Cost of Principal Turnover*. Retrieved from http://connectleadsucceed.org/sites/default/files/principal_turnover_cost.pdf

Seirawan, H., Faust, S., & Mulligan, R. (2012). The impact of oral health on the academic performance of disadvantaged children. *American journal of public health, 102*(9), 1729–1734. Retrieved from http://www.ncbi.nlm.nih.gov/pmc/articles/PMC3482021/pdf/AJPH.2011.300478.pdf

Shields, D. J. (2009). *Keeping Urban Teachers: A National Necessity*.

Simon, N., & Johnson, S. M. (2013). Teacher turnover in high-poverty schools: What we know and can do. *Teachers College Record*.

Sparks, S. (2012). *Poverty, other risks explain asthma's link to poor achievement*.

Strayhorn, T. L. (2009). Different folks, different hopes the educational aspirations of black males in urban, suburban, and rural high schools. *Urban Education, 44*(6), 710–731.

Texas Education Agency. (2015). Snapshot 2014 summary tables: community type. Retrieved from http://ritter.tea.state.tx.us/perfreport/snapshot/2014/commtype.html. from Texas Education Agency http://ritter.tea.state.tx.us/perfreport/snapshot/2014/commtype.html

The Federal Bureau of Investigations. (2015). Uniform Crime Reports: Table 12 Crime in the United States 2013 Retrieved from (https://www.fbi.gov/about-us/cjis/ucr/crime-in-the-u.s/2013/crime-in-the-u.s.-2013/tables/table-12/table_12_crime_trends_by_population_group_2012-2013 .xls). from The Federal Bureau of Investigation (https://www.fbi.gov/about-us/cjis/ucr/crime-in-the-u.s/2013/crime-in-the-u.s.-2013/tables/table-12/table_12_crime_trends_by_population_ group_2012-2013.xls)

The Texas Education Agency. (2015). 2013 School District Snapshot. from The Texas Education Agency.

Theoharis, G. (2010). Jaded Optimism and Other Critical Elements for 21st Century Educational Leaders. *Scholar-Practitioner Quarterly, 4*(4), 361–363.

Theoharis, G., & Causton-Theoharis, J. N. (2008). Oppressors or emancipators: Critical dispositions for preparing inclusive school leaders. *Equity & Excellence in Education, 41*(2), 230–246.

Wilder Research. (2014). *Nutrition and Students' Academic Performance*. Minnesota: Saint Paul.

WorldBank. (2011). Urban Poverty and Slum Upgrading Retrieved from http://web.worldbank .org/WBSITE/EXTERNAL/TOPICS/EXTURBANDEVELOPMENT/EXTURBANPOVER TY/0,,contentMDK:20227679~menuPK:7173704~pagePK:148956~piPK:216618~theSite PK:341325,00.html. from WorldBank http://web.worldbank.org/WBSITE/EXTERNAL/TOPICS/ EXTURBANDEVELOPMENT/EXTURBANPOVERTY/0,,contentMDK:20227679~menuPK:71 73704~pagePK:148956~piPK:216618~theSitePK:341325,00.html

COMPREHENSIVE SCHOOL REFORM IN TEXAS

Alternative Education Programs

Alfredo Ramirez, Jr. ◆ *Maria de Lourdes Viloria*

In the United States of America, it is a widely acknowledged and almost undisputed fact that the need for comprehensive school reform has existed for several decades (Andrews, Basom, & Basom, 2001; Austin & Reynolds, 1990; Duffy, 1997; Edmonds, 1979; Ovando & Cavazos, 2004; Reyes, Scribner, & Scribner, 1999; Valverde & Scribner, 2001). The urgency of this need has been well-informed by scholars, practitioners, policymakers, and, most recently, private industry leaders. Scholars such as Glickman (1999), Glickman, Gordon, and Ross-Gordon (2007), and Raywid (1990) have suggested that the need for comprehensive school reform is so grave that America is at a crossroads, and democracy is at stake. Scheurich (1998) has stated that while it is "gravely dangerous" to invoke the use of a construct such as democracy to highlight the need for school improvement, nevertheless, this need exists (p. 55). Scholars on all sides argue that one of the most important reasons behind the urgency for comprehensive school reform is that traditional forms of schooling have desperately failed to educate students from low-socioeconomic status (SES) backgrounds and students of color, mainly Latino students, who are gradually, but steadily, becoming the majority in America's public schools. Additionally, those who are charged with this daily task, practitioners, attempt to implement innovative educational practices aimed at improving the teaching and learning process. Despite these efforts, the attempts made to achieve comprehensive school reform that have demonstrated the most visible effects have been sponsored by policymakers. The most common have been legislatively sanctioned alternative forms of schooling.

◆ NATIONAL COMPREHENSIVE SCHOOL REFORM LEGISLATION

While the federal government's authority in administering public school education is significantly limited by constitutional omission, in the last decade, the federal government has attempted to leave its mark in school reform efforts through the enactment of comprehensive national legislation. Traditionally, the federal government has attempted to regulate public school education through fiscal policies that regulate the expenditures of federal funds in education. In the last decade, however, the federal administration under President George W. Bush was successful in enacting nontraditional comprehensive school reform legislation known as the No Child Left Behind Act (NCLB) of 2001. This legislation significantly impacted the administration of the day-to-day operation of schools through the enactment of increased accountability measures and teacher certification requirements. The pervasiveness of national educational reform efforts continues today under President Barrack Obama who sponsored the Race to the Top Legislation. Today, however, many states have applied for and received flexibility waivers from the Department of Education, making a significant majority of the states exempt from federal accountability demands in exchange for assurances leading to the development of stronger individualized state policy reform and accountability demands. Some of these have included the creation and adoption of value-added teacher and principal evaluation systems, assessment and curriculum systems.

Additionally, at the national and state levels, several educational trends have characterized educational reform efforts. These include alternative schools of choice, voucher programs, and most recently, the private industry's College Readiness Standards and the Common Core.

◆ STATE EDUCATIONAL REFORM EFFORTS

Many of these comprehensive school reform initiatives have been operationalized at the state level. The charter school movement, for example, began in 1991 in Minnesota followed by Arizona, California, and Michigan (Noll, 2001). In recent years, voucher programs in several states have attempted to refuel the public debate in these types of comprehensive school reform efforts, and early college readiness programs have emerged as the private industry's choice for revitalizing American education in 24 states. In 2015 with House Bill 1842, the Texas Legislature passed legislation further impacting the regulation of charter schools in the state and expanding their reach across the state.

◆ COMPREHENSIVE EDUCATIONAL REFORM EFFORTS IN TEXAS

The focus of this chapter will center upon both the historic as well as the most current comprehensive school reform efforts in Texas. The author will demonstrate, through a comprehensive review of alternative structural models of schooling, that in Texas, school improvement efforts have come about mainly through the development, implementation, and sustainability of alternative school structures. Additionally, the reader will gain an understanding of alternative school models in Texas. The chapter is organized into seven major parts, each of which will review the relevant characteristics of (1) home schooling, (2) charter schools, (3) disciplinary alternative education schools, (4) special legislation schools, (5) magnet schools, (6) for profit alternative education schools, and (7) early-college high schools. The author will begin with an examination of the concept of home schooling in Texas.

◆ HOME SCHOOLS

Perhaps the earliest attempts to reform public school education in Texas emerged in the form of home-school education. According to the Texas Education Agency (TEA), "for most of this century, Texas has exempted children enrolled in a private or parochial school from compulsory school attendance" (M. L. Williams, personal communication, April 08, 2013). This being the case, the concept of home schooling as an alternative to traditional structures of schooling has been in existence for the greater part of the last 100 years.

This historical record suggests that the existence of home-schooling opportunities for the last 100 years in Texas have left a traceable rich history in the state. Ironically, the opposite is true. The concept of home schooling derives its legitimacy in Texas from the Texas Education Code (TEC). According to the TEC Section 25.086, "a child is exempt from the requirements of compulsory school attendance if the child attends a private or parochial school that includes in its course a study of good citizenship" (p. 149). While this section does not specifically address the topic of home schooling, it implies that it is an option to families in Texas. This implication is informed by the fact that, in Texas, home schooling is considered to be a form of private education. The establishment of that fact is grounded in case law. According to the TEA, in the case of *Leeper et al. v. Arlington ISD et al.*, the Supreme Court of Texas affirmed a decision by District Judge Charles J. Murray holding that a school age child residing in Texas who is pursuing, under direct supervision of his/her parents, a curriculum designed to meet basic education goals is attending a private school within the meaning of Section 25.086(a)(1) of the Texas Education Code and is therefore exempt from compulsory school attendance. (M. L. Williams, personal communication, April 08, 2013)

Because the state of Texas has no legal authority to regulate or administer private schools, it, therefore, has no authority to regulate home schools. As a result, very little to no data are held by the state directly relating to the operation of home schools.

This is not intended to suggest that little is known about the operation of home schooling in Texas. Home-school participants are a well-organized group. Participants in the home-school experience include, but are not limited to, first and foremost, (1) the home-schooled student and their parent or legal guardian, (2) independent home-school providers who are usually content area specialists with advanced degrees in the field, (3) privately owned education agencies, (4) in large metropolitan communities, well-organized and defined cooperatives known as co-ops that pool educational resources for the purposes of providing home-school education, and (5) interest groups.

One of the more popular and well-established home-school interest groups in Texas is the Texas Home School Coalition (THSC). In the absence of a state centralized regulatory agency that regulates home schools, this group holds the most current and accurate statistical and demographic data regarding the composition and operation of Texas home schools. According to THSC, approximately 300,000 home-school families exist in the state of Texas (Texas Home School Coalition, 2007b). It is important to note that some families home school more than one child, and therefore, the actual number of home-schooled students may be much larger. Additionally, the National Home Education Research Institute (NHERI) serves as the nation's most organized interest group for home-school education. NHERI was founded in 1985 and provides research, serves as a national clearinghouse for all interested home-school constituencies, and conducts ongoing research projects regarding the home-school experience (National Home Education Research Institute, NHERI, 2007).

The state commissioner of education has issued the following policy statements directing home-school education in Texas. Pursuant to the Texas Supreme Court decision in *Leeper et al. v. Arlington ISD et al.*, the commissioner of education has maintained policies that are consistent with the court ruling that "students who are home schooled are exempt from the compulsory attendance requirement to the same extent as students enrolled in private schools" (M. L. Williams, personal communication, April 08, 2013). Further, the commissioner has clearly stated that all that is needed for a parent to home school their child is a curriculum and a written notice from the parent or legal guardian regarding their intent to home school their child. This notice can take the form of a letter of withdrawal or by the signing of withdrawal forms, and the parent is not required to appear before school officials or to have the curriculum that they intend to use reviewed. Additionally, the commissioner has also held that students transferring from a home school to a public school should receive the same academic matriculation process as students transferring from private schools. To determine appropriate grade level placement, school districts are recommended to administer previously administered TAKS examinations or nationally norm-referenced exams (M. L. Williams, personal communication, April 08, 2013).

Current research and demographic data indicate the following characteristics of home schools in Texas. It is estimated that from the 5.1 million Texas public school students, approximately 300,000 home-school families participate in home-school education in Texas. These families, generally (1) earn an average income of $25,000 to $50,000 per year, (2) either attended college or hold a college degree, and (3) are at least 90% white, 75% of which are active in the religious community. In these home-schooled families, the mother is usually the education provider, the families are larger than average-size families, and reside in stable marriages. Findings of the research further indicate that parents surveyed prefer home-school education as an alternative to public school education for religious and moral purposes, expressed deeply rooted concerns about school overcrowding that can lead to unsafe school environments, and expressed a high degree of dissatisfaction with the quality of public school education (Alvarez et al., 2007). Legal findings reported by the Heritage Foundation (2004) stated,

> In general, home-schooled students achieve at higher levels than their public school peers on nationally normed standardized tests in all subjects. Home-schooled students are active outside of school, with the average home-school student participating in five extracurricular activities such as dance, sports, music, and volunteerism. Nearly all home-schooled students participate in at least two extracurricular activities. In 1999, home-schooled students even started their own honor society, ETA Sigma Alpha. The society has grown to 20 chapters nationwide. (p. 5)

Contrary to popular myths, home-schooled children enjoy a healthy and socially active school experience. According to the THSC (2007a), one of the most popular and pedagogically sound field trips for home-schooled children in Texas is the state-sponsored Capitol Days. This is an activity that is sponsored and hosted by Texas state legislators in which home-schooled children meet and lobby through face-to-face interactions with legislators who are sponsoring legislation that is either in favor or against Texas home-school education. Despite the perceived success of these programs, there are those who are less optimistic.

No treatment of home-school education would be complete without mention of critics' views toward home-school education. Several views dominate opponents' thinking regarding the perceived benefits of home-school education. According to critics, home schooling does not lead to adequate socialization skill development, lacks exposure to high level instruction, leads to intolerance of diverse populations, reduces public funding for schools, and places students at a disadvantage when home-school families do not possess adequate financial and time resources (Alvarez et al., 2007).

◆ NATIONAL CHARTER SCHOOL MOVEMENT

Despite this criticism, home schooling remains a popular alternative to traditional school structures. Another fairly new alternative to traditional forms of schooling is the concept of the charter school. This section will focus upon charter schools in Texas. Probably, no attempt directed at comprehensive school reform in Texas has received as much attention and has gained in popularity as the charter school movement. According to Noll (2001), "the hottest idea for providing alternatives to the usual public school offering is the charter school movement" (p. 212). In the United States, it is believed that charter schools began in 1991 in the state of Minnesota and received their authority to operate through legislative action. The popularity of these schools was so intense that shortly after the first charter schools began to operate in Minnesota, the states of Arizona, California, and Michigan all passed legislation that enacted the creation and administration of charter schools in these states. Charter schools as a vehicle for reform have gained so much popularity that in one state, a wide variety of charter school structures exist. Generally speaking, however, most state-sanctioned charter schools (1) are mainly funded from state and national sources, (2) operate with a great deal of flexibility with regard to the credentialing of teachers, (3) are exempt from traditional accountability measures, and (4) operate independent of traditional state budgetary requirements.

Charter schools began in the United States as a direct result of the general public's dissatisfaction with the results of public education. According to Noll (2001),

> The movement has certainly brought variety to the school system menu and has expanded parental choice. Community groups, activists, and entrepreneurs seem to be clamoring for available charters for Core Knowledge schools, Paideia schools, fine arts academies, Afrocentric schools, schools for at-risk students and dropouts, technology schools, character education-based schools, job-training academies, and so on. (pp. 212–213)

It is also believed that charter schools may provide low-SES students of color with greater opportunities for success (McNeil, 1999; Weiher & Tedin, 2002). According to Raspberry, "it isn't because I harbor any illusions that there is something magical about those alternatives, it is because I am increasingly doubtful that the public schools can do (or at any rate will do) what is necessary to educate poor minority children" (as cited in Noll, 2011, p. 213). Additional reasons for the emergence and popularity in the American charter school movement include: (1) the use of innovative teaching methods, (2) specialized curriculums, (3) innovative school structures, (4) culturally sensitive school settings, and (5) the freedom to operate independent of state regulatory requirements.

◆ TEXAS CHARTER SCHOOL MOVEMENT

Consistent with the popularity of the national charter school movement, charter schools in Texas have experienced equal popularity, probably because of the growth of a large racial minority student population that has not been effectively served by traditional schools. Charter schools began in Texas in 1995 (Estes, 2004), and the statistics regarding their existence in the state suggest that the movement has been embraced as a successful option to traditional structures of schooling. The state operates a total of 194 approved charter operators (TEA, 2014). Additionally, a total of 437 charter campuses are operational in Texas, thus indicating that some charter programs operate multiple charter campuses. These numbers indicate with a high degree of accuracy that only three other states—California, Arizona, and Florida—operate a larger number of charter schools (Smith, 2005). Thus, Texas is ranked as the fourth largest state in the number of approved charters (Smith, 2005).

Several additional facts reflect the general composition of charter schools in Texas. Out of 5.1 million school children in Texas, more than 102,000, or 2% of the school age population, attend charter schools (Smith, 2005). These schools are mainly concentrated in large urban communities and the majority of students come from elementary backgrounds. Charter schools are mainly populated by low-SES students of color. Class size and student-to-teacher ratios are smaller than at traditional schools, and the campus populations also tend to be smaller in terms of student enrollment (Smith, 2005).

Charter schools in Texas are sanctioned through statutory authority by the Texas State Legislature. This authority can be found in Chapter 12 of the Texas Education Code. The Code establishes four distinct types of charter school structures in Texas. These structures include (1) a Home-Rule School District Charter, (2) a Campus or Campus Program Charter, (3) an Open-Enrollment Charter School, and (4) a College or University Charter School. According to Estes (2004), "although Texas law grants charters to four types of sponsoring entities, most have gone to tax-exempt nonprofit corporations with no ties to local school districts" (p. 259). Therefore, the most popular charter school structure in Texas is the open-enrollment charter school.

◆ OPEN-ENROLLMENT CHARTER SCHOOLS

Other important features are common and distinguish the open-enrollment charter school from the other three types of charter schools. These schools operate through a type of contract called a charter. These contracts are granted to private individuals who are interested in obtaining a charter to provide educational services to students, and these services come in a variety of open enrollment charter structures. For example, some open-enrollment charter schools operate solely for the purposes of providing educational opportunities to students in at-risk situations as defined by the Texas Education Code while others exist for populations of students from accelerated backgrounds. Regardless of the structural arrangement, open-enrollment charter schools are granted to individuals who present a successful application to the state for a period of 5 years. It is important to note that this period is for the initial award of the charter. Subsequent renewals of the charter are for a period of 10 years. Because charter schools are under the direct supervision of the commissioner of education who administers and regulates these schools through the Charter School Division of the TEA, during either one of these two terms, the commissioner may revoke the charter to operate a school if it is deemed that (1) the administration of the school has committed a material violation of the charter; (2) has failed to satisfy accounting standards of fiscal management; (3) has failed to protect the health, safety, or welfare of students enrolled at the school and or has failed to comply with the Texas Education Code Chapter 12, Subchapter D or other applicable laws. In recent years, the commissioner has authorized the revocation of a few charters. Out of a total of 194 charter schools in operation, the majority operate as open-enrollment charter schools. In 2013, the 83rd Texas State Legislative Session awarded authority to the commissioner of education to approve all charter schools in Texas. This power was transferred from the Texas State Board of Education (SBOE) to the commissioner of education. Therefore, the commissioner now has sole authority over the approval and administration of all charter schools.

◆ HOME-RULE SCHOOL DISTRICT CHARTER

In contrast to the open-enrollment charter school structure, a public school district in Texas or a nonprofit organization, such as a city or county, may adopt a home-rule school district charter pursuant to TEC Section 12.011. In this charter school structure, the board of trustees of a school district is authorized to grant a charter to operate a home-rule school district. The home-rule school district is subject to all applicable federal and state laws, and the adoption of this type of charter does not affect a school district's boundaries and/or taxes.

Additionally, the operation of a home-rule school district is somewhat similar to that of a traditional state-sponsored school district. For example, employees of these charter schools may be members of the Texas Teacher Retirement System and may be eligible to receive all of the applicable and related member benefits. The home-rule school district cannot discriminate against students with disabilities, and home-rule school districts enjoy the same taxing authority as that which is possessed by local public school boards.

Academically, home-rule school districts also operate similar to local public school districts. A sampling of these,

> Must describe the educational program to be offered, must maintain acceptable compliance with other applicable accountability provisions, describe the governance structure of the campuses, and provide all related support educational programs such as bilingual education, special education, graduation plans, student attendance, student admissions, and subscribe to the Public Education Information Management System (PEIMS). (TEC, 2004, p. 52)

In Texas, no home-rule school districts are currently in operation (K. L. Johnson, personal communication, July 10, 2015). Home-rule charters are different and more advantageous than traditional public school districts for several reasons. The advantages of these types of charter schools include, mainly, the financial generating revenue potential for local governments and public school districts while at the same time providing innovative educational settings that operate somewhat independent of traditional state accountability measures (K. L. Johnson, personal communication, July 10, 2015).

In 2015 with the passage of House Bill 1842, the Texas Legislature enacted new statutes allowing for public school districts in Texas to operate Districts of Innovation. Currently, five school districts in the state have expressed an interest possibly operating such alternatives (K. L. Johnson, personal communication, July 10, 2015).

◆ CAMPUS OR CAMPUS PROGRAM CHARTER SCHOOLS

Campus or campus program charter schools comprise the third type of charter school structure in Texas. Campus or campus program charter schools make up the second most popular type of charter school structure in the state. As of 2005, 41 campus or campus program charters were in operation in Texas. Unlike the open-enrollment charter schools that, as previously stated, account for the most popular type of charter school, campus or campus program charter schools operate under the direct supervision of a sponsoring public school district.

> Pursuant to TEC Section 12.052, the board of trustees of a school district or the governing body of a home-rule school district may grant a charter to parents and teachers for a campus or a program on a campus if the board is presented with a petition signed by: (1) the parents of a majority of the students at that school campus; and (2) a majority of the classroom teachers at that school campus. (p. 56)

The purpose of these charter schools is to promote innovative curriculum and teaching methods within the school district structures. To maintain the spirit and intent of this charter school option as stipulated by the Texas Education Code, neither teachers nor students may be assigned to these schools. Student attendance at these schools is based upon parental choice, and teachers must elect to teach at these campuses.

The school districts in the state that operate campus or campus program charter schools typically only operate one such program in the district, and they are also typically situated in large urban school district communities such as Dallas ISD. Again, these are unique because of their ability to operate independent of most state and district requirements. Opponents of these schools include mainly local school district personnel and administrators who oppose such school structures because they provide options that are in direct competition with the schools that they lead. As these innovative school structures experience and are highlighted for their student successes, they serve to illuminate the performance of less successful schools which also provides the basis for opponents' opposition to campus and campus program charter schools.

◆ COLLEGE OR UNIVERSITY CHARTER SCHOOLS

The fourth and final charter school structure in Texas is the college or university charter school. The authority to operate such schools is provided to public senior colleges or universities by the commissioner of education upon the submission and approval of an application. While the operation of college or university charter schools remains very closely congruent to the spirit and intent of the previous three charter structures, the Texas Education Code delineates several statutory requirements guiding the operation of such schools. According to the Texas Education Code Section 12.154, a college or university charter school's curriculum and instruction program,

> Must include innovative teaching methods, the college or university charter school's educational program must be implemented under the direct supervision of a member of the teaching or research faculty of the public senior college or university, the faculty member supervising the college or university charter school's educational program must have substantial experience and expertise in education research, teacher education, classroom instruction, or educational administration, the college or university charter school's educational program must be designed to meet specific goals described in the charter, including improving student performance, and each aspect of the program must be directed toward the attainment of the goals, the attainment of the college or university charter school's educational program goals must be measured using specific, objective standards set forth in the charter, including assessment methods and a time frame, and the financial operations of the college or university charter school must be supervised by the business office of the public college or university. (p. 74)

Similar to the driving forces that provided the impetus for the creation of the previously stated charter school forms, college and university charter schools were further looked upon for the potential they possessed to provide effective educational alternatives to traditional educational structures. The implication of this possibility is that while the more popular charter school structures, such as the open enrollment charter school, provide alternative educational opportunities for students, college and university charters can help to further provide richer educational opportunities. Essentially, colleges and universities are seen as the nation's educational organizations that are at the cutting edge in the teaching and learning process. Two university charters are in operation in the state of Texas (K. L. Johnson, personal communication, November 02, 2013). These include The University of Houston and The University of Texas at Austin Charter Schools. The University of Texas at Austin's Charter School was developed for the purpose of providing alternative and innovative programs to low-SES students of color within one of the city's historically underserved communities. The school has operated successfully and has been recognized for its work.

Research focusing upon the effect that charter schools have made on student learning has yielded mixed results. According to Smith (2005), when one asks the question of whether or not charter schools have made a successful impact upon student learning,

> The answer is a qualified yes. There is reason for encouragement if you look at the whole picture rather than the snapshot. Some charters are doing spectacular work and deserve all the applause they get. A few are failing, however, and should be shut down. Overall, charter schools are currently behind other public schools in average performance, but are making impressive gains and closing the gap. (p. 14)

In recent years, student performance data have not been available due to the fact that the state has recently updated its state accountability system, and this update has interrupted the state's student performance reporting activities. Unlike the traditional schools in Texas, charter schools performance is monitored by an alternative state accountability system. The recent revamping of the state accountability system has also affected the reporting activities of charter schools through this alternative accountability system.

Despite these performance reporting challenges, several facts are known. According to the Texas Center for Educational Research (TCER), student performance in charter schools is weaker than their traditional public school counterparts, and in grades 7–12, charter school students have lower completion rates, weaker end-of-course exam rates, lower attendance rates, and higher dropout rates (as cited in Smith, 2005). Also, evidence exists to suggest that when public school district schools are located nearby charter schools, the public schools' student performance increases as a result of the academic competition that is created by the charter school student's academic performance (Greene & Forster, 2002).

❖ MANDATORY PLACEMENT ALTERNATIVE EDUCATION PROGRAMS

We will now turn our attention toward two alternative education program structures created by the Texas State Legislature for students who are removed from traditional public school campuses and are required to attend a disciplinary alternative education program (Carpenter-Aeby, Salloum, & Aeby, 2001; Houston ISD, 1997; IDRA, 1996, 1999; Maughan, 1999). Prior to

1995, in Texas, students who engaged in criminal activities as defined by the Texas Penal Code or who engaged in conduct that was considered to be persistently disruptive as defined by local school boards of education were eligible to be removed from the traditional educational setting and were not allowed to continue their attendance at any public school in the state. These removals, which probably numbered in the thousands, were leading to high dropout rates. Recognizing that these dismissals would inevitably affect the larger society by creating a group of citizens that would not be educated, the Texas State Legislature enacted Senate Bill 1, known as the Safe Schools Act, which created disciplinary alternative educational programs.

DISCIPLINARY ALTERNATIVE EDUCATION PROGRAMS

In Texas, two types of disciplinary alternative education programs exist. The first is called a disciplinary alternative educational program (DAEP). The Texas Education Code requires all school districts within certain geographical boundaries with prescribed student enrollment totals to operate DAEPs. Additionally, statutory authority also allows public school districts to form co-ops with neighboring school districts in order to allow these districts to pool their financial resources for the purposes of operating DAEPs.

Student attendance in these programs is strictly mandatory, and required attendance is based upon a set of behavioral criteria that is customarily found in local school districts' student codes of conduct. In order for a student to attend a DAEP, the student must have engaged in behavior, either on or off campus, which the administration of a school district has determined is against the school district's student code of conduct. Once the student is given satisfactory due process and it is determined that the student has engaged in conduct that requires for him or her to be removed from a traditional academic setting and placed in a DEAP, the student is assigned to attend the DAEP for a predetermined amount of time. Restrictions on the number of days required for attendance are based upon state and federal policy requirements. Upon the completion of the given assignment, the student is eligible to return to their home campus.

In most cases, students are assigned to these campuses for several reasons, and while in attendance, certain academic requirements apply to them. The most commonly cited reason for students attending DAEPs is that they have engaged in minor criminal activity as defined by the Texas Penal Code and/or for engaging in persistent minor misbehavior as defined by the school district's student code of conduct. During their assignment, students are engaged in academic activities that are similar, if not equal, to those of the traditional school setting, and they are also subject to all state-sanctioned student performance measures of accountability in the state. Usually, the student performance on state standardized assessments is aggregated to the student's home campus regardless of their assignment in the DAEP.

JUVENILE JUSTICE ALTERNATIVE EDUCATION PROGRAMS

The second disciplinary alternative education program structure is known as the Juvenile Justice Alternative Education Program commonly referred to in Texas as JJAEP. Similar to the DAEPs, JJAEPs were created by Senate Bill 1 in 1995, and they are usually operated and administered by county governments throughout the state. In counties where large numbers of school districts with small student enrollments and thus limited financial resources exist, counties are allowed to operate JJAEP co-ops that are created and designed to serve multiple school districts' students. Student attendance at these schools is also mandatory. When the administration of a public school district in Texas has determined that a student has engaged in behavior that is considered to be a serious crime, either on or off campus, as defined by the Texas Penal Code, the student is required to attend a JJAEP for a predetermined amount of time. In many cases, students attending JJAEPs have received adjudication for committing a serious crime out of the school campus. For those public school district students who commit Title V offenses from the Texas Penal Code, known as "crimes against people," the Texas Education Code in Chapter 37 requires for these students to be immediately removed from the local public school campus. Additionally, they are required to attend a JJAEP for a predetermined amount of time. As with DAEPs, JJAEPs are also restricted by time limits imposed by state and federal policy requirements. Most of these crimes include, but are not limited to, assaults or aggravated assaults with a deadly weapon.

Obviously, since most of these crimes are committed outside of the normal operating hours of a school district and outside of the school campus, school district officials are not always informed that a student has committed such an offense. Therefore, in most cases, local governmental authorities such as probation officers, county officials, or judicial officials are required to report to school officials when a student of a local public school district has committed such a crime.

Many who have been interested in the operation of these two types of mandatory attendance disciplinary alternative education programs in Texas have conducted and reported the findings of research studies aimed at defining the success or lack thereof regarding these programs. In several cases, the research has been highly critical. For example, several have suggested that these structures of schooling have served to allow school districts to marginalize low-SES students of color. They argue that when one looks at the student composition of these schools, those who are required to attend are those students for whom school districts label as difficult to educate and who present the greatest academic challenges, and they happen to represent low-SES Hispanic and African-American students. Additionally, while the federal special education program prohibits the discrimination of students from disabled backgrounds, others have also argued that at disciplinary alternative education programs, students from disabled backgrounds are overrepresented.

Proponents of these educational programs commonly cite several reasons that support the creation and operation of these schools. Most supporters of DAEPs come from public school district employees, mainly teachers and administrators as well as some community members. These stakeholders argue that DAEP options to remove students from a campus foster a safe and healthy school climate. They also cite the perceived effect that removing students with disciplinary problems from a classroom, and thus a campus, also improves the overall quality of the teaching and learning process in the classroom. School district officials also capitalize upon the public's perception that these programs promote school safety so they promote disciplinary approaches such as zero-tolerance programs, which go hand and hand with DAEPs.

While no one can argue that operating a school campus that strives to achieve the highest level of student safety is the most important goal that any school district official should focus on achieving, the unanticipated effects of such a goal do not outweigh the benefits. It does not take policy officials, practitioners, and researchers much effort to recognize that mainly low-SES students of color populate many of these schools or that students from special education backgrounds are overrepresented. Taking note of these institutionalized forms of discrimination, the federal government through the enactment of national legislation (No Child Left

Behind) has implemented policy safeguards aimed at preventing the systemic discrimination of students from minority backgrounds. Currently, this legislation requires public reporting requirements by school districts as to the number of campuses within a district that are considered to be unsafe as measured by the number of documented disciplinary incidents that take place in any given year within the campus. This has forced school officials to seriously examine their student placement policies in DAEPs, thus preventing the structural aspects of the system from discriminating against the academically challenged students. Of course, some argue that these reporting requirements only lead to school district officials not reporting certain student offenses to prevent the school from being labeled as unsafe and thus actually creating a potentially dangerous situation. For now, these schools have been in existence for at least 20 years and their existence appears as if they will continue to operate in Texas.

◆ SPECIAL LEGISLATION SCHOOLS

This section will now focus upon special legislation schools in Texas. Of all the different comprehensive school reform structures in Texas probably no school type is less-known than that of as special legislation schools.

In Texas, the State Legislature has created four special legislation schools. Of these, three are currently in operation and one has been approved but has not yet opened it doors. The Texas Academy of Leadership in the Humanities (TALH) at Lamar University, the Texas Academy of Mathematics and Science (TAMS) at University of North Texas, the University of Texas at Brownsville Math and Science Academy, and the Texas Academy of International and STEM Studies at Texas A&M International University (TAMIU) comprise these schools.

They were created by special legislation passed in the Texas Legislature. As such, several operating features of these schools make them unique. First, each of these schools was created to promote an interest in students in particular academic disciplines such as the humanities, math, science, and internationalization. To achieve these goals, each of these schools is actively involved in aggressive and unique student recruitment efforts. While students from the local community are eligible to apply for acceptance into these programs, admission into these schools are open to all students throughout the state of Texas. This means that while local public school districts in Texas set local community boundaries to define those students who are eligible to attend certain schools in a given community, the attendance boundary for these schools is the entire state.

In addition to these attendance features, student enrollment at these schools is dependent upon a demonstrated level of success within the academic area of interest for the school. Students, for example, seeking to attend TALH must demonstrate the potential to develop or must possess leadership skills that will help them become successful future local, state, and national leaders. In contrast, students attending the TAMS must demonstrate a measurable degree of academic success in the areas of math and science. Focusing on the development of a globalized or an international society, the TAMIU Texas Academy of International and STEM Studies seeks to attract students with an interest in becoming leaders in the international and global job markets.

This academy was inaugurated and opened its doors to received public school students for the first time in the Fall 2014 Semester. Admission to the academy was based upon a competitive process for eligible high school junior and senior students. The inaugural class attracted 42 students with enrollment today steadily increasing to 94 students.

These schools hold high school diploma granting authority by the state. Typically, students attending these schools are upper-level high school juniors and seniors who are gaining college-level course credit while at the same time earning a high school diploma. The curriculum at these schools also reflects a strong component for cultivating not only their academic skills but also their civic duties through community volunteer programs. In turn, the development of these skills not only makes a positive contribution to the different communities in the state but also successfully prepares students for competitive admissions to public and private universities for the remainder of their academic experience.

◆ MAGNET SCHOOLS

Unlike charter schools that usually operate independent of local and state accountability structures, magnet schools are operated by local school districts. For this reason, they are also commonly referred to as schools within a school. Magnet schools began as a state movement in which the individual states created specialized schools with specialized curriculums. States created these schools with the hope that by offering a more attractive curriculum, magnet schools would end *de facto* segregation, and by schools being located within public school districts, this would also help to stop racial segregation.

Texas joined the magnet school movement for many of the same reasons. Magnet schools in the state operate under the same type of conditions. Many of these schools are operated by local school districts, and they are usually located within public school campuses. They offer the state curriculum with a specialization in particular areas of study. In some school districts, for example, magnet schools are located within large high school campuses, and these schools typically have medical, engineering, legal, or other specialized academic foci.

Admissions to these schools are only open to those students who attend the school district based upon attendance boundaries, and once in the district, students are eligible to apply for admission. Similar to the admissions process of special legislation schools, the process is a competitive one in which students must demonstrate a certain level of competence in the area of focus for the magnet school. One of the features that differentiate these schools from other types of alternative school forms is that admissions to these schools are typically based upon voluntary attendance. Unlike DAEPs where students' attendance is mandatory, attendance in magnet schools is voluntary.

Additionally, some school districts utilize these school structural options to create magnet schools for students for whom the traditional school setting is not a "good fit." For example, the Del Valle Independent School District in Austin, TX, operates a magnet school for working students, students with familial responsibilities, and/or students whose academic performance is stronger in alternative school settings. The school, which is called the Del Valle Opportunity Center, also operates a daycare center for students in attendance at the magnet school, a DAEP, and the alternative school of choice all under one roof.

Critics of magnet schools have raised several concerns regarding the operation of magnet schools in the state. As with other forms of alternative schooling, critics underscore the fact that through the competitive admissions process and the offering of specialized curriculums and geographical constraints, magnet schools may actually promote institutionalized forms of racial segregation. They suggest the possibility that these schools become magnets for students of majority and privileged backgrounds who are situated at an advantage when students go through the competitive admissions process to gain acceptance into these schools. This, they argue, causes the direct opposite effect of what these schools were intended to create—end racial segregation in public schools as well as offer competitive and rigorous academic programs to students who have traditionally been underserved in these areas. Despite these objections, magnet schools continue to thrive in the state as school districts continue to open and offer various academic options.

◆ FOR-PROFIT ALTERNATIVE SCHOOLS

While all forms of alternative schooling in Texas cause a certain degree of tension between these schools and their traditional public school counterparts, for profit alternative schools of choice create an even higher degree of tension, and these schools form our next section.

Known as the Edison Project, the Educational Management Organization is a private for-profit school structure. Edison schools were envisioned by and created by Christopher Whittle in 1991, and his aim was to create schools that attempted to provide new approaches to the teaching and learning process in both elementary and secondary schools. In addition to this focus, Whittle also envisioned these schools as helping students to move forward and operate more efficiently financially, while at the same time providing more academic services for students from low SES and minority backgrounds.

The academic program in Edison Schools focuses upon four different types of pedagogical methods and the school structures are organized around an academy structure. The school day in Edison schools is divided into a 7-h, 90-min, 200-day school calendar. Students who attend Edison schools must master five academies that consist of a primary academy for students in K-2 grades, an elementary academy for students in grades 3–5, a junior academy for students in grades 6–8, a senior-level academy for students in grades 9–10, and a collegiate academy for students in grades 11–12. Similar to the Student Success Initiative (SSI) in Texas public schools, students in Edison schools must master each academy before they are eligible to be promoted to the next academy. In addition to these, the learning techniques at these schools center around four types of learning—project-based learning, cooperative learning, differentiated learning, and direct instruction. The curriculum at these schools is composed of traditional core subjects, and it is supplemented by enrichment classes in the areas of character and ethics education, physical fitness and health, music and dance, visual arts, drama, and practical arts and skills. Despite the obvious tension that Edison schools foster, they continue to operate in various communities throughout the state.

◆ EARLY COLLEGE HIGH SCHOOLS

The Early College High School movement began as a reform movement to increase the number of students who can demonstrate college readiness (A Report, 2006). Through the funding of the Bill & Melinda Gates Foundation, the Carnegie Foundation of New York, the Ford Foundation, and the W. K. Kellogg Foundation, Early College High Schools work to annually increase the number of students who are ready to attend senior level universities.

The Early College High School initiative is designed to provide high-quality education that allows for student groups who have been underrepresented in college to get postsecondary credit at no cost (ECHS, 2015).

Early College High Schools began in 2002. Since 2002, it is estimated that these schools have served over 72,000 students in 28 states. The student population is two-thirds from

African-American and Latino backgrounds. In many cases, these students will be the first generation in a family to graduate from college, and nearly 60% are students from low-SES backgrounds.

◆ TEXAS VIRTUAL SCHOOL NETWORK

As we have already seen, over the course of the last several decades, the state of Texas has been engaged in a comprehensive school reform process that has seen the creation of several state school structures aimed at improving the quality of public school education. And, as we have also already noted, most of these appear to be top down state-driven initiatives rather than bottom up school district or practitioner-led efforts. As we will now see, the Texas Virtual School Network (TxVSN) is no exception.

Consistent with most other state-driven comprehensive school reform efforts, the 80th Texas Legislative Session sanctioned the creation of a state network to begin the process of delivering online courses to students in Texas public schools in grades 9–12. To ensure the success of this program, the state has carefully enlisted the expertise of several of its closely related state educational agencies. These agencies include the Region 10 Education Service Center, the Harris County Department of Education, Region 4 Education Service Center, and the iNACOL organization, which is responsible for the administration of the National Standards of Quality for Online Courses (TxVSN, 2013).

Each of these state educational agencies plays a vital role in the administration and the course delivery that make up the TxVSN. Region 10 Education Service Center and the Harris County Department of Education serve primarily as central operating hubs for the, "coordination of course registration and students enrollments, as well as to ensure eligibility of virtual school providers (TxVSN, 2013)." Additionally, these agencies also, "provide an online catalog of approved courses and they coordinate reporting requirements (TxVSN, 2013)." Region Education Service Center 4 is primarily responsible for reviewing the content of the online courses that are provided through the TxVSN.

To qualify for enrollment, students need only be enrolled in a Texas public school or open enrollment charter school and their sponsoring school district or charter school must be a member of the TxVSN. Membership in the virtual school network is achieved through an annual school district or charter school application process. Those school districts and open enrollment charter schools that are eligible to be a part of this network receive a $400 allotment for each student enrolled as well as an $80 reimbursement for administrative and student mentoring costs. Also, once approved as TxVSN members, school districts and open enrollment charter schools must provide personnel who are dedicated to the administration of these online courses at each of the approved school districts and open enrollment charter schools.

While the aims of the State Texas legislature in creating the TxVSN are implicit, the success of the network and its future is a well-coordinated effort that appears to be in its infancy and one that will depend upon the sustainability of its current recruitment structures. Currently, school district and open enrollment charter schools through the employment of several "TxVSN site coordinators," identify students whose learning needs can be better met through an online course delivery format allowing the student some degree of flexibility in their school schedule while assisting public school districts and open enrollment charter schools to get one step closer to successfully educating and graduating almost all of its students.

◆ REFERENCES

Carpenter-Aeby, T, Salloum, M., & Aeby, V. G. (2001). A process evaluation of school social work services in a disciplinary alternative educational program. *Children & Schools, 23*(3), 171–181.

Alvarez, R., Cognata, B., Dominguez, J., Gonzalez, A., Gutierrez, O., Lopez, M., et al. (2007, June). *Schools of choice for Texas public schools.* Symposium conducted at the meeting of the College of Education Annual Graduate Student Conference, Texas A&M International University, Laredo, TX.

Andrews, R. L., Basom, M. R., & Basom, M. (1991). Instructional leadership: Supervision that makes a difference. *Theory into Practice, 30*(2), 97–101.

Austin, G., & Reynolds, D. (1990). Managing for improved school effectiveness. An international survey. *School Organization, 10*(2/3), 167–178.

Duffy, F. M. (1997). Supervising schooling, not teachers. *Educational Leadership*, 78–83.

ECHS. (2015). Texas early college high school. *Education Service Center Region 13*. Retrieved from www.txechs.com

Edmonds, R. (1979). Effective schools for the urban poor. *Educational Leadership, 37*(1), 15–24.

Estes, M. B. (2004). Choice for all? Charter schools and students with special needs. *The Journal of Special Education, 37*(4), 257–267.

Glickman, C. D. (1999). Commentary a response to the discourse on democracy: A dangerous retreat. *International Journal of Leadership in Education, 2*(1), 43–46.

Glickman, C. D., Gordon, S. P., & Ross-Gordon, J. M. (2007). *Supervision and instructional leadership: A developmental approach* (7th ed.). Boston, MA: Allyn and Bacon.

Greene, J. P., & Forster, G. (2002, October). *Rising to the challenge: The effect of school choice on public schools in Milwaukee and San Antonio.* New York, NY: Center for Civic Innovation.

Intercultural Development Research Association. (1996, August). *Alternative schools: Short-term solution with long-term consequences.* San Antonio, TX: North Carolina Education and Law Project.

Intercultural Development Research Association. (1999). *Disciplinary alternative education programs in Texas: What is known; What is needed.* San Antonio, TX: Albert Cortez and Maria Robledo Montecel.

Kafer, K. (2004). School choice in 2003: An old concept gains new life. Legal Memorandum Published by The Heritage Foundation, 9, 1–13.

Maughan, S. (1999). Policy interpretation and implementation of the juvenile justice alternative programs throughout the state of Texas. *Journal of Correctional Education, 50*(4), 124–129.

McNeil, J. J. (1999). A university and charter school collaboration born out of great need. *Education, 119*(3), 438–446.

National Home Education Research Institute. (2007). *Welcome to the national home education research institute!* Retrieved from http://www.nheri.org/

Noll, J. W. (2001). *Taking sides: Clashing views on controversial educational issues* (11th ed.). City, CT: McGraw-Hill.

Ovando, M. N., & Cavazos, M. (2004). Principals' instructional leadership in successful Hispanic majority high schools. *Scholar-Practitioner Quarterly, 2*(2), 7–24.

Smith, N. (2005, February).*Texas roundup: Charter schooling in the lone star state*. Washington, DC: Progressive Policy Institute.

Raywid, M. A. (1990). Rethinking school governance. In R. F. Elmore and Associates (Eds.), *Restructuring Schools: The Next Generation of Educational Reform*. San Francisco, CA: Jossey-Bass.

A Report to the 80th Legislature from the Texas Education Agency. (2006, December). *Improving Texas high schools: School improvement strategies implemented under rider 59, the Texas high school initiative*. Austin, TX: Division of Planning and Grant Reporting Office for Planning, Grants and Evaluation and Office of Education Initiatives.

Reyes, P., Scribner, J. D., & Paredes-Scribner, A. (1999). *Lessons from high-performing Hispanic schools: Creating learning communities*. New York, NY: Teachers College Press.

Scheurich, J. J. (1998). The grave dangers in the discourse on democracy. *International Journal of Leadership in Education, 1*(1), 55–60.

Texas Education Agency. (2014). *Pocket edition: 2013–2014 Texas public school statistics*. Retrieved from http://tea.texas.gov/communications/pocket-edition/

Texas Home School Coalition. (2007a). *Capitol days in the 2007 Texas legislative session*. Retrieved from http://www.thsc.org/capdays.asp

Texas Home School Coalition. (2007b). *Frequently asked questions*. Retrieved from http://www.thsc.org/FAQ/default.asp

Texas School Law Bulletin. (2004). Austin, TX: Texas Education Agency.

Texas Virtual School Network. (2013). *TxVSN frequently asked questions*. Retrieved from http://www.txvsn.org/portal/AboutUS/FAQ.aspx

Valverde, L. A., & Scribner, K. P. (2001). Latino students: Organizing schools for greater achievement. *NASSP Bulletin, 85*(24), 22–30.

Weiher, G. R., & Tedin, K. L. (2002). Does choice lead to racially distinctive schools? Charter schools and household preferences. *Journal of Policy Analysis and Management, 21*(1), 79–92.

Appendix A

STANDARDS FOR THE PRINCIPAL CERTIFICATE

TAC §241.15

The knowledge and skills identified in this section must be used by educator preparation programs in the development of curricula and coursework and will be used by the State Board for Educator Certification as the basis for developing the assessments required to obtain the Provisional and Standard Principal Certificates. These standards must also serve as the foundation for the individual assessment, professional growth plan, and continuing professional education activities required by TAC 241.30 of this chapter (relating to Requirements to Renew the Standard Principal Certificate).

◆ LEARNER-CENTERED VALUES AND ETHICS OF LEADERSHIP

A principal is an educational leader who promotes the success of all students by acting with integrity and fairness and in an ethical manner. At the campus level, a principal understands, values, and is able to:

1. Model and promote the highest standard of conduct, ethical principles, and integrity in decision making, actions, and behaviors.
2. Implement policies and procedures that encourage all campus personnel to comply with Chapter 247 of this title, relating to Code of Ethics and Standards Practices for Texas Educators.
3. Model and promote the continuous and appropriate development of all learners in the campus community.
4. Promote awareness of learning differences, multicultural awareness, gender sensitivity, and ethnic appreciation in the campus community.
5. Articulate the importance of education in a free democratic society.

◆ LEARNER-CENTERED LEADERSHIP AND CAMPUS CULTURE

A principal is an educational leader who promotes the success of all students and shapes campus culture by facilitating the development, articulation, implementation, and stewardship of a vision of learning that is shared and supported by the school community. At the campus level, a principal understands, values, and is able to:

1. Create a campus culture that sets high expectations, promotes learning, and provides intellectual stimulation for self, students, and staff.
2. Ensure that parents and other members of the community are an integral part of the campus culture.
3. Utilize strategies to ensure the development of collegial relationships and effective collaboration of campus staff.
4. Respond appropriately to the diverse needs of individuals within the community in shaping the campus culture.
5. Utilize emerging issues, trends, demographic data, knowledge of systems, campus climate inventories, student learning data, and other information to develop a campus vision and plan to implement the vision.
6. Facilitate the collaborative development of a shared campus vision that focuses on teaching and learning.
7. Facilitate the collaborative development of a plan in which objectives and strategies to implement the campus vision are clearly articulated.
8. Align financial, human, and material resources to support the implementation of the campus vision.
9. Establish processes to assess and modify the plan of implementation to ensure achievement of the campus vision.
10. Support innovative thinking and risk-taking efforts of everyone within the school community and view unsuccessful experiences as learning opportunities.
11. Acknowledge, recognize, and celebrate the contributions of students, staff, parents, and community members toward the realization of the campus vision.

◆ LEARNER-CENTERED HUMAN RESOURCES LEADERSHIP AND MANAGEMENT

A principal is an educational leader who promotes the success of all students by implementing a staff evaluation and development system to improve the performance of all staff members, selects and implements appropriate models for supervision and staff development, and applies the legal requirements for personnel management. At the campus level, a principal understands, values, and is able to:

1. Collaboratively develop, implement, and revise a comprehensive and ongoing plan for professional development of campus staff that addresses staff needs and aligns professional development with identified goals.
2. Facilitate the application of adult learning and motivation theory to all campus professional development, including the use of appropriate content, processes, and contexts.

3. Ensure the effective implementation of the professional development plan by allocation of appropriate time, funding, and other needed resources.

4. Implement effective, legal, and appropriate strategies for the recruitment, selection, assignment, and induction of campus staff.

5. Utilize formative and summative evaluation processes to further develop the knowledge and skills of campus staff.

6. Diagnose and improve campus organizational health and morale through the implementation of strategies designed to provide ongoing support to campus staff members.

7. Engage in ongoing, meaningful, professional growth activities to further develop necessary knowledge and skills, and to model lifelong learning.

◆ LEARNER-CENTERED COMMUNICATIONS AND COMMUNITY RELATIONS

A principal is an educational leader who promotes the success of all students by collaborating with families and community members, responding to diverse community interests and needs, and mobilizing community resources. At the campus level, a principal understands, values, and is able to:

1. Demonstrate effective communication through oral, written, auditory, and nonverbal expression.

2. Utilize effective conflict management and group consensus building skills.

3. Implement effective strategies to systematically gather input from all campus stakeholders.

4. Develop and implement strategies for effective internal and external communications.

5. Develop and implement a comprehensive program of community relations utilizing strategies that will effectively involve and inform multiple constituencies, including the media.

6. Provide varied and meaningful opportunities for parents to be engaged in the education of their children.

7. Establish partnerships with parents, businesses, and other groups in the community to strengthen programs and support campus goals.

8. Respond to pertinent political, social, and economic issues that exist in the internal and external environment.

◆ LEARNER-CENTERED ORGANIZATIONAL LEADERSHIP AND MANAGEMENT

A principal is an educational leader who promotes the success of all students through leadership and management of the organization, operations, and resources for a safe, efficient, and effective learning environment. At the campus level, a principal understands, values, and is able to:

1. Implement appropriate management techniques and group processes to define roles, assign functions, delegate authority, and determine accountability for campus goal attainment.

2. Gather and organize information from a variety of sources for use in creative and effective campus decision making.

3. Frame, analyze, and creatively resolve campus problems using effective problem-solving techniques to make timely, high-quality decisions.

4. Develop, implement, and evaluate change processes for organizational effectiveness.
5. Implement strategies that enable the physical plant, equipment, and support systems to operate safely, efficiently, and effectively to maintain a conducive learning environment.
6. Apply local, state, and federal laws and policies to support sound decisions while considering implications related to all school operations and programs.
7. Acquire, allocate, and manage human, material, and financial resources according to district policies and campus priorities.
8. Collaboratively plan and effectively manage the campus budget.
9. Utilize technology to enhance school management.
10. Utilize effective planning, time management, and organization of work to maximize attainment of district and campus goals.

◆ LEARNER-CENTERED CURRICULUM PLANNING AND DEVELOPMENT

A principal is an educational leader who promotes the success of all students by facilitating the design and implementation of curricula and strategic plans that enhance teaching and learning; alignment of curriculum, curriculum resources, and assessment; and the use of various forms of assessment to measure student performance. At the campus level, a principal understands, values, and is able to:

1. Use emerging issues, occupational and economic trends, demographic data, student learning data, motivation theory, learning theory, legal requirements, and other information as a basis for campus curriculum planning.
2. Facilitate the use of sound research-based practice in the development and implementation of campus curricular, cocurricular, and extracurricular programs.
3. Facilitate campus participation in collaborative district planning, implementation, monitoring, and revision of curriculum to ensure appropriate scope, sequence, content, and alignment.
4. Facilitate the use and integration of technology, telecommunications, and information systems to enrich the campus curriculum.
5. Facilitate the effective coordination of campus curricular, cocurricular, and extracurricular programs in relation to other district programs.

◆ LEARNER-CENTERED INSTRUCTIONAL LEADERSHIP AND MANAGEMENT

A principal is an educational leader who promotes the success of all students by advocating, nurturing, and sustaining a campus culture and instructional program conducive to student learning and staff professional growth. At the campus level, a principal understands, values, and is able to:

1. Facilitate the development of a campus learning organization that supports instructional improvement and change through an ongoing study of relevant research and best practice.
2. Facilitate the implementation of sound, research-based instructional strategies, decisions, and programs in which multiple opportunities to learn and be successful are available to all students.

3. Implement special campus programs to ensure that all students are provided quality, flexible instructional programs and services to meet individual student needs.
4. Utilize interpretation of formative and summative data from a comprehensive student assessment program to develop, support, and improve campus instructional strategies and goals.
5. Facilitate the use and integration of technology, telecommunications, and information systems to enhance learning.
6. Facilitate the implementation of sound, research-based theories and techniques of classroom management, student discipline, and school safety to ensure an environment conducive to teaching and learning.
7. Facilitate the development, implementation, evaluation, and refinement of student activity programs to fulfill academic, developmental, social, and cultural needs.
8. Acquire and allocate sufficient instructional resources on the campus in the most equitable manner to support and enhance student learning.

Appendix B

STANDARDS FOR THE SUPERINTENDENT CERTIFICATE

TAC §242.15

The knowledge and skills identified in this section must be used by the Board as the basis for developing the assessment(s) required to obtain the superintendent certificate.

◆ LEARNER-CENTERED VALUES AND ETHICS OF LEADERSHIP

A superintendent is an educational leader who promotes the success of all students by acting with integrity, fairness, and in an ethical manner. A superintendent understands, values, and is able to:

1. Model and promote the highest standard of conduct, ethical principles, and integrity in decision making, actions, and behaviors.
2. Implement policies and procedures that encourage all district personnel to comply with Chapter 247 of this title, relating to the Code of Ethics and Standard Practices for Texas Educators.
3. Serve as an articulate spokesperson for the importance of education to a free democratic society.
4. Enhance teaching and learning by participation in quality professional development activities, study of current professional literature and research, and interaction with the district's staff and students.
5. Maintain personal physical and emotional wellness.
6. Demonstrate the courage to be a champion for children.

◆ LEARNER-CENTERED LEADERSHIP AND DISTRICT CULTURE

A superintendent is an educational leader who promotes the success of all students and shapes district culture by facilitating the development, articulation, implementation, and stewardship of a vision of learning that is shared and supported by the school community. A superintendent understands, values, and is able to:

1. Establish and support a district culture that promotes learning, high expectations, and academic rigor for self, student, and staff performance.
2. Facilitate the development and implementation of a shared vision that focuses on teaching and learning.
3. Implement strategies for the involvement of all stakeholders in planning processes and facilitate planning between constituencies.
4. Conduct and analyze district/school climate inventories for effective, responsive decision making.
5. Institute and monitor planning processes that include strategies designed to ensure the accomplishment of district goals and objectives to achieve the district's vision.
6. Facilitate the use and allocation of all available resources to support the implementation of the district's vision and goals.
7. Recognize and celebrate contributions of staff and community toward realization of the district's vision.
8. Demonstrate an awareness of emerging issues and trends affecting the education community.
9. Encourage and model innovative thinking and risk-taking and view problems as learning opportunities.
10. Promote multicultural awareness, gender sensitivity, and the appreciation of diversity in the education community.

◆ LEARNER-CENTERED HUMAN RESOURCES LEADERSHIP AND MANAGEMENT

A superintendent is an educational leader who promotes the success of all students by implementing a staff evaluation and development system to improve the performance of all staff members, selects appropriate models for supervision and staff development, and applies the legal requirements for personnel management. A superintendent understands, values, and is able to:

1. Develop, implement, and evaluate a comprehensive professional development plan designed specifically to address areas of identified district, campus, and/or staff need.
2. Facilitate the application of adult learning principles to all professional development activities, including the use of relevant issues and tasks and the use of support and follow-up strategies to facilitate implementation.
3. Implement strategies to enhance professional capabilities at the district and campus level to ensure support for a continuum of services and programming.
4. Deliver effective presentations and facilitate the learning of both small and large groups.

5. Implement effective strategies for the recruitment, selection, induction, development, and promotion of staff.
6. Develop and institute comprehensive staff evaluation models that include both formative and summative assessment and appraisal strategies.
7. Demonstrate use of district and staff evaluation data for personnel policy development and decision making.
8. Demonstrate and apply knowledge of certification requirements and standards.
9. Diagnose and improve organizational health/morale by the implementation of strategies and programs designed to provide ongoing assistance and support to personnel.

◈ LEARNER-CENTERED POLICY AND GOVERNANCE

A superintendent is an educational leader who promotes the success of all students by understanding, responding to, and influencing the larger political, social, economic, legal, and cultural context and by working with the board of trustees to define mutual expectations, policies, and standards. A superintendent understands, values, and is able to:

1. Define and apply the general characteristics of internal and external political systems to the educational organization.
2. Demonstrate and apply appropriate knowledge of legal issues affecting education.
3. Provide leadership in defining superintendent and board roles, mutual expectations, and effective superintendent-board working relationships.
4. Determine the political, economic, and social aspects and/or needs of groups in the community, and those of the community at large, for effective and responsive decision making.
5. Prepare and recommend district policies to improve student learning and district performance in compliance with state and federal requirements.
6. Utilize legal systems to protect the rights of students and staff and to improve learning opportunities.
7. Apply laws, policies, and procedures fairly, wisely, and considerately.
8. Access state and national political systems to provide input on critical educational issues.

◈ LEARNER-CENTERED COMMUNICATIONS AND COMMUNITY RELATIONS

A superintendent is an educational leader who promotes the success of all students by collaborating with families and community members, responding to diverse community interests and needs, and mobilizing community resources. A superintendent understands, values, and is able to:

1. Develop and implement an effective and comprehensive district internal and external communications plan and public relations program.
2. Analyze community and district structures and identify major opinion leaders and their relationships to district goals and programs.
3. Establish partnerships with parents, area businesses, institutions of higher education, and community groups to strengthen programs and support district goals.

4. Implement effective strategies to systematically communicate with and gather input from all stakeholders in the district.
5. Communicate effectively with all social, cultural, ethnic, and racial groups in the school district and community.
6. Develop and utilize formal and informal techniques to obtain accurate perceptions of the district staff, parents, and community.
7. Use effective consensus building and conflict management skills.
8. Articulate the district's vision and priorities to the community and to the media.
9. Influence the media by utilizing proactive communication strategies that serve to enhance and promote the district's vision.
10. Communicate and articulate positions on educational issues.
11. Demonstrate effective and forceful writing, speaking, and active listening skills.

◆ LEARNER-CENTERED ORGANIZATIONAL LEADERSHIP AND MANAGEMENT

A superintendent is an educational leader who promotes the success of all students by leadership and management of the organization, operations, and resources for a safe, efficient, and effective learning environment. A superintendent understands, values, and is able to:

1. Implement appropriate management techniques and group processes to define roles, assign functions, delegate effectively, and determine accountability for goal attainment.
2. Implement processes for gathering, analyzing, and using data for informed decision-making.
3. Frame, analyze, and resolve problems using appropriate problem-solving techniques and decision-making skills.
4. Develop, implement, and evaluate change processes for organizational effectiveness.
5. Implement strategies that enable the physical plant, equipment, and support systems to operate safely, efficiently, and effectively to maintain a conducive learning environment throughout the district.
6. Apply legal concepts, regulations, and codes for school district operations.
7. Perform effective budget planning, management, account auditing, and monitoring and establish district procedures for accurate and effective fiscal reporting.
8. Acquire, allocate, and manage resources according to district vision and priorities.
9. Manage one's own time and the time of others to maximize attainment of district goals.
10. Use technology to enhance school district operations.

◆ LEARNER-CENTERED CURRICULUM PLANNING AND DEVELOPMENT

A superintendent is an educational leader who promotes the success of all students by facilitating the design and implementation of curricula and strategic plans that enhance teaching and learning; alignment of curriculum, curriculum resources and assessment; and the use of various forms of assessment to measure student performance. A superintendent understands, values, and is able to:

1. Apply understanding of pedagogy, cognitive development, and child and adolescent growth and development to facilitate effective district curricular decisions.
2. Implement curriculum planning methods to anticipate and respond to occupational and economic trends and to achieve optimal student learning.
3. Implement core curriculum design and delivery systems to ensure instructional continuity and instructional integrity across the district.
4. Develop and implement collaborative processes for the systematic assessment and renewal of the curriculum to ensure appropriate scope, sequence, content, and alignment.
5. Evaluate and provide direction for improving district curriculum in ways that are based upon sound, research-based practices.
6. Facilitate the use of technology, telecommunications, and information systems to enrich the school district curriculum and enhance learning for all students.
7. Facilitate the use of creative, critical thinking, and problem-solving tools by staff and other school district stakeholders.
8. Facilitate the effective coordination of district and campus curricular and extracurricular programs.

◆ LEARNER-CENTERED INSTRUCTIONAL LEADERSHIP AND MANAGEMENT

A superintendent is an educational leader who promotes the success of all students by advocating, nurturing, and sustaining a district culture and instructional program conducive to student learning and staff professional growth. A superintendent understands, values, and is able to:

1. Apply knowledge and understanding of motivational theories to create conditions that empower staff, students, families, and the community to strive to achieve the district's vision.
2. Facilitate the implementation of sound, research-based theories and techniques of classroom management, student discipline, and school safety to ensure a school district environment conducive to learning.
3. Facilitate the development of a learning organization that supports instructional improvement, builds and implements an appropriate curriculum, and incorporates best practice.
4. Facilitate the ongoing study of current best practice and relevant research and encourage the application of this knowledge to district/school improvement initiatives.
5. Plan and manage student activity programs to fulfill developmental, social, cultural, athletic, leadership, and scholastic needs.
6. Institute a comprehensive school district program of student assessment, interpretation of data, and reporting of state and national data results.
7. Apply knowledge and understanding of special programs to ensure that students with special needs are provided quality, flexible instructional programs and services.

8. Analyze and deploy available instructional resources in the most effective and equitable manner to enhance student learning.
9. Develop, implement, and evaluate change processes to improve student and adult learning, and the climate for learning.
10. Create an environment in which all students can learn.

INDEX